D0851190

MUSIC'S BROKEN WINGS

Fifty Years of Aviation Accidents in the Music Industry

Also by William P. Heitman:

Flying & Learning: Basics For Every Pilot

MUSIC'S BROKEN WINGS

Fifty Years of Aviation Accidents in the Music Industry

William P. Heitman

Illustrations by Carla Osborne
Foreword by J.P. Richardson, son of the "Big Bopper"

Dreamflyer® Publications, LLC
Durham, North Carolina

MUSIC'S BROKEN WINGS
Fifty Years of Aviation Accidents in the Music Industry

©2003 William P. Heitman
All rights reserved.

No part of this book may be reproduced or transmitted in any form or by any means, electronic, mechanical, including photocopying, recording, or by any information storage and retrieval system, except in the case of reviews, without the express written permission of the publisher, except where permitted by law.

Every effort has been made to ensure that permission for use of all pertinent material was obtained. In addition, every effort has been made to ensure that all material within this book is accurate, up to date, and acknowledged where necessary. Any material not formally acknowledged, or changes in governmental determination and policy, may be corrected and/or included in all future editions of this work subsequent to notification by any appropriate sources. Any and all liabilities will be limited wholly to such editorial and textual changes. Our goal is to convey factual information to enhance aviation education and safety.

ISBN # 0-9660156-2-2

Front cover crash site photo is courtesy of Bill Griggs at www.rockin50s.com.
Front cover angel photo was taken by the author at a cemetery in Salisbury, North Carolina.
Front cover composite art and all artist illustrations are by Carla Osborne.
Rear cover photos are courtesy of Gary T. Whitford at www.n2flight.com.
Photos within the body of the text are credited where applicable.

For special orders and bulk quantities, contact:

Dreamflyer® Publications, LLC
P.O. Box 11583
Durham, NC 27703-0583

www.Dreamflyer.com

Manufactured in the United States of America

First Edition

Dedications:

This book is dedicated to all those within it
who lost their lives.

W. P. H.

Thanks to Tim and my family for their love and patience.
For my big brother David—may all your dreams take flight.

C. R. O.

*The angel of the Lord encampeth round
about them...and delivereth them.*

Psalms 34:7

Table of Contents

Acknowledgements

As with any body of work of this magnitude, a number of people contributed to its completion. I was fortunate to have had some of the nicest and most patient people volunteer their time and expertise. My special thanks go out to the family members, musicians and people close to the events who contributed invaluable information, and whose lives were directly affected by some of these particular accidents.

By no means is the following list absolutely complete. I spoke with hundreds of people during the research process who were gracious with their time, but were unable to provide new facts or information. Even though they are not mentioned here, I thank all of them for their time.

Sources:

Melba D. Moye (NTSB Records Management), Roger D. Cain (Aviation Photographer who supplied numerous photos), Thomas W. Myrick (Glen Miller), Steven M. Hutton (Glen Miller), Bob Grimes (Tamara), George Moquin, University of Maryland (William Kapell), Dr. Anna Lou Dehavenon (William Kapell), Dr. James Blackwood (Blackwood Brothers Quartet), Rev. Cecil Little (Blackwood Brothers Quartet), Gary Lane (Blackwood Brothers Quartet), Jimmy and Norma Martin, Martin Funeral Home (Blackwood Brothers Quartet), Bob and Nell Tucker, Chilton County News (Blackwood Brothers Quartet), Rita Wilson (Pedro Infante), Bill Griggs (Buddy Holly), Jay P. Richardson (the "Big Bopper"), Larryann Willis (Audie Murphy), Morton Lester (Audie Murphy), Mary E. Nowak (Maury Muehleisen), John Osterberg (Bill Chase), Marvin C. Frame, Jr. (Doobieliner), Miles Lumbard (Doobieliner), Brian and Mary Nash (Lynyrd Skynyrd), Artimus Pyle (Lynyrd Skynyrd), Magdalena Maria Ostas (Anna Jantar), Jeffrey Strunk (Jud Strunk), Mike Douglas (John Felten), the Tyler Morning Telegraph (Keith Green), Ariel Rogers (Stan Rogers), Hidekatsu Mizukami (Kyu Sakamoto), Masahiko Takeda (Kyu Sakamoto), Ed Frank (Rick Nelson), Joni Marie Hewitt (Rick Nelson), James Intveld (Rick Nelson), Jack Bertron (Rick Nelson), Tom Ingram (Rick Nelson)

Proofreaders:

David J. Ivey, NTSB Senior Air Safety Investigator
Larry F. Lambert, FAA Aviation Safety Program Manager
Joseph Algranti, NASA-JSC Chief Pilot (Retired)
T. Byron Smith, Attorney
Gary T. Whitford, Private Pilot
Carla Osborne, Graphic Artist
Catherine K. Heitman, Ph.D, Clinical Research Director
Thomas M. Krebs, Retired Business Executive
Ann K. Packer, Health Care Manager

General Thanks:

Steve Fred, Vladislav Oleynik and the staff at Umbrella Technologies and finally to Dr. Paul A. Craig for the challenge in April 1998 that directly led to this body of work.

Foreword

A plane goes down. An investigation is done. Several months later a report on the accident is made public. These reports are sometimes as thick as a bad novel. Even if you are an avid traveler or a seasoned veteran pilot you may not understand exactly what this report is saying, even after reading it several times. In my experience, at least, this is true.

You see, I lost my father, J.P. Richardson, also known as the "Big Bopper," to an air crash before I was born, and for many years I wondered about the accident. Even though I had read the Civil Aeronautics Board report and I knew what had happened, I still did not understand why it happened. I believe this to be the case with many accident reports. Whether you've lost a loved one to an accident or you are an experienced pilot, the question of why the accident happened can be a nagging one. Finding out why can help you put closure to the loss of someone loved, or can prevent you from making the same mistake if you are a pilot.

When Mr. Heitman asked me to write the foreword for his book I thought, why me? Certainly there were others more qualified to do this than I. Then, after reflecting back through the years and all the research I had done trying to understand why my father had died, I realized that I probably was more qualified than most. You see, I knew from personal experience what one goes through when dealing with the question of why. Though I've had many years to look into the crash that took my father's life, and though I understand what happened, the chapter in this book on my father has made it even clearer to me why it happened.

If you have an interest in aviation, or the accidents that have taken the lives of some of the greatest entertainers over this fifty year period, I know you will find this book to be enlightening reading. If you are a pilot, reading this book could help save your life and the lives of your passengers.

J. P. Richardson

Introduction

Aviation can be defined as the art (or science) of operating and navigating an aircraft. An aircraft can take many forms. There are hot air balloons, airships, ultralights, gliders, gyroplanes, helicopters and airplanes. Within the realm of airplanes, there is a huge range of designs. There are single-seat and multiple-seat; bi-wing and single-wing, including both high-wing and low-wing craft; and there are single-engine and multi-engine airplanes. The Federal Aviation Administration (FAA) defines an airplane as "an engine-driven fixed-wing aircraft heavier than air, that is supported in flight by the dynamic reaction of the air against its wings."

Over the past 100 years, aviation has grown exponentially from one short milestone take-off and landing on the sands of Kitty Hawk to a global network of private aircraft, corporate flight departments and airlines that have shrunk our concept of distance on the planet earth considerably. More than once I will say that aviation is exceedingly safe, but since aircraft are machines the possibility of malfunction and human error in their operation always exists. Fortunately, in the era of modern aviation there are very strict federal guidelines that demand the regular inspection and maintenance of aircraft. In addition, there are federal guidelines that dictate that pilots receive regular proficiency training. These Federal Aviation Regulations (FARs) form the backbone of air safety.

There is an element of danger in nearly everything in our lives, from taking a bath, to engaging in sports, to crossing the street as a pedestrian. In 1972, the United States Supreme Court stated profoundly that, "Safe is not the eqivalent of risk free." Certainly driving an automobile has substantial risk. In fact, it has been said wryly that the most dangerous part of flying is the drive to the airport. Still, it is natural and correct to assume that there is risk when flying. Any machine has risks associated with it, right down to the swing set on which a child plays. Risk does not guarantee injury or make an activity unsafe, but risk should not be ignored. The only way for a person to eliminate risk from their life's activities is to avoid any participation in them. However, few people will alter their lifestyle in order to avoid every potential risk.

There are two basic types of aviation. First, there is the airline industry, also known as the commercial air carrier, which runs its operations based on a flight schedule. An airline must fly on its own published timetable, even if there is only one passenger aboard. This is the nature of a scheduled airline. The down-side of this type operation is that the airline will not fly on the passenger's preferred schedule. The passenger has to adhere to the airline's own published time constraints. Flying on the airlines is very safe and mostly predictable. In fact, it is well known that aviation as a whole is the world's safest mode of transportation. During the years 1998 and 2002, despite several accidents, airlines in the United States flew without a single passenger fatality.

Of note, the events that occurred on September 11, 2001 should not be viewed as aviation accidents, per se. The tragedies of that day were deliberate criminal acts that took advantage of holes which existed in airport security policies and measures at the time. Air travel security is continually being improved upon and it would be a mistake to equate terrorism with natural human error. Furthermore, it would be a mistake to refrain from flying on any airline in the United States due to fear from a terrorist action. Terrorism must not be allowed to influence, hinder or paralyze any person's freedom to decide on how, when and where to travel.

Second, there is the general aviation domain, which includes literally everything else in aviation, other than military flying. General aviation is the largest and most active group in the air transportation realm.

Corporate flight departments fall under the heading of general aviation. It is also within general aviation that pilots with private licenses fly and fly-for-hire operators conduct banner towing operations, carry out pipeline patrol, spray crops and perform on-demand charter flights. Even if a rock band were to fly to a concert location on a large chartered transport-type of aircraft such as a Boeing, if this flight were not an air-carrier scheduled operation then it still would be considered a general aviation operation.

General aviation has no set flight schedule. There is no demand or pressure that a flight be conducted at all, aside from that which a pilot or corporate boss places on himself. General aviation has the flexibility to go when the pilot, charter customer or corporate executive wants to go. This flexibility is very appealing when it applies to business and pleasure. Without a rigid schedule the passenger doesn't have to rush to catch a flight. There is great ease of management with arrivals and departures, changes in scheduling and even canceling a flight. Celebrities often travel using this freedom of agenda. It is a necessary part of their business. This freedom is the advantage that general aviation offers.

The number of general aviation aircraft greatly exceeds the number of airliners. Moreover, general aviation aircraft fly three-fourths of all hours flown in the world. As a result, it is easy to see why, as far as statistics are concerned, most accidents will occur in the general aviation ranks. General aviation pilots can take-off into the sky even when better judgment would say, "No!" These pilots are not bound by all the additional restrictions and regulations which govern the airlines. Neither do general aviation pilots always have access to the modern full motion flight simulators and rigid training to which airline pilots are subjected. Therefore, general aviation pilots may have an overall weaker combination of experience, recent flight time and recurrent proficiency training, although this is not always the case. For the most part, general aviation pilots are well trained, highly skilled and very safe in our skies.

The human element, with its potential for bad decision-making, coupled with the possibility of a machine developing a malfunction, leads to almost all general aviation accidents. However, if you eliminate the malfunctioning machine scenario (because of the good maintenance laws in place) you are left simply with human error. Indeed, human error does account for 80 percent of all general aviation accidents. Bad decisions, bad judgment and bad pilot technique are the culprits that most frequently lead to aviation accidents. Lost lives can be the price paid for the freedom to decide for oneself how to conduct a general aviation flight. Once again, this freedom is the double-edged sword that general aviation provides.

Nonetheless, general aviation is very safe when compared to other forms of travel. On average, about 1,000 people die every year in all the aviation accidents in the United States, including the airlines. Compare this number with the thousands of people who die each year in bathtub accidents or bicycle accidents, the thousands who die in boating accidents and the tens of thousands who die every year from drowning, fires, poisoning, choking and job-related accidents. Think about the many thousands who die each year from murders and in highway accidents and it becomes evident that aviation as a whole is very safe.

I never take flying for granted and aviation still holds me in awe. Even though I am a very fortunate individual in that I am able to undertake as my profession exactly what I would do for fun, aviation remains an unnatural realm for this humble, gravity-defined creature. We are not born with the ability to fly like birds are. Rather, humans need a man-made machine to take them into the air. To commit oneself to enter into the understanding of aviation is to commit to a lifetime of learning. The greatest pilot who has ever flown, or will ever fly, will never know all, see all or do all within the unlimited expanse of aeronautical endeavors. Every day the clouds, temperature and winds are different. Every minute in the air is a live performance demanding learned motor skills stored within the neural synapses of our brain. Moreover, every flight calls for decision-making attributes that constantly challenge human intellect to counter natural forces. No one is capable of performing this technical dance perfectly every single time.

Obviously, not everyone wants to learn to fly. The journey into aviation is a personal one for each individual. As a flight instructor, I cannot instill in someone the desire to fly, nor can I simply grant the ability. That desire to manipulate a flying machine has to come from within and success has to be earned one lesson at a time. Aviation is totally indiscriminate, unbiased and non-prejudicial, and will accept anyone who has the ambition and persistence to learn the ways of the air. Likewise, flight accidents are similarly indiscriminate and can involve the rich, poor, famous and obscure alike. However, when one considers that celebrities must travel frequently to adhere to hectic and demanding performance schedules, it becomes clear that the laws of probability dictate that a performer could be more likely to become involved in an aviation accident. Even so, despite that higher probability, the overall evidence indicates that the likelihood of an aviation accident occurring at all remains very low.

The celebrities involved in the crashes described in this book were public figures who led public lives and sometimes died public deaths. Whenever an air crash involves an airliner going down, or a significant loss of life, or a flight with a celebrity aboard, the media scramble to cover the story. Sometimes an eager media corps, wanting to scoop the story and unwilling to wait for all the facts, will broadcast initial speculation. This sensationalism, supplied to a public who on the whole knows little about aviation except for sound bites, can misrepresent rather than inform. Yet this is the nature of the media in the world in which we live. Accidents are "human interest" events. Many times when one of our music superstars dies in an aviation-related crash, controversy, rumor and inaccuracy surround that death. Unfortunately, it is the mad rush for a headline that sometimes fuels the speculation and rumors that then take on lives of their own and never seem to fully dissipate.

By selecting and compiling information about this group of aviation accidents, I am in no way implying that any death of any performer involved was more tragic than some of the other great performers who have been killed by automobile accident, drug overdose, homicide, suicide or other fateful events. Nor am I suggesting that their deaths are more tragic than those of non-celebrities. Furthermore, by compiling this text I am not attempting to imply that this is an all-inclusive group of events or performers. I know for a fact that there are other aviation-related events that occurred within this time period which involved other music artists.

One example of an aviation misunderstanding involves Little Richard, who in October of 1957 believed that the plane in which he was a passenger was going to catch fire because he saw the wing glowing red during a flight at night. The plane landed safely with no fire. Little Richard only percieved that a fire was going to occur due possibly to a red-hot glowing turbocharger or exhaust stack. Other examples of aviation-related events with celebrities on board include Tex Ritter, who was on a scheduled airline flight sometime around 1970, bound for Miami, Florida, that was hijacked to Havana, Cuba. He later wrote a song about this event. In 1976, Paul Kossoff, guitarist for the band Free, died of a heart attack during a flight from Los Angeles to New York City. In 1965, Alan Price, of the British group The Animals, reportedly left that band because of his fear of flying. However, these examples do not constitute accidents and thus fall outside the scope of this body of research.

I know full well that in writing this book about aviation accidents and incidents involving celebrities, I am venturing into a realm where rumors often take on a life of their own. Those who believe the popular hearsay may not be easily swayed from their beliefs. I remember that once upon a time I believed I knew the truth about some of these accidents. I once believed that Jim Croce died in a Cessna 172, and that the

Lynyrd Skynyrd band went down in a Boeing 727. I saw the Patsy Cline movie where the Cessna crashes into the side of a cliff. There are still people out there who will swear that the song "Fire and Rain" by James Taylor tells of a plane crash. In fact, none of these anecdotes is true. While reading these pages keep in mind that, more than anything else, this is a book about the facts. Also, note that this book attempts to focus more on aviation than it does on celebrity itself.

I have tried very hard to achieve accuracy and completeness in reconstructing the accounts in this book. Some of my research has brought me into personal contact with survivors or relatives of victims involved in some of the events described. The support and cooperation of many of the families and individuals who were most affected by these events is perhaps the greatest reward in this whole endeavor. Perhaps this text will even serve to help put closure on an event for some of these good people. And while I have tried to structure the text to allow the non-pilot to learn something about aviation while reading through a particular accident report, the pilot-reader also can take away factual information about an accident and hopefully can learn something about aviation safety. Each chapter has been presented as a stand-alone story as much as possible, but in some cases it will be necessary for the reader to reference the included investigative report in order to gain full insight.

For anyone who wants the simplest answer as to why I wrote this book, it was to find the truth. Just as in a court of law, any search begins with the facts. From those facts a truth emerges (hopefully) and the best possible history of the case is developed from which the judge and/or jury then must make a final determination. The process was similar with this book with one exception. Although I have researched the facts from the most reliable sources, looked at as many aspects of the story as possible and presented my thoughts about each event from the perspective of a professional pilot, I am neither a judge nor a jury and I will refrain from offering any definitive statement regarding the cause of an accident. This compilation is not a Monday-morning-quarterback textbook or tabloid-type speculation. All the information presented within is based on solid aviation and scientific foundations. I have simply attempted to pull the information together into this single reference and unique body of work.

The recording business and modern aviation grew together as industries in the twentieth century. There is a certain mystique associated with superstars in the entertainment industry. In the case of musicians, I believe this is true because their voices and songs are an integral part of our lives every day, whether heard on our favorite radio station, cassette, compact disc or digital recording. We as listeners sometimes tend to live vicariously through our favorite artists' music and/or lyrics. Music is incredibly powerful in its ability to convey sadness and joy all at the same time. Music also can evoke distant memories and it can have great healing power. This complexity within music can mysteriously reach into our souls and bring forth emotions that we never knew existed.

There also is a mystique surrounding aviation that fascinates many of those among us. From a very young age, airplanes flying overhead seize our imagination. Interestingly, I have been told that the same areas of the brain associated with musical talent are also the ones integral to flying skills. Yet, while an air crash is always terribly tragic, there is also something strangely mesmerizing and captivating about this type of event. Perhaps it is morbid curiosity or the need to know what happened that drives our fascination. Perhaps it is empathy for the loss of human life. Regardless of the source of the mystique, I have tried to remain objective throughout the process of investigation and thus treat each of the accidents described in this book as a historical event.

In the event of an airplane crash, the United States is fortunate to have an investigative branch of our government called the National Transportation Safety Board (NTSB). This organization is a board of inquiry that is totally independent of the government and the judicial system. Just like aviation itself, the NTSB investigative process does not care who you are, how much money you have, what political ties you have, where you come from, or what your social status is. The NTSB investigators are absolutely, positively non-biased in their determinations. They only care about the facts. They only want to know what the accident can tell them from the evidence that is collected.

Their investigative work is so good and so detailed that they can actually tell whether or not a light bulb was burning when an aircraft hit the ground. Their job is to look at such things as configuration and loading of the aircraft, assess whether or not the aircraft engines were turning and/or producing power, gather eyewitness statements and ultimately to issue a report which states the determining factors that caused the accident or incident. From this report, the NTSB can make recommendations involving future safety concerns with regard to aircraft of the type involved in the accident, and issue statements regarding the existing weather conditions and/or pilot involvement. These facts can be used to debunk and dispel any hastily generated rumors and misconceptions revolving around a crash. The NTSB investigator only wishes to know what caused the accident or incident, what can be learned from it, and what can be done to prevent another one like it in the future.

We have lost some of the original documentation about some of the crashes in this book. The NTSB long ago decided to purge many of the reports from its system. From January 1, 1978 to 1993, the full reports that do remain are mainly on the information storage and retrieval system known as microfiche. Having been through thousands of pages of microfiche reports, I can regretfully confirm that the quality is sometimes poor, especially with photographs. This shortcoming results from the fact that the microfiche system is essentially a negative system. By the time an original photograph is put onto microfiche as a negative and then retrieved and printed on paper by essentially the same process as photocopying, the details of the photograph are lost. For this reason I have decided to eliminate most of the original investigative photographs from this text. However, the textual body of each report written after Jan. 1, 1978, is generally intact.

For almost every accident that occurred prior to 1978, almost all that remains of the original reports is a very brief one-page synopsis of the crash itself. I have searched high and low to try to find those reports from independent sources. On some occasions I was successful; on others I was not. In every case, the report found was not retyped for this book. Rather, it was scanned into the computer. In this way you are able to read as much of the original report as possible as it appeared, or currently appears, in a public document. However, these spartan reports must be accompanied by at least some additional background in order that all readers can understand the larger scenario as it may have unfolded. I want aviators and non-aviators alike to feel comfortable while reading this body of information.

It must be reiterated that, after having presented the facts in this book, no perfect or ideal conclusions, definitive or otherwise, should be drawn about the capability of any person, living or dead, nor the functionality of any type of aircraft, its systems or its parts, from any page of this book. Additionally, the documentation and thoughts contained within this manuscript should be considered by each reader as solely for his or her own personal interest, as well as for casual information gathering. Should anyone wish to find out more information about the lives of the music celebrities involved in these reports, he or she need only tap into this very modern world in which we live. There are literally thousands of web sites that are dedicated to your favorite musical performers. A multitude of books exists as well, both biographies and autobiographies. While I encourage you to seek any additional information you wish to find through some other source, I also caution you that there is a lot of misinformation available as well. In your own search, seek the truth and help dispel the myths and rumors.

It remains an obvious uncertainty as to if and when another aviation accident will occur involving a music celebrity. Whether it is as a pilot-in-command of his or her own plane, in a chartered jet, or even on a scheduled airliner, these singers, songwriters and musicians literally pass over our heads every day. While we all hope that none of these types of crashes ever happens again, the law of averages says that sometime, somewhere, most likely one will happen in the future. Then the process of media hype, professional investigation and rumor quenching begin anew. Indeed we enjoy their music, but I believe we should also respect our favorite artists' private lives, especially in times of great loss, while we thank them for giving us the great songs that they write and perform. Through it all, triumph and tragedy, it really is the music itself that remains and endures. Ultimately, every music artist will live forever through the body of music he or she leaves as a legacy. My only consolation at the loss of any music artist, under any circumstance, is the belief that there are other worlds in which to make music.

It is interesting to mention that while I was accumulating material for this manuscript, conducting many hours of research, review, writing, word processing and collating of the text, it seemed that each time I needed some bit of information or resource to rely upon, it mysteriously seemed to present itself. I would like to think that somehow, someway, in some manner or form, there was a good dose of divine intervention that played a hand, and kept me going, throughout the entire long and tedious process. To those forces unseen yet distinctly felt and believed in, I offer a "Thank you." For those of us who seek the truth, it is out there for each of us if only we have the desire, objectivity and perseverance to discover it.

W. P. H.
February 2003

The National Transportation Safety Board (NTSB)

The National Transportation Safety Board (NTSB) is an independent federal accident investigation agency. Since its creation in 1967, the NTSB's mission has been to determine the "probable cause" of transportation accidents and to formulate safety recommendations to improve transportation safety.

The NTSB determines the probable cause of:
- All United States civil aviation accidents and certain public-use accidents
- Selected highway accidents
- Railroad accidents involving passenger trains or any train accident that results in at least one fatality or major property damage
- Major maritime accidents and any marine accident involving a public and a nonpublic vessel
- Pipeline accidents involving a fatality or substantial property damage
- Selected transportation accidents that involve problems of a recurring nature

On September 17, 1908, when Army Lieutenant Thomas Selfridge was the first to die in an airplane crash, the face of aviation was changed irrevocably. Before there was a NTSB, Congress passed the Air Commerce Act of 1926. This legislation gave the Commerce Department the authority to determine the cause of airplane accidents. A small unit within the Commerce Department, known as the Aeronautics Branch, carried out this function.

By 1933, the Aeronautics Branch had become the Bureau of Air Commerce, which in turn was replaced by the Independent Air Safety Board. In 1938, the Air Safety Board became the Civil Aeronautics Administration, which two years later became the Civil Aeronautics Board (CAB). The CAB's Bureau of Safety formed the nucleus of the NTSB, which was established in 1967 as an independent agency within the newly created United States Department of Transportation.

It was at this time that Congress expanded the NTSB's authority to include accident investigation in four other modes: rail, highway, marine and pipeline. Then, in 1974, Congress passed the Independent Safety Board Act, which severed the NTSB's ties to the Department of Transportation and gave the NTSB increased authority in accident investigations.

The Independent Safety Board Act of 1974 is in effect to this day and gives the NTSB authority over, and responsibility for:
- Conducting special studies on safety problems
- Maintaining the official United States census of aviation accidents
- Evaluating the effectiveness of government agencies involved in transportation safety
- Evaluating the safeguards used in the transportation of hazardous materials, as well as the effectiveness of emergency responses to hazardous material accidents
- Reviewing appeals from airmen and merchant seamen whose certificates have been revoked or suspended
- Reviewing appeals from airmen, mechanics and repairmen who have been assessed civil penalties by the Federal Aviation Administration (FAA)
- Leading any United States teams on foreign airline accident investigations to assist foreign authorities under the provisions of the International Civil Aviation Organization (ICAO) agreements in effect

The NTSB's headquarters is in Washington, D.C. Regional offices are located in Chicago, Illinois; Dallas-Fort Worth, Texas; Los Angeles, California; Seattle, Washington and Parsippany, New Jersey. Field offices are located in Anchorage, Alaska; Atlanta, Georgia and Denver, Colorado. It is important to remember that the NTSB has no legislative or legal authority to make changes in the transportation system. It can only make recommendations. Think of it as a board of inquiry. It is important to note that the NTSB was established as an independent agency because, during the course of its investigations, it often must investigate any role that a particular Department of Transportation (DOT) agency might have played in the accident scenario. This independence keeps politics out of the investigation process. Yet, many times there is intense pressure shouldered by the NTSB to solve and explain certain high-profile accidents very quickly.

One of the best-known aspects of the NTSB's accident investigation process is the "Go-Team." The "Go-Team" is a group of NTSB personnel on 24-hour alert who possess a wide range of accident investigation skills. In aviation, a "Go-Team" roster includes an investigator-in-charge and a half dozen or more specialists and experts trained in witness interviews, aircraft systems and structures, maintenance, operations, air traffic control and meteorology. In addition, an actual Board member (one of five total appointees) usually accompanies the "Go-Team" to the scene of an accident. A public affairs officer also is assigned to the team to coordinate media activities.

The length of time a "Go-Team" remains on a site varies with need, but generally a team completes its on-scene work in 7 to 10 days. The NTSB takes its responsibility to keep the public informed very seriously. At a major accident site it follows a policy of providing factual information on the progress of the investigation at press briefings. Often, when a major accident occurs and the probable cause is not readily apparent, there is considerable speculation by the press about what happened. To minimize this speculation, the NTSB issues periodic press statements, and a Board member often meets directly with the press to brief the media and to answer questions in the days following an accident. These briefings convey only the known facts of the investigation. No one at the NTSB engages in speculation about possible causes of an accident.

With the completion of the fact-finding phase, the accident investigation process enters into the phase known as the analysis of the factual findings. The analysis of the factual findings results in what is known as the "probable cause of the accident." Usually within three to six months after the accident, factual reports, written by the NTSB investigators themselves, are made available in a public document at NTSB headquarters in Washington, DC. If additional, relevant factual material is revealed later, it also is added to the public document of the accident. The entire process, from accident investigation to final report, normally takes nine to twelve months, but can take longer in some investigations. Accidents investigated by the NTSB's regional field investigators generally are reported in a "brief" format.

The board investigates thousands of accidents annually, including all air carrier, commuter, air-taxi (charter) and fatal general aviation accidents. Many times, the result of an accident investigation is a safety recommendation. The safety recommendation is the NTSB's most important product. It is vital to the NTSB's basic goal of accident prevention since it is the lever by which changes and improvements regarding safety are made in our nation's transportation system. It is not unusual for the NTSB to issue safety recommendations as soon as a problem is identified, once the probable cause is unquestionably determined, even if the investigation is not fully completed .

The majority of the NTSB's air safety recommendations are directed to the FAA. These recommendations have resulted in a wide range of safety improvements in areas such as pilot training, aircraft maintenance and design, air traffic control procedures and post accident survival. The NTSB also is authorized to conduct safety studies of transportation problems. A safety study allows the NTSB to go beyond the single accident investigation to examine an underlying safety problem from a broader perspective.

Legislation enacted in late 1996 gave the NTSB a new responsibility of coordinating support services for the families of victims of aviation accidents resulting in major loss of life. In addition, a memorandum signed by President William J. Clinton requested that the Board assume the same responsibilities for major surface transportation accidents and directed Executive Branch agencies to provide their assistance. The NTSB coordinates the provision of federal services to the families, including providing speedy and accurate information about the accident, assisting in victim identification and ensuring that the families receive all necessary assistance and opportunities for counseling.

The NTSB maintains a public docket at its headquarters in Washington, DC. The docket contains the records of all Board investigations, safety recommendations and enforcement proceedings. These records are available to the public and may be reviewed or duplicated for public use. The Analysis and Data Division manages the computer database for aviation accidents that have occurred since 1962. The information, in brief form, lists the probable cause and contributing factors as determined by the Safety Board.

Author's note:

The Public Inquiries Branch of the NTSB, Washington, DC, is where much research for the reports included in this book was conducted. While there, I found that there are very few briefs remaining prior to 1964. Most of the reports prior to 1978 have been destroyed except for the briefs. Most full accident reports or briefs from January 1, 1978 to 1993 are now on microfiche only, and from 1993 to the present all information is stored in the main computer only. In October 2002, the NTSB extended its Internet database back to 1962. Prior to this, only reports back to 1982 were accessible through this website. Access to selected NTSB reports can be gained through the NTSB's website at http://www.ntsb.gov.

NTSB 830

The NTSB has its own set of federal regulations which govern whether an accident is classified as an accident or an incident, and how an accident site is to be overseen and acted upon according to the law. These federal regulations are known as NTSB 830. The following two pages are exact representations of the federal regulations which comprise NTSB 830.

I urge you to read these pages. Not only will they help you understand the nuances that define the differences between an aviation accident versus an incident regarding such measures as serious injury to a person and substantial damage to an aircraft, but they will also inform you about what priorities you should establish if ever you are a witness to an aviation accident or incident.

The main phone number for the NTSB in Washington, DC is (202) 314-6000. Their office hours of operation are 8:30 a.m. to 5:00 p.m. Eastern time, Monday through Friday. There also is a 24-hour phone number to the FAA where accidents can be reported. This phone number is (202) 267-3333.

PART 830-NOTIFICATION AND REPORTING OF AIRCRAFT ACCIDENTS OR INCIDENTS AND OVERDUE AIRCRAFT, AND PRESERVATION OF AIRCRAFT WRECKAGE, MAIL, CARGO, AND RECORDS.

Subpart A - General
Sec.

830.1   Applicability.
830.2   Definitions.

Subpart B - Initial Notification of Aircraft Accidents, Incidents, and Overdue Aircraft

830.5   Immediate notification.
830.6   Information to be given in notification.

Subpart C - Preservation of Aircraft Wreckage, Mail, Cargo, and Records.

830.10   Preservation of aircraft wreckage, mail, cargo, and records.

Subpart D - Reporting of Aircraft Accidents, Incidents, and Overdue Aircraft

830.15   Reports and statements to be filed.

Authority: Federal Aviation Act of 1958, as amended (49 U.S.C. 40101 et seq.), Independent Safety Board Act of 1974, as amended (49 U.S.C. 1101 et seq.).

SUBPART A - GENERAL

§ 830.1 Applicability.

This part contains rules pertaining to:

(a)   Initial notification and later reporting of aircraft incidents and accidents and certain other occurrences in the operation of aircraft, wherever they occur, when they involve civil aircraft of the United States; when they involve certain public aircraft, as specified in this part, wherever they occur; and when they involve foreign civil aircraft where the events occur in the United States, its territories, or its possessions.

(b)   Preservation of aircraft wreckage, mail, cargo, and records involving all civil and certain public aircraft accidents, as specified in this part, in the United States and its territories or possessions.

§ 830.2 Definitions.

As used in this part the following words or phrases are defined as follows:

Aircraft accident means an occurrence associated with the operation of an aircraft which takes place between the time any person boards the aircraft with the intention of flight and all such persons have disembarked, and in which any person suffers death or serious injury, or in which the aircraft receives substantial damage.

Civil aircraft means any aircraft other than a public aircraft.

Fatal injury means any injury which results in death within 30 days of the accident.

Incident means an occurrence other than an accident, associated with the operation of an aircraft, which affects or could affect the safety of operations.

Operator means any person who causes or authorizes the operation of an aircraft, such as the owner, lessee, or bailee of an aircraft.

Public aircraft means an aircraft used only for the United States Government, or an aircraft owned and operated (except for commercial purposes) or exclusively leased for at least 90 continuous days by a government other than the United States Government, including a State, the District of Colombia, a territory or possession of the United States, or a political subdivision of that government. "Public aircraft" does not include a government-owned aircraft transporting property for commercial purposes and does not include a government-owned aircraft transporting passengers other than: transporting (for other than commercial purposes) crewmembers or other persons aboard the aircraft whose presence is required to perform, or is associated with the performance of, a governmental function such as firefighting, search and rescue, law enforcement, aeronautical research, or biological or geological resource management; or transporting (for other than commercial purposes) persons aboard the aircraft if the aircraft is operated by the Armed Forces or an intelligence agency of the United States. Notwithstanding any limitations relating to use of the aircraft for commercial purposes, an aircraft shall be considered to be a public aircraft without regard to whether it is operated by a unit of government on behalf of another unit of government pursuant to a cost reimbursement agreement, if the unit of government on whose behalf the operation is conducted certifies to the Administrator of the Federal Aviation Administration that the operation was necessary to respond to a significant and imminent threat to life or property (including natural resources) and that no service by a private operator was reasonably available to meet the threat.

Serious injury means any injury which: (1) Requires hospitalization for more than 48 hours, commencing within 7 days from the date of the injury was received; (2) results in a fracture of any bone (except simple fractures of fingers, toes, or nose); (3) causes severe hemorrhages, nerve, muscle, or tendon damage; (4) involves any internal organ; or (5) involves second- or third-degree burns, or any burns affecting more than 5 percent of the body surface.

Substantial damage means damage or failure which adversely affects the structural strength, performance, or flight characteristics of the aircraft, and which would normally require major repair or replacement of the affected component. Engine failure or damage limited to an engine if only one engine fails or is damaged, bent fairings or cowings, dented skin, small punctured holes in the skin or fabric, ground damage to rotor or propeller blades, and damage to landing gear, wheels, tires, flaps, engine accessories, brakes, or wingtips are not considered "substantial damage" for the purpose of this part.

SUBPART B - INITIAL NOTIFICATION OF AIRCRAFT ACCIDENTS, INCIDENTS, AND OVERDUE AIRCRAFT

§ 830.5 Immediate notification.

The operator of any civil aircraft, or any public aircraft not operated by the Armed Forces or an intelligence agency of the United States, or any foreign aircraft shall immediately, and by the most expeditious means available, notify the nearest National Transportation Safety Board (Board) field office[1] when:

(a)   An aircraft accident or any of the following listed incidents occur:

(1)   Flight control system malfunction or failure;

(2)   Inability of any required flight crewmember to perform normal flight duties as a result of injury or illness;

(3)   Failure of structural components of a turbine engine excluding compressors and turbine blades and vanes;

(4)   In-flight fire; or

(5)   Aircraft collide in flight.

(6)   Damage to property, other than the aircraft, estimated to exceed $25,000 for repair (including materials and labor) or fair market value in the event of total loss, whichever is less.

(7)   For large multiengine aircraft (more than 12,500 pounds maximum certificated takeoff weight):

(i)   In-flight failure of electrical systems which requires the sustained use of an emergency bus powered by a back-up source such as a battery, auxiliary power unit, or air-driven generator to retain flight control or essential instruments;

(ii)   In-flight failure of hydraulic systems that results in sustained reliance on the sole remaining hydraulic or mechanical system for movement of flight control surfaces;

(iii)   Sustained loss of the power or thrust produced by two or more engines; and

(iv)   An evacuation of an aircraft in which an emergency egress system is utilized.

(b)   An aircraft is overdue and is believed to have been involved in an accident.

§ 830.6 Information to be given in notification.

The notification required in § 830.5 shall contain the following information, if available:

(a)   Type, nationality, and registration marks of the aircraft;

(b)   Name of the owner, and operator of the aircraft;

(c)   Name of the pilot-in-command;

(d)   Date and time of the accident;

(e)   Last point of departure and point of intended landing of the aircraft;

---

[1]   The Board field offices are listed under U.S. Government in the telephone directories of the following cities: Anchorage, AK, Atlanta, GA, West Chicago, IL, Denver, CO, Arlington, TX, Gardena (Los Angeles), CA, Miami, FL, Parsippany, NJ (metropolitan New York, NY), Seattle, WA, and Washington, DC.

(f) Position of the aircraft with reference to some easily defined geographical point;

(g) Number of persons aboard, number killed, and number seriously injured;

(h) Nature of the accident, the weather and the extent of damage to the aircraft, so far as is known; and

(i) A description of any explosives, radioactive materials, or other dangerous articles carried.

SUBPART C - PRESERVATION OF AIRCRAFT WRECKAGE, MAIL, CARGO, AND RECORDS

§ 830.10 Preservation of aircraft wreckage, mail, cargo, and records.

(a) The operator of an aircraft involved in an accident or incident for which notification must be given is responsible for preserving to the extent possible any aircraft wreckage, cargo, and mail aboard the aircraft, and all records, including all recording mediums of flight, maintenance, and voice recorders, pertaining to the operation and maintenance of the aircraft and to the airmen until the Board takes custody thereof or a release is granted pursuant to § 831.12(b) of this chapter.

(b) Prior to the time the Board or its authorized representative takes custody of aircraft wreckage, mail, or cargo, such wreckage, mail, or cargo may not be disturbed or moved except to the extent necessary:

(1) To remove persons injured or trapped;

(2) To protect the wreckage from further damage; or

(3) To protect the public from injury.

(c) Where ir is necessary to move aircraft wreckage, mail or cargo, sketches, descriptive notes, and photographs shall be made, if possible, of the original positions and condition of the wreckage and any significant impact marks.

(d) The operator of an aircraft involved in an accident or incident shall retain all records, reports, internal documents, and memoranda dealing with the accident or incident, until authorized by the Board to the contrary.

SUBPART D - REPORTING OF AIRCRAFT ACCIDENTS, INCIDENTS, AND OVERDUE AIRCRAFT

§ 830.15 Reports and statements to be filed.

(a) *Reports.* The operator of a civil, public (as specified in § 830.5), or foreign air craft shall file a report on Board Form 6120.½ (OMB No. 3147-0001)[2] within 10 days after an accident, or after 7 days if an overdue aircraft is still missing. A report on an incident for which immediate notification is required by § 830.5(a) shall be filed only as requested by an authorized representative of the Board.

(b) *Crewmember statement.* Each crewmember, if physically able at the time the report is submitted, shall attach a statement setting forth the facts, conditions, and circumstances relating to the accident or incident as they appear to him. If the crewmember is incapacitated, he shall submit the statement as soon as he is physically able.

(c) *Where to file the reports.* The operator of an aircraft shall file any report with the field office of the Board nearest the accident or incident.

Issued in Washington, DC, on this 1st day of August, 1995.

Jim Hall,
Chairman

[FR Doc. 95-19356 Filed 8-4-95; 8:45 am]
BILLING CODE 7533-01-P

---

[2] Forms are available from the Board field offices (see footnote 1), from Board headquarters in Washington, DC, and from the Federal Aviation Administration Flight Standards District Offices.

Carlos Gardel   **Alfredo Le Pera**

June 24, 1935

It is somehow appropriate that this text begins with an aviation mystery. Certainly the plot twists, speculation, eyewitness testimonies and expert opinions in this story appear to be straight out of a Hollywood writer's wildest imagination. However, the truth is that this was a real event and that the full extent of probable causes will never be known about this particular accident. Too much time has passed and too much disagreement hovers over what the evidence really is, which story is the correct version and what those who were there that day really saw. Perhaps it is also appropriate that the first event discussed in this book is one in which human error seems to have played a direct part. While it is true that human error does contribute to at least eighty percent of all aviation accidents, and most of these human factors are simply bad decisions based on schedule pressures or overconfidence, there is a part of the human psyche that is perhaps more frightening. Some call it bravado or machismo. Others may call it a type A personality. It is probably related to the group of hormones that leads to road rage, but within the ranks of the professional aviator, it has no place.

What we know to be factual is that this accident occurred on the property of Olaya Herrera Airfield in the city of Medellin, Colombia in South America. Two aircraft, both Ford Tri-Motors, collided violently and erupted into an intense inferno. One was barely off the ground and one was still on the ground at the time of the collision. There were three survivors, one of whom was José Plaja, who was the personal secretary of Latin tango singer Carlos Gardel, a casualty in the collision. Plaja was badly burned in the fireball and subsequently lost all of the fingers on both of his hands. This accident is recorded as occurring at 2:56 p.m. on June 24, 1935.

The official report issued by the authorities of Colombia allegedly states that only two factors were the cause of this accident. The first factor was the topography, geographical location and layout of the airport itself. The second factor was a meteorological phenomenon where sudden, strong gusts of wind take place in the afternoon hours and last only a few minutes. The report further alleges that on June 24, 1935, the phenomenon we now know as wind shear occurred about ten seconds before the crash. The implied explanation here is that the departing aircraft literally could have been blown into the other aircraft still on the ground. While these seem to be the facts from the official record, there is more documented evidence in this scenario that must be addressed.

It is reasonably well known that there was a fierce rivalry between the pilots of the two aircraft, and the two companies involved. Captain Ernesto Samper Mendoza was the pilot of the Tri-Motor that carried Gardel and Alfredo Le Pera, his lyricist. Mendoza owned the company Servicio Aereo Columbiano (SACO) and, as an aviation pioneer in Colombia, he was a source of national pride. The other company was the Colombian-German Society of Air Transportation (SCADTA). SCADTA was a German company and was operated at a time when Nazism was spreading and gaining footholds in certain parts of the world. The pilot for the SCADTA flight involved in this accident was Captain Hans Ulrich Thom.

As the two pilots flew mostly the same routes, to the same cities, and probably were engaged in ticket price wars as well, the rivalry and taunting between these two pilots had been building for some time. The strict laws we have now, prohibiting some of what must have been standard practices at the time, were probably not in place in Colombia, South America in 1935. On June 20, 1935, four days before the accident, the taunting reportedly came to a head. It has been said that on this day, at an airfield other than where the crash took place, Captain Thom executed a deliberate low-level buzzing pass directly above Captain Mendoza's airplane, which was still on the ground at the time. If this did indeed occur, it would have been difficult to misinterpret this aerial challenge. Certainly such a stunt would have infuriated Mendoza, inciting his self-pride to respond to this display of supposedly great skill.

On June 24, both men were preparing to depart Olaya Herrera Airfield in Medellin. Captain Mendoza taxied out first and prepared for take-off. However, at this point different versions of the story seem to emerge. According to some testimony, upon liftoff, Captain Mendoza turned his plane directly toward Thom's plane, as if to respond to the challenge issued several days earlier, and failed to clear the other Tri-Motor completely as he tried to pass just inches overhead. Certainly if this was the case, and if there was wind shear on the airfield at that moment, the accident could have happened so fast that Mendoza could not have compensated in time. Wind shear was not well known or understood at the time. There were no weather sensing devices to warn of adverse winds. These pilots were stick and rudder men who flew by the feel of the airplane in real time. It is not hard to envision that one of them could have been caught off guard with a sudden shearing wind gust.

Yet there is more to the rumor mill that must be brought out in order to completely tell the story. Sabotage is one theory. It is believed by some that Mendoza's plane may have been tampered with in some way, and this could have affected his flight control mechanisms. Another theory says that Mendoza's plane was heavily overloaded with cargo, and thus had too much weight for the wings to successfully lift the Tri-Motor off the ground for more than a few feet. This type of flight, where an aircraft cannot lift itself higher into the air and achieve true sustained flight, is known as ground effect. Ground effect is a cushion of air that occurs between the ground and the plane's wings. If a plane is too heavy, too slow, or both, the wings cannot successfully lift it out of this cushioning force.

Another theory is one that, within itself, takes numerous twists and turns. This is the gunshot theory. Some have postulated that because of a live concert performance dispute between Gardel and La Pera, they were arguing on the plane. It is said that La Pera pulled a pistol and shot at Gardel, the bullet missing him but hitting Captain Mendoza and causing him to lose control of the plane. However, this theory is vigorously denied by Gardel's personal secretary, who was a survivor and direct eyewitness to events in the cabin.

José Plaja said that there was not an argument, nor any gunshot within the airplane. Yet, the autopsy of the pilot Mendoza reportedly did reveal evidence of a gunshot wound to the head. If this is the case, then no one really knows where it actually could have come from.

Speculation about this gunshot wound has postulated that the co-pilot on the SCADTA plane stuck his hand out of a side window and shot at the SACO plane out of panic or anger when it came towards them. Further speculation as to where the gunshot may have originated suggests that Mendoza committed suicide when he found himself hopelessly trapped in the burning wreckage. We will never know the whole truth of what happened on that day when aviation took its first recorded victim from what was at that time a fledgling music industry.

But amidst nearly all of the investigations and speculative essays that have focused on this accident, one fact is conveyed over and over. The SACO Tri-Motor did veer towards the SCADTA Tri-Motor. Whether aided by wind shear, an overloaded plane and/or a disabling gunshot, it does appear that personal pride, and perhaps some national pride, may have played a very large role in this tragedy. It has been said that the two most dangerous words ever spoken in aviation are "Watch this." Most people who truly understand the discipline of aviation, and the laws of physics that govern it without prejudice, feel that those two words are still very dangerous within the context of flesh and flying machine.

Carlos Gardel was born poor and illegitimate in Toulouse, France. His mother immigrated to Buenos Aires, Argentina when he was two years old. Starting out as a theater actor, he eventually became an extremely popular Uruguayan nightclub tango singer in the 1920s and 30s. Mostly he toured the Latin-American countries and Spain, but came to Hollywood in the early 1930s to make a few Spanish-speaking motion pictures. It was during his most ambitious promotional tour that he died in the collision of the two Ford Tri-Motor airplanes in Medellin, Columbia. A total of 17 lives were lost in this accident, including Gardel and his lyricist, Alfredo Le Pera. To many Latin Americans, Gardel remains one of the greatest rags-to-riches stories of the twentieth century, personifying and giving certain legitimacy to tango. Originally perceived as low class and vulgar to watch, the tango gained widespread acceptance by all classes of people thanks to Gardel's popularity and influence.

Alfredo Le Pera worked as a theater critic before beginning a playwright career. His first theater play debuted in 1927. By 1931 Le Pera had moved to Paris, France and shortly thereafter began devoting most of his time to writing cinema script and songs almost exclusively for Carlos Gardel. Shortly after traveling to New York in 1935 for their new recording label, RCA Victor, they embarked on the fateful musical tour, which included stops in Puerto Rico, Venezuela, Colombia, Panama, Cuba and Mexico. Although the popular belief is that the two first met in Paris, it stands to reason that they had met earlier since they operated in the same circles in South America. There is evidence that as early as 1923 Gardel and Le Pera had met after one of Gardel's theater performances. There also is evidence that Le Pera was writing tango lyrics at this time.

Roger D. Cain

Aircraft addenda:

Common name: Tri-Motor, Tin Goose
Manufacturer: Ford
First flight of type: June 12, 1926
Total number built: 199
Air Carriers in this accident: Servicio Aereo Columbiano (SACO)
Colombian-German Society of Air Transportation (SCADTA)
Registration number for Gardel's airplane: C-31
Registration number for the SCADTA airplane: F-31
Serial number for Gardel's airplane: 5-AT-112
Serial number for the SCADTA airplane: 5-AT-006
Seats: 14 to 15 passenger
Length: 49 feet, 10 inches
Wingspan: 77 feet, 10 inches
Engines: (3) Pratt & Whitney "Wasp" nine cylinder, air-cooled, radial, piston
Horsepower: 420 hp each
Empty weight (approximate): 7,800 lbs
Gross weight: 13,250 lbs
Service ceiling: 20,000 ft
Cruising range: 515 miles
Cruising speed: 122 mph

* The above photo represents the type of aircraft and not necessarily the exact model involved in the accident.

Personal addenda:

Carlos Gardel: actor, singer
b. December 11, 1890: Toulouse, France
d. June 24, 1935: Medellin, Columbia, South America
Buried: Cemeterio De La Chacarita, Buenos Aires, Argentina, South America

Alfredo Le Pera: lyricist
b. June 8, 1900: Sao Paulo, Brazil
d. June 24, 1935: Medellin, Columbia, South America
Buried: South America

Jane Froman

Tamara

February 22, 1943

As a flight instructor, I tell my students before their first night flight that if they find it hard to navigate or land the airplane in the daytime, then it will be ten times harder at night. There are fewer visual cues at night to help the pilot discern height and judge distance (known as depth perception) as well as numerous illusions that can fool the eye. These illusions that fool the eye, in turn, fool the brain and can adversely affect the pilot's judgment. Over water, depth perception is difficult even in daylight. Under certain conditions, waves from a height of 50 feet can deceptively look the same as those from a height of 1,000 feet. It could therefore, certainly be held to reason that a water landing at night, which was the scenario surrounding this accident, can harbor significant risk. Along with other factors such as adverse weather and pilot fatigue, a depth perception problem could have been a contributing factor that led to this aviation tragedy.

Jane Froman studied voice at the Cincinnati Conservatory of Music from 1928 to 1930. Even before her graduation she began singing on the radio and doing commercials. Her singing career soared and in 1933 she moved to New York to allow greater opportunities to bear fruit. They did. By 1938 she had performed with the Ziegfield Follies and starred in musical films. In May 1941 Froman began performing in USO shows for United States troops and was one of the first performers to entertain troops overseas. On February 22, 1943, while on a trip to Europe to do a USO show, she was a passenger on board the famous Pan American World Airways B-314 flying boat, the "Yankee Clipper."

The Yankee Clipper was one of six long-distance flying boats built by the Boeing Aircraft Company specifically for Pan Am. Each of the B-314s had "Clipper" in the name. The Yankee Clipper was the first airplane to begin transatlantic airmail service on May 20, 1939, but it was the Dixie Clipper that inaugurated transatlantic passenger service on June 28, 1939. However, all of the Clipper ships were to transport passengers as well as airmail on their intercontinental flights. None of the flying boats was able to land on dry ground, thus restricting them to over-water flights only. They were the largest commercial planes to fly until Boeing's 747 jumbo jet took to the air in the 1970s.

On the night of February 22, 1943, the Yankee Clipper was approaching to touch down on the Tagus river in Lisbon, Portugal, arriving after a long but routine transatlantic trip. It was night and the crew was most likely tired. Additionally, there was a storm in progress. While making a descending left turn to settle on the river, the left wingtip contacted the water. The plane probably began to cartwheel immediately and it was destroyed in the crash. The pilot, Captain Rod Sullivan, died in the accident. Of the 39 people on board this plane, 25 perished, including singer/actress Tamara and novelist Ben Robertson. Froman exited the plane with a compound fracture to her right leg, her left leg gashed severely below the knee, two broken ribs and multiple fractures to her right arm. Physicians actually wanted to amputate one of her legs, but were able to save it.

Froman remained unable to walk for some time as a result of her injuries but continued to perform in a wheelchair. In 1945 she performed with the USO in Europe on crutches for the United States' occupation forces. She underwent numerous operations to repair injuries sustained in the crash and in late 1948 she finally was able to walk without crutches for the first time in more than five years. However, she was never able to walk as well as she had before the accident. It is interesting to note that on the night of the Yankee Clipper accident, the airplane's co-pilot, John Curtis Burn, kept Froman afloat. She married Flight Officer Burn on March 12, 1948. They divorced in 1956.

The other musical performer aboard this flight was a young, up-and-coming starlet who went by the stage-name Tamara. In 1914, during the Bolshevik revolution, Tamara Drasin's father Boris, a tailor, escaped to New York City. Her mother Hinda, an amateur singer, fled first with their two children to relatives in another region of their native Ukraine, then to eastern Poland, surviving many hardships and terror-filled moments. The family was finally reunited in 1922 in New York after eight years of separation. Young Tamara had learned many Russian folksongs during her childhood and she had perfected her voice. By the age of 17, Tamara Drasin had become a bright student and was also an accomplished guitarist and singer. However, when faced with the decision as to whether to take her high school final exams or rehearse for a small-time musical playing in the Bronx, she chose to rehearse. The gamble paid off when the musical moved to Broadway. It is believed that her high school eventually awarded her a diploma despite her decision.

Between 1927 and 1933, Drasin performed in numerous Broadway musicals. The most famous of these was Max Gordon's 1933 production of Jerome Kern's "Roberta." For the first time Tamara performed using only her first name, playing the role of Stephanie, a Russian princess. "Roberta" ran for a year on Broadway, some saying that the long run was because of the incredible way Tamara sang the new song, "Smoke Gets In Your Eyes." This particular song is probably best known today from the 1959 number 1 hit version recorded by the vocal group, The Platters. Tamara entered films in 1935 when she appeared in the movie "Sweet Surrender." In what was to be a short-lived musical called "Right This Way," Tamara introduced another song titled "I'll Be Seeing You." This song became a huge ballad hit during World War II and later was recorded by many famous artists. As was Froman, Tamara also was enroute to Europe to entertain troops with the USO show. She was 34 years old when this accident took her life.

Archives & Special Collections, Otto G. Richter Library,
University of Miami, Coral Gables, Florida

Aircraft addenda:

Common name: Boeing 314, (Yankee) Clipper, Clipper Ship, Flying Boat
Manufacturer: Boeing
Date the type began service: 1939
Air Carrier for this flight: Pan American World Airways
Registration number for this airplane: NC18603
Serial number for this airplane: 1990
Seats: 74 daytime passenger seats, 40 recliner seats for long night flights
Length: 106 feet, 0 inches
Wingspan: 152 feet, 0 inches
Engines: (4) Wright GR-2600 Twin Cyclone, 14 cylinder, air-cooled, radial, piston
Horsepower: 1,600 hp each
Empty weight (approximate): 50,268 lbs
Gross weight: 82,500 lbs
Service ceiling: 13,400 ft
Range: 3,500 miles
Cruising speed: 180 mph

* The above photo represents the type of aircraft and not necessarily the exact model involved in the accident.

Personal addenda:

Ellen Jane Froman: singer, actress
b. November 10, 1907: St. Louis, Missouri
d. April 22, 1980: Columbia, Missouri
Buried: Columbia Cemetery: Columbia, Missouri

Tamara Drasin (Tamara): singer, actress
b. January or February 1909: near Odessa, Russia (currently the country of Ukraine)
d. February 22, 1943: Lisbon, Portugal
Cremated. The ashes rest at Roosevelt Cemetery in Roosevelt, New Jersey

Glenn Miller

December 15, 1944

Next to the disappearance of Amelia Earhart, the vanishing of Glenn Miller is perhaps one of the greatest of all aviation mysteries. If there was an official aviation accident investigation into the death of Major Glenn Miller, there certainly is no accident report to document that inquiry. It is possible that since a war was raging at the time of the disappearance, there were no expendable resources to allow any large scale investigation. However, it is likely that once the military command realized that Major Miller's plane was missing, they searched as best they could. Nevertheless, to this day, neither the airplane, its passengers nor any irrefutable evidence from a wreck site has ever been found and positively identified. Consequently, there are very few facts known other than those few that were documented before, during and after the flight.

The time was World War II. The place of departure was a small airfield called Twinwood Farm, three miles north of Bedford, England. The first landing was scheduled to be made at Villacoublay, 25 miles west-southwest of Paris, France. Somewhere in between, the plane seemingly vanished without even a single radio message ever being received from it. The military eventually classified it as a missing aircraft.

Glenn Miller was a huge star of his day. His civilian band was one of the most popular dance bands of the Swing Era. After some ups and downs in the business, Miller finally signed with RCA Victor in 1939. In 1941 one of his songs, "Chattanooga Choo Choo," became the first record to sell a million copies in nearly 20 years. RCA Victor rewarded Miller with a gold lacquered version of the record to celebrate the event. This occurrence marked the first awarding of a "gold record." The symbolic gesture of the gold record was adopted by the recording industry over ten years later and has continued ever since. However, the gold record award is now given to recognize records that have sold only a half million copies.

When America entered the war in Europe in 1941, Miller wanted to serve his country. Too old to be drafted, he tried to volunteer with the United States Navy. The Navy turned him down but Miller promptly went to the Army and persuaded them to let him form a morale-building band for them. He entered the United States Army Air Corps as a Captain in late 1942 and proceeded to select for his band those servicemen who had belonged to the best bands in America prior to that time. He put together the 50-member band at Yale University, officially called the 418th Army Air Force Band.

In 1944, his band was dispatched to England as "The American Band of the Supreme Allied Command." They were attached to the Supreme Headquarters of the Allied Expeditionary Forces in London and initially were quartered at 25 Sloane Court. This location turned out to be right in the middle of "Buzz Bomb Alley," an area where nights were sleepless due to the nearly constant barrage of German V-1 bombs.

Realizing the extreme risk, Captain Miller arranged to have his band moved to Milton Ernest near Bedford, England. The move turned out to be just in time as the morning after the group's evacuation, a German V-1 "buzz bomb" hit their old quarters, destroying the building and killing more than a hundred people. None were Miller band members. Captain Miller reportedly told his band manager, Lieutenant Don W. Haynes, something on the order of, "As long as luck stays with us, we have nothing to worry about."

Miller and his band spent 18-hour days broadcasting, recording and performing for the troops. In August 1944 he was promoted to the rank of Major. On August 25 he christened a Boeing B-17 Flying Fortress bomber with nose art painted and named after his famous theme song, "Moonlight Serenade." However, this plane was shot down during a combat bombing mission over Europe shortly thereafter on September 5, 1944. The luck would not get better as Miller himself would end up missing, and presumed lost, only slightly more than three months later.

By December of 1944, the allied forces were pushing well into the heart of Europe and the Germans were on the retreat for the most part. Hitler, however, had a counter-attack brewing. This last major offensive by the Nazis, known as the Battle of the Bulge, started just a day after what was to be Miller's fateful flight. Major Miller and his band had been ordered to travel to Paris, France to be closer to the fighting troops. Lieutenant Haynes had already gone ahead of the band to arrange sleeping quarters but had subsequently returned to England. On December 14, Lieutenant Haynes apparently ran into a Lieutenant Colonel named Norman F. Baessell. The two men agreed that Major Miller could ride to Paris with Baessell on General Donald R. Goodrich's utility plane. Glenn Miller left on this flight on December 15, bound for Paris, to finalize the arrangements for his band. Lieutenant Haynes was one of the last people to see Miller alive as recorded by Haynes in his personal diary titled "Minus One." This diary should be considered part of the factual record, as it is a firsthand eyewitness account. It reads in part:

"As the Colonel talked, the sound of the motor over the far end of the field indicated the plane was in a turn, and a couple minutes later it came through the heavy overcast directly over the center of the field. . .circled the field once, and evidently Morgan [John R.S. Morgan, the plane's pilot] *had taken a look at the windsock on the control tower, and came down into the wind which was blowing from West to East, and driving the drizzle in an easterly direction. . .We climbed back into the staff car and drove out to the end of the airstrip and Morgan taxied back down the strip and turned around alongside the car. . .leaving the motor running he opened the door of this small nine-place cabin job and greeted us with a wave. "Hi", he said. "Sorry I'm late, - ran into heavy squalls, but the weather is supposed to be clearing over the continent".....The Colonel handed his bag to Morgan, and went back to the car for the case of empty champagne bottles he was taking to Paris (bottles are scarce in Paris and unless you have the empties they won't sell anyone a case of champagne to take out). . .I shook hands with Morgan as I tossed Glenn's B-4 bag through the open cabin door. . .Glenn and the Colonel climbed aboard, - the Colonel seated himself in the co-pilot's seat and Glenn sat in a bucket seat directly back of the Colonel facing the side of the ship. . .Morgan climbed into the pilot's seat, and as they all fastened their seat belts I waved a goodbye and, "Happy landings and good luck, - I'll see you in Paris tomorrow" I said as Glenn replied "Thanks Haynsie, - we may need it!". . .I closed the door, secured the catch*

and stepped away from the prop wash, as Morgan waved and revved-up the motor. . .he released the brakes and they started down the runway gaining speed, and were airborne, . . .in less than a minute they climbed into the overcast and out of sight. . .I got back into the staff car and drove back to Bedford and the ARC Officer's Club. . .it was 0145 [p.m.] when they took off and should arrive at Orly Field, Paris in two-and-a-half to three hours."

The plane was a Noorduyn Norseman, a Canadian built aircraft manufactured in Montreal, Canada. The type had been used as a civilian aircraft before the war and later as a Royal Canadian Air Force (RCAF) trainer for radio and navigational purposes. The Norseman was a large, single-engine airplane with non-retractable landing gear, a high-wing design and was constructed with the well-known tube and fabric method. The plane was built to be very strong and could handle very rugged working conditions. It could carry a ton of freight or eight passengers. The engine was considered a very reliable powerplant. The paint scheme was silver, with black painted on the top of the nose to reduce glare on the pilot's eyes.

From Lieutenant Haynes' detailed diary, we know that Major Glenn Miller boarded the plane that was to take him and Lieutenant Colonel Norman F. Baessell to Paris but that is where much of the known story ends. Initially, the fact that Miller's plane was not even reported missing for days was puzzling to me. However, the reasons for this seem obvious now. First, it was wartime and the plane itself was a small, single-engine transport mostly used by army brass. As such, it had to be considered as a small part of the overall war effort. This fact is especially significant considering that the German counter-offensive diverted so much attention so soon after Miller's plane went missing.

Second, Major Miller was listed as a passenger under the name Major Alton G. Miller, so his famous name may not have been recognized right away. Finally, the flight apparently was regarded as a type A mission, or a non-operational flight. There has always been some speculation that the pilot, Flight Officer John R. S. Morgan, was not adept with flight by instruments, although from the diary we know that he certainly found Twinwood Farm and descended through a heavy overcast to land there without any known problems. Also from the diary we can assume that Flight Officer Morgan was aware of not only the immediate weather, but also the forecast along his route of flight. Still, no flight plan has ever been found and he apparently did not tell anyone the exact route he intended to follow.

There is another eyewitness account from Captain Joseph R. Dobson, a C-47 pilot who also was at Twinwood Farm on December 15, 1944. The account not only has Glenn Miller being at Twinwood Farm but also departing that airfield. Captain Dobson stated that just after noon on December 15, he was in the weather shack on the field getting briefed about the weather for his executive priority flight mission, with which he had orders to proceed even without a weather clearance (a directive that only a General could issue). He looked around when three men walked into the building.

The three men were Lieutenant Colonel Baessell, Major Miller and Lieutenant Haynes. According to Dobson, he and Baessell engaged in a heated conversation about flying in the worsening weather conditions that day (contrary to Morgan's comment about the forecast of clearing, which may have been said more for calming his passengers than anything else) but Baessell assured Dobson that he had a priority mission authorization from General Goodrich. Dobson also remembered that he saw a look on Miller's face that supposedly turned from worry to dread when Baessell decided to continue with the flight despite the weather. Captain Dobson remembers saying "Goodbye and good luck." to Major Miller, who replied, "Thanks, we're going to need it." Dobson watched as the three men got back into their car and drove out to meet Morgan's plane. He then watched as the plane departed and climbed into the overcast layer of clouds.

Rumors abounded after Glenn Miller vanished. One report supposedly stated that Glenn Miller made it to France only to die of a heart attack in the arms of a French prostitute in a Paris brothel. It was alleged that this situation precipitated a cover-up by United States intelligence to keep his good name and legend alive. Additionally, and more importantly, the alleged cover-up was to protect the morale of the allied troops. Another theory had him defecting to the Germans. Still another theory had him surviving the crash with a mutilated body, and then living in seclusion. Some said he was a secret agent. Yet another theory had Miller faking his death, then being seen by many people for years to come, after which he allegedly died in England of lung cancer. Finally, some said an enemy fighter had shot down his plane over the English Channel. These colorful theories underscore the fact that no one really knows for sure what actually happened. However, we do know that on Christmas Eve, 1944, the official news was released: Major Alton Glenn Miller was lost. All that remains to this day, as far as official documentation, are the "missing aircraft" and "missing air crew" reports from the military archives.

So, what could have happened? There is a question about the plane's lack of de-icing equipment for the flight. Could the airframe or the engine's carburetor have iced up? Certainly the conditions were ripe for carburetor icing because there was visible moisture and the outside air temperature was documented at about 34 degrees Fahrenheit, but the airplane was equipped with carburetor heat and a pilot's training does include how, when and where to use it. Once the plane had climbed to just 1,000 feet above the ground, the atmospheric temperature would have been below the freezing mark. Inside the clouds, and with the temperature below freezing, the airframe ice build-up could have been rapid, and this certainly would have been a significant factor. Airplanes do not fly very well with large amounts of ice clinging to them.

Another lingering question surrounds the plane's actual route from England to France, over the English Channel. Did Flight Officer Morgan go east of London, or west of London for his flight? Which route seems the most likely? Some people believe they know, but no one knows for sure. All of these questions will remain unanswered until the plane is actually found, and even then some answers might remain elusive. There is an account from a British flight of bombers which, after aborting their mission over Germany, returned to England, but not before jettisoning the deadly payload of bombs into the English Channel. Among all the rumors and questions, this bomber flight is one of a limited number of available first-hand accounts. It is an eyewitness account that supports Morgan's route west of London. The bomber account goes like this:

On December 15, 1944, a total of 138 British Lancaster four-engine bombers took off from various bases in England to bomb the German town of Siegen. Flight Lieutenant Victor Gregory piloted one of the Lancasters, serial number NF973 of the 149 Squadron, out of Methwold in Norfolk. It was his, and his crew's, first mission. Gregory has stated in interviews after the war that the weather conditions on that particular day were misty, with ground fog, but a clear sky was just above the fog layer. Unfortunately, the 100 or so P-51 Mustangs that were scheduled to escort the Lancaster formation could not take off, so the mission was aborted while the bombers were enroute. This meant that the cargo of bombs had to be jettisoned into the English Channel because a landing could not be safely made with the heavy, sometimes sensitive and very dangerous payload of bombs aboard.

The Avro Lancaster carried some of the heaviest bomb loads during World War II, the heaviest being a single 22,000-pound "Grand Slam" bomb. On most missions, however, it carried about 12,000 to 14,000-pounds of bombs. Four liquid-cooled Rolls Royce Merlin V-12 engines powered the plane, each producing almost 1,600 horsepower. On this particular flight the bomb load consisted of one 4,000-pound "cookie," also known as a "blockbuster," and 8,000 pounds of other bombs that consisted mainly of 500-pound containers of 4-pound incendiary bombs. The 4-pound incendiaries, packed in honeycomb-like clusters of

30 bombs each, would spread out in all directions during their release and descent. There were three Channel areas designated for jettisoning bombs. One of these "prohibited areas" was centered at 50° 15′ N, 00° 15′ E. The center of this "Southern Jettison Area" was located just 35 miles south of a prominent Great Britain landmark known as Beachy Head. The diameter of this circular bomb jettison area was about 20 miles across. It is possible that a total of 100,000 to 200,000 of the incendiary bombs fell into the Southern Jettison area from all the bombers during this aborted mission.

When Lancaster NF973 reached this area, bombardier Ivor Pritchard looked through his bombsight at the fog below to see if any planes or ships had strayed into the area. When he saw none, he dropped the bombs and then reported that they were exploding. Navigator Fred Shaw wanted to see the bombs explode, so he moved from his assigned position to a small "bubble" window in the side of the fuselage (Figure 3-1). Suddenly, Pritchard shouted, "There's a kite down there!" The term "kite" was used in the Royal Air Force (RAF) as slang to describe any unidentifiable aircraft. Shaw recognized the plane immediately as a Norseman because he had trained in them in Canada. Shaw then watched as the southbound Norseman dropped its left wing and seemed to dive just before he lost sight of it under the Lancaster's wing. He then heard the rear gunner Harry Fellows shout, "There's a kite gone in! Did you see it?" Shaw replied, "I saw it."

When the Lancaster returned to Methwold, the Gregory crew did not undergo a formal debriefing. This aborted mission was not considered an operational flight, so they were not required to report to the Operations Room. Instead, weary and disappointed from the thought that their first mission would not count toward their total, they dispersed. No one in command was told about the small plane's possible demise. With this delay in time the strong currents and tides must have washed away any specific evidence, even though the wings and other debris of the Norseman may have floated for a while. With no official record in the Operations Record Books, we are left with only first-person recollections like that of the Gregory crew. However, most of the survivors of this bomber flight remembered the events that unfolded very clearly. Yet, only later did they piece together the puzzle and begin to believe that they not only saw, but also actually destroyed or mortally damaged, Glenn Miller's plane. Was the "kite" that they saw plunge into the cold, dark water of the southern English Channel really the Norseman in which Glenn Miller was riding? Consider this next story.

This next eyewitness testimony comes from a group of World War II combat glider pilots who were ordered to ferry seven airplanes from England to Chartres, France. The glider pilots were all combat veterans of the 74th Troop Carrier (T.C.) Squadron, 434th T.C. Group, who had landed their gliders during D-Day and other campaigns. The planes to be ferried on this mission were two-seat L-1C liaison airplanes made by the Stinson Aircraft Company. This airplane type commonly was known as the "Vigilant" and was used for medical evacuation, aerial observation and artillery spotting. The group of eight pilots, led by Lieutenant David J. Kull, was ordered from its home base in Aldermaston, England to Burtonwood, England, where on December 11, 1944, they would pick up the Vigilants and begin their journey to France (Figure 3-2). That first day they made it to a P-38 aircraft reconnaissance base at Hempstead, northwest of London, where they refueled and stayed overnight.

The next day, December 12, they flew back to their base at Aldermaston, which is near Oxford, to eat breakfast and then proceeded to Bexhill, which is an RAF base on the English Channel coast near Eastbourne. It was at Bexhill where they were grounded for a few days due to bad weather, and it also was at Bexhill where they would get their clearance to cross the Channel. On the morning of departure, the pilots arrived at the flight line to see a UC-64 Norseman parked on the ramp close to their L-1Cs. The weather was not ideal but they were told to continue with their mission and follow the Norseman, which in turn was going to follow a (still to this day) unidentified RAF amphibian that supposedly had good instrumentation. Shortly after departure on a southerly heading, the entire flight procession was over the Channel and forced to descend to less than 300 feet to stay under the overcast. Only a short time after this descent to low altitude, heavy explosions, shock waves and columns of water all around began to rock and buffet the light planes. Immediately there was chatter over the radio between the planes asking what was going on. It was then that one or two of the glider pilots saw, through a break in the overcast, heavy Lancaster bombers jettisoning their bombs.

When the barrage of explosions finally ended, everyone in the liaison aircraft was badly shaken but unhurt, and their airplanes were soaked with water. They then noticed that the Norseman and amphibian were gone from the formation, but there was nothing that could be done except to continue on towards the French coast. Sometime soon after this "friendly fire" encounter, one of the L-1Cs developed an oil leak and had to land at Rouen, France for repairs. All eight pilots allegedly remained in Rouen that night and delivered their aircraft to the airfield in Chartres the next day (Figure 3-3). However, the question remains as to whether or not the Norseman they flew with that day was the plane that was carrying Glenn Miller. Once again there is no definitive answer. Certainly the time of day between Miller's flight (afternoon) and the departure of the liaison aircraft (morning) is inconsistent. Yet this story corroborates the Lancaster crew's story about a similar type of plane being seen and possibly disappearing in the Southern Jettison Area. People will continue to argue the scenario until indisputable proof is found.

If a Norseman did crash into the English Channel in the Southern Jettison Area, there is only an outside chance that discovery will ever be attempted. Shipping traffic now uses that area very heavily. In fact, there are two one-way shipping lanes near the old jettison area in which over 100 large vessels pass each day. Considering this modern-day, narrow, busy shipping corridor, along with the very real possibility of live bombs still lying on the bottom, and you have the ingredients for an extremely dangerous underwater search environment. Still, while it is entirely feasible that someone with modern sonar and underwater imaging equipment might brave the Channel's hazards, one must still take into consideration the reality that this was a tube and fabric aircraft. If one of the Lancaster's bombs had damaged the plane and it subsequently crashed hard into the water, surely the airframe was badly broken up. The swift, corrosive, salt-water currents of the Channel most likely have had time to eat away at any remnants of the plane, such that it is doubtful if much of the wreckage still exists. Couple all of the above with the fact that no one knew Morgan's flight path and no one even knows where to begin looking for Miller's plane. There are arguments to suggest that the pilot actually could have taken an easterly direction, before turning south, in order to reach Paris. Based on this theory, one salvage diver has claimed that he actually found Miller's plane in the eastern part of the Channel, although no hard evidence has ever proved that supposition.

While we will never really know what happened to Glenn Miller's plane until it is actually located, it is a very real possibility that the plane may never be found. Surely if the plane went down anywhere into the icy December waters of the English Channel, Miller and the two others most likely would have died from hypothermia within 20 minutes, even if they had survived the impact. Their bodies have long since been consumed by time. Certainly having no closure to the obscurities of this story only serves to compound and feed the speculation surrounding this aviation mystery. Still, no matter how one perceives this event, one irrefutable fact is that the world lost Glenn Miller during World War II. The United States Army officially declared Major Glenn Miller dead on December 18, 1945. Why it took one year and three days to do so is yet another unexplained and puzzling aspect to possibly consider in this whole enigmatic tale.

Miller's military awards include the Bronze Star, the World War II Victory Medal, the American Campaign Medal, the European, African and Middle Eastern Campaign Medal, and the Marksman Badge with Carbine and Pistol Bars. His Bronze Star Medal Citation reads: "Major Glenn Miller (Army Serial No.

0505273), Air Corps, United States Army, for meritorious service in connection with military operations as Commander of the Army Air Force Band (Special), from 9 July 1944 to 15 December 1944. Major Miller, through excellent judgment and professional skill, conspicuously blended the abilities of the outstanding musicians, comprising the group, into a harmonious orchestra whose noteworthy contribution to the morale of the armed forces has been little less than sensational. Major Miller constantly sought to increase the services rendered by his organization, and it was through him that the band was ordered to Paris to give this excellent entertainment to as many troops as possible. His superior accomplishments are highly commendable and reflect the highest credit upon himself and the armed forces of the United States."

USAF

Aircraft addenda:

Common name: Norseman
USAAF designation: UC-64A (U.S. Navy Designation: JA-1)
Manufacturer: Noorduyn Aircraft Ltd., Montreal, Canada
First flight of prototype: November 1935
Total production: 904 were built between 1937 and 1959
Serial number for this plane: 44-70285 (44 being the year of manufacture)
Mission: Cargo or personnel transport
Length: 32 feet, 0 inches
Height: 10 feet, 3 inches
Wingspan: 51 feet, 6 inches
Engine (Mk. IV): (1) Pratt & Whitney Wasp, R-1340-AN-1
Horsepower: nine-cylinder radial producing 600 h.p.
Empty weight (approximate): 4,680 lb.
Gross weight: 7,400 lb.
Service ceiling: 17,000 ft
Range: 1,150 miles
Cruising speed: 148 mph

* The above photo represents the type of aircraft and not necessarily the exact model involved in the accident.

Personal addenda:

Alton Glenn Miller: Trombonist and bandleader
b. March 1, 1904: Clarinda, Iowa
d. December 15, 1944: Location unknown
As there was not a body recovered, there was never a formal burial. However, a cenotaph was erected in the American Military Cemetery in Hamm, Luxembourg with the name Alton Miller. In April 1992, a memorial headstone was placed in Arlington National Cemetery in Glenn Miller's memory. It is located in Memorial Section H, Number 464-A on Wilson Drive.

LT DON W. HAYNES (CHAUFFEUR)
MAJOR ALTON GLENN MILLER (PASSENGER)
LT/COL NORMAN F. BAESSELL (PASSENGER)
F/O JOHN R. S. MORGAN (PILOT)

PRELUDE TO FATAL FLIGHT OF UC-64 "NORSEMAN" #470286 DECEMBER 15, 1944

Note: This is a composite photograph. Composite photo courtesy of Thomas W. Myrick.

Date	Hour	Aircraft Type and No.	Pilot	Duty	Remarks (Including results of bombing, gunnery, exercises, etc.)	Flying Times Day	Flying Times Night
					Time Carried Forward:—	124.50	70.45
14.12.44	1500	N.F. 970 Lancaster	F/o Gregory	Navigator.	Air Test	1.15	
15.12.44	1200	N.F. 973 Lancaster	F/o Gregory	Navigator	Ops. Siegen. Cancelled. Jettison Southern Area	2.45	
17.12.44	1900	H.K. 652 Lancaster	F/o Gregory	Navigator	Bullseye London.		3.15
18.12.44	1500	H.K. 646 Lancaster	F/o Gregory	Navigator,	G.H., Ely, Av. Error 316 yds.	1.40	
19.12.44	1130	N.G. 355 Lancaster	F/o Gregory	Navigator	Ops. Trier, Landed Manston	4.50	
23.12.44	1130	N.G. 355 Lancaster	F/o Gregory	Navigator	Elevators Holed.—Landed Fido. Manston – Base	0.35	
24.12.44	1700	Lancaster	F/o Gregory	Navigator	Ops. Bonne–Hangelar Airfield (Fighter Attack over ▲)		5.25
28.12.44	1400	H.K.652. Lancaster	F/o Gregory	Navigator	G.H., Friday Bridge., G.H.—U/S	1.05	
29.12.44	1230	H.K. 699 Lancaster	F/o Gregory	Navigator	Ops.-Koblentz Flak Hits Landed Manston (Tank Holed)	4.55	
31.12.44	1430	H.K. 699 Lancaster	F/o Gregory	Navigator	Manston – Base	0.35	
					Total Time:—	142.30	79.25

Figure 3-1
Actual page from Navigator Fred Shaw's logbook

HEADQUARTERS
434TH TROOP CARRIER GROUP
APO 133 U S Army

E/H/3

11 December 1944

OPERATIONS ORDER)

NUMBER   128   )

_E X T R A C T_

1.   The following Officers will proceed to BURTONWOOD by MA on or about 11 December 1944 reporting to Maj Ott for further instructions. Purpose of ferrying aircraft to Far Shore.

    1st LT DAVID J. KULL, O-674271, AC
    2nd LT KENNETH R. COFFMAN, O-1996164, AC
    2nd Lt ROY B. MEYERS, O-1998199, AC
    2nd LT IRWIN J. MORALES, O-1996165, AC
    1st LT LESLIE L. VAN PELT, O-521590, AC
    2nd LT HENRY W. STAPLES, O-887204, AC
    F/O VALTON H. BRAY, T-123363, AC
    2nd Lt ROBERT C. KIRCHMAN, O-887185, AC

    Upon completion of temp dy pers will return to their proper station, 467. Auth: VOCO 53rd TCW.

    *   *   *   *   *   *   *   *

    By order of Colonel WHITACRE:

MARVIN W. HEATH,
Major, Air Corps,
Group S-3.

OFFICIAL: *Clarence G. Weishar*
CLARENCE G. WEISHAR,
1st Lt., Air Corps,
Ass't. S-3.

C O N F I D E N T I A L

- 1 -

Figure 3-2

AIRCRAFT DELIVERY RECEIPT   SPECIAL INSTRUCTIONS

_____

_____

Capt. David J. Kull   12-16-44   L/C
FROM PILOT   DATE   AIRCRAFT TYPE

41-18957   590-   ~~~~~ FLIGHT TEST
AIRCRAFT NO.   STATION AND UNIT

Pfc McKinnis A-40   12-12-44 BURTONWOOD
SIGNATURE OF RECIPIENT   DATE   PLACE

DESTINATION _____
                    STATION AND UNIT
                    MY FLYING TIME WAS ____7____ HRS. __05__ MIN.

_____   FERRYING SQUADRON
            OPERATIONS OFFICER
            SIGNATURE OF PILOT ___*David J Kull Capt AC*___

326 FS FORM
NO. 327   1 ST COPY RETURNED TO FERRYING SQUADRON OPERATIONS

Figure 3-3

C O P Y

SUBJ: MISSING AIRPLANE

    HQ VIII AFSC

    AAF Sta 506, APO 636

G-1 SECTION, SHAEF (MAIN)
  Attn GEN BARKER   P

  thru: Eighth AF, AAF Sta 101, APO 634

                                     20 Dec 44

Info copy: SHAEF (REAR)
            CG, US Strategic AF in Europe

    VIII AFSC-D-832-G-27-A

CONFIRMING VERBAL INFORMATION TO G-1 SHAEF REAR C-64 AIRPLANE

NUMBER 44-70285 MISSING AND UNREPORTED SINCE DEPARTURE

TWINWOOD FIELD 1355 HOURS 15 DECEMBER FOR FRANCE PILOT FLIGHT

OFFICER MORGAN TWO PASSENGERS INCLUDING MAJOR GLENN MILLER.

                                      EARLY

OFFICIAL:

ALBERT G. BUELOW
Major, AGD
Adjutant General

C O P Y

DECLASSIFIED BY AUTHORITY OF NND DECLASSIFICATION PROJECT 785072,
H. D. MAYER, NARS, SEPTEMBER 10, 1982.

HEADQUARTERS
2D STRATEGIC AIR DEPOT
APO 636

G—A—4

AAF Sta 547.
22 December 1944.

704

SUBJECT: Missing Air Crew Report.

TO: Commanding Officer, VIII Air Force SvC, AAF Sta 506, APO 636, US Army.

Inclosed herewith ETO CAS Form 2 and Missing Air Crew Report per verbal request Lt Colonel Traester, 21 December 1944.

For the Commanding Officer:

50848

RALPH S. CRAMER
Capt, Air Corps
Adjutant.

2 Incls:
Incl 1 - ETO Cas Form 2
Incl 2 - Missing Air Crew Report

704   1st Ind.   C—C—2
HQ VIII AFSC AAF STA 506 APO 636 US ARMY.   23 DEC 1944

TO: Commanding General, Eighth Air Force, AAF Station 101, APO 634, US Army.

1. Forwarded in compliance with Cir 94, Hq European T of Opns US Army, dated 31 August 1944.

2. Paragraph 10a(4) cited circular complied with per TWX VIIIAFSC-D-832-G-27-A, this Hq, 20 Dec 44, copy attached.

For the Commanding Officer:

ALBERT G. BUELOW,
Major,   AGD,
Adjutant General.

4 Incls:
Added - 2 Incls.
Incl. 3-ETO Cas Form 2(Lt Col Baessell)(trip)
Incl. 4-Cy TWX VIIIAFSC-20 Dec 44

23310

(Ltr Hq 2d Strategic Air Depot, subj: "Missing Air Crew Report." dtd 22 Dec 44)

319.1.   2nd Ind.   SCU-D-17

HEADQUARTERS EIGHTH AIR FORCE, APO 634, U. S. ARMY.   3 JAN 1945

TO: Commanding General, European Theater of Operations, APO 887, U. S. Army.

    Forwarded in accordance with letter, War Department, TAGO, AG 704 (5 Jul 44)
OB-S-AAF-M, 7 July 1944, subject: "Missing Air Crew Reports".

        For the Commanding General:

                                    H. S. WILSON, Jr.
                                    Major, A.G.D.,
                                    Asst. Adjutant General.

1 Incl:
  Incl.1. Missing Air Crew Report, 2d SAD,
         UC-64A, 44-70285, 15 Dec 44 (in trip)

WAR DEPARTMENT
HEADQUARTERS ARMY AIR FORCES
WASHINGTON

Classification changed
~~by~~ R. A. BRADUNAS, Lt. Col., AC
by P. M. MUENCH, Capt., AC
Date MAR 18 1946

MISSING AIR CREW REPORT

IMPORTANT: This Report will be compiled in triplicate by each Army Air
Forces organization within 48 hours of the time an air crew
member is officially reported missing.

Ripton
1. ORGANIZATION: Location, by Name **Abbotts** ; Command or Air Force **VIII Air Force** SvC
   Group **35th ADG** ; Squadron **Repair** ; Detachment **2d Strategic Air Depot**
2. SPECIFY: Place of Departure **Abbotts Ripton** Course Bordeaux Via A-42
   Target or Intended Destination **Bordeaux** ; Type of Mission **A**
3. WEATHER CONDITIONS AND VISIBILITY AT TIME OF CRASH OR WHEN LAST REPORTED: _
   Unknown
4. GIVE: (a) Day **15** Month **Dec** Year **44** ; Time **1355** ; and Location **Twinwood**
   of last known whereabouts of missing aircraft.
   (b) Specify whether aircraft was last sighted ( ); ~~xxxxxxxxxxxxxxx~~
   ~~xxxxxxxxxxxxxxxxxxxxxxxxxxxxxxxxxxxxx~~ Information not Available ( )
5. AIRCRAFT WAS LOST, OR IS BELIEVED TO HAVE BEEN LOST, AS A RESULT OF: (Check
   only one) Enemy Aircraft ( ); Enemy Anti-Aircraft ( ); Other Circumstances
   as Follows: **Unknown**

6. AIRCRAFT: Type, Model and Series **UC-64A** ; AAF Serial Number **44-70285**
7. NICKNAME OF AIRCRAFT, If Any **Norseman**
8. ENGINES: Type, Model and Series **Radial - 1340 P&W** ; AAF Serial
   Number (a) **Unknown** ; (b) _____ ; (c) _____ (d)
9. INSTALLED WEAPONS (Furnish below Make, Type and Serial Number); **None**
   (a) _____ ; (b) _____ ; (c) _____ ; (d) _____ ;
   (e) _____ ; (f) _____ ; (g) _____ ; (h) _____ ;
   (i) _____ ; (j) _____ ; (k) _____ ; (l) _____ ;
   (m) _____ ; (n) _____ ; (o) _____ ; (p) _____ ;
10. THE PERSONS LISTED BELOW WERE REPORTED AS: ~~xxxxxxxxxxxxxxx~~ _____
    ~~xxxxx~~ Non Battle Casualty

11. NUMBER OF PERSONS ABOARD AIRCRAFT: Crew **1** ; Passengers **2** ; Total **3**
    (Starting with Pilot, furnish the following particulars: If more than 11
    persons were aboard aircraft, list similar particulars on separate sheet
    and attach original to this form.)

Crew Position	Name in Full (Last Name First)	Rank	Serial Number	Current Status
1. Pilot w/	Morgan, John R.S.	F/O	T-190776	Missing AC
2. Passenger w/	Baessell, Norman F.	Lt Col	0-905387	Missing AC
3. Passenger w/	Miller, Alton G.	Major	0-505273	Missing AC
4.				
5.				
6.				
7.				
8.				
9.				
10.				
11.				

12. IDENTIFY BELOW THOSE PERSONS WHO ARE BELIEVED TO HAVE LAST KNOWLEDGE OF AIR-
    CRAFT, AND CHECK APPROPRIATE COLUMN TO INDICATE BASIS FOR SAME:

| | | | Check Only One Column | | | |
Name in Full (Last Name First)	Rank	Serial Number	Contacted by Radio	Last Sighted	Saw Crash	Saw Forced Landing
1. Unknown						
2.						
3.						

13. IF PERSONNEL ARE BELIEVED TO HAVE SURVIVED, ANSWER YES TO ONE OF THE
FOLLOWING STATEMENTS: (a) Parachutes were used ___ ; (b) Persons were seen
walking away from scene of crash ___ ; or (c) Any other reason (Specify)
_____ Unknown
14. ATTACH AERIAL PHOTOGRAPH, MAP, CHART, OR SKETCH, SHOWING APPROXIMATE
LOCATION WHERE AIRCRAFT WAS LAST SEEN OR HEARD FROM.
15. ATTACH EYEWITNESS DESCRIPTION OF CRASH, FORCED LANDING, OR OTHER CIRCUM-
STANCES PERTAINING TO MISSING AIRCRAFT.
16. GIVE NAME, RANK AND SERIAL NUMBER OF OFFICER IN CHARGE OF SEARCH, IF ANY,
INCLUDING DESCRIPTION AND EXTENT ___ None

Date of Report __23 December 1944__

For the Commanding Officer:

(Signature of Preparing Officer)

RALPH O. CRAMER
CAPT, F.A.
ADJUTANT

17. REMARKS OR EYEWITNESS STATEMENTS: None

JAN 22 1945

RECEIVED

Grace Moore

January 26, 1947

In the course of flying an airplane, the two phases of flight which present the largest possibility for danger are the take-off and the landing. It is in these phases where the plane is closest to the ground and flying at the slowest airspeeds. During the take-off phase in a multi-engine transport airplane where the fuel loads are heaviest, one possible risk is the sudden loss of power in one engine, which can seriously affect how the airplane behaves. Another risk is related to visual illusions associated with entering instrument meteorological conditions (IMC) during the take-off and climb-out. Clouds, fog and/or rain can cause IMC, thereby obscuring a pilot's view of the world. Another risk comes from nothing more than outright pilot error. Where does this pilot error come from? It can come from the panic that occurs when a pilot faces an adverse situation. However, most of the time it comes from complacency and/or haste in the cockpit when a pilot is not disciplined enough to take the time to perform his or her job properly.

Flying an airplane with a professional attitude takes discipline. One very important aspect of this discipline is to follow what is known as a checklist. The take-off checklist is used to ascertain that all items have been taken care of properly so that when the aircraft is launched into the air, it will be flyable. Even if the checklist is so well known to a pilot that he or she can go through it from memory, the checklist should be used as a backup to verify that no important item has been missed. The checklist is an insurance item.

All pilots are taught certain basic tasks early in their training. One of these tasks is to check the flight controls throughout their range of motion to make sure that they are not obstructed from moving correctly. These flight controls include the ailerons on the wings and the elevator and rudder on the tail. Installing wind gust locks, or control locks when a plane is parked is a normal practice because this prevents the flight controls from being randomly slammed about by the wind. The checking of flight controls for freedom and full range of motion before flight is on every checklist I have ever seen. While it may become instinctive over time to check flight controls before departure, failure to verify range of motion with a checklist is to break one of the absolute fundamental rules of flight.

Grace Moore was a well-known American opera singer in the second quarter of the twentieth century. Her voice and singing style earned her the nickname "The Tennessee Nightingale." In the 1930s she also starred in some Hollywood operatic musical films. During and after World War II she helped entertain United States troops in occupied Europe. Moore received many honors for her service even though she was a non-combatant during the war. These honors included being decorated as a Chevalier of the Legion of Honor from France. In the United States she also was a commissioned Colonel on the staff of the governor of Tennessee. Miss Moore married Valentin Parera in Cannes, France on July 15, 1931.

On January 26, 1947, following a concert in Copenhagen, Denmark, which reportedly ended in multiple standing ovations and encores, Moore boarded a converted wartime C-47 transport airplane in the livery of KLM Royal Dutch Airlines enroute to Stockholm, Sweden. According to some accounts, the plane climbed to an altitude of approximately 150 feet after take-off where it apparently was found to be uncontrollable. The plane crashed and exploded into a raging fireball only a very short distance from Kobenhavn-Kastrup airport. All 18 passengers and the four crewmembers on board were killed. The probable cause of the crash was determined to be failure by the pilots to remove the elevator control locks. When the pilots took off, they had no ability to properly control the airplane.

Author

Aircraft addenda:

Common names: C-47, Gooney Bird, Dakota, Skytrain
Manufacturer: Douglas Aircraft Company
First flight of prototype: December 17, 1935
Air Carrier for this flight: KLM Royal Dutch Airlines
Registration number for this airplane: PH-TCR
Serial number for this airplane: 25479
Seats: 28 passenger
Length: 64 feet, 6 inches
Wingspan: 95 feet, 0 inches
Engines: (2) Wright Cyclone R-1820, 9 cylinder, air-cooled, radial, piston
Horsepower (approximate): 1200 hp
Empty weight (approximate): 16,970 lbs.
Gross weight: 28,000 lbs.
Service ceiling: 23,200 feet
Fuel capacity: 804 gallons
Range (approximate): 1500 miles
Cruising speed: 160 mph

* The above photo represents the type of aircraft and not necessarily the exact model involved in the accident.

Personal addenda:

Grace Moore: singer, actress
b. December 5, 1898: Slabtown, Cocke County, Tennessee
d. January 26, 1947: Copenhagen, Denmark
Buried: Forest Hills Cemetery, Chattanooga, Tennessee

Buddy Clark

October 2, 1949

The three things that made the Wright Brothers' first flight achievement so monumental were power, control and the sustainment of that flight over level ground. In all of aviation there are very few things which can be spoken of as absolute. One truism of aviation is that gravity always wins. Another truism is that powered aircraft need fuel on board and readily available to stay in the air. Should an airplane run out of fuel, or if the fuel supply is blocked from reaching the engine, powered and sustained flight ceases. At this point, the force of gravity takes over and the airplane begins its return to earth. Takeoffs are optional but landings are not. When an engine quits the landing simply becomes imminent at an unplanned destination.

Such a situation with fuel loss does not necessarily mean that an airplane will drop straight down as if it were a rock dropped off a building. Rather, every airplane has a glide characteristic that determines how far it can fly, usually based on its altitude at the time of the engine loss. Additionally, the pilot still has the ability to control the airplane so that positioning can be attempted for the emergency off-airport landing. In all actuality, there are no excuses for running out of fuel in an airplane. With proper calculation and in-flight management, fuel consumption can be closely monitored. Based upon this fuel consumption, planned re-fueling stops are a way of life to the pilot of a powered airplane.

Buddy Clark and four of his friends were passengers in the chartered Cessna twin-engined airplane that took them for a day of fun and festivities at a college football game north of Los Angeles, California. During the return trip from the game all was going as planned until the pilot, James L. Hayter, found himself with a sputtering engine problem, which was possibly from fuel starvation. To make matters worse, the plane reportedly had to glide down through an overcast cloud layer. Supposedly the pilot admitted later that when the plane emerged below the cloud deck, he did not know exactly where he was.

Where the pilot happened to be was directly over Beverly Boulevard in downtown central Los Angeles. With everything happening very quickly and without much time to do anything but make a hasty decision, he was left with few options. Pilot Hayter decided that Beverly Boulevard was the best choice for the emergency landing. This decision was made despite the fact that the city street was heavily laden with automobile traffic. However, before the aircraft struck power lines and treetops, the motorists were somehow able to see the plane and had time to pull off the main traffic lanes.

Portions of the tail section were torn off the plane before it hit the ground and, according to accounts, one parked truck was struck by some parts of the plane. Fortunately, no one was in the truck at the time and, miraculously, the hurtling debris and wreckage hurt no one on the ground. The time was approximately 9 p.m. PST. By all accounts, the passengers of the plane were thrown clear of the crash and almost everyone survived. Buddy Clark was not so fortunate. He was the only person killed in this accident.

The young Buddy Clark, born Samuel Goldberg, was smart and athletic. At one time in his youth he had plans to become a professional baseball player and an attorney, but it was his love of music and singing ability that exerted the stronger pull. By the time he was 17 he was singing at local Boston pubs, weddings and other gatherings. It was at one of these events that he was offered a chance to take music lessons, which led directly to his professional career as a vocalist. Appearing for nine years at a Boston radio station singing on morning programs six days a week and two evening shows, Samuel Goldberg's performing name was changed to Buddy Clark.

His smooth baritone voice eventually allowed him to take a chance and venture to New York City where he hoped to join a big band as a vocalist. He was not disappointed when he was invited to debut as a singer with the Benny Goodman Band on the "Let's Dance" radio show in 1934. Between 1936 and 1939, Buddy Clark was billed on several other top radio shows including the "Hit Parade." It was at this time that he began another activity that would eventually lead to his most famous work, yet ironically it was this job that would make him more obscure to the public. This work was as a sometimes-unaccredited studio recording artist and "ghost singer" for film productions. By all accounts, he was well liked, extremely talented and easy to work with.

Between 1937 and 1942, Clark was hired to do the singing in a number of films where the audience saw only the face of the billed movie star. Despite his lack of movie star good looks, his smooth crooner-type voice always carried him through and got him the job. Clark made a few hit records with the big bands and famous orchestras of the time. By 1942, World War II was raging and Buddy Clark wanted to do his part. He enlisted in the United States Army and served as a singer with many of the morale boosting military bands for three years until the war's end. After the war he resumed his career as a recording artist and "movie voice." His most successful song, "Linda," was recorded at this time and became a number 1 hit in 1946. He also recorded big hit duets with Dinah Shore and Doris Day. He was 37 years old when he died.

Roger D. Cain

Aircraft addenda:

Common name: T-50, Bobcat, Bamboo Bomber, Crane, C-78, UC-78, AT-17, JRC-1
Manufacturer: Cessna
First flight of type: 1939
Total number built: 5,399
Registration number for this airplane: unknown
Seats: 5 passenger
Length: 32 feet, 9 inches
Wingspan: 41 feet, 11 inches
Engines: (2) R-755-9 Jacobs, seven cylinder, radial, piston
Horsepower: 245 hp each
Empty weight (approximate): 3,500 lbs
Gross weight: 5,700 lbs
Service ceiling: 15,000 ft
Cruising range: 750 miles
Cruising speed: 150 mph

* The above photo represents the type of aircraft and not necessarily the exact model involved in the accident.

Personal addenda:

Samuel Goldberg (Buddy Clark): actor, singer
b. July 26, 1912: Dorchester, Massachusetts (suburb of Boston)
d. October 2, 1949: Los Angeles, California
Buried: Forest Lawn Cemetery: Glendale, California

Ginette Neveu

October 28, 1949

All was as it should have been as the pilots of a Lockheed Constellation departed Paris-Orly airport for a flight to New York City, with an intermediate stop at Santa Maria airport in the Azores. Everything seemed routine for the flight when the crew checked in with 150 nautical miles left before landing at Santa Maria airport. Descending to an altitude of 3,000 feet and reporting the airfield in sight, the crew received and acknowledged their landing instructions. Nothing more was heard from anyone on board as the plane hit Redondo Mountain at approximately 2,950 ft.

Anytime a perfectly good and flyable aircraft is flown into the ground and the crew is flying with control of the aircraft, the situation is known as controlled flight into terrain (CFIT). This term is used whether the event occurs on flat land or on a jutting mountainside. Because CFIT should be one of the most preventable accidents due to the fact that the plane is mechanically airworthy, it is one of the most puzzling and disturbing of all aviation accident types.

A child prodigy is a child who is remarkably brilliant in some respect. Certainly Ginette Neveu was a child prodigy among violinists. Her formal debut occurred when she was seven years old at a concert in Paris, France. After winning nearly every award in every competition in which she played, she was invited to receive instruction from the best instructors available at the time and entered the Paris Conservatory of Music at age 11. After only eight months of study at the Conservatory she had taken the highest student honors. In 1935, at age 16, she won the prestigious Wienawski Competition in Poland, defeating 180 competitors, including the top seed who was 27 years old. Following this win, Neveu was on her way to debuts in Russia and the United States where her status as an international virtuoso was cemented.

Despite the fact that Ginette Neveu was a well-known, prestigious, award winning, classical French violinist before the hostilities of World War II began, during the war she played very little. Perhaps she chose this course in protest to her country's occupation, and purportedly lived reclusively within France during that time. After the liberation of Europe from Germany's aggression, she resumed her touring and recording career. She was on her way to America to begin a new tour when, just as her career seemed to be reaching new levels, she was killed as a passenger in this accident. With her when she died was her beloved and priceless Stradivarius violin. Because of her short career, very few recordings exist from her performances. Also aboard this flight was her brother, Jean Neveu, a pianist, who had become her permanent accompanist by that time.

Certainly the crew of this airplane was well trained and qualified to make this flight. According to the International Civil Aeronautics Organization (ICAO) report, the probable cause of this accident is quoted as, "Failure to carry out either of the approach procedures for Santa Maria airport. False [incorrect] position reports given by the crew (and) inadequate navigation. Failure to identify Santa Maria airport when flying in VFR [visual flight rules] conditions." All 11 crew members and 37 passengers aboard the flight perished. So why did this accident happen? We may never know. Why do good pilots sometimes make bad decisions or simply get caught off guard or unaware? Sometimes there are no easy answers for those who are left to ask the questions.

Roger D. Cain

Aircraft addenda:

Common name: Constellation L-749 (Connie)
Manufacturer: Lockheed Aircraft Corporation
Date the type began service: 1946
Air Carrier for this flight: Air France
Registration number for this airplane: F-BAZN
Serial number for this airplane: 2546
Seats: 60 to 81 passengers
Length: 95 feet, 2 inches
Wingspan: 123 feet, 0 inches
Engines: (4) Wright R-3350, 18-cylinder, air-cooled, radial, piston
Horsepower: 2,500 hp each
Empty weight (approximate): 56,000 lbs.
Gross weight: 94,000 lbs.
Service ceiling: 25,000 ft
Fuel capacity: 6,245 gal.
Cruising speed: 320 mph

* The above photo represents the type of aircraft and not necessarily the exact model involved in the accident.

Personal addenda:

Ginette Neveu: violinist
b. August 11, 1919: Paris, France
d. October 28, 1949: Sao Miguel, Azores (Portugal)
Buried: La Pere Lachaise: Paris, France (She is buried near the grave of Chopin.)

Jacques Thibaud

September 1, 1953

Many aspects of this accident are remarkably similar to the crash that took the life of Ginette Neveu. The performer's country of origin, the musical instrument, the air carrier, the specific make of airplane involved and the phase of flight are all eerily the same. While interesting, these similarities are attributed to coincidence and nothing else. Although the exact meteorological conditions at the time of this accident are not known, we do know that the area of the French Alps where the accident occurred certainly is prone to sudden and abrupt weather changes.

This scheduled passenger flight took off from Paris, France with an ultimate destination of Hong Kong. The scheduled enroute stop in Nice, France was supposed to be a routine one. While on approach and preparing to land at Nice-Cote d'Azur airport, the plane struck mountainous terrain near Mt. Cemet, France. Everyone on board perished with nine crew fatalities and 33 passenger deaths. Most likely, this was another controlled flight into terrain (CFIT) accident, but of all the records found to date none has documented or determined the official probable cause.

Jacques Thibaud was a world-famous classical French violinist, known mostly for his fine tonal performances of Mozart, Beethoven and 19th century French arrangements. However, he also was known for the dynamic expressiveness he conveyed in his playing. He studied at the Paris Conservatory and then, according to accounts, honed his skill and personal playing style by performing in a small Paris Cafe. As early as 1898 he appeared with orchestras as a soloist and toured widely thereafter, but in 1905 he formed a trio with two friends, Pablo Casals, a Spanish cellist and Alfred Cortot, a French pianist. They toured the world together for many years in the early part of the twentieth century and made some of the earliest recordings of chamber music.

Roger D. Cain

Aircraft addenda:

Common name: Constellation L-749A (Connie)
Manufacturer: Lockheed Aircraft Corporation
Date the type began service: 1946
Air Carrier for this flight: Air France
Registration number for this airplane: F-BAZZ
Serial number for this airplane: 2674
Seats: 60 to 81 passengers
Length: 95 feet, 2 inches
Wingspan: 123 feet, 0 inches
Engines: (4) Wright R-3350, 18-cylinder, air-cooled, radial, piston
Horsepower: 2,500 hp each
Empty weight (approximate): 56,000 lbs.
Gross weight: 107,000 lbs.
Service ceiling: 25,000 ft
Fuel capacity: 6,245 gal.
Cruising speed: 320 mph

* The above photo represents the type of aircraft and not necessarily the exact model involved in the accident.

Personal addenda:

Jacques Thibaud: violinist
b. September 27, 1880: Bordeaux, France
d. September 1, 1953: near Mt. Cemet, near Barcelonnette, France
Buried: France

William Kapell

October 29, 1953

William Kapell was an American pianist traveling on a regularly scheduled passenger flight from Honolulu, Hawaii to San Francisco, California. Honolulu had been an intermediate stop, as the plane's flight route had originated in Sydney, Australia. Kapell was returning from a musical tour of Australia. The airplane crashed about 7.5 miles southeast of Half Moon Bay, California while the crew was conducting the initial phases of an instrument approach into the San Francisco International Airport (SFO). According to the investigation report, the pilot basically failed to follow the prescribed instrument approach procedure. Everyone on board perished, including eight crew fatalities and 11 passenger fatalities, when the plane crashed into mountainous terrain. This was another CFIT accident.

On September 24, 1929, a major advancement in aviation took place. On that day Lieutenant James H. Doolittle safely flew a specially equipped biplane over a 15 mile course without any reference to the outside world and shortly afterward made the world's first "blind" landing. Flying by reference to cockpit instruments where an accurate artificial representation of the natural horizon was depicted to the pilot was the true breakthrough that allowed safe flights in bad weather. Flight by reference to instruments only is a disciplined task. The pilot must learn to quickly, accurately and efficiently scan, interpret and react to subtle changes in indicator needle deflections and movements on no less than six different flight monitoring instruments. To alleviate some of the pilot's workload and subsequent fatigue, the autopilot was developed. Autopilots date back to the 1930s and most likely there was an autopilot on board William Kapell's airplane. But more importantly, there were at least two professional, well-trained pilots aboard also. How could an accident like this happen? There are some thoughts to ponder in considering the answer to this question.

The whole purpose of an instrument approach is to fly an aircraft through less than ideal weather and have the aircraft end up in a position where a normal landing on the desired runway can be accomplished. The mechanics of flying any instrument approach is to fly a prescribed set of headings and altitudes, descending only when safe margins from terrain, tall towers and any other obstructions are satisfied. Eventually the pilot arrives through the clouds with the plane at a level only a few hundred feet and mere seconds from a safe touchdown. Aircraft performance based upon time, speed and distance calculations are vital factors to consider during the course of an instrument approach. When all factors of the approach are assessed, including altitudes to be flown during a prescribed segment, this information then becomes part of an approach procedure that is published by the government. Today, there are basically two categories of instrument approaches. One category has only one type of approach known as a "precision approach," which is also known as an Instrument Landing System or ILS. The other category comprises all the other types of instrument approaches and these are known as "non-precision approaches."

The main difference between the two categories of approaches is that precision approach equipment consists mainly of two highly directional transmitting systems that emit electronic signal beams. These signals not only provide guidance for exact runway centerline alignment (localizer), but also for the precise rate of descent (glideslope) of the aircraft to the runway threshold (Figure 8-1). The other components of the ILS are an outer marker and a middle marker, which are positioned at a fixed distance from the runway. The ILS signals are received by equipment in the plane and displayed on the instrument panel so the pilot can intercept the desired course and manipulate the aircraft accordingly for the precise flight path. It is this glideslope, or glidepath, that allows the pilot to fly his or her airplane closer to the ground without compromising safety margins. Non-precision approach equipment does not have glideslope capability, therefore a non-precision approach does not allow a pilot to descend as close to the ground due to the lack of vertical guidance. While it does take trust in one's instruments to actually fly any instrument approach amidst rising terrain, I want to emphasize that it is not dangerous when performed properly with equipment that is working as designed.

In 1953, the precision approach, or ILS, had only been used in the industry for about seven years, so the technology was relatively new at the time. Additionally, only the larger airports worldwide were equipped with the expensive ILS equipment. Most likely San Francisco had an ILS approach, but it cannot be verified that the pilots were flying on an ILS course. Radar would not have helped very much in 1953 because the air traffic control system at that time could not monitor the plane's descent and maneuvering as is done regularly in today's modern flight environment.

Fatigue also could have been a factor while flying this particular instrument approach before the accident occurred. After a long flight across the Pacific Ocean, these pilots must have been ready to end their duty time. While an ILS approach can be flown by manual pilot input, a properly working and engaged autopilot does reduce a pilot's workload. The ability to fly an approach solely by autopilot was virtually non-existent in 1953, but these pilots could have used an autopilot to assist them in this approach. Did the pilots get complacent? Did they misread the instrument approach procedure? Did they misread the instruments? Did they not have their instruments set properly? Did the weather cause faulty readings in their instruments? The details will never be known, but the final determination of the investigation into this crash laid the responsibility squarely upon pilot error.

Aircraft designers and engineers have long wanted to design a fully automated airplane. In other words, they would like to eliminate the human error factor and take the pilot right out of the cockpit. For the most part, our modern airliners have nearly achieved this. There are new planes right now with electronic systems so sophisticated that all the pilot has to do is take the airplane off the ground. After that the autopilot has the capability to get the airplane to its pre-determined altitude, fly the assigned route, descend the plane at the appropriate time and place, and actually land the airliner in almost any weather without any further input from the pilot. In fact, the first autoland approach by an airplane carrying passengers was made in 1965. The technology required to accomplish this action was amazing enough even back then, but the advancement and complexity of today's on-board flight systems, and their total control of nearly every aspect of flight, is enough to stagger the imagination of any neoteric technophile.

However, as the pilot is increasingly taken out of the control loop and fatigue is no longer a major factor, the possibility of boredom increases. Psychologists are now beginning to hypothesize that the pilot may be too far removed from the flying process and that automation may be flying the airplane too much. One thing is sure: the human element, even with its prospect for mistakes, will likely never be designed out of the loop. Ironically, even though human error accounts for 80 percent of all aviation accidents, human judgment is also vital to safety in flying. I firmly believe that there have been more accidents averted due to human action and intervention than have been caused by it. Unfortunately for our society, we don't often hear about any of the flights that were saved by pilot input. It is mainly the disasters and errors that are splattered on our headlines and evening news telecasts. More unfortunately still—somehow, sometime, somewhere, most assuredly—a CFIT accident will happen again.

William Kapell was born on the Upper East Side of New York to parents of Spanish, Russian and Polish descent. He learned to play the piano at an early age and proved to be a child prodigy, as six weeks after his first lesson he won a music contest for children. At age 12 he was already playing private and public recitals and only a few years later he was awarded a scholarship to the Philadelphia Conservatory of Music. In 1940, at age 18, he was awarded a fellowship at the Juilliard Graduate School. Kapell began his professional concert career in 1942, and in 1944 the Philadelphia Orchestra offered him a three-year contract. By 1953 he had traveled to many parts of the world, known best for his performances of late nineteenth century classical music. He also performed works by American composers, most notably the music of Aaron Copeland. Kapell was the finest American pianist of his time and his legacy is his example of total devotion to, and passion for, excellence in his music. The William Kapell International Piano Competition and Festival is held once every four years at the University of Maryland.

Author

Aircraft addenda:

Common name: Douglas DC-6
Manufacturer: Douglas Aircraft Company
First flight of type: 1946
Air Carrier: British Commonwealth Pacific Airways
Registration number for this airplane: VH-BPE
Serial number for this airplane: 43125/131
Year built for this airplane: 1948
Seats: 89
Length: 100' 7"
Wingspan: 117' 6"
Engines: (4) Pratt & Whitney R-2800-34, 18-cylinder, air-cooled, radial, piston
Horsepower: 2,100 hp (each)
Empty weight (approximate): 49,767 lbs.
Gross weight: 97,200 lbs.
Service ceiling: 25,000 ft
Fuel capacity: 4,260 gal.
Cruising speed: 290 mph

* The above photo represents the type of aircraft and not necessarily the exact model involved in the accident.

Personal addenda:

William Kapell: pianist
b. September 20,1922: New York, New York
d. October 29, 1953: Half Moon Bay, California
Buried: Mt. Ararat Cemetery, Farmingdale, New York

Basic Components of an Instrument Landing System (ILS)

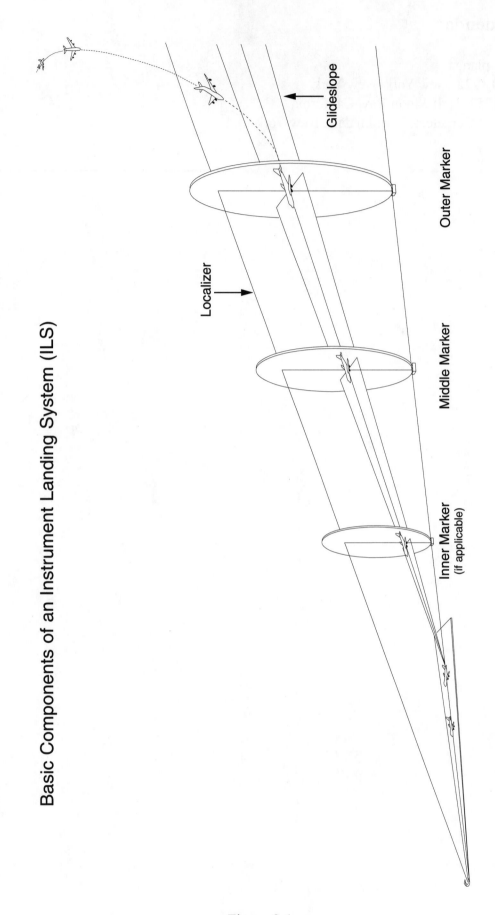

Figure 8-1

R. W. Blackwood   **Bill Lyles**

June 30, 1954

As discussed previously in the chapter about Grace Moore, the take-off and the landing are the two phases of aviation that pose the most risk. During each of these phases, it is critical for the pilot to properly configure the airplane for the task at hand. However, there should always be the fall-back position that, if something does not look right or feel right, a decision to abort the take-off or the landing can be made and accomplished safely. In the case of an aborted landing, this would necessitate that the plane be re-configured by the pilot for what would subsequently become a take-off situation.

On the control surfaces of an airplane there are smaller control surfaces called trim tabs. A trim tab acts to relieve the control pressure the pilot feels in his hands and arms. Think about it: if a pilot were to fly for hours constantly having to hold strong forces on the control column with his muscles, he or she would become physically exhausted. This pressure relief is what the trim tabs provide. They allow the plane to be flown with the slightest touch by the pilot.

The elevator on an airplane is the horizontal control surface that allows a pilot to control the pitch of the nose. The elevator is one such control surface that has a trim tab. During the approach for landing phase of flight, it is not uncommon for a pilot to configure a plane for the landing and then set the trim tab on the elevator in preparation to assist with the final nose-up landing attitude. Once again, this practice reduces the control pressure that a pilot feels during the critical part of the landing phase, where he or she must utilize control inputs without heavy resistance. This is the narrow window of the landing called the "round out," where the plane must transition from the descent phase to the horizontal flight path, parallel to the runway. It is at this time where the ground can seem to rush up very fast, and indeed things do happen quickly during these brief seconds.

Should an aborted landing become necessary, where the engines are throttled up to greater power, if the pilot does not take some of the elevator trim out quickly, the sudden rush of airflow over the elevator will allow the trim tab to become even more powerful in its assigned duty. The nose-up trim configuration then becomes a surprisingly strong force that can easily overpower the pilot's ability to counteract. If the pilot is not able to overcome the trim tab's authority quickly enough, the plane can become too nose high and an aerodynamic stall can be the result. This sudden, nose-high attitude caused by the configuration of the airplane's trim tab is called an elevator trim stall. Should any plane stall too close to the ground, there usually is very little room for recovery.

The Blackwood Brothers Quartet originated when oldest brother and evangelist Roy Blackwood organized his brothers, Doyle and James, along with his own oldest son, R.W. Blackwood, into a gospel singing group. It is interesting to note that when they were formed in 1934, R.W. Blackwood was just 13 years old at the time. The vocal group soon gained a strong following around the south central United States right up until World War II, when the family dismantled the quartet so they each could help with the war effort by working in defense plants. In 1946 the group reformed and set out to rekindle its popularity. In 1950 Roy, the group's founder, retired and was replaced by Bill Lyles. The group moved to Memphis, Tennessee, where they soon signed and recorded with RCA Victor. This national exposure led to an appearance on the Arthur Godfrey television show where they won the talent contest. Only 18 days later, R.W. Blackwood and Bill Lyles were killed in a plane crash, which seems to have been caused by an elevator trim stall.

Three people died in this particular accident. Piloting the plane was R.W. Blackwood. His co-pilot was Bill Lyles. The third person on board was 20 year old John Ogburn, who had come along for a short plane ride. Mr. Ogburn was the son of a local banker who had founded and promoted the annual Chilton County Peach Festival, a five-day gala, which was the event where the Blackwood Brothers were to sing their gospel songs. With perhaps as many as 1,000 people looking on, it is possible that R.W. Blackwood was distracted by the impromptu show he was putting on for the rural Alabama crowd. According to some descriptions, the plane rose to an altitude of about 300 feet, "did a complete loop" and crashed roughly 250 yards from the airport hangar where the quartet was to perform. Although there is no existing accident report to be found, I was able to contact an eyewitness to the event who is also one of the original Blackwood Brothers Quartet. Dr. James Blackwood was kind enough to relay what he so tragically saw on that fateful day (Figure 9-1).

Shortly after the plane crash, the remaining members said they would never perform again. Despite this proclamation, a short time later, saying that God was leading them, the group reformed and regained its former stature as gospel ministry artists. Shortly thereafter they organized the National Quartet Convention and the Gospel Music Association. Since then the Blackwood Brothers Quartet has traveled the world for their musical evangelistic ministry and performed with such notables as the late Tennessee Ernie Ford, Reverend Billy Graham and Barbara Mandrell, as well as hosting their own television specials. As a group, they have won nine Grammy Awards, 27 Dove Awards and were inducted into the Gospel Music Hall of Fame on April 12, 1998. Although the group's members have changed over the years, the Blackwood Brothers Quartet continues to perform their harmonizing gospel music to adoring fans around the world.

Author

Aircraft addenda:

Common name: Beech 18, C-45 (military designation)
Manufacturer: Beechcraft
First flight of type: 1937
Registration number for this airplane: unknown
Seats: 7 to 9
Length: 35 feet, 2 inches
Wingspan: 49 feet, 8 inches
Engine: (2) Pratt & Whitney R-985, nine cylinder, air-cooled, radial, piston
Horsepower: 450 h.p. (each)
Empty weight (approximate): 5,910 lbs.
Gross weight: 9,700 lbs.
Service ceiling: 21,000 ft.
Fuel capacity: 198 gal.
Cruising speed: 200 mph

* The above photo represents the type of aircraft and not necessarily the exact model involved in the accident.

Personal addenda:

R. W. Blackwood: tenor (early years) and baritone singer
b. October 23, 1921: Ackerman, Mississippi, (Choctaw County)
d. June 30, 1954: Clanton, Alabama
Buried: Memorial Gardens, Memphis, Tennessee
Note: A granite memorial commemorates the crash at the airport in Clanton, Alabama.

James W. Lyles (Bill Lyles): bass singer
b. December 7, 1920: Rossville, Georgia
d. June 30, 1954: Clanton, Alabama
Buried: Memorial Gardens, Memphis, Tennessee

James Blackwood, D. Mus.

4411 SEQUOIA ROAD

MEMPHIS, TENNESSEE 38117

(901) 683-5711

4-3-2000

Dear William:

The lady in Calif. who does my web page sent me your
message.

The plane   a twin Beech that the navy called C-18
I dont know any other designation..

We had landed at the little airstrip at Clanton,AL
shortly before noon June 30th 1954 and were to sing
along with the Statesmen Quartet that night in a
concert to be held in the airport hanger seated with
folding chairs...after singing for the Lions Club at
their noon luncheon(they were the sponsros for that
night)..we in the little town all afternoon..shortly
before dusk..R.W,.my nephew and baritone in our group
said he thought he should take the plane up to check
how much room he had on take off As we planned to fly
home to Memphis that night after the concert..The
strip was not lighted but we would sometimes line up cars
along the runway and have them turn their lights on..
On landing earlier R.W. set the plane down almost on the end
of the runway..I think it was only 3300 feet..when landing
there was no obstruction to the approach...Bill Lyles,the
bass and copilot got in the plane along with a friend and
took off...in coming back to land,the wind had shifted so
that he was approaching from the oposite end of the run way.
at that approach there was a hill..in clearing the hill he
would pick u p airspeed so that when he got near the grould
he was going too fast to land..he never touched and lifted
the gear..pushed the throttleand went around again..on the
2nd approach I saw he was having the same problem..about a
4th of the way up the runway he gave the plane a"drop" but
it bounched too bad to keep it on the ground..he lifted the
gear..pushed the throttleand this time the plane went straight
up until it stalled..came back and crashed and went up in
flames...pilots who have flown that type plane think perhaps
the 2nd time he forgot to re-trim the tabs from landing to
take off.... I hope this answers your questions..

James Blackwood

Figure 9-1

Guido Cantelli

November 24, 1956

This accident suggests a scenario where a heavily loaded, fully fueled transport airplane was in the take-off phase of flight and something went terribly wrong. We do not know what the pilots saw or perceived, but we can assess the atmospheric conditions that prevailed at the time and we can draw upon similar scenarios that have been investigated since that offer some insight. This extrapolation of information should not be misconstrued as speculation. Without facts and evidence we are always left with questions that we may never be able to answer. Yet, the information presented is well-known and factual and should be considered as educational.

One illusion that can be associated with the take-off phase of flight is called a somatogravic illusion. This occurs during the rapid acceleration of the airplane, after throttling the engines up and rapidly gaining airspeed in preparation to fly. This rapid acceleration can lead the pilot to believe he or she is in a nose-up attitude, and to respond by pushing the nose down. Obviously this illusion, if it takes over the senses of a pilot during the critical time he or she is still close to the ground, can leave no room for recovery. A pilot who is disoriented in this way can easily fly an airplane right into the ground or into an unseen obstruction before he or she ever realizes exactly what is happening.

Certainly when there is a low cloud ceiling and the pilot has to transition from outside reference to instrument reference, there may be a small fraction of time when the perceived sensations that a pilot feels can dominate the physical actions taken. This misperception can occur before the eyes have time to re-focus and the brain can subsequently interpret instrument information and dictate the proper actions for aircraft control. Proper practice and training for flight into instrument conditions reduces the risk that this potential problem will become overwhelming to the pilot.

Guido Cantelli was an orchestra and opera conductor of monumental promise. As a child, he was playing the piano by age six and by age nine he was directing the local church choir. He made his initial debut as a conductor in 1943, but World War II re-directed his career. Refusing to enlist in the Italian army, he was imprisoned in a Nazi labor camp on the Baltic coast. Somehow escaping, he managed to survive the rest of the war in hiding under an assumed name. Resuming his conducting career immediately after the war, he made his professional debut in 1945 at La Scala in Milan, Italy. In 1948, he was "discovered" by the great conductor, Arturo Toscanini, who immediately arranged for Cantelli to guest conduct the NBC Symphony Orchestra in New York City.

Throughout Cantelli's career he was known as a man obsessed with perfection. With this intensity came the occasional burst of temper, but the orchestral members who worked under him respected him greatly. He would eventually conduct most of the great orchestras in the world, and possibly was in line to succeed the much older Toscanini as the conductor of the NBC Symphony. He was even rumored to be a potential candidate for the New York Philharmonic's chief conductor position. His recording career spanned only eight years, but to those who appreciate symphony music, his ability to get the absolute best and most brilliant performances from his musicians is legendary.

The flight that took the life of Guido Cantelli was departing Orly Field, Paris, France, for New York, New York as a regularly scheduled passenger flight when it crashed. Ten crew members and 24 of the 25 passengers aboard were killed. After arriving from Rome on its normal stop in Paris, the airplane departed Orly Airfield runway 26. About 10 to 15 seconds later, the plane lost altitude and struck a house almost 2000 feet past the runway end. A post-crash fire erupted. The weather at the time of the accident was reported as misty, with a visibility of 2.2 miles. Wind direction was from 320 degrees at 6 knots. The cloud ceiling was registered as 4/8ths coverage, just less than 800 feet, with a temperature of about 28 degrees Farenheit.

Although the original document was unavailable for a complete review, no apparent mechanical malfunctions were believed found during the accident investigation. The ICAO determination for the probable cause of this accident is described in part: "The aircraft's slight loss of altitude soon after take-off was the main cause of the accident. There is no explanation for this loss of altitude. Although the regulations in force were observed, the presence of unmarked obstructions in the take-off path constituted an aggravating factor. The initial and direct cause of the accident remains unknown."

Certainly the atmospheric conditions that existed at the time of this airplane's departure were conducive to the flight crew succumbing to somatogravic illusion. It is difficult to conceive that this could happen to two professionally trained pilots, but we must remember that flight physiology was not understood as well in 1956 as it is today. While this illusion could have been the catalyst that led to this accident, we will never know all the contributing factors pertaining to this particular aviation disaster.

Author

Aircraft addenda:

Common name: Douglas DC-6B
Manufacturer: Douglas Aircraft Company
First flight of type: 1946
Air Carrier: Linee Aeree Italiane
Registration number for this airplane: I-LEAD
Serial number for this airplane: 45075/731
Year built for this airplane: 1956
Seats: 102 passengers, 7 crew
Length: 106 feet, 6 inches
Wingspan: 117 feet, 6 inches
Engines: (4) Pratt & Whitney R-2800 CB17, 18 cylinder, air cooled, radial, piston
Horsepower: 2,500 hp (each)
Empty weight (approximate): 58,300 lbs.
Gross weight: 107,000 lbs.
Service ceiling: 21,900 feet
Fuel capacity: 5,525 gal.
Cruising speed: 315 mph

* The above photo represents the type of aircraft and not necessarily the exact model involved in the accident.

Personal addenda:

Guido Cantelli: music conductor
b. April 27, 1920: Novara, Italy
d. November 24, 1956: Paris, France
Buried: Paris, France

Pedro Infante

April 15, 1957

Pedro Infante Cruz was a colorful character, and some might say that he still is. He was born into a lower middle class Mexican family in Guamuchil, Mazatlan, Sinalóa where his father was a music teacher and performer. Learning to sing at a young age, Cruz performed in various local town squares into his teens. Apparently needing more money he became an apprentice carpenter, where he reportedly built his own guitar over a two year period. Giving up as a carpenter, Cruz briefly tried his hand at becoming a barber before his move in 1939 to Mexico City in pursuit of a career as an entertainer. He also was married by this time.

Cruz arrived in Mexico City with little money but found work as a singer for radio station XEB. Shortly thereafter Cruz became a regular night club performer where he was discovered by patrons who were also motion picture producers. By 1943 Infante had ceased using his last name Cruz, had starred in five films and had also signed an exclusive recording contract. His name, his voice and his face were everywhere in Mexico's media and entertainment scenes. He was quickly becoming a pivotal and influencial figure in defining Mexican culture during this period, which has since become known as Mexico's golden age of cinema.

Infante often credited his first wife, Maria Luisa Leon, as the person who made him an actor. However, with his widening fame came temptations from other women. Throughout the course of his career he became known as a great womanizer, had affairs with numerous mistresses and fathered a few illegitimate children. Despite this upheaval in his personal life, he still accomplished his dream of becoming a star, an icon and a millionaire within ten years of arriving in Mexico City. He also became a pilot. In fact, it is often stated that Infante felt it was God's calling that had directed him to become a pilot. He eventually earned his commercial pilot's certificate in his spare time, but other pilots who knew him sometimes described his flying as "crazy" or "loco."

His first airplane accident occurred in 1947 and, although not much is known about this event, it is known that Infante was not badly injured. His second aviation accident occurred on May 22, 1949 while he was flying a twin-engine Cessna, which most likely was a T-50 Bobcat (see Chapter 5 *Buddy Clark*), from Acapulco to Mexico City with his mistress at the time, Lupita Torrentera, a dancer whom he had initially met while she was only 14 years old. Twenty minutes after departure Infante encountered worsening weather conditions. Not long after this he apparently got lost and the plane's radio reportedly failed. Flying until the airplane's fuel supply was exhausted, he maneuvered the aircraft in a glide down to a crash landing near Zitacuaro, Michoacan in Mexico. His girlfriend was not hurt, but Infante suffered serious trauma to his head that required surgery. That operation left him with a permanent platinum plate in his head, which was used to identify his body in the later accident that took his life.

Infante's fatal aviation accident occurred in a converted World War II troop and cargo transport called a LB-30 Liberator. This particular Liberator was owned by the airline Transportes Aéreos Mexicanas S.A. (TAMSA), was given the Mexican registration number XA-KUN and was known to have frequent mechanical problems. On Monday, April 15, 1957, the Captain for this flight was Victor Manuel Vidal and the scheduled co-pilot was Gerardo de la Torre Limón. However, Pedro Infante asked the co-pilot to allow him to fly this flight because he needed to get to Mexico City to take care of a legal mess with his marriage. It seems that Infante had thought that his divorce to his first wife was final, so he went ahead and married Irma Dorantes, an actress. However, the courts decided that there was sufficient evidence to warrant a declaration that the divorce was not valid, thus nullifying his marriage to Dorantes, which had taken place in Mérida, Yucatan on April 10th.

The purpose of the flight was to transport a load of fish, cloth and packages from Mérida to Mexico City. It is estimated that the plane was carrying approximately six and a half tons of cargo, but some speculate that the plane had been loaded with much more weight than that. The departure was at 7:45 a.m. on a clear day and all was normal for several minutes. Eyewitnesses stated that the plane then apparently ceased to gain altitude and also appeared to lose airspeed. Coming down rather quickly, it clipped some trees and crashed in Mérida between 54th and 87th streets. Because the plane was fully loaded with fuel, it erupted in to a huge fireball that enveloped numerous houses. Those killed in the crash included Captain Vidal, Infante, the flight engineer Marciano Bautista and an 18 year-old girl on the ground whose name was Ana Ruth Rosel Chan. Another teenager, Baltazar Martín Cruz, died the next day from his serious injuries.

If the plane had been loaded to its maximum gross weight for takeoff, and if the plane experienced an engine failure soon after takeoff, certainly the pilots would have had their hands full controlling this airplane. Since lift is a force that directly counteracts weight, and since the wings produce the lift based on airflow over them (airspeed), if the plane had not accelerated to a sufficiently safe airspeed there would have been insufficient lift to offset the weight. Certainly if the plane had been overloaded and subsequently had an engine failure, this would explain the plane's rapid drop from the sky. In this scenario, the engines that remained operational would have been even more hampered to keep the plane at a sufficient airspeed for the wings to create the lift to hold the plane and all its weight in the air. It is important to remember that the physics of the world we live in absolutely rule what is possible for man and machine to accomplish. One thing that one can never argue is that gravity always wins.

Roger D. Cain

Aircraft addenda:

Common names: B-24, LB-30, Liberator
Manufacturer: Consolidated Aircraft
First flight of type: December 29, 1939
Air Carrier for this flight: TAMSA
Registration number for this airplane: XA-KUN
Length: 66 feet, 4 inches
Wingspan: 110 feet, 0 inches
Engines: (4) Pratt & Whitney R-1830, supercharged, air-cooled, 14 cylinder, radial
Horsepower: 1,200 hp (each)
Empty weight (approximate): 37,000 lbs.
Maximum take-off weight: 56,000 lbs.
Service ceiling: 25,000 ft.
Fuel capacity: 3,000 gal.
Cruising speed: 210 mph

* The above photo represents the type of aircraft and not necessarily the exact model involved in the accident.

Personal addenda:

Pedro Infante Cruz (Pedro Infante): singer, actor
b. November 18, 1917: Sinalóa, Mexico
d. April 15, 1957: Mérida, Yucatan
Buried: Panteón Jardin (Garden Cemetery): Mexico City

Buddy Holly   **Ritchie Valens**   **J. P. Richardson**

February 3, 1959

As a professional pilot and a flight instructor who on occasion has had the opportunity to teach people to fly an airplane by reference to their cockpit instruments only, I find this flight scenario heart breaking. This is the story of a pilot, his flight qualifications and his three famous passengers. It has been described by some as the day on which the music died, but it may be just the opposite of that. It may very well be the day that music came to live forever. During the course of writing this book, whenever I had the opportunity to talk about the premise of my manuscript, the listener often spoke up and almost always said something similar to, "Oh, like Buddy Holly." This tragedy is perhaps the most famous aviation accident that has occurred within the music industry.

Occurring towards the end of the 1950s, this accident was a turning point in more ways than one. It defined the magnitude of just how deeply felt the loss of a music star could be and also changed the way Rock and Roll music was viewed as an influence on society. I believe that many of us still feel the effect of this accident whether we realize it or not. This is because of the way in which we view Buddy Holly's image today and how we regard the library of music he left behind. It is widely recognized that Holly's music has influenced multitudes of artists. This accident has also become symbolic, whether subconsciously or not, as an example of the tragic loss of the rising star. We can only imagine how popular Ritchie Valens and J. P. Richardson, also known as the "Big Bopper," would have become in their rising careers. Now their immortality is forever tied to that of Buddy Holly and this particular aviation event.

Of the three famous passengers actually on this ill-fated flight, two were not originally scheduled to be on board. Initially Buddy Holly had booked Waylon Jennings, a bass player, and Tommy Allsup, a guitarist, to accompany him on the chartered plane. Both musicians had been enlisted for the winter 1959 tour to fill in when Buddy and the members of the original Crickets band had a falling out. The flight followed the eleventh stop of a 24 day Midwest tour. The whole tour was known as the "Winter Dance Party."

Between the musical acts playing that night at the Surf Ballroom dance hall in Clear Lake, Iowa, J.P. Richardson approached Waylon Jennings and asked him if he could have his seat on the plane. Richardson said he was physically uncomfortable on the bus due to his large size, and he had a cold as well. Jennings agreed to the switch as long as Holly didn't mind. According to Jennings himself, Holly jokingly said to him after approving the passenger switch that he hoped the tour bus froze up again. Jennings is known to have quipped back that he hoped Holly's plane crashed. This off-the-cuff comeback by Jennings, although said in light-hearted jest, haunted his memory for many years.

At about this same time, Ritchie Valens and Tommy Allsup had struck up a conversation regarding who would get the other seat on the chartered flight. Apparently they ended up engaging in a coin toss to decide the matter. Valens called heads and won. He would accompany Buddy and the Big Bopper on the late night charter flight to Fargo, North Dakota. So, just what was it that took Buddy Holly, Richie Valens and the "Big Bopper" from us and immortalized their music? From the facts presented in the Civil Aeronautics Board (CAB) investigation, it appears to be a simple and clear-cut case of pilot disorientation.

Disorientation is an insidious and progressively swift process. It starts with a pilot feeling that all is fine. Then a tense anxiety that something is just not right steadily creeps up on the pilot and rapidly progresses into a total loss of situational awareness. Disorientation can lead directly to panic, and panic in an airplane can quickly lead to disaster. Sometimes referred to as spatial disorientation, it renders the pilot as little more than a helpless passenger. Gravity takes over when the pilot becomes spatially lost and gravity always wins. In fact, it is because of the absolute law of gravity that it can be said truthfully, "Take-offs are optional, landings are mandatory." In the case of this accident, gravity took over very quickly and the result was a violent and deadly crash.

It has been well-known for many years that spatial disorientation, once developed, can cause an accident within minutes. Of course, while a pilot's flying altitude, skill level and aircraft type are factors in the equation, it was found in a research study conducted by the University of Illinois that the average time for a pilot to become spatially disoriented was less than three minutes. In a publication called "FAA Aviation News," a realistic scenario was laid out for all to read. In this chilling scenario titled "178 Seconds to Live" it is assumed that an airplane has just entered the clouds and the pilot is subject to spatial disorientation. This is how the authors described it:

"You now have 178 seconds to live!
Your aircraft feels on an even keel, but your compass turns slowly. You push a little rudder and add a little pressure on the controls to stop the turn, but this feels unnatural and you return the controls to their original position. This feels better, but your compass is now turning a little faster and your airspeed is increasing slightly. You scan your instrument panel for help, but what you see looks unfamiliar. You are sure this is just a bad spot. You will break out in a few minutes (but you do not have a few minutes left...).

You now have 100 seconds to live!
You glance at your altimeter and are shocked to see it unwinding. You are already down to 1,200 feet. Instinctively you pull back on the controls, but the altimeter still unwinds. The engine RPM is into the red and the airspeed nearly so.

You now have 45 seconds to Live!
Suddenly you see the ground. The trees rush up at you. You can see the horizon if you turn your head far enough, but it is at an unusual angle-you are almost inverted. You open your mouth to scream but...

You have just become a victim of spatial disorientation."

Spatial disorientation is a natural enemy to nearly every animal. One over-simplified example of disorientation within nature occurrs when dolphins and whales occasionally beach themselves. However, for humans disorientation was mostly lurking in the shadows until aviation became a reality. Once our species entered into the three dimensional world of the sky, we quickly had to learn how to adapt within the all-enveloping ocean of air that makes up our atmosphere. To understand spatial disorientation, one must first understand that sight is the most important sense to a pilot. Without seeing a horizon, the brain can be fooled into thinking that down is up, and up is down.

When a pilot is looking out of the cockpit in an airplane, not only is he or she looking for other air traffic, but that pilot is using the horizontal line in the distance, where the earth and sky meet, to keep the wings level. This line is known as the horizon. The horizon is the most powerful outside visual reference that a pilot can use to fly an aircraft. In fact, vision is the dominant coordinating sense that a pilot will ever use to stabilize an aircraft. When this sense is taken away because of darkness or reduced visibility, or fooled due to false horizons and aerial illusions, even the best pilot can quickly become disoriented.

The reason for this disorientation is physiological in nature. It is not the environment that is at fault for spatial disorientation; rather, it is the natural physiology of the human inner ear. Even though the inner ear is about the size of a dime, this sensory organ is the key to our sense of balance while on the ground and certainly in the air. The inner ear consists largely of a spiral-shaped cochlea (the main hearing organ) and three semi-circular canals. It is these semi-circular canals which send signals to the brain to define our balance and our orientation as to which way is up and which way is down.

The semi-circular canals are oriented in the same three axes in which a plane moves (Figure 12-1). Even though we essentially move in a two dimensional world on the ground, we still live in a three dimensional world. Within each canal is fluid which moves over fine hair-like cilia that detect movement. Any movement or rotation of the body tends to move the fluid in one or more of the canals, thereby causing displacement of the hair cells. It is these cells which transmit messages to the brain, telling it which way they are displaced, and the brain figures out the movement or rotation required.

A simple example to illustrate this point is to think of each canal like a bucket with grass growing in the bottom. Now pour water in the bucket just over the top of the grass. Sitting stationary on the ground, the water naturally seeks the bottom of the bucket because of the law of gravity. Now tip the bucket from side to side and watch as the blades of grass sway back and forth with the motion of the water. The water represents the fluid within our ears, and the grass represents the hair-like cells.

So how can the brain be fooled? Imagine tying a string to the handle of the bucket and swinging the bucket in a circle. The water will stay in the bottom of the bucket because of the outward force exerted during the process. Because of this steady state, chances are good that the grass will not move very much either. Stop the bucket suddenly, however, and the water quickly will find its natural driving forces: momentum and gravity. The grass will also move with the water's rapid rush as it flows suddenly. When flying in an airplane, all of the natural forces which dominate and dictate our lives are very much at work. At work too are these insidious forces which can ultimately fool the brain.

The "seat-of-the-pants" flying that you may have heard about refers to how a pilot feels when a plane turns. A coordinated turn will leave the pilot feeling like the turning forces run straight down his spine and through the seat of his pants, right through the floor of the airplane. The coordination of the turn directly relates to how well the pilot uses the rudder pedals with his feet to make the tail of the airplane track the same in the turn as the nose of the airplane. An uncoordinated turn will make the pilot feel like he is slipping or sliding in his seat to either one side or the other. Yet, the pilot still relies totally on vision for returning the plane's wings to level flight based on orientation to a visible horizon, whether that horizon is the natural horizon outside the cockpit or the artificial horizon on an instrument inside the cockpit.

Take away the visual cues, however, and "seat-of-the-pants" flying becomes very dangerous even in a well-coordinated turn. This is because the pilot, without visual backup, will have little or no sensation of being in a turn due to the fact that the pressure in the seat will feel much like it does during straight-and-level flight. Gravity is sensed at the floor of the aircraft, not the center of the earth, and is a false cue for estimating right side up. In other words, the "perceived gravity" feels normal, just like the water in the bucket did not know it was being swung around.

This means that in a change of roll, pitch or yaw without visual cues, the action may be too slow for the pilot to perceive. The senses in the inner ear feel right. However, when a sense of movement is finally received, the pilot without visual confirmation, either through natural or artificial horizon, will have ambiguous information with which to return to level flight. Additionally, even if a constant turn is perceived by the pilot, the initial fluid motion in his or her inner ear will compensate by equalizing the motion and eventually, as well as inaccurately, send a signal that level flight has resumed when in fact a turn is still ongoing. The graveyard spiral begins this way.

In a graveyard spiral, the senses of a pilot begin to perceive that the plane in a descent. In effect the plane is in a descent, but not with wings level. The pilot without normal visual cues compensates for the descent by pulling back on the yoke, which is a very natural tendency. However, by pulling back on the yoke when the plane is in a turn, the pilot in effect tightens the radius of the turn and steepens the spiral. Now the forces on the plane and its occupants reach even greater proportions, whereby the pilot loses all orientation where the sky and ground are located. Altitude is lost at an alarming rate at this point and because of the high airspeed and high stresses on the plane's airframe, it is entirely possible to exceed the designed stress limits. The plane could possibly begin to break up even before it hits the ground.

In the case of the crash which took the lives of Buddy Holly, Ritchie Valenzuela, and J.P. Richardson, a well-developed graveyard spiral would not seem to be plausible because there may not have been enough time after take-off to gain sufficient altitude for a steep spiral to develop. However, pilot disorientation does seem to be a major factor in this crash and it is possible that a graveyard spiral was in the beginning stages. There also is a possibility that an illusion called flicker vertigo could have contributed to this accident. Flicker vertigo is caused by the strobe-like effect that the propeller can create when spinning through the beam of a landing light. The term landing light is somewhat misleading because this light is normally turned on for departures as well. The hypnotic effect of flicker vertigo is more likely to occur in a single engine airplane and certainly something like falling snow flakes could enhance the effect.

When a pilot loses visual reference with the earth's natural horizon, he or she must rely on an instrument known as an artificial horizon. The artificial horizon is exactly what it sounds like. It is an artificial representation of what a pilot would see out of the windshield. The artificial horizon has an artificial sky, an artificial ground, an artificial horizon line and an artificial depiction of the airplane as viewed from the rear of the plane. When a pilot banks the wing of the plane to turn, the artificial horizon depicts that turn

Music's Broken Wings

on the face of the instrument in direct correlation to what the plane is actually doing in relation to the Earth's horizon. Additionally, the artificial horizon will also depict very accurately the plane's climbs and descents. Using this exact artificial representation of the plane's attitude, along with his other instruments, the pilot can fly an airplane precisely and safely even when the weather is not very good.

In order to gain the privilege to fly by instruments only, a pilot must undergo additional flight instruction with an approved instrument instructor, pass a written examination on instrument flying, then pass both an oral and flight examination with a designated instrument pilot examiner. Only after all of these requirements have been met may the pilot launch his or her plane into the air to fly without outside visual references. In the case of this flight, the pilot, Roger Peterson, had taken and failed his instrument flight test.

You will additionally read in the CAB report that Roger Peterson had performed all of his instrument training with one particular type of artificial horizon. This artificial horizon is a more modern type of instrument where the bank angle of the airplane is depicted directly above, or perpendicular to, the artificial plane's wings. On the particular night of this flight, the pilot was flying a plane with an older style of artificial horizon where the bank angle is depicted by an indicator that moves opposite to the one with which he was familiar (Figure 12-2). The mental confusion caused by this unfamiliarity must have contributed to the pilot's spatial disorientation.

There are many rumors that persist about this accident. There is, first of all, the fact that Buddy Holly had taken some flight lessons with the ultimate goal of becoming a licensed pilot. Since Holly was in the front right passenger seat of the plane, which is a traditional co-pilot's seat in some airplanes, the rumor exists that perhaps Buddy was at the controls of the plane when it went down. The reality is that this airplane was not equipped with controls on both sides of the cockpit. Instead, the plane had what is known as a "throw-over yoke," which means that it could be swung over from one side of the cockpit to the other. If the control yoke had been on Holly's side of the plane, the wreckage would have preserved this evidence and the investigation would have documented it. Because the official accident report does not describe this finding, we must conclude that pilot Peterson had the airplane's controls in front of him at all times during the short length of time that this plane was in the air. Buddy Holly was not the pilot, nor the co-pilot.

One of the other rumors that persists stems from the fact that Buddy Holly was carrying a small handgun with him at the time. Some have speculated that perhaps the gun discharged and incapacitated or frightened the pilot. Interestingly, the gun was not found until a few weeks after the accident and then only because of a request by Holly's widow. Supposedly, the farmer who found the weapon fired it to see if it worked. What is unfortunate is the fact that the CAB report never addressed the gun to put the rumors of any in-flight gun firing to rest. Although the available data may not convince some people who believe the theory of a discharged firearm, there was no evidence from inspection of the wreckage or autopsy of the pilot to support the supposition that the gun discharged on board the airplane.

The last rumor to be addressed is the suggestion that this airplane was named or called "American Pie." Apparently, this rumor surfaced on the Internet and is based on the incorrect notion that there was an American flag emblem on the airplane with the center cut out like a piece of pie. While it was popular during World War II to name a warplane and have artwork on the side, this practice was never embraced by the civilian industry. Certainly some aircraft owners do put American flag decals on their planes, but this is more a show of patriotism. Once again, there is no evidence to support any speculation or rumor that this particular airplane ever was named anything whatsoever. However, there is a song titled "American Pie," written by Don McLean, and this song is reportedly dedicated to Buddy Holly. However, that seems to be as far as that connection goes.

The genius and career of Buddy Holly is well known and documented. He was a groundbreaker for the Rock and Roll movement, and his influence in music is still felt to this day. Holly was one of the first inductees into the Rock and Roll Hall of Fame in 1986. Ritchie Valens was the first Hispanic-American rock star, and actually was considered the hottest performer on the Winter Dance Party tour. His ballad single "Donna" was number 3 on the Billboard charts during the tour, and ultimately reached number 2. He was only 17 years old when he died. Ritchie Valens was inducted into the Rock and Roll Hall of Fame in 2001.

The "Big Bopper" began his career in music as a disc jockey and this delay from recording made him the "old man" of the Winter Dance Party tour at 28 years old. During his deejay days at KTRM in Beaumont, Texas, he was always looking to push the envelope for ratings and while there he purposely set an on-the-air world endurance record of 1,821 records in 6 days. When he did finally emerge as a songwriter and performer, he proved to be more than a one-hit-wonder. While it is a fact that he was on the Winter Dance Party tour because of his huge hit, "Chantilly Lace," which was actually released as a "B" side single, he also wrote other great songs. Two of these songs, released after his death, reached number 1 on the charts. George Jones' version of "White Lightning" went to number 1 in the spring of 1959, and Johnny Preston took "Running Bear" to number 1 in 1960. Both songs are credited to J. P. Richardson.

Author

Aircraft addenda:

Common name: Bonanza, "V" tail Bonanza
Manufacturer: Beechcraft
First flight of prototype: 1945
Registration number for this airplane: N3794N
Seats: 4
Length: 26 feet, 5 inches
Wingspan: 33 feet, 6 inches
Height: 8'3"
Engine: (1) Continental E185-8, four-cylinder, horizontally opposed, piston
Horsepower: 185 h.p.
Empty weight (approximate): 1,458 lb.
Gross weight: 2,550 lb.
Service ceiling: 18,000 ft.
Fuel capacity: 39 U.S. gal.
Cruising speed: 172 mph

* The above photo represents the type of aircraft and not necessarily the exact model involved in the accident.

Personal addenda:

Charles Hardin Holley (Buddy Holly): guitar player, singer, songwriter
b. September 7, 1936: Lubbock, Texas
d. February 3, 1959: near Clear Lake, Iowa
Buried: City of Lubbock Cemetery, Lubbock, Texas

Richard Steven Valenzuela (Ritchie Valens): guitar player, singer, songwriter
b. May 13, 1941: Pacoima, California
d. February 3, 1959: near Clear Lake, Iowa
Buried: San Fernando Mission Cemetery, Mission Hills, California

Jiles Perry Richardson, Jr. (the "Big Bopper"): singer, songwriter
b. October 24, 1930: Sabine Pass, Texas
d. February 3, 1959: near Clear Lake, Iowa
Buried: Forest Lawn Memorial Park, Beaumont, Texas

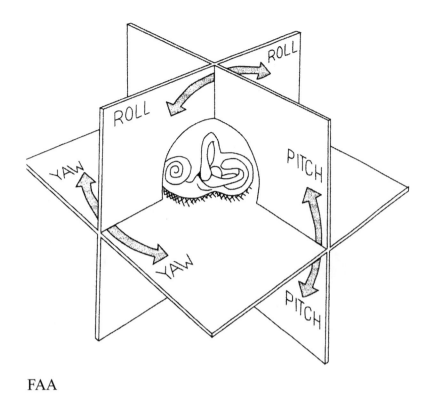

FAA

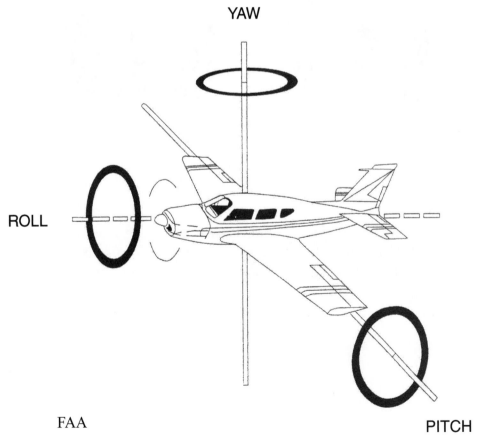

FAA

Figure 12-1

Conventional
Artifical
Horizon

Straight and Level   Left Turn (or Bank)

Sperry
Attitude Gyro

In the conventional artificial horizon, the bank angle indicator stays perpendicular to the instrument's wings. In the Sperry attitude gyro, the bank angle indicator stays perpendicular to the instrument's horizon.

Figure 12-2

Music's Broken Wings

Bill Griggs Collection

Actual photo of the February 3, 1959 crash site.

Bill Griggs Collection

Actual photo of the February 3, 1959 crash site.

Bill Griggs Collection

Actual photo of the February 3, 1959 crash site.

INCIDENT REPORT

CSDO #4

228 Administration Building

Municipal Airport, Des Moines, Iowa

FROM: Air Route Traffic Control Center
Federal Aviation Agency
Wold Chamberlain Field
Minneapolis 50, Minnesota

The following is a description of an incident which affected the operation of this Airways Operations Facility. It is forwarded to acquaint you with the particulars of the incident, and it is requested that it be immediately brought to the attention of the pilot or other individual(s) involved. It is hoped that a review of these facts will result in recommendations which will prevent recurrence of incidents of this type. No reply is required; however, if desired, the undersigned will be glad to answer any questions at your convenience. Any action which you can take to assist the Airways Operations Division to provide more efficient service will be appreciated.

TYPE OF INCIDENT	TIME OF INCIDENT			INCIDENT NO.
☒ PRIMARY ☐ SECONDARY	DATE: February 3, 1959	☐ DAY	☒ NIGHT	MSP ARTCC 629

AGENCY/AIRCRAFT IDENTIFICATION

N3794N Beechcraft Bonanza

NAME(S) OF PERSONNEL OR PILOT

Roger Peterson, Clear Lake, Iowa

SUMMARY OF INCIDENT

1. An alert notice was received on Beechcraft Bonanza N3794N, pilot Roger Peterson, enroute from Mason City, Iowa to Fargo, North Dakota. The aircraft, a charter flight with three passengers, departed Mason City at approximately 0055C without filing a flight plan with FAA facilities.

2. The alert notice was issued at 0515C by Mason City ATCS at the request of Dwyer Flying Service, Mason City, Iowa, owner of the aircraft. A communications search along the route of flight produced no information.

3. The 10th Air Force Search and Rescue Coordinatiln Center was alerted at 0641C by the Minneapolis Center.

4. Mason City sent a cancellation of the alert notice at 0955C along with a report that wreckage of the aircraft was located five miles north northwest of Mason City. All four occupants were killed.

5. The 10th Air Force Coordination Center was de-alerted at 1015C.

CIVIL AERONAUTICS BOARD

I have compared this and certify it to be a true copy.

CHAS F TRUMOND _C. F. Ellwanger_

Signature

AIR SAFETY INVESTIGATOR

Title

Bureau of Safety

REMARKS

cc: KC-520
    W-520

ATTACHMENTS	FORWARDED	
	DATE	SIGNATURE OF FACILITY CHIEF
	2/3/59	/s/ C. I. Bates
		C. I. Bates

U.S.G.P.O. ☆ 213267

Form ACA-304A
(6-52)

U. S. [DEPARTMENT] OF COMMERCE
CIVIL AERONAUTICS ADMINISTRATION

Form approved.
Budget Bureau No. 41-R1744.1

FOR CAA USE ONLY
ACCIDENT NO.

PILOT/OPERATOR AIRCRAFT ACCIDENT REPORT

1. LOCATION, DATE, AND TIME OF ACCIDENT

City, or Place and State	MASON CITY, IOWA	Date FEBR. 3, 1959
If on airport, name of airport	7 MILES N.W. OF AIRPORT	Time 0100 A.M. P.M.

Checkboxes: ☐ Dawn ☐ Daylight ☐ Dusk ☒ Night | ☐ On Airport ☐ In Traffic ☐ Pattern ☒ Other

2. PILOT AT THE CONTROLS

Name and Address
ROGER ARTHUR PETERSON
CLEAR LAKE, IOWA

Business or Profession: COMMERCIAL PILOT
Age 21   Telephone No. FL-74364

PILOT CERTIFICATE

CAA Certificate No. 1324428

☐ Student ☐ Private ☒ Commercial
☐ Airline Transport ☐ Flight Instructor ☐ Lighter-Than-Air

PILOT RATINGS

☒ Airplane ☐ Rotorcraft ☐ Glider ☐ Instrument
☒ Single Engine ☐ Multi-Engine ☒ Land ☐ Sea
Type Rating

AERONAUTICAL EXPERIENCE (Hours)

Pilot Time in This	Last 90 Days	Total
Make and Model	48:10	126:30
Instrument Pilot Time	7 HRS.	52:25
Night Pilot Time	14:40	37:35
Total Pilot Time	208:50	710:45

Medical Certif.—Class ☐ I ☒ II ☐ III
Date Issued 3-29-58
Certif. Limitations: Defective Hearing R. EEAR Waiver issued 4/29/58

Were you flight tested for your present Pilot Certificate within 12 months prior to accident?
☒ YES ☐ NO   If "Yes," who gave the test?

	Name	Date of Test	Where Given
☒ CAA Insp. ☐ Desig. Pilot Examiner	JOHN HUNT	1/27/59	DES MOINES

3. PURPOSE AND TYPE OF FLIGHT (Check each applicable item)

☐ Local ☒ Cross-Country ☐ Pleasure ☐ Business ☐ Commercial ☐ Noncommercial ☐ Training ☐ Dual Instruction
☒ Air Taxi/Charter ☐ Aerial Application ☐ Patrol ☐ Other (Describe)

4. AIRCRAFT

Name and Address of Owner
HUBERT J. DWYER
DWYER FLYING SERVICE
MASON CITY, IOWA

Aircraft Make BEECHCRAFT
Model 35
Registration No. N3794N
Serial No. D-1019

Engine Make CONTINENTAL
Model C185-8
Horsepower 185
Serial No.(s) 25470D-1-8

LAST INSPECTION
☐ 100 Hour ☒ Periodic ☐ Progressive
Date JAN. 10, 1959

AIRCRAFT DAMAGE
Describe: DEMOLISHED
Est. Cost, $
Will it be rebuilt or repaired? ☐ YES ☒ NO
Where is it located now?

PROPERTY DAMAGE—Other than aircraft
Describe
Est. Cost, $

5. OCCUPANTS AND OTHERS AND THEIR INJURIES (Include Pilot and Persons on the ground, if injured)

Name and Address	Crew	Passenger	Other	Fatal
CHARLES HARDIN (BUDDY) HOLLY		X		X
J. P. RICHARDSON		X		X
RICHARD VALENZUELA		X		X
ROGER ARTHUR PETERSON	X			X

6. WEATHER AND GENERAL CONDITIONS AT TIME OF ACCIDENT (Approximate as closely as possible)

Ceiling 3000 ft.; Visibility 6 mi.; Temperature 18 °F.; Wind direction 5 Velocity 25 m.p.h.; Eleva. 1216 ft.;
☐ Clear ☐ Gusty ☐ Turbulent ☐ Clouds ☐ Fog ☐ Rain ☐ Snow ☒ Other (Specify) BLOWING LIGHT SNOW

7. COLLISION ACCIDENTS (Complete only on other aircraft involved)

Name and Address of Owner
Aircraft Make
Model
Registration No.
Damage
Est. Cost, $

8. WHAT HAPPENED? (Describe events and circumstances leading to accident and present when it occurred. Use a diagram if desired. If mechanical failure occurred before impact please identify parts involved.)

(IF MORE SPACE REQUIRED CONTINUE ON REVERSE OF THIS FORM)

Signature of Pilot or Operator
HUBERT J. DWYER, OPER.
Date of this Report FEBRUARY 4, 1959

For CAA Inspector: GSDO of Accid. _____ GSDO of Res. _____
☐ Report accepted without detailed investigation
☒ Detailed investigation made of this accident

C. E. Stillwagon
Air Safety Investigator, CAB
CAA Inspector   Date 2/3-6/59

Form ACA-2400 (4-57)

4

8. WRECKAGE DISTRIBUTION (To be completed if airframe failure occurred prior to impact.)

DRAW A ROUGH PICTURE OF WRECKAGE DISTRIBUTION ON GRID SHOWING RELATIVE LOCATION OF VARIOUS COMPONENTS OF AIRFRAME. CENTER OF GRID INDICATES POINT OF IMPACT WITH GROUND. INDICATE APPROXIMATE SCALE USED

WRECKAGE·DISTRIBUTION·CHART

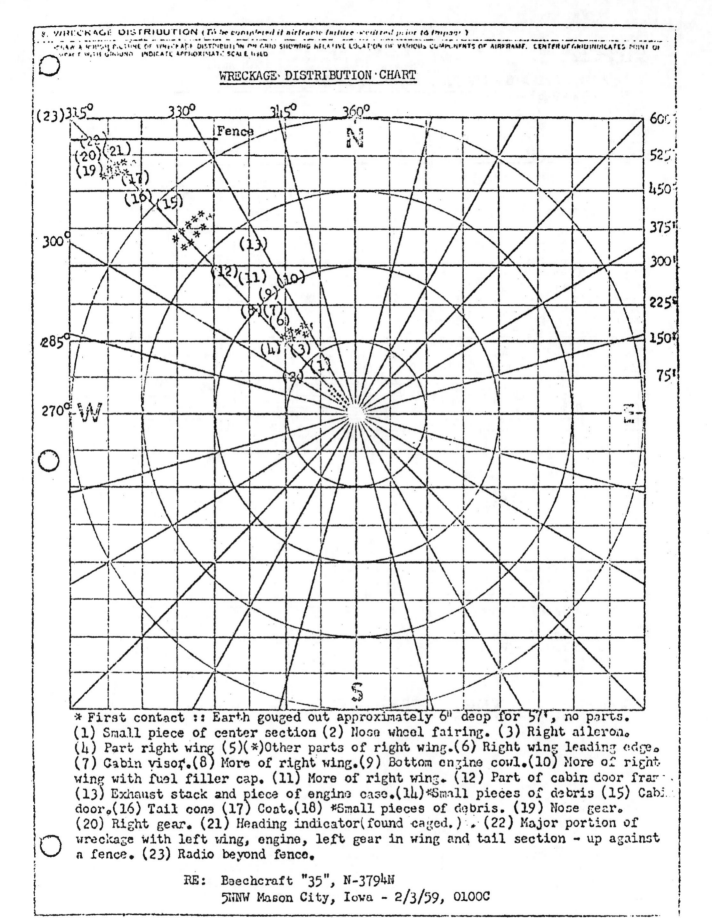

* First contact :: Earth gouged out approximately 6" deep for 57', no parts.
(1) Small piece of center section (2) Nose wheel fairing. (3) Right aileron.
(4) Part right wing (5)(*)Other parts of right wing.(6) Right wing leading edge.
(7) Cabin visor.(8) More of right wing.(9) Bottom engine cowl.(10) More of right
wing with fuel filler cap. (11) More of right wing. (12) Part of cabin door frame.
(13) Exhaust stack and piece of engine case.(14)*Small pieces of debris (15) Cabin
door.(16) Tail cone (17) Coat.(18) *Small pieces of debris. (19) Nose gear.
(20) Right gear. (21) Heading indicator(found caged.) . (22) Major portion of
wreckage with left wing, engine, left gear in wing and tail section - up against
a fence. (23) Radio beyond fence.

RE: Beechcraft "35", N-3794N
     5NNW Mason City, Iowa - 2/3/59, 0100C

I am Hubert J. Dwyer. I live at 409 18th St. W., Clear Lake, Iowa. I am the owner and fixed base operator at the Mason City Municipal Airport. This is in regards to the fatal flight of Bonanza N3794N on February 3, 1959. These are the events that I remember to the best of my knowledge. I worked at the office until approximately 6:00 P.M. February 2, 1959, at which time I left for a Jr. Chamber of Commerce meeting at Mason City, Iowa. I left the meeting and arrived home at approximately 9:45 P.M. At this time, our baby sitter asked me if I had been contacted about the charter flight. She told me that Mr. Carroll Anderson of the Surf Ballroom had called earlier that evening about a trip to Fargo, North Dakota and that she had called the Roger Peterson residence to see if they could reach me. I then called Mrs. Peterson on the telephone to find out if they had taken care of the trip. She told me that she had talked to Roger and he was going to take a trip at 12:30 A.M. to Fargo, North Dakota. I told her to have Roger call me if he needed help getting the plane out, due to the fact that we had a 170 Cessna parked in front of it.

I then went over to a Church meeting and picked up my wife. I would say that we went to bed approximately at 10:30 P.M. I received a call from Roger at approximately 11:15 to 11:30 P.M. Roger called me asking me if I would help him get the plane out. I dressed and drove directly to the airport following Roger into the drive. The first thing we did was to go to the Tower to check the weather conditions. Roger told me that he had checked several times earlier. To the best of my knowledge the weather conditions were approximately a 3000 ft. ceiling, 6 miles visibility, temperature approximately 18 degrees above zero. Wind direction was almost straight south and the anamometer was indicating about 22 knots. We had a very light snowing condition. As far as weather for the whole trip was concerned, we both agreed that he might have to stay overnight at Fargo, North Dakota due to the fact that they predicted a front to move in to Fargo at approximately 3:00 A.M. We then went over to Dwyer Flying Service, turned on the lights in the hangar and began an inspection of the aircraft. Roger personally opened both sides of the cowling, checked the engine compartment and accessories over and checked the oil. I watched him and as far as I remember, the oil was on about 8 3/4. We then both checked the airplane over completely and then rolled the plane outside.

The airplane was parked heading East by our 80 Oct. gas pump. Roger got in and started the airplane to warm it up and I would say he ran it approximately 8 or 10 minutes. I was in our office at this time. When he shut it off, I went out and personally filled both tanks with 80 Oct. gas. Then Roger put chocks under both main wheels and then got back in and started the airplane again. I would say the time was

About 12:20 A.M. he ran the airplane a few minutes more and then shut
it off around 12:30. We went in the office and wrote a ticket for the
trip. Roger then told me that the passengers were supposed to be there
at about 12:30. It was approximately 12:40 when Carroll Anderson drove in.
The fellows got out and Mr. Anderson introduced them to Roger. He did
not introduce them to me, but I heard the introductions and this was
the first time I realized who our passengers were to be. We all went
back into the office and they paid individually for the trip. We talked
for about 4 or 5 minutes, basically about where the boys were from and
one thing I specifically remember is that Buddy Holley mentioned that
he had been taking flying lessons and that he had hoped one of these days
to buy a Cessna and fly these trips himself when he was completely capable.

We then went outside and the fellows got in the airplane. I don't
recall how they sat in the back seat, but I do remember that Mr. Holley
sat in the right front seat. I remember specifically because Buddy
Holley got in the plane before Roger and then had to get out to let Roger
in first. They started the airplane and then taxied North out of our
taxi strip and then turned West and taxied up toward our terminal building. I got in my car and drove over to the terminal building and then
I went upstairs into the tower. Mr. Bryan was on duty and I asked him
if Roger had filed a flight plan yet as "one of my requirements of
charter flying is that the pilot should always file a flight plan". Mr.
Bryan said he had not filed a flight plan as yet, but had contacted him
by radio and said that he would file a flight plan as soon as he got into
the air. He sat on the North end of the North-South runway and sat there
for several minutes. I would say that at this time it was approximately
12:50 or 12:55 A.M. on the morning of February 3.

He turned on both landing lights and I stepped outside the tower
onto the platform and watched them take off. I would say it was a very
normal take off. He broke ground about one-third the way down the runway
and turned his landing lights off at approximately 150 feet of altitude.
I would say the climb out was quite normal and he leveled off South of
the field at approximately 800 feet. This is higher than usual for a
daytime pattern, but quite normal for night time flying. He made a 180°
(degree) turn to the left and took up about a straight North heading. I
stepped back inside the tower and asked if Roger had filed a flight plan
yet. He told me that he had not. So I asked Mr. Bryan to give him a
call on the radio and tell him I wanted him to file a flight plan both
ways. There was no answer. He tried another time or two and once more
throwing the master switch so that all the transmitters would be transmitting as he thought Roger might have changed frequencies. I again
stepped outside of the tower and could still see the white tail light
of the airplane northeast of the field.

The airplane still appeared to be approximately at the same altitude. The airplane took up what looked like a North West heading and I could still see the white tail light. When the airplane was directly North of the field, I noticed by watching the white tail light in reference to the red lights on the two towers on the North edge of the field the airplane appeared to be going down at a very slow rate of decent (descent) as it went farther away from us. I would guess that it was approximately 4 miles north of us. I thought at the time that probably it was an optical illusion due to the plane going away from us at an angle. I went back into the tower and Mr. Bryan was just coming out to shoot a new fix on the ceiling. We then went back into the tower and then tried for the next 10 or 15 minutes to reach Roger by radio. I couldn't figure why he didn't file a flight plan. So I asked Mr. Bryan if he would teletype ahead to Redwood Falls, Minnesota and to Alexandria, Minnesota and have them call me as soon as Roger made contact. These towns were both on his route and had Omni stations. I then went home at I guess approximately 1:30 A.M. I again contacted Bryan by telephone around 2:00 A.M. He told me that one station had acknowledged the teletype message and that they had not been contacted by our Beechcraft and the other did not acknowledge at all. I again asked him if he would teletype to Redwood Falls, Minn., Alexandria, Minnesota and Fargo, North Dakota. He said he would and would notify me as soon as he heard anything. I called Mr. Bryan again at approximately 3:00 A.M. as that was the time I felt Roger should be in Fargo. He said as yet he had received no word. I called him again about 3:30 A.M. and he said there was still no word of contact. I then called person to person by telephone for Roger Peterson the pilot of the Beechcraft N3794N.

The man at the tower informed us that he had not had a contact from the airplane and he did not expect one, due to a heavy snowstorm going on. I again called Mr. Bryan and asked him if he had contacted Minneapolis. He said no, but he would right away. I checked back with him around 4:00 A.M. and he told me that Minneapolis had no word either. I then called Charles McGlothlen our head mechanic to see if he could possibly give me any information as to where Roger might have gone. I believe this was about 4:10 A.M. He didn't have any information so I called Mr. Bryan again and asked him what I should do next. He said the only thing left was to contact Minneapolis and issue an alert. This I asked him to do and he said they would have it by 5:00 A.M. and that Minneapolis would take it from there and do whatever necessary to find the airplane. I went out to the airport at approximately 8:00 A.M. and the first place I went was up to the tower and they still had no news whatsoever. I didn't know what to do, so I stayed around the terminal building approximately until 9:15. I decided I just couldn't sit there and decided I would go fly and try to follow the same course that I thought Roger would have taken. I was only approximately 8 miles northwest of the field when I spotted the wreckage. I believe the time was approximately 9:35 A.M.

I called the tower by radio and told them I had fo nd the wreckage and told them to send the police and two ambulances immediately. I kept circling over the field until they got there, so as to help guide them in. That is about all I can tell you about the accident.

As to the condition of the airplane, I feel that it was in perfect condition with approximately 35 or 40 hours on a major and a periodic inspection run approximately January 10, 1959. This airplane made a flight to West Virginia and back Saturday January 31st and also to Des Moines and back and to Minneapolis and back on Sunday, February 1st, and we all felt that the airplane was in real good condition.

As to the pilot, Roger Peterson, he had quite a lot of experience and I feel that he was a very competent pilot. He had flown around 200 hours in the last 90 days.

These are the facts to the best of my knowledge.

/s/ Hubert J. Dwyer

CIVIL AERONAUTICS BOARD
I have compared this and certify it to be a true copy.

_____
Signature

_____
Title
Bureau of Safety

51

DWYER FLYING SERVICE

MUNICIPAL AIRPORT

Mason City, Iowa

Feb. 4, 1959

This is in regardes (regard) to the log book entries on Beechcraft N3794N. We purchased this plane on about 7/1/58 to the best of our knowledge the time on the airplane was 2004:03 on our periodic inspection on 1/10/59 we computed the time to be 2154:51 we arived (arrived) at this figure by cross refrence (reference) with the engine and aircraft log books this is true to the best of my knowledge.

Hubert J. Dwyer

/s/ Hubert J. Dwyer

CIVIL AERONAUTICS BOARD
I have compared this and certify it to be a true copy.

C. C. Stillwagon
Signature   AIR SAFETY
              INVESTIGATOR
Title
Bureau of Safety

ESTIMATED WEIGHT AND BALANCE ON BEECHCRAFT N3794N
ON ITS LAST FLIGHT FEB. 3, 1959

	WEIGHT	ARM	MOMENT
Empty Weight	1590	77.5	123225
Gas 39 Gal	234	75	17550
Oil 21/2 Gal.	19	43	817
Pilot	165	85	14035
F. Pass	190	85	16150
R. Pass	145	117	16965
R. Pass	165	117	19305
Baggage Est.	43	140	6020
	2551 lbs.		214057

Range for this flight / 82.4 to / 84.8

Loaded C.G. / 83.09
This is an estimate to the best of my knowledge.

/s/ Hubert J. Dwyer
Hubert J. Dwyer

CIVIL AERONAUTICS BOARD
I have compared this and certify it to be a
true copy.

C. E. Stillwagon
Signature   AIR SAFETY
             INVESTIGATOR
Title
Bureau of Safety

BEECHCRAFT N3794N
ENGINE LOG ENTRIES AND TIME
CORRECTIONS

4/11/52   636:45 Hrs. in Aircraft log showing engine
           change. Tac set at zero hours. Continental
           Reconditioned engine installed in Beech Model
           35 - Serial #D1019
           Engine Serial #25470D-1-8, Model E-185-8
                        Entry by: Mr. Robert Gorman
                                  A & E 147293

4/11/52   Annual inspection certificate issued
                        Entry by: William DeBlonk
                                  DAMI 5225

6/28/52   Aircraft time should be 728:25
           Tac time 91:40
           100 hr. inspection
                        Entry by: Glen R. Jones
                                  A & E 337164

10/8/52   Tac time 207:25. Aircraft time should be
           844:10. Entry shows it as certified as
           inspected, but doesn't say what kind of
           inspection.
                        Entry by: Glen R. Jones
                                  A & E 337164

11/12/52   Tac time 244:20. Aircraft time should be
           881:05. Installed crankcase breather
           modification kit #35-550 as per print.
                        Entry by: Robert Gorman
                                  A & E 149293

4/2/53   Tac time 273:20. Aircraft time should be
           910:05. Entry certified that it was inspected
           but doesn't say what kind of inspection.
                        Entry by: Glen R. Jones
                                  A & E 337164

4/2/53   No tac time entries or aircraft entries, but
           must be the same as above. Annual inspection
           & certified airworthy.
                        Entry by: William De Blonk
                                  DAMI 5225

6/5/53   Tac time 373:20. Aircraft time should be
           1010:05. 100 hr. periodic inspection. Engine
           Airworthy.
                        Entry by: Robert Gorman
                                  A & E 149293

9/15/53   TAC TIME 491:30. AIRCRAFT TIME SHOULD BE 1128:15. 100 HR. INSPECTION. INTAKE SEAL REPLACED IN #1 CYL. ENTRY BY: MACE A. COOLEY
A & E 568961

12/28/53   TAC TIME 579:25. AIRCRAFT TIME SHOULD BE 1216:10. 100 HRS. INSPECTION.
ENTRY BY: MACE COLLEY
A & E 568961

3/15/54   TAC TIME 614:05. AIRCRAFT TIME SHOULD BE 1250:50. 100 HR. INSPECTION.
ENTRY BY: ROBERT GORMAN
A & E149293

10/20/54   TAC TIME 789:00. AIRCRAFT TIME SHOULDBE 1425.45. COMPLETE MAJOR OVERHAUL ON ENGINE & ACCESSORIES. ENTRY BY: MACE A.COOLEY
A &E 568961

10/20/54   789:00 HRS. TAC SET TO "0" (THIS NOT IN LOG BUT EVIDENTLY SO AS THE NEXT ENTRY SHOWS ONLY 2:20 ON 10/26/54.) AIRCRAFT TIME SHOULD BE 1425:45.
ENTRY BY: MACE A. COOLEY
A & E568961

4/21/55   TAC TIME 142 HRS. SINCE MAJOR. TOTAL TIME THIS ENGINE 931:00. AIRCRAFT TIME SHOULD BE 1567:45. 100 HRS. INSPECTION. OIL TANK REPAIRED GASKETS REPLACED ON #3 CYL.
ENTRY BY:MACE A. COOLEY
A&E568961

10/29/55   TAC TIME 281:02 SINCE MAJOR. TOTAL TIME SHOULD BE 1070:02. AIRCRAFT TIME SHOULD BE 1706:47 100 HR. PERIODIC INSPECTION.
ENTRY BY:ROBERT GORMAN
A & E149293

4/2/56   TAC TIME 373:00 SINCE MAJOR. TOTAL TIME THIS ENGINE 1162:00. AIRCRAFT TIME SHOULD BE 1798:45. 100 HR. PERIODIC INSPECTION.
ENTRY BY: ROBERT GORMAN
A & E 149293

4/2/56   SAME TIMES AS ABOVE. FUEL PUMP REPLACED. REFER TO ATTACHED OVERHAUL RECORD.
ENTRY BY: ROBERT GORMAN
A & E 149293

12/12/56   TAC TIME 488:00 SINCE MAJOR. TOTAL TIME THIS ENGINE 1277:00. AIRCRAFT TIME SHOULD BE 1913:45 100 HR. INSPECTION. ENTRY BY: WILLIAM E HOGA.
A & E 305122

BEECHCRAFT N3794N
ENGINE LOG ENTRIES AND TIME
CORRECTIONS

4/11/57   TAC TIME 525:00, SINCE MAJOR. TOTAL TIME
           THIS ENGINE 1314:00. AIRCRAFT TIME SHOULD
           BE 1950:45. 100 HR. INSPECTION. NEW COIL
           & POINTS IN LEFT MAG. AIRWORTHY.
                        ENTRY BY: L.L. PRICE
                                  A P1167829

4/11/57   SAME TIME AS ABOVE. PERIODIC INSPECTION.
           AIRWORTHY.   ENTRY BY: JAMES COOPER
                                  AP 11844456

3/12/58   TAC TIME 625 SINCE MAJOR. TOTAL TIME THIS
           ENGINE 1414:00. AIRCRAFT TIME SHOULD BE
           2050:45. PERIODIC INSPECTION. INSTALLED
           NEW PUSH ROD TUBE - OIL SEALS & NEW ROCKER
           BOX GASKETS. INSTALLED NEW EXHAUST GASKETS
           NEW EXHAUST GASKERS ON RIGHT SIDE. AIRWORTHY.
                        ENTRY BY: JAMES COOPER
                                  A & P 1184456

7/11/58   TAC TIME 667:8 SINCE MAJOR. TOTAL TIME THIS
           ENGINE 1456:8. AIRCRAFT TIME SHOULD BE
           2093:25. 100HR INSPECTION. ENGINE AIRWORTHY/
                        ENTRY BY: CHARLES E. MCGLOTHLEN
                                  A & P 1395830

8/14/58   TAC TIME 696.9 SINCE MAJOR. OIL CHANGE WASHED
           COWLING & NOSE GEAR.
                        ENTRY BY: NO NAME

9/12/58   TAC TIME 720:50
                        ENTRY BY: ROGER PETERSON

10/4/58   TAC TIME 754.0
                        ENTRY BY: ROGER PETERSON

10/13/58   TAC TIME 761.8 SINCE MAJOR. TOTAL TIME THIS
           ENGINE 1550:8. AIRCRAFT TIME SHOULD BE 2187:25
           100 HR. INSPECTION. ENGINE AIRWORTHY
                        ENTRY BY: H. J. DWYER
                                  A P 1172704

11/22/58   TAC TIME 818.6. ENGINE TORN DOWN FOR MAJOR
           OVERHAUL.

1/3/59   TOTAL TIME SINCE MAJOR "0" HOURS. TOTAL TIME
           THIS ENGINE 1607.6. AIRCRAFT TOTAL TIME SHOULD
           BE 2244:05. COMPLETE ENGINE MAJOR & 100 HR.
           INSPECTION.
                        ENTRY BY: CHARLES E. MCGLOTHLEN
                                  A & P 1395830

1/10/59   SAME TIMES AS ABOVE. PERIODIC INSPECTION.
           AIRWORTHY.
                        ENTRY BY: H. J. DWYER AP 1172704

Chapter 12: Buddy Holly   111

BEECHCRAFT N3794N
ENGINE LOG ENTRIES AND TIME
CORRECTIONS

1/14/59   TIME ON TAC 817.8.   OIL CHANGED.
                        ENTRY BY: RICHARD CAREY

1/26/59   TIME ON TAC 840.9.   OIL CHANGED.
                        ENTRY BY: ROGER PETERSON

2/3/59   TIME ON TAC 858.6   TOTAL TIME SINCE MAJOR
            40 HRS.   TOTAL TIME THIS ENGINE 1647.6.   AIRCRAFT
            TOTAL TIME SHOULD BE 2284:05

2/3/59   AIRCRAFT COMPLETELY DEMOLISHED IN ACCIDENT.

                        H.J. DWYER 1172704

○ *BEECHCRAFT N3794N* ○
AIRCRAFT LOG ENTRIES AND TIME
CORRECTIONS

4/30/48   TIME ON TAC 93.7.   T.T. ON AIRCRAFT THIS DATE
          SHOULD BE 92.7 THIS DATE.   SER. #D-1019
          AIRCRAFT GIVEN 100 HR. INSPECTION.
                    ENTRY BY: RALPH F. HOLM
                              A & E 17685

9/29/48   TIME ON TAC 208.   TOTAL TIME ON AIRCRAFT SHOULD
          BE 208 THIS DATE.   100 HR ANNUAL INSPECTION
          PLUS CONTROL WHEEL CHAINS TIGHTENED, NEW STYLE
          LANDING GEAR SAFETY SWITCH INSTALLED, NEW STYLE
          FUEL UNIT HANDLE INSTALLED, SHIMMEY DAMPENER
          REBUILT, UP FLAP POSITION LIGHT REPLACED.   WING
          BOLTS TIGHTENED.
                    ENTRY BY: ALBERT DEWING
                              A & E 168748

7/7/49   NO TIME ENTRY THIS DATE.   AD49-4-1 COMPLIED
          WITH.   CHAIN OK.
                    ENTRY BY: HAROLD W. HATHEWAY
                              A & E 819840

11/1/49   NO TIME ENTRY THIS DATE.   ROUTINE ANNUAL INSP-
          TION PERFORMED PLUS BRAKE BLOCKS REPLACED XXXX
          BOTH WHEELS, INSTALLED ANTENNA RAIL BUMPER
          BLOCK.   ENTRY BY: PAUL W. CROWLEY
                              A & E 425146

11/17/50 TIME ON TAC 519.   TOTAL TIME ON AIRCRAFT SHOULD
          BE 519.   §ROUTINE 100 HRS. INSPECTION PERFORMED
          PLUS AD 50-5-2 COMPLIED WITH.
                    ENTRY BY: CURTIS D. REIBER
                              A & E 16534

12/12/51 TAC TIME 612.   TOTAL TIME THIS DATE SHOULD BE
          612.   ROUTINE 100 HR. INSPECTION PERFORMED PLUS
          AD 51-8-2 NEW HEAT TREATED CONTROL RODS INSTALLED
                    ENTRY BY: CURTIS D. REIBER
                              A & E 16534

4/11/52   TIME ON TAC 636:45.   TOTAL TIME SHOULD BE 636:45
          ROUTINE 100 HRS. INSPECTION PERFORMED. PLUS STEP
          RETRACT CABLE REPLACED, ENGINE SERIAL #347D
          REMOVED AND CONTINENTAL RECONDITIONED ExXXx ENGIN
          SER. #25470D-1-8 INSTALLED.   ECLIPSE MODEL E-80
          STARTER INSTALLED, NET WEIGHT DECREASE 3 LBS AT/
42", WIRING CIRCUIT (STARTER) & FIREWALL MODIFIED AS PER
          BEECH SERVICE BULLETIN.   NEW PROP CONTROL SWITCH
          INSTALLED.   NEW "O" RING INSTALLED AT WOBBLE
          PUMP SHAFT.   TAC RESET TO ZERO HOURS.
                    ENTRY BY: ROBERT GORMAN
                              A & E 149293

4/11/52   TAC TIME 0.   TOTAL TIME ON AIRCRAFT SHOULD BE
          636:45.   ANNUAL INSPECTION PERFORMED. AIRWORTHY.
                    ENTRY BY: WILLIAM DEBLANK
                              DAMI 5225

BEECHCRAFT N5794N
AIRCRAFT LOG ENTIRES AND TIME
CORRECTIONS

6/3/52   TOTAL TIME 694. DOUBLE "O" RING ASSY. INSTALLED
ON WOBBLE PUMP AS PER AD NOTE 49-31-1
ENTRY BY: ROBERT GORMAN
A & E 149293

6/28/52   NO TIME ENTRY. TOTAL TIME SHOULD BY 727:25. ROUTINE
100 HR. INSPECTION PERFORMED. AIRWORTHY.
ENTRY BY: GLEN R. JONES
A & E 337164

10/8/52   NO TIME ENTRY. TOTAL TIME SHOULD BE 844:10.
ROUTINE CHECK AS REQUIRED BY CAR & AIRWORTHY.
ENTRY BY: GLEN R. JONES
A & E 337164

3/20/53   NO TIME ENTRY. AD NOTE 53-1-2 COMPLIET WITH.
ENTRY BY: ROBERT GORMAN
A & E 149293

4/2/53   NO TIME ENTRY. TOTAL TIME SHOULD BE 910:05
ROUTINE CHECK AS REQUIRED BY CAR. AIRWORTHY.
NEW BRAKE DISC & BLOCKS & ANTI-RATTLER CLIPS,
BATTERY CHARGED.
ENTRY BY: GLEN R. JONES
A & E 337164

4/2/53   NO TIME ENTRY. TOTAL TIME SHOULD BE 910:05.
ROUTINE ANNUAL INSPECTION PERFORMED.
ENTRY BY: WILLIAM DeBLANK
DAMI 5225

6/4/53   NO TIME ENTRY. TOTAL TIME SHOULD BE 1010:05
ROUTINE 100 HR. INSPECTION PERFROMED & AIRWORTHY.
ENTRY BY: GLEN R. JONES
A & E 337164

7/10/53   NO TIME ENTRY. AD 53-11-1 COMPLIED WITH.
ENTRY BY: OTTO HOEIGEN
A & E 492232

9/15/53   NO TIME ENTRY. TOTAL TIME SHOULD BE 1128:15
ROUTINE 100 HR. INSECTION.
ENTRY BY: MACE A. COOLEY
A & E 568961

12/28/53   NO TIME ENTRY. TOTAL TIME SHOULD BE 1216:10
ROUTINE 100 HR. INSPECTION PERFORMED & AIRWORTHY.
AD 53-20-2 COMPLIED WITH.
ENTRY BY: MACE A. COOLEY
A & E 568961

3/15/54   NO TIME ENTRY. TOTAL TIME SHOULD BE 1250:50
ROUTINE 100 HR. INSPECTION PERFORMED. AIRWORTHY.
ENTRY BY: ROBERT GORMAN
A & E 149293

3/15/54   NO TIME ENTRY. TOTAL TIME SHOULD BE 1250:50.
ANNUAL INSPECTION. ACA1362 ISSUED
ENTRY BY: ROBERT GORMAN
DAMMKX
DAMI 5345

10/20/54   NO TIME ENTRY. TOTAL TIME SHOULD BE 1425:45. ENGINE SER. #25470D-1-8 REMOVED, OVERHAULED & RE-INSTALLED IN AIRCRAFT.
ENTRY BY: MACE A. COOLLEY
A & E 568961

10/20/54   TAC TIME 789.0. TOTAL TIME SHOULD BE 1425:45. ROUTINE 100 HR. PERIODIC INSPECTION PERFORMED & AIRWORTHY. ENTRY BY: ROBERT GORMAN
A & E 149293

10/20/54   NO TIME ENTRY. TOTAL TIME SHOULD BE 1425:45. ANNUAL INSPECTION PERFORMED & ACA1362 ISSUED.
ENTRY BY: ROBERT GORMAN
DAMI 5345

1/16/55   NO TIME ENTRY. NARCO OMNIGATOR INSTALLED. PANEL UNIT 7.5 LBS. @ ≠ 67" & AMPLIFIER 7.0 LBS. @ ≠ 47". ENTRY BY: ROBERT GORMAN
A & E 149293

4/21/55   NO TIME ENTRY. TOTAL TIME SHOULD BE 1567:45 ROUTINE 100 HR. PERIODIC INSPECTION PERFORMED & AIRWORTHY. ENTRY BY: ROBERT GORMAN
A & E 149293

4/21/55   NO TIME ENTRY. TOTAL TIME SHOULD BE 1567:45. ANNUAL INSPECTION PERFORMED & ACA 1362 ISSUED.
ENTRY BY: ROBERT GORMAN
DAMI 5345

7/5/55   TIME ON TAC 187. ONE SET FA203-219-88AD PROP BLADES INSTALLED. SER. #1BLADE 3533, #2 BLADE 5282. HUB ASSEMBLY TORN DOWN, CLEAN & INSPECTED. NEW PITCH CHANGE BEARINGS, NEW INTERMEDIATE DRUM BLADE SEAL, INSTALLED NEW PITCH CHANGE RETAINER RING. PROP BALLANCED AND PTTCH RESET WITHIN 1/8 DEGREE EACH OTHER. NOSE GEAR REMOVED & REBUILT. NEW TIRES & TUBE INSTALLED. BOTH BRAKE MASTER CYLINDERS REBUILT.
ENTRY BY: OWEN H. GASSAWARY (?)
A & E 457174

10/28/55   NO TIME ENTRY. TOTAL SHOULD BE 1706:47. ROUTINE 100 HR PERIODIC INSPECTION PERFORMED. AIRWORTHY.
ENTRY BY: ROBERT GORMAN
A & E 149293

10/28/55   NO TIME ENTRY. TOTAL TIME SHOULD BE 1706:47. ANNUAL INSPECTION PERFORMED & ACA 1362 ISSUED.
ENTRY BY: ROBERT GORMAN
DAMI 5345

4/2/56   TAC TIME 373 HRS. TOTAL TIME SHOULD BE 1798:45. ROUTINE 100 HR. INSPECTION PERFORMED. AIRWORTHY.
ENTRY BY: ROBERT GORMAN
A & E 149293

4/2/56   NO TIME ENTRY. TOTAL TIME SHOULD BE 1798:45. ANNUAL INSPECTION PERFORMED & ACA 1362 ISSUED.
ENTRY BY1 ROBERT GORMAN ,DAMI 5345

4/2/56   No time entry. Total time should be 1798:45
Piston assembly & selector cone assembly replaced
in wobble pump.
> Entry by: Robert Gorman
> A & E 149293

7/6/56   Tac time 416:00. Wobble pump assembly replaced.
> Entry by: Robert Gorman
> A & E 149293

8/2?/56   No time entry. Beech S.B. #35-32 C/W
> Entry by: Robert Gorman
> A & E 149293

8/2/56   No time entry. Cabin door outer skin reinforced
at lower hinge.
> Entry by: Robert Gorman
> A & E 149293

12/12/56   Time on tac 488:00. Total time should be 1913:45.
Routine 100 hr. inspection performed plus striped
paint. Balanced aelerons & repainted entire
aircraft. Installed new battery.
> Entry by: William Hogan
> A & E 305122

2/7/57   No time entry. Prop overhauled by Flottorp.
Refer to ACA 337.
> Entry by: Robert Gorman
> A & E 149293

3/22/57   No time entry. Installed vacuum system incorporatin
one regulator, directional gyro 4.0 lbs. @ 66.0",
Sperry artificial horizon 3.0 lbs. @ 66.0".
Vacuum set at 4.2" & 2.2" H.G.
> Entry by: Robert Gorman
> A & E 149293

4/11/57   Time on tac 525 hrs. Total time on aircraft
should be 1950:45. Normal routine maintenance
for periodic plus new safety belts installed
on fron seat, new assist step cable. New safety
bunge & new bumpers.
> Entry by: James Cooper
> A P 1184456

9/27/57   No time entry. Checked stabilizer. Front &
rear bulkheads for cracks or distortion in
compliance with AD57-18-1
> Entry by: James Cooper
> AP 1184456

9/27/57   No time entry. Installed item 409, Lear Arcon
& Lear Radio. ADF-14. ACA 337 issued. Dated
9/21/57.   Entry by: Robert Gorman
> A E 149293

3/12/58   Tac time 625. Total time on aircraft should be
2050:45 this date. Installed new brake blocks
both wheels, adjusted landing gear warning horn.
> Entry by: James Cooper AP 1395830

BEECHCRAFT N3794N
AIRCRAFT LOG ENTRIES AND TIME
CORRECTIONS

7/8/58   TIME ON TAC 667. TOTAL TIME ON AIRCRAFT SHOULD
BE ~~20:22:45~~ 2092:45. (AIRCRAFT PURCHASED BY
DWYER THIS DATE) 100 HRS INSPECTION & ROUTINE
MAINTENANCE PERFORMED.
ENTRY BY: CHARLES E. MCGLOTHLEN
A P 1395830

9/13/58   TIME ON TAC 761.8 TOTAL TIME ON AIRCRAFT SHOULD
BE 2187:25. 100 HR. PERFORMED & AIRWORTHY.
ENTRY BY: CHARLES E. MCGLOTHLEN
A P 1395830
H. J. DWYER AI 1172704

1/3/59   TIME ON TAC 818.6 TOTAL TIME ON AIRCRAFT SHOULD
BE 2244:05. ROUTINE MAINTENANCE PERFORMED ON
100 HR. INSPECTION PLUS REPLACE BULB IN FLAP
INDICATOR & NEW MAIN TIRES.
ENTRY BY: CHARLES E. MCGLOTHLEN
A P 1395830

1/10/59   TIME ON TAC 818.6 TT. 2244:05. PERIODIC
INSPECTION PERFORMED.
ENTRY BY: H. J. DWYER
A P 1172704

2/3/59   TIME ON TAC AT TIME OF ACCIDENT 858.6. TOTAL
TIME ON AIRCRAFT SHOULD BE 2284:05.

Form CAB-457
(3-7-55)

UNITED STATES OF AMERICA
CIVIL AERONAUTICS BOARD
BUREAU OF SAFETY
WASHINGTON, D. C.

BUDGET BUREAU No. 39-R024.2
APPROVAL EXPIRES 3-1-58

STATEMENT OF WITNESS

Place ...... Mason City, Ia. ......

Date ...... 2/4/59 ......

I. Place of accident ...... Mason City, Iowa ...... Date ...... 2/3/59 ...... Hour ...... 0100 CST. ......

II. Aircraft ...... Beechcraft ...... CAA Certificate No. and Symbol ...... N-3794N ......

III. What is your name ...... Dalbert Juhl ...... Address ...... Clear Lake ...... Age ...... 22 ......

IV. Occupation ...... Farmer ...... By whom employed ...... Albert Juhl ......

V. Where were you at the time of the accident ...... At home 1/2 mile East. ......

VI. Tell in your own words what you saw before and at the time the accident occurred.

We got home about 10:15. The weather was pretty good, it was snow(ing) a little bit now and then. We went to bed, then between 12 and 1 we heard a plane go over. To me the motor was working good and he had it going pretty good and that was the last we heard of it. To me I think the plane went somewhere near our place. It was pretty low then and it keep (kept) right on going. The wind was blowing from Southwest.

CIVIL AERONAUTICS BOARD
I have compared this and certify it to be a true copy.

_____
Signature

_____
Title
Bureau of Safety

_____ /s/ Dalbert Juhl
Dalbert Juhl (Signature)

(Use reverse side of sheet for diagram and additional statement)

USComm-DC 30073

81

Music's Broken Wings

Form CAB-457
(3-7-55)

UNITED STATES OF AMERICA
CIVIL AERONAUTICS BOARD
BUREAU OF SAFETY
WASHINGTON, D. C.

BUDGET BUREAU NO. 39-R024.2
APPROVAL EXPIRES 3-1-58

STATEMENT OF WITNESS

Place ..... Clear Lake .....

Date ..... Feb. 4, 1959 .....

I. Place of accident ..... Mason City, Iowa ..... Date ..... February 3, 1959 ..... Hour ..... App. 1:00

II. Aircraft ..... Beechcraft ..... CAA Certificate No. and Symbol ..... N-3794N .....

III. What is your name ..... Reeve Eldridge ..... Address ..... Rt. 3 ..... Age ..... 35 .....

IV. Occupation ..... Farmer ..... By whom employed ..... self .....

V. Where were you at the time of the accident ..... In bed. .....

VI. Tell in your own words what you saw before and at the time the accident occurred.

Woke out of a sound sleep by motor roar. Sounded smooth but pulling as though climbing. Couldn't see nothing (anything) because of darkness, but was low from sound. Strong wind blowing with a southeasterly direction. Woke my wife succenly & scared her & child.

There is a hall light left on all night that shows out of window.

CIVIL AERONAUTICS BOARD
I have compared this and certify it to be a true copy.

Signature
_____

Title
Bureau of Safety

/s/ Reeve Eldridge
_____
Reeve Eldridge (Signature)

(Use reverse side of sheet for diagram and additional statement)

USComm-DC 30073

9

Form CAB-457
(3-7-55)

UNITED STATES OF AMERICA
CIVIL AERONAUTICS BOARD
BUREAU OF SAFETY
WASHINGTON, D. C.

BUDGET BUREAU NO. 39-R024.2
APPROVAL EXPIRES 3-1-58

STATEMENT OF WITNESS

Place ... Mason City, Iowa

Date ... 2/4/59

I. Place of accident ... Mason City, Iowa ... Date ... 2/3/59 ... Hour ... 0100 CST

II. Aircraft ... Beechcraft ... CAA Certificate No. and Symbol ... N3794N

III. What is your name ... Charles E. McGlothlen ... Address ... 804 N. 13th St. ... Age ... 31
Commercial Pilot &

IV. Occupation ... A & E Mechanic ... By whom employed ... Dwyer Flying Service

V. Where were you at the time of the accident ....

VI. Tell in your own words what you saw before and at the time the accident occurred.

On the morning of Monday, Feb. 2, 1959 when I arrived for work at about 8:00 a.m., Roger Peterson was walking from the office to the shop. We cleaned the shop then started riveting on a 120 Cessna. We worked together most of the day on the 120. He left work at about 5:15.

At about 7:30 p.m., my wife & I went to his house to pick him up. My wife stayed with his while Roger & I went to the local Jatcee meeting, of which we were both members. It was at the meeting that Roger received a phone call about the trip. He borrowed my car to go to the airport to check the weather and mileage. He returned shortly, made a phone call and then told me he had a trip to make at about 12:00 or 12:30 that night. The meeting was over soon & we returned to Roger's home at about 9:30 p.m. We had coffee & pie with our wives and talked e while, then my wife & I left about 10:00. He seemed to be in a very good mood all the time.

CIVIL AERONAUTICS BOARD

I have compared this and certify it to be a true copy.

Signature _____

Title _____
Bureau of Safety

/s/ Charles E. McGlothlen
(Signature)

(Use reverse side of sheet for diagram and additional statement)

USComm-DC 30073

Music's Broken Wings

Coroner's investigation
Air crash, Feb. 3, 1959
SW¼ Section 18, Lincoln Twp.
Cerro Gordo County, Iowa

Jiles P. Richardson, Charles Holley, Richard Valenzuela and Roger A. Peterson, pilot of the plane, were killed in the crash of a chartered airplane when it fell within minutes of takeoff from the Mason City Airport. The three passengers were members of a troupe of entertainers who appeared at the Surf Ballroom at Clear Lake, Iowa, the evening of Feb. 3, 1959, bound for Fargo, N. D. and was headed northwest from the airport at the time of the crash in a stubble field, 5¼ miles north of Clear Lake, Iowa. The plane was discovered about 9:00 A.M., February 3, 1959, when Mr. H. J. Dwyer, owner of the crashed plane, made aerial search because he had received no word from Peterson since his takeoff.

The wreckage had been approached only by Deputy Sheriff Bill McGill in his sheriff's car before I arrived about 11:15 A.M. At this time two sheriffs' cars, two highway patrol cars and cars carrying members of the press, both reporters and photographers, and representatives of TV and radio stations and a few spectators were allowed to pass through the gate into the field where the crash occurred. Approach was made in a circuitous route to avoid disturbing wreckage and debris from the crash.

The wreckage lay about 1/2 mile west from the nearest north-south gravel road and the farmhomes of the Albert Juhl's and Delbert Juhl's. The main part of the plane lay against the barbed wire fence at the north end of the stubble field in which it came to earth. It had skidded and/or rolled approximately 570 feet from point of impact directed northwesterly. The shape of the mass of wreckage approximated a ball with one wing sticking up diagonally from one side. The body of Roger Peterson was enclosed by wreckage with only the legs visible sticking upward. Richard Valenzuela's body was south, lying prone, head directed south 17 feet from the wreckage; Charles Holley's body, also in the prone position, was lying southwest, head directed southwest, 17 feet from the wreckage; and J. P. Richardson's body, lying partly prone and partly on the right side, was northwest of the wreckage, head directed south 40 feet from the wreckage, across the fence in a picked cornfield. Fine snow which fell lightly after the crash had drifted slightly about the bodies and wreckage. Some parts of each body had been frozen by the ten hours' exposure in temperature reported to have been near 18 degrees during that time. The three bodies on the ground were removed before I left. Peterson's body was removed after permission was granted by the inspector for the Civil Aeronautics Board and Federal Aviation Agency. This was done by Deputy Sheriffs Wm. McGill and Lowell Sandquist using metal cutting tools to open a space in the wreckage.

At the scene of the crash Mr. Carroll Anderson was helpful in tentatively identifying the bodies from the clothing.

A large brown leather suitcase with one catch open lay near one leg of Charles Holley, and about 8 ft. north of the same body lay a travel case with brown leather ends and sides of a light plaid color. This measured approximately 15 in. x 12 in. x 6 in.

A billfold containing the name of Tommy Douglas Allsup and a leather pocket case marked with the name, "Ritchie Valens", were brought to me at the scene by Deputy Sheriffs inspecting the ground over which the wreckage had skidded and rolled.

Glen Kellogg of Clear Lake took photos of the scene at the request of Sheriff Jerry Allen and me. News and TV photographers also took still pictures and movies of the scene.

The plane was a Beach-Craft Bonanza, No. N3794N, painted red, with white and black trim. Deputy Sheriff Lowell Sandquist, an experienced pilot, who has flown in and out of the Mason City airport, was present when the radio and navigational equipment from the plane was examined. He reports the radio to have been set for listening and talking to the Mason City Airport Station MCW, and the navigational equipment to have been correctly set for a course from Mason City to Fargo, N. D.

Arrangements for the flight were made by Mr. Carroll Anderson, Manager of the Surf Ballroom at Clear Lake, Iowa, with Mr. H. J. Dwyer, fixed base operator for the Mason City Airport. The reasons given to Mr. Anderson for the flight were that all three passengers wished to reach their next destination in their itinerary ahead of the chartered bus which carried the rest of the troupe in order to have some laundry done. Mr. Anderson drove the three passengers to the airport in his family automobile. Accompanying him were his wife and 8-year-old son. They saw the plane take off and make its circle to take up its course.

The Air Traffic Communication Center of the Federal Aviation Agency at the Mason City Municipal Airport reported to me that at 0058 on February 3rd, the wind was south, gusty to 20 M.P.H., temperature 18 degrees F., dew point 11. In takeoff, the plane followed a normal procedure using the runway toward the south and turning in a counterclockwise direction. The amount of now falling from midnight to 6:30 A.M. on February 3rd was listed as a trace.

Further information from them was that as the pilot taxied down the runway he communicate by radio with the tower and secured additional information about the weather en route. He told the officer in charge in the tower he would file a flight plan after getting in the air. When this information did not come in, the officer tried to reach the pilot without getting a reply.

An official investigation was carried on by a crew of field representatives headed by Mr. C. E. Stillwagon of the Civil Aeronautics Board, Bureau of Safety Investigation, 4825 Troost Avenue, Kansas City, Missouri, and Mr. A. J. Prokop, Federal Aviation Agency, Des Moines office. This group spent three days on the investigation arriving here the evening of February 3rd. They visited the scene of the crash for preliminary survey before dark that day.

I, Ralph E. Smiley, M. D., Acting Coroner of Cerro Gordo County, Iowa, on the 4th day of February, 1959, hereby certify that the above facts are made of record after diligent investigation and I believe them to be correct.

Ralph E. Smiley, md
Acting Coroner

CIVIL AERONAUTICS BOARD

BUREAU OF SAFETY

NOTIFICATION

re

Aircraft Accident involving Beechcraft N-3794N
which occurred 5 NW Mason City, Iowa on Febru-
rary 3, 1959 at approximately 0100 CST.

Notification of the accident was received in the Kansas City
office of the Civil Aeronautics Board at approximately 10:45 a.m.,
CST, on February 3, 1959 by a long distance telephone call from
Mr. A. J. Prokop, Supervising Inspector of the Federal Aviagion
Agency GSDO #4 at Des Moines, Iowa. Mr. Prokop informed our office
that an accident had occurred near Mason City, Iowa early that morning and involved Beechcraft N-3794N, owned by the Dwyer Flying Service,
Mason City, Iowa and that the pilot, Roger Peterson, and three passengers were fatally injured.

This investigator made arrangements to depart Kansas City by the
first available means of transportation, which was Braniff Airways
Flight 66, and so notified Mr. Prokop by telephone. At this time
arrangements were completed to meet and accompany him and other inspectors from his office at Des Moines to the scene of the accident.
I proceeded to Des Moines as scheduled and accompanied Inspectors
Prokop, Anderson and Becchetti to Mason City in a FAA rental aircraft.

Arrival at the scene was approximately 5:00 p.m. that same afternoon and the investigation was begun. Investigation at the scene continued until February 6, 1959.

C. E. Stillwagon
C. E. Stillwagon
Air Safety Investigator
2/9/59

Hartley, Iowa
February 10, 1959

Federal Aviation Agency
Municipal Airport
Des Moines, Iowa

Gentlemen: Re: Roger Arthur Peterson
                          Aircraft Accident (Fatal)
                          February 3, 1959

        According to my records, I gave Roger Arthur
Peterson 8 hours of instrument dual flight instruction
in preparation for his Commercial Pilot Certificate.

        Mr. Peterson was below average at the end of
this time in that he had tendencies up into the 6th
hour of developing severe vertigo, and allowing the
aircraft to go into diving spirals to the right.

                          Sincerely yours,

                          Lambert L. Fechter
                          Flight Instructor Certificate -
                             Airplanes and Instrument
                          CFI 51511

UNITED STATES OF AMERICA
CIVIL AERONAUTICS BOARD
WASHINGTON, D. C.

```
* * * * * * * * * * * * * * * * * *
                                  *
In the Matter of Investigating of *
Accident Involving Aircraft of U. S. *
Registry N3794N, Which Occurred   *   Accident File No. 2-0001
Near Mason City, Iowa, February 3, 1959 *
                                  *
* * * * * * * * * * * * * * * * * *
                                  *
```

ORDER TO TAKE DEPOSITIONS

Pursuant to the authority conferred by Order of the Civil

Aeronautics Board adopted December 28, 1951, Mr. Van R. O'Brien,

Assistant Chief, Hearing and Reports Division, Bureau of Safety,

is hereby designated to take such depositions as are necessary

in connection with the above-entitled matter, with authority to

sign and issue subpena, administer oaths and affirmations, and

designate the time and place of the taking of the depositions.

Dated this 11th day of February 1959.

_____
Acting Director, Bureau of Safety

Office Memorandum • UNITED STATES GOVERNMENT

FEDERAL AVIATION AGENCY

Sioux Falls, South Dakota

DATE: February 12, 1959

AIR MAIL

TO   : Inspector-in-charge, CAB

FROM : Supervising Inspector, GSDO 3-9

SUBJECT: Instrument Rating Flight Test — Roger A. Peterson, Alta, Iowa
March 21, 1958

       The subject flight test was conducted by the writer at Sioux Falls, South Dakota. The applicant's flight instructor, Leonard G. Ross, Box 26, Boulevard Station, Sioux City, Iowa was on board in the capacity of safety observer during the flight.

       Following are the results of the flight test, which was disapproved:

1. Aircraft used in test was a Piper PA-22, N8406D.

2. Phase I — Oral Operational Examination — accomplished satisfactorily.

3. Phase II — Instrument Flying — accomplished satisfactorily.

4. Phase III — Radio Navigation and Approach Procedures — unsatisfactory for the following reasons:
   a. Applicant had difficulty copying and interpreting ATC Clearances. Failed to orientate himself and comply with Air Traffic Control instructions given by Sioux Falls Approach Control.
   b. Failure to properly tune and use his omni radio, became confused and was unable to establish on course.
   c. Failed to establish holding procedures and identify station passage.
   d. Lost control of the aircraft, on two occasions, while reading approach charts and descended below his assigned altitude in a spiral attitude. At this point the flight test was discontinued, and no approach procedure, missed approach procedure or emergency procedure was accomplished.

       This applicant was very susceptible to distractions and became upset and confused during Phase III of the flight test.

       The applicant's deficiencies were thoroughly discussed with him and his flight instructor.

Melvin O. Wood, 3-9

CIVIL AERONAUTICS BOARD
DOCKET No. _____ EXHIBIT No. _____
WITNESS _____
DATE _____

c — GSDO 3-
KC-250

CIVIL AERONAUTICS BOARD

BUREAU OF SAFETY

FACTUAL SUMMARY OF INVESTIGATION

RE

Aircraft Accident involving Beechcraft N-3794N
which occurred 5 NW Mason City, Iowa Airport on
February 3, 1959 at approximately 0100 CST.

ACCIDENT

Beechcraft 35, N-3794N, was involved in an accident on February 3, 1959
approximately 5 miles Northwest of the Mason City, Iowa Municipal Airport
at approximately 0100 CST. The accident resulted in fatal injuries to
the pilot and the three passengers. The aircraft was completely demolished.

INVESTIGATION

History of Flight

During the early evening of February 2, 1959, Roger Peterson, employed as pilot for the Dwyer Flying Service at Mason City, Iowa was contacted regarding a cross-country charter flight later that evening from
Mason City to Fargo, North Dakota. Purpose of the flight was to take
three entertainers to Fargo upon completion of their show at Clear Lake,
estimating the time to be about 12:30 a.m. on February 3, 1959.

In order to obtain the current weather conditions for the trip, Peterson
visited the Mason City Air Traffic Communications Station in person and obtained the Mason City, Iowa; Minneapolis, Redwood Falls, Alexandria and
Fargo, and the terminal forecast for Fargo. All stations were reporting
Ceilings of at least 5000 and visibility of 10 miles. The terminal forecast called for light snow showers at Fargo as of 030200 CST. It also
indicated a cold front passage at Fargo at 0400 CST.

At 022200 CST, Mr. Peterson again called the ATCS and requested weather
along his route to Fargo. At that time Alexandria and Fargo were giving
clear weather conditions. At 2300 CST, Mr. Peterson again called ATCS
and requested weather along his route and the new terminal forecast at
Fargo. All stations were reporting lowering ceilings at 4200 feet and
visibility of 10 miles. Light snow was being reported at Minneapolis.
The terminal forecast at Fargo, his destination, called for a frontal
passage at 0200 CST instead of 0400 CST. 9

At 022355 CST, Mr. Peterson and Mr. Hubert Dwyer, owner of the operation, personally checked the current weather conditions and forecasts for the trip.

The aircraft was then rolled out and warmed up by Mr. Peterson for eight to ten minutes. It was then refueled and made ready for the trip. At 030020 CST prior to loading the passengers, the aircraft was again warmed up for a few minutes and shut off at 0030 CST.

At approximately 0040 the passengers appeard and boarded the aircraft preparatory to take-off. Mr. Peterson did not file a flight plan on the ground but stated that he would file one after getting into the air. At approximately 0055 CST a normal take-off was made from runway 17, and the aircraft climbed straight ahead to 800 feet. A 180 degree turn was made to the left to about a north heading, which would be in the direction of Minneapolis, Minnesota. The aircraft was last seen after it had turned and was taking what appeared to be a northwest heading, which would place it on a direct course to Fargo, its intended destination.

Mr. Dwyer stated he was watching the airplane's tail light and it appeared to be going down at a very slow rate of descent as it went farther away. He thought it was an optical illusion. Mr. Dwyer had the ATCS operator on duty try to contact the flight but to no avail.

After repeated attempts to contact the flight, ATCS instituted an INFORMATION REQUEST to Redwood Falls, Alexandria, Minneapolis and Fargo, with negative results from all stations.

At 030416C, an Alert Notice was sent out from Mason City to all Stations. Nothing further was heard from the flight and after standing watch throughout the night and early morning, Mr. Dwyer took off from the airport shortly after 030815C to fly the probable course to Fargo in search of the missing aircraft. He discovered the wreckage of N-3794N at approximately 0935 CST about 5 miles northwest of the airport.

Investigation at the Scene

Investigation revealed that the aircraft made first contact with the ground on the right wing, completely disintegrating it and then strewed segments of its various components on a heading of about 315 degrees for some 540 feet. The only large component attached to the aircraft was the left wing. A check of the instrument panel showed that instrument readings were stopped in place by the sudden impact and indicated normal engine temperature and other readings. The RPM was approximately 2200. The directional gyro stopped on a heading of northwest, which was the direction of travel from the place of impact. The spherical horizon indicated a 90 degree bank to the right and a nose down attitude. The climb indicator read 3000 feet per minute descent and the air speed indicator was in the yellow, reading approximately 167 to 170 miles per hour.

Examination of the Wreckage

Examination of the wreckage disclosed no evidence of malfunctioning of the aircraft or engine prior to impact. Investigation of the radio equipment showed that the radio was set up to the proper communication frequencies and navigation frequency of Mason City.

Weather

Weather at the time of take-off was: Ceiling 3000 feet Indefinite; Visibility 6 miles, light snow; Temperature 18, Dew Point 11, Wind South from 20 to 30 knots. Weather at Fargo, the intended destination, was at the time of take-off at Mason City: High, thin, scattered; Visibility 10 miles; Temperature 16, Dew Point 7, Wind South at 16 knots.

General

Mr. Eldridge, who lives 1½ miles East of the accident scene, stated that an aircraft came over his farm home very low and awakened him and his wife out of a sound sleep.

Mr. Juhl, on whose farm the aircraft was found, stated that he also heard the aircraft going over.

Investigation revealed that the aircraft was properly certificated and within gross weight and c.g. limits. The pilot was currently certificated for Commercial VFR flying day or night.

Subsequent to the accident, Dr. Smiley, the coroner, performed an autopsy on the pilot and stated that there was no physical deficiency which could have caused the accident.

Mr. Peterson, the pilot, had been up for about 17 or 18 hours. He had worked all day in the airport shop, had a short rest period before his supper, then went to a Jaycee meeting, and afterward made preparation for the flight. The pilot's medical certificate was in order and current.

The Dwyer Flying Service was properly certificated for charter operations, day and night, under Air Taxi Certificate #31141 issued June 21, 1957 for Day VFR, and October 29, 1957 for Night VFR.

Further details of the accident are contained in the basic Factual Report of Investigation.

C. E. Stillwagon
C. E. Stillwagon
Investigator-in-Charge
2-16/59

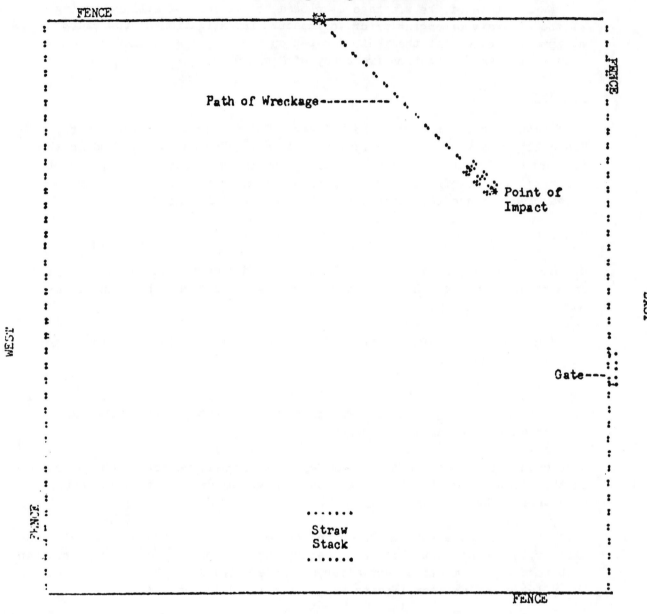

NORTH

Site of Major Portion of
Wreckage - against fence

FENCE

Path of Wreckage----------

Point of
Impact

FENCE

WEST

EAST

Gate---

FENCE

Straw
Stack

FENCE

FENCE

SOUTH

Field is approximately one-quarter mile square

PROBABLE GROUND PATH OF N-3794N

CIVIL AERONAUTICS BOARD

BUREAU OF SAFETY

FACTUAL REPORT OF INVESTIGATION

A. ACCIDENT

Location: Approximately 5 miles NW of Mason City, Iowa
           Municipal Airport on February 3, 1959 at 01.00 CST.

Aircraft: Beechcraft Bonanza, Model 35, S/N D-1019, Identifi-
           cation N-3794N. The aircraft was owned and operated
           by the Dwyer Flying Service, Mason City, Iowa.

Pilot: Roger Arthur Peterson, age 21, 514 North Shore Drive,
           Clear Lake, Iowa. Fatally injured.

Passengers: Charles Hardin (Buddy) Holly, age 22, Lubbock, Texas
            J. P. Richardson, age 28, Beaumont, Texas
            Richard Valenzuela, age 17, San Fernando, California

            The passengers were members of a group of entertainers
            who had presented a show at the Surf Club earlier in
            the evening at Clear Lake, Iowa. All received fatal
            injuries.

B. FLIGHT DETAILS

The aircraft made a normal take-off from the Mason City, Iowa Municipal Airport at approximately 0055C on February 3, 1959 as a charter
operation to Fargo, North Dakota. There was no contact with the
flight after departure. Wreckage of the aircraft was subsequently
located approximately 5 miles northwest of the Mason City Airport.

C. INVESTIGATION

History of Flight

Early in the evening of February 2, 1959, while attending a local
Junior Chamber of Commerce meeting, pilot Peterson was contacted

with reference to a charter trip from Mason City, Iowa to Fargo,
North Dakota. At the conclusion of the meeting, which was about
9:30 p.m., Mr. Peterson drove to the airport where he personally
checked with ATCS regarding the current weather conditions at
Mason City, Minneapolis, Redwood Falls, Alexandria and Fargo. He
was advised that new terminal forecasts would be available at 2300C
and would present a better picture of the weather conditions to be
expected. At this time the Fargo forecast indicated the possibility
of light snow showers at about 0200C, and a cold frontal passage at
about 0400C. Mason City to Fargo is approximately 3:30 hours flying
time in the aircraft involved.

At approximately 2200C, pilot Peterson telephoned ATCS and again
requested current weather conditions and the terminal forecast for
Fargo, North Dakota. At this time all of these stations were reporting ceilings of at least 6000 ft. and visibilities of at least
10 miles. Alexandria and Fargo were clear.

At 2320C, Mr. Peterson requested and received the latest weather information. At this time ceilings had lowered slightly to about
4200 ft. and visibility was at least 10 miles. Light snow was
reported at Minneapolis.

The terminal forecast for Fargo remained essentially the same except
the frontal passage had been changed from 0400C to 0200C.

At 2350C, pilot Peterson visited the ATCS with Mr. Dwyer, owner of
N-3794N and again checked the current weather and terminal forecasts,
after which they pre-flight checked the aircraft and moved it outside
the hanger. The engine was started and allowed to warm up, then was
shut down. The fuel tanks were topped off and it was again started
and run a few minutes, until approximately 0030C. Shortly thereafter
the passengers arrived at the airport and prepared to depart. Mr.
Dwyer asked pilot Peterson if he had filed a flight plan. Peterson
replied that he had not but would do so by radio after take-off.

Take-off was at approximately 0055C from runway 17⁵ in what appeared
to observers to be normal. Following take-off the aircraft was
observed to make a left turn and normal climb to an estimated altitude
of 800 ft. South of the field. It was then turned about 180° to the
left and took up a heading of approximately 360°. No flight plan had

been filed up to this time, therefore, Mr. Dwyer was uninformed as
to the route chosen by Mr. Peterson.

From the platform outside the tower, Mr. Dwyer saw the white tail
light of the aircraft northeast of the airport at approximately the
same 800 ft. level. It then took up what appeared to be a northwest
heading. Dwyer stated that while he was watching the aircraft after
it had turned northward, it appeared to pass through a patch of snow,
fog, or clouds. The tail light became visible again and as he watched
it, an estimated four miles or more away, it appeared to gradually
descend and finally go out of sight. Mr. Dwyer stated that he
thought the apparent gradual descent of the aircraft was possibly an
optical illusion and the distance made the light appear to be going
down but was in reality just increasing distance from him. At no
time after take-off was a flight plan filed for N-3794N. This fact
worried Mr. Dwyer and he remained on at ATCS. Approximately fifteen
minutes after N-3794N departed Mason City and no radio contacts, flight
plan or other were made despite repeated efforts to make contact with
the flight, ATCS instituted an INFORMATION REQUEST to Redwood Falls,
Alexandria, Minneapolis and Fargo, with negative results from all
stations.

At .0304:00 an Alert Notice was sent out from Mason City to all Stations.
After standing watch throughout the night and early morning, Mr. Dwyer
took off from the airport shortly after 0815 in another aircraft to
fly the probable course to Fargo in search of the missing aircraft. He
sighted the wreckage at approximately 0935 in open farm country about
5 miles northwest of the Mason City Airport.

The aircraft made impact with the ground while on a heading of about
315°. Disintegration began at impact and continued about 540 ft.
until finally coming to rest by a fence. All occupants were found to
have been fatally injured and the aircraft demolished. There was no
fire.

Operator

The Dwyer Flying Service, owned and operated by Hubert J. Dwyer, is a
fixed base operation at the Mason City, Iowa Municipal Airport. The
Service operates a charter and taxi service under Air Taxi Certificate
No. 31141 issued on June 21, 1957 for Day VFR. Night VFR Certificate
was issued on October 20, 1957.

Aircraft

The aircraft was a Beech Bonanza, Model 35, S/N D-1019, Identification
N-3794N, manufactured October 17, 1947. It was powered by a Continental
Model E185-8 engine, S/N 25470D-1-8, equipped with Beech Model R-203-100
propeller, S/N 1849, Blade Model R-203-208-82H, Serial Numbers 6521H
and 6481H. According to the hour-recording tachometer the engine at
the time of the accident had operated a total of 838.6 hours since a
major overhaul, October 20, 1954, at which time the tachometer was
zeroed. It had operated 40 hours since the most recent major overhaul
dated January 3, 1959, tachometer reading 818.8 hours. Tachometer was
not zeroed at this overhaul.

According to Mr. Dwyer, owner of N-3794N, he purchased the aircraft
about July 1, 1958 and it had operated a total of 2154:51 hours since
new, to the date of the accident. Examination of the aircraft records
disclosed discrepancies in the manner in which flight times were recorded.
Subsequent to April 1956 no flight time entries were recorded in the
aircraft flight log. Times were computed by reference to the engine
recording tachometer. The most recent entries in the aircraft log
are Tach time rather than aircraft flight operating time.

Facilities for the maintenance of aircraft at Dwyer Flying Service
were found to be satisfactory.

Records of Mr. Dwyer indicate that the aircraft was loaded within the
allowable gross weight and c.g. limits at time of take-off prior to
the subject accident. As a result of the accident the aircraft was
demolished.

Pilot

Roger Arthur Peterson, age 21, resided at Clear Lake, Iowa and was
regularly employed by the Dwyer Flying Service. He possessed
Commercial Pilot Certificate #1324428, ASEL and Flight Instructor
ratings. Peterson's pilot log indicates that he had accumulated
approximately 710:45 hours flight time including about 128:30 hours
in the type equipment involved. He recorded 43:10 hours flight time
in the last ninety days. He also recorded 318:00 hours air taxi
flying and 37:35 hours night flying as pilot-in-command. Peterson
received his Student Pilot Certificate on October 11, 1954, Private

Certificate October 16, 1955, and Commercial ASEL on April 2, 1958.
It was endorsed Non-ICAO, night requirements. Mr. Peterson passed
his Flight Instructor test on January 27, 1959 and his Instrument
written test with a grade of 74 on February 12, 1958. He failed
his Instrument check on March 21, 1958, given by CAA Inspector Melvin
O. Wood, GSCO #9, Sioux Falls, South Dakota.

Mr. Peterson's most recent medical examination is dated March 29,
1958, Second Class. Due to a hearing deficiency in his right ear,
he was flight tested and a waiver was issued November 29, 1958.

Available records indicate that Mr. Peterson had received approximately 52:25 hours Instrument training under a hood. Records further
indicate that he received no Link training and no actual Instrument
experience other than hood time.

On the morning of February 2, 1959 preceding the accident, pilot
Peterson arrived at the Dwyer Flying Service at approximately 8:00
a.m., where he met Charles McGlothlen, Chief Mechanic for the flying
service. Together they went to the service shop and throughout
most of the day they worked in the shop. At approximately 5:15 p.m.,
Peterson left for home. At about 7:30 p.m., McGlothlen and Peterson
attended a local Junior Chamber of Commerce meeting. While the meeting
was in progress Mr. Peterson received a telephone call regarding a proposed cross-country trip to Fargo later that night. According to
Mr. McGlothlen's statement, Mr. Peterson made a trip to the airport
after receiving the telephone call and checked the weather and mileage,
after which he returned to the meeting. The meeting was concluded at
approximately 9:30 p.m., and the two men returned to Mr. Peterson's
home.

The remainder of the evening, prior to take-off at approximately
0300°5C, was spent in preparation for the trip. It is indicated that
Peterson had no actual rest, as such, from the time he arose on the
morning of the Second, until departure of the flight at 0300°5C. This
would indicate that he had put in approximately 18 hours without
appreciable rest; in addition to which he was preparing to begin a night
flight of two or more hours.

The local County Coroner, Dr. Smiley, ordered an autopsy performed
on Mr. Peterson as a part of the investigation. The results indicated
no physical deficiency which could have been a factor in the accident

such as monoxide poisoning, coronary, or other. His death was the
result of injuries received in the accident.

Examination of Wreckage

Examination of the wreckage at the scene disclosed the following:
The wreckage was found in a field on the Gilbert Juhl farm, Clear Lake,
Iowa. The field was level and the surface consisted of a stubble growth.
The ground was frozen and covered with approximately 4 inches of soft snow.

The wreckage and scattered parts indicated the aircraft made impact with
the ground in a steep right bank and nose low attitude at a high rate of
speed on an approximate 315° (Ref. Photo #1).

The three passengers were thrown clear of the wreckage, one about 40 ft.
northwest of the main wreckage, and the other two about 13 ft. South and
southwest of the wreckage. The body of pilot Peterson was found in the
cockpit.

The right wing and flap were found entirely disintegrated along the path
following the first ground contact. There were no large sections of the
wing (Ref. Photo #3) at the wreckage site. With the wing segments were
found a few pieces of the engine cowling. The right wheel cell was torn
in small pieces. The right aileron was fairly complete but badly distorted.
Close examination disclosed no evidence of in-flight failure of the controls.

The main airframe structure was found approximately 540 feet from the point
of first impact. The left wing, with left main gear in the gear well,
was complete but buckled and distorted (Ref. Photo #4). Close examination
of the aileron and fuselage-wing point of separation indicated only impact
damage. Position of the landing gear and related parts indicated the gear
was retracted at time of impact.

The fuselage was found to have buckled immediately behind the cabin
approximately 90 degrees (Ref. Photo #2). The cabin portion of the structure
was completely broken open and mutilated. All seats were in the cabin but
had broken loose from their attach points. The safety belts were of a 360
type, the webbings intact, but the attach fittings were broken on two belts.
The other two showed no evidence of strain. The exact seat from which each
belt came was not determined. Both center section steel trusses were found
generally intact. The wings were torn loose from the center section trusses
by the wing spars tearing close to the attach points.

The empennage was fairly intact, both stabilizers and elevator-rudder, controls were still attached to the fuselage. The elevator trim tab position could not be established because both trim tab fittings were broken by impact and the trim tab control disintegrated (Ref. Photo #5).

Generally, the airframe was in a severely mutilated and disintegrated condition. Important stressed areas and controls throughout the structure were badly damaged or broken. A close examination of these items did not indicate an in-flight failure. All damage had occurred as a result of ground impact forces (Ref. Photo #6).

The engine was found under the cabin and fuselage wreckage. It was taken to the shop of the Dwyer Flying Service, partially disassembled, and examined. The carburetor was broken off and damaged. The left magneto was also broken off. The rear accessories case was broken open. The front cylinder of the right bank had the top of the head broken off. Part of the head of the next cylinder was torn off and the last one had the rocker box off. The case was split at the nose section. All components of the engine were examined and there was no evidence of lack of engine response, malfunctioning, or failure in flight. The cabin heater showed no evidence of leakage.

Both propeller blades (laminated wood) were found broken sharply at the hub, giving evidence of power at ground impact (Ref. Photo #7).

The hub pitch change mechanism was found operative. Position of the propeller pitchange drive and pinion gears indicated the blade pitch to be in the cruise range. There was no evidence of in-flight malfunctioning of the propeller or its controls.

The aircraft was equipped with a "Lear" auto pilot and its switch was found in the "off" position. The engine throttle was forward and bent. The following cockpit instrument readings were noted:

    Magneto switches were "off" both
    Battery and generator switch "on"
    Tachometer total time was 853.6
    RPM needle at 2200
    Fuel pressure, oil temperature and pressure gauges were stuck
        on the normal or green range.
    Attitude indicator stuck on 90 degree right bank and nose down
        position.

Climb indicator read 3000 ft. per minute descent.
Air Speed 165-170 mph
Directional Gyro was caged
Omni Selector 114.9
Course Selector 360°
Transmitter set to Mason City Range, 122.1

All settings were normal for transmitting and receiving.

Generally, the aircraft was in an extremely mutilated condition. Practically all airframe and power plant components received some form of substantial damage, but from a close examination of all parts there was no evidence of an in-flight malfunctioning or failure.

All components of the aircraft were accounted for at the wreckage site.

There was no fire.

Weather

The Official weather observation at Mason City Airport at 0300580 (Take-off was at 0055C) was as follows: Ceiling 3000, Precipitation, Obscuration; Visibility 6 miles with light blowing snow; Barometric pressure 135, Temperature 18°; Dew Point 11, Wind South 20-30 knots; Altimeter Setting 2985.

Complete weather data including Terminal Forecasts for en route and terminal stations is a separate part of this report.

Participants in the Investigation

The following participated in the investigation of this accident:

Andrew J. Prokop, Supervising Inspector, GADO #4, FAA, Des Moines
Eugene Anderson, Operations Inspector, GADO #4, FAA, Des Moines
Fred Bacchetti, Maintenance Inspector, GADO #4, FAA, Des Moines
Ott Aycock, Technical Representative, Beech Aircraft Corporation
Leo F. Sander, Technical Representative, Beech Aircraft Corporation

C. C. Stillwagon

C. E. Stillwagon
Investigator-in-Charge
2/16/59

Exhibit 2

UNITED STATES DEPARTMENT OF COMMERCE
WEATHER BUREAU

Pilot Reports

No pilot reports for the Mason City-Fargo route were received during the period 0500Z-0800Z, February 3, 1959.

P. W. Kenworthy
Meteorologist in Charge
Weather Bureau Airport Station
Minneapolis, Minnesota

Exhibit 3

UNITED STATES DEPARTMENT OF COMMERCE
WEATHER BUREAU

AREA FORECASTS ISSUED BY MSP NIGHT OF FEBRUARY 2, 1959:

FA MSP 030052Z
19C MON-07C TUE

MINN NDKT SDKT

CLDS AND WX. PAC FRONT SSW ACRS XTRM WRN NDKT AT 19C MOVG SE
30-35KTS ACPYD BAND ABT 100-150 WIDE OF C30-60⊕3SW- CNDS RPDLY
VRBL TO C8X3/4SW-BS WITH MST FQT RSTNS IN THE BAND AS IT CROSSES
WRN NDKT SDKT SRN MINN. PRECDG THIS BAND IN DIST CLR MST SDKT
TO C50-100⊕ RMNDR DIST WITH CNDS OCNLY C20X2S-BS CNDN BDR RGNS
OF MINN AND ERN NDKT AHD OF FRONT. FLWG THIS BAND OF WX WITH
PAC FRONT 25⊕ TO ⊕ ABV GND WITH MORE GENL C80⊕ ABV.

ICG. GENLY MDT ICGIC AND OCNLY IN PCPN IN BAND OF WX ACPYG
PAC FRONT ACRS DIST AND OCNLY IN NE NDKT XTRM NRN MINN AHD
FRONT. FRZG LVL SFC XCP SML LYR ABV FRZG BTN 35-60 AHD FRONT
IN NDKT NRN AND CNTRL MINN.

TURBC. GENLY MDT BLO 120 VCNTY AND FLWG PAC FRONT. LCLY MDT
BLO 50 OTHERWISE.

OTLK. 07C-19C TUE. FRONT CONTG EWD WITH SNW ACPYG RECEDG SEWD
MSTLY OUT OF DIST BY ERY AFTN WITH LTLCG WX FLWG FRONTAL BAND.

I hereby certify that the above is an official true copy of a United States
Weather Bureau record.

Weather Bureau Airport Station
Minneapolis, Minnesota

P. W. Kenworthy
Meteorologist in Charge

FA MSP 030652Z
01C-13C TUE

MINN NDKT SDKT

CLDS AND WX. PAC FRONT IN TROF FM CNTRL NDKT THRU WRN SDKT
AND ARCTIC COLD FRONT FM XTRM NWRN MINN WSWWD OVR NRN NDKT
AT 01C. PAC FRONT MOVG ESEWD ABT 25KTS AND ARCTIC COLD
FRONT MOVG SEWD ABT 35KTS DCRG TO 20KTS BY 13C. IN BAND
ABT 100 MIS WIDE IN VCNTY OF PAC AND ARCTIC FRONTS CIGS
GENLY 8-15 VSBYS 3/4-2 IN SNW AND BLWG SNW DCRG CLDNS ABT
100 MIS N OF ARCTIC FRONT NRN NDKT. SERN MINN CIGS 30-60
LWRG TO 10-30 WITH VSBYS 1-3 IN SNW BY 02C. SFC WNDS FLWG
ARCTIC FRONT ↓↘30+ AND FLWG PAC FRONT →↘20+.

ICG. LCLY MDT ICGIC AND ICGIP IN PCPN AREAS AND FRONTS
OTHERWISE LGT ICGIC. FRZG LVL SFC.

TURBC. LCLY MDT TURBC IN VCNTY OF FRONT AND FLWG ARCTIC
FRONT ESPCLY SFC TO 40.

OTLK. 13C TUE-01C WED. ARCTIC FRONT MOVG BYD AREA WITH
CLRG MINN AND XTRM ERN DKTS BY SNST AND SNW WITH CIGS
8-15 VSBYS 3/4-2S- DVLPG WRN DKTS BY EVE AND SPRDG INTO
CNTRL DKTS BY 01C. DCRG SFC WNDS LATE AFTN AND EVE.

I hereby certify that the above is an official true copy of a United
States Weather Bureau record.

Weather Bureau Airport Station   P. W. Kenworthy
Minneapolis, Minnesota   Meteorologist in Charge

Exhibit 4

UNITED STATES DEPARTMENT OF COMMERCE
WEATHER BUREAU

FLASH ADVISORIES ISSUED BY MSP FEB. 2, 1959:

URGENT CKTS 6 7 & 10
FL MSP 030145Z
FLASH ADVISORY NR 4. NW AND XTRM NRN NDKT AREA LGT SNW VSBYS FQTLY
LESS THAN 2 CIGS OCNLY BLO 1 THSD IN PCPN AT 1930C AREA MOVG SEWD
ABT 30KTS IN DKTS AND MINN DURG EVE WITH IPVT BGNG NW NDKT BY 23C.
MDT ICGIC IN SNW AREA. VALID TIL 2345C.
FILED 021951C

URGENT CKTS 6 7 & 10
FL MSP 030535Z
FLASH ADVISORY NR 5. A BAND OF SNW ABT 100 MIS WD AT 2335C FM XTRM
NWRN MINN NERN NDKT THRU BISMARCK AND SSWD THRU BLKHLS OF SDKT WITH
VSBYS GENLY BLO 2 MIS IN SNW. THIS AREA OR BAND MOVG SEWD ABT 25KTS.
COLD FRONT AT 2335C FM VCNTY WINNIPEG THRU MINOT WILLISTON MOVG SEWD
25 TO 30 KTS WITH SFC WNDS FLWG FRONT ↓↘25G45. VALID TIL 0335C.
FILED 022340C

I hereby certify that the above is an official true copy of a United States
Weather Bureau record.

Weather Bureau Airport Station   P. W. Kenworthy
Minneapolis, Minnesota   Meteorologist in Charge

KANSAS CITY, MO.
FEBRUARY 3, 1959

STATEMENT OF H. R. MARTIN, FORECASTER ON DUTY (0000-0800C)
FEBRUARY 3, 1959 - DISTRICT METEOROLOGICAL OFFICE, KANSAS CITY, MO.

MY TOUR OF DUTY BEGAN AT MIDNIGHT, SOME 35 MINUTES PRIOR TO
THE OCCURRENCE OF THE ACCIDENT INVOLVED. AS SOON AS THE MIDNIGHT
SEQUENCES WERE AVAILABLE A MAP WAS MADE OF THE MIDWEST AND PLAINS
AREA WHICH INCLUDED CLOUD HEIGHTS, PRECIPITATION, VISIBILITIES
AND SURFACE WINDS. THIS MAP GAVE SOME INDICATION OF INCREASING
CLOUDINESS, SLIGHTLY LOWERING OF CEILINGS AND SPREADING OF LIGHT
SNOW OVER MOST OF IOWA. THEREFORE, IN ISSUING FLASH ADVISORY
NO. 1, ICING IN THE CLOUDS WAS EXTENDED TO INCLUDE MOST OF IOWA.
CEILINGS AND VISIBILITIES OVER NORTHERN IOWA WERE WELL ABOVE
LIMITS OF A FLASH ADVISORY AND WERE NOT INCLUDED.

HAVING RECHECKED THE WEATHER FOR THE NIGHT IN QUESTION,
AN AFTERCAST WOULD NOT HAVE CHANGED THE FORECAST AS ISSUED.
THIS RECHECK OF WEATHER CONDITIONS FOR NORTHERN IOWA DID NOT
REVEAL ANY RAPID DETERIORATION IN WEATHER DURING THE PERIOD
CONCERNED IN THIS REPORT.

HOWARD R. MARTIN
FORECASTER

KANSAS CITY

120

GRAHAM FLYING SERVICE

[TELEPHONE 3-9451]
GRAHAM-RICKENBACKER FIELD
N. SIOUX CITY, S. DAK.

BEECHCRAFT AIRPLANES
SALES & SERVICE
AIRCRAFT & ENGINE REPAIRS
AVIATION SUPPLIES
COMPLETE SERVICE & STORAGE
CHARTER SERVICE
AIRPLANE RENTALS

BOX 26, BOULEVARD STATION --- SIOUX CITY 6, IOWA

February 19, 1959

Civil Aeronautics Board
4825 Troost Avenue
Kansas City 10, Missouri

Gentlemen:

This letter is in response to Mr. Stillwagon's request for
testimony on the Roger A. Peterson case.

Roger Peterson enrolled in the Instrument Course at our
school and flew with us during February and March of 1958,
and worked as lineman in his spare time. Roger received
most of his training in light aircraft at a country airport and had had no radio training before coming here.
When he began his training he seemed to be slightly over-
confident of his own ability. We gave him his instrument
training in a Piper Tri-Pacer. He handled the airplane
well on instruments but when things would go badly with a
flying lesson he would become disoriented in his radio
procedure. All of this harked back to his lack of radio
experience.

We gave him 42 hours of training while he was here and
during that time we did not notice that there was any tendency to fall off to the right in his flying.

Yours very truly,

GRAHAM FLYING SERVICE

Charles F. Meyer C1127279 FI-A&I

CFM;dr

C. A. A. APPROVED FLYING SCHOOL

Mason City, Iowa,
February 21, 1959.

Mr. C. E. Stillwagon,

Civil Aeronautics Board,

4825 Troost Ave.,

Kansas City, Mo.

Dear sir:

I herewith return to you notification and factual
summary of investigation re aircraft accident involving
Beechcraft N-3794N which occurred 5 NW Mason City, Iowa
on February 3, 1959 . Also order to take depositions.

With personal regards, I remain

Yours truly,

R E Holder

3/2/59

TO WHOM IT MAY CONCERN:

Re: Roger A. Peterson - Accident in Vicinity of Mason City, Iowa,
     February 3, 1959

On January 6, 1959, I gave Roger A. Peterson 3:15 hours of instrument dual instruction at Mason City, Iowa in my Tri-Pacer, N3763P.

After takeoff, I had the colored goggles (which are used in instrument training) on my lap, and shortly thereafter, Mr. Peterson
reached over and put them on. He had trouble orientating himself
and flying the aircraft for at least 15 minutes after putting on
the goggles. I would say that he had a false courage or was a
little over-confident.

Mr. Peterson had previously come to the Eagle Grove airport to
make arrangements for the above-mentioned instruction. I was not
present at the time, but he informed my wife that he wouldn't
need much time, and that he had received high grades on his written
and also had received previous instrument time, and stated that
all he would need was a little brushing up. My wife related to
me what he had said, and I thought he would be pretty good, so the
first thing I was going to have him do was some holdings.

However, after taking off, I felt it was necessary to practice
considerable straight and level flying for some time before practicing turns and holdings. Then after the 3:15 hours of instruction,
given by me, I think Mr. Peterson was disappointed in himself and
may have thought I was a little rough as a flight instructor on
instruments.

On the afternoon, previous to the aircraft accident, I called Mr.
Peterson at the Dwyer Flying Service, Mason City, Iowa on the
telephone and he told me that he had been busy getting his flight
instructor rating but planned to take additional instrument
instruction from me the next week.

(I definifely feel that Mr. Peterson got "vertigo" at the time of
the accident, and that the aircraft got away from him.)

Lawrence A. DenHartog
Eagle Grove, Iowa

24

CIVIL AERONAUTICS BOARD   File No. 2-0001

AIRCRAFT ACCIDENT REPORT

ADOPTED: September 15, 1959   **RELEASED:** September 23, 1959

BEECH BONANZA, N 3794N
MASON CITY, IOWA
FEBRUARY 3, 1959

SYNOPSIS

A Beech Bonanza, N 3794N, crashed at night approximately 5 miles northwest of the Mason City Municipal Airport, Mason City, Iowa, at approximately 0100, February 3, 1959. The pilot and three passengers were killed and the aircraft was demolished.

The aircraft was observed to take off toward the south in a normal manner, turn and climb to an estimated altitude of 800 feet, and then head in a northwesterly direction. When approximately 5 miles had been traversed, the tail light of the aircraft was seen to descend gradually until it disappeared from sight. Following this, many unsuccessful attempts were made to contact the aircraft by radio. The wreckage was found in a field later that morning.

This accident, like so many before it, was caused by the pilot's decision to undertake a flight in which the likelihood of encountering instrument conditions existed, in the mistaken belief that he could cope with en route instrument weather conditions, without having the necessary familiarization with the instruments in the aircraft and without being properly certificated to fly solely by instruments.

Investigation

Charles Hardin, J. P. Richardson, and Richard Valenzuela were members of a group of entertainers appearing in Clear Lake, Iowa, the night of February 2, 1959. The following night they were to appear in Moorhead, Minnesota. Because of bus trouble, which had plagued the group, these three decided to go to Moorhead ahead of the others. Accordingly, arrangements were made through Roger Peterson of the Dwyer Flying Service, Inc., located on the Mason City Airport, to charter an aircraft to fly to Fargo, North Dakota, the nearest airport to Moorhead.

At approximately 1730,[1] Pilot Peterson went to the Air Traffic Communications Station (ATCS), which was located in a tower on top of the Administration Building, to obtain the necessary weather information pertinent to the flight. This included the current weather at Mason City, Iowa; Minneapolis, Redwood Falls, and Alexandria, Minnesota; and the terminal forecast for Fargo, North Dakota. He was advised by the communicator that all these stations were reporting ceilings of 5,000 feet or better and visibilities of 10 miles or above; also, that the Fargo terminal forecast indicated the possibility of light snow showers after 0200 and a cold frontal passage about 0400. The communicator told Peterson that a later terminal forecast would be available at 2300. At 2200 and again at 2320 Pilot Peterson called ATCS

---

[1] All times herein are central standard and based on the 24-hour clock.

concerning the weather. At the latter time he was advised that the stations en route were reporting ceilings of 4200 feet or better with visibilities still 10 miles or greater. Light snow was reported at Minneapolis. The cold front previously reported by the communicator as forecast to pass Fargo at 0400 was now reported to pass there at 0200. The Mason City weather was reported to the pilot as: ceiling measured 6,000 overcast; visibility 15 miles plus; temperature 15 degrees; dewpoint 8 degrees; wind south 25 to 32 knots; altimeter setting 29.96 inches.

At 2355, Peterson, accompanied by Hubert Dwyer, a certificated commercial pilot, the local fixed-base operator at the Mason City Airport, and owner of Bonanza N 3794N (the aircraft used on the flight), again went to ATCS for the latest weather information. The local weather had changed somewhat in that the ceiling had lowered to 5,000 feet, light snow was falling, and the altimeter setting was now 29.90 inches.

The passengers arrived at the airport about 0040 and after their baggage had been properly stowed on board, the pilot and passengers boarded the aircraft. Pilot Peterson told Mr. Dwyer that he would file his flight plan by radio when airborne. While the aircraft was being taxied to the end of runway 17, Peterson called ATCS and asked for the latest local and en route weather. This was given him as not having changed materially en route; however, the local weather was now reported as: Precipitation ceiling 3,000 feet, sky obscured; visibility 6 miles; light snow; wind south 20 knots, gusts to 30 knots; altimeter setting 29.85 inches.

A normal takeoff was made at 0055 and the aircraft was observed to make a left 180-degree turn and climb to approximately 800 feet and then, after passing the airport to the east, to head in a northwesterly direction. Through most of the flight the tail light of the aircraft was plainly visible to Mr. Dwyer, who was watching from a platform outside the tower. When about five miles from the airport,2/ Dwyer saw the tail light of the aircraft gradually descend until out of sight. When Peterson did not report his flight plan by radio soon after takeoff, the communicator, at Mr. Dwyer's request, repeatedly tried to reach him but was unable to do so. The time was approximately 0100.

After an extensive air search, the wreckage of N 3794N was sighted in an open far field at approximately 0935 that morning. All occupants were dead and the aircraft was demolished. The field in which the aircraft was found was level and covered with about four inches of snow.

The accident occurred in a sparsely inhabited area and there were no witnesses. Examination of the wreckage indicated that the first impact with the ground was made by the right wing tip when the aircraft was in a steep right bank and in a nose-low attitude. It was further determined that the aircraft was traveling at high speed on a heading of 315 degrees. Parts were scattered over a distance of 540 feet, at the end of which the main wreckage was found lying against a barbed wire fence. The three passengers were thrown clear of the wreckage, the pilot was found in

2/ See map attached.

the cockpit. The two front seat safety belts and the middle ones of the rear seat were torn free from their attach points. The two rear outside belt ends remained attached to their respective fittings; the buckle of one was broken. None of the webbing was broken and no belts were about the occupants.

Although the aircraft was badly damaged, certain important facts were determined. There was no fire. All components were accounted for at the wreckage site. There was no evidence of inflight structural failure or failure of the controls. The landing gear was retracted at the time of impact. The damaged engine was dismantled and examined; there was no evidence of engine malfunctioning or failure in flight. Both blades of the propeller were broken at the hub, giving evidence that the engine was producing power when ground impact occurred. The hub pitch-change mechanism indicated that the blade pitch was in the cruise range.

Despite the damage to the cockpit the following readings were obtained:
Magneto switches were both in the "off" position.
Battery and generator switches were in the "on" position.
The tachometer r. p. m. needle was stuck at 2200.
Fuel pressure, oil temperature, and pressure gauges were stuck in the normal or green range.
The attitude gyro indicator was stuck in a manner indicative of a 90-degree right bank and nose-down attitude.
The rate of climb indicator was stuck at 3,000 feet per minute descent.
The airspeed indicator needle was stuck between 165-170 m. p. h.
The directional gyro was caged.
The omni selector was positioned at 114.9, the frequency of the Mason City omni range.
The course selector indicated a 360-degree course.
The transmitter was tuned to 122.1, the frequency for Mason City.
The Lear autopilot was not operable.

The Aircraft

The aircraft, a Beech Bonanza, model 35, S/N-1019, identification N 3794N, was manufactured October 17, 1947. It was powered by a Continental model E185-8 engine which had a total of 40 hours since major overhaul. The aircraft was purchased by the Dwyer Flying Service, July 1, 1958, and, according to records and the testimony of the licensed mechanic employed by Dwyer, had been properly maintained since its acquisition. N 3794N was equipped with high and low frequenc radio transmitters and receivers, a Narco omnigator, Lear autopilot (only recently installed and not operable), all the necessary engine and navigational instruments and a full panel of instruments used for instrument flying including a Sperry F3 attitude Gyro.

Pilot

Roger Arthur Peterson, 21 years old, was regularly employed by the Dwyer Flying Service as a commercial pilot and flight instructor, and had been with them about one year. He had been flying since October of 1954, and had accumulated 711 flying hours, of which 128 were in Bonanza aircraft. Almost all of the Bonanza time was acquired during charter flights. He had approximately 52 hours of dual instrument training and had passed his instrument written examination. He failed an instrument flight check on March 21, 1958, nine months prior to the accident. His last CAA second-class physical examination was taken March 29, 1958. A hearing deficiency of his right ear was found and because of this he was given a flight test. A waiver noting this hearing deficiency was issued November 29, 1958. According to his associates he was a young married man who built his life around flying. When his instrument training was taken, several aircraft were used and these were all equipped with the conventional type artificial horizon and none with the Sperry Attitude Gyro such as was installed in Bonanza N 3794N. These two instruments differ greatly in their pictorial display.

The conventional artificial horizon provides a direct reading indication of the bank and pitch attitude of the aircraft which is accurately indicated by a miniature aircraft pictorially displayed against a horizon bar and as if observed from the rear. The Sperry F3 gyro also provides a direct reading indication of the bank and pitch attitude of the aircraft, but its pictorial presentation is achieved by using a stabilized sphere whose free-floating movements behind a miniature aircraft presents pitch information with a sensing exactly opposite from that depicted by the conventional artificial horizon.

The Weather

The surface weather chart for 0000 on February 3, 1959, showed a cold front extending from the northwestern corner of Minnesota through central Nebraska with a secondary cold front through North Dakota. Widespread snow shower activity was indicated in advance of these fronts. Temperatures along the airway route from Mason City to Fargo were below freezing at all levels with an inversion between 3,000 and 4,000 feet and abundant moisture present at all levels through 12,000 feet. The temperature and moisture content was such that moderate to heavy icing and precipitation existed in the clouds along the route. Winds aloft along the route at altitudes below 10,000 feet were reported to be 30 to 50 knots from a southwesterly direction, with the strongest winds indicated to be closest to the cold front.

A flash advisory issued by the U. S. Weather Bureau at Minneapolis at 2335 on February 2 contained the following information: "Flash Advisory No. 5. A band of snow about 100 miles wide at 2335 from extreme northwestern Minnesota, northern North Dakota through Bismarck and south-southwestward through Black Hills of South Dakota with visibility generally below 2 miles in snow. This area or band moving southeastward about 25 knots. Cold front at 2335 from vicinity Winnipeg through Minot, Williston, moving southeastward 25 to 30 knots with surface winds following front north-northwest 25 gusts 45. Valid until 0335." Another advisory issued by the U. S. Weather Bureau at Kansas City, Missouri, at 0015 on February 3, was: "Flash Advisory No. 1. Over eastern half Kansas ceilings are locally below one thousand feet, visibilities locally 2 miles or less in freezing drizzle, light snow and fog. Moderate to locally heavy icing areas of freezing drizzle and locally moderate icing in clouds below 10,000 feet over eastern portion Nebraska, Kansas, northwest Missouri, and most of Iowa. Valid until 0515." Neither communicator could recall having drawn these flash advisories to the attention of Pilot Peterson. Mr. Dwyer said that when he accompanied Pilot Peterson to ATCS, no information was given them indicating instrument flying weather would be encountered along the route.

Analysis

There is no evidence to indicate that very important flash advisories regarding adverse weather conditions were drawn to the attention of the pilot. On the contrary there is evidence that the weather briefing consisted solely of the reading of current weather at en route terminals and terminal forecasts for the destination. Failure of the communicators to draw these advisories to the attention of the pilot and to emphasize their importance could readily lead the pilot to underestimate the severity of the weather situation.

It must be pointed out that the communicators' responsibility with respect to furnishing weather information to pilots is to give them all the available information, to interpret this data if requested, but not to advise in any manner. Also, the pilot and the operator in this case had a definite responsibility to request and obtain all of the available information and to interpret it correctly.

Mr. Dwyer said that he had confidence in Pilot Peterson and relied entirely on his operational judgment with respect to the planning and conduct of the flight.

At Mason City, at the time of takeoff, the barometer was falling, the ceiling and visibility were lowering, light snow had begun to fall, and the surface winds and winds aloft were so high one could reasonably have expected to encounter adverse weather during the estimated two-hour flight.

It was already snowing at Minneapolis, and the general forecast for the area along the intended route indicated deteriorating weather conditions. Considering all of these facts and the fact that the company was certificated to fly in accordance with visual flight rules only, both day and night, together with the pilot's unproven ability to fly by instrument, the decision to go seems most imprudent.

It is believed that shortly after takeoff Pilot Peterson entered an area of complete darkness and one in which there was no definite horizon; that the snow conditions and the lack of horizon required him to rely solely on flight instruments for aircraft attitude and orientation.

The high gusty winds and the attendant turbulence which existed this night would have caused the rate of climb indicator and the turn and bank indicator to fluctuate to such an extent that an interpretation of these instruments so far as attitude control is concerned would have been difficult to a pilot as inexperienced as Mr. Peterson. The airspeed and altimeter alone would not have provided him with sufficient reference to maintain control of the pitch attitude. With his limited experience the pilot would tend to rely on the attitude gyro which is relatively stable under these conditions.

Service experience with the use of the attitude gyro has clearly indicated confusion among pilots during the transition period or when alternating between conventional and attitude gyros. Since Peterson had received his instrument training in aircraft equipped with the conventional type artificial horizon, and since this instrument and the attitude gyro are opposite in their pictorial display of the pitch attitude, it is probable that the reverse sensing would at times produce reverse control action. This is especially true of instrument flight conditions requiring a high degree of concentration or requiring multiple function, as would be the case when flying instrument conditions in turbulence without a copilot. The directional gyro was found caged and it is possible that it was never used during the short flight. However, this evidence is not conclusive. If the directional gyro were caged throughout the flight this could only have added to the pilot's confusion.

Conclusion

At night, with an overcast sky, snow falling, no definite horizon, and a proposed flight over a sparsely settled area with an absence of ground lights, a requirement for control of the aircraft solely by reference to flight instruments can be predicated with virtual certainty.

The Board concludes that Pilot Peterson, when a short distance from the airport, was confronted with this situation. Because of fluctuation of the rate instruments caused by gusty winds he would have been forced to concentrate and rely greatly on the attitude gyro, an instrument with which he was not completely familiar. The pitch display of this instrument is the reverse of the instrument he was accustomed to; therefore, he could have become confused and thought that he was making a climbing turn when in reality he was making a descending turn. The fact that the aircraft struck the ground in a steep turn but with the nose lowered only slightly, indicates that some control was being effected at the time. The weather briefing supplied to the pilot was seriously inadequate in that it failed to even mention adverse flying conditions which should have been highlighted.

Probable Cause

The Board determines that the probable cause of this accident was the pilot's unwise decision to embark on a flight which would necessitate flying solely by instruments when he was not properly certificated or qualified to do so. Contributing factors were serious deficiencies in the weather briefing, and the pilot's unfamiliarity with the instrument which determines the attitude of the aircraft.

BY THE CIVIL AERONAUTICS BOARD:

/s/ JAMES R. DURFEE

/s/ CHAN GURNEY

/s/ HARMAR D. DENNY

/s/ G. JOSEPH MINETTI

/s/ LOUIS J. HECTOR

NOTE: See attachment entitled "Safety Message for Pilots."

USCOMM—DC

S U P P L E M E N T A L   D A T A

Investigation and Depositions

The Civil Aeronautics Board was notified February 3, 1959, of this accident and an investigation was immediately begun in accordance with the provisions of Section 701 (a) (2) of the Federal Aviation Act of 1958. Depositions were taken at Mason City, Iowa, February 18, 1959.

The Aircraft

N 3794N, a Beech Bonanza, model 35, S/N-1019, was manufactured October 17, 1947. It was equipped with Continental model E 185-8 engine and a Beech model R-203-100 propeller. The aircraft had accumulated a total of 2,154 flying hours and the engine had 40 hours since overhaul. The aircraft was purchased by the Dwyer Flying Service July 1, 1958.

The Operator

The Dwyer Flying Service, owned and operated by Mr. Hubert J. Dwyer, was started in 1953. The business consisted of a fixed-base operation engaged in charter flying, student instruction, and aircraft maintenance and sales. The service had an air carrier operating certificate with an air taxi rating issued by the Federal Aviation Agency. The certificate permitted the carrying of passengers for hire within the continental limits of the United States in accordance with visual flight rules, both day and night.

The Pilot

Roger Peterson, age 21, held airman certificate No. 1324428, with single-engine land and flight instructor ratings. He took his last second-class physical examination March 29, 1958.

A SAFETY MESSAGE FOR PILOTS

To the pilot who has not been exposed to instrument flight utilizing both the attitude gyro and the artificial horizon, the fact that pitch information is displayed in an opposing manner on these instruments does not appear particularly significant. The assumption may be that, providing one is aware of this difference, no difficulty should be experienced in utilizing either instrument. This assumption, however, is true only if the pilot has had sufficient training on both instruments to interpret pitch information from either with equal facility. In the absence of such training or experience the habit patterns generated by training and repetitive experience in interpreting pitch information displayed in an identical manner each time causes an instinctive reaction in the application of control pressures to achieve a desired result. When this information is then displayed in an opposite manner, the instinctive reaction will cause an improper application of control pressures, a change in attitude contrary to that anticipated, and at least momentarily, a period of disorientation follows. Unless the pilot is highly skilled in instrument flying and can reorient himself by use of the other instruments in the cockpit, this period of disorientation can be fatal.

All pilots who have received instrument training utilizing the artificial horizon are advised not to rely upon the attitude gyro unless sufficient experience has been gained under simulated instrument conditions to insure competence with this instrument.

While this message deals primarily with flight instruments, it is equally applicable to other equipment in the aircraft including radio navigation and approach aid equipment.

KNOW YOUR AIRCRAFT EQUIPMENT, ITS CAPABILITIES AND LIMITATIONS. DO NOT RELY UPON ANY EQUIPMENT UNDER CIRCUMSTANCES REQUIRING ITS USE FOR THE SAFE CONDUCT OF THE FLIGHT UNTIL YOU HAVE ACQUIRED SUFFICIENT EXPERIENCE UNDER SIMULATED CONDITIONS TO INSURE YOUR ABILITY TO USE IT PROPERLY.

GENERAL HIGHWAY AND TRANSPORTATION MAP
CERRO GORDO COUNTY
IOWA
PREPARED BY THE
IOWA STATE HIGHWAY COMMISSION
IN COOPERATION WITH THE
U.S. DEPARTMENT OF COMMERCE
BUREAU OF PUBLIC ROADS
DATA OBTAINED FROM
HIGHWAY PLANNING SURVEY
SCALE IN MILES

1956

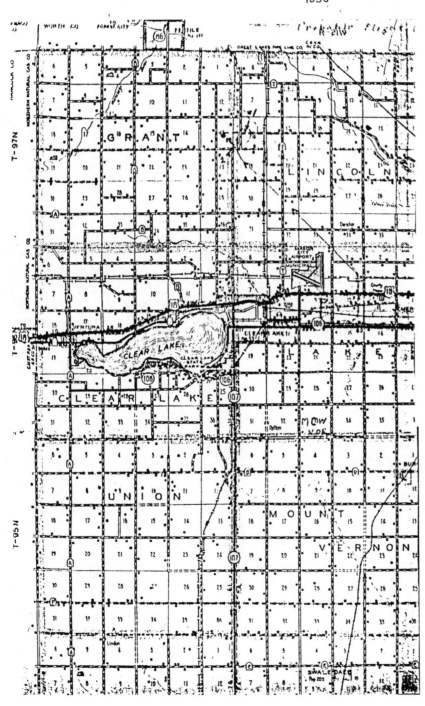

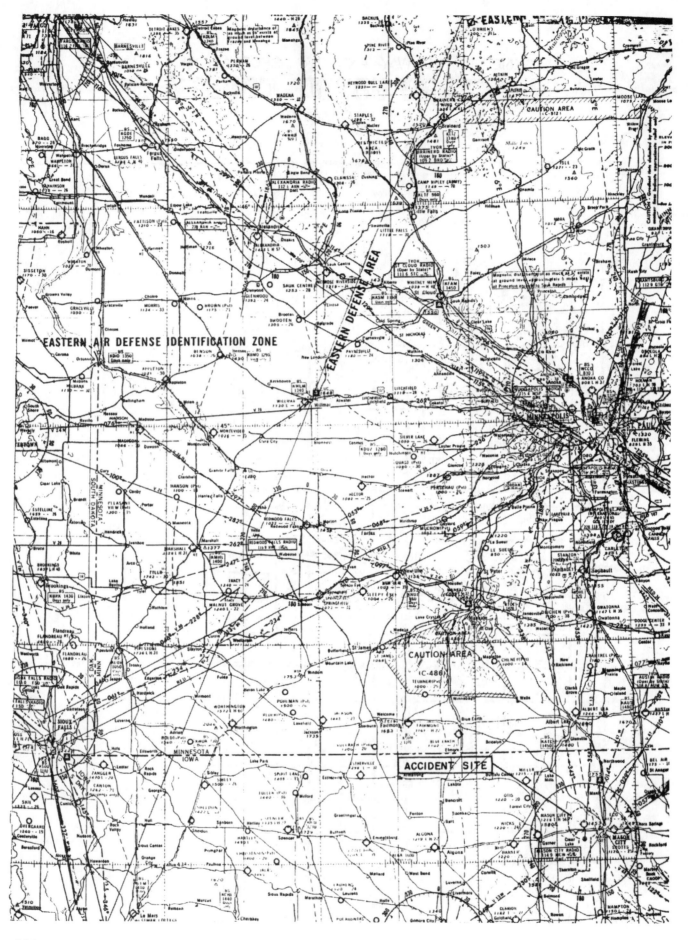

The United States Navy Band

February 26, 1960

A mid-air collision is probably the most feared of all aviation disasters. Fortunately, it is one of the more rare occurrences in aviation. At the moment when one aircraft collides with another aircraft, the usual result is two non-flyable aircraft. Such was the case in this accident. After the airplanes involved in this disaster collided in the air, all hope that remained was that any helpless survivors encased in various parts of the airplanes, would survive gravity's horrible ride to the ground or waters of the earth. The words "catastrophic" and "horrific" do little to accurately describe the magnitude of an event such as a mid-air collision.

Studies of mid-air collisions alert researchers to definite danger zones for pilots. While it may be surprising to some people that nearly all mid-air collisions occur during daylight hours and in very good weather conditions, it should not be surprising that the majority of mid-air accidents occur within five miles of an airport. This fact makes sense when you think that on good weather flying days, when more leisure flying is in progress, the result is greater air traffic concentration close to the home airport. In fact, three quarters of all mid-air collisions occur below 3,000 feet and, more specifically, in the airport traffic pattern. These collisions occur, not surprisingly, mostly at airports where there is not an operating control tower. However, this is not to say that non-towered airports are not safe. They are.

The possibility of a mid-air collision is exacerbated by the various makes and models of manufactured aircraft. For instance, the pilot of a low wing airplane in a descent may have his or her traffic scan blocked by the fuselage or wings. Concurrently, the pilot of a high wing aircraft may not be able to see traffic above. Without this visual avoidance, each pilot may be totally unaware of the other until the startling sound of the collision takes place. The flight rule that every pilot uses during good weather flying is, "See and avoid." The rationale is that you must see the hazard before you can avoid it. Additionally there is the recognition and reaction time needed to avoid a collision, should one become imminent. A United States Naval Aviation Safety Bulletin estimates that the recognition and reaction time needed to avoid a collision once another aircraft is spotted is 12.5 seconds.

Pilots learn very early in their training that a division of attention is necessary to effectively fly a plane. The student learns to dedicate as much as 70 percent of his or her time to looking outside the aircraft. Don't be fooled. Effective scanning for traffic is more difficult than it sounds. Bad habits such as only glancing out a plane's windshield or staring into one spot for too long are easy traps. It takes time and practice to develop good scanning technique. However, collision avoidance involves much more than proper eye utilization. You could be the most conscientious scanner in the world and still have an in-flight collision if other important factors are neglected in the see-and-avoid concept. In order to retain a high degree of air safety, it is vital that all pilots follow the same rules of the air. Unfortunately, there are times when the rules are breached either through neglect, carelessness or logistical traps. During those times the risk of an accident increases greatly.

The United States Navy Band is steeped in history. From the early seaman's songs, sung to relieve the rigors of shipboard life, to the addition of drummers and fifers who were carried aboard to sound calls and perform at funerals, the nautical musician became an integral part of life on the sea. It was in the 1800s that shore-based bands led to the creation of the Naval Academy Band, which grew to prominence in the Civil War. President Calvin Coolidge, in 1925, signed a bill into law stating that, "hereafter the band now stationed at the Navy Yard, known as the Navy Yard Band, shall be designated as the United States Navy Band."

The United States Navy Band made its first national tour in 1925, shortly after it became a national treasure. Under the baton of the band's first leader, the Navy Band was featured at many historic occasions. These events included non-naval functions as well. Two of these functions were the aviation events of Charles Lindbergh's return to the United States after his historic 1927 solo flight across the Atlantic Ocean and the return of Admiral Richard E. Byrd from his South Pole crossing flight in 1929. However, there is one day in the United States Navy Band's history that is forever dark and austere. The event was the band's accompaniment of President Dwight D. Eisenhower for his official visit to Brazil.

On February 26, 1960, a United States Navy R6D-1, bureau #131582, (commercially known as a DC-6B) airplane departed Buenos Aires, Argentina with an instrument flight rules (IFR) flight plan for Galeao Airport in Rio de Janeiro, Brazil. The plane traveled on a northeast heading, and on board were 31 American servicemen passengers, including members of the Navy Band. As the transport plane was in its initial turn to begin the descent to land, little did the flight crew know that another plane was flying a path that would eventually converge with the diplomatic flight. This other airplane was a Brazilian registered DC-3 (registration: PP-AXD), operated by Consorcio REAL Aerovias Nacional. This civilian flight had departed Vitoria, Espitito Santo on scheduled domestic service, flying southwest with a VFR flight plan, for Santos-Dumont Airport in Rio de Janeiro.

While English is the recognized language for aviation communications all over the world, it is well-known that thick accents can impair the comprehension of pilot/controller dialogue. What is known in this case is that, while the air-traffic controller was speaking to the American pilots in English, that same controller was speaking to the Brazilian pilots in Portuguese. This meant that the R6D crew had no way of knowing the altitude, location, direction of flight nor the intentions of the DC-3 crew. It was a recipe for disaster.

To make matters worse, weather at the time was reported as a broken layer of strato-cumulus clouds at 2,300 feet, with a solid overcast at 10,000 feet. This was one of those times when the conditions could have seemed blurred between VFR and IFR flight. Although technically VFR conditions were in effect, one has to suspect that there were various clouds and cloud layers in between the two reported layers. It would seem that this IFR flight and the VFR flight were both operating appropriately for the weather conditions that existed, but the timing could have not been worse.

Music's Broken Wings

Just after the American military plane turned to a new heading approximately 60 degrees to the left over the south Atlantic and began its initial approach to land (now flying wings-level almost on a heading of north), the REAL DC-3 began its initial approach to land by turning left over Santos-Dumont airport. As the commercial flight reached a heading of approximately east, not quite completing its entire turn (i.e., in a right-wing high attitude), the right wing of the Brazilian plane sliced into the aft fuselage section of the military transport at an estimated altitude of 5,000 feet. The time of the mid-air collision was approximately 1:00 p.m. (Figure 13-1).

As pieces of both aircraft plunged into Guanabara Bay, two and a half miles south of Santos-Dumont airport, the tail section of the U.S. Navy plane apparently went into a spinning motion like a falling leaf. This lucky oscillation caused the tail of the U.S. plane to strike the water more gently than the rest of the wreckage, and three American personnel survived the accident. They were the only ones.

It is speculated that none of the flight crewmembers on either plane ever saw each other. Certainly, if they did, there was no time to react and take sufficient evasive action. As a result, 35 military servicemen and band members, including the crew of seven, and all 26 people on the commercial flight, including the crew of four, perished. Most of the sixty-one bodies were recovered from Guanabara Bay, as were most of the demolished remains from both aircraft.

The Brazilian and United States governments conducted subsequent investigations into this mid-air collision. Brazilian aviation investigators eventually blamed the crew of the U.S. Navy R6D for the accident, saying that those pilots had disobeyed the Rio air-traffic controller's instructions to descend. Later testimony by that air-traffic controller revealed that he apparently had told the R6D crew to disregard that instruction to descend. He apparently also testified that he believed the American military plane's altitude to be "considerably" higher than the commercial plane.

The United States military accident investigation team came to a different conclusion, disagreeing with the Brazilian government and placing no blame on either pilot. The contributing factors cited by the United States' government report stated that the factors involved in this accident were:

- the air-traffic controller's lack of certainty as to the positions of both airplanes,
- the air-traffic controller's inability to recognize the potential closure rate of both aircraft, as well as the additional reaction times of the pilots,
- the communication difficulties associated with an air-traffic controller who spoke to two different crews in different languages,
- the absence of modern navigational aids and air-traffic control facilities on the ground.

The United States Navy Band continues to perform all over the world.

Roger D. Cain

Aircraft addenda:

United States Navy designation: R6D-1 (U.S. Air Force Designation: C-118)
Common name: Liftmaster
Manufacturer: Douglas Aircraft Company
First flight of type: 1946
Total production: 74 were built for commercial and military use
Bureau number for this airplane: 131582
Mission: Cargo or personnel transport
Length: 105 feet, 7 inches
Wingspan: 117 feet, 6 inches
Engines: (4) Pratt & Whitney R-2800 CB16, 18-cylinder, air cooled, radial, piston
Horsepower: 2400 h.p. (each)
Empty weight (approximate): 45,800 lbs.
Gross weight: 107,000 lbs.
Service ceiling: 22,000 ft.
Range: 4,900 miles
Cruising speed: 315 mph

* The above photo represents the type of aircraft and not necessarily the exact model involved in the accident.

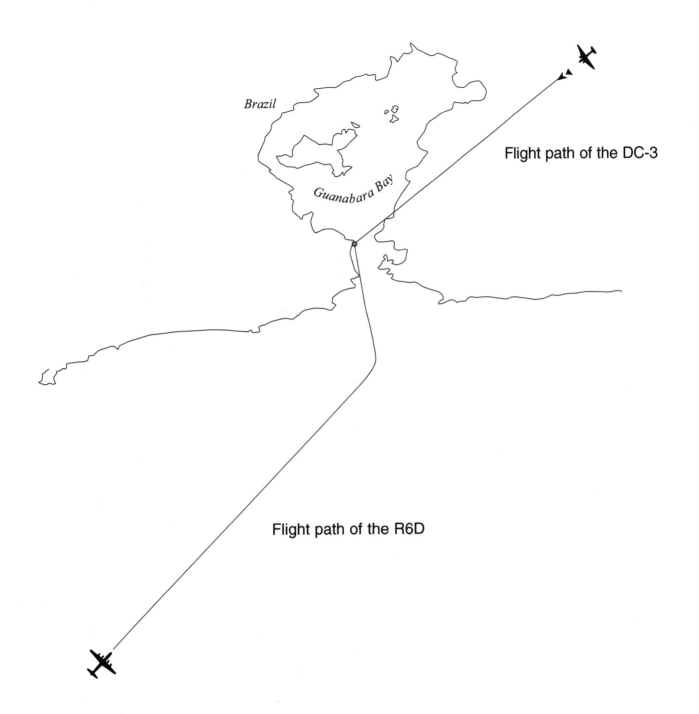

Brazil

Guanabara Bay

Flight path of the DC-3

Flight path of the R6D

Figure 13-1

Patsy Cline

Hawkshaw Hawkins

Cowboy Copas

Randy Hughes

March 5, 1963

This accident was a case of a pilot who was qualified only for VFR conditions but who continued a flight into a deteriorating weather situation. The spatial disorientation experienced by a pilot not rated for flight conditions by reference to instruments is described in the previous chapter discussing the Buddy Holly accident. The only differences in this scenario appear to be that the pilot was one of the musicians (also the manager of singer Patsy Cline) and that a different make of airplane was involved. The fact that the pilot's disorientation did not occur until well into the final stages of the cross-country flight is irrelevant since the accident would have occurred shortly after the pilot actually became disoriented, making this accident very similar to the Holly accident.

What makes a pilot decide to continue on a flight when an appropriate qualification is lacking? The answers are varied but well-known. The first reason that travelers might feel they absolutely must complete a journey is the "get-there-itis" syndrome. This is the feeling that one must get to a destination at any cost due to a meeting or some other time-sensitive engagement. Most of us have witnessed this type of attitude many times with drivers on the highway. The second reason that one feels compelled to continue a journey is the "pride factor." The person making the decisions in the flight feels that if the journey cannot be completed, he or she will be perceived as having inadequate skills.

Another aspect of the "pride factor" for some pilots is the urge to prove the utility and versatility of owning and operating a general aviation aircraft. The owner may feel that if the flight cannot be completed, the business expense of the aircraft may not be apparent or justified to the non-pilot occupants. Therefore, the pilot feels he or she is responsible for proving that the choice to fly, as opposed to driving, is a good one. All of this self-imposed pressure can create a very strong conflict between perception and reality. In this conflict, the pilot convinces himself or herself that the flight will go better than predicted, or that the weather will not be as bad as forecasted. Worse still is the possibility that the pilot has become deluded that his or her skill level is greater than it actually is.

As a last minute addition to her schedule, Patsy Cline performed at a benefit concert in Kansas City, Missouri for the family of disc jockey "Cactus" Jack Call, who had been killed in an automobile accident. She had flown there with her pilot/manager, Randy Hughes, in the single-engine Piper Comanche airplane that he owned. Accompanying them for the concert were the performers Hawkshaw Hawkins and Cowboy Copas, both well-known Nashville artists. The concert took place on the evening of March 3, 1963, in the Kansas City Memorial Hall.

Wearing a white dress and white high-heeled shoes, Cline held a small handkerchief in her hand while singing most of her big hits. One of her songs that night had only been recorded a month earlier. This song, "Sweet Dreams," would later become one of her posthumous hits. It is said that Cline held a finger to her ear during some high notes and actually apologized to the audience once between songs because she felt her performance was not up to par. If she was off her top form, it was due to her fatigue and a touch of the flu. Patsy Cline was the final performer at the concert and she did receive a standing ovation. Dottie West, who also was there performing that night, recalled that Patsy Cline told the crowd, "I love you all," during the ovation. These may have been the last words she ever spoke on stage.

Delayed by inclement weather, the foursome finally departed Kansas City two days after the concert. Their final destination that day was Nashville, Tennessee, but they had to make a stop in Dyersburg, Tennessee to obtain fuel. Randy Hughes supposedly had successfully dodged some spotty bad weather during the leg from Kansas City to Dyersburg. Perhaps this airmanship success was a confidence booster and may have been a factor in his decision to depart Dyersburg at approximately 6:07 p.m.

The pressure Hughes felt to get Cline and the others back to Nashville must have been great. Although both Dyersburg and Nashville were clear, a wall of clouds stood between the two cities. Almost exactly halfway through the last leg of their journey, the plane caught up with the backside of a strong storm front that had passed through Dyersburg shortly before Hughes landed to refuel. Rather than turning back and returning to Dyersburg to stay the night, Hughes pressed on. The plane crashed a few miles west of Camden, Tennessee. No one survived.

Once Randy Hughes became disoriented only a few minutes would have passed before he lost control of the plane, cut through a dense stand of trees and slammed into the ground. The 500 foot cloud ceiling would not have been high enough for Hughes to have recovered the plane from its earthward plunge.

After the misfortune of this airplane accident, the public was stunned as the news spread that another group of music industry legends had lost their lives to an aviation tragedy only four years after the Holly, Valens and "Big Bopper" accident in 1959.

The CAB accident report brief that was found in the NTSB archives apparently spanned two pages of a larger case book, such that the actual copy of this particular brief is left as somewhat confusing to read. In this case only, I have rearranged the brief to allow a more clear viewing to the reader. Both versions of the brief, original and rearranged, appear at the end of this chapter.

Virginia Patterson Hensley was born in the Winchester Memorial Hospital, in Winchester, Virginia, in the Shenandoah Valley of the Appalachian Mountains in 1932. Her family's home was in nearby Gore, Virginia. By age three it is said that she already was singing and entertaining her neighbors. In 1946, Hensley auditioned for a Winchester radio station and secured a regular spot on disc jockey "Joltin" Jim McCoy's Saturday broadcast. In 1948, she traveled to Nashville, Tennessee, but was unsuccessful in her audition efforts and had to return to Winchester where she performed in local clubs and taverns. In 1952 Hensley was urged to change her name to "Patsy," a derivative of "Patterson," her middle name. In 1953, Patsy married Gerald Cline and her to-be famous name was established. Although she and Gerald Cline divorced around September 1957, by that time Patsy Cline had solidified her stage name.

Patsy Cline's big break had come earlier in January 1957, when she won an "Arthur Godfrey's Talent Scouts" program singing "Walkin' After Midnight." Her rapid rise to fame brought her to perform at the Grand Ole Opry in 1958. She signed with her manager, Randy Hughes, in 1959. In 1960, Patsy Cline became a full member of the Grand Ole Opry. During 1961, Decca, her record label released two of her best-known hits, "I Fall To Pieces" and "Crazy." Leading industry publications such as Billboard and Cashbox named Patsy Cline the favorite female vocalist in 1961, 1962 and posthumously in 1963.

Patsy Cline was inducted as the first female solo artist into the Country Music Hall of Fame in 1973. In 1992, Patsy Cline received an induction into the Grammy Awards Recording Hall of Fame for the song "Crazy." In 1993, the United States Postal Service released a commemorative Patsy Cline stamp, and in 1994 she was inducted into the National Cowgirl Hall of Fame in Fort Worth, Texas. In 1995, Patsy Cline received another Grammy Award for Creative Contribution of Outstanding Artistic Significance to the Field of Recording.

Hawkshaw Hawkins and Cowboy Copas also were stars at the Grand Ole Opry, but Hawkins had other talents as well. He was an accomplished horse rider and performed rope tricks and stand-up comedy, as well as sang, during his performances at western shows. Copas taught himself to play the guitar and fiddle at a very young age and the music business became his whole life soon thereafter. Randy Hughes, the pilot-in-command of the flight, was Patsy Cline's former guitar player-turned manager and Cowboy Copas' son-in-law.

Author

Aircraft addenda:

Common name: Comanche, PA-24
Manufacturer: Piper
First flight of type: 1958
Registration number for this airplane: N7000P
Seats: 4
Length: 24 feet, 9 inches
Wingspan: 36 feet, 0 inches
Engine: (1) Lycoming 0-540-A1A5, six-cylinder, air-cooled, horizontally opposed, piston
Horsepower: 250 h.p.
Empty weight (approximate): 1,600 lb.
Gross weight: 2,800 lb.
Service ceiling: 20,000 ft
Fuel capacity: 60 gal.
Cruising speed: 180 mph

* The above photo represents the type of aircraft and not necessarily the exact model involved in the accident.

Personal addenda:

Virginia Patterson Hensley (Virginia H. Dick, Patsy Cline): singer
b. September 8, 1932: Winchester, Virginia
d. March 5, 1963: Camden, Tennessee
Buried: Shenandoah Memorial Park, Winchester, Virginia
Note: A bell tower, erected in Patsy Cline's memory, is in the Shenandoah Memorial Park.

Lloyd Estel Copas (Cowboy Copas): musician, singer
b. July 15, 1913: near Muskogee, Oklahoma (or) Adams County, Ohio
d. March 5, 1963: Camden, Tennessee
Buried: Forest Lawn Memorial Gardens, Goodlettsville, Tennessee

Harold Franklin Hawkins (Hawkshaw Hawkins): musician, singer
b. December 22, 1923: Huntingdon, West Virginia
d. March 5, 1963: Camden, Tennessee
Buried: Forest Lawn Memorial Gardens, Goodlettsville, Tennessee

Ramsey D. Hughes (Randy Hughes): country musician, manager
b. 1928
d. March 5, 1963: Camden, Tennessee
Buried: Forest Lawn Memorial Gardens, Goodlettsville, Tennessee

Docket	Location	Date	Aircraft	Injury			Probable Cause
				F	S	M/N	
2-1324	Camden, Tenn.	3/5/63	Piper PA-24 N-7000P (D)	CR 1 PX 3	0 0	0 0	Noninstrument pilot attempted visual flight in adverse weather conditions, resulting in a loss of control. Judgment of the pilot in in initiating flight in the existing conditions. (see next page)

(BUSINESS) Private; age 34; 160 total hours; 117 in type; not instrument rated.

At 1705 c.s.t., the pilot landed N-7000P at Dyersburg, Tennessee to obtain weather information for the remaining portion of his flight from Kansas City, Missouri to Nashville, Tennessee. The pilot received a thorough weather briefing based upon reports of existing and forecast

- 573 -

Docket	Location	Date	Aircraft

2-1324
(Cont'd.)

terminal and area weather, current SIGMET's and current Advisories to Light Aircraft. He was informed that the en route weather was unfavorable and the destination weather was below VFR minima with further deterioration indicated before any improving trends could be expected. After receiving the weather briefing, the pilot talked with his wife in Nashville by telephone, and she informed him that the sun was shining in Nashville. The pilot then indicated his intention to continue the flight and would return if he found it necessary. Shortly thereafter, at 1807, the pilot taxied out and took off. During taxi, the pilot was again furnished weather information by the tower operator. After takeoff, there were no further radio contacts with N-7000P.

About 1830, an aviation qualified witness near Camden, Tennessee, heard the sounds of an aircraft flying at low altitude, and directed his attention in the direction of the sounds. He then observed the aircraft as it descended out the the low overcast in an estimated 45° nosedown dive, and then heard a dull crash.

Investigation revealed that N-7000P had crashed on a wooded, swampy area about five miles west of Camden. Inspection of the wreckage disclosed that the aircraft was intact and the engine was developing substantial power at initial impact with trees. There was no evidence of preimpact failure or malfunction. Post-mortem examination of the pilot disclosed nothing that could have been a factor in the accident. The weather at Camden was reported as, "Ceiling 500 feet; visibility 5 miles."

Docket	Location	Date	Aircraft	Injury			Probable Cause
					F S M/N	
2-1324	Camden, Tenn.	3/5/63	Piper PA-24 N-7000P (D)	CR	1 0 0	Noninstrument pilot attempted visual flight in adverse weather conditions, resulting in a loss of control.
				PX	3 0 0	Judgment of the pilot in in initiating flight in the existing conditions.

(BUSINESS) Private; age 34; 160 total hours; 117 in type; not instrument rated.

At 1705 c.s.t., the pilot landed N-7000P at Dyersburg, Tennessee to obtain weather information for the remaining portion of his flight from Kansas City Missouri to Nashville, Tennessee. The pilot received a thorough weather briefing based upon reports of existing and forecast terminal and area weather, current SIGMETs and current Advisories to Flight Aircraft. He was informed that the en route weather was unfavorable and the destination weather was below VFR minima with further deterioration indicated before any improving trends could be expected. After receiving the weather briefing, the pilot talked with his wife in Nashville by telephone, and she informed him that the sun was shining in Nashville. The pilot then indicated his intention to continue the flight and would return if he found it necessary. Shortly thereafter, at 1807, the pilot taxied out and took off. During taxi, the pilot was again furnished weather information by the tower operator. After takeoff, there were no further radio contacts with N-7000P.

About 1830, an aviation qualified witness near Camden, Tennessee, heard the sounds of an aircraft flying at low altitude, and directed his attention in the direction of the sounds. He then observed the aircraft as it descended out the the low overcast in an estimated 45° nosedown dive, and then heard a dull crash.

Investigation revealed that N-7000P had crashed on a wooded, swampy area about five miles west of Camden. Inspection of the wreckage disclosed that the aircraft was intact and the engine was developing substantial power at initial impact with trees. There was no evidence of preimpact failure or malfunction. Post-mortem examination of the pilot disclosed nothing that could have been a factor in the accident. The weather at Camden was reported as, "Ceiling 500 feet; visibility 5 miles."

Jim Reeves

July 31, 1964

At first glance this accident might be quickly attributed to the same spatial disorientation that caused the Buddy Holly and Patsy Cline crashes. The brief report reprinted in this chapter, which is all that remains of this accident in the NTSB records, clearly states that the pilot continued VFR flight into adverse weather conditions. However, upon looking closer at this case report one can see that VFR conditions prevailed at the time of the crash. How can this be? The first clue lies in the word found at the bottom right of the report. This word is thunderstorm. The second clue lies in the time of the year, late July. Summer thunderstorms can build in intensity at an alarmingly rapid pace. Ask any pilot about a summer's day weather forecast and he likely will tell you that it includes the chance of thunderstorms.

Thunderstorms are one of the most severe forces in nature. They contain wind shear, which is defined as a sudden change in wind direction or velocity that can occur anywhere in the atmosphere. The wind shear hazard associated with a thunderstorm is one of the worst weather hazards known to flight. The unseen violence of wind shear within a thunderstorm is real and it is deadly. These winds can take even a large airplane out of the sky, or they can rip an airplane apart in mid-air. Pilots who have flown through a thunderstorm and received little damage to their airplane should consider themselves extremely fortunate. The possibility and severity of wind shear in close proximity to a thunderstorm is not to be taken lightly either. This is true of jet airliners, and it is especially true of light aircraft. Ultimately, however, it boils down to pilot decision-making to prevent an aircraft from being battered by a thunderstorm.

Thunderstorms vary in intensity from level 1, the lowest intensity, to the level 5 thunderstorm, the most severe. They all should be given a wide berth by all pilots. The first rule of thumb for a pilot is to avoid all thunderstorms. The minimum recommended distance to avoid a thunderstorm is twenty miles in every direction from any visible storm cloud. Pilots should be extremely cautious if attempting to fly beneath a thunderstorm where the visibility may sometimes be good. The destructive potential of wind shear and microbursts always exists when in close proximity to a thunderstorm. The microburst is a very strong, yet localized, downdraft column of air, usually short in duration, that can occur well in advance of a thunderstorm's arrival. The microburst is hard to detect and is a phenomenon for which it is nearly impossible for a pilot to compensate. A microburst could cause the plane to be slammed into the ground despite any control attempt by the pilot.

However, it is not always the wind shear that pilots should fear in a thunderstorm. The frozen precipitation known as hail can do significant damage to an airplane as well. Further, icing conditions can lead to diminished aircraft flight characteristics due to reduced lift capability of the wings. In addition, heavy turbulence can lead to decreased ability by the pilot to control the airplane as a whole. All of these factors working together are a true recipe for disaster. Still, it is the wind shear within a thunderstorm, in the form of strong updrafts and rapid downbursts, that has the most capability to divert an aircraft from its intended flight path. The thunderstorm is an indiscriminate and mighty ruler in its domain.

Jim Reeves was a country music ballad singer. His success is best measured by the fact that almost every record he released hit the Billboard charts. He is more frequently thought of as Gentleman Jim Reeves, a name that he likely earned because of his rich, soothing, baritone voice. Behind the records he was known as a perfectionist and personal accounts indicate that he was sometimes difficult to work with or to work for. Reeves' hobby was flying and he used his airplane for concert engagements and business trips. On this particular flight he was returning from Batesville, Arkansas where he had been engaged in a business deal regarding some land. His passenger, Dean Manuel, was Reeves' manager at the time, as well as the pianist for the Blue Boys Band.

The accident occurred about ten miles south of Nashville, Tennessee, just a few minutes before 5:00 p.m., on Friday, July 31, 1964. The area where the crash happened is known as the Brentwood area, and at the time it was very heavily wooded. Even though there was a post-crash fire, it still took two days for search parties to find the wreckage. The plane was demolished and the evidence showed that the plane went into the ground in a nearly vertical attitude. While it is possible that Reeves did indeed fly into instrument meterological conditions (IMC) and experience vertigo, which led to the crash, certainly thunderstorms played a part in the accident. Most likely we will never know the complete sequence of events that led to this crash.

It is interesting to note that as a result of Jim Reeves' private recording sessions, he left many demo tapes. These were coveted by his wife, Mary, even while they were being recorded, and she closely guarded them after her husband's death. It was Mary Reeves, in association with RCA records, who continued to release Jim Reeves' songs long after his death. This continued release of fresh, original material led to some rumors by many fans and record executives alike that Jim Reeves was still alive. However, the cache of new tracks dried up eventually and the truth of Reeves' death became evident.

In 1981, one of the most amazing recordings to ever be produced was a duet between Jim Reeves and Patsy Cline. It was found that not only had they both recorded some of the same songs, but the songs were of nearly the same tempo and key. The posthumous duet in the song, "I Fall to Pieces," is haunting when you realize that both artists shared the same violent fate. Gentleman Jim Reeves was inducted into the Country Music Hall of Fame in 1967.

Author

Aircraft addenda:

Common name: Debonair (35-B33, this was a straight tail version of the series type)
Manufacturer: Beechcraft
First flight of prototype: 1945 (this was for the original "V" tail version of the series)
Registration number for this airplane: N8972M
Seats: 4
Length: 25 feet, 5 inches
Wingspan: 32 feet, 10 inches
Engine: (1) Continental IO-470-J, four-cylinder, horizontally opposed, air-cooled, piston
Horsepower: 225 h.p.
Empty weight (approximate): 1,730 lb.
Gross weight: 2,900 lb.
Service ceiling: 19,800 ft
Fuel capacity: 50 gal.
Cruising speed: 185 mph

* The above photo represents the type of aircraft and not necessarily the exact model involved in the accident.

Personal addenda:

James Travis Reeves (Gentleman Jim, Gentleman Jim Reeves): country music artist
b. August 20, 1923: 10 miles east of Carthage, Texas
d. July 31, 1964: 10 miles south of Nashville, Tennessee
Buried: Jim Reeves Memorial Park, Galloway, Texas

Dean Manuel: manager, pianist
b. unknown at this time
d. July 31, 1964: 10 miles south of Nashville, Tennessee
Buried: unknown at this time

FILE	DATE	LOCATION	AIRCRAFT DATA	INJURIES F S M/N	FLIGHT PURPOSE	PILOT DATA
2-0613	64/7/31 TIME - 1652	NR.NASHVILLE TENN	BEECHCRAFT 35-B33 N8972M DAMAGE-DESTROYED	CR- 1 0 0 PX- 1 0 0 OT- 0 0 0	NONCOMMERCIAL BUSINESS	PRIVATE, AGE 39, 200 TOTAL HOURS, UNK/NR IN TYPE, UNK/NR INSTRUMENT RATED.

TYPE OF ACCIDENT
COLLISION WITH GROUND/WATER.: UNCONTROLLED

PHASE OF OPERATION
IN FLIGHT: UNCONTROLLED DESCENT

PROBABLE CAUSE(S)
PILOT IN COMMAND - CONTINUED VFR FLIGHT INTO ADVERSE WEATHER CONDITIONS
WEATHER - RAIN
WEATHER BRIEFING - BRIEFED BY WEATHER BUREAU PERSONEL, BY PHONE
WEATHER FORECAST - FORECAST SUBSTANTIALLY CORRECT
MISSING AIRCRAFT - LATER RECOVERED

SKY CONDITION
BROKEN
CEILING AT ACCIDENT SITE
3800
VISIBILITY AT ACCIDENT SITE
5 OR OVER(UNLIMITED)
PRECIPITATION AT ACCIDENT SITE
RAIN SHOWERS, THUNDERSTORM
OBSTRUCTIONS TO VISION AT ACCIDENT SITE
HAZE
TYPE OF WEATHER CONDITIONS
VFR
TYPE OF FLIGHT PLAN
NONE
FIRE AFTER IMPACT
REMARKS- RECOVERY DATE-08/02/64

David Box

October 23, 1964

It is essential to locate the right person or report when finding factual details about a story. Look closely at the available brief. Although it is the best information we have, there is very little information to give insight into this accident. Even the NTSB identification number is listed as "Unknown." What we can see is that this pilot had a total of 100 hours flight time and 25 hours in this type of airplane, which can be considered low time for experience level. We also can see that there was an "uncontrolled descent" and that the probable cause remains "unknown."

What is believed is that Bill Daniels, the drummer for the "Buddy and the Kings" band, had a pilot's certificate and that he was the pilot of the Cessna 172. However, it cannot be definitively stated that Daniels was the pilot for this flight. It is further believed that the plane was rented, rather than owned, by the musicians. One bit of information gleaned from deeper research suggested that the plane had crashed nose first. This aspect would be consistent with an uncontrolled descent.

As a general statement when one looks back upon aviation's history, it can be safely said that pilots rarely find new ways of crashing airplanes. It usually boils down to a selection from the same set of well-known probable causes over and over again. That said, I am left with the opinion that the proper thing to do is give this pilot the benefit of doubt and suggest that it could have been a mechanical problem that perhaps led to this accident.

Taught by his father, David Box learned to play the guitar at an early age. He was a big Buddy Holly fan, and in 1958 formed his own group called the Ravens. The Ravens were styled after Holly's Crickets, and after Holly died they cut a few demo songs at Mitchell Studio in Lubbock, Texas. When Box heard that the Crickets were looking for a vocalist to replace Sonny Curtis, a demo tape was sent to the Crickets through a family friend. In 1960 David was rewarded for his efforts by being asked to sing the lead vocal tracks on the single, "Peggy Sue Got Married," based on some of the surviving demo songs that Holly recorded in his home just before Christmas, 1958. This was the last single released by the Crickets on the Coral label.

Box returned to school shortly thereafter, and in 1962 he enrolled in the School of American Art in Westport, Connecticut where he studied under the great Norman Rockwell. Longing to get back into the recording studio, Box traveled to Nashville, Tennessee where he stayed with Roy Orbison and recorded with Orbison's band. Box toured with the Everly Brothers as an opening act, and in 1964 he again returned to Nashville to record his best known song, "Little Lonely Summer Girl." Based on the prospect of this song becoming a hit he toured mostly on the East Coast, but returned to Houston, Texas where the single had a strong following. Working with a local band, Buddy and the Kings, Box and his new band mates were presumably enroute home following a concert in Harris County, Texas when the plane went down. All four musicians on board were killed. It is both sad and ironic that two lead singers for the Crickets were lost to aviation accidents.

Author

Aircraft addenda:

Common name: Skyhawk, 172 (the description below is for older model Cessna 172s.)
Manufacturer: Cessna
First flight of type: 1956
Registration number for this airplane: N2142Y
Seats: 4
Length: 26 feet, 6 inches
Wingspan: 36 feet, 2 inches
Engine: (1) Continental, O-300-D, four cylinder, horizontally opposed, air-cooled, piston
Horsepower: 145 hp
Empty weight (approximate): 1,260 lbs.
Gross weight: 2,300 lbs.
Service ceiling: 13,100 ft
Fuel capacity: 42 gal.
Cruising speed: 130 mph

The above photo represents the type of aircraft and not necessarily the exact model involved in the accident.

Personal addenda:

Harold David Box (David Box): singer, songwriter, guitarist
b. August 11, 1943: Sulphur Springs, Texas
d. October 23, 1964: Harris County, Texas
Buried: Sulphur Springs, Texas

Buddy Groves: guitarist, singer (Buddy and the Kings)
b. unknown at this time
d. October 23, 1964: Harris County, Texas
Buried: unknown at this time

Carl Banks: Bass guitar (Buddy and the Kings)
b. unknown at this time
d. October 23, 1964: Harris County, Texas
Buried: unknown at this time

William Daniels (Bill Daniels): drummer (Buddy and the Kings)
b. unknown at this time
d. October 23, 1964: Harris County, Texas
Buried: unknown at this time

NTSB Identification: Unknown

Incident occurred Friday, October 23, 1964 at HOUSTON TEXAS, TX
Aircraft:CESSNA 172, registration: N2142Y
Injuries: Unavailable

FILE	DATE	LOCATION	AIRCRAFT DATA	INJURIES F S M/N	FLIGHT PURPOSE	PILOT DATA
2-0751	64/10/23	NR.HOUSTON TEXAS	CESSNA 172	CR- 1 0 0	NONCOMMERCIAL	NO CERTIFICATE, AGE 19,
	TIME - 1155		N2142Y	PX- 3 0 0	PLEASURE/PERSONAL TRANSP	100 TOTAL HOURS, 25 IN
			DAMAGE-DESTROYED	OT- 0 0 0		TYPE, UNK/NR INSTRUMENT
						RATED.

TYPE OF ACCIDENT
   COLLISION WITH GROUND/WATER: UNCONTROLLED
PROBABLE CAUSE(S)
   MISCELLANEOUS - UNDETERMINED
MISSING AIRCRAFT - LATER RECOVERED
REMARKS- RECOVERY DATE-10/23/64.

PHASE OF OPERATION
   IN FLIGHT: UNCONTROLLED DESCENT

Otis Redding   **The Bar-Kays**

December 10, 1967

All that remains of the NTSB investigation into this accident is a brief version of the report. Almost as unfortunate is the fact that the probable cause of the accident is reported as "MISCELLANEOUS - UNDETERMINED." In other words, this tragedy presents another mystery. However, there are certain things that can be ascertained from the factual report in existence. Using this information I will progress as far as I can with a "reverse engineering" analysis of the accident. From this perspective, you may be able to see a clearer picture of how this accident might have happened.

Here is what we know. The airplane was a Beechcraft Model H18, a medium, twin-engine transport that can be configured for cargo hauling or executive travel. It is logical to assume that the plane's interior was laid out in a manner that would allow Redding and his band, or guests, to ride in comfort. We know also that the plane was in the landing phase of flight. The weather must have been less than ideal because the plane was on an instrument approach into Madison, Wisconsin, Dane County Regional airport (also known as Truax Field). We know that the plane crashed into Lake Monona, three miles from the runway, and that the left engine and propeller were not recovered, indicating that they both must have separated from the airplane at some point in time. Finally the report tells us that the pilot, despite relatively few hours logged in the Beech 18, appeared to be qualified to fly this airplane.

If you draw a straight line from the approach end of Truax Field's runway 36 to a point three miles south, you do indeed end up in the middle of Lake Monona's largest and northernmost bay. From this fact we can assume that the plane was approaching in a direction from the south, in order to land to the north on runway 36. We know that the temperature was cold and probably dropping due to the late time of day, and we know that something happened to the flight just about the time that the plane crossed over the water. What we do not know is whether the left engine and propeller separated before or after impact with the water. Although these clues leave seemingly little to go on, they do provide us with enough information to allow some insight into what might have occurred to cause this tragic loss of such a great collection of talent.

There are multiple scenario variations on this accident to possibly assess, but I will attempt to address briefly some of the more obvious ones. The first of the possibilities involves an airborne emergency. Since we know that the engine and propeller separated from the airplane, the first possible scenario is one in which the airplane experienced a structural failure in the mechanism of the left engine mount. If it indeed was the engine mount that experienced failure first, then this was an exceedingly rare event. Engine mounts are known to be very strong structures, and their evolution in aviation is a well-documented process. They simply do not break by themselves unless something has very seriously weakened them over a long period of time. Therefore, although I acknowledge this possibility, I seriously doubt that this is what happened.

The second scenario to ponder is the possibility that the engine itself experienced a failure. However, this may not have been enough in and of itself to cause the plane to go down. Pilots are taught early in their multi-engine training how to handle engine-out situations. Thus, assuming that the pilot was capable of handling a left engine problem (such as a cylinder going bad, loss of oil or an ignition problem) while attempting an instrument approach, we can probably discount this theory as a possibility. Still, the Beech 18 is known to be demanding of a pilot during an engine-out situation. If a pilot's skills are not well-honed in compensating for the loss of an engine in a Beech 18, an engine-out situation could turn for the worse very quickly. If the pilot of this airplane was insufficiently experienced in this type of airplane to quickly handle an engine-out emergency, then one might have to attribute the accident to pilot error.

Another mechanical aspect to consider with regards to an airborne failure that could have caused the flight to terminate tragically is the possibility that a propeller malfunctioned in some way. Whether a propeller has two, three or more blades, they are balanced to eliminate vibration and allow the smooth operation of a crankshaft within the bearings that surround the crankshaft. A small but insidious imbalance could cause excessive bearing wear in the engine that could, over time, lead to an engine failure. If, however, there was a catastrophic failure of a propeller blade, then this could lead to a very heavy vibration that could in turn lead to the engine being shaken right off its engine mount. Obviously anything as catastrophic as this would be of special interest to the NTSB because, if the problem were indicative of potential dangers within the fleet of similar equipment, other accidents might be avoided by suggesting mandatory inspections. Perhaps one day the missing engine and propeller will be recovered from Lake Monona and some of these questions may be answered.

Finally, we must consider the possibility that the pilot flew a perfectly good airplane into the ground or, in this case, a lake. As described in a previous chapter, controlled flight into terrain, or CFIT, occurs when the pilot is caught unaware that a collision status exists and then flies inadvertently, under complete control, into the ground. It is easy to see how CFIT can occur when a pilot is flying too low in mountainous territory, but it becomes rather mysterious when the plane flies into water, which obviously is flat. The key to understanding how this can happen is to consider one of the illusions that can fool the eye. The culprits that could have been at work in this case are the "featureless terrain" and "atmospheric" illusions. The featureless terrain illusion comes into play where there is an absence of ground features, such as when approaching to land over water. What happens is that the pilot is insidiously overtaken by the perception that he or she is at a higher altitude than he actually is. This misperception leads to the tendency to fly a lower than normal approach. The situation can be further complicated by the fact that depth perception can become nearly non-existent over a body of water.

Atmospheric illusion occurs when rain falling on a windshield causes a sensation of greater height. The pilot who experiences this illusion will tend to fly a lower approach than normal. Any penetration of fog or other impediment to visibility would only exacerbate the problem with the illusion of the nose of the airplane pitching up. A pilot who does not recognize this illusion of falsely pitching up can steepen an approach, sometimes abruptly. Nonetheless, all these illusions do not explain why a pilot would deviate from the precision guidance of an ILS approach. This is, unless, of course, the pilot had reached a point in the approach when he broke out of the clouds and reached what he believed to be visual conditions. In any case the passengers were helpless to change the event that unfolded. Ben Cauley, of the Bar-Kays, was the only survivor of the crash. The other five performers and the pilot died either upon impact or drowned in the frigid lake waters.

Otis Redding burst onto the national scene after his breakthrough performance at the June 1967 Monterey International Pop Festival. He was the closing act on June 17 and he was backed by the band Booker T. & the MGs during this engagement. His style was passionate and charismatic, blending soul, rhythm and blues and pop. Other performers recorded his songs, including Aretha Franklin, whose rendition of "RESPECT" is considered to be a true classic. His biggest hit, "(Sittin'On) The Dock Of The Bay," was recorded on December 7, 1967. Following this recording session he flew to Cleveland, Ohio, on December 9, in his newly purchased twin-engine Beech 18H, to appear on a television show. The next day he and his band, the Bar-Kays, were flying to Madison, Wisconsin to perform a concert at a venue called "The Factory" when the accident occurred. In March 1968, the ironically titled, "(Sittin' On) The Dock Of The Bay," hit number 1 and stayed there for four weeks. Redding was inducted into the Rock and Roll Hall of Fame in 1989.

The Bar-Kays were formed in the mid-1960s in Memphis, Tennessee. They were a big part of the Stax recording company and in 1967 had their biggest hit with a party effect instrumental track titled, "Soul Finger." After this song hit its peak at number 17 on the charts, the Bar-Kays went on tour with Otis Redding following his smashing appearance at the Monterey International Pop Festival. James Alexander, the bass player with the Bar-Kays, was not on board the plane when it crashed. Alexander and Cauley, the lone survivor of the crash, re-formed the Bar-Kays in 1968 and went on to record with many great songwriters, including Isaac Hayes on his number 1 hit "Theme From Shaft" in 1971.

Author

Aircraft addenda:

Common names: Beech 18, H model
Manufacturer: Beechcraft
First flight of type: 1937
Registration number for this airplane: N390R
Seats: variable up to about 9 passengers
Length: 35 feet, 2 inches
Wingspan: 49 feet, 8 inches
Engines: (2) Pratt & Whitney R-985, nine cylinder, radial, air cooled, piston
Horsepower: 450 hp (each)
Empty weight (approximate): 5,910 lbs.
Gross weight: 9,700 lbs.
Service ceiling: 21,000 ft
Fuel capacity: 198 gal.
Cruising speed: 210 mph

* The above photo represents the type of aircraft and not necessarily the exact model involved in the accident.

Personal addenda:

Otis Redding: singer, songwriter
b. September 9, 1941: Dawson, Georgia
d. December 10, 1967: Madison, Wisconsin
Buried: His family home, Round Oak, Georgia

Ronald Caldwell (Ronnie Caldwell): keyboards
b. 1948
d. December 10, 1967: Madison, Wisconsin
Buried: unknown at this time

Carl Cunningham: drums
b. 1949
d. December 10, 1967: Madison, Wisconsin
Buried: unknown at this time

Phalin Jones: saxophone
b. 1949
d. December 10, 1967: Madison, Wisconsin
Buried: unknown at this time

James King (Jimmy King): guitar
b. 1949
d. December 10, 1967: Madison, Wisconsin
Buried: unknown at this time

BRIEFS OF ACCIDENTS

FILE	DATE	LOCATION	AIRCRAFT DATA	INJURIES F S M/N	FLIGHT PURPOSE	PILOT DATA
2-1109	67/12/10	MADISON,WIS	BEECH H18	CR- 1 0 0	NONCOMMERCIAL	COMMERCIAL, FL.INSTR.,
	TIME - 1525		N390R	PX- 6 0 1	CORP/EXEC	AGE 26, 1290 TOTAL HOURS,
			DAMAGE-DESTROYED	OT- 0 0 0		118 IN TYPE, INSTRUMENT
						RATED.

PHASE OF OPERATION
LANDING: FINAL APPROACH

NAME OF AIRPORT - TRUAX
TYPE OF ACCIDENT
    UNDETERMINED

PROBABLE CAUSE(S)
    MISCELLANEOUS - UNDETERMINED
FACTOR(S)
    MISCELLANEOUS ACTS,CONDITIONS - AIRCRAFT CAME TO REST IN WATER
REMARKS- ACFT CRASHED IN LAKE 3 MILES FROM RNWY. LEFT ENG AND PROP NOT RECOVERED.

Audie Murphy

May 28, 1971

This accident is another example of a controlled flight into terrain (CFIT) and the region where this flight crashed was mountainous. It would appear that this pilot got into a situation well over his head. Thunderstorms were everywhere. The cloud ceilings and flight visibility were horrible with fog, rain and drizzle obscuring the mountains. There was only one crewmember (the pilot), meaning there was no backup person to help with decision-making in the cockpit, and there were five passengers. With the ceiling so low, the temptation may have been to fly at a lower altitude so that the ground could be seen continually. This kind of flying is known as "scud running" and it is dangerous at anytime. From the accident brief we can see that this pilot's apparent insufficient flight qualifications for the conditions, coupled with low flying in the vicinity of mountainous terrain in poor visibility, proved deadly. The most well-known of all the people who died on this flight was Audie Murphy, who came from simple beginnings to become the most decorated combat soldier of World War II.

Although Audie Murphy was a licensed pilot and owned and flew his own single-engine plane, he did not own the airplane in which he was killed as a passenger. Murphy was trying to raise capital to finish a movie he was producing, so he was very busy at the time of the accident. The airplane involved in this crash was an Aero Commander 680 owned by Colorado Aviation, based in Denver, Colorado. Murphy's business deals had brought him together with three business executives who were arranging the purchase of a company, Modular Properties, Inc., a Georgia-based manufacturer of prefabricated homes. They had departed from Atlanta, Georgia in the chartered plane for Martinsville, Virginia to tour a manufacturing plant of prefabricated components.

The story is best told in a correspondence from the Audie Murphy Research Foundation:

Dear Mr. Heitman:

The flight was purely a business trip.

It is my understanding that Audie Murphy was acting as a middleman arranging financing for the possible purchase of Modular Homes (aka Modular Properties, Inc.) by a Denver, CO based company named Telstar, Inc. Upon completion of the transaction, Murphy was to receive a finder's fee in the neighborhood of $300,000. He was planning to use this money to complete a film he was producing titled "A TIME FOR DYING." (This film was never really finished. After Audie Murphy's death Budd Boeticher tried to salvage the existing footage by editing it together and releasing it in Europe and on video. However, key scenes involving Murphy had not been shot. Without them the film wasn't commercial so it never made back the production costs.)

The plane was rented by Telstar, Inc. from Colorado Aviation, Inc. Telstar was a regular customer of Colorado Aviation, Inc. and had rented this particular plane on many occasions.

The people who got on the plane in Denver, CO were:

1. *Audie Murphy, who was acting as the broker.*
2. *Jack Littleton, an attorney representing Telstar, Inc.*
3. *Herman Butler, the pilot*
4. *Kim Dody, a gift shop owner who apparently was just going along for the ride. We know of no connection between him and Telstar or the deal or anyone else on the plane. I understand that after the meeting at the Modular Home plant Murphy was going to a charity golf tournament being held on the East Coast that weekend. Perhaps Mr. Dody was along for that. We simply don't know. We do know that the Murphy family had never heard of Mr. Dody before the accident.*

In fact, the Murphy family did not know any of the people who were killed along with Audie Murphy in the plane crash.

Butler, Murphy, Littleton, and Dody flew to Atlanta, GA on Thursday, May 27, 1971 where they spent the night. In the morning at the Airport they met Mr. Claude Crosby, the President of Modular Properties, Incorporated, and Raymond Prater a Chattanooga, TN attorney representing the financial institution that was considering making the loan to Telstar, Inc. for the proposed purchase.

On Friday, May 28, 1971 a little after 9:00 a.m. all 6 took off from Peachtree DeKalb Airport (PDK), Atlanta, GA with the intent of traveling to Martinsville, VA. The plane never arrived.

This was purely a business trip. While Audie Murphy may have known Jack Littleton, Raymond Prater and Herman Butler before the flight, they were not close personal friends. I don't believe Audie Murphy knew Dody or Crosby before this particular business trip.

It is my understanding that both Telstar and Colorado Aviation have long been out of business. I believe Colorado Aviation went bankrupt as a direct result of this crash. The Foundation has not been able to locate anyone from either of those companies to interview.

I hope this has helped answer your questions about the purpose and path of the trip.

Sincerely,
Larryann Willis
Executive Director
Audie Murphy Research Foundation

It is believed that approximately 60 miles from Martinsville, Virginia, Herman Butler, a non-instrument rated pilot, encountered deteriorating weather conditions. Eventually deciding that the situation was bad enough to request help, he contacted the Roanoke, Virginia airport control tower, where the conditions apparently were more favorable for a safe landing. Roanoke is 45 miles north of Martinsville. While it is understandable that a non-instrument pilot would try to avoid instrument conditions, this is most likely where the scud running began. Perhaps the pilot felt pressure to complete the trip.

According to some witnesses interviewed by the accident investigators, the pilot made several emergency landing attempts on a highway, and possibly in a field, all unsuccessful. If true, then apparently the pilot knew he was in a very bad situation and was making every effort to get the airplane on the ground any way possible. It is doubtful that Audie Murphy tried to assist the pilot in any way. Mr. Murphy was not familiar with, nor rated in a more complex twin-engine airplane and therefore he most likely chose to ride the situation out and allowed the pilot to handle the condition.

Finally, at some point during the pilot's attempts to scud-run below, between and in-and-out-of the rain, fog and low-lying clouds, this perfectly flyable airplane, with no mechanical or electrical problems, collided with the ground. It is believed that Audie Murphy was riding in the rear seat of the airplane when the aircraft struck the mountainside at approximately 3,100 feet elevation. Immediately the plane burst into flames. Everyone on board perished, most likely from the high speed impact itself. Ironically for Murphy, a well-known war veteran, it was Memorial Day weekend. It was discovered later that Colorado Aviation's Part 135 charter flying certificate had been suspended before this trip began. Unfortunately, due to the nature and duration of the bad weather, the wreckage was not found for three days. Audie Murphy was buried on June 7, 1971 in Arlington National Cemetery with full military honors. His gravesite overlooks the tomb of the unknown soldiers and is one of the most visited headstones in Arlington, along with that of John F. Kennedy.

Murphy's wartime record, by way of his medals and citations for valor, is noteworthy. Simply stated, he received every medal the United States Army could award, including the Bronze Star with Oak Leaf Clusters, the Silver Star, which he earned twice in three days, three Purple Hearts, the Distinguished Service Cross and the Congressional Medal of Honor. France and Belgium also decorated him for valor. His French decorations include the Legion of Merit, the French Legion of Honor, the Croix de Guerre with Silver Star and the Croix de Guerre with Palm. Belgium also awarded him its version of the Croix de Guerre with Palm. In all, Audie Murphy received 33 awards and decorations for bravery and valor in combat during his World War II service. Not only was he the most decorated United States combat soldier in that war, his documented courage and heroism have also made him a genuine role model for all generations to come.

After World War II, actor James Cagney invited Murphy to Hollywood where the young veteran promptly landed bit parts in two films. His Hollywood film career took off from there. Today, we best know Audie Murphy through his autobiography, "To Hell and Back," which documents his World War II experiences. It is worth noting that Murphy was known as a humble man and in his autobiography he never once mentioned receiving any of his medals. The movie detailing Murphy's World War II exploits and heroism, which bears the same title as his autobiography, was released in 1955 and actually starred Audie Murphy as himself. By that time Murphy had already established himself as a successful star. The movie "To Hell and Back" was Murphy's 16th film, and held the record as Universal Pictures highest grossing film until it was finally surpassed by the movie "Jaws" in 1975. Murphy made a total of 44 feature films. Thirty-two of his movies were westerns. However, it is a little known fact that Audie Murphy was also a successful songwriter.

During the war, Audie Murphy started writing poetry. This beginning led to his songwriting. He worked in conjunction with other talented artists and composers to refine his songs and instrumentals. Some of the composers he collaborated with include Scott Turner, Jimmy Bryant, Guy Mitchell, Coy Ziegler and Terry Eddleman. Many of Murphy's songs were recorded and released by well-known performers such as Jerry Wallace, Jimmy Bryant, Dean Martin, Eddy Arnold, Jimmy Dean, Charley Pride, Porter Waggoner, Roy Clark and Harry Nilsson, to name just a few. His two biggest hits were "Shutters and Boards," which has been recorded in over 60 versions since 1962, and "When the Wind Blows in Chicago," which was recorded and released in 1993 by Eddy Arnold. Murphy co-wrote both of these songs with Scott Turner in 1962. In all, Audie Murphy wrote at least 17 songs that were copyrighted and recorded before his death. In actuality, however, Audie Murphy wrote far more than 17 songs, most of which remain unpublished. He was inducted into the Country Music Association of Texas Hall of Fame in 1996.

Author

Aircraft addenda:

Common names: Aero Commander 680, Commander
Manufacturer: Aero Commander Company
First flight of prototype: 1951 (model 520)
Registration number for this airplane: N601JJ
Serial number for this airplane: 491-161
Seats: 5 to 7
Length: 35' 1"
Wingspan: 44' 1"
Engines: (2) Lycoming GSO-480-B1A6, six-cylinder, horizontally-opposed, gear-driven,
    air cooled, piston
Horsepower: 290 hp
Empty weight (approximate): 4,300 lbs.
Gross weight: 6,750 lbs.
Service ceiling: 28,600 ft
Fuel capacity: 223 gal.
Cruising speed: 200 mph

* The above photo represents the type of aircraft and not necessarily the exact model involved in the accident.

Personal addenda:

Audie Leon Murphy (Audie Murphy): war hero, movie actor, songwriter
b. June 20, 1924: Hunt County, near Kingston, Texas
d. May 28, 1971: Brush Mountain, 15 miles northwest of the Roanoke, Virginia airport
Buried: Arlington National cemetery (near the Amphitheater): Arlington, Virginia
Note: There is a memorial marker near the site of the airplane crash, along a short leg of the Appalachian Trail. The walk is a 1.5 mile loop and not difficult to traverse. The memorial marker was erected by VFW post 5311, in Christiansburg, Virginia.

BRIEFS OF ACCIDENTS

FILE	DATE	LOCATION	AIRCRAFT DATA	INJURIES F S M/N	FLIGHT PURPOSE	PILOT DATA
3-1752	71/5/28 NR.ROANOKE, VA TIME - 1108		AERO COMDR 680E N601JJ DAMAGE-DESTROYED	CR- 1 0 0 PX- 5 0 0 OT- 0 0 0	NONCOMMERCIAL BUSINESS	PRIVATE, AGE 43, 8000 TOTAL HOURS, UNK/NR IN TYPE, NOT INSTRUMENT RATED.

DEPARTURE POINT
ATLANTA, GA
                        INTENDED DESTINATION
                        MARTINSVILLE, VA
TYPE OF ACCIDENT
  COLLISION WITH GROUND/WATER: CONTROLLED

                        PHASE OF OPERATION
                          IN FLIGHT: NORMAL CRUISE

PROBABLE CAUSE(S)
  PILOT IN COMMAND - CONTINUED VFR FLIGHT INTO ADVERSE WEATHER CONDITIONS
  PILOT IN COMMAND - ATTEMPTED OPERATION BEYOND EXPERIENCE/ABILITY LEVEL
  WEATHER - LOW CEILING
  WEATHER - RAIN
  WEATHER - FOG
  TERRAIN - HIGH OBSTRUCTIONS
  WEATHER BRIEFING - BRIEFED BY FLIGHT SERVICE PERSONNEL, BY PHONE
  WEATHER FORECAST - FORECAST SUBSTANTIALLY CORRECT
  MISSING AIRCRAFT - LATER RECOVERED

SKY CONDITION
  BROKEN/LOWER SCATTERED
VISIBILITY AT ACCIDENT SITE
  ZERO
OBSTRUCTIONS TO VISION AT ACCIDENT SITE
  FOG
TYPE OF FLIGHT PLAN
  VFR
FIRE AFTER IMPACT

                        CEILING AT ACCIDENT SITE
                          0
                        PRECIPITATION AT ACCIDENT SITE
                          RAIN
                        TYPE OF WEATHER CONDITIONS
                          IFR

REMARKS- RCVRY DATE 5/31/71.PLT CONTD FLT INTO ADVERSE WX.ENTERED INST WX AT ALT TOO LO TO CLEAR MT.

Mike Jeffrey

March 5, 1973

Often when I am engaged in conversation with a non-pilot, that person, upon learning what I do for a living, will ask about any near-misses I may have had with other aircraft. First of all, such incidents are "near hits" in my opinion and I would venture to say that many pilots have experienced at least one such event during their careers. Still, I try to use these conversations to illustrate a point to the listeners. I remind them that they routinely drive their automobiles down a two-lane road, going at least 55 miles per hour, and that other cars pass in the opposite lane going at least as fast. I then point out that nothing separates this 110 mile per hour "near miss" except for a few feet and perhaps a couple of painted lines. Yet, while most people don't think twice about this everyday occurrence in their cars, it suddenly becomes a different picture when they think about an everyday separation between two aircraft by 1,000 feet.

As mentioned in the chapter describing the crash of the plane carrying the United States Navy Band, there may be nothing more feared in aviation than a mid-air collision. The ageless method to avoid colliding with another aircraft is the simple technique of "see and avoid." See and avoid means that to avoid another aircraft, the pilot first has to look out of the cockpit and see it. Under some circumstances such as bad weather, radar coverage does help pilots avoid other aircraft through the assistance of air traffic control (ATC) personnel, but during flights of good weather, the see and avoid responsibility is that of the pilot.

For air carriers and many air charter operations, modern technology has allowed more advanced methods of mid-air collision avoidance such as the cockpit installed "Traffic Collision and Avoidance System" (TCAS). However, before there was such a thing as TCAS to help a pilot with the avoidance of other aircraft, the use of radar service, together with the "see and avoid" method, were most critical. To this day, the see and avoid aspect of collision avoidance forms the backbone of every pilot's early basic training.

The "big sky" theory is the assumption that even though hitting another airplane is possible the probability is extremely low because the sky is so vast. To be sure, the mid-air collision is a very rare event. However, sometimes there are external factors that add to the total package of contributing factors. At the time of this particular crash, there was a civil ATC strike in France. Military ATC personnel had filled in during negotiations as a contingency effort, but they were working from different control centers. Because of the different duties of military controllers and the extended workloads due to the strike, two airplanes ended up on the same flight route. Incomplete radar coverage did not help the situation. Adding to the mix was the fact that both planes involved in the collision had deviated from their normal air carrier time schedule. The Iberia DC-9 flight departed late and the Spantax Convair 990 "Coronado" jetliner had departed early. The two Spanish registered planes collided at 29,000 feet at about 1:50 p.m. local time over Nantes, France, in a cruise flight environment.

At least one flight crewmember apparently saw the other plane because it is reported that the Spantax crew had initiated a right turn, most likely to avoid the Iberia flight. Even a radio call would appear to have been too late because the collision course of the two airliners was set and the two planes struck. It may be surprising to think that pilots could not judge a collision hazard, but non-pilots probably do not realize the alarming rate at which two fast moving planes can approach each other. Amazingly, although the Spantax Coronado, flight number BX400, with 114 people on board, was damaged after the mid-air collision, the pilots were able to land the plane safely shortly thereafter at Cognac, France. The Iberia plane crashed and all 68 people on board were killed. The final investigative determination was that the Spantax crew had improperly assessed the in-flight collision course. This error, coupled with the poor radio communications both transmitted and received, ultimately led to the accident.

Chas Chandler, formerly a bass player with the Animals band, met Jimi Hendrix in mid 1966, signed Hendrix as a client and was instrumental in the formation of the Jimi Hendrix Experience. Chandler needed help with finances so he entered into an agreement with Mike Jeffrey to help manage the band as a 50/50 partner. Mike Jeffrey had been in the intelligence corps in the army, was college educated and became a successful nightclub owner whose popular nightspots occasionally featured live bands such as the Rolling Stones and the Animals. Eventually, Jeffrey became full owner/manager of the Jimi Hendrix Experience band during the recording of 1968's "Electric Ladyland" album.

The ever-present problems and disputes between Hendrix and the money-conscious Jeffrey are well documented. Hendrix had tried desperately to escape from the confines of Jeffrey's managerial style throughout 1969, and reportedly would often simply become inaccessible because of his dislike for any kind of personal confrontation. After Hendrix's sudden tragic death in September 1970, Jeffrey became the much-disputed owner of the musician's estate. He was in London to attend a trial that would finally settle the Hendrix estate when he received word that his nightclub in Majorca, Spain was having some problems. Jeffrey and an associate departed London's Heathrow International Airport on Iberia flight 504, bound for Palma de Mallorca Airport in Majorca. They never arrived.

According to people who knew him, Mike Jeffrey had an intense fear of flying and he would literally grasp the armrests until his knuckles turned white. In fact, some that knew him say that he believed for many years that he would actually die in a plane crash. The laws of probability which govern the big sky theory and the simple see and avoid rule did not work in favor of the pilots and passengers of these two airplanes. Even though one plane miraculously kept flying, too many lives were lost in this terrible aviation disaster.

Author

Aircraft addenda:

Common names: DC-9 (this airliner was a DC-9-32)
Manufacturer: McDonnell Douglas
First flight of prototype: 1965 (initial prototype, DC-9-10), 1966 (DC-9-30 version)
Air Carrier for this flight: Iberia
Registration number for this airplane: EC-BII
Serial number for this airplane: 47077/148
Year built for this airplane: 1967
Crew on board this flight: 7
Passengers on board this flight: 61
Length: 119 feet, 3 inches
Wingspan: 93 feet, 5 inches
Engines: (2) Pratt & Whitney, JT8D-7, jet turbofan
Thrust: 14,000 lbs. (each)
Empty weight (approximate): 57,190 lbs.
Maximum take-off weight: 121,000 lbs.
Service ceiling (approximate): 45,000 ft.
Fuel capacity: 3,682 gal.
Cruising speed: 575 mph

* The above photo represents the type of aircraft and not necessarily the exact model involved in the accident.

Personal addenda:

Michael Jeffrey (Mike Jeffrey): Manager of Jimi Hendrix
b. 1940s
d. March 5, 1973: near Nantes, France
Buried: presumably in Spain or England

Jim Croce

Maury Muehleisen

September 20, 1973

At first glance, this accident report makes little sense to me. The pilot had over 14,000 hours of flight time. He had over 2,000 hours in this type of airplane, and he possessed the highest certificate that the FAA can issue, the Airline Transport Pilot (ATP) certificate. But when the time of day (or more accurately, the time of night) is taken into consideration, the probable cause becomes clearer. This 57-year-old pilot most likely and quite simply did not see the large row of old pecan trees looming just off the end of the runway as he lifted off and made a shallow climb-out. When one of the plane's wings struck one of the pecan trees, the plane went out of control and all on board perished. The question remains: why did the pilot make a shallow climb-out?

The effectiveness of night vision is influenced by the fact that the human eye cannot instantly adapt from light to dark. This means that the pilot should wait at least a half-hour to allow his or her eyes to fully adapt to night vision. In the cockpit, the instrument lights should be turned down as low as possible, and possibly illuminated with red light, so as not to upset the eye's night vision capability. Did this pilot walk out of a lighted environment and start his engines without allowing his eyes to adapt? The answer is not known.

Certainly, there are a host of illusions at night that can fool the eye. In discussing earlier accidents, I already have mentioned the fact that depth perception is greatly reduced at night. There is a related illusion that also could have been at work in this case. This illusion is called "focus fixation" and occurs when few outside images are available to the eye. When this illusion takes over, the eye focuses on objects closer at hand and is unable to see distant obstacles clearly. Taking off into an unlighted horizon can create this illusion. Another illusion that could have been a contributing factor in this accident is somatogravic illusion (described in the chapter on Guido Cantelli).

There is yet another illusion called "false horizon" that might have contributed directly to this accident. While a pilot must rely on a horizon to keep a plane's wings level, a false horizon can appear when scattered ground lights deceptively look like stars above a horizon. The result may be the illusion of being at a greater height than the pilot actually is. A false horizon also can occur at night when certain shapes of the ground, such as a hillside, meet a starlit sky. When this happens the pilot may incorrectly interpret the sloping horizon to be a level horizon, and as a result, could place the airplane in a wing-down attitude. Also, when the runway lights are dim, as they probably were at this small airport, a pilot also can experience the illusion of being higher than he actually is. This illusion most often occurs when the nose is held in a nose high attitude and the pilot looks at the runway lights below him. The pilot believes that if the lights are dim, he or she must be high. Also, we should consider this particular pilot's age of 57 years old. Although not an overall good marker for one's flying competence, it is a known fact that the eyes lose some ability to see clearly as a person ages.

Unfortunately, these nighttime illusions could possibly have been avoided. According to the court hearing that followed this accident, the pilot elected to depart the runway not only in the direction of reduced lighting, but also in a direction that was with the wind. According to eyewitnesses, taking off in the other direction would have provided a better-lit horizon. In addition, the plane would have been accelerating into the wind. Even a student pilot with few hours in the air can tell you that, unless extenuating circumstances prevail, all airplane departures should be performed into the wind. So why would this experienced pilot expose himself, and his passengers, to multiple risk factors? The answer may lie in the fact that this pilot had overslept and ended up running about three miles toward the airport before a police car stopped and offered him a ride. Quite simply, he may have been in a hurry and did not take time to assess all the parameters of the departure. According to at least one story, he did not perform a pre-flight inspection of the airplane. Because he was late arriving and probably felt bad about keeping everyone waiting, he may have felt a self-imposed pressure to get going.

There is one more thing to mention, which may seem to be in the pilot's defense. While this pilot was considered to be a health nut and probably was not a smoker, the owners of the airplane and the defense lawyers argued at the court hearing that the pilot suffered from a serious heart condition. They speculated that he had succumbed to a heart attack and that this incapacitation directly led to the crash. Certainly if he did have a heart attack, then this accident should be considered an act of God. But if this was the case, if he did have a serious heart condition, then why was he able to get an FAA flight medical certificate? While an aviation medical exam is required for pilot-in-command duties and is designed to pick up this kind of health condition, it is possible that a health flaw not detected could manifest itself at a later time. Additionally one must further ask that if he were able to get a valid medical certificate to allow him to fly, then why would he have consciously run three miles with a heart condition? The answer will probably remain unknown. The Federal Court jury ruling on this case did find "that the pilot failed to observe the highest degree of care in takeoff."

Jim Croce was a master storyteller with his songs. He brought characters and feelings to life through his interwoven words and perfectly matched music. But before he had become a music superstar he, like almost every performer, had toured on a smaller circuit. He was scheduled early in his career to perform at Northwestern State University in Natchitoches, Louisiana, but had to unexpectedly cancel due to an illness. Because of his strong work ethic, he promised the promoters that he would make up the concert at a later date.

By mid-1973, Croce was touring feverishly and filling major coliseums for his performances. Because his marriage and family life were suffering back home from this hectic schedule, it was his intent to finish the tour and take a well-deserved break. By this time he had become a huge celebrity. Despite his fame, Croce never forgot his promise to the university and as the 1973 tour was in its last stages he saw the opportunity to make good on his word. He finished his last performance that night with his prophetic song, "Time in a

Bottle." Shortly afterward, he boarded the fateful flight that took his life, bound for a show in Texas on the chartered Beech aircraft. "Time in a Bottle" hit number 1 on the charts a few weeks later. Jim Croce was at the peak of his career when he lost his life.

Accompanying Croce on this tour was guitarist and singer/songwriter Maury Muehleisen. Muehleisen was an accomplished performer in his own right and had recorded an album prior to embarking on the tour with Croce. The two were perfectly matched on stage and many who knew him believe that Muehleisen would have become a well-known recording music star eventually. The other passengers on board the ill-fated flight were comedian George Stevens from Colorado, Croce's tour manager Dennis Rast (whose business name was Morgan Tell), and Croce's booking agent Kenneth Cortese. Both Rast and Cortese were from Chicago. Sometime after this crash, the airport at Natchitoches was rebuilt and the pecan trees were cut down.

Author

Aircraft addenda:

Common names: Beech E18S
Manufacturer: Beechcraft
First flight of type: 1937
Registration number for this airplane: N50JR
Seats: variable up to about 9 passengers
Length: 35 feet, 2 inches
Wingspan: 49 feet, 8 inches
Engines: (2) Pratt & Whitney R-985, nine cylinder, radial, air cooled, piston
Horsepower: 450 hp (each)
Empty weight (approximate): 5,910 lbs.
Gross weight: 9,700 lbs.
Service ceiling: 21,000 ft
Fuel capacity: 198 gal.
Cruising speed: 210 mph

* The above photo represents the type of aircraft and not necessarily the exact model involved in the accident.

Personal addenda:

James Joseph Croce (Jim Croce): musician, singer, songwriter
b. January 10, 1943: Philadelphia, Pennsylvania
d. September 20, 1973: Natchitoches, Louisiana
Buried: Hyam Salomon Cemetery, section B/B: Frazer, Pennsylvania

Maurice Thomas Muehleisen (Maury Muehleisen): musician, singer, songwriter
b. January 14, 1949: Trenton, New Jersey
d. September 20, 1973: Natchitoches, Louisiana
Buried: St. Mary's Cemetery: Trenton, New Jersey

BRIEFS OF ACCIDENTS

FILE	DATE	LOCATION	AIRCRAFT DATA	INJURIES F S M/N	FLIGHT PURPOSE	PILOT DATA
3-3541	73/9/20 TIME - 2245	NATCHITOCHES, LA	BEECH E18S N50JR DAMAGE-DESTROYED	CR- 1 0 0 PX- 5 0 0 OT- 0 0 0	COMMERCIAL, AIR TAXI-PASSG	AIRLINE TRANSPORT, AGE 57, 14290 TOTAL HOURS, 2190 IN TYPE, INSTRUMENT RATED.

NAME OF AIRPORT - NATCHITOCHES MUNI
DEPARTURE POINT   INTENDED DESTINATION   LAST ENROUTE STOP
  NATCHITOCHES,LA   DALLAS,TEX   SHERMAN,TEX
TYPE OF ACCIDENT   PHASE OF OPERATION
  COLLIDED WITH: TREES   TAKEOFF: INITIAL CLIMB

PROBABLE CAUSE(S)
  PILOT IN COMMAND - FAILED TO SEE AND AVOID OBJECTS OR OBSTRUCTIONS
FACTOR(S)
  PILOT IN COMMAND - PHYSICAL IMPAIRMENT
  WEATHER - FOG
  WEATHER - OBSTRUCTIONS TO VISION
  TERRAIN - HIGH OBSTRUCTIONS

SKY CONDITION   CEILING AT ACCIDENT SITE
  CLEAR   UNLIMITED
VISIBILITY AT ACCIDENT SITE   PRECIPITATION AT ACCIDENT SITE
  5 OR OVER(UNLIMITED)   NONE
OBSTRUCTIONS TO VISION AT ACCIDENT SITE   TEMPERATURE-F
  HAZE   69
WIND VELOCITY-KNOTS   TYPE OF WEATHER CONDITIONS
  CALM   VFR
TYPE OF FLIGHT PLAN
  NONE
REMARKS- PLT HAD SEV CORONARY ARTERY DISEASE.RAN FRM MOTEL TO NEAR ARPT,ABT 3MI.

Bill Chase

August 9, 1974

In bad weather when the ground is obscured by rain and fog, there is nothing for a pilot to use to get safely on the ground except for the cockpit instruments and his or her skill interpreting them. It is an amazing and rewarding thing to launch a machine into the air, maneuver it under complete control to a destination that cannot be seen and place it on the ground exactly where the pilot wants it without bending or breaking any pieces. In order for any heavier-than-air machine to fly there must be sufficient airspeed. The airspeed, or simply stated, the air flowing over the wings, is necessary for those wings to produce the lift that carries the weight of the plane, passengers, fuel and baggage into the sky. In short, airspeed is life. Should a plane get into the air and then have the airflow over its wings diminish below the threshold where lift is attainable, the wings will cease to produce lift. This scenario is called a stall. In this accident it appears that the qualified charter pilot performed all tasks correctly, with one major exception: he may have allowed his airspeed to decay below the critical airspeed threshold.

An instrument approach is a very structured and regulated procedure. The types of instrument approaches vary from the least accurate, non-precision, non-directional beacon (NDB) variety to the very accurate Instrument Landing System (ILS). Only pilots who have undergone the required training and testing can legally fly in bad weather when an instrument approach would be required to safely get an aircraft back on the ground. When a pilot performs an instrument approach to land at an airport, there are headings and altitudes to fly during specific segments in the approach. Variations of these altitudes and headings at times other than specified in the published instrument approach for that particular airport are not an option. This is exactly why instrument rated pilots must possess strong discipline. They willfully continue to get closer to the ground without seeing it, all the while knowing that if they follow the rules they will arrive safely. Finally, there is a final altitude for every bad weather instrument approach beyond which a pilot should not descend if the runway environment is not seen. Doing so could result in disaster.

It is entirely possible that if the weather is bad at a destination, an instrument approach will not necessarily result in a successful landing at the desired airport. The pilot then has the option of trying the approach again, following the procedure from its beginning through to the minimum descent altitude, or perhaps diverting to another airport where the weather or another approach might be better. This is a decision time for the pilot. If the pilot is chartered, there might be some self-imposed, get-there pressure. A pilot may feel the need to complete his assigned flying task and not inconvenience his passengers by having to divert to an alternate airport. You can call it pride in a job well done. Call it anything you wish. The bottom line is pressure to perform.

The probable cause of this accident is listed as a stall in a phase of flight sometimes referred to as the low approach. It appears as if this pilot successfully completed the instrument portion of the approach and was in the process of trying to see the runway or runway environment, such as a runway lighting system. However, an approach is not fully complete until the tires are on the ground. As the approach would have been conducted at a lower than cruise power setting, the pilot would have had to increase the power eventually in order to execute what is known as a missed approach. If this pilot were so intent on seeing the ground during the low pass that he momentarily forgot to increase the power, which allowed the airspeed to decay, then this would explain the stall that occurred. As with many of the other accidents discussed in this text, there are aspects of this flight that we may never understand. However, the weather conditions that prevailed in this case were bad enough that the wreckage was not found until the next day.

As a child and adolescent, Bill Chase experimented with many musical instruments. After finally settling on the trumpet playing jazz, he attended the prestigious Berklee School of Music in Boston. He loved jazz and the big band sounds. Soon after, he was hired by Woody Herman and toured with Woody's Herd until 1966. He then settled in Las Vegas performing on the hotel show circuit, with orchestras, as a studio musician and occasionally touring with Herman's band. In 1970 he formed his own band and landed a recording contract with Epic records. His biggest hit was "Get It On," which originally was written without a vocal part, but eventually made it to the number 1 spot on the Pop charts in the summer of 1971. His band was nominated for a "Best New Artist" Grammy Award in 1971. On this particular flight, he and his band had just performed for a week in Texas and were headed for the Jackson County Fair in Jackson, Minnesota. Everyone on board died in the accident. Chase is remembered for his jazz and rock performances, as well as his jazz-rock fusion.

Author

Aircraft addenda:

Common names: Twin Comanche, PA-30
Manufacturer: Piper
First flight of type: 1962
Registration number for this airplane: N8129Y
Seats: 6 (4 seats up to 1965 models)
Length: 25 feet, 2 inches
Wingspan: 36 feet, 9 inches
Engines: (2) Lycoming, IO-320-B1A, four cylinder, horizontally opposed, piston
Horsepower: 160 hp each
Empty weight (approximate): 2,270 lbs.
Gross weight: 3,600 lbs.
Service ceiling: 20,000 ft.
Fuel capacity: 90 gal.
Cruising speed: 195 mph

* The above photo represents the type of aircraft and not necessarily the exact model involved in the accident.

Personal addenda:

William Edward Chiaiese (Bill Chase): trumpet musician, songwriter
b. October 20, 1934: Squantum, Massachusetts (A suburb of Boston on Quincy Bay)
d. August 9, 1974: Jackson, Minnesota
Buried: Cedar Grove Cemetery: Squantum, Massachusetts

Walter J. Clark: drummer
b. January 24, 1949
d. August 9, 1974: Jackson, Minnesota
Buried: Cross Keys Methodist Cemetery: Cross Keys, New Jersey

John T. Emma: guitar
b. April 30, 1952: Geneva, Illinois
d. August 9, 1974: Jackson, Minnesota
Buried: Lincoln Memorial Park: Aurora, Illinois

Wallace Keith Yohn (Wally Yohn): organ
b. January 12, 1947: Phoenix, Arizona
d. August 9, 1974: Jackson, Minnesota
Buried: Greenwood Cemetery: Phoenix, Arizona

FILE	DATE	LOCATION	AIRCRAFT DATA	INJURIES F S M/N	FLIGHT PURPOSE	PILOT DATA
3-3102	74/8/9 JACKSON,MINN TIME - 1700		PIPER PA-30 N8129Y DAMAGE-DESTROYED	CR- 1 0 0 PX- 5 0 0 OT- 0 0 0	NONCOMMERCIAL PLEASURE/PERSONAL TRANSP	AIRLINE TRANSPORT, AGE 41, 2600 TOTAL HOURS, UNK/NR IN TYPE, INSTRUMENT RATED.

NAME OF AIRPORT - JACKSON MUNI
DEPARTURE POINT   INTENDED DESTINATION
  WATERLOO,IOWA   JACKSON,MINN
TYPE OF ACCIDENT   PHASE OF OPERATION
  STALL   IN FLIGHT: LOW PASS

PROBABLE CAUSE(S)
  PILOT IN COMMAND - FAILED TO OBTAIN/MAINTAIN FLYING SPEED
  PILOT IN COMMAND - IMPROPER IFR OPERATION
  PILOT IN COMMAND - INADEQUATE PREFLIGHT PREPARATION AND/OR PLANNING
FACTOR(S)
  WEATHER - LOW CEILING
  WEATHER - RAIN
  WEATHER - TURBULENCE, ASSOCIATED W/CLOUDS AND/OR THUNDERSTORMS
  WEATHER BRIEFING - NO RECORD OF BRIEFING RECEIVED
  WEATHER FORECAST - FORECAST SUBSTANTIALLY CORRECT

SKY CONDITION   CEILING AT ACCIDENT SITE
  OVERCAST   400
VISIBILITY AT ACCIDENT SITE   PRECIPITATION AT ACCIDENT SITE
  3 MILES OR LESS   RAIN SHOWERS
OBSTRUCTIONS TO VISION AT ACCIDENT SITE   WIND DIRECTION-DEGREES
  FOG   130
WIND VELOCITY-KNOTS   TYPE OF WEATHER CONDITIONS
  3   IFR
TYPE OF FLIGHT PLAN
  IFR
REMARKS- ACFT STRUCK GND ABT 3/8 MILE NE OF ARPT.OBSVD INFLT AT LO ALT,DSCNDG.

the doobie liner

The Doobie Brothers' Doobieliner

September 1, 1974

This accident involved an airplane that was not in motion at the time. Because of this fact, in addition to the fact that there were no injuries, there was never a NTSB accident report. The accident was a fire, caused by an unknown origin, while all personnel and passengers were away from the plane. The event occurred at what was then called the Norfolk Regional Airport, in Norfolk, Virginia. The airplane was destroyed, but the accident yielded an improved fire control system for the airport and a practice airplane for fire drills.

The plane which carried the world famous Doobie Brothers band was a Martin 404, a pressurized and air-conditioned 1950s era airliner. It had been aptly dubbed the "Doobieliner" in honor of its duty at the time. On Sunday, September 1, 1974, the Doobie Brothers band landed at the Norfolk Regional Airport for a concert at a local stadium. The Doobie Brothers were the headline act, accompanied by the bluegrass oriented Earl Scruggs Revue and pop/rock Ozark Mountain Daredevils.

Back at the airport, just before 7:00 p.m., an airline agent on the airport ramp saw smoke seeping from the chartered airplane that was parked in front of what was then the Terminal Building. The airport volunteer fire department was called and, upon arriving on the scene, they went to work on what proved to be a hopeless cause. The combination of the fuselage and the open rear "airstair" door allowed the plane to act as a chimney. What had begun as a small fire somewhere in the rear of the plane, near the galley area, soon erupted into a full-scale blaze. Before it was over, a half dozen Norfolk fire units responded to the call. The plane burned to the window line. It was fortunate that the fire was extinguished before it could reach the wings because, for the band's flight out of Norfolk, approximately 800 gallons of high-octane aviation fuel had been pumped into the wing's fuel tanks only a short time before the fire started.

The plane's owner/pilot, Sam Stewart, believed that someone might have set the fire because he was sure that he had turned off all electrical power before leaving the custom-outfitted airliner. The chartered plane's flight attendant, Fay Stephens, stated that she was confident that no equipment in the galley could have caused the flare-up. Others speculated that a still-lit cigarette, either accidentally left or dropped on a seat, was the cause of the inferno. Of course the running joke was that it was a marijuana cigarette, also known as a "doobie," that was the fire's origin. Fire officials eventually listed the cause of the fire as undetermined. No matter what the cause, the plane was a total loss.

The plane's fire-gutted hulk sat in place for a time while everyone waited for Stewart to do something with his ruined airplane. After a while, it became an eyesore, so the plane was towed to the other side of the airfield where it continued to sit. During this time, an internal airport board determined that the airport volunteer fire department had run its course and three permanent Norfolk Airport fire-fighter positions were established. Not wanting to let a good opportunity pass, the newly formed airport fire department towed the plane to a practice fire area and used the carcass as a training aid. Eventually an aircraft salvager from Texas came and removed the 404's engines, wheels, brakes and other salvageable components, leaving only the plane's shell. The last time the plane was moved, it was shamelessly dragged on its axles through the dirt, yet it still was to serve as a fire fighting practice tool for a few years to come.

The Doobie Brothers finished their last two concerts of the 1974 tour without any known further excitement in their aviation travels. The Doobie Brothers went on to achieve super-stardom in the 1970s, 1980s and 1990s. To this day they still have the ability to sell out their concerts.

Norfolk Airport Fire Department

Norfolk Airport Fire Department

Aircraft addenda:

Common name: Martin 404
Manufacturer: Glenn L. Martin Company
First flight of prototype: 1950
Total number built: 103
Charter company in this accident: GSD Aircraft Leasing
Registration number for this airplane: N40427
Serial number for this airplane: 14133
Seats: 40 to 44 as an airliner - this airplane was custom configured and held 24 seats.
Length: 74' 7"
Wingspan: 93' 3.5"
Engines: (2) Pratt & Whitney R-2800-CB-16, 18 cylinder "Double Wasp," radial
Horsepower: 2400 hp each
Empty weight (approximate): 29,126 lbs
Gross weight: 44,900 lbs
Service ceiling: 29,000 ft
Fuel capacity: 1,370 gal.
Cruising speed: 275 mph

* The photos represent the exact aircraft involved in the accident.

Luciano Pavarotti

December 22, 1975

The one thing that will nearly always prevent a pilot from seeing the ground and thus prevent a successful landing is a thick, low-lying fog. On the occasion of this accident there was just such a fog. In fact, the fog was below the weather minimums required for the approach. Yet despite the advice of air traffic control not to attempt a landing, the Captain decided otherwise and continued his descent toward the Milano-Malpensa Airport in Milan, Italy. Even though the NTSB accident brief lists this accident as a "controlled" collision, the aircraft basically crash landed beside, and parallel to, the intended runway, hitting electronic equipment.

The landing gear and all four engines were torn away from the plane and the nose section broke off just behind the forward cabin door as the plane slid punishingly to a stop. There were no fatalities in this mishap, but there were some injuries. Luciano Pavarotti was one of the passengers on this flight and he was slightly injured. The airplane was damaged beyond repair and the captain of this scheduled flight reportedly was fired after this accident.

Luciano Pavarotti is arguably the most famous tenor in the world. He made his singing debut in Italy in 1961, in London in 1963 and in the USA in 1965. He has appeared regularly at the New York Metropolitan Opera since 1968, but it was his performance there in 1972 that catapulted him to become what can only be described as a vocal phenomenon. His beautiful tenor voice and crystal clear pronunciation have led to sold out concerts at the venues where he performs all over the world. Fortunately, no lives were lost in this accident, which was a non-stop flight from New York City to Milan, Italy.

Roger D. Cain

Aircraft addenda:

Common names: 707 (this airplane was a 707-331B model)
Manufacturer: Boeing
First flight of prototype: 1954
Air Carrier for this flight: Trans World Airlines (TWA)
Registration number for this airplane: N18701
Serial number for this airplane: 18978/465
Year built for this airplane: 1966
Crew on board this flight: 8
Passengers on board this flight: 117
Length: 152 feet, 11 inches
Wingspan: 142 feet, 5 inches
Engines: (4) Pratt & Whitney JT-3D, jet, turbofan
Power: 18,000 pounds of thrust (each)
Empty weight (approximate): 137, 500 lbs.
Gross weight: 328,000 lbs.
Service ceiling: 45,000 ft
Fuel capacity: 22,800 gal.
Cruising speed: 590 mph

* The above photo represents the type of aircraft and not necessarily the exact model involved in the accident.

Personal addenda:

Luciano Pavarotti: tenor opera singer
b. October 12, 1935: Modena, Italy
Luciano Pavarotti continues to perform.

NTSB Identification: **DCA76RZ015**

Incident occurred Monday, December 22, 1975 at MILAN, ITALY, OF
Aircraft: BOEING 707, registration: N18701
Injuries: Unavailable

FILE	DATE	LOCATION	AIRCRAFT DATA	INJURIES F S M/N	FLIGHT PURPOSE	PILOT DATA
1-0044	75/12/22	MILAN, ITALY	BOEING 707	CR- 0 0 9	SCHED INTERNATL PASSG SRV	AIRLINE TRANSPORT, AGE
	TIME - 1029		N18701	PX- 0 3110		52, 25303 TOTAL HOURS,
			DAMAGE-SUBSTANTIAL	OT- 0 0 0		7316 IN TYPE, INSTRUMENT
						RATED.

NAME OF AIRPORT - MILAN-MALPENSA
OPERATOR - TRANS WORLD AIRLINES, INC.
DEPARTURE POINT   INTENDED DESTINATION
  NEW YORK, NY   MILAN, ITALY
TYPE OF ACCIDENT
  COLLISION WITH GROUND/WATER: CONTROLLED   PHASE OF OPERATION
PROBABLE CAUSE(S)   LANDING: LEVEL OFF/TOUCHDOWN
  PILOT IN COMMAND - FAILED TO FOLLOW APPROVED PROCEDURES, DIRECTIVES, ETC.
  MISCELLANEOUS ACTS, CONDITIONS - NOT ALIGNED WITH RUNWAY/INTENDED LANDING AREA
REMARKS- INVESTIGATED & REPORTED BY THE GOVT OF ITALY.

Orfeon University Choir

September 3, 1976

Once any object or creature departs what could be metaphorically considered the atmospheric shoreline, that entity has entered into and is subject to the effects of an ocean of air. Just like any large body of water, the air is full of all types of currents. There are eddy currents, whirlpool currents, rising currents and descending currents. These currents can occur horizontally or vertically. Some are mild, some are strong and some are violent. Any sudden change in the direction or velocity of wind current, no matter where or in what orientation, is called wind shear. Also, like fluid, air has density and thus has the capability of force. This effect can be illustrated by sitting beside a swimming pool and running your arm through the water. The resistance felt is due to the water's density. Now imagine driving fast in your car and reaching your arm out of the window. Once again a force is felt. The difference is that air, being thinner than water, needs more speed to create the same force.

It has been established in previous chapters that the take-off and landing phases of flight have the most risk associated with them. This fact is not surprising when one considers that there is little room for human error or machine malfunction with the ground so close and gravity so absolute. Hurricane hunter aircrews purposely and routinely fly into some of the most violent weather on earth to extract data that will assist in saving lives. Yet even the most seasoned of hurricane hunter pilots would not dare to attempt a take-off or a landing in the fierce and tricky winds of a hurricane.

Additionally, it is not only the strong winds in a hurricane that should be feared. A hurricane can also harbor severe embedded thunderstorms and freakish tornadoes. Yet, an attempted landing in hurricane-like conditions led directly to this accident. An aircrew, flying the same kind of airplane that is used to hunt hurricanes, attempted a landing while two storms (one a hurricane) were near. This action was the primary contributing factor that led to this tragic accident. Additional risk factors were a hilly terrain close by and a nighttime instrument approach.

The purpose of the trip was to transport the world-renowned choir of the Central University of Venezuela to participate in the 12th International Day of Choral Singing competition in Barcelona, Spain. The University had approached the Venezuelan government for help in transporting the 19 to 20 year old boys since the expense was too great for the school. Many of the young men were from the interior of the country and this was their first trip abroad. The President of Venezuela obliged and found an experienced Venezuelan Air Force pilot for the task, Lieutenant Colonel Manuel Aureliano Vasquez Ocanto. He was on vacation at the time in Maracay, but agreed to fly the trip if he could bring his wife along. He also knew the route well because he had flown it before.

The plane departed Simon Bolivar Airport, serving Caracas, early on September 3, 1976 for the long transatlantic flight. Surely the crew had obtained a weather briefing and they certainly must have been aware of Hurricane Emmy and the other storm named Frances, but for some reason they continued to their destination of Lajes Air Base, near the city of Praira da Vitoria. This base is on Terceira Island, which is part of the Azores Islands Archipelago belonging to Portugal. Perhaps the crew thought that since the main body of Hurricane Emmy had already passed, it did not pose a significant a risk. They were wrong.

Just after 9:40 p.m. the crew was on its final descent path to runway 16, with very little visibility, in heavy rain and raging winds gusting from 35 mph to as much as 70 mph. Reportedly, the approach control personnel attempted to tell the pilots that the plane was not aligned with the runway, but it may have been too late. The military transport slammed into a hill just under a mile from the runway threshold. The victims included the flight crew, the entire university choir, the choir's conductor Vinicio Adames, its vocal advisor Leyla Mastroccola and its coordinator Mercedes Ferrer. There were no survivors.

The Central University of Venezuela was founded in 1725 and the main campus is in Caracas. Currently it comprises a whole educational system of forty-five schools and institutes that dot this South American country. Of these schools, the Orfeon Universitario was founded in 1943 to pioneer Venezuelan choral groups. The choir is the oldest active choir in the country and performed at the 1st International Festival of College Choirs in the Lincoln Center of New York in 1965. Following this terrible accident that wiped out the entire group of student and staff talent, it took more than six months of hard work to re-establish the choir. The choir made its re-emergent debut in the main amphitheater of the Central University on March 27, 1977. Since that time the choir has traveled extensively for regional and international competitions and performances. In 1987 at the 23rd international contest and in 1990 at the 26th event, both held in Montreaux, Switzerland, the choir took first place in the judging.

The Orfeon University Choir continues to perform.

Roger D. Cain

Aircraft addenda:

Common names: C-130H, Hercules
Manufacturer: Lockheed
First flight of prototype: 1953
Operator of this flight: Venezuelan Air Force
Registry number for this airplane: 7772
Crew on board this flight: 10 (normal crew is 5)
Passengers on board this flight: 58
Length: 97 feet, 8 inches
Wingspan: 132 feet, 6 inches
Engines: (4) Allison turbine, turboprop
Horsepower: 4,824 hp each
Empty weight (approximate): 75,927 lbs.
Gross weight: 175,428 lbs.
Service ceiling: 35,000 feet
Range: 4886 miles
Cruising speed: 375 mph

* The above photo represents the type of aircraft and not necessarily the exact model involved in the accident.

Ronnie Van Zant

Steve Gaines

Cassie Gaines

Dean Kilpatrick

October 20, 1977

In the course of flying an airplane there is an absolute that no one can argue. Fuel left on the ground does absolutely no good whatsoever. Fuel is a necessary component for combustion within the engine(s). It is the "go" juice. In this accident we know that the plane ran out of fuel. What we do not know is exactly why. It is known, however, that there was a malfunction in the fuel flow system of the right engine. The right engine on a two-engine airplane is also known as the number two engine. The pilots were aware of this malfunctioning fuel delivery system to the number two engine, yet decided to continue with the flight. Personally, I have never met any pilot who would deliberately fly an airplane with a fuel malfunction such as this. A malfunction can lead to an unknown, and to fly with an unknown is to risk flying as a test pilot.

Interestingly, the accident report describes the claim by the firm leasing the plane to the Lynyrd Skynyrd band that it was the band's responsibility to have any malfunctions fixed during the lease agreement. If this is the case, then why didn't the pilots tell the band of the arrangement and have the plane fixed at the departure point in Greenville, South Carolina? We know from interviews with the surviving band members that the band and their families were concerned about the plane's condition just before the flight departed on its course. Perhaps if the band had known that they were responsible for the decision to have the plane fixed, they would have done so. However, it is not unreasonable to assume that the band would have left any flight decisions, as well as any mechanical considerations, to the flight crew and trusted their judgment to continue with the flight. It should be noted that the rock band Aerosmith turned down the use of this same airplane about one month before the accident, but the reasons for this decision are not documented.

The Lynyrd Skynyrd band was jokingly named after the most notoriously disliked coach and teacher at Lee High School during the band members' high school days in Jacksonville, Florida. His name was Leonard Skinner. The heart, soul, founder, leader, main songwriter and lead singer for the band was Ronnie Van Zant. Van Zant had the reputation of being a roughneck street brawler, yet he unwaveringly believed that music was his ticket out of the rough side of town. He was a masterful songwriter/storyteller who wrote about people and events in his life.

The band's unique southern style rocketed them from garage band to international superstars in the 1970s. Their only top ten hit was "Sweet Home Alabama," but the true rock anthem that the band recorded was the song "Free Bird." In an interview, Van Zant stated that the lyrics were based on the idea that everyone is free, symbolized by the ultimate freedom that a bird has to be able to fly wherever it wants to go. This individual freedom, lived vicariously through the flight of a bird, struck a chord in the hearts of people everywhere.

On October 17, 1977, the band released its sixth album, titled "Street Survivors." This was an appropriate name for the album because almost all the band members had survived the mean streets while growing up. On the album cover some of the band members were depicted as being surrounded in flames. Two days later the band played at the Greenville Memorial Auditorium in Greenville, South Carolina. The next afternoon they were to begin a flight to Baton Rouge, Louisiana where they were to perform at the Louisiana State University Assembly Center on October 21st. The plane departed the Greenville airport around 5:00 p.m. on the 20th. Soon the band was relaxing by playing poker and telling jokes while the pilots went about their tasks. Just a short distance from their destination, they knew something was terribly wrong when the right engine quit. Then, except for the sound of rushing air, everything became quiet when the number one, or left engine, stopped producing power. It was at this time that the co-pilot came back and told everyone to take a seat because the plane was going to crash.

Very quickly after the plane hit the ground, it broke apart. Still strapped into his seat, Ronnie Van Zant died instantly when he was thrown free of the wreckage and his head hit a tree. Steve Gaines, a guitar player, apparently also died quickly. Gaines' sister, Cassie Gaines, a back-up singer who was the person who helped Steve get into the band, either died upon impact or shortly thereafter. Dean Kilpatrick, one of the original roadies for the band who had become an assistant road manager, was also killed. Billy Powell, pianist for the band, had severe facial lacerations; Artimus Pyle, drummer, sustained compound rib fractures with other internal injuries; Leon Wilkeson, bass player, had severe internal injuries; Allen Collins, a guitar player, had a fractured neck. The most severely injured surviving member of the band was guitar player Gary Rossington. Rossington sustained multiple broken bones and punctured organs, along with other bodily injuries. In fact, of the 26 people aboard only one received injuries that could be classified as minor.

Just a few days after the plane crash, after receiving requests from surviving band members and the victim's families, MCA records recalled the "Street Survivors" album with the "flames" cover. Even though there was not a post crash fire resulting from the accident, this action was believed by all involved to be the right thing to do as a gesture of respect for those who perished. The album was quickly re-released with only a black background for the pictured band members.

Just over a year after the plane crash, the members of the band, still healing from the injuries, found the mental and physical strength to begin playing again. In January 1979, at a concert organized by Charlie Daniels, the Lynyrd Skynyrd band played publicly for the first time since October of 1977. During that performance they played the song "Free Bird" as an instrumental while a lone spotlight shone on an empty microphone where Ronnie Van Zant would have stood. The original free bird himself would not be forgotten as his band took on the form of a mythical bird, a Phoenix rising from the ashes.

Sadly, it was Allen Collins who perhaps indirectly became the fifth casualty of the crash when he was never able to fully recover from the psychological effects of the plane accident and subsequent personal tragedy within his family. In 1980 his wife died due to complications of childbirth just as some of the band members began a resurgence in the form of the Rossington Collins Band. That band fell apart in 1983. In 1986 Collins' girlfriend was killed, and he was left paralyzed from the waist down, when he crashed his car while driving intoxicated. During the 1987 tour for the resurrected Lynyrd Skynyrd band he served as the musical director, selecting arrangement of songs and the stage. However, this role proved to be very painful for him because as his band mates performed he could only watch from the sidelines. He used his wheelchair-bound situation as positively as he could by warning young people of the dangers of drunk driving, but in 1989 Collins developed pneumonia as a result of paralysis-related decreased lung capacity. He died in a Jacksonville, Florida hospital in January 1990.

It is interesting to note that a young Artimus Pyle nearly became a licensed pilot himself until his father was tragically killed in a mid-air airplane accident. In addition, Pyle was involved in a military helicopter accident while he was in the Marines. Although he never completed the training necessary to become an FAA certified pilot, he did understand enough about flying that it was not uncommon for him to be at the controls of the Lynyrd Skynyrd band's various airplanes from time to time under supervision of the plane's captain. It was Pyle who, despite his painful injuries, went for help when the Convair went down in Mississippi in 1977. After the Lynyrd Skynyrd accident, Pyle chose not to reunite with his former band for personal reasons. He now tours the world with his own band called APB, for the "Artimus Pyle Band."

Author

Aircraft addenda:

Common names: Convair 240, CV-240
Manufacturer: Convair
First flight of type: March 16, 1947
Registration number for this airplane: N55VM
Seats: 44 in an airliner configuration
Length: 74 feet, 8 inches
Wingspan: 91 feet, 9 inches
Engines: (2) Pratt & Whitney R2800, eighteen-cylinder, air-cooled radial
Horsepower: 2,400 hp each
Empty weight (approximate): 27,000 lbs.
Gross weight: 41,790 lbs.
Service ceiling: 30,000 feet
Cruising speed: 270 mph

* The above photo represents the type of aircraft and not necessarily the exact model involved in the accident.

Personal addenda:

Ronald Wayne Van Zant (Ronnie Van Zant): lead singer, songwriter, musician
b. January 15, 1948: Jacksonville, Florida
d. October 20, 1977: near Gillsburg, Mississippi
Buried: Jacksonville Memory Gardens, Orange Park, Florida
Note: Van Zant was buried with one of his trademark "Texas Hatters" hats and his favorite fishing pole, named "murder." On February 13, 1982, a 300-pound marble bench next to Ronnie Van Zant's tomb was stolen. Police found it in a dry riverbed about two weeks later. On June 29, 2000, Van Zant's mausoleum itself was broken into. Grave robbers shattered the two-inch thick rear marble wall of his crypt and when police arrived, his unopened casket was found on the ground. As a result of this vandalism, Van Zant's family has moved the entertainer's remains from Jacksonville Memory Gardens to an undisclosed and private location. The mausoleum will remain standing where it is.

Steve Earl Gaines (Steve Gaines): singer, songwriter, guitar player
b. September 14, 1949: Miami, Oklahoma
d. October 20, 1977: near Gillsburg, Mississippi
Cremated. The ashes were interred in a vault at Jacksonville Memory Gardens, Orange Park, Florida
Note: During the June 29, 2000 break-in of Van Zant's tomb, the urn containing Gaines' cremated remains was taken out of its vault. By the time police arrived the ashes had been separated from the urn, but both were found on the ground nearby. Fortunately, Gaines' ashes were in a plastic bag, however a small hole in the bag allowed some ashes to spill out. Following this desecration, Gaines' ashes also were relocated to an undisclosed and private location.

Cassie LaRue Gaines: (Cassie Gaines): back-up singer
b. January 9, 1948: Miami, Oklahoma
d. October 20, 1977: near Gillsburg, Mississippi
Cremated. The ashes rest at Jacksonville Memory Gardens, Orange Park, Florida
Note: During the June 29, 2000 break-in of Van Zant's tomb, the ash remains of Cassie Gaines remained undisturbed.

Dean Arthur Kilpatrick (Dean Kilpatrick): assistant band manager
b. May 30, 1949, Canada
d. October 20, 1977: near Gillsburg, Mississippi
Buried: Arlington Memorial Park: Jacksonville, Florida

Larkin Allen Collins, Jr. (Allen Collins): singer, songwriter, guitar player
b. July 19, 1952: Jacksonville, Florida
d. January 23, 1990: Jacksonville, Florida
Buried: Riverside Cemetery, Jacksonville, Florida
Note: Collins is included here as an indirect victim of the aviation accident.

U.S. DEPARTMENT OF COMMERCE
National Technical Information Service

NTISUB/D/104-006

Aircraft Accident Report - L and J Company, Convair 240, N55VM, Gillsburg, Mississippi, October 20, 1977

U.S. National Transportation Safety Board, Washington, D C

19 Jun 78

1. Report No. NTSB-AAR-78-6	2. Government Accession No.	3. Recipient's Catalog No.
4. Title and Subtitle Aircraft Accident Report — L & J Company, Convair 240, N55VM, Gillsburg, Mississippi, October 20, 1977		5. Report Date June 19, 1978
		6. Performing Organization Code
7. Author(s)		8. Performing Organization Report No.
9. Performing Organization Name and Address National Transportation Safety Board Bureau of Accident Investigation Washington, D.C. 20594		10. Work Unit No. 2365
		11. Contract or Grant No.
12. Sponsoring Agency Name and Address NATIONAL TRANSPORTATION SAFETY BOARD Washington, D. C. 20594		13. Type of Report and Period Covered Aircraft Accident Report October 20, 1977
		14. Sponsoring Agency Code
15. Supplementary Notes		

16. Abstract

About 1852 c.d.t., on October 20, 1977, a Convair 240, N55VM, owned and operated by L & J Company and transporting the Lynyrd Skynyrd Band from Greenville, South Carolina, to Baton Rouge, Louisiana, crashed 5 miles northeast of Gillsburg, Mississippi.

There were 24 passengers and 2 crewmembers on board the aircraft. The 2 crewmembers and 4 of the passengers were killed; 20 others were injured. The aircraft was destroyed by impact; there was no fire.

The flight had reported to the Houston Air Route Traffic Control Center that it was "low on fuel" and requested radar vectors to McComb, Mississippi. The aircraft crashed in a heavily wooded area during an attempted emergency landing.

The National Transportation Safety Board determines that the probable cause of this accident was fuel exhaustion and total loss of power from both engines due to crew inattention to fuel supply. Contributing to the fuel exhaustion were inadequate flight planning and an engine malfunction of undetermined nature in the right engine which resulted in higher-than-normal fuel consumption.

17. Key Words Flight planning; fuel consumption; power loss; fuel exhaustion; lease agreements; operational control.	18. Distribution Statement This document is available to the public through the National Technical Information Service, Springfield, Virginia 22151
19. Security Classification (of this report) UNCLASSIFIED	20. Security Classification (of this page) UNCLASSIFIED	21. No. of Pages 26	22. Price

NTSB Form 1765.2 (Rev. 9/74)

TABLE OF CONTENTS

ii

NATIONAL TRANSPORTATION SAFETY BOARD
WASHINGTON, D.C. 20594

AIRCRAFT ACCIDENT REPORT

Adopted: June 19, 1978

L & J COMPANY
CONVAIR 240, N55VM
GILLSBURG, MISSISSIPPI
OCTOBER 20, 1977

SYNOPSIS

About 1852 c.d.t. on October 20, 1977, a Convair 240 (N55VM) owned and operated by L & J Company and transporting the Lynyrd Skynyrd Band from Greenville, South Carolina, to Baton Rouge, Louisiana, crashed 5 miles northeast of Gillsburg, Mississippi.

There were 24 passengers and 2 crewmembers on board the aircraft. The 2 crewmembers and 4 of the passengers were killed; 20 others were injured. The aircraft was destroyed by impact; there was no fire.

The flight had reported to the Houston Air Route Traffic Control Center that it was "low on fuel" and requested radar vectors to McComb, Mississippi. The aircraft crashed in a heavily wooded area during an attempted emergency landing.

The National Transportation Safety Board determines that the probable cause of this accident was fuel exhaustion and total loss of power from both engines due to crew inattention to fuel supply. Contributing to the fuel exhaustion were inadequate flight planning and an engine malfunction of undetermined nature in the right engine which resulted in higher-than-normal fuel consumption.

1. FACTUAL INFORMATION

1.1   History of the Flight

On October 20, 1977, L & J Company Convair 240 (N55VM) operated as a charter flight to transport the Lynyrd Skynyrd Band from Greenville, South Carolina, to Baton Rouge, Louisiana. The aircraft was owned by L & J Company of Addison, Texas, and the flightcrew was employed by Falcon Aviation of Addison. A lease agreement had been entered into by Lynyrd Skynyrd Productions, Inc., and the L & J Company for the period October 11, 1977, to November 2, 1977.

At 0430 c.d.t. 1/ on October 18, N55VM had arrived at the Greenville Downtown Airport, Greenville, South Carolina, from Lakeland, Florida. While on the ground at Greenville, the aircraft had been refueled with 400 gallons of 100-octane, low-lead fuel.

On October 20 at 1602 c.d.t., the flight had departed Greenville Downtown Airport for Baton Rouge, Louisiana. The pilot had filed an IFR flight plan by telephone with the Greenville Flight Service Station. The route of flight was to be Victor 20 Electric City, direct Atlanta, direct La Grange, direct Hattiesburg Victor 222 McComb, V194 and to Baton Rouge. The pilot requested an altitude of 12,000 ft m.s.l. 2/ and stated that his time en route would be 2 hours 45 minutes and that the aircraft had 5 hours of fuel on board. The pilot was also given a weather briefing.

The flight was initially cleared as filed, except the pilot was told to maintain 5,000 ft. Shortly after takeoff, the flight was cleared to 8,000 ft and was asked to report when leaving 6,000 ft. When the flight reported leaving 6,000 ft, it was issued a frequency change. The pilot did not adhere to the 8,000-ft restriction but continued to climb to 12,000 ft. The flight was allowed to continue its climb to 12,000 ft and the clearance was so amended.

After reaching 12,000 ft, N55VM proceeded according to flight plan and at 1839:50 was cleared to descend to and maintain 6,000 ft. This clearance was acknowledged. At 1840:15 the flight told Houston Air Route Traffic Control Center (ARTCC), "We're out of one two thousand for six thousand." About 1842:00 N55VM advised Houston Center, "Yes, sir, we need to get to a airport, the closest airport you've got, sir." Houston Center responded by asking the crew if they were in an emergency status. The reply was, "Yes, sir, we're low on fuel and we're just about out of it, we want vectors to McComb, post haste please, sir."

1/ All times herein have been converted to central daylight based on the 24-hour clock.

2/ All altitudes herein are mean sea level, unless otherwise indicated.

1. FACTUAL INFORMATION

1.1   History of the Flight

On October 20, 1977, L & J Company Convair 240 (N55VM) operated as a charter flight to transport the Lynyrd Skynyrd Band from Greenville, South Carolina, to Baton Rouge, Louisiana. The aircraft was owned by L & J Company of Addison, Texas, and the flightcrew was employed by Falcon Aviation of Addison. A lease agreement had been entered into by Lynyrd Skynyrd Productions, Inc., and the L & J Company for the period October 11, 1977, to November 2, 1977.

At 0430 c.d.t. 1/ on October 18, N55VM had arrived at the Greenville Downtown Airport, Greenville, South Carolina, from Lakeland, Florida. While on the ground at Greenville, the aircraft had been refueled with 400 gallons of 100-octane, low-lead fuel.

On October 20 at 1602 c.d.t., the flight had departed Greenville Downtown Airport for Baton Rouge, Louisiana. The pilot had filed an IFR flight plan by telephone with the Greenville Flight Service Station. The route of flight was to be Victor 20 Electric City, direct Atlanta, direct La Grange, direct Hattiesburg Victor 222 McComb, V194 and to Baton Rouge. The pilot requested an altitude of 12,000 ft m.s.l. 2/ and stated that his time en route would be 2 hours 45 minutes and that the aircraft had 5 hours of fuel on board. The pilot was also given a weather briefing.

The flight was initially cleared as filed, except the pilot was told to maintain 5,000 ft. Shortly after takeoff, the flight was cleared to 8,000 ft and was asked to report when leaving 6,000 ft. When the flight reported leaving 6,000 ft, it was issued a frequency change. The pilot did not adhere to the 8,000-ft restriction but continued to climb to 12,000 ft. The flight was allowed to continue its climb to 12,000 ft and the clearance was so amended.

After reaching 12,000 ft, N55VM proceeded according to flight plan and at 1839:50 was cleared to descend to and maintain 6,000 ft. This clearance was acknowledged. At 1840:15 the flight told Houston Air Route Traffic Control Center (ARTCC), "We're out of one two thousand for six thousand." About 1842:00 N55VM advised Houston Center, "Yes, sir, we need to get to a airport, the closest airport you've got, sir." Houston Center responded by asking the crew if they were in an emergency status. The reply was, "Yes, sir, we're low on fuel and we're just about out of it, we want vectors to McComb, post haste please, sir."

1/ All times herein have been converted to central daylight based on the 24-hour clock.
2/ All altitudes herein are mean sea level, unless otherwise indicated.

Houston Center gave the flight vectors to McComb and at 1842:55 advised it to turn to a heading of 025°. N55VM did not confirm that a turn was initiated until 1844:12. At 1844:34, the pilot of N55VM said, "We are not declaring an emergency, but we do need to get close to McComb as straight and good as we can get, sir."

At 1845:12 N55VM advised Houston, "Center, five victor Mike we're out of fuel." The center replied, "Roger, understand you're out of fuel?" N55VM replied, "I am sorry, it's just an indication of it." The crew did not explain what that indication was. At 1845:47 Houston Center requested N55VM's altitude. The response was, "We're at four point five." This was the last recorded communication between N55VM and the ARTCC. Several attempts were made by Houston Center to contact the flight but there was no response. At 1855:51 an aircraft reported picking up a weak transmission from an emergency locator transmittor (ELT).

The aircraft had crashed in heavily wooded terrain, during twilight hours, at an elevation of 310 ft, and at latitude 31° 04' 19" and longitude 90° 35' 57" near the town of Gillsburg, Mississippi.

1.2 Injuries to Persons

Injuries	Crew	Passengers	Others
Fatal	2	4	0
Serious	0	19	0
Minor/None	0	1	0

1.3 Damage to Aircraft

The aircraft was destroyed.

1.4 Other Damage

Trees in the impact area were damaged.

1.5 Aircraft Information

N55VM was purchased by the L & J Company in April 1977. The aircraft was manufactured in 1947 and had accumulated 29,013.6 flight-hours. The aircraft was certificated and equipped in accordance with current regulations and procedures.

1.6 Meteorological Information

At 1855, the weather at McComb, Mississippi, was 5,000 ft a.g.l. scattered, 12,000 ft a.g.l. scattered, 25,000 ft a.g.l. thin broken, visibility—15 mi, temperature—62°F, dewpoint—57°F, wind—calm, altimeter setting—30.12 in.Hg.

At 1900, the winds aloft observation at 12,000 ft for Athens, Georgia, was 335° at 10 kn; at Centerville, Alabama, 310° at 15 kn; and at Jackson, Mississippi, 320° at 6 kn. The radiosonde observations for Athens, Centerville, and Jackson showed dry air at 12,000 ft and below. The temperature at Athens and Centerville at 12,000 ft was near 0° C, 9° C warmer than International Standard Atmosphere (ISA) temperature. The temperature at Jackson at 12,000 ft was about -1° C, 8° C warmer than ISA temperature.

1.7   Aids to Navigation

The Houston ARTCC was equipped with ARSR-1E and ATC BI-4 radar; the ATC BI-4 was equipped with NAS Stage-A automation. All radar equipment was operating normally when radar vectors were given to N55VM.

1.8   Communications

Communications between N55VM and any facility contacted were not a factor in this accident.

1.9   Aerodrome and Ground Facilities

The McComb-Pike County Airport was the closest facility available to N55VM when the pilot asked for vectors to the closest airport. Runway 15/33 is 5,000 ft long. Runway 15 is equipped with medium intensity runway lights, a medium intensity approach light system, sequence flashers, and abbreviated approach slope indicators. Runway 33 is similarly equipped except it does not have an approach lighting system and sequence flashers.

The runway lights and the rotating beacon were controlled by a light-sensitive photo cell. It could not be determined if the runway lights were on the night of the accident. However, 2 days later, the lights were monitored and they illuminated at 1822.

The localizer had been out of service for several months and was transmitting without identification; a Notice to Airmen (NOTAM) to this effect had been issued. The outer marker, a nondirectional beacon, was out of service and was not transmitting at the time of the accident.

1.10   Flight Recorders

The aircraft was not equipped with either a flight data or cockpit voice recorder, nor were they required.

1.11   Wreckage and Impact Information

The aircraft crashed in a heavily wooded area. The descent angle through the trees was about 5° initially. The angle steepened after the aircraft hit the second tree and continued the steeper angle until it hit the ground. The wreckage path was about 495 ft long. Trees as high as 80 ft and as large as 3 ft in diameter were struck during the final 300 ft of flight. The left horizontal stabilizer and the outboard section of both wings were torn from the aircraft and found 100 ft from the main wreckage along the wreckage path. The right outboard wing panel separated from the aircraft after initial contact with trees. The left horizontal stabilizer and the left outboard wing panel also struck trees and separated along the wreckage path. The wreckage distribution was on a magnetic heading of 012°. The fuselage continued forward on that heading and came to rest about 140 ft from the point of initial impact. The fuselage separated forward of the bottom leading edge of the vertical stabilizer. The center wing and engine nacelles were twisted to the left of the forward fuselage. The cockpit structure was crushed against trees. Cabin seats separated during the impact sequence. (See Appendix D.)

All of the fuel crossfeed and fuel dump valves were in the closed position. Both fuel tank filler caps were in place. Fuel tank selector valves were in the closed position.

Both engines remained within their nacelles; the left propeller separated from the engine, while the right propeller remained attached. The propeller blades were not extensively damaged.

The cylinder heads and most of the accessories of both engines remained intact, attached, and undamaged. The cooling fins on several cylinders had been damaged slightly.

The spark plugs of both engines were intact and generally undamaged. The spark plug electrodes were not damaged nor did they bear any evidence of a combustion chamber malfunction. The carburetor fuel strainers of both engines were free of contamination; no entrapped or pressurized fuel was found in either carburetor. The landing gear and flaps were retracted. Both landing lights were in the retracted position.

Positions of cockpit switches and controls were as follows:

SWITCH	SETTING
Left generator	On
Right generator	On
Battery switch	On
Left magneto	Both
Right magneto	Both
Gear handle	Up Position
Fuel quantity indicator (position unknown)	Pointer (Missing)
Left fuel boost pump switch	On
Right fuel boost pump switch	On

Radio master switch	Off
Left engine blower switch	High
Right engine blower switch	High
Left and right throttles	Full Forward
VHF Comm 1	125.20 MHz. Baton Rouge ATIS
VHF Nav 1	109.10 MHz. McComb Localizer
ADF	272 kHz. Undetermined
VHF Comm 2	123.80 MHz. Houston Approach-W.
VHF Nav 2	116.50 MHz. Baton Rouge VOR
Transponder 1	3,171
Transponder 2	3,281
Fire extinguishers	Normal
Left fuel tank selector switch	Closed
Right fuel tank selector switch	Closed
Fuel crossfeed lever	Off

1.12 Medical and Pathological Information

Post-mortem examinations of the flightcrew and passengers were made to determine cause of death and to identify types of injuries. Toxicological examination of the flightcrew disclosed no evidence of drugs, alcohol, or elevated levels of carbon monoxide in the blood. Both flightcrew members and the four passengers died as a result of traumatic injuries sustained at impact.

All surviving passengers were hospitalized. Most of the passengers received multiple fractures and severe lacerations. However, three passengers received only contusions and abrasions. Two of these passengers were hospitalized over 48 hours and were, therefore, listed as seriously injured.

1.13 Fire

There was no fire.

1.14 Survival Aspects

Warning was given to the passengers before the crash landing. Most passengers assumed the crash position after being told by a flightcrew member that an emergency landing was imminent.

The accident was survivable for passengers in the cabin because there was no fire and some sections of the fuselage retained their integrity during impact. However, other sections, particularly the cockpit area, sustained massive impact deformation and therefore the accident, for occupants of these sections, was nonsurvivable. No fire erupted during the crash sequence because there was no fuel in the wing tanks when wing sections separated from the main structure. Survival was also enhanced by the six medical doctors and 20 corpsmen and emergency medical technicians at the crash site who diagnosed, treated, and helped stabilize crash victims during the evacuation and en route to hospitals.

Chapter 25: Lynyrd Skynyrd

At 1855, the United States Coast Guard Station at New Orleans notified an airborne HH3F helicopter of the accident. The helicopter arrived in the general area of the accident 30 minutes later. After receiving an ELT signal, the helicopter located the wreckage at 1936. The helicopter hovered at 25 ft above the trees over the crash site and illuminated the area. Ground parties and emergency vehicles reached the wreckage area about 30 minutes later. At 2055 and 2100 Coast Guard helicopters landed within yards from the accident site with personnel, communications equipment, and medical supplies. A Coast Guard C-131 aircraft arrived over the accident site at 2010 and assumed on-scene command duties.

Pike County Civil Defense Council, Pike and Amite Counties Sheriffs' Departments, Mississippi Highway Patrol, and Southwest Mississippi Regional Medical Center jointly implemented disaster plans and helped to rescue aircraft occupants.

The crash rescue personnel had displaced the wreckage in order to rescue injured passengers and to recover bodies. The fuselage was fractured aft of the trailing edge of the wings and forward of the leading edge of the wings. The fractured portions of the fuselage were completely displaced and pointed in different directions. The cockpit and center portion of the aircraft was upright and essentially level.

The cabin was partitioned into three passenger compartments with seating for 24 persons. Two aft facing seats were located in the aft section on the right side of the aircraft; between these two seats a table had been installed. An executive-type swivel seat had been installed on the left side of the aircraft facing forward. Facing it (aft facing) another swivel-type seat had been installed. A collapsible table was located between these two seats. In this section of the aircraft, the floor was completely disrupted and all seats had torn loose. No deformation from impact was noted on any of these seats. All passengers in this section survived, but were injured seriously.

In the center section of the aircraft, six double-unit, forward - facing seats had been installed; only one of these units remained attached to the floor. Although this unit had been bent and deformed to the right, the seat legs were not fractured. The other seats in this section of the aircraft were completely displaced and scattered about the cabin; the floor also broke up. One passenger in this section was killed, while others in the section received minor to serious injuries.

In the forward section of the aircraft on the right side a four-place side-facing couch had been installed. The couch was damaged extensively; however, investigators could not differentiate between damage from impact and damage from rescue operations. On the left side of this section were two swivel seats; one aft facing, the other forward facing with a table installed in between them. Although both seats separated from the floor, no impact load damage to either seat was obvious. The cockpit seats were in place, however, they were damaged extensively by impact forces. The major loads on these seats appeared to be to the right. Both crewmembers were killed.

All seats in the aircraft were fitted with slip-through, metal-to-fabric seatbelts. There were no shoulder harnesses installed. The seatbelts in the aircraft did not fail, although some had been cut by rescue personnel to remove the occupants. The buffet, both the forward and aft lavatory, and the aft storage compartment were extensively damaged by impact. The aft stairway entry door was closed and locked. The forward service door directly behind the cockpit was bent and the handle was in the locked position. The two overwing exits on the left side of the aircraft and the forward overwing exit on the right side were in place. The aft right overwing exit was outside the aircraft about 26 ft forward and to the right of the wreckage.

1.15   Tests and Research

Under the direction of Safety Board investigators, functional tests of fuel, ignition system, and propeller control components were conducted at various test facilities.

1.16   Carburetors

Both carburetors were flow tested. The density values obtained were slightly over limits. The right carburetor's automatic mixture control was disassembled and examined; there was no evidence of corrosion or contamination. The control wear pattern was normal.

Results of the left carburetor flow test indicated that most flow test points were within the manufacturer's specifications. The altitude compensation feature of the automatic mixture control was slightly lean. At low operating ranges the right carburetor produced fuel flow rates above manufacturer's specifications. At or above cruise operating ranges, the fuel flow rates were within manufacturer's specified limits.

1.16.1   Propeller Governors and Blade Angles

The selected positions of the governor's head rack were determined to be 1,200 rpm.

Since the auxiliary check valve on the left propeller governor was broken away from the governor housing, the governor could not be tested "as received." Therefore, the governor head, the high-pressure valve, and the cut-out solenoid switch were removed from the hydraulic governor "as received" and installed on an equivalent governor housing. These components functioned satisfactorily when tested.

The right propeller governor was intact and undamaged. Results of the propeller governor functional test were satisfactory, except that the propeller feathering cutoff switch would not allow high pressure to build up for the feathering/unfeathering cycle. The clearance between the hydraulic governor body base bore and the governor drive shaft was measured; the bore measured 0.8762 inch, while the governor drive shaft measured 0.8726 inch. The manufacturer's allowable tolerance for the bore dimension is 0.8745 to 0.8750 inch. The gear shaft bushing, P/N 322565F, was not installed.

Propeller blade impact angle measurements were obtained from the spider shim plates which were removed from both propellers. Average readings were +30°.

1.16.2   Magnetos and Distributors

The left magneto was not damaged externally. The magneto rotor shaft turned freely. The "E" (timing) gap locating pin functioned normally. A resistance check of the four coils showed normal electrical continuity. A high voltage check to the ground of the magneto primary cable showed no leakage. A trace of depolymerized potting material had leaked onto the low tension coil in the "L1" position of the magneto. No other mechanical or electrical discrepancies were present.

The right magneto was not damaged externally. The magneto rotor shaft turned freely. The resistance check of the four coils showed normal electrical continuity. A high voltage check to the ground of the magneto primary cable disclosed no leakage. Normal operating voltage is 200 volts; test voltage was 500 volts. No mechanical or electrical discrepancies were found during the examination of the right magneto.

1.16.3   Distributors

Left Engine. Neither the left nor right distributor was damaged and the individual carbon distributor brushes were intact. Both distributor shafts turned freely.

The distributor timing was checked. The opening duration of the No. 1 breaker point was 17° for the left distributor and 15° for the right distributor. The opening duration of the No. 2 breaker point was 15 1/2° for the left distributor and 15° for the right distributor. Bendix Publication Form L-242-4 specifies tolerances of 16° ± 1/2° for the No. 1 breaker, and ± 2° for the No. 2 breaker point. The static timing angular relationship between the left distributor's No. 1 breaker point assembly and its No. 2 breaker point assembly was 260° after the No. 1 breaker point assembly opened. The same relationship on the right distributor's breaker opening was 258°. Specified tolerances are 260° ± 15'.

The two capacitors installed in the left and right distributors were tested with a Bendix 11-1767-3 primary condenser tester for series resistance, leakage, and capacitance; these capacitors were all within service overhaul manual specifications. The carbon brush free heights were 13/64 inch for the left distributor and 17/64 inch for the right distributor. The service overhaul manual specifies 1/8 inch minimum free brush height. The breaker point contacts were in normal condition. No mechanical or electrical discrepancies were found in either distributor. All distributor primary wiring was intact and undamaged.

Right Engine. The left distributor was extensively damaged; primarily, the housing had cracked and collapsed and attaching bolt blanges had broken. The lower section of both capacitors were crushed inward about 1/4 inch. The distributor rotor had cracked over its cross-sectional area. The No. 1 breaker point assembly was displaced from its installed position. The No. 2 breaker point assembly was not damaged and remained in its installed position. The distributor shaft turned freely.

Because the No. 1 breaker point assembly was displaced, opening duration and angular relationship could not be determined. The No. 2 breaker point's opening duration was 13°.

The two capacitors were within service overhaul manual tolerances for series resistance, leakage, and capacitance. Free brush height for the carbon brushes was 1/4 inch. The condition of the breaker points was normal with respect to the distributor's operating time.

The right distributor was not damaged externally. The distributor shaft turned freely and the distributor brushes were intact. The breaker point opening duration for the No. 1 breaker point assembly was 17° and the angular relationship between the No. 1 breaker point and the No. 2 breaker point was 261°. The breaker point opening duration for the No. 2 breaker point was 18 1/2°. The two capacitors were within service tolerances for series resistance, leakage, and capacitance. Carbon brush free heights were 13/64 inch. Distributor operating time was normal. No electrical or mechanical discrepancies were found in the distributor. Because of impact deformation and displacement, distributor to engine timing could not be determined.

1.16.4   Fuel Pumps and Gages

Both the left and right fuel boost pumps and engine-driven fuel pumps were functionally tested and operated normally. The fuel quantity gages were examined at the Safety Board's Laboratories in Washington, D.C.; the following resulted:

One gage, S/N 508C, had been crushed upward on the lower forward end. The case was dented, distorted, and cut on the right side. The rear cover and some of the internal components were missing. The glass face was broken and the graduated-dial face was buckled; its pointer was missing. The pointer pivot shaft was in place and was examined under a 10-power magnifying glass, which disclosed the outline of the pointer's position on the pivot shaft. By placing a pointer in the outline, the Safety Board determined that the pointer was indicating either 100 pounds or 4,000 pounds.

The other gage, serial number unknown, had been crushed on the aft end and the electrical connector had been broken off. The case was distorted and gouged. The glass face was broken and the graduated dial-face had been crushed inward and gouged. The pointer was attached to its shaft and was indicating zero pounds. The long side of the pointer as bent inward and could not be moved above zero pounds, the pointer could be moved below zero pounds.

1.17   Additional Information

1.17.1   Aircraft Fuel Consumption

Normal average fuel consumption for the Convair 240 aircraft powered with the Pratt & Whitney R2800CB-16 engine is about 183 gallons per hour.

A surviving pilot-qualified passenger stated that he had seen torching from the right engine on the flight from Lakeland, Florida, to Greenville, South Carolina. Flames had extended from the engine as far as 10 feet for a period of about 5 minutes. This passenger had also visited the cockpit and noted that the right engine was being operated with the mixture control in the auto-rich position. The crew had explained that they were operating in this manner in order to alleviate a rough operating condition of the engine.

Based on carburetor flow specifications obtained from the engine manufacturer, the difference in fuel flow between the auto-rich (650 lbs/hr) and the auto-lean fuel flow (500 lbs/hr) at 12,000 feet and 1,100 brake horsepower is about 150 lbs./hr. or 25 gallons/hr.

The aircraft departed Addison, Texas, with 1,300 gallons of fuel; its fuel capacity was 1,550 gallons. At it's first stop, Jacksonville, Florida, 200 gallons of fuel were added. At Statesboro, Florida, 200 gallons were added; at Miami, 400 were added; at St. Petersburg, 250 gallons were added, at Lakeland, 200 gallons were added, and at Greenville, 400 gallons were added. The total flight time for this itinerary, including the 2.8 hours from Greenville to the accident site, was 13.5 hours. Based on the average fuel consumption of 183 gallons per hour and 82.5 gallons for each of the seven taxi, takeoff, and climb operations, sufficient fuel should have been on board the aircraft to reach its destination. Fuel consumption calculations, based on available operational data, disclosed that 2.8 hours (512 gallons) of fuel was available from Greenville to

the accident site. Best estimates indicate that 207 gallons of fuel
should have been on board at the accident site. The Safety Board could
not determine why the flight plan reflected 5 hours of fuel on board.
Fuel consumption data, based on fuel added at each intermediate stop
after the flight left Addison, cannot support the presence of a 5-hour,
or 900-gallon, supply at Greenville. However, the precise number of
hours during which the right engine was operated with the mixture in
"auto-rich" could not be established. It is, therefore, impossible to
calculate exactly how much fuel was on board the aircraft after 400
gallons were added at Greenville.

1.17.2   Leasing Data

On October 11, 1977, a lease agreement was made between the
L & J Company and Lynyrd Skynyrd Productions, Inc.   (See Appendix E.)
Federal Aviation Regulations 14 CFR 91, "General Operating and Flight
Rules," 91.54 paragraph (a)(2), requires:

> "Identification of the person the parties consider
> responsible for operational control of the aircraft
> under the lease or contract of conditional sale and
> certification by that person that he understands his
> responsibilities for compliance with applicable
> Federal Aviation Regulations."

Further, 14 CFR 91.54 (c) (1) requires that:

> "The lessee or conditional buyer, or the registered
> owner if the lessee is not a citizen of the
> United States, has mailed a copy of the lease or
> contract that complies with the requirements of
> paragraph (a) of this section, within 24 hours of
> its execution, to the Flight Standards Technical
> Division, Post Office Box 25724, Oklahoma City,
> OK 73125."

Examination of the aircraft records on file with the
Federal Aviation Administration (FAA) in Oklahoma City disclosed that
the lease agreement for N55VM executed on October 11, 1977, was received
by FAA on October 25, 1977. The envelope in which the lease agreement
was mailed had affixed to it Pitney Bowes Meter postage, dated
October 17, 1977, at Addison, Texas. The Pitney Bowes postage was
cancelled by the Dallas, Texas, Post Office during "pm" of October 21,
1977.

1.18   New Investigative Techniques

None

- 13 -

2. ANALYSIS

The flightcrew was properly certificated and trained in accordance with applicable regulations. There was no evidence of pre-existing medical problems that might have affected the flightcrew's performance.

The aircraft was certificated and equipped according to applicable regulations. The gross weight and c.g. were within prescribed limits. The aircraft's structure and components were not factors in this accident. There was no evidence of any malfunction of the aircraft or its control system. The propulsion system was operating and was producing power until fuel was exhausted. The right engine had been malfunctioning for some time and caused the flightcrew to operate that engine on auto-rich fuel mixture during the accident flight and during previous flights in order to obtain an acceptable level of performance from it.

Although examination of the engine and its components did not identify the exact discrepancy, the Safety Board believes that the discrepancy was of a general nature, such as an ignition or induction problem, and was not a major mechanical failure. Components of the right engine's ignition system were so badly damaged by impact that engine to distributor timing could not be determined. Consequently, the pre-impact condition of the ignition system could not be determined from the evidence available.

Based on wreckage examination, the Safety Board concludes that both engines ceased producing power because of fuel exhaustion. Only one quart of fuel was recovered from both engines. Evidence obtained from the fuel quantity gages indicates that both fuel tanks were empty at the time of impact.

According to the best estimates, the aircraft should have had about 207 gallons of fuel on board at the time of the accident. This figure is based on a normal cruise configuration with both engines operating with "auto-lean" fuel mixture.

In order to determine the reason for the discrepancy between calculated fuel on board and actual fuel on board, the Safety Board analyzed the following three explanations:

First, there could have been a fuel leak. However, no evidence of fuel leakage, such as stains or loose fuel tank caps or lines, was found in the wreckage. Although this possibility cannot be discounted completely, because there is a remote possibility that leakage evidence could have been obliterated at impact, the Safety Board does not believe it to be the most viable explanation.

Secondly, the aircraft may not have been fueled with the amount shown on the fuel slips. The Safety Board considers this explanation relatively remote because the fuel meters on refueling trucks cannot be reset and, if functioning properly, will reflect the total amount of fuel dispensed to a given aircraft.

Finally, the engines or an engine could have been burning more fuel than specified and more than the flightcrew expected to be burned. The witnesses report of torching from the right engine would indicate a rich fuel mixture or other discrepancy associated with inadequate combustion. Operating an engine in the auto-rich configuration would increase the fuel consumption by about 25 gallons per hour for that engine, from 183 gal/hr to 208 gal/hr. During the accident flight of 2.8 hours this would have amounted to about 70 gallons. It is impossible to determine how long the aircraft was operated with the right engine in auto-rich, but it was evidently long enough to exhaust the useable fuel on board the aircraft. Regardless of the high fuel consumption of the right engine, the 5-hour, or 900+ gallon, fuel supply listed on the flight plan would have been sufficient to reach the destination. Considering the increased fuel consumption on the right engine, 583 gallons would have been required to complete 2.8 hours of flight from Greenville to the accident site. Therefore, the Safety Board concludes that the right engine was burning more fuel than anticipated because it was being operated in the auto-rich fuel mixture.

The crew was either negligent or ignorant of the increased fuel consumption because they failed to monitor adequately the engine instruments for fuel flow and fuel quantity. Had they properly monitored their fuel supply and noted excessive fuel consumption early in the flight, they could have planned an alternate refueling stop rather than attempting to continue flight with minimum fuel. In addition, the Safety Board believes that the pilot was not prudent when he continued the flight with a known engine discrepancy and did not have it corrected before he left Greenville.

This accident involves another operation where the party which had operational responsibility is in controversy. It appears that it was the intent of L & J Company to have the operational responsibility assumed by the lessee, Lynyrd Skynyrd Productions. The lessee, however, appears to have had no understanding that it was the operator and had assumed the responsibilities thereby imposed. The question of who was the legal operator of this flight is currently being litigated by the FAA in an enforcement action against L & J Company and will be addressed in civil litigation arising out of this accident.

In examining this relationship, the Board reviewed the lease for this flight. The lease was not drafted to meet the "letter of the regulations" in that the "truth in leasing provisions" were not in the concluding paragraph or in "large print" as required by 14 CFR 91.54.

However, it did contain the information required by 14 CFR 91.54(a)(1)(2) and (3), particularly paragraphs 4 and 5 of the lease which clearly indicate the lessee was to be the operator and thereby have "paramount and complete responsibility for the supervision and direction of the flightcrew...."

There may have been sufficient information in the lease for the lessee to understand his status, if he read it and if he did, understood it. However, the lessee did not understand what his role was on the basis of the lease, nor would he have had any better understanding if the provision had been drafted as intended by the regulations.

It therefore appears to the Safety Board that whether this lease was or was not adequate is not the primary safety problem, but how does the system in such a case protect a lessee who is uninformed either by design, by inadvertence, or by his own carelessness. The requirement that a copy of the lease be sent to FAA within 24 hours of its execution has not been effective. In this case, this requirement was not even met. However, in November 1977, FAA amended CFR 91.54 to require that lessees notify the nearest FAA office 48 hours prior to the first flight under a lease and provide information concerning (1) the departure airport, (2) time of departure, and (3) the registration number of the aircraft. In adopting the amendment, the FAA stated that the purpose of the new requirement was to give the FAA notice prior to the flight and thereby an opportunity to conduct preflight surveillance of lease and contract operations. This requirement should serve to protect innocent lessees if (1) they comply with the requirement and contact the FAA office, and (2) the FAA office takes action to assure that there is a clear understanding by the lessee as to who is the operator and what responsibilities and obligations are thereby assumed. If this occurs, it should be a step toward resolving the problem of the uninformed lessee.

3. CONCLUSIONS

3.1   Findings

1. Both engines of N55TM ceased to produce power because the aircraft's useable fuel supply was exhausted.

2. The crew failed to monitor adequately the fuel flow, en route fuel consumption, and fuel quantity gages.

3. The crew failed to take appropriate preflight and maintenance action to assure an adequate fuel supply for the flight.

4. The crew operated the aircraft for an indeterminate amount of time before the accident with the right engine's mixture control in the auto-rich position.

5. There were no discernible discrepancies between the amounts of fuel added to the aircraft and the amounts shown on the fuel receipts from the servicing facilities.

6. There was no evidence of a fuel leak.

7. There was no fire after impact because little fuel remained in the aircraft's fuel system.

8. The survival of many passengers was due to the lack of severe 'mpact deformation in the center of the fuselage and the absence of a postcrash fire.

9. The provisions of the lease intended to satisfy the requirement for a "truth in leasing clause" did not result in this lessee having an adequate understanding as to who was the operator of this flight and what that means.

3.2   Probable Cause

The National Transportation Safety Board determines that the probable cause of this accident was fuel exhaustion and total loss of power on both engines due to crew inattention to fuel supply. Contributing to the fuel exhaustion were inadequate flight planning and an engine malfunction of undetermined nature in the right engine which resulted in higher-than-normal fuel consumption.

4.   SAFETY RECOMMENDATIONS

No safety recommendations were submitted as a result of this accident. FAA issued Advisory Circular 91-37A on January 16, 1978, with detailed guidance relative to leasing of aircraft.

BY THE NATIONAL TRANSPORTATION SAFETY BOARD

/s/ JAMES B. KING
Chairman

/s/ FRANCIS H. McADAMS
Member

/s/ PHILIP A. HOGUE
Member

/s/ ELWOOD T. DRIVER
Member

June 19, 1978

5. APPENDIXES

APPENDIX A

INVESTIGATION

Investigation

At 2025 e.s.t. on October 20, 1977, the National Transportation Safety Board was notified of the accident by the FAA Communications Center in Washington, D.C. An investigative team was dispatched immediately to McComb, Mississippi, and working groups were established for operations, human factors, structures, systems, powerplants, air traffic control, witnesses, weather, and aircraft records.

The Federal Aviation Administration, Convair Division of General Dynamics, and Pratt & Whitney Aircraft Group of United Technologies participated in the investigation.

APPENDIX B

PERSONNEL INFORMATION

Captain Walter W. McCreary

Captain Walter W. McCreary, aged 34, held a first-class medical certificate dated September 19, 1977, with no waivers or restrictions. He also held Airline Transport Pilot Certificate No. 1804920, dated September 12, 1977, with multiengine land ratings in the DC-3, Convair 240, 340, and 440 aircraft. He also had commercial privileges, airplane single-engine land. He had accrued a total of 6,801.6 flight-hours, 68 of which were in the Convair aircraft.

First Officer William J. Gray, Jr.

First Officer William J. Gray, Jr., aged 32, held a second-class medical certificate dated December 30, 1976, with the restriction that "holder shall wear correcting glasses while exercising the privileges of his airman's certificate." He also held Commercial Pilot Certificate No. 75224, issued March 4, 1976, with airplane single- and multi-engine land and instrument ratings. He had accrued 2,362 flight-hours, 38 of which were in the Convair aircraft.

APPENDIX C

AIRCRAFT INFORMATION

The aircraft, a Convair 240, serial No. 3, United States registry N55VM, was manufactured in 1947 by Convair in San Diego, California. N55VM had accumulated 29,013.6 flight-hours as of October 16, 1977. The aircraft was equipped with one Pratt & Whitney R2800-CB-16 engine, one R2800-CB-17 engine, and two Hamilton Standard 43E60 propellers.

Engine serial numbers and vital data were as follows:

Engine Position	Serial No.	Date Installed	TSO
No. 1	P 36878	5/7/73	922 hrs
No. 2	P 31683	4/24/70	1,807 hrs

Although the aircraft registration certificate carried U. S. registry marks N55VM, the airworthiness certificate carried in the aircraft carried U. S. Registry marks N55VX.

At the time of the accident, the aircraft was leased to Lynyrd Skynyrd Production, Inc., and was being operated under provisions of 14 CFR 91.

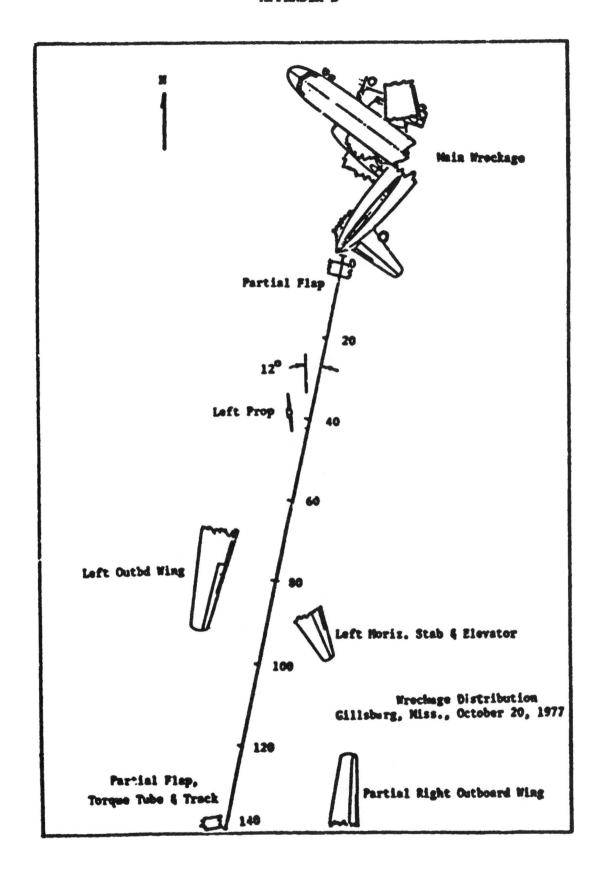

Wreckage Distribution
Gillsburg, Miss., October 20, 1977

APPENDIX E

AIRPLANE LEASE AGREEMENT

THIS LEASE AGREEMENT, made and executed on this ___11th___ day of __October 19 77__, by and between _____L&J Company_____, (hereinafter LESSOR)

with principal offices at __Addison__, ___Texas___ and __Lynyrd-Skynyrd Prod, Inc.__, (entity) __Corporation__ with principal offices in the State of __New York__.

WITNESSETH:

(1) LESSEE is desireous of leasing from LESSOR, and LESSOR is desireous of leasing to LESSEE, subject to the terms and conditions set forth herein, and for the consideration hereinafter set out, an aircraft known as __Convair 240__, whose registration number issued by the Federal Aviation Administration (FAA) is___N-55VM___.

(2) LESSOR is the sole__owner__of the aforementioned civil aircraft number__N-55VM__, and is duly empowered and authorized to make and execute this lease.

NOW THEREFORE, the parties hereto, for the mutual covenants and conditions contained herein, do hereby agree as follows:

(1) The LESSOR shall LEASE unto LESSEE civil aircraft number __N-55VM__.

(2) The parties hereto agree that the term of this LEASE shall commence on the __11th__ day of __October__, 19__77__, and shall be continuous until the proposed date of __Nov. 2 1977__,

Reproduced from best available copy.

APPENDIX B

19___77___. At the expiration of this lease, civil aircraft number _____N-55VM_____ shall be returned to LESSOR in as good or in the same condition as when received by LESSEE, normal wear excepted.

(3) LESSOR agrees, understands, and acknowledges that the scheduling usage and operation of civil aircraft number _____N-55VM_____, when operated under this LEASE, shall be under the supervision and control of LESSEE. LESSEE hereunder shall have the exclusive right to use the aircraft leased hereunder. Full operational control of the aircraft shall rest with LESSEE, (including arrangements for the performance of required maintenance).

(4) LESSEE agrees that it will be the operator of civil aircraft number _____N-55VM_____ during the times and flight hours said aircraft is utilized for and on account of its own business and will not utilize civil aircraft number _____N-55VM_____ for the purpose of providing transportation of cargo or passengers in air commerce for compensation or hire, unless it holds appropriate authority to do so, and complies with all regulations, both state and federal, in exercising that authority.

(5) LESSEE; in executing this LEASE, covenants, agrees, acknowledges and certifies that it is to have paramount and complete responsibility for the supervision and direction of of the flight crew engaged, employed, hired or leased by it to fly civil aircraft number _____N-55VM_____, and shall pay crew and expenses of same throughout the duration of the lease.

Reproduced from best available copy.

(6) LESSOR AND LESSEE agree and understand that title to civil aircraft number ____x-55174____ shall and does remain vested in LESSOR.

(7) LESSEE WARRANTS and agrees by execution of this LEASE to conduct all its operations under and during the term of this LEASE in accordance with all applicable regulations from whereever derived, in a good, safe and reasonable manner.

(8) The parties hereto agree that this LEASE shall not be assigned.

(9) In consideration of the above LEASE, LESSEE agrees to pay LESSOR the sum of ▮▮▮▮ per running statute mile flown. Based on itinerary presented said sum shall be paid in increments as follows:

1st. Increment   ▮▮▮▮▮▮▮ in advance

2nd. Increment   days after beginning of LEASE

3rd. Increment   days after beginning of LEASE

Total amount of this LEASE shall be   ▮▮▮▮▮▮▮

(10) This LEASE may be continued on an indefinite basis by prior arrangement with LESSOR at the same monetary consideration shown above.

(11) LESSOR shall supply $2,000,000 Liability Insurance: $100,000.00 per seat Liability and Hull insurance for the total value of the aircraft.

(12) LESSEE shall hold LESSOR harmless in any event that drugs or narcotics of any kind should be brought aboard this aircraft for any purpose.

APPENDIX E

(13)   LESSEE shall be responsible for any unusual damage incurred
       to interior of aircraft due to LESSEE or person or persons
       transported or employed by LESSEE.

(14)   The aircraft referred to in this lease is maintained under
       FAR 91-217-B4 and is accepted and certified to be current
       as of the date of this LEASE under said maintenance program

(15)   An explanation of factors bearing on operational control
       and pertinent Federal Aviation Regulations can be obtained
       from the nearest FAA Flight Standards District Office,
       General Aviation District O-fice, or Air Carrier District
       Office.

IN WITNESS WHEREOF, the parties hereto have placed their
hands and seals on this ___11th___ day of ___October___, 19_77_.

WITNESS

L&J   Co.
LESSOR

P.O. Box 2, Addison, Texas
ADDRESS
By _____
Title: President

WITNESS

Lynyrd Skynyrd Prod. Inc.
LESSEE:

130 W. 57th St., Suite 6D
New York, New York 10019
ADDRESS:
By: _____
Title: THE MANAGER

FILE	DATE	LOCATION	AIRCRAFT DATA	INJURIES F S M/N	FLIGHT PURPOSE	PILOT DATA
3-3896	77/10/20 TIME - 1852	GILLSBURG,MS	CONVAIR 240 N55VM DAMAGE-DESTROYED	CR- 2 0 0 PX- 4 19 1 OT- 0 0 0	COMMERCIAL AIR TAXI-PASSG	AIRLINE TRANSPORT, AGE 34, 6802 TOTAL HOURS, 68 IN TYPE, INSTRUMENT RATED.

DEPARTURE POINT
  GREENVILLE,SC
TYPE OF ACCIDENT
  ENGINE FAILURE OR MALFUNCTION
  COLLIDED WITH: TREES

INTENDED DESTINATION
  BATON ROUGE,LA

PHASE OF OPERATION
  IN FLIGHT: NORMAL CRUISE
  LANDING: FINAL APPROACH

PROBABLE CAUSE(S)
  PILOT IN COMMAND - MISMANAGEMENT OF FUEL
  MISCELLANEOUS ACTS,CONDITIONS - INATTENTIVE TO FUEL SUPPLY
  MISCELLANEOUS ACTS,CONDITIONS - FUEL EXHAUSTION
FACTOR(S)
  PILOT IN COMMAND - INADEQUATE PREFLIGHT PREPARATION AND/OR PLANNING
  POWERPLANT - MISCELLANEOUS: OTHER
COMPLETE POWER LOSS - COMPLETE ENGINE FAILURE/FLAMEOUT-2 ENGINES
EMERGENCY CIRCUMSTANCES - FORCED LANDING OFF AIRPORT ON LAND
REMARKS- R ENG MALFUNCTION OF UNDETERMINED NATURE RESULTED IN HIGHER THAN NORMAL FUEL CONSUMPTION.

Anna Jantar

March 14, 1980

There are times when in-flight problems arise over which the pilot has little control. There are also times when things go from bad to worse very quickly. Such was the case with this accident. Apparently after a routine flight from New York's John F. Kennedy airport, and while on final approach to Warsaw, Poland's Warszawa-Okecie airport, the crew of LOT flight 007 experienced a problem with the landing gear failing to lock in the down position. The crew initiated a rejected landing, also known as a go-around, which would be the correct procedure in this situation. The next proper procedure for the crew would be to gain altitude to troubleshoot the problem with the landing gear.

However, when power was applied to accomplish the go-around, the number two engine disintegrated. The number two engine on this 4-engine airplane was the inboard engine on the left side of the plane. Jagged fragments from this rare engine explosion immediately caused damage to two of the other engines and damaged the rudder and elevator control cables. Without power and without control, the airliner entered an uncontrolled descent at around 11:00 p.m. local time. Hitting the ground only a half mile from the runway threshold at an estimated 20-degree nose down attitude, the plane exploded, killing all 87 people on board. The probable cause of the engine failure was attributed to metal fatigue in a turbine disc in the number two engine. Anna Jantar, a Polish singer, died in the accident. Additionally, 22 members of the United States amateur boxing team, on their way to two tournaments in Poland, perished as well.

Anna Jantar began her singing career in 1968 at a Polish student music festival. Between the years 1970 and 1972, she recorded and performed with a band called Waganci. In 1972 she began a successful solo career, singing many of the songs written by her husband, Jaroslawa Kukulski. Her biggest hit came in 1973 with a song titled, "The Hardest First Step." She maintained her popularity throughout the 1970s and toured extensively outside of her native Poland during that time. Although not well known in the west, Anna Jantar is revered in Poland. It is estimated that as many as 40,000 fans gathered at her funeral. There is a highly coveted award given for native Polish music that is named in her honor.

LOT

Aircraft addenda:

Common names: IL-62, NATO codename "Classic"
Manufacturer: Ilyushin
First flight of prototype: 1963
Air Carrier for this accident: LOT Polish Airlines, (Polskie Linje Lotnicze)
Registration number for this airplane: SP-LAA
Serial number for this airplane: 11004
Year built for this airplane: 1971
Crew on board: 10
Passengers on board: 77
Length: 174 feet, 3 inches
Wingspan: 142 feet, 0 inches
Engines: (4) Zuznetsov NK-8-4, jet turbofan
Power: 23,150 pounds of thrust each
Empty weight (approximate): 146, 390 lbs.
Gross weight: lbs. 368,000 lbs.
Service ceiling: 50,000 ft.
Range: 6,400 miles
Cruising speed: 535 mph

The above photo represents the type of aircraft and not necessarily the exact model involved in the accident.

Personal addenda:

Anna Jantar: singer
b. 1950
d. March 14, 1980, Warsaw, Poland
Buried: Warsaw, Poland
Note: Every year on All Saint's Day, fans reportedly burn hundreds of candles on Anna Jantar's grave.

Jud Strunk

October 5, 1981

Regardless of whether or not we choose to think about it, each one of us is going to die one day. And unless we happen to be on death row or under some kind of direct and immediate threat, none of us knows exactly when or where we are going to pass on from this world. The pilot and owner of this airplane, Jud Strunk, made a mistake by taking off with the flaps in the full down position. Flaps by definition add lift to a plane's wing, but they also can add copious amounts of drag. Under many circumstances flaps are not used during a plane's departure unless they are set in a relatively shallow deployment. This partial extension of flap can be used to add some lift when it is needed to clear an obstruction in a departure path, or when the air is so thin that the plane simply needs that extra lift to get off the ground.

Full flaps can actually impede the departure capability of most light aircraft. The drag is too great in most cases for the engine's power to overcome and a safe take-off is improbable. Whether or not the usage of flaps in this case may have directly led to the accident is arguable. It may have been possible for Strunk to successfully complete the take-off and recover from the full-flap departure. But perhaps the more relevant aspect of this accident is the fact that the autopsy revealed that Jud Strunk had suffered a heart attack just after the plane took off. Whether his heart attack came before or as a result of the realization that he was going down is speculative. Certainly, if his coronary attack occurred before the accident, there would have been no one to control the flight and the resultant crash would have been unavoidable. The passenger who perished with Strunk in the plane accident was Carrabassett Valley's mayor-in-residence Dick Ayotte. They had only planned to take a short sight-seeing flight when the accident occurred. The plane was named the "Spirit of Peace."

Jud Strunk was a folk hero to the people of his adopted state of Maine. His reputation was one of a socially and environmentally conscious citizen, who also gained popularity as a singer/songwriter and comedian. He recorded one top 15 hit, titled "Daisy a Day," in 1973. He appeared in a Broadway musical, was a semi-regular guest on the television show, "Rowan and Martin's Laugh-In," and also appeared on shows such as "Hee Haw," "Bewitched," the "Merv Griffin Show" as well as his own "Jud Strunk Specials." Strunk made a run for the Maine State Senate in 1970 and lost by only one vote. He toured with such stars as Andy Williams, Eddy Arnold, Glen Campbell, Jim Stafford and with his own group called the Coplin Kitchen Band. He was planning to tour with Glen Campbell when he died. Jud Strunk was inducted into the Maine Country Music Hall of Fame on April 28, 1985.

Author

Aircraft addenda:

Common name: M-62A, PT-19A, Cornell (World War II primary trainer)
Manufacturer: Fairchild
First flight of type: 1940
Registration for this airplane: N60542
Seats: 2
Length: 27 feet, 8 inches
Wingspan: 36 feet, 0 inches
Height: 7 feet, 7.5 inches
Engine: (1) Ranger L-440-C2, 6 cylinder inverted inline piston
Horsepower: 200 hp
Empty weight (approximate): 2,022 lbs.
Gross weight: 2,736 lbs.
Service ceiling: 13,200 feet
Range: 400 miles
Cruising speed: 101 mph

* The above photo represents the type of aircraft and not necessarily the exact model involved in the accident.

Personal addenda:

Justin R. Strunk, Jr. (Jud Strunk): singer, songwriter, banjo and guitar player, humorist
b. June 11, 1936: Buffalo, New York
d. October 5, 1981: Carrabassett, Maine
Cremated. In 1985 two of his three sons, along with a family friend, retraced Strunk's last 1979 performance route, driving the same 1974 VW "Thing" which Strunk used on that tour. During stops along the 8,000-mile trip, they scattered Strunk's ashes at his favorite places, which included Ottawa, Canada, the Rocky Mountains, the Southwest and Midwest United States and along the route back to Maine.

FACTUAL AIRCRAFT ACCIDENT REPORT
– GENERAL AVIATION –

NTSB FORM 6120 1 SUBMITTED	NTSB ACCIDENT IDENT NO. NIC-82-F-A001	
☒ NO ☐ YES	REGISTRATION MARK N 60542	DATE OF ACCIDENT 10-5-81

DISTANCE AND DIRECTION FROM NEAREST CITY OR PLACE STATE Carrabassett, Maine	ELEVATION 623 MSL	TIME (Local) 1545	TIME ZONE e.d.c.

Part A – WHEN ACCIDENT OCCURRED DURING APPROACH TO OR DEPARTURE FROM AN AIRPORT—COMPLETE FOLLOWING:

AIRPORT NAME Sugarloaf Regional	RUNWAY IN USE DIRECTION: 350° MAG. LENGTH: 2800 FT.	ON AIRPORT ☐ OFF AIRPORT ☒	FROM AIRPORT DEGREES. 355° MILES: 1/2	RUNWAY SURFACE TYPE: Asphalt CONDITION: Good

Part B – AIRCRAFT DATA

AIRCRAFT MAKE AND MODEL Fairchild M-62A	SERIAL NO. T42-3758	AIRCRAFT TOTAL TIME 1992.9 hr.	DATE LAST ANNUAL OR ~~XXXXXXXXX~~ INSP. 8-15-80	TIME SINCE ANNUAL OR ~~XXXXXXXXX~~ INSP. 15 hour

ENGINE MAKE AND MODEL Fairchild Eng. Corp. Ranger - 6-440C-2	ENGINE TOTAL TIME TIME SINCE O.H. NO. 1 545.0 / 545.0 NO. 2 ___ / ___	TIME SINCE LAST ~~XXXX~~ ~~XXXXX~~ INSPECTION 15 hour

NAME AND ADDRESS OF OWNER OR OPERATOR Justin R. Strunk, Jr. Box 23, Eustis, Maine	CATEGORY OF AIRWORTHINESS CERTIFICATE Standard

PURPOSE AND TYPE OF OPERATION *(Check all applicable boxes)*

☒ LOCAL	☐ SCHEDULE	☐ PASSENGER	☐ PRACTICE	☐ _____
☒ PLEASURE	☐ MAIL	☐ BUSINESS	☐ INSTRUCTIONAL	
☐ AIR TAXI	☐ CARGO	☐ CORP./EXEC.	☐ AERIAL APPLICATION	

Part C – PILOT-IN-COMMAND DATA

NAME AND ADDRESS Justin R. Strunk, Jr. Box 23 Eustis, Maine	SEAT OCCUPIED Front	PILOT CERTIFICATE NO. 106282785
	DEGREE OF INJURY Fatal	SOCIAL SECURITY NO.
	OCCUPATION	NATIONALITY U.S.A.

		TYPE RATINGS OR STUDENT ENDORSEMENTS	MEDICAL CERTIFICATE	
☐ AIRLINE TRANSPORT	☒ AIRPLANE		DATE OF ISSUE 6-12-81	CLASS Third
☐ COMMERCIAL	☐ HELICOPTER			
☐ FLT. INSTRUCTOR	☐ ROTORCRAFT			
☒ PRIVATE	☐ GYROPLANE	AUTOPSY	LIMITATIONS/WAIVERS Corrective lenses	
☐ STUDENT	☐ GLIDER	☐ NO ☒ YES		
☐ OTHER	☐ INSTRUMENT			
☐ MULTI ENGINE LAND ☐ SEA ☐		TOXICOLOGY		
☒ SINGLE ENGINE LAND ☒ SEA ☒		☐ NO ☒ YES	DATE OF BIRTH 6-21-36	

PILOT TIME		LAST 24 HOURS		LAST 90 DAYS		TOTAL TO DATE		
		DUAL	PIC	DUAL	PIC	DUAL	PIC	TOTAL
1 THIS MAKE AND MODEL		N/O	N/O	N/O	N/O	N/O	N/O	20.00
2. NIGHT (All Models)								
3. DAY (All Models)								
4. INSTRUMENTS	ACTUAL							
	SIMULATED							

SOURCE OF TIME		
☐ PILOT FLIGHT TIME	5. SINGLE ENG. FIXED WING	
	6. MULTI ENG. FIXED WING	
☐ PILOT/OPERATOR EST.	7. GLIDER	
☐ FAA RECORDS	8. ROTORCRAFT	QUALITY CONTROL CHECK
☒ OTHER *(Specify)* Flt. Inst. and Medical Records	9. OTHER	
	TOTAL FLIGHT TIME (5, 6, 7, 8, 9)	315.00

NTSB Form 6120.4 PAGE 1 (Rev. 9/80)

NOTE: N/A-NOT APPLICABLE. N/O-NOT OBTAINED

Chapter 27: Jud Strunk

NAME AND ADDRESS	SEAT OCCUPIED	PILOT CERTIFICATE NO.
	DEGREE OF INJURY	SOCIAL SECURITY NO.
	OCCUPATION	NATIONALITY

☐ AIRLINE TRANSPORT ☐ AIRPLANE
☐ COMMERCIAL ☐ HELICOPTER
☐ FLT. INSTRUCTOR ☐ ROTORCRAFT
☐ PRIVATE ☐ GYROPLANE
☐ STUDENT ☐ GLIDER
☐ OTHER ☐ INSTRUMENT

☐ MULTI-ENGINE: LAND ☐ SEA ☐
☐ SINGLE ENGINE: LAND ☐ SEA ☐

TYPE RATINGS OR STUDENT ENDORSEMENTS

AUTOPSY ☐ NO ☐ YES

TOXICOLOGY ☐ NO ☐ YES

MEDICAL CERTIFICATE

DATE OF ISSUE	CLASS

LIMITATIONS WAIVERS

DATE OF BIRTH

PILOT TIME	LAST 24 HOURS		LAST 90 DAYS		TOTAL TO DATE		
	DUAL	PIC	DUAL	PIC	DUAL	PIC	TOTAL
1 THIS MAKE AND MODEL							
2. NIGHT (All Models)							
3. DAY (All Models)							
4. INSTRUMENTS ACTUAL							
SIMULATED							

SOURCE OF TIME						
☐ PILOT FLIGHT TIME	5. SINGLE ENG. FIXED WING					
☐ PILOT/OPERATOR EST.	6. MULTI-ENG. FIXED WING					
☐ FAA RECORDS	7. GLIDER					
☐ OTHER (Specify)	8. ROTORCRAFT					
	9. OTHER:					
	TOTAL FLIGHT TIME (5, 6, 7, 8, 9)					

NAME	ADDRESS (CITY AND STATE)	Other Crew	Pass-enger	Non-occu-pant	DEGREE OF INJURY			
					Fatal	Serious	Minor	None
Richard J. Ayotte	Valley Crossing Carrabassett, Maine		X		X			

QUALITY CONTROL CHECK

IF ADDITIONAL SPACE IS NEEDED – ATTACH SUPPLEMENTAL SHEET

MAKE AND MODEL	REGISTRATION MARK	DAMAGE
	N	☐ DEMOLISHED ☐ SUBSTANTIAL ☐ MINOR ☐ NONE

NTSB Form 6120.4 PAGE 2 (Rev 9/80)

NOTE: N/A = NOT APPLICABLE. N/O = NOT OBTAINED.

Part G — WEATHER AT TIME AND PLACE OF ACCIDENT

SOURCE OF INFORMATION	SKY COVER	WIND
Airport Manager	☒ CLEAR ☐ CEILING _____ FT. ☐ OTHER _____ FT.	FROM 345° _____ TRUE DIRECTION VELOCITY 5 XTS., GUSTS 10 KTS. LIGHT & VARIABLE ☐

TURBULENCE	LIGHT CONDITIONS	VISIBILITY	ALTIMETER SET.
☒ NONE ☐ LIGHT ☐ MODERATE ☐ SEVERE ☐ EXTREME	☐ DAWN/DUSK ☒ DAYLIGHT ☐ BRIGHT NIGHT ☐ DARK NIGHT	20 MILES	N/O HG.

WEATHER CONDITIONS AND VISIBILITY RESTRICTIONS	TEMPERATURE	DEW POINT
☐ FOG ☐ RAIN ☐ SNOW ☐ SLEET ☐ FREEZING RAIN ☐ THUNDERSTORMS ☐ HAZE ☐ HAIL ☐ SMOKE ☐ DUST ☐ ICING CONDITIONS	65 °F	N/O °F

Part H — FLIGHT PLAN INFORMATION

DEPARTURE POINT	DATE AND TIME OF DEPARTURE	DESTINATION	ETA (if any)
Carrabassett, Maine	10-15-81 1542	Local	N/O

INTERMEDIATE POINTS OF LANDING	SERVICE PRIOR TO LAST TAKEOFF	FUEL ON BOARD LAST TAKEOFF
None	Full fuel service	49 gallons

FLIGHT PLAN FILED: ☒ NONE ☐ VFR ☐ IFR ☐ SPECIAL VFR ☐ OTHER:

DESCRIBE WEATHER BRIEFINGS OBTAINED (From whom, when, where and how received) AND ENROUTE WEATHER REPORTS REC'D.

It is not known if the pilot may have utilized self-help automatic recorded radio or telephone briefing services.

Part I — COMPONENT/SYSTEM FUNCTIONAL FAILURE

☒ NO ☐ YES (If "Yes", give part name, mfr., part no., serial no., etc.)	TIME ON PART	
	TOTAL	SINCE OVERHAUL

Part J — AIRCRAFT AND GROUND DAMAGE

DEGREE OF AIRCRAFT DAMAGE	FIRE	
☒ DEMOLISHED ☐ SUBSTANTIAL ☐ MINOR ☐ NONE	☒ NO ☐ YES	☐ IN FLIGHT ☐ ON GROUND

DESCRIBE GROUND DAMAGE (If any)

Several trees broken in a wooded area

QUALITY CONTROL CHECK

NTSB Form 6120.4 PAGE 3 (Rev. 9/80)   NOTE: N/A = NOT APPLICABLE. N/O = NOT OBTAINED.

Part K – AIRPLANE WRECKAGE EXAMINATION
IF WRECKAGE WAS MOVED PRIOR TO EXAMINATION – PROVIDE DETAILS IN NARRATIVE

COMPONENT DAMAGE			TYPE OF LANDING GEAR	FUEL SELECTOR POSITIONS	VACUUM SELECTOR POSITION
I – IMPACT	F – FIRE		Conventional		
D – DEMOLISHED	S – SUBSTANTIAL		Fixed	Left tank	N/A
M – MINOR	N – NONE				

			RETRACTABLE GEAR AT IMPACT	UP OR DOWN	LOCKED OR INTERMEDIATE
PROPELLER	NO. 1	I–D			
	NO. 2				
ENGINE	NO. 1	I–S	LEFT		
	NO. 2		RIGHT	N	N
FUSELAGE		I–D	NOSE/TAIL	/	/
FLIGHT CONTROL SYSTEM		I–D	LANDING GEAR CONTROL	A	A
ENGINE CONTROLS		I–D			
LANDING GEAR SYSTEM		I–S	LANDING GEAR INDICATOR		
HORIZONTAL STABILIZERS		I–S			

			POSITION OF WING FLAPS	WING FLAP POSITION INDICATOR	WING FLAP CONTROL POSITION
ELEVATORS/STABILATORS		I–S			
VERTICAL STABILIZERS		I–D	☐ UP	Control in up pos.	Up
RUDDER/RUDDERVATORS		I–D			

TRIM TABS	RUDDER		☒ DOWN (Amount)	DUAL CONTROLS			
	ELEVATOR	N	Full	INSTALLED		OPERATIVE	
	AILERON			☐ NO ☒ YES		☐ NO ☒ YES	

		TRIM TAB POSITIONS (Deflection Angle)	NEUTRAL	RIGHT OR UP	LEFT OR DOWN	FIXED	TRIM INDICATOR SETTINGS
LEFT WING	I–D						
LEFT FLAP	I–S						
LEFT AILERON/SPOILER	I–S	RUDDER				N/A	
LEFT WING STRUTS		ELEVATOR			Down		6–Up
RIGHT WING	I–D	AILERON					
RIGHT FLAP	I–S						
RIGHT AILERON/SPOILER	I–S		No. Install	No. Used	No. Separated	Failure Description	
RIGHT WING STRUTS		SEAT BELTS	2	2	0		

SYSTEMS	FUEL	I–D					
	OIL	I–S					
	ELECTRIC		SHOULDER HARNESS	0	0	0	
	HYDRAULIC						
	ANTI-ICE						
	VACUUM		SEATS	2	2	0	
	PNEUMATIC						
CABIN HEATER							
OTHER (Specify)			OXYGEN	ON BOARD ☒ No ☐ Yes	USED ☒ No ☐ Yes	REMARKS (Quantity)	

CABIN PRESSURIZATION	INSTALLED ☒ No ☐ Yes	REMARKS		
EMERGENCY LOCATOR TRANSMITTER	ON BOARD ☒ No ☐ Yes	AIDED SEARCH/LOCATION ☒ No ☐ Yes	REMARKS	Local flight

Part L – COCKPIT DOCUMENTATION
COMMUNICATIONS AND NAVIGATION SETTINGS

ITEM	REMARKS	ITEM	REMARKS
NO COMMUNICATION AND NAVIGATION EQUIPMENT INSTALLED			

QUALITY CONTROL CHECK

086

NTSB Form 6120.4 PAGE 4 (Rev. 9/80)

NOTE: N/A = NOT APPLICABLE. N/O = NOT OBTAINED.

Part O — INSTRUMENT READINGS

ITEM	REMARKS	ITEM	REMARKS
Altimeter Pressure	29.91Hg	Oil Pressure	Pointer missing
Altimeter Elev.	988 ft.	Fuel Pressure	Pointer missing
Front RPM	950	Oil Temperature	Pointer missing
Rear RPM	700		
Front Recording Tach	92 hour		
Turn & Bank	1/2 needle width – left		
	Ball displaced right		
Airspeed Front	Zero		
Airspeed Rear	Zero		
Ammeter	Zero		
Right fuel gauge	Full		
Compass	100 degrees		

Part P — POWER PLANT CONTROL SETTINGS

ITEM	REMARKS	ITEM	REMARKS
Mixture	– one inch from full rich position		
Throttle	Forward		

Part Q — FLIGHT CONTROL - DEICER - ANTI-ICER SETTINGS

ITEM	REMARKS	ITEM	REMARKS
Carburetor Heat Cont.	Cold		

Part R — ELECTRIC PANEL - LIGHT SWITCHES

ITEM	REMARKS	ITEM	REMARKS
Magneto Switch	Both		

QUALITY CONTROL CHECK

Chapter 27: Jud Strunk

AIRCRAFT GROSS WEIGHT		AIRCRAFT CENTER OF GRAVITY	
AT TAKEOFF	AT OCCURRENCE	AT TAKEOFF	AT OCCURRENCE

AT TAKEOFF	AT OCCURRENCE
☒ WITHIN MAX.	☒ WITHIN MAX.
☐ OVER MAX.	☐ OVER MAX.
☐ UNKNOWN	☐ UNKNOWN
REMARKS:	REMARKS

AT TAKEOFF (Center of Gravity):
☒ WITHIN LIMITS ☒ FORE ☒ LATERAL
☐ AFT ☐ LEFT
☐ BEYOND LIMITS ☐ FORE
☐ UNKNOWN ☐ AFT ☐ RIGHT

AT OCCURRENCE (Center of Gravity):
☒ WITHIN LIMITS ☒ FORE ☒ LATERAL
☐ AFT ☐ LEFT
☐ BEYOND LIMITS ☐ FORE
☐ UNKNOWN ☐ AFT ☐ RIGHT

Part T – ACCIDENT SITE EXAMINATION

TERRAIN FEATURES
(Check more than one if necessary)

☒ LEVEL	☒ WOODED	☐ PLOWED FIELD	☐ LAKE
☐ ROLLING	☐ BRUSH	☐ CROPS	☐ CITY AREA
☐ HILLY	☐ SWAMP	☐ OPEN WATER	☐ OTHER (Specify)
☐ MOUNTAINOUS	☐ DESERT	☐ RIVER	

GROUND CONDITIONS: ☐ SOFT ☐ HARD ☒ ROCKY ☐ OTHER (Specify):

OBSTACLES STUCK BEFORE PRINCIPAL IMPACT
☐ WIRES ☐ OTHER (Specify)
☒ TREES
☐ BRUSH
☐ BUILDING

COMPONENT INVOLVED WITH OBSTACLE IMPACT (Describe)
Both wings

MOVED AFTER PRINCIPAL IMPACT
☐ NO
☒ YES → DISTANCE ___54___ FT.
DIRECTION ___175___ °MAG.

GRADE OF TERRAIN AT IMPACT
☒ LEVEL
☐ UP ☐ DOWN
_____° OF SLOPE

SKETCH OF IMPACT POINTS: (Sketch gouge marks with dimensions and magnetic headings; include obstacle and principle impact points, pertinent landmarks, buildings, runways, reconstructed flight and ground paths, wreckage distribution, etc.)

25 FEET

LEFT WING   15'   RIGHT WING TIP

18 FEET

QUALITY CONTROL CHECK

175°

▼ SKETCH. Indicate Magnetic Direction and Scale

SCALE

NTSB Form 6120.4 PAGE 7 (Rev. 9/80)

NOTE: N/A = NOT APPLICABLE. N/O = NOT OBTAINED.

History of Flight

On October 5, 1981, at 1545 hours, N60542, a Fairchild PT19A aircraft operated by Justin Strunk, the owner pilot, crashed uncontrolled shortly after takeoff from the Sugarloaf Regional Airport, Carrabassett, Maine. Visual meteorological conditions prevailed at the time. No flight plan was filed. The aircraft was destroyed. The pilot and passenger were fatally injured.

The flight originated at the Sugarloaf Regional Airport, Carrabassett, Maine on October 5, 1981 at 1542 hours. Prior to departure, the fuel tanks were "topped" after which the aircraft was taxied to Runway 35. The aircraft was observed by the airport manager, who assisted in fueling and oiling, watched the aircraft taxi out and reported that all appeared normal. Subsequently, it was learned from a photograph supplied by the airport manager that both flaps were down (extended). When the climbing aircraft reached an altitude of approximately 400 feet, it was observed to turn left and then it descended in a left turn. The descent continued into a wooded area. Both occupants were fatally injured. The aircraft was destroyed.

Mr. A. Lewiski observed the departing aircraft and noticed that the aircraft appeared to be in a climbing attitude, but did not appear to be climbing. Approximately one-half mile beyond the runway, the aircraft was observed to turn some 90 degrees to the left. The aircraft appeared to be in a climbing attitude, although the altitude remained about the same. It continued for a short distance before another left turn was observed. At that time, the nose appeared to descend and the aircraft continued turning and descending below the tree line.

Crew Information

This airman satisfactorily accomplished the requirements of FAR 61.57, Biennial Flight Review, having received a satisfactory check out in the Fairchild M62A by a certificated flight instructor in June 1981.

Aircraft Information

The aircraft was certificated, equipped and maintained in accordance with existing Federal Aviation Regulations.

Meteorological Information

Visual meteorological conditions prevailed at the time and place of the accident. The pertinent weather observed and reported by the airport manager of the Sugarloaf Regional Airport, Carrabassett, Maine was:

1545 e.d.t.

Sky clear; visibility 20 miles;
temperature 65°F; wind northwest
5-10 miles per hour

QUALITY CONTROL CHECK

Wreckage

The aircraft entered a wooded area on a heading of 175 degrees and came to rest in an inverted position. Thirty feet north of the main wreckage, a 12-inch shattered Fir Tree was observed.

A five-inch Fir Tree was laying across the inverted fuselage. A portion of the left wing was laying parallel to the fuselage. The left flap was extended. The right wing with its flap extended remained attached to the center section of the wing. Eighteen feet aft of the fuselage, the aircraft's right wing tip, which had separated eight inches from the aileron cutout was found. The airspeed pitot tube was still in position on the right wing tip. A ten-foot portion of the left wing was found 15 feet beyond the right wing tip. The left aileron and counterweight were in place. The aileron was in the down position.

The right stabilizer was damaged and the right elevator trailing edge was buckled inward to the stabilizer. The elevator trim tab was deflected down. This measured 1/2 inch from the elevator trailing edge. The left stabilizer was destroyed. The elevator was still attached to the remaining structure. The rudder was destroyed with 18 inches of the lower portion remaining. The vertical stabilizer was destroyed to within 22 inches of the lower portion.

The left landing gear assembly was found in the main wreckage area. The right landing gear assembly was in place in the right wing. The tail wheel was aligned with the aircraft's longitudinal axis.

Numerous pieces of the aircraft's wing structure were found in the crash path.

The Ranger engine remained attached to its mounts. The engine case was broken with internal parts visible through the breaks. The sparkplugs were removed and examined. These showed some signs of sooting. The engine oil screen was removed and examined. No metal particles were found. The screen was clean. Compression noted on the engine as recorded from front to rear was 75, 66, 60, 78, 64 and 78. There were no signs of engine distress or evidence of a catastrophic failure of the engine components examined. Both blades of the wood propeller were shattered.

Fuel was found in the right engine fuel tank.

Some discoloration was evident in the plywood wing structure. No "dry rot" was found. The glued joints were examined. The glued members that had separated, did not exhibit any tearing of the wood structure that mated the surfaces.

QUALITY CONTROL CHECK

Medical and Pathological

The postmortem examination of the pilot was performed at the Franklin General Hospital, Farmington, Maine · Dr. Richard Taylor, Pathologist. The immediate cause of death was onary thrombosis.

Toxicological examination of the pilot was performed at the Civil Aeromedical Institute, Oklahoma City, Oklahoma. The results were negative for acidic and neutral drugs, basic drugs and ethyl alcohol. The carbon monoxide test revealed 5 percent saturation on a sample of blood containing 12.2 gm percent hemoglobin.

Survival Report

The cockpit area was crushed by tree penetration. The front and rear seats remained attached to the fuselage structure. Both front and rear seat belt restraints were used. No failure was found in either the belts or the seats. The rear seat was equipped with a bottom and back cushion. The pilot's seat was not cushion equipped, as he had used a parachute.

The aircraft was equipped with a turn over structure, which was positioned between the front and rear cockpits.

Test and Research

The engine cowling was removed and an external examination of the engine was made. There were no signs of a catastrophic failure. The engine case split, producing oil spill. A visual examination of the internal mechanism through the breaks, revealed that these components were well lubricated and oil was present in the area. The sparkplugs were removed and examined. They were clean with signs of normal useage. Some sooting was found in several of the exhaust stacks. No oil was found in any exhaust stacks. The engine oil screen was clean, with no particles attached to the screen.

An inspection of basic engine, its component parts, accessories and systems did not reveal any evidence of failure.

Additional Data

The Fairchild M62A was equipped with a split flap. The split flap consists of a lower control surface that can be deflected from the lower surface of the wing structure. When extended, the hinged portion of the wing trailing edge causes a significant increase in lift by changing the camber of the wing.

QUALITY CONTROL CHECK

Additional Data (con't)

This also results in a large increase in drag from the turbulent wake produced by the flap. The first half of flap deflection causes more than half the total change in drag. Principally, it is to accomplish a steeper landing approach, over obstacles.

Wreckage Release

The aircraft wreckage was released to Mr. D. Maramant, the Airport Manager of Sugarloaf Regional Airport upon authorization from Mr. Jeff Strunk, the pilot owner's son. The wreckage was subsequently removed from the crash site and stored at the Sugarloaf Regional Airport, Carrabassett, Maine.

QUALITY CONTROL CHECK

THIS REPORT CONSISTS OF   PAGES.

Part V – ADDITIONAL PERSONS PARTICIPATING IN THIS INVESTIGATION

NAME, ADDRESS, AND AFFILIATION

Mr. D. L. Crook   FAA-GADO #15
                       Portland International Jetport
                       Portland, Maine

Mr. P. Simpson   Bureau of Aeronautics,
                       Dept. of Transportation
                       Augusta, Maine

Part W – INVESTIGATED BY

DATE	AGENCY	SIGNATURE
12-3-81	National Transportation Safety Board	Michael T. Kuzenko, Air Safety

Music's Broken Wings

TOXICOLOGY REPORT (RIS: AC 8025-2)

DATE:	CASE:	PILOT:
October 14, 1981	4179	Justin Strunk

ACCIDENT OR EVENT:

An aircraft accident which occurred at Carrabassett Valley, Maine, on October 5, 1981.

RECEIVED BY:

Jim Sershon from TWA Air Freight at 9:46 a.m. on October 12, 1981.

SAMPLES:

One bottle each of blood, urine, and gastric contents, one bag each of liver, lung, and kidney identified with the name Justin Strunk.

One tube of blood, identified with the name Richard Ayotte.

Specimens were frozen after arrival.

RESULTS:

ACIDIC & NEUTRAL DRUGS (Acid-Ether Extractions, UV Scan):	BASIC DRUGS (Alkaline-Ether Extraction, UV Scan):
Strunk - None detected - blood & urine Ayotte - None detected - blood	Strunk - None detected - blood & urine Ayotte - None detected - blood

ETHYL ALCOHOL (Gas Chromatography):	CARBON MONOXIDE (Conway Diffusion Palladium Chloride):
Strunk - None detected - blood & urine Ayotte - None detected - blood	Strunk - 5% saturation in blood containing 12.2 gm% hemoglobin. Ayotte - None detected in blood containing 10.0 gm% hemoglobin.

QUALITY CONTROL CHECK

SIGNATURE AND TITLE:

DELBERT J. LACEFIELD, Ph.D.
CHIEF, FORENSIC TOXICOLOGY RESEARCH UNIT, AAC-114B

cc: AAC-132
AC Form 8025-2-1 (4-80)

FILE	DATE	LOCATION	AIRCRAFT DATA	INJURIES F S M/N	FLIGHT PURPOSE	PILOT DATA
3-3664	81/10/5 TIME - 1545	CARRABASSETT,ME	FAIRCHILD M-62A N60542 DAMAGE-DESTROYED	CR- 1 0 0 PX- 1 0 0 OT- 0 0 0	NONCOMMERCIAL PLEASURE/PERSONAL TRANSP	PRIVATE, AGE 45, 315 TOTAL HOURS, 20 IN TYPE, NOT INSTRUMENT RATED.

NAME OF AIRPORT - SUGERLOAF RGNL.
DEPARTURE POINT   INTENDED DESTINATION
  CARRABASSETT,ME   LOCAL
TYPE OF ACCIDENT
  COLLISION WITH GROUND/WATER: UNCONTROLLED

PHASE OF OPERATION
  TAKEOFF: INITIAL CLIMB

PROBABLE CAUSE(S)
  PILOT IN COMMAND - INCAPACITATION
  MISCELLANEOUS ACTS,CONDITIONS - PILOT SUFFERED HEART ATTACK
FACTOR(S)
  PILOT IN COMMAND - MISUSED OR FAILED TO USE FLAPS
REMARKS- EVIDENCE OF CORONARY THROMBOSIS.FULL FLAP TKOF.

Music's Broken Wings

Randy Rhoads

March 19, 1982

Of all the accidents described in this book, this one has to be one of the most bizarre, heartbreaking and senseless. Every two years, a private pilot has to get a flight physical from a medical doctor who is specifically authorized to perform pilot exams. Additionally, by today's requirements, each pilot must at the absolute minimum have a ground knowledge lesson and flight competency check every two years. This proficiency check is conducted by an FAA authorized flight instructor and is known as the flight review. Furthermore, there is an FAA regulation that states no pilot may take any passengers aloft unless he or she has made three take-offs and landings within the prior 90 days.

There is no proof to document if this particular pilot was within the 90-day proficiency window to take passengers. Likewise there is no proof to indicate if the pilot was current within his 2-year flight review. However, we do know that he was not current with his flight physical so without a doubt, it was illegal for him to conduct this flight. We also know he had driven all night, so he certainly must have been fatigued. It is a fact that he did not have permission to use the plane. From eyewitness accounts we know that he was "buzzing" or showing off at a very low altitude, and finally we know from the toxicology report that he had cocaine in his system. These factors did not add up to a good combination for safe flight.

Early in his career Randy Rhoads became a local rock guitar legend in the Los Angeles area. He then became an international celebrity in 1976 and through 1979 with a band he formed called Quiet Riot. The band Quiet Riot recorded two albums for CBS/Sony records and was widely regarded as a powerhouse of Rock and Roll. As Quiet Riot began to break apart in the late summer of 1979, Rhoads auditioned for a band being formed by Ozzy Osbourne, the former lead singer of Black Sabbath. Osbourne recognized Rhoads' talent and quickly hired him for the job of lead guitarist. Osbourne would later say that Randy Rhoads turned out to be his musical soul mate.

In March of 1980, the band recorded Osbourne's comeback album, "Blizzard of Ozz," on which on the track "Crazy Train" showcased Rhoads' absolute mastery of the rock lead guitar. The band toured from

September 1980 and throughout much of 1981 on the "Blizzard of Ozz" tour, but had taken time in March of 1981 to record a second album, "Diary of a Madman." During the break from touring, Rhoads had the third of his custom built "Flying V" guitars made. Even though the Flying V guitar had actually been introduced in 1958, it was to become synonymous with the name and style of Randy Rhoads. After the release of the "Diary of a Madman" album in November of 1981, the band began a European tour to promote the album. That tour had to be cancelled after three shows because Osbourne was mentally and physically exhausted. After a month of rest, the band resumed the tour in San Francisco, California. At this concert Rhoads was awarded Guitar Player Magazine's "Best New Talent" award. Yet while the album sold well, the concerts were fraught with problems, mainly due to Osbourne's alleged animal abuse on stage.

On March 18, 1982, the band played a show at the Civic Coliseum in Knoxville, Tennessee. From Knoxville the band traveled all night by bus to Orlando, Florida where they were to play at the Rock Super Bowl XIV along with Foreigner, Bryan Adams and UFO. The bus driver, Andrew Aycock, wanted to stop at his home in Leesburg, Florida where the bus could undergo some minor repairs and he could drop off his ex-wife, whom he had picked up at one of the concerts. It just so happened that a small private airport bordered Aycock's home. Not long after arriving at his home, Aycock proceeded to invite Don Airey, keyboardist for the band (and the band's manager), to fly and then simply took an airplane for the purpose of joyriding and buzzing. After successfully completing this flight, Aycock then invited Randy Rhoads and make-up artist Rachel Youngblood for some of the same flying excitement. The driver/pilot apparently made a few passes with these passengers, at times below treetop level, and then maneuvered himself into a position from which there was no recovery (see actual photo reproduction on page 285).

From a vantage point just outside the tour bus eyewitnesses watched helplessly as the plane's left wing slammed into the bus and tore off. The impact awakened Osbourne and the other sleeping occupants of the bus, who thought at first they had been involved in an accident while traveling on the road. After the plane hit the bus, the fuselage, along with its helpless occupants, was propelled by the momentum and snapped a tree halfway down the trunk. Everything finally came to a halt when the plane crashed into a nearby house. A post-crash fire ensued. The bus was moved very quickly to protect it from the fire, but the band members were in shock at what had just happened. Later that day the band checked into a local hotel to wait for family members to arrive. The Rock Super Bowl XIV, scheduled for later that day, was not cancelled. However, the Ozzy Osbourne band did not perform.

Author

Aircraft addenda:

Common name: V35 Bonanza
Manufacturer: Beechcraft
First flight of prototype: 1945
Registration number for this airplane: N567LT
Seats: 5 passengers
Length: 25 feet, 1 inch
Wingspan: 32 feet, 9 inches
Engine: (1) Continental IO-520-B, six-cylinder, horizontally opposed, air cooled, piston
Horsepower: 285 hp
Empty weight (approximate): 1,970 lbs.
Gross weight: 3,400 lbs.
Service ceiling: 20,000 feet
Cruising speed: 180 mph

* The above photo represents the type of aircraft and not necessarily the exact model involved in the accident.

Personal addenda:

Randall William Rhoads (Randy Rhoads): rock guitar player
b. December 6, 1956: Santa Monica, California
d. March 19, 1982: Leesburg, Florida
Buried: Mountain View Cemetery, San Bernadino, California

National Transportation Safety Board

PRELIMINARY REPORT OF AVIATION

☒ Accident ☐ Incident

| M | I | A | 8 | 2 | F | A | 0 | 7 | 8 |

NTSB Accident/Incident No.

	Registration(N)Number	Make(Manufacturer)	Model Number
1 AIRCRAFT	N567LT	Beech	F35

2 LOCATION	City	State	Zip	Airport Identifier
	Leesburg	FL		☐ 9X2

3 DATE AND TIME	Date	Flight Number	Time(Local)	Zone
	Mar. 19, 1982		1000	e.s.t.

4 NUMBER OF INJURIES	3 Fatal	_____ Serious	_____ Minor	_____ None	_____ Unknown

5 AIRCRAFT DAMAGE	☒ Destroyed	☐ Substantial	☐ Minor	☐ None	☐ Unknown

6 FIRE	☐ None	☐ In-flight	☒ On Ground	☐ Unknown

7 ITINERARY	Last Departure Point	Time 0955	Destination
	☐ 9X2 Leesburg, FL		☐ Local
	Ident and City State		Ident and City State

8 OPERATOR	Name Mike Partin (Owner)	Address 1510 Henry Partin Drive Kissimmee, FL 32741
	dba	

9 DAMAGE TO PROPERTY	☐ None	☐ Residential Area	☒ Vehicle	☒ Trees	☐ Wires/Poles
	☒ Residence	☐ Commercial Bldg	☐ Airport Facility	☐ Crops	☐ Other

10 FLIGHT PLAN	☒ None	☐ VFR	☐ IFR	☐ Unknown

11 WEATHER DATA	At Accident ☐ Site	☒ VMC ☐ Precipitation	Ceiling UNL. Ft.	7 SM 79 °F
	Other Area ☒ Ident ORL.	☐ IMC ☒ No Precipitation	☐ BKN ☐ -X ☐ Unk	Visibility Temp
			☐ OVC ☐ X	170 ° 7
				Winds Kts

12 TYPE OF OPERATING CERTIFICATE	Air Carrier Operating Certificate	Operating Certificate	Neither Certificate (General Aviation)
	☐ Domestic/Flag Air Carrier	☐ Commercial Operator	Personal Use/Business Transportation
	☐ Supplemental Air Carrier	☐ Air Travel Club	☒ Personal ☐ Business ☐ Unk
	☐ All Cargo Air Service Air Carrier (Section 418)	☐ Corporate (14 CFR 125)	☐ Executive/Corporate Transportation
		☐ Other	☐ Instructional
	Air Taxi Operator		☐ Aerial Application
			☐ Aerial Observation
	☐ Commuter Air Carrier		☐ Other Work Use
	☐ On-Demand Air Taxi		☐ Other
			☐ Foreign Registered Aircraft ☐ Public

13 TYPE OF OPERATION	☐ Scheduled	☐ Domestic	☐ Passenger	☐ Passenger + Cargo	☐ Training	☐ Other
	☐ Non-Scheduled	☐ International	☐ Cargo	☐ Mail Contract Only	☐ Ferry	

14 FLIGHT CONDUCTED UNDER	☒ 14 CFR 91	☐ 14 CFR 121	☐ 14 CFR 127	☐ 14 CFR 135	☐ 14 CFR 137
	☐ 14 CFR 91D	☐ 14 CFR 125	☐ 14 CFR 133	☐ 14 CFR 123	☐ Other

15 PHASE OF OPERATION	☐ Static	☐ Takeoff	☐ Cruise	☐ Approach	☒ Maneuvering	☐ Other
	☐ Taxi	☐ Climb	☐ Descent	☐ Landing	☐ Hover	☐ Undetermined

16 TYPE OF ACCIDENT	During an In-flight Phase of Operation Collided With	Personal Injury	Aircraft Damage	☐ Undetermined
	☒ Ground/Water/Obstacle	☐ On Ground	☐ On Ground	
		☐ In-flight	☐ In-flight	☐ Missing Aircraft
	During an On Ground Phase of Operation Collided With			☐ Other
	☐ Obstacle			

PRELIMINARY INFORMATION — Subject to change; Pertinence to Accident/Incident not positively established at this time.

NTSB Form 6120.19a
(Rev. 1/82)

BEST COPY AVAILABLE

00/

17 CREW (Names and Injuries) (Pilot-Address)	PASSENGERS (Names and Injuries)
Andrew C. Aycock - fatal Leesburg, FL	Randall Rhoads - fatal
	Rachel Youngblood - fatal

18 Narrative This occurrence involved personnel associated with Ozzy Osbourne's rock band that had traveled in their bus from Knoxville, TN to Leesburg, FL on the night preceding the accident. The pilot was employed as the driver of the bus and the group had arrived at the Flying Baron Estates private airport at Leesburg at about 0900 e.s.t. Prior to the fatal flight, he completed a short flight with 2 members of the group aboard during which he made several low passes over the area. After taking off again with 2 other members of the group aboard, he made more low passes. The group's bus was parked in front of a Georgian type mansion adjacent to the airstrip and on the final low pass the left wing collided with the bus. The bulk of the aircraft crossed over the bus and severed a large pine tree before crashing through the roof of the garage on the west end of the mansion. The 3 occupants sustained fatal injuries and the aircraft was destroyed. There were no injuries to persons on the ground but 2 automobiles in the garage were destroyed and the mansion was extensively damaged when the post crash fire spread to the main part of the structure.

The weather was VFR and not a factor in the accident.

The pilot possessed an expired second class medical certificate dated 11-16-79. His private pilot airman certificate, that was not valid without a current medical certificate, showed ratings in airplanes single and multi engine land, instruments airplanes and helicopters

The owner of the aircraft reported that the plane was flown without proper authority.

NTSB Acc/Inc No.	M	I	A	8	2	F	A	0	7	8	

ADMINISTRATIVE DATA

NOTIFICATION FROM FAA, FSDO-64	DATE 3-19-82	LOCAL TIME 1020
OTHER FEDERAL AGENCIES INVOLVED FAA		FAA DISTRICT OFFICE FSDO-64, St Petersburg, FL
NTSB PERSONNEL ASSIGNED T. W. Watson		
DATE THIS FORM PREPARED 3-22-82	INVESTIGATOR IN CHARGE *T.W. Watson*	
DATE THIS FORM RECEIVED BY NTSB/FAA		

☒ Initial   ☒ Preliminary

BEST COPY AVAILABLE

65 SKETCH OF CRASH SITE - Show distribution of major components, ground and aircraft components involved in fire, obstacles struck, occupants, wind direction and velocity vectors, magnetic north. Sketch is "NOT TO SCALE" and distances are approximate.

PLAN VIEW

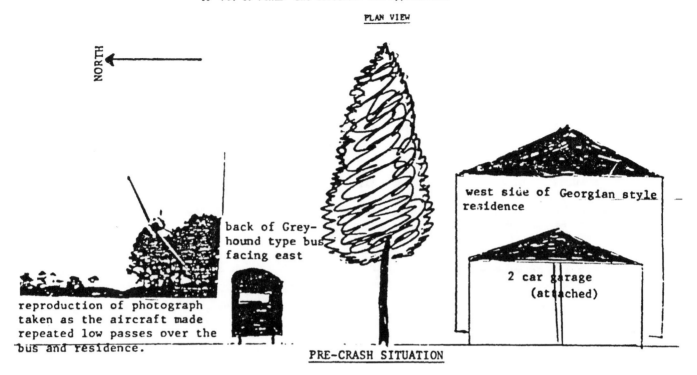

NORTH ←

back of Grey-
hound type bus
facing east

west side of Georgian style
residence

2 car garage
(attached)

reproduction of photograph
taken as the aircraft made
repeated low passes over the
bus and residence.

PRE-CRASH SITUATION

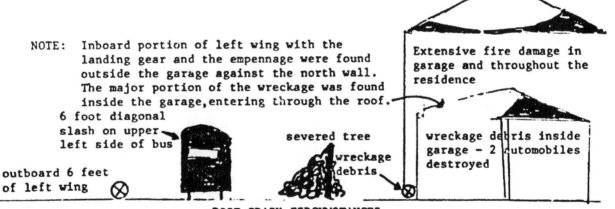

NOTE: Inboard portion of left wing with the
landing gear and the empennage were found
outside the garage against the north wall.
The major portion of the wreckage was found
inside the garage, entering through the roof.

6 foot diagonal
slash on upper
left side of bus

Extensive fire damage in
garage and throughout the
residence

wreckage debris inside
garage - 2 automobiles
destroyed

severed tree

wreckage
debris

outboard 6 feet
of left wing   ⊗

POST CRASH CIRCUMSTANCES

NTSB Form 6120.4F(1/82)

- 3 -

QUALITY CONTROL CHECK

Chapter 28: Randy Rhoads

DEPARTMENT OF TRANSPORTATION
FEDERAL AVIATION ADMINISTRATION
MIKE MONRONEY AERONAUTICAL CENTER

TOXICOLOGY REPORT (RIS: AC 8025-2)

DATE	CASE	PILOT
8/2/02	4332	Andrew Aycock

ACCIDENT OR EVENT

On aircraft accident which occurred near Leesburg, Florida, on March 29, 1982.

RECEIVED BY

"Mac" McCabe from American Air Freight at 12:55 p.m. on March 22, 1982.

SAMPLES

Three tubes of blood, one bottle of urine, one tube of bile, one bag each of liver and kidney identified with the name Andrew Aycock. Three tubes of blood, one bottle of urine, one tube of bile, one bag each of liver, kidney, and brain identified with the name Randall Rhoades. Specimens were cold.

RESULTS

ACIDIC & NEUTRAL DRUGS (Acid Ether Extractions, UV Scan):

Aycock - None detected - blood and urine

Rhoades - None detected in blood
        Salicylates found in urine

BASIC DRUGS (Alkaline Ether Extraction, UV Scan)

Aycock - None detected - blood
        Cocaine found in urine

Rhoades - None detected in blood
        Nicotine and a metabolite of
        propoxyphene found in urine

ETHYL ALCOHOL (Gas Chromatography):

Aycock - None detected - blood and urine

Rhoades - 0.017% (17mg%) blood
        0.020% (20mg%) urine
        0.009% (9mg%) bile

CARBON MONOXIDE (Conway Diffusion Palladium Chloride):

Aycock - less than 1% saturation in
        blood containing a hemoglobin
        concentration of 19.3 gm%

Rhoades - 6% saturation in blood contain-
        ing a hemoglobin concentration
        of 13.4 gm%.

A culture of the blood of Rhoades produced a heavy growth of mixed enteric bacilli and 0.038% (38mg%) ethyl alcohol in BHI after 24 hours incubation.

QUALITY CONTROL CHECK

SIGNATURE AND TITLE

Delbert J. Lacefield

Delbert J. Lacefield, Ph.D.
CHIEF, FORENSIC TOXICOLOGY RESEARCH UNIT, AAC-114B

cc AAC 132, T. Inglima, SO-FSDO-64, St. Petersburg, FL; T. Watson, NTSB, Miami, FL; FL.

AC Form 8025-2 (14 80)

Music's Broken Wings

Mike Partin
1510 Henry Partin Road
Kissimmee, Florida 32741

Mr. T. Watson
BUREAU OF ACCIDENT INVESTIGATION
National Transportation Safety Board
4471 N.W. 36th Street, Suite 230
Miami Springs, Florida 33166

Dear Mr. Watson:

Enclosed is the Aircraft Accident Report, which you mailed to me.

I was unable to answer most of the questions due to the fact that I didn't know any particulars about the pilot.

The plane was being stored in a hangar at the Flying Baron Ranch. No one was given permission to fly the plane.

If you need anymore information pertaining to the plane, please advise me.

Yours truly,

Mike Partin

MP:jp

(Brady M. Fidler 3/19/82
2018 Holms. Ave.
Leesburg, Fl. 32748

My name is Brady M. Fidler and I was at the West end of The runway when I heard an airplane takening off so I went out of the shop to watch this plane & Then they came back & started buzzing on the East end of the runway. They made several ~~passes~~ & then they ~~landing~~ landed. So I went back in the Shop. Than someone came to the shop & I talk to him awhile & when he was ~~fixing~~ fixing to leave, we was standing out by his truck & the plane took off again. And at that time I thought That they were going to leave the feild, but then they started buzzing the house again & they went out to the South East, & make a turn to the Left to come back going to the West, & then I guess they couldn't pull out in time, & the airplane went out of sight from this end. And the man I was talking to said "thats all lets go. So we jumped in The truck & went down there. But there wasn't anything we could do to help anyone in the plane.

00100113
QUALITY CONTROL CHECK G

NARRATIVE STATEMENT OF PERTINENT FACTS, CONDITIONS AND CIRCUMSTANCES RELATING TO THE ACCIDENT AT LEESBURG, FL ON MARCH 19, 1982, INVOLVING A BEECH MODEL F35, AIRCRAFT, N567LT.

History of Flight

At 1000 e.s.t. on March 19, 1982, aircraft N567LT, a Beech model F35, collided with a vehicle, tree and residence while the pilot was executing low passes over a residence on the south side of the eastern end of Runway 11 at the Flying Baron Estates airport, Leesburg, FL. The pilot and 2 passengers were killed and the aircraft was destroyed by impact forces and fire. There were no injuries to persons on the ground but the bus with which the aircraft collided was damaged, the tree was severed, 2 automobiles in the garage of the Georgian type residence were destroyed and the residence was extensively damaged when the post crash fire spread to the main part of the structure.

The accident involved personnel associated with Ozzy Osbourne's rock band who had traveled to Leesburg in their private Greyhound type bus after completing a concert in Knoxville, TN on the evening of March 18th. The pilot was employed as the driver of the bus and the group had arrived at the Flying Baron Estates private airport at about 0900 on the accident date. Prior to the fatal flight, the pilot made a short local flight with 2 members of the group aboard during which he made several low passes over the area. After taking off on the second flight with 2 other members of the group on board, the pilot made more low passes over the area. The group's bus was parked about 60 feet in front of the north facing residence and on the final low pass the left wing collided with the bus. The aircraft was in a left bank at the time of the collision and the bulk of the aircraft structure crossed over the bus and severed a large pine tree before crashing through the roof of the garage on the west end of the residence where post crash fire erupted.

Pilot Information

The pilot possessed a private pilot certificate with ratings in airplanes single and multi-engine land, instruments airplanes and helicopters. The latest medical certificate on file for the pilot was dated November 16, 1979. That medical certificate had expired and no record was found that the pilot possessed a current medical certificate. The pilot's flight logbooks were not received and his recent flight experience was not determined. His application for a medical certificate dated 11-16-79 showed 1,500 flying hours.

Aircraft Information

The aircraft records were reported to have been on board at the time of the crash and the aircraft history was not determined. The owner remarked that he did not remember whether an annual inspection had been performed within the preceding 12 months. In a cover letter received with his partially completed accident report, NTSB Form 6120.1, he stated the following: "....The plane was being stored in a hangar at the Flying Baron Ranch. No one was given permission to fly the plane...."

Meteorological Information

The weather was VFR and not a factor in the accident. The 0950 surface weather observation at the nearest reporting station in Orlando, FL showed 1,500 feet scattered, visibility 7 miles with surface winds from 170° at 7 knots.

I

QUALITY CONTROL CHECK

Aircraft Wreckage

There was a 5 to 6 foot diagonal slash on the upper left side of the bus about 1/3rd of the way aft from the front. The bus was parked on an easterly heading in front of the north facing residence and a pine tree standing between the bus and the residence was severed about 10 feet above the ground. The separated outer portion of the left wing that collided with the bus was adjacent to the rear of the bus and outside the post crash fire pattern. The inboard portion of the left wing including the landing gear and portions of the empennage and "V" tail were outside the garage adjacent to the north wall. The remainder of the aircraft slammed through the garage roof and came to rest inside.

The wreckage was almost totally consumed in the post crash fire and the readings or settings of the various cockpit instruments, switches, levers, etc. were not obtained. The engine sustained extensive fire and impact damage and all of the accessories were destroyed. The propeller was attached to the crankshaft and the outer portions of the blades were consumed in the fire.

Medical and Pathological Information

Autopsies were performed by the State of Florida's district medical examiner in Leesburg and toxicological studies were conducted at the Federal Aviation Administration's civil aeromedical institute in Oklahoma City, OK. The post mortem studies showed no evidence of human factors involvement.

Other Information

None of the witnesses noted anything unusual in the operation of the powerplant prior to the accident. One of the witnesses, a member of the rock group, related that in aviation terminology it would be said that the pilot was "buzzing".

II

QUALITY CONTROL CHECK

Music's Broken Wings

National Transportation Safety Board
Washington, D.C. 20594

Brief of Accident

File No. - 2450	3/19/82	LEESBURG,FL	A/C Reg. No. N567LT		Time (Lcl) - 1000 EST		

---Basic Information---
Type Operating Certificate-NONE (GENERAL AVIATION)

		Aircraft Damage		Injuries			
		Destroyed		Fatal	Serious	Minor	None
Type of Operation	-Personal use	Fire		Crew 1	0	0	0
Flight Conducted Under	-14 CFR 91	ON GROUND		Pass 2	0	0	0
Accident Occurred During	-MANEUVERING						

---Aircraft Information---
Make/Model	- BEECH F35	Eng Make/Model - CONTINENTAL E225-8	ELT Installed/Activated - UNK/NR
Landing Gear	- Tricycle-retractable	Number Engines - 1	Stall Warning System - YES
Max Gross Wt	- 2750	Engine Type - Reciprocating-carburetor	Weather Radar - NO
No. of Seats	- 4	Rated Power - 225 HP	

---Environment/Operations Information----
Weather Data		Itinerary	Airport Proximity
Wx Briefing	- No record of briefing	Last Departure Point	Off airport/strip
Method	- N/A	SAME AS ACC/INC	
Completeness	- N/A	Destination	Airport Data
Basic Weather	- VMC	LOCAL	
Wind Dir/Speed	- 170/007 KTS		Runway Ident - N/A
Visibility	- 7.0 SM	ATC/Airspace	Runway Lth/Wid - N/A
Cloud Conditions(1st)	- 1500 FT SCATTERED	Type of Flight Plan - None	Runway Surface - N/A
Cloud Conditions(2nd)	- NONE	Type of Clearance - None	Runway Status - N/A
Obstructions to Vision	- None	Type of Apch/Lndg - None	
Precipitation	- None		
Condition of Light	- Daylight		

---Personnel Information---
Pilot-In-Command

		Medical Certificate - Non-valid medical		
Age - 33			Flight Time (Hours)	
Biennial Flight Review		Total - 1500	Last 24 Hrs - 0	
Certificate(s)/Rating(s)		Make/Model- UNK/NR	Last 30 Days- UNK/NR	
Current - UNK/NR		Instrument- UNK/NR	Last 90 Days- UNK/NR	
Private	Months Since - UNK/NR	Multi-Eng - UNK/NR	Rotorcraft - UNK/NR	
SE land,ME land	Aircraft Type - UNK/NR			

Instrument Rating(s)   - Airplane

---Narrative----
THE PILOT, WHO WAS A ROCK GROUP DRIVER, TOOK AN AIRCRAFT FROM THE HANGAR WITHOUT PERMISSION TO JOY RIDE MEMBERS OF
THE GROUP. DURING THE 2ND FLIGHT, THE AIRCRAFT WING HIT THE BUS DURING ONE OF SEVERAL LOW PASSES OVER THE AREA. THE
AIRCRAFT THEN HIT A TREE AND A RESIDENCE. A POST CRASH FIRE OCCURRED. THE PILOT'S LAST MEDICAL CERTIFICATE WAS DATED
11/16/79.

PAGE   1

Brief of Accident (Continued)

File No. - 2450   3/19/82   LEESBURG,FL   A/C Reg. No. N567LT   Time (Lcl) - 1000 EST

Occurrence #1   IN FLIGHT COLLISION WITH OBJECT
Phase of Operation   MANEUVERING

Finding(s)
1. STOLEN AIRCRAFT/UNAUTHORIZED USE - PERFORMED - PILOT IN COMMAND
2. JUDGEMENT - POOR - PILOT IN COMMAND
3. BUZZING - PERFORMED - PILOT IN COMMAND
4. CLEARANCE - MISJUDGED - PILOT IN COMMAND
5. OBJECT - VEHICLE
6. OBJECT - TREE(S)
7. OBJECT - RESIDENCE

Occurrence #2   IN FLIGHT COLLISION WITH TERRAIN
Phase of Operation   MANEUVERING

-----Probable Cause-----

The National Transportation Safety Board determines that the Probable Cause(s) of this accident
is/are finding(s) 2,3,4

Factor(s) relating to this accident is/are finding(s) 5,6,7

Music's Broken Wings

PAGE   2

John Felten

May 17, 1982

In the course of flying, every pilot is going to hear the term "get-there-itis." This powerful psychological tug can be a dangerous foe to a pilot. It may lead him to push himself beyond his, and the plane's, capabilities. Get-there-itis is a pull most often experienced by a pilot on his own business or personal schedule, but can also be a motivator to a chartered pilot. There is another strong psychological motivator, which has been addressed in previous chapters, that can also play havoc with one's ability to make good decisions. This stress inducer is known as "pressure-to-perform."

"Pressure-to-perform" is probably experienced most by those in the medical field, where seconds count when it comes to saving lives. This is especially true with ambulance drivers. I have experienced this emotion myself during flights when our crew was carrying a medical team for an organ transplant operation. It is our human nature to want to be successful in these critical situations. We also want to be able to perform our jobs. According to this accident report, "get-there-itis," as well as "pressure-to-perform," may both have contributed to the pilot's decision to depart an airport when logic demanded that he stay on the ground.

The Diamonds were a mid-1950's vocal quartet who had a unique harmony during the doo-wop era. Mostly they covered other vocal groups' songs, but they did record a few original songs. Canadian by birth, the group's members found their initial success through a Cleveland, Ohio disc jockey who helped them get a recording contract with Mercury Records in August of 1955. The Diamonds had numerous top 40 hits, television appearances and cameo appearances in films during their career. However, their biggest hit came in April 1957 with a song originally sung by the Gladiolas titled "Little Darlin'." According to some sources, this song was recorded at 4:00 a.m., after a long night in the studio, in one take. "Little Darlin'" by the Diamonds topped out at number 2 on the American charts for eight weeks. The original version by the Gladiolas made it only briefly to number 41.

In 1959, two original members, Ted Kowalski (tenor) and Bill Reed (bass) left the group. Two California vocalists, Evan Fisher (tenor) and John Felten (bass) soon replaced them. By the close of 1960, the group's appeal had run its course and the quartet disbanded in 1961. Subsequently, there were recurring reunion appearances by the group. It was during a return from a Diamonds reunion concert in Reno, Nevada that John Felten was killed along with his wife, Linda Felten. The pilot and his wife were also killed.

In all likelihood, if this pilot had decided to stay on the ground and had waited until the weather conditions were aligned with his skill level, no one would have perished during this flight. Furthermore, if he had made an in-flight decision to return to his point of departure when he saw that the weather was worsening along his route, the accident probably would never have happened. This is another unfortunate example of a fair weather pilot who decided to continue into worsening weather conditions, allowing the potential for disaster to increase with the passing of each second.

Author

Aircraft addenda:

Common names: Sierra, A24R
Manufacturer: Beechcraft
First flight of type: 1969
Registration number for this airplane: N9715L
Seats: 6
Length: 25 feet, 9 inches
Wingspan: 32 feet, 9 inches
Engines: (1) Lycoming, IO-360-A1B6, four cylinder, horizontally opposed, piston
Horsepower: 200 hp
Empty weight (approximate): 1,610 lbs.
Gross weight: 2,750 lbs.
Service ceiling: 14,350 ft.
Fuel capacity: 59 gal.
Cruising speed: 150 mph

* The above photo represents the type of aircraft and not necessarily the exact model involved in the accident.

Personal addenda:

John Palmer Felten (John Felten): Bass vocalist
b. November 16, 1936: Seattle, Washington
d. May 17, 1982: 2 miles south of Duck Lake, near Tennant, California
Cremated. Felten's ashes were scattered on his ranch in Grants Pass, Oregon.

National Transportation Safety Board

PRELIMINARY REPORT OF AVIATION

ICAO REPORT: ___ Yes X No

X Accident   ☐ Incident

| L | A | X | 8 | 2 | F | A | L | 8 | 3 |

NTSB Accident/Incident No.

| 1 AIRCRAFT | Registration(N)Number N97LSL | Make(Manufacturer) BEECH | Model Number A24R |

| 2 LOCATION | City MT. SHASTA | State CA | Zip N/O | Airport Identifier ☐ N/A |

| 3 DATE AND TIME | Date 5-17-82 | Flight Number N/A | Time(Local) 1315 | Zone PDT |

4 NUMBER OF INJURIES   4 Fatal   Ø Serious   Ø Minor   Ø None   Ø Unknown

5 AIRCRAFT DAMAGE   X Destroyed   ☐ Substantial   ☐ Minor   ☐ None   ☐ Unknown

6 FIRE   X None   ☐ In-flight   ☐ On Ground   ☐ Unknown

7 ITINERARY   Last Departure Point ☐ RDD REDDING CA   Time 1245   Destination ☐ 35S GRANTS PASS OR
Ident and City State   Ident and City State

8 OPERATOR   Name DANIEL L. JACKSON   Address 5291 RIVERBANK RD.
dba   GRANTS PASS, OR. 97526

9 DAMAGE TO PROPERTY   X None   ☐ Residential Area   ☐ Vehicle   ☐ Trees   ☐ Wires/Poles
☐ Residence   ☐ Commercial Bldg   ☐ Airport Facility   ☐ Crops   ☐ Other

10 FLIGHT PLAN   ☐ None   X VFR   ☐ IFR   ☐ Unknown

11 WEATHER DATA
At Accident ☐ Site   X VMC   ☐ Precipitation   Ceiling 3200 Ft.   25 SM Visibility   55 °F Temp
Other Area X Ident SIY   ☐ IMC   X No Precipitation   X BKN ☐ -X ☐ Unk   360° Winds 15 Kts
☐ OVC ☐ X

12 TYPE OF OPERATING CERTIFICATE

Air Carrier Operating Certificate
☐ Domestic/Flag Air Carrier
☐ Supplemental Air Carrier
☐ All Cargo Air Service Air Carrier (Section 418)

Air Taxi Operator
☐ Commuter Air Carrier
☐ On-Demand Air Taxi

Operating Certificate
☐ Commercial Operator
☐ Air Travel Club
☐ Corporate (14 CFR 125)
☐ Other

Neither Certificate (General Aviation)
Personal Use/Business Transportation
X Personal   ☐ Business   ☐ Unk
☐ Executive/Corporate Transportation
☐ Instructional
☐ Aerial Application
☐ Aerial Observation
☐ Other Work Use
☐ Other
☐ Foreign Registered Aircraft   ☐ Public

13 TYPE OF OPERATION   ☐ Scheduled   ☐ Domestic   ☐ Passenger   ☐ Passenger + Cargo   ☐ Training   ☐ Other
☐ Non-Scheduled   ☐ International   ☐ Cargo   ☐ Mail Contract Only   ☐ Ferry

14 FLIGHT CONDUCTED UNDER   X 14 CFR 91   ☐ 14 CFR 121   ☐ 14 CFR 127   ☐ 14 CFR 135   ☐ 14 CFR 137
☐ 14 CFR 91D   ☐ 14 CFR 125   ☐ 14 CFR 133   ☐ 14 CFR 123   ☐ Other

15 PHASE OF OPERATION   ☐ Static   ☐ Takeoff   X Cruise   ☐ Approach   ☐ Maneuvering   ☐ Other
☐ Taxi   ☐ Climb   ☐ Descent   ☐ Landing   ☐ Hover   ☐ Undetermined

16 TYPE OF ACCIDENT
During an In-flight Phase of Operation Collided With
X Ground/Water/Obstacle

Personal Injury
☐ On Ground
☐ In-flight

Aircraft Damage
☐ On Ground
☐ In-flight

☐ Undetermined

During an On Ground Phase of Operation Collided With
☐ Obstacle

☐ Missing Aircraft

☐ Other

PRELIMINARY INFORMATION — Subject to change; Pertinence to Accident/Incident not positively established at this time.

NTSB Form 6120.19a
(Rev. 1/82)

BEST COPY AVAILABLE   001

17 CREW (Names and Injuries) (Pilot-Address)	PASSENGERS (Names and Injuries)
DANIEL L. JACKSON (FATAL)	PEGGY JACKSON (FATAL)
	JOHN FELTEN (FATAL)
	LINDA FELTEN (FATAL

18 Narrative   THE AIRCRAFT WAS ENROUTE FROM RENO, NV. TO GRANTS PASS, OR. UPON BEING TOLD BY RED BLUFF, CA. FSS IN AN IN-FLIGHT WEATHER BRIEFING THAT THE PASSES WERE CLOSED AND VFR FLIGHT WAS NOT RECOMMENDED, THE AIRCRAFT LANDED AT REDDING, CA. AFTER ANOTHER BRIEFING THE PILOT FILED A VFR FLIGHT PLAN AT 1213 PDT WHICH WAS ACTIVATED AT 1245 PDT. THE PILOT WAS TOLD THREE TIMES THAT VFR FLIGHT WAS NOT RECOMMENDED. HE TOLD FLIGHT SERVICE THAT THERE WAS AN ENTERTAINER ABOARD WHO WAS ANXIOUS TO GET HOME AND THAT IF HE ENCOUNTERED ANY PROBLEMS WITH THE WEATHER HE WOULD HEAD WEST. THE AIRCRAFT WRECKAGE WAS LOCATED ON 5-18-82 AT 7,000 FEET MSL IN 5 FEET OF SNOW.

NTSB Acc/Inc No. | L | A | X | 8 | 2 | F | A | L | 8 | 3 |

ADMINISTRATIVE DATA

NOTIFICATION FROM FAA DO DOYLE	DATE 5-18-82	LOCAL TIME 1220
OTHER FEDERAL AGENCIES INVOLVED NONE		FAA DISTRICT OFFICE
NTSB PERSONNEL ASSIGNED MJ PYATT		
DATE THIS FORM PREPARED 5-18-82		INVESTIGATOR IN CHARGE MJ PYATT
DATE THIS FORM RECEIVED BY NTSB/FAA		

☒ Initial   ☒ Preliminary

BEST COPY AVAILABLE 004

HISTORY OF FLIGHT

The flight of N9715L, a Beech A24R, Sierra, Aircraft originated on May 17, 1982, in Redding, California, at 1242 PDT * A VFR flight plan to Grants Pass, Oregon, was activated with Red Bluff, California, Flight Service Station (FSS) at 1249. The aircraft had departed Reno, Nevada, at 0815 bound for Grants Pass and, following an inflight weather briefing, the pilot elected to land at Redding at 1142. A telephone briefing was obtained from Red Bluff FSS at 1207 at which time VFR flight was not recommended due to mountain pass obscurement. The pilot filed a VFR flight plan after stating that he had three people on board who were really nervous, including an entertainer from Reno, who was anxious to get home. He said that if it was himself he would stay put.

INJURIES TO PERSONS

All four persons aboard the aircraft were fatally injured.

DAMAGE TO AIRCRAFT AND OTHER DAMAGE

The aircraft was demolished. Numerous trees were damaged over a 420 foot path from the first tree strike to the principal impact site.

CREW INFORMATION

The pilot, Daniel Larry Jackson, held private pilot certificate #554580649 issued September 11, 1979, with airplane and single engine land ratings. There was no notation of a biennial flight review in the pilot's logbook. A third class medical certificate with no limitations was issued June 10, 1980. The pilot had a total of 208 hours of flight time, 154 as pilot in command, and 115 in a Beech A24R.

AIRCRAFT INFORMATION

N9715L was a Beech A24R, Serial # MC92, manufactured in 1971. A Lycoming IO-360-A1B Engine, Serial # L-7396-51A, was installed. The aircraft and engine had a total time of 1351.71 hours. It had been 25.96 hours since the most recent annual and 100-hour inspections which were completed on February 24, 1982. The engine had been overhauled 114.38 hours prior to the accident.

METEOROLOGICAL INFORMATION

According to a weather study prepared by the Bureau of Technology of the NTSB, Northern California was under the influence of a weak low over northwestern Nevada with a cold front extending southward. The area forecast contained flight precautions for mountain obscurement near the Oregon border, occasional moderate turbulence below 18,000 feet, and occasional moderate icing in clouds and in precipitation below 18,000 feet. Broken cloud bases were forecast to be between 5,000 and 8,000 feet with tops at 12,000 feet. The forecasts were substantially correct.

---

*/ All times appearing herein are Pacific Daylight based on the 24-hour clock.

-I-

According to the study there would have been extensive cloudiness in the vicinity of Mt. Shasta between 5,500 and 10,000 feet with scattered rain showers. There would have been light, possibly moderate turbulence in the vicinity of mountains. There would have been mixed rime and clear icing in clouds and rain showers above approximately 6,300 feet.

AIDS TO NAVIGATION

A radio test at an altitude of 8,500 feet, as filed in a VFR flight plan by the pilot of N9715L, indicated that VOR reception was not possible in the vicinity of the accident site from Redding VOR/DME; Fort Jones, California, VORTAC; or Montague, California, VOR. All facilities were operational.

COMMUNICATIONS

N9715L was cleared to taxi by the Redding Air Traffic Control tower at 1239 and cleared to take off at 1242. A VFR flight plan was activated with Red Bluff FSS at 1249. There were no further communications between N9715L and any known facility or aircraft.

WRECKAGE

The wreckage was located on May 18, 1982, at 1106 by a California Highway Patrol helicopter. A tree strike was found at 7,000 feet MSL, 50 feet above ground level (AGL). The aircraft was traveling south and continued on that heading for approximately 420 feet before coming to rest in a clump of trees. The terrain was descending at a 30 degree incline. The right horizontal stabilizer was located in a tree approximately 60 feet AGL, 150 feet along the path. The outboard panel of the right wing, left main gear, and outboard panel of the left wing, were all found on the ground. The right main gear was in a tree near the principal impact site. The fuselage was split behind the luggage compartment at Station #181. The engine was turned at right angles to the fuselage. The trim tab was torn off of the elevator. The right flap was separated and the left flap was attached at the in-board side. The rudder was separated as was the only door on the aircraft. The control cables were broken on impact. All seats remained on their tracks. The back rest was twisted off of the rear platform seat. All seats were attached to the floor which had moved forward. The left control wheel was broken off and the right was intact with the torque tube bent 90 degrees to the left.

The engine was clean and well-oiled. All valves were working and the drive train was intact. There was compression on all cylinders. The top spark plugs were new. The left magneto sparked on all four leads. There was fuel in the spider, the injector, fuel pump, filter, gascolater, and in the fuel line forward of the firewall. There were bark stains on the propeller and wood was embedded in the spinner. Branches up to 13 inches in diameter had been chopped off and were strewn along the entire wreckage path.

MEDICAL AND PATHOLOGICAL INFORMATION

According to the Siskiyou, California, County Sheriff-Coroner the pilot and front seat passenger died of multiple traumatic injuries. The two rear seat passengers died of cervical spinal fractures. There were no pre-existing conditions revealed in the autopsy examination of the pilot which would have prevented the normal operation of the aircraft. A toxicology examination of the pilot was requested and performed; however, according to the Siskiyou County Sheriff-Coroner's Office, the report was lost by the laboratory.

ADDITIONAL PERSONS PARTICIPATING IN THIS INVESTIGATION - Name, Address, and affiliation

MIKE H. McCLURE, Staff Engineer
Beech Aircraft Corp, Dept 290
Box 85
Wichita, Kansas 67201

INVESTIGATED BY - SIGNATURE	AGENCY	DATE
MARY JEAN PYATT	NATIONAL TRANSPORTATION SAFETY BOARD	12/23/82

NTSB Form 6120.4F(1/82)

QUALITY CONTROL CHECK

National Transportation Safety Board
Washington, D.C. 20594

Brief of Accident

File No. - 2456   5/17/82   NEAR MT. SHASTA,CA   A/C Reg. No. N9715L   Time (Lcl) - 1315 PDT

---Basic Information---
Type Operating Certificate-NONE (GENERAL AVIATION)

		Injuries		
Aircraft Damage		Fatal	Serious	Minor	None
DESTROYED					
Fire	Crew	1	0	0	0
NONE	Pass	3	0	0	0

Type of Operation   - PERSONAL
Flight Conducted Under   - 14 CFR 91
Accident Occurred During   - CRUISE

---Aircraft Information---
Make/Model   - BEECH A24R
Landing Gear   - TRICYCLE-RETRACTABLE
Max Gross Wt   - 2750
No. of Seats   - 4

Eng Make/Model - LYCOMING IO-360-A1B
Number Engines - 1
Engine Type   - RECIP - FUEL INJECTED
Rated Power   - 200 HP

ELT Installed/Activated - YES/YES
Stall Warning System - YES
Weather Radar - NO

---Environment/Operations Information---
Weather Data
Wx Briefing   - FSS
Method   - TELEPHONE
Completeness   - FULL
Basic Weather   - VMC
Wind Dir/Speed- 310/012 KTS
Visibility   - 15.0   SM
Cloud Conditions(1st) - UNK/NR
Cloud Conditions(2nd) - UNK/NR
Obstructions to Vision- NONE
Precipitation   - NONE
Condition of Light - DAYLIGHT

Itinerary
Last Departure Point
  REDDING,CA
Destination
  GRANTS PASS,OR

ATC/Airspace
Type of Flight Plan - VFR
Type of Clearance   - NONE
Type of Apch/Lndg   - NONE

Airport Proximity
  OFF AIRPORT/STRIP

Airport Data
Runway Ident   - N/A
Runway Lth/Wid - N/A
Runway Surface - N/A
Runway Status   - N/A

---Personnel Information---
Pilot-In-Command
Certificate(s)/Rating(s)
  PRIVATE
  SE LAND

Age   - 39
Biennial Flight Review
  Current   - NO
  Months Since - 32
  Aircraft Type - UNK/NR

Medical Certificate - VALID MEDICAL-NO WAIVERS/LIMIT

Flight Time (Hours)		
Total	203	Last 24 Hrs - 0
Make/Model-	115	Last 30 Days- 5
Instrument-	3	Last 90 Days- 19

Instrument Rating(s) - NONE

---Narrative---
THE FLIGHT ORIGINATED AT RENO, NV, BUT THE PILOT LANDED AT RED BLUFF, CA AFTER RECEIVING AN IN-FLIGHT WEATHER
BRIEFING. AFTER LANDING, HE OBTAINED ANOTHER WEATHER BRIEFING AND WAS ADVISED THAT VFR FLIGHT WAS NOT RECOMMENDED.
HE THEN FILED A VFR FLIGHT PLAN AFTER REPORTING THAT THE PASSENGERS WERE ANXIOUS TO GET HOME. OTHERWISE HE WOULD
STAY. THE FLIGHT PLAN WAS FILED FOR 8500 FT. THERE WERE NO KNOWN COMMUNICATIONS WITH THE AIRCRAFT AFTER THE PILOT
ACTIVATED HIS FLIGHT PLAN. THE PLANE COLLIDED WITH TREES AND CRASHED ON DOWNSLOPING TERRAIN ABOUT 12 MI NORTHEAST
OF MT SHASTA. THE IMPACT OCCURRED ON A SOUTHERLY HEADING AT ABOUT 7000 FT MSL. ACCORDING TO A WEATHER STUDY, THERE
WOULD HAVE BEEN EXTENSIVE CLOUDS BETWEEN 5500 AND 10,000 FT WITH SCATTERED RAIN SHOWERS. ALSO, THERE WOULD HAVE BEEN
MIXED RIME AND CLEAR ICING IN CLOUDS AND RAIN SHOWERS ABOVE APPROXIMATELY 6300 FT AND TURBULENCE WAS FORECASTED
BELOW 18,000 FT.

PAGE 56

BEST COPY AVAILABLE

Brief of Accident (Continued)

File No - 2456   5/17/82   NEAR MT SHASTA,CA   A/C Reg No. N9/15L   Time (Lcl) - 1315 PDT

Occurrence #1   IN FLIGHT ENCOUNTER WITH WEATHER
Phase of Operation   CRUISE - NORMAL

Finding(s)
1. WEATHER CONDITION - CLOUDS
2. WEATHER CONDITION - TURBULENCE
3. WEATHER CONDITION - LOW CEILING
4. WEATHER CONDITION - ICING CONDITIONS
5. FLIGHT INTO KNOWN ADVERSE WEATHER   CONTINUED - PILOT IN COMMAND
6. IMPROPER DECISION,PRESSURE INDUCED BY OTHERS - PILOT IN COMMAND
7. VFR FLIGHT INTO IMC - CONTINUED - PILOT IN COMMAND
8. IMPROPER DECISION,LACK OF TOTAL INSTRUMENT TIME - PILOT IN COMMAND

Occurrence #2   IN FLIGHT COLLISION WITH OBJECT
Phase of Operation   CRUISE

Finding(s)
9. TERRAIN CONDITION - MOUNTAINOUS/HILLY
10. TERRAIN CONDITION - HIGH TERRAIN
11. OBJECT - TREE(S)

Occurrence #3   IN FLIGHT COLLISION WITH TERRAIN
Phase of Operation   DESCENT - UNCONTROLLED

----Probable Cause----

The National Transportation Safety Board determines that the Probable Cause(s) of this accident
is/are finding(s) 1,2,3,4,6,8,9,10,11

Factor(s) relating to this accident is/are finding(s) 5,7

PAGE 57

BEST COPY AVAILABLE

NTSB Identification: **LAX82FA183**

Accident occurred Monday, May 17, 1982 at NEAR MT. SHASTA, CA
Aircraft:BEECH A24R, registration: N9715L
Injuries: 4 Fatal.

THE FLIGHT ORIGINATED AT RENO, NV, BUT THE PILOT LANDED AT RED BLUFF, CA AFTER RECEIVING AN IN-FLIGHT WEATHER BRIEFING. AFTER LANDING, HE OBTAINED ANOTHER WEATHER BRIEFING AND WAS ADVISED THAT VFR FLIGHT WAS NOT RECOMMENDED. HE THEN FILED A VFR FLIGHT PLAN AFTER REPORTING THAT THE PASSENGERS WERE ANXIOUS TO GET HOME, OTHERWISE HE WOULD STAY. THE FLIGHT PLAN WAS FILED FOR 8500 FT. THERE WERE NO KNOWN COMMUNICATIONS WITH THE AIRCRAFT AFTER THE PILOT ACTIVATED HIS FLIGHT PLAN. THE PLANE COLLIDED WITH TREES AND CRASHED ON DOWNSLOPING TERRAIN ABOUT 12 MI NORTHEAST OF MT SHASTA. THE IMPACT OCCURRED ON A SOUTHERLY HEADING AT ABOUT 7000 FT MSL. ACCORDING TO A WEATHER STUDY, THERE WOULD HAVE BEEN EXTENSIVE CLOUDS BETWEEN 5500 AND 10,000 FT WITH SCATTERED RAIN SHOWERS. ALSO, THERE WOULD HAVE BEEN MIXED RIME AND CLEAR ICING IN CLOUDS AND RAIN SHOWERS ABOVE APPROXIMATELY 6300 FT AND TURBULENCE WAS FORECASTED BELOW 18,000 FT.

The National Transportation Safety Board determines the probable cause(s) of this accident as follows.

FLIGHT INTO KNOWN ADVERSE WEATHER..CONTINUED..PILOT IN COMMAND
VFR FLIGHT INTO IMC..CONTINUED..PILOT IN COMMAND

Contributing Factors

WEATHER CONDITION..CLOUDS
WEATHER CONDITION..TURBULENCE
WEATHER CONDITION..LOW CEILING
WEATHER CONDITION..ICING CONDITIONS
PILOT IN COMMAND
PILOT IN COMMAND
TERRAIN CONDITION..MOUNTAINOUS/HILLY
TERRAIN CONDITION..HIGH TERRAIN
OBJECT..TREE(S)

Keith Green

July 28, 1982

Because airplanes have weight, the lift produced by an airplane's wings is measured by weight in the form of pounds. If an airplane is loaded too heavily, the power of the engines cannot pull the airplane fast enough to allow the airplane's wings to produce enough lift to take the weight of the aircraft into the air. In other words, if the generated lift does not exceed aircraft weight then flight cannot occur. If only enough lift is produced to just barely get an airplane off the ground, chances are good that the airplane will not climb very well, or perhaps not at all. The consequence of such a situation can be a disastrous crash.

Additionally, in the course of assessing an airplane's weight, there must also be consideration of balance. Like a seesaw on a playground, if the weights of the children on each end are not balanced, the heaviest child will go down while the lightest child will be forced up. There is a way to balance two children of different weights on a seesaw, however, so the two can play happily. The way to accomplish this is to move the heavier child closer to the fulcrum of the seesaw. In doing so, balance is achieved. Just like weight, balance is critical to the safety of an airplane's flight. Balance in an airplane is referenced by what is known as the center of gravity (cg). The cg is the fulcrum, or that place where, if a pivot point supported the plane, the airplane would balance (Figure 30-1). The cg is measured in inches from the front of the plane towards the rear. The higher the number of inches aft of the measuring point (called the datum), the more rearward the cg.

The balance in an airplane has limits, also known as the cg range. Should the cg be too far forward or too far aft, the aerodynamic forces normally generated by the flight control surfaces that allow the pilot to control the airplane may not have enough force to effect positive control. In other words, if there is too much weight forward the pilot may not be able to get the airplane's nose up to begin flight. If there is too much weight rearward, or if some of the correctly distributed weight shifts to the rear, the pilot may not have enough control force to get the nose of the plane back down to a safe angle. If the angle of attack of the wings gets too great from a nose-high condition, the plane may stall. If the plane stalls with a rearward cg, the pilot may not be able to recover the wings from the stalled condition and the plane would then descend with very little control. These simple rules of weight and balance apply to every airplane that has ever been built and flown, from the smallest to the largest.

In the case of this accident there was one eyewitness who also was a pilot. That kind of eyewitness is exceedingly valuable to an accident investigator. Someone knowledgeable in general flight characteristics can accurately describe what occurred. What this eyewitness related were oscillations in the airplane's nose pitch attitude before it hit tall trees in a densely wooded area. A non-pilot might have described the accident differently. If the eyewitness had been an adult unfamiliar with aeronautics, he or she might have described the plane's actual oscillations as "flips," which would mean something very different to the assigned investigator. It is vital that the professionally trained investigator receive a description that is as aeronautically correct as possible in order to properly assess what actually happened.

As a side note, it is interesting to point out that sometimes a more true representation of what happened to an airplane just before an accident can come from a child eyewitness. It is not uncommon for an accident investigator, during an adult consented interview with a child eyewitness, to have the child hold an airplane model and use it in a show-and-tell form. The child, not being pre-conditioned to common misconceptions of aviation, will show exactly what he or she remembers seeing. This innocent knowledge is very valuable to the investigator, keeping in mind that factual knowledge is critical when it comes to finding the truth during an investigation.

In the final moments of this accident, the airplane struck a tree very hard and then traveled another 150 feet before coming to rest. At some point during the process of hitting that first tree, other trees, and finally the ground, the fuel tanks were badly damaged enough to allow raw fuel to spew out in a highly combustible mist. This fuel somehow ignited and Keith Green, along with two of his children, the pilot and eight additional passengers (all from one family), were killed and burned nearly beyond visible recognition. Twelve people died in this accident in an airplane that was equipped with only seven passenger seats. It would appear that this plane was overloaded and out of balance for safe flight.

As amazing as it sounds, Keith Green apparently began his professional songwriting career at the age of 13. He had a Jewish background but converted to Christianity in 1973. While in the San Fernando Valley in the mid-1970s, he began what can be considered a Christian musical career playing in a small Christian nightclub north of Los Angeles called the "Daisy Club." Putting into practice the Christian teachings he and his wife (also a songwriter) studied, they opened their home to anyone who needed a place to stay. Their Woodland Hills, California, home became a refuge from drugs and the hardcore street lifestyle. By 1978, Green had a successful recording career (his first album sold over 250,000 copies in the first two years) and a full ministry going with six houses that sheltered as many as 40 Christian converts. His music can be described as Christian Rock, but his songs were always ministry oriented.

In 1979 the entire ministry was transplanted to the Lindale, Texas, area where some other music-oriented and youth ministries had already been established. Green named his ministry "Last Days Ministries," and called his property Garden Valley. Sometime during 1980, Green pioneered the controversial concept of practically giving albums away by telling people that they could pay for them only as they were able to. He wanted people to get his records and listen to them for the message they conveyed, not necessarily for the money they put in his own pocket. Soon his concert schedule necessitated that he travel by airplane, and a runway was constructed on the Garden Valley ministry property. This particular flight began as an aerial tour of the ministry property for a visiting family of eight, six of whom were children. The Cessna 414 involved in this crash was operated under a lease agreement. It was found by the NTSB investigators to have no mechanical or structural malfunction.

Author

Aircraft addenda:

Common names: Chancellor, Cessna 414
Manufacturer: Cessna Aircraft Company
First flight of type: 1965
Registration number for this airplane: N110VM
Seats: 7
Length: 36 feet, 5 inches
Wingspan: 44 feet, 2 inches
Engines: (2) TSIO-520-NBs, six cylinder, horizontally opposed, air cooled, piston
Horsepower: 310 hp each
Empty weight (actual): 4,786 lbs.
Gross weight: 6,350 lbs.
Service ceiling: 30,800 ft.
Range: 1,200 miles
Cruising speed: 230 mph

* The above photo represents the type of aircraft and not necessarily the exact model involved in the accident.

Personal addenda:

Keith Gorden Green (Keith Green): singer, songwriter, keyboard player
b. October 21, 1953: Brooklyn, New York
d. July 28, 1982: Garden Valley, Texas
Buried: Garden Valley Baptist Church, Garden Valley, Texas
Note: Green's two children, Josiah, nearly four years old and Bethany, two and a half years old, were buried with him in the same coffin.

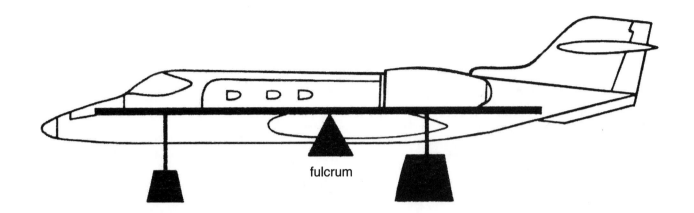

The balance of an aircraft in flight can be compared to that of a playground seesaw.

Figure 30-1

ICAO REQ'D. ☒ Tx
ICAO NOT REQ'D. ☐

National Transportation Safety Board

PRELIMINARY REPORT OF AVIATION

☒ Accident   ☐ Incident

| F | T | W | 8 | 2 | A | A | 2 | 9 | 9 |

NTSB Accident/Incident No.

1 AIRCRAFT	Registration(N)Number N110VM	Make(Manufacturer) CESSNA	Model Number 414	
2 LOCATION	City Lindale	State TX	Zip 75771	Airport Identifier ☐
3 DATE AND TIME	Date Jul 28, 82	Flight Number N/A	Time(Local) 1925	Zone CDT

4 NUMBER OF INJURIES	12 Fatal	Ø Serious	Ø Minor	Ø None	Ø Unknown

5 AIRCRAFT DAMAGE	☒ Destroyed	☐ Substantial	☐ Minor	☐ None	☐ Unknown

6 FIRE	☐ None	☐ In-flight	☒ On Ground	☐ Unknown

7 ITINERARY

Last Departure Point: ☐ ___ Lindale   Time 1925   City ___ TX State

Destination: ☐ ___ Local Ident and City State

8 OPERATOR — Name Last Days Ministries   Address P.O. Box 40   Lindale, TX 75771

dba

9 DAMAGE TO PROPERTY	☐ None	☐ Residential Area	☐ Vehicle	☒ Trees	☐ Wires/Poles
	☐ Residence	☐ Commercial Bldg	☐ Airport Facility	☐ Crops	☐ Other

10 FLIGHT PLAN	☒ None	☐ VFR	☐ IFR	☐ Unknown

11 WEATHER DATA

At Accident Site ☐   Other Area ☐ Ident TYR

☒ VMC   ☐ IMC

☐ Precipitation   ☒ No Precipitation

Ceiling 2000 Ft.   ☒ BKN ☐ -X ☐ Unk   ☐ OVC ☐ X

Visibility 10 SM   Temp 90 °F   Ø ° Winds Ø Kts

12 TYPE OF OPERATING CERTIFICATE

Air Carrier Operating Certificate
- ☐ Domestic/Flag Air Carrier
- ☐ Supplemental Air Carrier
- ☐ All Cargo Air Service Air Carrier (Section 418)

Air Taxi Operator
- ☐ Commuter Air Carrier
- ☐ On-Demand Air Taxi

Operating Certificate
- ☐ Commercial Operator
- ☐ Air Travel Club
- ☐ Corporate (14 CFR 125)
- ☐ Other

Neither Certificate (General Aviation)
Personal Use/Business Transportation
- ☒ Personal   ☐ Business   ☐ Unk
- ☐ Executive/Corporate Transportation
- ☐ Instructional
- ☐ Aerial Application
- ☐ Aerial Observation
- ☐ Other Work Use
- ☐ Other
- ☐ Foreign Registered Aircraft   ☐ Public

13 TYPE OF OPERATION	☐ Scheduled ☐ Non-Scheduled	☐ Domestic ☐ International	☐ Passenger ☐ Cargo	☐ Passenger + Cargo ☐ Mail Contract Only	☐ Training ☐ Ferry	☐ Other

14 FLIGHT CONDUCTED UNDER	☒ 14 CFR 91	☐ 14 CFR 121	☐ 14 CFR 127	☐ 14 CFR 135	☐ 14 CFR 137
	☐ 14 CFR 91D	☐ 14 CFR 125	☐ 14 CFR 133	☐ 14 CFR 123	☐ Other

15 PHASE OF OPERATION	☐ Static ☐ Taxi	☐ Takeoff ☒ Climb	☐ Cruise ☐ Descent	☐ Approach ☐ Landing	☐ Maneuvering ☐ Hover	☐ Other ☐ Undetermined

16 TYPE OF ACCIDENT

Personal Injury AND A/C Damage
- ☒ On Ground
- ☒ In-flight

Personal Injury Only
- ☐ On Ground
- ☐ In-flight

Aircraft Damage Only
- ☐ On Ground
- ☐ In-flight

Mid-air Collision "N" NO. _____

- ☐ Undetermined
- ☐ Missing Aircraft
- ☐ Other

PRELIMINARY INFORMATION — Subject to change; Pertinence to Accident/Incident not positively established at this time.

NTSB Form 6120.19a
(Rev. 1/82)

BEST COPY AVAILABLE

17 CREW (Names and Injuries) (Pilot-Address)	PASSENGERS (Names and Injuries)
Don A. Burmeister (Fatal) P.O. Box 1032 Lindale, TX 75771	11 Passengers (Fatal)

18 Narrative

This aircraft was destroyed by impact forces and post crash fire when it settled into trees shortly after takeoff from a 3163' private airstrip near Lindale, TX. The aircraft, owned by a private individual and operated by the Last Days Ministries, was on a local sightseeing flight and there was no flight plan filed. There were some isolated thunderstorms north and west of the airstrip at the time of the accident. However, pilot witnesses stated that none came close to the airstrip or the accident site.

Witnesses stated that the aircraft departed on runway 33 and appeared to over rotate at lift off. The aircraft was observed to climb to about 75 to 100 feet AGL, then begin to sink until it disappeared behind some trees. Smoke was seen rising from the area immediately thereafter. The witnesses indicated that the aircraft deck angle oscillated several times throughout the 20 to 30 second flight. The point of initial impact with the trees is about 700 yards from the departure end of the runway.

Initial investigation revealed that the aircraft impacted at a 11° flight path angle in 30° nose up, wings level attitude. The main fuselage came to rest about 157 feet from the point of initial impact. Both tip tanks, horizontal stabilizers and elevators and the right wing separated during the impact sequence. Significant prop slash marks were found through the prop paths of both the left and right engines. Measurements of the slash marks indicated that both engines were operating a 2760 RPM and that the aircrafts ground speed would have been in the area of 76 knots. Preliminary weight and balance calculations indicate that the aircraft was overloaded by 200 to 300 pounds and the C.G. was between 3 and 5 inches aft of the aft limit. These calculations were based on aircraft records, refueling slips and witness statements regarding passenger seat locations and weights. There were 6 seats and 1 toilet seat on board. More investigation in this area is in progress. The gear was found in a transient position as were the flaps. The aircraft is equipped with a Robertson STOL modification.

Initial investigation into the pilots background indicates that he is ex-military with Commercial, ADMEL, instrument rating with about 11000+ hours total time. On 6-9-82, he received his standard multi-engine rating from a FAA designated examiner. Prior to that, he was limited to centerline thrust only. The pilot was not the full time pilot for the operator and it is not known at this time how much time he had in this make and model or if he had

(continued)

NTSB Acc/Inc No.	F	T	W	8	2	A	A	2	9	9

ADMINISTRATIVE DATA

NOTIFICATION FROM FAA Com Ctr	DATE Jul 28, 82	LOCAL TIME 2022 CDT
OTHER FEDERAL AGENCIES INVOLVED		FAA DISTRICT OFFICE FAA-SW-GADO-11 (Brooks)
NTSB PERSONNEL ASSIGNED W.V. Wandel G. Braden		
DATE THIS FORM PREPARED Aug 2, 82		INVESTIGATOR IN CHARGE W.V. Wandel
DATE THIS FORM RECEIVED BY NTSB/FAA		BEST COPY AVAILABLE

☐ Initial   ☒ Preliminary

NTSB Form 6120.19a - FTW 82-A-A299

18 Narrative (Cont'd.)

received a formal checkout.

Preliminary autopsy results indicate that all of the occupants died as a result of thermal injuries and smoke inhalation.

The engines, turbochargers and props will be torn down at a later date.

BEST COPY AVAILABLE

Disc IBM-33

NATIONAL TRANSPORTATION SAFETY BOARD
Bureau of Technology
Washington, D.C. 20594

March 10, 1983

HUMAN FACTORS SPECIALIST REPORT OF THIS INVESTIGATION

A.   Accident

Operator   :   Last Days Ministries
Aircraft   :   Cessna 414, N110VM
Location   :   Near Lindale, Texas
Date   :   July 28, 1982
Time   :   About 1930 CDT
NTSB No.   :   FTW-82-A-A299

B.   Human Factors Group

No group formed.

C.   Summary

At about 7:30 p.m. on July 28, 1982, the Cessna 414, N110VM departed from the Last Days Ministries private airstrip near Garden Valley, Texas. The aircraft was configured with 7 seats but 12 people were onboard when the crash occurred. The aircraft was observed after takeoff in an erratic pitch changing climb to an altitude of 75 or 100 feet before sinking out of sight behind some trees. The aircraft crashed and burned after it impacted with trees and the ground about 2,300 feet from the departure end of the runway. All occupants died in the postcrash fire.

Postmortem examination of the occupants revealed that their cause of death was from thermal burns and smoke inhalation. No evidence was found in any of the examination what would indicate impact trauma.

D.   Details of the Investigation

1.   Aircraft Configuration

The cockpit was equipped with two pilot seats and the cabin had five passenger seats. The two forward passenger seats were aft facing units positioned one on either side of the cabin separated by a center aisle. These seats faced two forward facing units. The remaining passenger seat was the potty chair which was positioned on the right side near the aft part of the cabin. It was positioned facing toward the airstair door.

2.   Crew Information

The pilot, Don Alan Burmeister was born December 3, 1945. He held a second class medical certificate which was issued on March 5, 1982, and showed no limitations.

He held a commercial pilot certificate #1981463 with the following rating and limitations:

> Airplane Single Engine Land
> Airplane Multiengine Land
> Instrument Airplane

His multiengine rating had been limited to center line thrust until the limitation was removed on June 9, 1982.

The following is a summary of Don Burmeister's activities 72 hours prior to the crash. He had just returned from 2 weeks vacation on Saturday before the crash on Wednesday. Consequently, he met with quite a few people who were involved in different projects which he was overseeing.

Monday, July 26

He talked with Lloyd Kelley concerning dirt-work to be done at various projects. He talked with Dean Snell about the "married-housing" and how the progress was. He talked with the foreman working on the hangar to check on its progress. Made phone calls concerning used trailers. He worked until dinner time. He got 8 to 9 hours a sleep that night.

Tuesday, July 27

He worked with Lloyd Kelley for about an hour and a half showing him different dirt-work that needed to be done on various projects. Then he talked with Dean Snell and his wife concerning carpet and tile samples for the "married-housing." He talked with James Rush concerning putting in septic tanks for the "married-housing." He looked at used trailers in Tyler for about 3 hours that afternoon. He flew the C-182 to Tyler for gas about 7:00 p.m. (about 8 min. there and 8 min. back). Returned to find that someone needed to be picked up at the Tyler Airport, and so took off again in the C-182 arriving back about 8:00 p.m. He then did paperwork until 11:00 or so that night.

He flew a total of about half an hour that day.
He got only about 5 hours of sleep that night.

Wednesday, July 28

He woke up about 4:30 a.m., so that he could depart in the C-182 by 5:00 for Dallas/Ft. Worth Airport to pick up two passengers by 6:00 arriving back about 7:30 p.m. He then met with Lloyd Kelley showing him how to do some dirt-work at one of the trailer sites. He did some surveying for the runway for leveling the dirt between the hangar and the runway. He checked on the hangar's progress. He went to our prayer meeting. . .about an hour and a half. He worked with Lloyd at the trailer site some more and showed him what needed to be done with dirtwork by the runway. He planned some concert/crusade details (i.e., albums tracts and programs they'd need.) He left for Dallas/Ft. Worth Airport about 4:00 p.m. to pick up another passenger. Returned by 7:15 p.m. or so. This brought his flying time for that day to about 4 hours. He took off again about 7:25 p.m. in the 414. He crashed on takeoff about one half mile from end of the runway.

3.   Passengers

There were 11 passengers onboard: 2 adult males; 1 adult female; 1 teenage male; 5 preteenage male children and 2 preteenage female children.

4.   Wreckage/Aircraft Damage

4.1   Description of Site

The crash site was about 1/2 mile from the runway and the crash path was through a moderately wooded area on a heading of about 320°. The ground at the impact area was sandy loom and had a slight downhill slope away from the direction of aircraft travel. The initial impact was to a tree limb about 29 feet above the ground. Other trees were struck before the airplane struck the ground about 135 feet from tree where the initial strike occurred. The airframe left a shallow ground scar about 42 feet in length. The scar indicated that the airplane was very near wings level with a slight noseup pitch attitude. The main fuselage wreckage came to rest and a heading of 340°.

4.2   Damage to the aircraft

The main wreckage consisted of the fuselage 3/4 of the left wing, including the No. 1 engine, which was still attached to the fuselage, and the vertical tail which had burned and had fallen away from the fuselage. The nose cone was still intact but had suffered some thermal damage. The cockpit and cabin area had been burned out along with the top and most of the cabin sidewalls. All other parts of airframe were shed during the crash sequence through the trees.

The seats were examined to determine damage, position and belt usage. Most of the steel tubular structure of the cockpit seats were recovered, none of which exhibited any impact damage. Neither seat position could be determined because of the extreme thermal damage. No seatbelt material survived the fire, but the buckle hardware did survive. This hardware indicated that the pilots shoulder harness and lapbelts were fastened during the fire. The copilot shoulder harness and lapbelts were unfastened during the fire.

There were five seats in the cabin. The two which were directly behind the cockpit seats were aft facing units. The unit on the left was found outside the cabin just forward of the left wing. It appeared that it had been moved there after having burned in position inside the cabin. Its inboard legs and floor level fore to aft structural member was separated from the seat pan framework. Its outboard forward leg had separated at its jucture with the floor level structural member. Bending was noted where the forward outboard leg was welded to the seat pan structure. The bending indicated a forward and down load on the seat pan. The lapbelt hardware found at this position showed the buckle was unfastened during the fire.

The seat unit on the right side of the cabin was securely attached to the floor track. All four legs exhibited bending but no fracture. The bending allowed the seat pan to move forward about 3 inches and downward about 1 inch at the forward end. No lapbelt hardware was found at this position.

Both of the above seats were aft facing. Their positions in the cabin were measured from the aft end of their respectively floor tracks to the back edge of their rear seat legs. This measurement for the left one was 9 inches; the right one was 10.75 inches.

Facing the above seats were two forward facing seat units. The unit on the right showed the same bending as the unit in front of it except the bending was in the opposite direction. This seat remained secured to the floor track. The position of this seat was measured as 9.50 inches from the front edge of the forward leg to the front of the seat track. The lapbelt hardware showed the buckle was fastened during the fire.

The left forward facing seat was positioned aft of the airstair door. It position was measured as 6 inches from the rear leg to the rear of the floor track. This seat was securely attached to its floor track. No damage was noted on the seat frame. No lapbelt buckle was found.

The fifth seat was a combination passenger seat potty chair. It is normally constructed of plywood and sheet metal and is positioned in the right aft part of the cabin. Fire had completely destroyed this seat. No lapbelt hardware was found at this position.

None of the seat tracks in the cabin exhibited impact damage.

A burned part of the right overwing exit was still in its fuselage exit frame. Part of the airstair door was still in the closed position. Its latching hardware was badly burned.

5.   Medical and Pathological

5.1   Injury Table

	Cockpit Crew	Passengers	Other	Total
Fatal	1	11	0	12
Serious	0	0	0	0
Minor	0	0	0	0
None	0	0	0	0
Total	1	11	0	12

5.2   Fatal Injuries

The pilot, Don Burmeister, was found laying in front of the copilot seat. His injuries were:

1.   Thermal burns of head, trunk, and extremities with pugilistic pose, charring of skin, and heat injury of internal organs.

2.   Smoke inhalation with:

   a.   Searing of upper airways.
   b.   Soot in airways

3.   No fractures of intact bones.

4.   No other injuries

Toxicology:

Blood: Alcohol - negative
             ABN drug screen - negative
             Alkaline drug screen - negative
             Cyanide - 6.6 mg/L. cyanide
             Carbon monoxide - 14% saturation
             Narcotics - negative by RIA
Urine: Alcohol - 0.02% ethanol
             Narcotics - negative by RIA

Keith Green was found sitting in the copilot seat. His injuries were:

1.   Thermal burns of head, trunk, and extremities with pugilistic pose, charring of skin, and heat injury of internal organs.

2.   Smoke inhalation with:

    a.   Searing of upper airways.
    b.   Soot in airways

3.   No fractures of intact bones

4.   Focal perihilar hemorrhage in spleen.

5.   No other injuries.

Toxicology:

Blood: Alcohol - negative
             ABN drug screen - negative
             Alkaline drug screen - negative
             Cyanide - 1.1 mg/L. cyanide
             Carbon monoxide - 24% saturation
             Narcotics - negative by RIA
Urine: Narcotics - negative by RIA

Chet Allen Hysell was found in the left front cabin seat. His injuries were:

1.   Thermal burns of head, trunk, and extremities with pugilistic pose, charring of skin, and heat injury of internal organs.

2.   Smoke inhalation with:

    a.   Searing of upper airways.
    b.   Soot in airways

3.   No fractures of intact bones

4.   No other injuries.

Toxicology:

Blood: Alcohol - negative
            ABN drug screen - negative
            Alkaline drug screen - negative
            Cyanide - 1.9 mg/L. cyanide
            Carbon monoxide - 35% saturation
            Narcotics - negative by RIA
Urine: Narcotics - negative by RIA

Josaiah Green was found on the floor just aft of the left front cabin seat. His injuries were:

1.   Thermal burns of head, trunk, and extremities with pugilistic pose, charring of skin, and heat injury of internal organs.

2.   Smoke inhalation with:

    a.   Searing of upper airways.
    b.   Soot in airways

3.   No fractures of intact bones

4.   No other injuries.

Toxicology:

Blood: Alcohol - negative
            ABN drug screen - negative
            Alkaline drug screen - negative
            Cyanide - 1.0 n g/L. cyanide
            Carbon monoxide - 36% saturation
            Narcotics - negative by RIA
Urine: Narcotics - negative by RIA

Timothy Neil Smalley was found in the right front cabin seat. His injuries were:

1.   Thermal burns of head, trunk, and extremities with pugilistic pose, charring of skin, and heat injury of internal organs.

2.   Smoke inhalation with:

    a.   Searing of upper airways.
    b.   Soot in airways

3.   No fractures of intact bones

4.   No other injuries.

Toxicology:

Blood: Alcohol - 0.01% ethanol
ABN drug screen - negative
Alkaline drug screen - negative
Cyanide - 0.7 mg/L. cyanide
Carbon monoxide - 50 % saturation
Narcotics - negative by RIA

Vitreous: Alcohol - negative

Urine: Narcotics - negative by RIA
Alcohol - negative

Daniel Henry Smalley was found in the right front cabin seat. His injuries were:

1.   Thermal burns of head, trunk, and extremities with pugilistic pose, charring of skin, and heat injury of internal organs.

2.   Smoke inhalation with:

    a.   Searing of upper airways.
    b.   Soot in airways

3.   No fractures of intact bones

4.   No other injuries.

Toxicology:

Blood (caked):   Alcohol - negative
ABN drug screen - negative
Alkaline drug screen - negative
Cyanide - 5.0 mg/kg. caked blood.
Carbon monoxide - sample unsuitable for analysis.
Narcotics - negative by RIA

James D. Smalley was found in either the right or left forward facing cabin seats. His injuries were:

1.   Thermal burns of head, trunk, and extremities with pugilistic pose, charring of skin, and heat injury of internal organs.

2.   Smoke inhalation with:

    a.   Searing of upper airways.
    b.   Soot in airways

3.   No fractures of intact bones

4.   No other injuries.

QUALITY CONTROL CHECK

Toxicology:

Blood: Alcohol - negative
               ABN drug screen - negative
               Alkaline drug screen - quantity not sufficient
               Cyanide - quantity not sufficient
               Carbon monoxide - 21% saturation
               Narcotics - negative by RIA
Urine: Narcotics - negative by RIA

John Daniel Smalley was found in either the right or left forward facing seats. His injuries were:

1. Thermal burns of head, trunk, and extremities with pugilistic pose, charring of skin, and heat injury of internal organs.

2. Smoke inhalation with:

    a. Searing of upper airways.
    b. Soot in airways

3. No fractures of intact bones

4. No other injuries.

Toxicology:

Blood: Alcohol - negative
               ABN drug screen - negative
               Alkaline drug screen - quantity not sufficient
               Cyanide - 0.3 mg/L. cyanide
               Carbon monoxide - 42% saturation
               Narcotics - negative by RIA

Bethany Green was found in the aisleway forward and inboard of the right forward facing cabin seat. His injuries were:

1. Thermal burns of head, trunk, and extremities with pugilistic pose, charring of skin, and heat injury of internal organs.

2. Smoke inhalation with searing of upper airways.

3. No fractures of intact bones

4. No other injuries.

Toxicology:

Blood (caked):   Alcohol - unsuitable
                      ABN drug screen - negative
                      Alkaline drug screen - negative
                      Cyanide - 1.0 mg/kg. caked blood.
                      Carbon monoxide - sample unsuitable for analysis.
                      Narcotics - negative by RIA

Deidre Lynn Smalley was found in the aisleway between the potty seat and the airstair door. Her injuries were:

1. Thermal burns of head, trunk, and extremities with pugilistic pose, charring of skin, and heat injury of internal organs.

2. Smoke inhalation with:

   a. Searing of upper airways.
   b. Soot in airways

3. No fractures of intact bones

4. Heat fracture of right leg.

5. Focal perihilar hemorrhage in right kidney.

6. No other injuries.

Toxicology:

Blood: Alcohol - negative
ABN drug screen - negative
Alkaline drug screen - negative
Cyanide - 2.8 mg/L. cyanide
Carbon monoxide - 29% saturation
Narcotics - negative by RIA
Urine: Narcotics - negative by RIA

Katherine Elizabeth Smalley was found in the aisleway between the two forward facing cabin seats. Her injuries were:

1. Thermal burns of head, trunk, and extremities with pugilistic pose, charring of skin, and heat injury of internal organs.

2. Smoke inhalation with:

   a. Searing of upper airways.
   b. Soot in airways

3. No fractures of intact bones

4. No other injuries.

Toxicology:

Blood: Alcohol - quantity not sufficient
ABN drug screen - 10 mg/L. phenobarbital
Alkaline drug screen - quantity not sufficient
Cyanide - 0.1 mg/L. cyanide
Carbon monoxide - 35% saturation
Narcotics - negative by RIA
Urine: Narcotics - negative by RIA
Bile: Alcohol - 0.02% ethanol

Chapter 30: Keith Green   321

John Charles Smalley was found in the aisleway inboard of the airstair door. His injuries were:

1. Thermal burns of head, trunk, and extremities with pugilistic pose, charring of skin, and heat injury of internal organs.

2. Smoke inhalation with:

    a. Searing of upper airways.
    b. Soot in airways

3. No fractures of intact bones

4. No other injuries.

Toxicology:

Blood: Alcohol - negative
        ABN drug screen - negative
        Alkaline drug screen - negative
        Cyanide - 1.3 mg/L. cyanide
        Carbon monoxide - 21% saturation
        Narcotics - negative by RIA
Urine: Narcotics - negative by RIA

6. Crash/Fire/Rescue (CFR) Response

    Not a factor.

The crash was observed by some of the employee/residents of Last Day Ministries but by the time they reached the scene the fire prevented any effective rescue effort.

Gale Braden
Human Factors Specialist

History of Flight

On 7-28-82, at 1922 CDT, a Robertson STOL Equipped Cessna 414, N110VM, crashed into a densely wooded area shortly after takeoff from a private airstrip near Lindale, TX. The aircraft, owned by William D. Jenkins (dba Junk Air) and leased to the Last Days Ministries, was departing on a local sightseeing flight. There was no flight plan filed and visual meteorological conditions prevailed at the accident site. The commercial pilot and all 11 passengers received fatal injuries and the aircraft was destroyed during impact and the postcrash fire.

The purpose of the flight was to show some visitors the Last Days Ministries properties from the air. According to witnesses, the pilot returned to the Ministries airstrip from a flight in a Cessna 172 to Dallas at approximately 1915. Immediately upon his return the pilot loaded his awaiting passengers into the accident aircraft, started the engines and conducted a runup.

About 1 minute later the aircraft was observed taking off on Runway 34. A pilot witness, who was located about 2000' down the runway stated that the aircraft rotated immediately in front of him. After liftoff, the aircraft started to climb in what was described as a flat nose high attitude. The pilot witness stated that as the aircraft passed him he noticed normal engine sounds and that the flaps were not extended. He further stated that the gear appeared to be down as long as he had the aircraft in sight. The witness stated that during the 20 to 30 second flight, the aircraft oscilated violently 2 or 3 times in the pitch axis. The maximum altitude gained throughout the flight was estimated between 75' and 100' AGL.

The aircraft settled into 30' trees, about 4,225 feet from the point of liftoff in a nose-high, wings level attitude. The postcrash fire errupted immediately after initial impact.

Injuries to Persons

All 12 people aboard the aircraft were fatally injured.

Damage to Aircraft

The aircraft was destroyed by impact forces and an intense postcrash fire.

Other Damage

Numerous trees were destroyed in the postcrash fire.

Crew Information

The PIC, Mr. Don Burmeister, held a commercial license with airplane single and multi-engine land and instrument ratings. He also held a current Class II medical certificate issued without limitations on 3-5-82. Mr. Burmeister had satisfied the biennial flight review requirements by upgrading his certificate on 6-9-82. On that date, he took a 2 hour check-ride to have a "centerline thrust only" restriction removed from his multi-engine rating.

A review of Mr. Burmeister's military and civilian logbooks indicated that he had a total of 758 hours flight time of which 44 were in the last 90 days with 4 hours in the previous 24 hours. He had logged 62 hours multi-engine time of which 59 were as copilot in the Cessna 414. This was to have been his first flight as pilot in command of the accident aircraft.

Investigation into Mr. Burmeister's training background revealed that he had received no formal training in the Cessna 414 and had only received 2 hours of instruction in conventional multi-engine aircraft. It was further revealed that he had never been required to perform weight and balance computations either in his military flying or on any FAA examinations or checkrides. It was also determined that the examiner who gave Mr. Burmeister his multi-engine checkride was refused renewal on his designation as an examiner on 7-10-82. The FAA stated that he was not renewed due to a history of incomplete or substandard checkrides.

NARRATIVE (Continued)

Aircraft Information
The aircraft was a Cessna 414, s/n 414-0590 which had been modified with a Robertson STOL kit in October of 1977. The purpose of the Robertson modification is to provide the aircraft with short field takeoff and landing ability and/or increase the aircraft's margin of safety in low speed flight regimes. The modification does not increase the certified gross weight of the aircraft nor does it change the allowable center of gravity envelope. The kit involves the installation of fowler flaps with drive system, aileron drooping mechanisms, a coordinated elevator trim spring and a rudder anti-servo.

The aircraft was properly certified and had received annual and 100 hour inspections on 5-28-82; 13.2 hours prior to the accident. On the same date as the annual inspection, the aircraft had suffered a gear collapse incident at Wichita Falls, TX. Only minor damage was sustained and the aircraft was repaired and placed back in service on 7-12-82.

A review of the recovered aircraft logbooks and maintenance records indicated that all applicable airworthiness directives had been complied with and there were no descrepancies noted which would have affected the airworthiness of the aircraft.

The weight and balance for the aircraft was calculated using the last recorded basic empty weight of the aircraft and know fuel weight. The aircraft had been topped off at Pounds Field in Tyler, TX, on 7-25-82. It had flown a total of 6 minutes from Tyler to the Last Days Ministries airstrip and remained parked until the date of the accident. Passenger weights were obtained from relatives and medical records. Passenger locations were obtained using information obtained from rescue personnel. There was no baggage aboard the aircraft. It was determined that the aircraft weighed 6795 2 pounds at takeoff with a corresponding center of gravity of 163.04 inches. The maximum allowable takeoff gross weight is 6350 pounds and the takeoff C.G. range is from 149.9 inches to 158.7 inches. The takeoff figures represent a 445.2 pound over gross condition with the C.G. 4.26 inches aft of the aft limit.

Meteorological Information
Tyler Tower, the closest reporting station, 1944 CDT observation, reported the weather as 10,000' scattered, 20,000' scattered, visibility 10 miles, temperature 90°F, dew point 72°F, winds calm, altimeter 29.93, TCU NW and NE - AC Accident Last Day Min. Density altitude would have been 2600'.

On the basis of the reported thunderstorms to the northwest through the northeast quadrants, overlays and radar photographs were ordered from the NWS radar facility at Longview, TX. The overlays and photographs indicate that there was no significant activity in the vicinity of the accident site.

Aerodrome and Ground Facilities
The Last Days Ministries Airstrip is a single runway private airstrip oriented 164°-344° with a field elevation of 595' MSL. The runway has a 3163' by 50' oiled iron ore base surface with a 601' dirt overrun at the north end. A windsock is mounted on the right side of the runway about 2000' from the head of Runway 34.

CONTINUED....

ADDITIONAL PERSONS PARTICIPATING IN THIS INVESTIGATION - Name, Address, and affiliation

FAA - Randy Brooks, Shreveport, LA

INVESTIGATED BY - SIGNATURE	AGENCY	DATE
Warren V. Wandel, ASI	Fort Worth Field Office-NTSB	5-31-83
TSB Form 6120.4F(1/82)	- 44 -	

Aerodrome and Ground Facilities Continued

During the investigation it was determined that a military low level VR route crossed the centerline of the runway about 1/2 mile north of the departure end. A check of the military usage schedule indicated that the route was not active at the time of the accident.

Wreckage

The aircraft crashed in a densely wooded area about 4225 feet north of the liftoff point and slightly left of the runway heading. It hit the first tree at the 29 foot level in a wings level, 17° nose high attitude. The flight path angle was about 140 down. These angles are based on impact marks on the wreckage and measurements taken on-scene. After initial impact with the trees, the aircraft continued descending and impacted the ground in a level attitude 135.5' from the initial impact point. After principal impact, the aircraft slid 12.2' and came to rest on a heading of about 340°

On initial impact with the trees the horizontal stabilizers and elevators separated from the tail. Early in the accident sequence, both main tip fuel tanks separated and split open allowing fuel to spray along the wreckage path. The right wing separated at the root when it struck a 26" tree about 110' from the initial impact point. The left wing remained attached throughout the impact sequence, despite hitting several large trees. The left engine remained attached to the wing while the right engine separated at the mounts and came to rest next to the right side of the fuselage. Both propellers sheared off of the engines at the flanges. Numerous cut branches and slash marks through tree trunks were found along both sides of the initial wreckage path. The length of these consistently measured around 11.25 inches. Based on required takeoff RPM, these measurements equate to a ground speed of 76 knots. Evidence indicated that the postcrash fire started immediately after fuel tank separation.

Examination of the airframe revealed control continuity from the cockpit back to the tail control surfaces. The breaks in the elevator cables appeared to be overload type breaks consistent with elevator separation. The rudder cables and rudder trim cables were intact. Continuity was established to the left aileron and the breaks in the right aileron cables appeared to be overload. Both elevator balance weights were accounted for. Trim settings and instrument readings could not be obtained due to the level of damage caused by the fire.

Examination of the flap drive system indicated that the flaps were in transit down from 0° to 10° down. The landing gear drive train indicated that the gear had cycled more than 50% up. The elevator trim spring was found in place in what appeared to be a neutral position.

The fuselage was destroyed by fire, however, with the exception of one tree strike along the right nose, it appeared to have survived the impact intact. There was very little horizontal crush except localized tree strikes on the wings. About 4 to 6 inches of vertical crush was noted on the bottom and the floor. Both the left main cabin door and the right emergency exit window were found in place. Most of the cabin door latching mechanism had melted down, but the emergency exit opened freely and the window removed easily when it was examined.

Fire

An intense postcrash fire errupted early in the impact sequence when the tip tanks separated. This allowed fuel to spray forward along the wreckage path. Although the exact ignition source was not determined, there would have been several available during the sequence. Evidence indicates that there was an initial flash fire and then a sustained fire around the fuselage. No evidence was found of an in-flight fire.

Firefighting efforts were hampered by the dense forest surrounding the accident site. Eventually a path was cut through the woods and fire trucks were able to approach the wreckage. The trucks only carried water, therefore, the efforts were relatively ineffective on the aircraft fire.

Medical and Pathological Information

Autopsies and toxicology studies were ordered on all of the occupants. No debilitating pre-existing condition was found that would have affected the pilot's performance and there were no significant findings or the toxicology tests.

Survival Aspects

This was a survivable accident in the sense that the impact forces did not exceed the levels of human tolerance. This was confirmed in the post mortem examination of the occupants which showed that their cause of death was from thermal burns and smoke inhalation. No evidence of impact trauma was found on any of the victims. A complete human factors report is contained as Enclosure 10 of this report.

Tests and Research

Engine Teardown Examinations: Both engines were removed and torn down at the Teledyne Continental Facilities in Mobile, AL. in September of 1982: Left engine: This was a Teledyne-Continental TSIO-520-N, factory remanufactured engine, serial number 176226-N. The engine was very heavily fire damaged externally, however, it showed little internal fire damage. The crankshaft flange was cracked radially around the bolt holes. A cold compression check was made and the lowest compression noted was on #4 cylinder which was 62/"0. All of the drive train was intact and showed no abnormal wear patterns. All of the bearing races appeared clean and normal. The magnetos were found capable of producing a spark and all of the plugs had normal wear and soot patterns. Ths pistons all had normal burn patterns. The oil pump appeared normal. No mechanical malfunctions or material defects were noted which would have prevented the engine from operating normally.

Right Engine: This was a Teledyne-Continental TSIO-520-N, factory remanufactured engine, serial number 176123-71N. Like the left engine, it was extensively fire damaged. The crankshaft flange was cracked radially on the front and aft faces. No compression check was performed. The drive train was intact throughout the engine and showed no abnormal wear patterns. The bearing races appeared clean with normal wear patterns. The magnetos were not bench checked as they had melted down internally due to heat exposure. All of the plugs appeared normal, however, it was noticed that some of the plugs were newer than others. The oil pump was destroyed by the fire, however, the pump drive shaft was found intact. The pistons all appeared to have normal burn patterns as did the cylinder domes and valves. No discrepancies were noted which would have prevented the engine from operating normally.

Turbocharger Teardown Examinations: Both turbochargers were disassembled in August of 1982. No discrepancies were noted with one exception. On the left turbocharger exhaust plenum cracks were found in the area of the right outlet part. These cracks would not have affected the aircraft's performance in the accident environment. A full report of the turbocharger teardown is located at Enclosure 14 of this report.

Propeller Teardown Examinations: Both propellers were disassembled and examined at the same time as the engines were examined. The left propeller was found on the low pitch latch and the right propeller was found slightly off the low pitch stop. A complete report is contained as Enclosure 15 to this report.

Aircraft Performance Data: On the basis of the overweight and out of C.G. conditions known to have been present during the accident, research was undertaken to determine what the aircraft's flight characteristics would have been. It was determined that the Robertson modification does not change the flight characteristics in any way in a no (0°) flaps takeoff configuration. Therefore, standard Cessna 414 performance data was used. The takeoff ground roll for the actual gross weight was computed to be about 2400'. Witnesses stated that the aircraft became airborne after a 2000' ground run, therefore, it is apparent that the aircraft took off at less than the normal takeoff speed of 84 knots IAS.

A computer simulation was undertaken using a Cessna 421 simulator which had been reprogrammed to perform like a C-414 through a software change. Several simulated takeoffs were flown at takeoff gross weight and full authorized aft C.G. using varying liftoff speeds and pilot techniques. Due to a software limitation, the aft C.G. conditions could not be duplicated. During takeoffs where rotation speed was varied from 100 knots to 60 knots, the aircraft showed a tendency to overrotate to a 25° nose high attitude which required up to 25 pounds forward stick pressure to overcome. As the liftoff speed was lowered, the aircraft became extremely unstable in the pitch axis and demonstrated a tendency to porpoise. The aircraft would then go into pre-stall buffet and ultimately crash.

Additional Data

Wreckage Release: Due to litigation between the leasor, leasee and the insurance carrier the legal owner has not been identified. A wreckage release was mailed to the registered owner and has not been returned.

ELT: The aircraft was equipped with an ELT, however, it was destroyed in the fire.

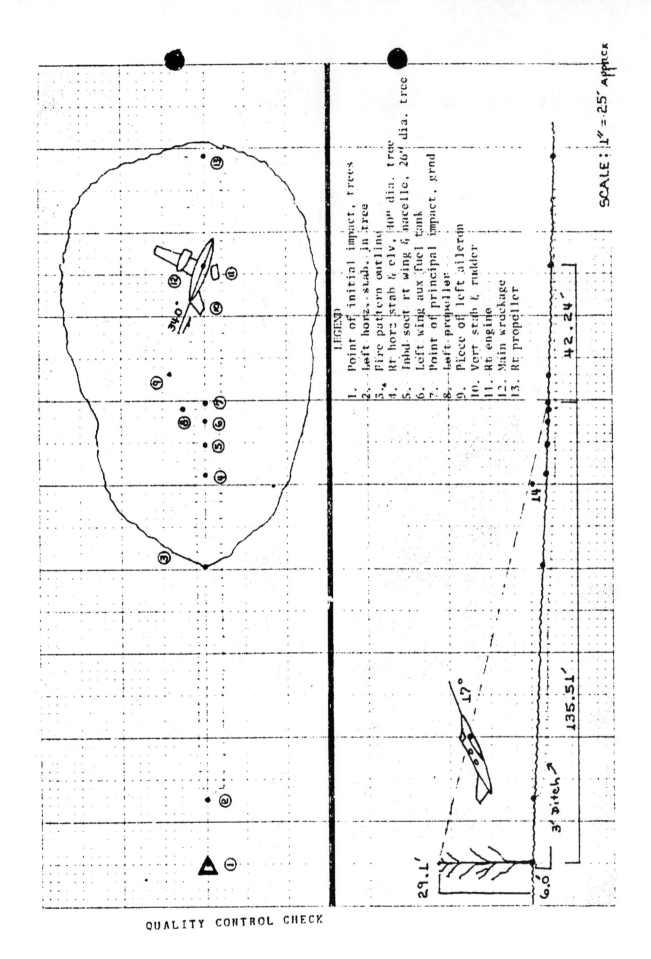

LEGEND

1. Point of initial impact, trees
2. Left horiz. stab. in tree
3. Fire pattern outline
4. Rt horz stab & elv, 40" dia. tree
5. Inbd sect rt wing & nacelle, 26' dia. tree
6. Left wing aux fuel tank
7. Point of principal impact, grnd
8. Left propeller
9. Piece of left aileron
10. Vert stab & rudder
11. Rt engine
12. Main wreckage
13. Rt propeller

SCALE: 1" = 25' approx

QUALITY CONTROL CHECK

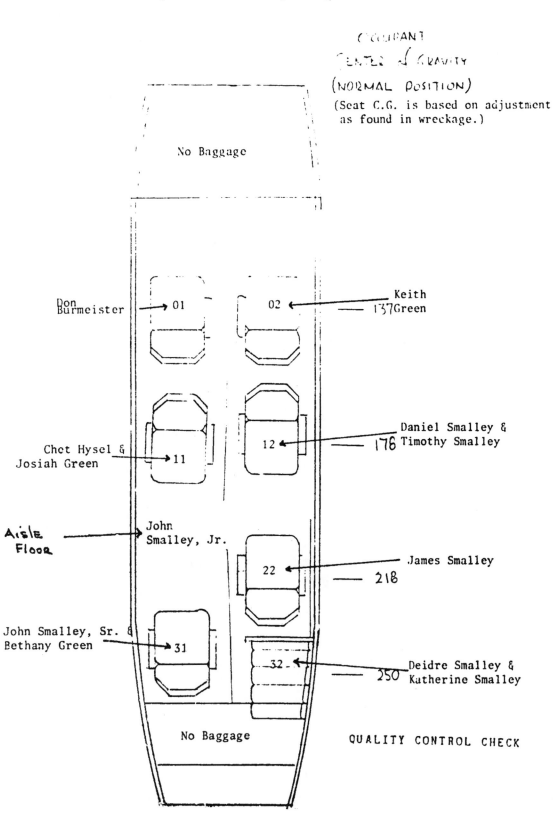

OCCUPANT
CENTER of GRAVITY
(NORMAL POSITION)
(Seat C.G. is based on adjustment as found in wreckage.)

No Baggage

Don Burmeister → 01

Keith Green → 02 — 137

Chet Hysel & Josiah Green → 11

Daniel Smalley & Timothy Smalley — 12 — 176

Aisle Floor → John Smalley, Jr.

James Smalley — 22 — 218

John Smalley, Sr. & Bethany Green → 31

Deidre Smalley & Katherine Smalley — 32 — 250

No Baggage

QUALITY CONTROL CHECK

Stan Rogers

June 2, 1983

When an in-flight fire erupts on an airplane it is always a very serious situation. Every pilot, whether flying a small aircraft as sole occupant or as part of an airline crew, should consider even a "small" fire to be an immediate emergency in an airplane. There are no other options.

Air Canada flight 797 originated in Houston, Texas, for a destination of Toronto, Canada, with a scheduled intermediate stop in Dallas-Fort Worth, Texas. The first signs of trouble on this flight were three circuit breakers that tripped, indicating something was wrong with the aft lavatory flush motor. The captain waited approximately eight minutes before trying to reset the breakers, at which time the reset proved to be unsuccessful. At about this same time a smoky odor apparently was detected in the aft of the plane, where the cabin attendant found the lavatory indeed to be filled with smoke. The cabin attendant discharged a fire extinguisher into the lavatory, although black smoke was still visible coming out of the lavatory's walls.

According to eyewitness accounts, the first officer was called to investigate the situation. He found too much smoke to see anything clearly so he returned to the cockpit to obtain a pair of goggles and then went back to inspect a second time. Upon returning to the cockpit the second time, the first officer advised the captain that it would be best to descend. It was around that time that the situation progressed from bad to worse as the airliner began developing serious electrical problems. The flight crew declared an emergency on the radio and a decision was made to land at the Cincinnati/Northern Kentucky International Airport, which is located south of Cincinnati, Ohio, in Covington, Kentucky.

During this emergency descent the passenger cabin began to fill with smoke. This smoke probably would have made its way to the cockpit very quickly, but the pilots were able to make a successful emergency landing on runway 27 at the airport. Shortly after the plane came to a stop the exit doors were opened to allow passenger evacuation. This action allowed the plane's fuselage to act as a chimney and a flash fire erupted. Because the blaze was so intense, the crash, fire and rescue personnel were not able to extinguish the fire and the flames gutted the aircraft's fuselage. Smoke inhalation and burns claimed the lives of 23 passengers who could not get out of the plane fast enough. No flight crew members were killed.

Stan Rogers was proud of his Canadian heritage. He was raised in rural Ontario, but spent his summers with his family in Nova Scotia. It was there that he was richly influenced by the way of life of the fishermen and the maritime environment. He was always surrounded and influenced by music during his childhood, and while still in his teens he started working as a rock bass guitar player. Sometime later he embraced the acoustic guitar and folk music, and began to write songs about the fishing industry people and experiences of his childhood. Later still, he would write about the other hard-working people of inland Canada. He was an avid reader who researched his songs diligently, and frequently he went out to visit with the people who later would become the essential element in his songs. In a sense, he gave a voice to people all across Canada by eloquently portraying their true lives in melodic poetry.

Rogers was a big man who stood 6 feet, 4 inches tall. He had a rich baritone voice that could just as easily mesmerize the listener as it could rumble the listener's seat. His work went a long way in helping to establish a national identity for working class Canadians and Canadian songwriting. He was traveling home from the Kerrville Folk Festival in Kerrville, Texas when he lost his life on the ill-fated Air Canada flight 797. In May 1984 he was posthumously awarded the DiplÙme d'Honneur by the Canadian Conference of the Arts. Garnet Rogers, Stan Rogers' younger brother who toured with him for ten years, continues to perform and carries the torch for Canadian folk music with the same great humanity as his big brother. Today there is a Stan Rogers Folk Festival that is held every year in Nova Scotia, around the time of Canada Day.

It should be noted that this accident was the catalyst for introducing and establishing the term "Crew Resource Management" (CRM) into the professional flight environment. Although NASA had originated the CRM concept as early as 1979, the aviation industry learned much about how flight crews interact with each other as a direct result of the studies that were done in the course of analyzing this accident. To this day, CRM is a significant part of the airline pilot and flight attendant initial and recurrent training regimen. The skies are safer because flight crews are now better trained in how to communicate and work together as a team. From the loss of life and the mistakes that were made during this accident, there came a greater good.

Author

Aircraft addenda:

Common names: DC-9 (This was a DC-9-32 variant.)
Manufacturer: McDonnell Douglas
First flight of prototype: 1965
Air Carrier for this flight: Air Canada
Registration number for this airplane: C-FTLU
Serial number for this airplane: 47196-278
Year built for this airplane: 1968
Crew on board this flight: 5
Passengers on board this flight: 41
Length: 119 feet, 3 inches
Wingspan: 93 feet, 5 inches
Engines: (2) Pratt & Whitney, JT8D-7, jet turbofan
Thrust: 14,000 lbs. (each)
Empty weight (approximate): 57,190 lbs.
Maximum take-off weight: 121,000 lbs.
Service ceiling (approximate): 45,000 ft.
Fuel capacity: 3,682 gal.
Cruising speed: 575 mph

* The above photo represents the type of aircraft and not necessarily the exact model involved in the accident.

Personal addenda:

Stanley Allison Rogers (Stan Rogers): Canadian folk singer, songwriter, guitar player
b. November 29, 1949: Hamilton, Ontario, Canada
d. June 2, 1983: Covington, Kentucky
Cremated. Stan Rogers' ashes were spread at Cole Harbor on the northeastern shore of Nova Scotia.
Note: Rogers' death certificate lists his place of death as Hebron, Kentucky. The Cincinnati/Northern Kentucky International Airport is located in Covington, Kentucky.

NTSB Identification: **DCA83AA028**. The docket is stored on NTSB microfiche number **20436A**.

Scheduled 14 CFR 129 operation of AIR CANADA
Accident occurred JUN-02-83 at COVINGTON, KY
Aircraft: DOUGLAS DC-9-32, registration: CFTLU
Injuries: 23 Fatal, 3 Serious, 13 Minor, 7 Uninjured.

AT ABOUT 1903 EDT, WHILE ENROUTE AT FL 330, THE CABIN CREW DISCOVERED A
FIRE IN THE AFT LAVATORY. AFTER CONTACTING ATC & DECLARING AN
EMERGENCY, THE FLT CREW MADE AN EMERGENCY DESCENT & ATC VECTORED
THE ACFT TO THE GREATER CINCINNATI INTL ARPT. AT 1920, THE ACFT WAS
LANDED ON RWY 27L. AS THE AIRCREW STOPPED THE PLANE, FIRE DEPT
PLERSONNEL MOVED IN PLACE & BEGAN FIREFIGHTING OPERATIONS. ALSO, AS THE
PLANE STOPPED, THE OCCUPANTS BEGAN EVACUATIONS THE ACFT. ABOUT 60 TO 90
SEC AFTER THE EXITS WERE OPENED, A FLASH FIRE ENVELOPED THE INTERIOR OF
THE ACFT. 23 PASSENGERS WERE UNABLE TO EXIT THE ACFT & DIED IN THE FIRE.
AN INVESTIGATION REVEALED THAT 3 FLUSH MOTOR CIRCUIT BREAKERS HAD
POPPED ABOUT 11 MIN BEFORE SMOKE WAS DETECTED. THE CAPTAIN
MISCONSTRUED REPORTS THAT THE FIRE WAS ABATING WHEN HE RECEIVED
CONFLICTING FIRE PROGRESS REPORTS. SUBSEQUENTLY, HE LANDED AT THE
CINCINNATI INTL ARPT RATHER THAN AT LOUISVILLE WHICH WOULD HAVE
ALLOWED HIM TO LAND 3 TO 5 MIN SOONER. WET TOWELS & BREATHING THRU
CLOTHING AIDED SURVIVAL. FIRE SOURCE UNK.

Probable Cause

Misc eqpt/furnishings,lavatories..Fire
Safety advisory..Conflicting..Other crewmember
Unsafe/hazardous condition..Not understood..Pilot in command

Contributing Factors

Fuselage,cabin..Smoke
Fuselage,crew compartment..Smoke
Flight to alternate destination..Delayed..no person specified

Kyu Sakamoto

August 12, 1985

Professional pilots of our modern age go to work dressed in uniforms that look much like business suits. Long gone are the days when a captain and/or first officer would get out of a passenger airplane with a rag hanging out of one back pants pocket and a wrench sticking out of the other. Pilots of airliners depend upon the expertise of professional aircraft mechanics to handle maintenance concerns. The only way a pilot would know that an item has been fixed, and fixed properly in most cases, is to read a resolution in the aircraft's maintenance log. The pilot does not supervise the work that has been done. Trust among professionals is normal and essential in today's aviation industry and it could be said theoretically that, as long as all the necessary maintenance is performed and performed correctly, nearly every production airplane ever built could be airworthy for many years to come.

Although rare, there are times when that professional trust is broken. Sometimes a repair is made that is not subject to double check by supporting maintenance personnel. Sometimes the faulty repair is not realized as a problem until time has passed and the repair begins to fail as a result of long term use. This insidious degradation is a true concern for a pilot. Such a problem cannot be identified through a pre-flight check of the aircraft. This is a problem that can unfortunately manifest itself at the worst possible time - while airborne. It catches the pilot unaware. It leaves the pilot helpless to control the machine that he or she has trustingly and skillfully launched into the air. It truly is a nightmare, not only for the pilot, but also for each individual passenger who has boarded the airplane with the trust, desire and expectation to arrive safely at an intended destination.

This story of this accident is one such nightmare. To this day, it is the worst disaster in aviation history to involve only a solitary airplane. It is the second worst accident in terms of fatalities in all of aviation (not including the deliberate criminal acts of September 11, 2001), with loss of life slightly less than the collision between two Boeing 747 Jumbo jets at Tenerife on a foggy runway in the Canary Islands in 1977, where 583 people died. The pilots of the Tenerife collision did not see each other until the last seconds, and the passengers were assuredly unaware. In contrast, the pilots involved in the accident described in this chapter actually fought hard for over 30 minutes to save the airplane, but fate was not on their side. Five hundred twenty people died in this crash, but not before they had time to write hurried farewell notes to their families and loved ones. Kyu Sakamoto, a Japanese recording and performing artist, was one of the passengers killed. Only four people survived.

The story begins back in 1978 in Osaka, Japan, where a greater than normal nose-high attitude during a landing caused a hard tail-strike, which damaged the rear fuselage and rear pressure bulkhead in this particular Japan Air Lines (JAL) Boeing 747-100SR (Short Range) Jumbo jet. Damage to the airplane was apparent at the time and JAL contracted with the Boeing factory to have the repair work done. The repair was finished, but apparently unknown to anyone the Boeing workers had constructed an improper repair joint to the Jumbo jet's aft pressure bulkhead. Without any suspicion or questions after the repair was made, the airplane was put back into service. In order to understand this accident, one must first look at what a pressure bulkhead is and how it affects the airplane.

In its simplest definition, the fuselage of an airliner is a pressurized aluminum can. Each time a plane of this type climbs to a high altitude it is pressurized since, at 25,000 feet and above, the available oxygen from the reduced atmospheric pressure is not enough to sustain human life. For this reason emergency oxygen masks are installed above passenger seats. They are there in case of a pressurization failure, which is itself a rare event. Passengers generally never realize the cabin is being pressurized because the process is gradual as the plane ascends. Additionally, at higher flight altitudes, the outside air temperature is brutally cold, somewhere between minus 60 to 70 degrees Fahrenheit. Each time an airliner descends, the pressurization must be adjusted so it will be acclimated with the atmospheric pressure at the destination airport. Otherwise the plane's cabin pressure would remain out-of-sync with the pressure surrounding it. This process of pressurizing and de-pressurizing is called a pressure cycle.

With each pressure cycle, the plane's fuselage is subject to expansion and contraction. Repeated pressure cycles conducted over a long period of time can lead to metal fatigue, which will usually find the weakest link in the structure. In the case of this airplane, the weak link was the improper repair splicing to the rear pressure bulkhead (Figure 32-1). Undetected fatigue cracks eventually propagated to the point of catastrophic failure. Given enough time and pressure cycles, the significantly reduced strength of the rear cone of the 747 became like a ticking bomb, and the only place it could go off was in the air during a pressurized flight. Everyone was caught unaware when it happened. Information from the flight data recorder and cockpit voice recorder helped investigators to fill in the blanks. Because the accident occurred in a foreign country, under foreign ownership, the actual accident report could not be located. Nonetheless, many details of the flight are known.

On August 12, 1985, JAL flight number 123 took off at 6:12 p.m. local time from Haneda International Airport, just south of Tokyo, for a relatively short flight to Osaka. At 6:24 p.m., while climbing through an altitude of 23,900 feet at a speed of nearly 350mph, an unusual vibration was detected. Suddenly a loud noise was heard and a strong force raised the nose of the Boeing 747 while the crew began experiencing control problems. Two minutes later, the flight control hydraulic pressure had dropped, leaving all of the aileron, elevator and rudder controls inoperative. The plane was then wandering with rolling and oscillating movements and ultimately began to descend. The pilots tried desperately to control the crippled plane and actually were able to partially control the 747 for some 32 minutes by using engine thrust. However, after a lengthy series of gyrating turns, climbs and descents, at around 6:56 p.m. the helpless airplane grazed against a tree covered ridge. It then continued and struck another ridge at approximately 5,400 feet elevation, on Mount Osutaka, in Gunma Prefecture, where it disintegrated.

The investigation into the cause of the airplane's crash found that the deterioration of flight characteristics and loss of primary flight controls were due to the rupture of the aft pressure bulkhead, which either blew off or severed the plane's tail control surfaces, vertical fin and all four of the hydraulic flight control systems. Indeed, a Japanese Navy Destroyer found a 15-foot section of the plane's vertical stabilizer floating in Sagami Bay. Several other tail assembly pieces were eventually found in the bay as well. Not only did the flight crew not see the failure coming, but once it happened they never really had a good chance of saving the airplane or the passengers on board. Of the four survivors, one was an off-duty flight attendant who recalled a sudden decompression in the cabin, which started in the rear of the airplane and tore off the ceiling tiles from the rear toilets. Another survivor was a small child. It is a miracle that anyone survived at all.

Japanese recording artist Kyu Sakamoto made his show business debut in 1960. His biggest hit came in 1961 with the release of a melodic, yet haunting love song titled, "Ue-o Muite Aruko." Roughly translated, this title means "I look up when I walk." The heartbroken person that the song portrays is looking up so tears won't drop from his eyes. The music was composed by Hachidai Nakamura and the words were written by Rokusuki Ei. It is said that songwriter Rokusuki composed the words to the song when the Japanese actress Meiko Nakamura broke his heart. Sakamoto's smooth voice was the perfect match and, once recorded, the song was destined for the top.

Finding success within his own country seemed natural for Sakamoto, but bigger surprises were to come. When Capitol Records executives in the United States listened to the song, they loved it and were sure that the American public would love it also. The problem for them was the artist's heritage and the foreign language in which the song was recorded. How were they going to promote an artist whose country had perpetrated a sneak-attack bombing on Pearl Harbor only 20 years before? The terrible memories of World War II were still fresh in the minds of many Americans in the early 1960s. To make matters worse, no one in America could even pronounce the title of the song as it was known.

Then the executives at Capitol got an idea and took a chance. They changed the name of the song to something that everyone on every main street could relate to: food. The title of the song became "Sukiyaki" even though neither the word itself, nor any mention of food, is within the lyrics. Newsweek magazine at the time compared the name change to releasing Andy Williams' "Moon River" in Japan and calling it "Beef Stew." Nevertheless, the gamble worked and eventually the easily pronounceable and recognizable "Sukiyaki" became a hit. The Capitol Records executives had been right about main street America loving this song.

The final rung in the ladder of success for Sakamoto's mournful love ballad came on June 15, 1963 when "Sukiyaki" bumped Leslie Gore's "It's My Party" to become number 1 on Billboard's chart. Against all odds, and even with an unintelligible language for American teenagers, this song not only made it to the top, but it stayed there for three weeks. Even more, "Sukiyaki" not only became the first song in Billboard's history to be sung in a foreign language to top the hot 100, it remains to this day the only Japanese hit song to reach number 1 in the United States.

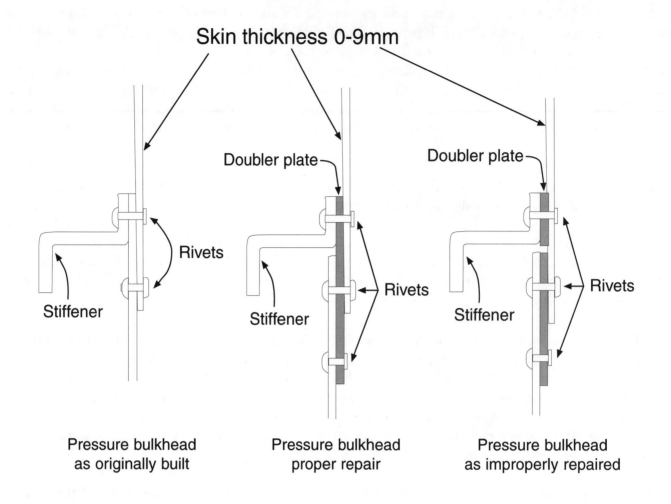

Figure 32-1

TWA

Aircraft addenda:

Common names: Jumbo jet, 747, 747SR, Boeing 747
Manufacturer: Boeing Aircraft Company
First flight of type: February 9, 1969
Note: There was no prototype for this airplane. Serial number 1 was the first 747 Jumbo Jet to leave the Boeing production line.
Air Carrier for this flight: Japan Air Lines (JAL)
Registration number for this airplane: JA-8119
Serial number for this airplane: 20783/230
Year built for this airplane: 1973 (This was the third of 29 total 747-100SRs built.)
Crew on board this flight: 15
Passengers on board this flight: 509
Length: 231 feet, 10 inches
Wingspan: 195 feet, 8 inches
Engines: (4) Pratt & Whitney, JT-9D-7A, jet turbofan
Note: Approximately one gallon of fuel is burned every four seconds in this engine. Thus, with 4 engines, the Boeing 747 carries more fuel than any other civil aircraft.
Thrust: 46,500 lbs. (each)
Empty weight (approximate): 345,000 lbs.
Gross weight: 735,000 lbs.
Service ceiling: 50,000 ft.
Fuel capacity: 48,445 gal.
Cruising speed: 555 mph.

* The above photo represents the type of aircraft and not necessarily the exact model involved in the accident.

Personal addenda:

Hisashi Oshima (Kyu Sakamoto, Kyu Chan): Japanese singer
Note: Kyu is pronounced 'Cue.'
b. November 10, 1941: Kawasaki City, Kanagawa Prefecture
d. August 12, 1985: Near Ueno Village, 60 miles northwest of Tokyo, Japan
Cremated. Kyu Sakamoto's ashes rest at the Chokoku-ji Temple, of the Buddhist denomination of Soto Zen, in the Minato-ku ward of central Tokyo.
Note: A cenotaph has been erected at the foot of Mount Osutaka that displays the names of all 520 people who died on JAL Flight 123.

Ray Charles

October 19, 1985

Landing accidents are part of the risk one must accept when launching a flying machine into the air. As has been mentioned previously, the most dangerous times when flying an airplane are the take-off and the landing. If the take-off is the most vulnerable time for a flying machine, the landing is the second most vulnerable time. With any flight, to any destination, there are risk factors. The pilot has to weigh numerous factors during every flight. However, when flying conditions are less than ideal, the mental workload of the pilot becomes one of focus and concentration. It is the job of the pilot-in-command to reduce the number of risk factors on any flight as much as possible.

Airspeed control is a very big part of safely landing an airplane. Approaching to land with a faster than normal speed will result in a longer landing distance. "Flying by the numbers" must be the rule for any professional pilot. While the pilot of this particular flight was most likely on his target indicated airspeed for this instrument approach, other factors for the landing should have been considered. The wet runway certainly gave the landing a higher risk. A slight tailwind may have been another factor. While anti-lock brakes became the newest and best innovation in automobiles in the late 1980s, anti-lock brake technology had been developed and was installed on heavy transport aircraft as early as the 1960s. On wet pavement, anti-lock brakes can be the difference between an accident and a successful stop. However, this airplane was not equipped with an anti-lock brake system and this fact should have been another consideration for the pilot.

Among a pilot's repertoire of decisions is one which involves discontinuing a landing and executing what is known as a rejected landing, or "go around." The go around is sometimes the wisest and safest decision a pilot can make, and every pilot should view each landing as though a go around is a possibility. The pilot for this flight was Gordon Smith. In his defense I will say that sometimes the decision window consists of only microseconds. In this miniscule timespan a pilot must either abort the landing and take action to go around, or commit to the landing roll. This exceedingly narrow window of time for decision-making is where the Monday-morning-quarterbacks love to dwell. Any pilot can be criticized after the fact for making a bad decision, but none of us can know how we would react to the same scenario until we have actually experienced a similar situation.

There is reason to suspect that the pilot lost sight of the runway briefly and this may have delayed his decision to place the landing gear tires on the runway. All reports and evidence obtained during this accident investigation did reveal that the airplane touched down at a considerable distance down the runway's usable length. This fact, coupled with the evidence of the plane's tires undergoing hydroplaning during the landing, leads one to believe that the pilots realized they were in trouble and tried desperately to stop the airplane's momentum. In the accident report, you will read the abbreviation "MLG." This stands for main landing gear. On board this airplane was the entertainer, Ray Charles. While it is reasonable to assume that Charles was shaken by the accident, he was apparently unhurt. No one was killed in the mishap.

Ray Charles is no stranger to airplanes and has always loved flying to his appearances. In fact, it is rumored that he would sometimes actually take the controls of his plane and fly by the sounds created by the old navigational aids, which indicated if the pilot was off to the left or right of the desired course by different tones. Given that Charles is blind, one would assume that the pilot kept close watch on him as he manipulated the controls. Ray Charles' first airplane was bought somewhere around the late 1950s to the early 1960s and was a used Cessna 310 that had the registration number N3657D. His pilot at the time was Tom McGarrity, a former United States Air Force veteran. After the success of his great song, "I Can't Stop Loving You," Charles purchased his second plane, which was a Martin 404 that he bought used in 1963 from American Airlines for $500,000 dollars. The third plane he owned was acquired in 1970, and this was the airplane involved in the accident. It was nicknamed the "Buzzard."

Ray Charles was not born blind, but rather he became blind as a result of glaucoma at age six. His parents had died by his early teens, and he learned to play many musical instruments at the St. Augustine School for the Deaf and Blind. He has worked as a professional musician since the middle of the 1940s. Charles has become a legend among legends. His list of awards would probably fill an entire book. I suspect that few individuals have been enshrined in as many Halls of Fame as Ray Charles. Some people believe that Ray Charles does not just sing soul music; he *is* the soul in soul music. Certainly Ray Charles is a musical treasure.

Origin Unknown

Aircraft addenda:

Common name: Viscount, VC-810
Manufacturer: Vickers Armstrong Aircraft, Ltd.
First flight of prototype: 1948 (for the 700 series)
Registration number for this airplane: N923RC (Charles' birth date and initials)
Serial number for this airplane: 320
Seats: Up to 70 as an airliner, but this particular airplane had custom seating.
Length: 85 feet, 8 inches
Wingspan: 93 feet, 8 inches
Engines: (4) Rolls-Royce Dart RDa7-525, four bladed, turboprop
Horsepower: 1990 hp (each)
Empty weight (approximate): 43,200 lbs.
Gross weight: 72,500 lbs.
Service ceiling: 29,000 ft
Range: 1,800 statute miles
Cruising speed: 350 mph

* The above photo represents the type of aircraft and not necessarily the exact model involved in the accident.

Personal addenda:

Ray Charles Robinson (Ray Charles): Singer, songwriter, musician
b. September 23, 1930: Albany, Georgia
Ray Charles continues to perform.

National Transportation Safety Board
PRELIMINARY REPORT
AVIATION

2 NTSB Accident/Incident No.	D C A 8 6 A A 0 0 1

3 Investigation By
1 [X] NTSB   2 [ ] FAA delegated

1 1 [X] Accident   2 [ ] Incident

4 I.C.A.O. Preliminary Report Submitted (NTSB only)
1 [ ] Yes   2 [X] No

5 Report Status
1 [X] Initial report   2 [ ] Preliminary Report

Location/Date

6 Nearest City/Place	7 State	8 Zip Code (First 5 Nos.)	9 Date (Nos. for M, D, Y)	10 Local time (24 hour clock)	11 Time Zone
Bloomington	IN	47401	10-19-85	1535	+5

Aircraft Information

12 Registration No.	13 Aircraft Manufacturer	14 Model/Series No.
N932RC N923RC	Vickers	Viscount VC-810

15 Type of Aircraft
1 [X] Airplane   3 [ ] Glider   5 [ ] Blimp/Dirigible   7 [ ] Gyroplane
2 [ ] Helicopter   4 [ ] Balloon   6 [ ] Ultralight   A [ ] Specify _____

16 Home Built
1 [ ] Yes   2 [X] No

Other Aircraft—Collision Between Aircraft

17 Registration No.	18 Aircraft Manufacturer	19 Model/Series No.
N/A	N/A	N/A

Accident Information

20 Aircraft Damage
1 [ ] None
2 [ ] Minor
3 [ ] Substantial
4 [X] Destroyed

21 Property Damage (Multiple entry)
1 [ ] None   6 [ ] Airport Facility
2 [ ] Residence   7 [ ] Trees
3 [ ] Residential area   8 [ ] Crops
4 [ ] Commercial Bldg.   9 [ ] Wires, Poles
5 [ ] Vehicle   10 [ ] Other property

22 Accident/Incident Phase of Operation
1 [ ] Standing   6 [ ] Descent
2 [ ] Taxi   7 [ ] Approach
3 [ ] Takeoff   8 [ ] Landing
4 [ ] Climb   9 [ ] Maneuvering
5 [ ] Cruise   10 [ ] Hover
A [ ] Specify

23 Injury Index (Most critical injury)
1 [ ] None
2 [ ] Minor
3 [ ] Serious
4 [ ] Fatal

Injury Summary	24 Fatal	25 Serious	26 Minor	27 None

Crew	A Name	B Address (City, State only)	C Certificate No.	D Injury Code	Passenger	A Name	B Injury Code
	Smith, Gordon F.,	2944 S. Versailles St., Springfield MO	85804	03	16		01
	Davies, Richard,	Rt 5 Box 845, Canyon Lake, TX 78130		01	10		00
					26 Total		

Injury Codes None—1   Minor—2   Serious—3   Fatal—4

Ground Personnel	A Name	B Injury Code

Operator Information

42 Name	43 Operator Designator Code	44 Doing Business as (dba)
Ray Charles Enterprises	N/A	Ray Charles Enterprises, Inc.

45 Street Address	46 City	47 State	48 Zip Code
2107 W. Washington Blvd.#200	Los Angeles	CA	90018

Type of Certificate(s) Held   49   None (Go to Block 53)

50 Air Carrier Operating Certificate (Check all applicable)
1 [ ] Flag carrier/domestic (121)   4 [ ] Large helicopter (127)
2 [ ] Supplemental   5 [ ] Commuter air carrier
3 [ ] All cargo (418)   6 [ ] On-demand air taxi

51 Operating Certificate
[ ] Other operator of large aircraft

52 Operator Certificate
1 [ ] Rotorcraft—external load operator (133)   2 [ ] Agricultural aircraft operator (137)

Regulation Flight Conducted Under

53
1 [XX] 14 CFR 91 (only)   4 [ ] 14 CFR 105   7 [ ] 14 CFR 127   10 [ ] 14 CFR 137   A [ ] Specify _____
2 [ ] 14 CFR 91D   5 [ ] 14 CFR 121   8 [ ] 14 CFR 133   11 [ ] 14 CFR 129
3 [ ] 14 CFR 103   6 [ ] 14 CFR 125   9 [ ] 14 CFR 135   (Foreign flag)

PRELIMINARY INFORMATION — SUBJECT TO CHANGE

NTSB Form 6120.19A (1-84) This form supersedes NTSB Form 6120.19 (Rev. 1-83)

Page 1

National Transportation Safety Board	NTSB Accident/Incident Number
PRELIMINARY REPORT **AVIATION** ACCIDENT/INCIDENT	D C A 8 6 A A 0 0 1

Type of Flight Operation Conducted

(Complete 54, 55, 56 ONLY if flight was a revenue operation conducted under 121, 125, 127, 129, 135)

54	55	56	
1 ☐ Scheduled	1 ☐ Domestic	1 ☐ Passenger	3 ☐ Passenger/cargo
2 ☐ Non-scheduled	2 ☐ International	2 ☐ Cargo	4 ☐ Mail contract ONLY

(Complete 57 ONLY if 54, 55, 56 not applicable)

57		
1 ☐ Personal	4 ☐ Executive/corporate	7 ☐ Other work use
2 ☐ Business	5 ☐ Aerial application	8 ☐ Public use 10 ☐ Positioning
3 ☐ Instructional *(Including air carrier training)*	6 ☐ Aerial observation	9 ☐ Ferry A Specify _____

Flight Plan/Itinerary

58 Flight Plan Filed

1 ☐ None   2 ☐ VFR   3 ☐ IFR   4 ☐ IFR/VFR   5 ☐ Company (VFR)   6 ☐ Military (VFR)

59 Itinerary—Last Departure Point	60 State	61 Airport I.D.	62 Destination *(If "local," mark X here 1 ☐)*	63 State	64 Airport I.D.
1 ☐ Same as accident/incident location Nearest city/place A _____			Nearest city/place A _____		

Weather Information

65 Source	67 Sky/Lowest Cloud Condition	68 Lowest Ceiling	69 Visibility (decimals)
1 ☐ Accident site (Pilot/witness)	1 ☐ Clear	1 ☐ None	1½ SM
2 X Weather Observation	2 ☐ Scattered	2 ☐ Broken	
Facility	3 ☐ Thin broken	3 X Overcast	**70 Temperature**
A Facility Identifier ___BMG___	4 ☐ Thin overcast	4 ☐ Obscured	66 °F
	5 X Partial obscuration		
66 Time of Weather Observation 2034 (local)	A 600 Ft. AGL	A 1,000 Ft. AGL	**71 Dew Point** 65 °F

72 Wind Direction	73 Wind Speed	74 Gusts	75 Altimeter	76 Weather Conditions (at accident site)	77 Precipitation
230 Degrees (Mag.)	05 Kts.	None Kts.	30.21 "Hg	1 ☐ VMC 2 X IMC	1 X Yes 2 ☐ No

Narrative

78 *(Brief resume of facts. The information shall not contain opinion, conjecture, or statements reflecting on the character or integrity of the persons involved.)*

The accident airplane, a Vickers Viscount (VC-810), N923RC, being operated under 14 CFR Part 91 rules (with full exemption from 14 CFR Part 125) departed Lexington, Kentucky (LXX) about 1450 c.s.t. with 26 passengers and entertainer Ray Charles aboard. All phases of the flight were normal until arriving at Bloomington Monroe County Airport from an ILS approach to runway 35. The weather at Bloomington (BMG) at the time of the accident, which was relayed to the airplane by Bloomington Tower (BMG), was sky -- partially obscurred, estimated ceiling -- 600 feet broken, 1,000 feet overcast, visibility -- 1 and 1/2 miles, moderate rain showers and fog, temperature -- 66 degrees, dew point -- 65 degrees F., winds -- 230 degrees at 5 knots, altimeter -- 30.21 inches Hg. Upon checking in with the Bloomington tower on final approach, the tower advised the airplane that the visibility had increased to 1 and 1/2 miles.

The copilot stated that the airplane touched down about 1,200 to 1,400 feet from the runway threshold and slightly left of the runway centerline. The captain called for and the copilot selected ground fine propeller pitch for aerodynamic braking. Normal braking was applied by both the PIC and the copilot with negative

(Please continue to next page.)

PRELIMINARY INFORMATION — SUBJECT TO CHANGE

National Transportation Safety Board

PRELIMINARY REPORT
AVIATION
ACCIDENT/INCIDENT

NTSB Accident/Incident Number

D C A 8 6 A A 0 0 1

Narrative (continued)

results. The airplane went off the upwind end of the runway and over a 25 foot embankment finally coming to rest in a field 320 feet from the upwind end of the runway. There was no fire. The airplane fuselage remained intact except for a full circumferential break and separation at fuselage station (F.S.) 262. The wing remained attached to the fuselage. All landing gear collapsed. All 16 propeller blades were bent aft. The captain received a lower vertibrae fracture and the copilot received minor injuries. Sixteen of the 26 passengers received minor injuries. The left forward entry stair was jammed in the up position. Entertainer Ray Charles was assisted from the airplane through the aft right exit door by his personal valet and a helper. Most of the passengers exited over the 6 over-wing exits.

The Van Buren Township Volunteer Fire Dept., located on the airport, responded to the accident in about 2 minutes and removed the captain from the airplane. The captain and passengers were transported to the Bloomington Hospital for examination and treatment.

Runway 17/35 at Bloomington is 150 feet wide and 5,200 long. Examination of the runway revealed tire marks associated with the tires of N923RC beginning about 2,400 feet and 2,800 feet from the upwind end of the runway for the left and right MLG tires, respectively. The footprint of the MLG tire marks on the runway placed the airplane about 25 feet left of the runway centerline at the point where the tire marks began. The two tires on the right MLG exhibited eliptical signatures of 'reverted rubber' which is characteristic of hydroplaning on wet runways. The two tires of the left MLG could not be examined on scene.

The flightcrew claimed no mechanical malfunction with the airplane; however, the copilot stated that about the time the airplane crossed the runway threshold, the PIC asked him if he still 'had the runway'. The copilot said that, to him, that meant that possibly the PIC's windscreen might have been fogged over, so he reached up and wipped his (the copilot's - RH side) windscreen clean and responded to the PIC that he still had the runway insight.

(Attach additional pages if necessary.)

Administrative Data

79 Notification From		80 Date (Nos. for M. D. Y)	81 Local Time (24 hour clock)	82 Time Zone
FAA (BMG-Tower)		10-19-85	1631 c.s.t	+5

83 FAA District Office/Coordinator	84 Other Federal Agencies Involved in Investigation			
FAA Hdqtrs ASF-100 R. Cook	1 ☐ FBI 2 ☐ USCG	3 ☐ DEA 4 ☐ DOD	5 ☐ Customs A Specify	None

Investigator(s) Assigned

85 Investigator-in-Charge	86 Form Preparation Date (Nos. for M. D, Y)	87 Form Receipt Date (For NTSB use only)
G. M. Dail	10-20-85	

88 Other NTSB Personnel Assigned

A	J. L. White	TE-20	D	G
B	E. F. Mudrowsky	TE-10	E	H
C	E. P. Wizniak	TE-20	F	I

PRELIMINARY INFORMATION — SUBJECT TO CHANGE

Page 3

NTSB Form 6120.19A (1-84) This form supersedes NTSB Form 6120.19 (Rev. 1-83)

National Transportation Safety Board
Washington, D.C. 20594

Brief of Accident

DCA86AA001
FILE NO. 2929   10/19/85   BLOOMINGTON, IN   AIRCRAFT REG. NO. N923RC   TIME (LOCAL) - 15:35 EDT

	FATAL	SERIOUS	MINOR/NONE
CREW	0	1	1
PASS	0	0	26

MAKE/MODEL   - VICKERS VISCOUNT VC-810
ENGINE MAKE/MODEL   - ROLLS ROYCE DART 525
AIRCRAFT DAMAGE   - Destroyed
NUMBER OF ENGINES   - 4

OPERATING CERTIFICATES   - None
TYPE OF FLIGHT OPERATION   - Business
REGULATION FLIGHT CONDUCTED UNDER - 14 CFR 91

LAST DEPARTURE POINT   - Same as Accident
DESTINATION   - Same as Accident

CONDITION OF LIGHT - Daylight

WEATHER INFO SOURCE- Weather observation facility

AIRPORT PROXIMITY   - On airport
AIRPORT NAME   - MONROE COUNTY
RUNWAY IDENTIFICATION   - 35
RUNWAY LENGTH/WIDTH (Feet)   - 5200/ 150
RUNWAY SURFACE   - Asphalt
RUNWAY SURFACE CONDITION   - Wet

BASIC WEATHER   - Instrument (IMC)
LOWEST CEILING   - 600 FT Broken
VISIBILITY   - 0001.500 SM
WIND DIR/SPEED   - 230 /005 KTS
TEMPERATURE (F)   - 66
OBSTR TO VISION   - Fog
PRECIPITATION   - Rain

PILOT-IN-COMMAND   AGE - 67

CERTIFICATES/RATINGS
   Airline transport
   Single-engine land, Multiengine land
INSTRUMENT RATINGS
   Airplane

FLIGHT TIME (Hours)

TOTAL ALL AIRCRAFT   - 27000
LAST 90 DAYS   - Unk/Nr
TOTAL MAKE/MODEL   - 6000
TOTAL INSTRUMENT TIME   - Unk/Nr

DRG AN ILS TO RWY 35, THE APCH WAS NORMAL UNTIL, THE ACFT WAS APRX 100' ABV THE DECISION HEIGHT, EXCEPT THERE WAS CONDENSATION ON THE WINDSHIELD. TOUCHDOWN WAS HARD. A WITNESS SAID THE ACFT LNDD APRX 1/3 OF THE WAY DOWN THE 5200' RWY. AFTER LNDG, WITH THE PROPS IN "GROUND FINE," BRAKING ACTION WAS INEFFECTIVE ON THE WET RWY. THE ACFT WAS NOT EQUIPPED WITH AN ANTI-SKID BRAKING SYS. SUBSEQUENTLY, THE ACFT CONTD OFF THE RWY & WENT DOWN AN EMBANKMENT INTO A FIELD. SCRUB MARKS ON THE RWY & REVERTED RUBBER ON THE TIRES INDICATED THE ACFT WAS HYDROPLANING. ACCORDING TO THE FLT MANUAL, 4500' (PLUS A 10% FACTOR FOR NO ANTI-SKID) WOULD HAVE BEEN REQUIRED TO STOP ON A DRY RWY IN THE PREVAILING WX CONDS, WHICH INCLUDED A SLIGHT TAILWIND. TWO PAX, ACTING AS FLT ATTENDANTS (F/A'S), ASSISTED THE OTHER PAX IN EVACUATING. AN INVESTIGATION REVEALED THE F/A'S WERE NOT PROPERLY TRAINED; THE PAX WERE NOT COMPLETELY BRIEFED BEFORE THE FLT; & THE PAX BRIEFING CARDS WERE INADEQUATE. THE ACFT WAS ON A BUSINESS FLT TO TRANSPORT AN ENTERTAINMENT TROUPE.

Brief of Accident (Continued)

DCA86AA001   10/19/85   BLOOMINGTON, IN   AIRCRAFT REG. NO. N923RC   TIME (LOCAL) - 15:35 EDT
FILE NO. 2929

Occurrence# 1   OVERRUN
Phase of Operation   LANDING - ROLL

Findings
1. - WEATHER CONDITION - TAILWIND
2. - WEATHER CONDITION - FOG
3. - WEATHER CONDITION - RAIN
4. - WINDOW,FLIGHT COMPARTMENT WINDOW/WINDSHIELD - DIRTY(FOGGY)
5. - PROPER TOUCHDOWN POINT - EXCEEDED - PILOT-IN-COMMAND
6. - Visual/aural perception - PILOT-IN-COMMAND
7. - IN-FLIGHT PLANNING/DECISION - IMPROPER - PILOT-IN-COMMAND
8. - MISSED APPROACH - NOT PERFORMED - PILOT-IN-COMMAND
9. - AIRPORT FACILITIES,RUNWAY/LANDING AREA CONDITION - WET
10. - AIRCRAFT PERFORMANCE,HYDROPLANING CONDITION - WATER

Occurrence# 2   ON GROUND/WATER ENCOUNTER WITH TERRAIN/WATER
Phase of Operation   LANDING - ROLL

Findings
11. - TERRAIN CONDITION - ROUGH/UNEVEN
12. - TERRAIN CONDITION - DOWNHILL

Occurrence# 3   MISCELLANEOUS/OTHER
Phase of Operation   OTHER

Findings
13. - PASSENGER BRIEFING - INADEQUATE - FLIGHT ATTENDANT
14. - INADEQUATE TRAINING(EMERGENCY PROCEDURE(S)) - FLIGHT ATTENDANT
15. - INFORMATION UNCLEAR - COMPANY/OPERATOR MANAGEMENT

---Probable Cause--

CAUSES   5 6 7 8 9 10 11 12 13 14 15
FACTORS   1 2 3 4

Format Revision 4/97

Rick Nelson

The Stone Canyon Band

December 31, 1985

There are times when even the most thorough and exhaustive investigation will not reveal all the facts of an airplane crash. This accident is one such example. As a result of rumors that illegal drug usage may have led to the fire that caused this crash, the FBI became directly involved in this investigation. After the investigating agencies were able to successfully analyze nearly all of the evidence surrounding this accident, all that could be concluded as a probable cause was the determination that a fire had started in the rear of the airplane near the airplane's heater. Even though the investigation was rigorous, the exact reason for the deadly fire remains unknown to this day.

It may surprise some people to know that the same aviation gasoline that powered the plane's engines also fueled the plane's heater, which was in the rear of this airplane. With this fact in mind, consider that there must be plumbing to route the fuel to the heater. As with any mechanical connection, it is possible that a break occurred in the fuel line, either before or after the moment of ignition, and this would have allowed the aviation gas to become an accelerant to the fire that erupted. We simply do not know the sequence of the events in this terrible accident. However, it is known that the heater on this plane was tested about two months prior to this flight, and that its proper operation might have been in question even at that time.

The accident report documents that the pilot of this airplane went back to inspect a temperamental heater and that the co-pilot protested the repeated re-firing of the heater. This scenario is an example of less than optimal cockpit resource management by the crew. The pilot probably should have taken the co-pilot's concerns more seriously. Looking back at the event, it does seem risky to try multiple times to ignite a device fueled with a highly combustible liquid after knowing that it had started malfunctioning while in the air. The prudent action would have been to get the airplane on the ground as soon as possible and have the problem checked.

There is something interesting and wholly positive recorded within this investigation report, however. Read carefully the transcript of the radio transmissions made by the Eagle Express flight crew (MEX1756) during the struggle of the crew of Nelson's airplane. Their willingness to leave a scheduled airline route and help a flight crew in distress is noteworthy. This is an unwritten code of conduct for pilots. Their action is best described as an example of good airmanship, but the term heroic would not be unjustified. Good Samaritan airmanship is still alive in the community of pilots. It is a professional ethic that all pilots are taught and accept from their first flight through their last when a fellow aviator is in distress. It would be a sad day in the skies if this comradeship and chivalrous code-of-the-air were to be broken. On this sad day for Rick Nelson and the Stone Canyon Band, it was alive and well.

The life of Rick Nelson is very well known. He entered show business in the late 1940s, before his tenth birthday, on his parents' radio show. He then literally grew up during the 1950s, throughout his teen years, before the eyes of the American public on his parents' television show. It was on the April 10, 1957 airing of the "Ozzie and Harriet" family show that Ricky Nelson made his musical debut. Not only did this wholesome young man give some much needed credibility to the new genre of music called Rock and Roll, he also became one of the first of many "teen idols." From 1957 to early 1963, Ricky Nelson's songs made the charts' top 40 on 33 occasions, and made the top 10 during 17 time frames. Only Elvis Presley's recordings outsold Nelson's records. It was on his 21st birthday that Ricky Nelson officially changed his performing name to Rick Nelson.

During the 1960s, the Rick Nelson phenomenon experienced a decline, leaving the star struggling to resurrect his career. He entered the country music phase of his career in 1966, and that same year his parents' popular television show ended its fourteenth, and last season. At the dawn of the 1970s, Rick Nelson formed the Stone Canyon Band. On October 15, 1971, he once again tried to re-define who he was onstage at the seventh annual Rock 'n' Roll Revival concert at New York's Madison Square Garden. After Nelson had finished his well-known early hits, he began to play some new material. During his rendition of "Honky Tonk Woman," the crowd of 22,000 people began booing and continued until he left the stage. This display by his "fans" hurt Nelson's feelings deeply. One year later Nelson released a new album titled "Garden Party." The autobiographical title track spoke back to the "fans" and conveyed how he felt about that particular concert event. Nelson's vindication was complete as "Garden Party" became his first million-seller since 1961, and eventually went platinum. It was to be his last major successful album.

In the mid-1970s, Rick Nelson's career once again went into the doldrums, and he seemingly drifted aimlessly. His personal life came apart also, as his wife divorced him and took their four children with her. Nelson tried to return to acting during this time, but his heart was just not in it. He returned to the road as a performing music artist and there he would stay, no matter what. In November of 1985, he was on a very successful nostalgia rock tour in Great Britain. Upon returning to the United States, Nelson promptly began a tour of the south, traveling in an airplane that he had purchased in May of that year. During the last weekend in 1985, Nelson and his band were playing multiple shows in a small but consistently packed nightclub in Guntersville, Alabama. He was there as a favor for his old friend Pat Upton, who had opened the nightclub. On the final night, the last song that he and his band played was Buddy Holly's "Rave On."

The following Tuesday, after some delays, Rick Nelson, his fiancé Helen Blair, five members of the Stone Canyon Band and Nelson's two pilots boarded the plane for a flight to their next concert venue in Dallas, Texas. During this flight, there apparently was a problem with the cabin heater mounted in the rear of the airplane. The heater apparently caught on fire, subsequently igniting the rest of the plane's tail section. The pilots tried to make it to an airport, but were forced to make an emergency landing in a field, amid a smoke-filled cockpit. Both pilots survived, but the co-pilot was burned severely. All the passengers on board died, most likely from smoke inhalation.

It is well known that smoke kills more people during fires than flames. The smoke will fill the lungs and choke the victim by not allowing a breath of fresh air to bring relief. Adding to the danger are the noxious fumes that can be produced when certain materials are burned. If any of the passengers had been mobile after the plane ended up in the field, they probably would not have been able to find the emergency exit. The smoke, acting as an extreme irritant, causes the eyes to shut so that the body's natural defense of producing tears can begin to wash the irritant out of the eyes. When there is no relief from the smoke, however, as in this case, the eyes remain shut and the victim is left disoriented. That noted, there is no supporting evidence that any of the people who died in this accident were still alive when the plane stopped moving.

It was alleged by some that Rick Nelson might have been using a form of cocaine called "freebase" on the airplane. The term freebase is an idiom used to describe the action of converting purified cocaine hydrochloride powder (regular cocaine), which is usually snorted or injected, into a form of the drug that is far more powerful and easily smoked. Smoking regular cocaine powder can be done, but to the drug user, this is a wasteful technique. In the early 1970s, it was found that to "free" the cocaine into its chemical "base" one had to first use a strong alkaloid solution such as ammonia and then add an organic solvent such as ethyl ether. The solid substance that separated from the solution was the cocaine base, or freebase. The problem with freebase is that if the user tries to smoke the drug too soon, before the highly flammable ether has entirely evaporated, the freebase can ignite violently, which can cause the butane lighter in the user's hand to explode.

The autopsy report does reveal that Rick Nelson had cocaine in his blood system. That much is undisputed, but how much cocaine did he have in his system? In short, the results show that Nelson had a very low level of cocaine in his blood at the time of the crash. This would be inconsistent with the level of cocaine that would have been found if freebase had been used. Incidentally, the form of cocaine known as "crack" came into vogue in the mid-1980s as an alternative to freebase because the method of processing was safer, using baking soda and water. Crack gets its name from the baking soda residue that makes a crackling sound when smoked. Although the freebase form of cocaine was still in use well into the mid-1980s, the FBI investigation found no evidence that any type of freebase smoking activity was in progress during this flight.

Ricky Intveld was the youngest to die in the accident. He started playing drums after James, his older brother, bought him a drum set. It did not take long for the Intveld brothers to form a band called The Rockin' Shadows. Rick Nelson was impressed when he saw them perform as his opening act during a gig in a Long Beach, California nightclub. Nelson promptly recruited Intveld, as well as Pat Woodward, the bass player, for his band. Andy Chapin was a veteran of the professional music stage. He had played keyboards for such bands as Steppenwolf and The Association before Rick Nelson brought him into the Stone Canyon Band. Bobby Neal had been a staff guitarist at Lyn-Lou Studios in Memphis, Tennessee when Nelson met him during some recording sessions. Neal joined the Stone Canyon Band in 1979.

Before purchasing the DC-3 in which he tragically died, Rick Nelson flew around in a Jet Commander that had the registration number N3335V. This was quite an expensive airplane to operate, which might have contributed to his decision to purchase the older transport. Whatever the reasons, the airplane that Rick Nelson did purchase was a veteran of musical ownership. This World War II vintage DC-3 actually was a converted military transport (C-47), previously owned by the wealthy DuPont family and subsequently by Jerry Lee Lewis. The plane also had some history with bad luck. On April 23, 1971, while in the possession of Jerry Lee Lewis, the DC-3 was parked at the Hi-Air general aviation terminal in Memphis, Tennessee when a strong storm hit. The storm caused much damage in the area and in the early hours of the morning the plane was torn from its tie-down spot and blown across the ramp where it allegedly smashed into three smaller airplanes. This damage was repaired, however, and in no way contributed to the crash that took the lives of Nelson and the others.

Another interesting fact about this airplane is that some of the fuselage was made of magnesium instead of aluminum. This practice was employed during World War II due to the shortage of aluminum. The drawback to magnesium as a manufacturing material is its low melting point when heated. Certainly this was a factor when the DC-3 caught fire, and most likely it was the melted magnesium that witnesses saw dripping from the plane as it descended.

In the accident documents this DC-3 is referred to as a DC-3C. This DC-3 "C" designation indicates that the DC-3 was converted from a military C-47 to civilian standards, including changing military radios, electrical systems and adding windows. Some of the photos and diagrams from the accident investigation are not reproduced here due to their poor quality as a result of microfiche retrieval. There is enough of the printed text included, however, to give the reader a good idea of what transpired and the complexity of this investigation. Additionally, there were multiple lawsuits that resulted from this accident. This body of work does not include those legal issues and court findings because they are beyond the scope of the facts of the accident investigation. There was no insurance on this plane so the NTSB released the aircraft wreckage back to Century Equipment Company, the company through which Nelson had purchased the plane.

Rick Nelson had a total of 24 gold records during his career and is the only Rock and Roll performer ever to have top-selling albums on the charts in the '50s, '60s, '70s and '80s. He was a pioneer in the fusion between Rock and Roll and country music, called "Rockabilly." For his accomplishments and contributions to music, Rick Nelson was inducted into the Rock and Roll Hall of Fame in 1987.

Author

Aircraft addenda:

Common name: DC-3, Military names: C-47, Gooney Bird, Dakota, Skytrain
Manufacturer: Douglas Aircraft Company
First flight of prototype: December 17, 1935
Registration number for this airplane: N711Y
Serial number for this airplane: 13650
Seats: 14 to 28 (this airplane was custom-configured and held 14 seats.)
Length: 64 feet, 6 inches
Wingspan: 94 feet, 7 inches
Engines: (2) Pratt & Whitney R-1830-75, 14-cylinder, air-cooled radial, "Twin Wasp"
Horsepower: 1,200 hp each
Empty weight (approximate): 20,610 lbs.
Gross weight: 26,900 lbs.
Service ceiling: 24,000 ft
Fuel capacity: 680 gal.
Range: 1,200 miles
Cruising speed: 180 mph

* The above photo represents the type of aircraft and not necessarily the exact model involved in the accident.

Personal addenda:

Eric Hilliard Nelson (Ricky Nelson, Rick Nelson): Singer, songwriter, musician
b. May 8, 1940: Teaneck, New Jersey
d. December 31, 1985: near DeKalb, Texas
Buried: Forest Lawn Memorial Park: Los Angeles, California

Rick Jason Intveld (Ricky Intveld): Drums
b. December 30, 1962: Compton, California
d. December 31, 1985: near DeKalb, Texas
Buried: Good Shepherd Cemetery: Huntington Beach, California

Andrew Chapin (Andy Chapin): Keyboards
b. Believed to be age 30 and birthplace believed to be Chicopee, Massachusetts
d. December 31, 1985: near DeKalb, Texas
Buried: unknown at this time

Robert Neal (Bobby Neal): Lead guitar
b. July 19, 1947: Parkin, Arkansas
d. December 31, 1985: near DeKalb, Texas
Buried: Dogwood Cemetery: Blytheville, Arkansas

Patrick Jack Woodward (Pat Woodward): Bass guitar
b. August 29, 1948: Fort Worth, Texas
d. December 31, 1985: near DeKalb, Texas
Buried: Greenwood Cemetery: Fort Worth, Texas

Donald Clark Russell (Clark Russell): Sound engineer
b. Believed to be age 35
d. December 31, 1985: near DeKalb, Texas
Buried: unknown at this time

CENTURY EQUIPMENT CO.

May 2, 1985

BILL OF SALE

RICK NELSON
Stone Canyon Band
Box 9528
Palm Springs, Calif. 92263
1 Douglas DC3C   Reg. No. 711Y

Serial No. 13658 $118,000.00

Downpayment   5,000.00

$113,000.00

Note: In the event there is any sales tax due on the selling price,
Purchaser will pay same.

Stell,

May 3
1) Rick Nelson will mail
   the note to you today
2) Call Martin Aviation
   We have vacated the DC3
   Ad just red
3) Bill of Sale given to R. Nelson

2126 COTNER AVENUE • LOS ANGELES 90025 • (213) 879-1415 • 478-1511

BEST COPY AVAILABLE

                                        LOS ANGELES   , California

$ 113,000.00   Date May 2, 1985

  Three (3) Years   , after date, for value received,

  I promise to pay to   Century Equipment Co.

_____, or order,

at 2126 Cotner Avenue, Los Angeles, Calif. 90025

the sum of One Hundred Thirteen Thousand and 00/100----------------------DOLLARS,

with interest from May 2, 1985   until paid, at the rate of
Prime plus 2% (Prime Bank of America as of the 1st of the month)
_____ per cent per annum, payable $1000.00 per month

Sales tax, if any, to be paid by purchaser.

     Should the interest not be so paid, it shall thereafter bear like interest
as the principal. Should default be made in the payment of any installment of
principal or interest when due, then the whole sum of principal and interest
shall become immediately due and payable at the option of the holder of this
note. The undersigned (jointly and severally) further promise to pay all costs
of collection, including attorney's fees, incurred in the collection of this
note. Principal and interest payable in lawful money of the United States; the
makers, sureties, guarantors, and endorsers of this note hereby consent to
extensions of time at or after the maturity hereof, and hereby waive diligence,
protest, demand and notice of every kind. Should this note be signed by more
than one person, firm or corporation, all of the obligations herein contained
shall be considered joint and several obligations of each signer hereof.

Address_____   RICK NELSON

_____   _____

_____   _____

_____   _____

_____   _____

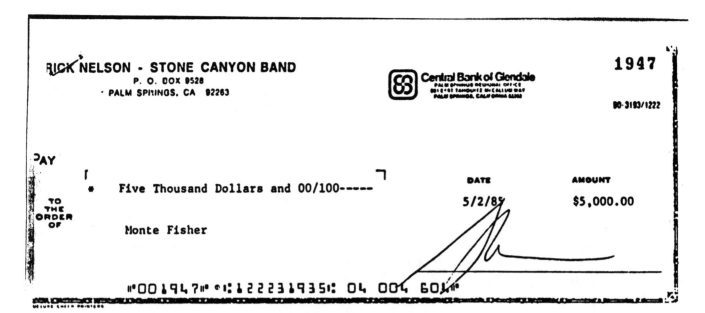

RICK NELSON - STONE CANYON BAND
P. O. BOX 9528
· PALM SPRINGS, CA 92263

Central Bank of Glendale

1947

80-3193/1222

PAY

Five Thousand Dollars and 00/100-----

DATE 5/2/85

AMOUNT $5,000.00

TO THE ORDER OF

Monte Fisher

⑈0019470⑈ ⑈1222319350⑈ 04 004 601⑈

RICK NELSON - STONE CANYON BAND

DETACH AND RETAIN THIS STATEMENT
THE ATTACHED CHECK IS IN PAYMENT OF ITEMS DESCRIBED BELOW
IF NOT CORRECT PLEASE NOTIFY US PROMPTLY   NO RECEIPT DESIRED

DELUXE FORM TWC-3   V-4

| INVOICE | | DESCRIPTION | TOTAL AMOUNT | DEDUCTIONS | | NET AMOUNT |
DATE	NO.			DISCOUNT	FREIGHT	
		DC-3				

BEST COPY AVAILABLE

FORM APPROVED
OMB NO. 04-R0070

UNITED STATES OF AMERICA
DEPARTMENT OF TRANSPORTATION FEDERAL AVIATION ADMINISTRATION

AIRCRAFT BILL OF SALE

FOR AND IN CONSIDERATION OF $ _____ THE
UNDERSIGNED OWNER(S) OF THE FULL LEGAL
AND BENEFICIAL TITLE OF THE AIRCRAFT DES-
CRIBED AS FOLLOWS:

UNITED STATES REGISTRATION NUMBER	N 711Y
AIRCRAFT MANUFACTURER & MODEL	Douglas DC3C
AIRCRAFT SERIAL No.	13658

DOES THIS **2nd** DAY OF **May** 19 **85**
HEREBY SELL, GRANT, TRANSFER AND
DELIVER ALL RIGHTS, TITLE, AND INTERESTS
IN AND TO SUCH AIRCRAFT UNTO:

Do Not Write In This Block
FOR FAA USE ONLY

PURCHASER

NAME AND ADDRESS
(IF INDIVIDUAL(S), GIVE LAST NAME, FIRST NAME, AND MIDDLE INITIAL.)

NELSON, RICK

DEALER CERTIFICATE NUMBER

AND TO their EXECUTORS, ADMINISTRATORS, AND ASSIGNS TO HAVE AND TO HOLD
SINGULARLY THE SAID AIRCRAFT FOREVER, AND WARRANTS THE TITLE THEREOF.

IN TESTIMONY WHEREOF We HAVE SET OUR HAND AND SEAL THIS 2nd DAY of May 19 85

SELLER

NAME (S) OF SELLER (TYPED OR PRINTED)	SIGNATURE (S) (IN INK) (IF EXECUTED FOR CO-OWNERSHIP, ALL MUST SIGN.)	TITLE (TYPED OR PRINTED)
Century Equipment Co.		Pres.

ACKNOWLEDGMENT (NOT REQUIRED FOR PURPOSES OF FAA RECORDING; HOWEVER, MAY BE REQUIRED
BY LOCAL LAW FOR VALIDITY OF THE INSTRUMENT.)

ORIGINAL: TO FAA

AC FORM 8050-2 (8-78) (0052-020-0002)

BEST COPY AVAILABLE

TO: Henley Leventhal
MSC

FROM: Century Equipment Co.

SUBJECT

DATE 5/24/85

MESSAGE

Enclosed note for Century Equipment from Rick Nelson, Stone Canyon Band.
Please set up for collection. Any question, please call me.

SIGNED   Stella Wissner

REPLY

SIGNED

DATE / /

REDIFORM® 4S 471

SEND PARTS 1 AND 3 WITH CARBON INTACT -
PART 3 WILL BE RETURNED WITH REPLY.

POLY PAK (50 SETS) 4P 471

DETACH AND FILE FOR FOLLOW-UP

Chapter 34: Rick Nelson

ICK NELSON' - STONE CANYON BAND
P. O. BOX 9528
PALM SPRINGS, CA 92263

Central Bank of Glendale
PALM SPRINGS BRANCH
901 EAST TAHQUITZ-McCALLUM WAY
PALM SPRINGS, CALIFORNIA 92262

2014

90-3193/1222

---One Thousand Dollars---00/xx

Century Equipment Co.
2126 Cotner Avenue
Los Angeles, Calif 90025

DATE
5/28/85

AMOUNT
$1,000.00**

⑈002014⑈ ⑆122231935⑆ 04 004 604⑈

NELSON - STONE CANYON BAND

DETACH AND RETAIN THIS STATEMENT
THE ATTACHED CHECK IS IN PAYMENT OF ITEMS DESCRIBED BELOW.
IF NOT CORRECT PLEASE NOTIFY US PROMPTLY   NO RECEIPT DESIRED

DELUXE FORM TWC-3   V-4

| INVOICE | | DESCRIPTION | TOTAL AMOUNT | DEDUCTIONS | | NET AMOUNT |
DATE	NO.			DISCOUNT	FREIGHT	

BEST COPY AVAILABLE

TO

HENLEY LEVENTHAL

MSC

FROM

Century Equipment Co.
2126 Cotner Avenue
Los Angeles, Ca. 90067

SUBJECT

DATE 5/30/85

MESSAGE

We received the check for Rick Nelson's payment. We are depositing same to our account today - please input into your computer setup. Thanks.

SIGNED   Stella Wissner

REPLY

SIGNED

DATE / /

REDIFORM ® 45 471

SEND PARTS 1 AND 3 WITH CARBON INTACT -
PART 3 WILL BE RETURNED WITH REPLY.

DETACH AND FILE FOR FOLLOW-UP

POLY PAK (50 SETS) 4P 471

BEST COPY AVAILABLE

OFFENSE REPORT
AND MULTI-PURPOSE REPORT FORM

17. UNIT	18. BEAT	19. DIST.	20. REP. AREA	1. VICTIM'S NAME (LAST, FIRST, MIDDLE)	2. COMPLAINT NO.
444	CID	West		NELSON, RICK	B-8563807

21. WATCH	3. VICTIM'S ADDRESS	4. RES. PHONE
II	Los Angeles, California	

22. DISPATCHED AS!	23. DISP. ACKN.	5. VICTIM'S PLACE OF EMPLOYMENT OR SCHOOL	6. BUS. PHONE
Plane Crash	5:15 A.M. XX	Self-employed	

24. ADDRESS DISPATCHED TO	25. REV'D. SERV.	7. VICTIM'S SEX, RACE, AGE	8. LOCATION OF OFFENSE (ADDRESS)
Southeast of DeKalb	A.M. P.M.	W/M/45	3/4 mile southeast of DeKalb

26. DESCRIBE LOCATION—TYPE PREMISES	9. REPORTING PERSON'S NAME	10. RES. PHONE
Pasture	John M. Chandler	N/A

27. VICT. OCCUPAT.	28. HOURS OF EMPLOY	29. SOBRIETY	11. REPORTING PERSON'S ADDRESS	CITY	12. BUS. PHONE
Entertain.	N/A	N/A	Bowie County Sheriff Dept.		798-3150

30. REQUESTED		
CORONER ☐	CRIM. INV. ☒	
NCIC CK ☐	AMB ☒	TOW ☐
OTHER ☒ Fire & NTSB & FAA	APB RADIO ☐	T. TYPE ☐

13. DATE AND TIME OCCURRED	14. DATE AND TIME REPORTED
12-31-85 5:15pm	12-31-85 5:15pm

15. CRIME OR INCIDENT	16. CLASSIFICATION
Airplane Crash	

WITNESS/PARENT/GUARDIAN

31. NAME	AGE	BEST CONTACT ADDRESS	BEST PHONE	OTHER PHONE
① See Attachments				
②				

SUSPECTS

32. NAME AND ADDRESS, SEX, RACE, AGE-DESCRIP.—ARR. NO.	NAME AND ADDRESS, SEX, RACE, AGE-DESCRIP.—ARR. NO.
① N/A	②
③	VEH. COLOR(S) YEAR MAKE MODEL LIC.-YEAR-STATE-NO.

STOLEN PROPERTY

33. QTY.	DESCRIPTION—(SIZE-COLOR-MODEL-STYLE-MATERIAL-CONDITION)	SERIAL NO.	WHERE LOCATED	VALUE, NEW	AGE	VALUE NOW
N/A						

PER.

34. VICTIM TAKEN TO	35. TRANSPORTED BY	36. DESCRIBE INJURIES	37. CONDITION
N/A	N/A	N/A	N/A

PERSON

38. HT.	WT.	HAIR	EYES	COMP.	HAT	COAT	JACKET	SWEATER	BLOUSE/SHIRT	SKIRT/TROUSERS	SHOES	JEWELRY
N/A												

39. POSSIBLE CAUSE OF ABSENCE	40. COMPETENCY: PHYSICAL	41. PAST RECORD, OTHER DATA-ID, MONEY CARRIED
N/A	N/A	
DESTINATION: N/A	MENTAL: N/A	N/A N/A

42. NARRATIVE: (1) CONTINUATION OF ABOVE ITEMS (INDICATE "ITEM NUMBER" CONTINUED AT LEFT.) INCLUDE ADDITIONAL VICTIMS, WITNESSES AND SUSPECTS AS OUTLINED ABOVE. (2) DESCRIBE DETAILS OF INCIDENT. (3) DESCRIBE EVIDENCE AND PROPERTY AND INDICATE DISPOSITION. (4) M.O. HOW DONE — FORCE USED — AT WHAT POINT — WITH WHAT TOOL OR WEAPON — OTHER ACTS OR TRADEMARK (5) IF COMPLAINT IS UNFOUNDED EXPLAIN WHY.

Investigator Chandler was assigned the crash of a privately owned DC-3. The plane crashed in Nolan Woddards pasture approximately 3/4 miles southeast of DeKalb, Texas. Witness's reported seeing smoke coming from the plane and that the plane attempted to land in the pasture. The plane struck several trees as it came to rest. Shortly after the plane was engulfed in flames. The plane carried seven

OFFICE USE ONLY	

43. REPORTING OFFICER	NO. 780
OFFICER	- NO.
SUPERVISOR APPROVING	NO.

44. CASE STATUS (STATUS MUST BE INDICATED FOR ALL CASES, INCLUDING NON-CRIMINAL INCIDENTS.)
☐ OPEN (PENDING) ☐ CLOSED ☐ SUSPENDED

CASE DISPOSITON (DISPOSITION OF CRIMINAL CASES MAY BE INDICATED AS APPROPRIATE)
☐ UNFOUNDED
☐ CLEARED BY ARREST ☐ CLEARED EXCEP.

45. DATE/TIME TYPED NO.	47. REPRODUCES BY NO.
48. UNIT REFERRED TO!	49. UCR DISPOSITION
50. REVIEWER	NO.	PAGE NO. OF

51. COMPLAINT NO.

SUPPLEMENTAL REPORT

1. EVIDENCE NUMBER	2. ARREST, CITATION, OR SUMMONS NO.	3. COMPLAINT NO

4. NAME OF COMPLAINANT, DRIVER #1, VICTIM OR ARRESTEE	5. DATE OF THIS REPORT	6. DATE OF ORIGINAL OCCURRENCE

7. FORM USED AS CONTINUATION SHEET FOR CURRENT REPORT ☐	8. OFFENSE, CHARGE OR INCIDENT ON ORIGINAL REPORT

9. FORM USED TO REPORT FOLLOWUP INVESTIGATION OR SUPPLEMENTAL INFORMATION ☐	10. CORRECT OFFENSE OR INCIDENT CLASSIFICATION	CHANGED ☐ YES

11. KIND OF REPORT CONTINUED ☐ OFFENSE ☐ TRAFFIC ACCIDENT ☐ ARREST ☐ VEHICLE ☐ OTHER _____	12. MULTIPLE CLEARANCE ☐ YES (LIST OTHER COMPLAINT NUMBERS IN NARRATIVE) ☐ NO

13. INSTRUCTIONS FOR FOLLOWUP OR SUPPLEMENTAL USAGE. UNDER NARRATIVE RECORD YOUR ACTIVITY AND ALL DEVELOPMENTS IN THE CASE SUBSEQUENT TO LAST REPORT. DESCRIBE AND RECORD VALUE OF ANY PROPERTY RECOVERED, NAMES AND ARREST NUMBERS OF PERSONS ARRESTED. EXPLAIN ANY OFFENSE CLASSIFICATION CHANGE. CLEARLY SHOW DISPOSITION OF RECOVERED PROPERTY AND INVENTORY NO. RECOMMEND TO SUPERVISOR CASE STATUS AND TO REVIEWER UCR DISPOSITION. INDICATE "ITEM NUMBER CONTINUED" AT LEFT, IF ANY.

ITEM NO.

passengers and a crew of two. The two crew members were the only survivors of the crash. The seven passengers bodies were recovered and identified as: Rick Nelson age 45, Helen Blair age 29, Patrick Woodard age 35, Bobby Neal age 38, Rick Intveld age 23, Andy Chapin age 30, and Clark Russell age 35.

CASH VALUE	14.	MONEY	JEWELRY	CLOTHING	FURS	AUTO ACCESS.	BICYCLES	MISCELL.
	STOLEN	$	$	$	$	$	$	$
	15.	MONEY	JEWELRY	CLOTHING	FURS	AUTO ACCESS.	BICYCLES	MISCELL.
	RECOVERED	$	$	$	$	$	$	$

16. REPORTING OFFICER NO. 780.	18. CASE STATUS (STATUS MUST BE INDICATED FOR ALL CASES, INCLUDING NON-CRIMINAL INCIDENTS) ☐ OPEN (PENDING) ☐ CLOSED ☐ SUSPENDED	OFFICE USE ONLY

2ND OFFICER NO.

	CASE DISPOSITION (DISPOSITION OF CRIMINAL CASES MAY BE INDICATED AS APPROPRIATE)	19. DATE/TIME TYPED NO.	20. REPRODUCED BY NC
17. SUPERVISOR APPROVING NO.	☐ UNFOUNDED ☐ CLEARED BY ARREST ☐ CLEARED EXCEP.	21. UNIT REFERRED TO:	22. UCR DISPOSITION
		23. REVIEWER NO.	PAGE NO. OF

SUPPLEMENTAL REPORT

1. EVIDENCE NUMBER	2. ARREST, CITATION, OR SUMMONS NO.	3. COMPLAINT NO

4. NAME OF COMPLAINANT, DRIVER #1, VICTIM OR ARRESTEE	5. DATE OF THIS REPORT	6. DATE OF ORIGINAL OCCURRENCE
Plane Crash	010186	12 31 85

7. FORM USED AS CONTINUATION SHEET FOR CURRENT REPORT ☐	8. OFFENSE, CHARGE OR INCIDENT ON ORIGINAL REPORT

9. FORM USED TO REPORT FOLLOWUP INVESTIGATION OR SUPPLEMENTAL INFORMATION ☐	10. CORRECT OFFENSE OR INCIDENT CLASSIFICATION	CHANGED ☐ YES

11. KIND OF REPORT CONTINUED ☐ OFFENSE ☐ TRAFFIC ACCIDENT ☐ ARREST ☐ VEHICLE ☐ OTHER	12. MULTIPLE CLEARANCE ☐ YES (LIST OTHER COMPLAINT NUMBERS IN NARRATIVE) ☐ NO

13. INSTRUCTIONS FOR FOLLOWUP OR SUPPLEMENTAL USAGE.	UNDER NARRATIVE RECORD YOUR ACTIVITY AND ALL DEVELOPMENTS IN THE CASE SUBSEQUENT TO LAST REPORT. DESCRIBE AND RECORD VALUE OF ANY PROPERTY RECOVERED, NAMES AND ARREST NUMBERS OF PERSONS ARRESTED. EXPLAIN ANY OFFENSE CLASSIFICATION CHANGE. CLEARLY SHOW DISPOSITION OF RECOVERED PROPERTY AND INVENTORY NO. RECOMMEND TO SUPERVISOR CASE STATUS AND TO REVIEWER UCR DISPOSITION. INDICATE "ITEM NUMBER CONTINUED" AT LEFT, IF ANY.

ITEM NO.

At approximatly 5:15 pm on 12-31-85 Investigator Chandler overheard Dekalb Police Department Patrolman Rick Riggs and Charlie Evans radio traffic that there was an apparent air plane crash southeast of Dekalb. Investigator Chandler checked in route to the area. Shortly there after the Dekalb Police dispatcher advised that she had a report of a plane being down approximately 3/4 mile south of the farm market road 1840 and farm market road 990 intersection, west of farm market road 990. Dekalb police patrolman Rick Riggs and Charlie Evans arrived at the scene and advised that they needed fire equipment at the scene. The radio channel became jumbled and congested at this time Investigator Chandler requested that the dispatcher clear the channel and keep it clear for emergency traffic. Investigator Chandler then requested fire units from New Boston, Simms Fire Departments. Dekalb P. D. ask if they shouldget an ambulance in route to the scene. Investigator Chandler advised yes. Investigator Chandler asked units at the scene if the plane was a civil or military aircraft. The patrolman at the scene advised that it was civilian. Investigator Chandler advised BIC Communications to advise the Texas Department of Public Safety and send all available units to the scene for security and traffic control. After this time Investigator Chandler arrived at the scene. Investigator Chandler set upon the road at Bob Jones residence and advised fire units how to get to the fire. Investigator Chandler

14.	MONEY	JEWELRY	CLOTHING	FURS	AUTO ACCESS.	BICYCLES	MISCELL.
STOLEN	$	$	$	$	$	$	$
15.	MONEY	JEWELRY	CLOTHING	FURS	AUTO ACCESS.	BICYCLES	MISCELL.
RECOVERED	$	$	$	$	$	$	$

16. REPORTING OFFICER NO. 780	18. CASE STATUS (STATUS MUST BE INDICATED FOR ALL CASES, INCLUDING NON-CRIMINAL INCIDENTS)	OFFICE USE ONLY
2ND OFFICER NO.	☐ OPEN (PENDING) ☐ CLOSED ☐ SUSPENDED	19. DATE/TIME TYPED NO. / 20. REPRODUCED BY NC
	CASE DISPOSITION (DISPOSITION OF CRIMINAL CASES MAY BE INDICATED AS APPROPRIATE)	21. UNIT REFERRED TO: / 22. UCR DISPOSITION
17. SUPERVISOR APPROVING NO.	☐ UNFOUNDED ☐ CLEARED BY ARREST ☐ CLEARED EXCEP.	23. REVIEWER NO. / PAGE NO. 1 OF 13

SUPPLEMENTAL REPORT

1. EVIDENCE NUMBER	2. ARREST, CITATION, OR SUMMONS NO.	3. COMPLAINT NO.

4. NAME OF COMPLAINANT, DRIVER #1, VICTIM OR ARRESTEE	5. DATE OF THIS REPORT	6. DATE OF ORIGINAL OCCURRENCE
Airplane Crash	01 01 86	12 31 85

7. FORM USED AS CONTINUATION SHEET FOR CURRENT REPORT ☐	8. OFFENSE, CHARGE OR INCIDENT ON ORIGINAL REPORT

9. FORM USED TO REPORT FOLLOWUP INVESTIGATION OR SUPPLEMENTAL INFORMATION	10. CORRECT OFFENSE OR INCIDENT CLASSIFICATION	CHANGED ☐ YES

11. KIND OF REPORT CONTINUED ☐ OFFENSE ☐ TRAFFIC ACCIDENT ☐ ARREST ☐ VEHICLE ☐ OTHER _____	12. MULTIPLE CLEARANCE ☐ YES (LIST OTHER COMPLAINT NUMBERS IN NARRATIVE) ☐ NO

13. INSTRUCTIONS FOR FOLLOWUP OR SUPPLEMENTAL USAGE.	UNDER NARRATIVE RECORD YOUR ACTIVITY AND ALL DEVELOPMENTS IN THE CASE SUBSEQUENT TO LAST REPORT. DESCRIBE AND RECORD VALUE OF ANY PROPERTY RECOVERED. NAMES AND ARREST NUMBERS OF PERSONS ARRESTED. EXPLAIN ANY OFFENSE CLASSIFICATION CHANGE. CLEARLY SHOW DISPOSITION OF RECOVERED PROPERTY AND INVENTORY NO. RECOMMEND TO SUPERVISOR CASE STATUS AND TO REVIEWER UCR DISPOSITION. INDICATE "ITEM NUMBER CONTINUED" AT LEFT, IF ANY.

ITEM NO.

Assigned units to stop traffic at F.M. 1840 and F.M. 990, South of the crash

area on F.M. 990 and on the dirt road west of the crash site. Also assigned

units to set up a security perimeter. At this time Investigator Chandler

requested that Chief Deputy Huggins be advised and that the FFA be advised.

Fire units at the scene requested that BIC Communications have a foam unit

located and put enroute. At this time Investigator Chandler moved Command Post

close to the scene of the crash. Chief Deputy Huggins advised that two survivors

had been located and there had been a total of 9 persons on board. Chief Deputy

Huggins took charge of the search for more survisors. One survisor was transported

by Airlife and one by Dekalb Police Department Ambulance. No other survivors

were found. The fire units had the fire contained to the fuselage of the plane,

all the grass fires had been extinguished. Investigator Chandler got with Chief

Deputy Huggins and Sgt Tad Estes of Department of Public Safety to exchange

information. The plane was burning except for the tail section. The tail numbers

of the plane were N711y. The plane was apparently white with a blue and

gold Strip down the middle of the fuselage. Also a blue and gold vertical Chevron

on the tail section. Part of the left wing was located in a tree and fence aprox

200 feet from the fuseloge. The rest of the left wing was next to several trees

approximately 15 ft from the fuseloge. the right wing was torn off and resting

14. CASE VALUE	MONEY	JEWELRY	CLOTHING	FURS	AUTO ACCESS.	BICYCLES	MISCELL.
STOLEN	$	$	$	$	$	$	$
15. RECOVERED	MONEY $	JEWELRY $	CLOTHING $	FURS $	AUTO ACCESS. $	BICYCLES $	MISCELL. $

16. REPORTING OFFICER	NO. 780	18. CASE STATUS (STATUS MUST BE INDICATED FOR ALL CASES, INCLUDING NON-CRIMINAL INCIDENTS)	OFFICE USE ONLY
2ND OFFICER	NO.	☐ OPEN (PENDING) ☐ CLOSED ☐ SUSPENDED	19. DATE/TIME TYPED NO. / 20. REPRODUCED BY NO.
17. SUPERVISOR APPROVING	NO.	CASE DISPOSITION (DISPOSITION OF CRIMINAL CASES MAY BE INDICATED AS APPROPRIATE) ☐ UNFOUNDED ☐ CLEARED BY ARREST ☐ CLEARED EXCEP.	21. UNIT REFERRED TO: / 22. UCR DISPOSITION / 23. REVIEWER NO. / PAGE NO. 2 OF 13

SUPPLEMENTAL REPORT

1. EVIDENCE NUMBER	2. ARREST, CITATION, OR SUMMONS NO.	3. COMPLAINT NO

4. NAME OF COMPLAINANT, DRIVER # 1, VICTIM OR ARRESTEE	5. DATE OF THIS REPORT	6. DATE OF ORIGINAL OCCURRENCE
Plane Crash	01 01 86	12 31 85

7. FORM USED AS CONTINUATION SHEET FOR CURRENT REPORT ☐

8. OFFENSE, CHARGE OR INCIDENT ON ORIGINAL REPORT

9. FORM USED TO REPORT FOLLOWUP INVESTIGATION OR SUPPLEMENTAL INFORMATION ☐

10. CORRECT OFFENSE OR INCIDENT CLASSIFICATION CHANGED ☐ YES

11. KIND OF REPORT CONTINUED ☐ OFFENSE ☐ TRAFFIC ACCIDENT ☐ ARREST ☐ VEHICLE ☐ OTHER

12. MULTIPLE CLEARANCE ☐ YES (LIST OTHER COMPLAINT NUMBERS IN NARRATIVE) ☐ NO

13. INSTRUCTIONS FOR FOLLOWUP OR SUPPLEMENTAL USAGE. UNDER NARRATIVE RECORD YOUR ACTIVITY AND ALL DEVELOPMENTS IN THE CASE SUBSEQUENT TO LAST REPORT. DESCRIBE AND RECORD VALUE OF ANY PROPERTY RECOVERED. NAMES AND ARREST NUMBERS OF PERSONS ARRESTED. EXPLAIN ANY OFFENSE CLASSIFICATION CHANGE. CLEARLY SHOW DISPOSITION OF RECOVERED PROPERTY AND INVENTORY NO. RECOMMEND TO SUPERVISOR CASE STATUS AND TO REVIEWER UCR DISPOSITION. INDICATE "ITEM NUMBER CONTINUED" AT LEFT, IF ANY.

ITEM NO.

in trees aprox 10ft from the fuseloge. Investigator Chandler was advised

to call BIC Immediatley. Investigator Chandler went to a near by house and called.

Sgt. Bill Moore stated that he had been called by U. S. Customs and that they

had tracked a plane out of Mexico and they had lost it over Laffeyette LA. and

this might be the plane. Customs advied to watch for anything unusual. When

Investigator Chandler was advised by Trooper Robby Stinson of Department of

Public Safety that DPS had just been told that the plane carried Rick Nelson

and his Band. Investigator Chandler ask for immediate conformationand then the

Command Post was asked to identify the survivors the only survivors command post

could identify was Brad Rank of San Juan Capistrano Cal. Trooper Stinson

advised Investigator Chandler that he had learned that the plane had taken off

from Guntersville Alabama and was enroute to Dallas, Tex. Trooper Stinson

advised also that he had the names of several witnesses who said they had seen

the plane in the air and it was trailing smoke. Also that Don Ruggles of Texarkana

had been in contact with the pilot told him the cockpit was filled with smoke

and he was having trouble breathing. Mr. Ruggles followed the plane in his helicopte

and landed at the crash site. The other witnesses were Don Lewis, Tim Cooper

address not known at this time. Leonzel Shaver Rt.2 Box 328 Dekalb, Texas, and

Tom Ward of Box 636 Dekalb, Texas. L. B. Barrett of Dekalb, Texas.

---

14. STOLEN	MONEY	JEWELRY	CLOTHING	FURS	AUTO ACCESS.	BICYCLES	MISCELL.
	$	$	$	$	$	$	$

15. RECOVERED	MONEY	JEWELRY	CLOTHING	FURS	AUTO ACCESS.	BICYCLES	MISCELL.
	$	$	$	$	$	$	$

16. REPORTING OFFICER NO.

2ND OFFICER NO.

17. SUPERVISOR APPROVING NO.

16. CASE STATUS (STATUS MUST BE INDICATED FOR ALL CASES, INCLUDING NON-CRIMINAL INCIDENTS)

☐ OPEN (PENDING) ☐ CLOSED ☐ SUSPENDED

CASE DISPOSITION (DISPOSITION OF CRIMINAL CASES MAY BE INDICATED AS APPROPRIATE)

☐ UNFOUNDED
☐ CLEARED BY ARREST ☐ CLEARED EXCEP.

OFFICE USE ONLY

19. DATE/TIME TYPED NO. **20. REPRODUCED BY NC**

21. UNIT REFERRED TO: **22. UCR DISPOSITION**

23. REVIEWER NO. **PAGE NO.** 3 OF 13

SUPPLEMENTAL REPORT

1. EVIDENCE NUMBER	2. ARREST, CITATION, OR SUMMONS NO.	3. COMPLAINT NO

4. NAME OF COMPLAINANT, DRIVER #1, VICTIM OR ARRESTEE	5. DATE OF THIS REPORT	6. DATE OF ORIGINAL OCCURRENCE
Plane Crash	01 01 86	12 31 85

7. FORM USED AS CONTINUATION SHEET FOR CURRENT REPORT ☐

8. OFFENSE, CHARGE OR INCIDENT ON ORIGINAL REPORT

9. FORM USED TO REPORT FOLLOWUP INVESTIGATION OR SUPPLEMENTAL INFORMATION ☐

10. CORRECT OFFENSE OR INCIDENT CLASSIFICATION — CHANGED ☐ YES

11. KIND OF REPORT CONTINUED ☐ OFFENSE ☐ TRAFFIC ACCIDENT ☐ ARREST ☐ VEHICLE ☐ OTHER _____

12. MULTIPLE CLEARANCE ☐ YES (LIST OTHER COMPLAINT NUMBERS IN NARRATIVE) ☐ NO

13. INSTRUCTIONS FOR FOLLOWUP OR SUPPLEMENTAL USAGE. UNDER NARRATIVE RECORD YOUR ACTIVITY AND ALL DEVELOPMENTS IN THE CASE SUBSEQUENT TO LAST REPORT. DESCRIBE AND RECORD VALUE OF ANY PROPERTY RECOVERED, NAMES AND ARREST NUMBERS OF PERSONS ARRESTED. EXPLAIN ANY OFFENSE CLASSIFICATION CHANGE. CLEARLY SHOW DISPOSITION OF RECOVERED PROPERTY AND INVENTORY NO. RECOMMEND TO SUPERVISOR CASE STATUS AND TO REVIEWER UCR DISPOSITION. INDICATE "ITEM NUMBER CONTINUED" AT LEFT, IF ANY.

ITEM NO.

At this time Investigator Chandler was told by Trooper Stinson that he had a passenger list and he would give it to Investigator Chandler. The list was as follows ... Rick Nelson, Helen Blair, Patrick Woodward, Rick Inveld, Andy Chapin, Clark Russell and Bobby Neal. The foam truck had arrived and pumped foam on the wreckage. Several loads were used to extinguish the fire. Reporters were on the scene asking about the passengers. Sheriff Hodge who had been on the scene for sometime fielded all questions, and told news people that we could not identify the people on board. At this time officers at this time began hearing that the news was saying that Rick Nelson was on board. Investigator Chandler ask Sgt. Estes and Trooper Stinson if someone had notified all the families involved. Investigator Chandler was advised that this had been taken care of. The command post learned that the other survivor was Kenneth Ferguson. Sheriff Hodge decided that removal of the dead would have to wait until the wreckage was cool enough to allow it to be done safely. The area was secured. Deputies and DPS Troopers were assigned security at the site. Investigator Chandler, Sheriff Hodge, Sgt. Estes and Chief Huggins left the crashsite. At 11:45 PM, Investigator Chandler was advised that National Transportation Safety Board Investigator was at the crash site and asking for Investigator Chandler to return to the site. Investigator Chandler returned to the site and met Tommy McFall of the N.T.S.B.

		MONEY	JEWELRY	CLOTHING	FURS	AUTO ACCESS.	BICYCLES	MISCELL.
CASH VALUE	**14. STOLEN**	$	$	$	$	$	$	$
	15. RECOVERED	MONEY $	JEWELRY $	CLOTHING $	FURS $	AUTO ACCESS. $	BICYCLES $	MISCELL. $

16. REPORTING OFFICER	NO.	**16. CASE STATUS** (STATUS MUST BE INDICATED FOR ALL CASES, INCLUDING NON-CRIMINAL INCIDENTS)	OFFICE USE ONLY
2ND OFFICER	NO.	☐ OPEN (PENDING) ☐ CLOSED ☐ SUSPENDED	19. DATE/TIME TYPED NO. 20. REPRODUCED BY NC
		CASE DISPOSITION (DISPOSITION OF CRIMINAL CASES MAY BE INDICATED AS APPROPRIATE)	21. UNIT REFERRED TO: 22. UCR DISPOSITION
17. SUPERVISOR APPROVING	NO.	☐ UNFOUNDED ☐ CLEARED BY ARREST ☐ CLEARED EXCEP.	23. REVIEWER NO. PAGE NO. 4 OF 13

SUPPLEMENTAL REPORT

1. EVIDENCE NUMBER	2. ARREST, CITATION, OR SUMMONS NO.	3. COMPLAINT NO.

4. NAME OF COMPLAINANT, DRIVER #1, VICTIM OR ARRESTEE	5. DATE OF THIS REPORT	6. DATE OF ORIGINAL OCCURRENCE
Plane Crash	01-01-86	12-31-85

7. FORM USED AS CONTINUATION SHEET FOR CURRENT REPORT ☐

8. OFFENSE, CHARGE OR INCIDENT ON ORIGINAL REPORT

9. FORM USED TO REPORT FOLLOWUP INVESTIGATION OR SUPPLEMENTAL INFORMATION ☐

10. CORRECT OFFENSE OR INCIDENT CLASSIFICATION   CHANGED ☐ YES

11. KIND OF REPORT CONTINUED ☐ OFFENSE ☐ TRAFFIC ACCIDENT ☐ ARREST ☐ VEHICLE ☐ OTHER

12. MULTIPLE CLEARANCE ☐ YES (LIST OTHER COMPLAINT NUMBERS IN NARRATIVE) ☐ NO

13. INSTRUCTIONS FOR FOLLOWUP OR SUPPLEMENTAL USAGE. UNDER NARRATIVE RECORD YOUR ACTIVITY AND ALL DEVELOPMENTS IN THE CASE SUBSEQUENT TO LAST REPORT. DESCRIBE AND RECORD VALUE OF ANY PROPERTY RECOVERED, NAMES AND ARREST NUMBERS OF PERSONS ARRESTED. EXPLAIN ANY OFFENSE CLASSIFICATION CHANGE. CLEARLY SHOW DISPOSITION OF RECOVERED PROPERTY AND INVENTORY NO. RECOMMEND TO SUPERVISOR CASE STATUS AND TO REVIEWER UCR DISPOSITION. INDICATE "ITEM NUMBER CONTINUED" AT LEFT, IF ANY.

ITEM NO.

Investigator Chandler and Investigator McFall went over the crash site and surrounding area. After Investigator Chandler and Investigator McFall discussed the matter, it was decided that sometime around 2:30 am or 3:00 am to remove the bodies. Investigator Chandler contacted Sheriff Hodge and it was agreed that the removal should be done then. Investigator Chandler and Investigator McFall returned to the site after making arrangements for needed equipment. Sheriff Hodge, Investigator Money, Chief Huggins, Deputy Phil Kennedy, Deputy Rick House, Investigator Chandler of Bowie County Sheriff's Office, Investigator McFall NTSB, David Rolf, Bill Radcliff of Bates Rolf Funeral Home removed the bodies. The bodies were located in the wreckage as follows:

Body #1 was found in the western most part of the wreckage. Body #1 was partially covering Body #2. Body #1 was lying with its head in a southern direction. Body #1 was removed and tagged "#1".

Body #2 was found partially under Body #1. Its head was lying in a southernly direction. Body #2 was removed and tagged "#2".

Bodies #3, #4 and #5 were found just inboard of the right engine. Body #3 being closest to the right engine. Body #4 was west of Body #3, lying parallel and touching Body #4. Body #5 was west of Body #4 with its' head resting on the lower portion of Body #4. All three bodies were lying on their right side and facing aft.

	14.	MONEY	JEWELRY	CLOTHING	FURS	AUTO ACCESS.	BICYCLES	MISCELL.
CASH VALUE	STOLEN	$	$	$	$	$	$	$
	15.	MONEY	JEWELRY	CLOTHING	FURS	AUTO ACCESS.	BICYCLES	MISCELL.
	RECOVERED	$	$	$	$	$	$	$

16. REPORTING OFFICER NO. 286	18. CASE STATUS (STATUS MUST BE INDICATED FOR ALL CASES, INCLUDING NON-CRIMINAL INCIDENTS)	OFFICE USE ONLY
2ND OFFICER NO.	☐ OPEN (PENDING) ☐ CLOSED ☐ SUSPENDED	19. DATE/TIME TYPED NO. / 20. PRODUCED BY NO.
	CASE DISPOSITION (DISPOSITION OF CRIMINAL CASES MAY BE INDICATED AS APPROPRIATE)	21. UNIT REFERRED TO: 22. UCR DISPOSITION
17. SUPERVISOR APPROVING NO.	☐ UNFOUNDED ☐ CLEARED BY ARREST ☐ CLEARED EXCEP.	23. REVIEWER NO. PAGE NO. 5 OF 13

SUPPLEMENTAL REPORT

1. EVIDENCE NUMBER	2. ARREST, CITATION, OR SUMMONS NO.	3. COMPLAINT NO

4. NAME OF COMPLAINANT, DRIVER #1, VICTIM OR ARRESTEE	5. DATE OF THIS REPORT	6. DATE OF ORIGINAL OCCURRENCE
Plane Crash	01-01-86	12-31-85

7. FORM USED AS CONTINUATION SHEET FOR CURRENT REPORT ☐	8. OFFENSE, CHARGE OR INCIDENT ON ORIGINAL REPORT

9. FORM USED TO REPORT FOLLOWUP INVESTIGATION OR SUPPLEMENTAL INFORMATION ☐	10. CORRECT OFFENSE OR INCIDENT CLASSIFICATION	CHANGED ☐ YES

11. KIND OF REPORT CONTINUED ☐ OFFENSE ☐ TRAFFIC ACCIDENT ☐ ARREST ☐ VEHICLE ☐ OTHER _____	12. MULTIPLE CLEARANCE ☐ YES (LIST OTHER COMPLAINT NUMBERS IN NARRATIVE) ☐ NO

13. INSTRUCTIONS FOR FOLLOWUP OR SUPPLEMENTAL USAGE. UNDER NARRATIVE RECORD YOUR ACTIVITY AND ALL DEVELOPMENTS IN THE CASE SUBSEQUENT TO LAST REPORT. DESCRIBE AND RECORD VALUE OF ANY PROPERTY RECOVERED, NAMES AND ARREST NUMBERS OF PERSONS ARRESTED. EXPLAIN ANY OFFENSE CLASSIFICATION CHANGE. CLEARLY SHOW DISPOSITION OF RECOVERED PROPERTY AND INVENTORY NO. RECOMMEND TO SUPERVISOR CASE STATUS AND TO REVIEWER UCR DISPOSITION. INDICATE "ITEM NUMBER CONTINUED" AT LEFT, IF ANY.

ITEM NO.

The Bodies were removed and tagged "#3", "#4", and "#5" as they were removed.

Body #6 and Body #7 were located aft of the right engine. Body #7 being closest to the engine and Body #6 being the farthest. Bodies #6 and #7 were lying with their heads in a northern direction. The Bodies were removed and tagged "#6" and "#7".

The removal of the bodies was completed at approximately 3:30 am on January 1, 1986.

Justice of the Peace Alfred Welch ordered autopsies and the bodies were transported to Dallas to the Florensic Lab.. At approximately 9:10 am Investigator Chandler talked with the Dallas County Medical Examiners office to see what was needed for the identification proceedure. The Lab stated that they needed dental records, medical records (if no dental records available) then physical descriptions and jewelry descriptions. Investigator Chandler advised the Medical Examiners office that he would have the families mail the dental records and phone the physical descriptions and jewelry descriptions. At 9:17 am Investigator Chandler started contacting the families of the deceased. David Nelson was called first. Investigator Chandler talked with John Nelson, David's 26 year old son. Investigator Chandler told John that the Lab would need Ricks' dental records to be shipped Express Mail to facilitate

	14.	MONEY	JEWELRY	CLOTHING	FURS	AUTO ACCESS.	BICYCLES	MISCELL.
	STOLEN	$	$	$	$	$	$	$
	15.	MONEY	JEWELRY	CLOTHING	FURS	AUTO ACCESS.	BICYCLES	MISCELL.
	RECOVERED	$	$	$	$	$	$	$

16. REPORTING OFFICER NO.	18. CASE STATUS (STATUS MUST BE INDICATED FOR ALL CASES, INCLUDING NON-CRIMINAL INCIDENTS)	OFFICE USE ONLY
2ND OFFICER NO.	☐ OPEN (PENDING) ☐ CLOSED ☐ SUSPENDED	19. DATE/TIME TYPED NO. 20. REPRODUCED BY NO.
17. SUPERVISOR APPROVING NO.	CASE DISPOSITION (DISPOSITION OF CRIMINAL CASES MAY BE INDICATED AS APPROPRIATE) ☐ UNFOUNDED ☐ CLEARED BY ARREST ☐ CLEARED EXCEP.	21. UNIT REFERRED TO: 22. UCR DISPOSITION
		23. REVIEWER NO. PAGE NO. 6 OF 13

SUPPLEMENTAL REPORT

1. EVIDENCE NUMBER	2. ARREST, CITATION, OR SUMMONS NO.	3. COMPLAINT NO.

4. NAME OF COMPLAINANT, DRIVER #1, VICTIM OR ARRESTEE	5. DATE OF THIS REPORT	6. DATE OF ORIGINAL OCCURRENCE
Plane Crash	01-01-86	12-31-85

7. FORM USED AS CONTINUATION SHEET FOR CURRENT REPORT ☐	8. OFFENSE, CHARGE OR INCIDENT ON ORIGINAL REPORT

9. FORM USED TO REPORT FOLLOWUP INVESTIGATION OR SUPPLEMENTAL INFORMATION ☐	10. CORRECT OFFENSE OR INCIDENT CLASSIFICATION	CHANGED ☐ YES

11. KIND OF REPORT CONTINUED ☐ OFFENSE ☐ TRAFFIC ACCIDENT ☐ ARREST ☐ VEHICLE ☐ OTHER	12. MULTIPLE CLEARANCE ☐ YES (LIST OTHER COMPLAINT NUMBERS IN NARRATIVE) ☐ NO

13. INSTRUCTIONS FOR FOLLOWUP OR SUPPLEMENTAL USAGE.	UNDER NARRATIVE RECORD YOUR ACTIVITY AND ALL DEVELOPMENTS IN THE CASE SUBSEQUENT TO LAST REPORT. DESCRIBE AND RECORD VALUE OF ANY PROPERTY RECOVERED, NAMES AND ARREST NUMBERS OF PERSONS ARRESTED. EXPLAIN ANY OFFENSE CLASSIFICATION CHANGE. CLEARLY SHOW DISPOSITION OF RECOVERED PROPERTY AND INVENTORY NO. RECOMMEND TO SUPERVISOR CASE STATUS AND TO REVIEWER UCR DISPOSITION. INDICATE "ITEM NUMBER CONTINUED" AT LEFT, IF ANY.

ITEM NO.

the identification process. Also, Investigator Chandler advised John Nelson that the Lab needed a complete description of Rick Nelson and a complete description of any jewelry that Rick might have been wearing. John Nelson stated that he would tell his dad and that his dad would probably call Investigator Chandler later in the day.

At 9:32 am Investigator Chandler contacted Mrs. Ruth Blair, Helen Blair's Mother, and advised her that the Lab would need Helen's dental records. Mrs. Blair stated that she knew that Helen had recently seen Rick's dentist but she did not know his name, but, she would attempt to find out and get the records. Investigator Chandler told her to call the Lab and give the Lab a physical description and jewelry description as soon as she could. Mrs. Blair stated that she would.

At 9:44 am Investigator Chandler called Frank Intveld, Rick Intveld's brother, and received no answer. Investigator Chandler returned the call at 10:15 am and talked with Frank Intveld. Frank was asked to Express Mail Rick's dental records to the Lab as soon as they could be located. Frank was also told to call the Lab with a physical description and jewelry description.

At 10:30 am Investigator Chandler called Bobby Neal's residence and received no answer. Recalled at 10:46 and talked with Phyllis Neal's sister. Investigator Chandler advised Mrs. Neal's sister of the need for the dental records and gave her

14. CASH VALUE	MONEY	JEWELRY	CLOTHING	FURS	AUTO ACCESS.	BICYCLES	MISCELL.
STOLEN	$	$	$	$	$	$	$
15. RECOVERED	MONEY $	JEWELRY $	CLOTHING $	FURS $	AUTO ACCESS. $	BICYCLES $	MISCELL. $

16. REPORTING OFFICER NO. 280	18. CASE STATUS (STATUS MUST BE INDICATED FOR ALL CASES, INCLUDING NON-CRIMINAL INCIDENTS) ☐ OPEN (PENDING) ☐ CLOSED ☐ SUSPENDED	OFFICE USE ONLY
2ND OFFICER NO.	CASE DISPOSITION (DISPOSITION OF CRIMINAL CASES MAY BE INDICATED AS APPROPRIATE) ☐ UNFOUNDED ☐ CLEARED BY ARREST ☐ CLEARED EXCEP.	19. DATE/TIME TYPED NO. / REPRODUCED BY NC
17. SUPERVISOR APPROVING NO.		21. UNIT REFERRED TO: / 22. UCR DISPOSITION
		23. REVIEWER NO. / PAGE NO. 7 OF 13

24. COMPLAINT NO.

SUPPLEMENTAL REPORT

1. EVIDENCE NUMBER	2. ARREST, CITATION, OR SUMMONS NO.	3. COMPLAINT NO

4. NAME OF COMPLAINANT, DRIVER #1, VICTIM OR ARRESTEE	5. DATE OF THIS REPORT	6. DATE OF ORIGINAL OCCURRENCE
Plane Crash	01-01-86	12-31-85

7. FORM USED AS CONTINUATION SHEET FOR CURRENT REPORT ☐	8. OFFENSE, CHARGE OR INCIDENT ON ORIGINAL REPORT

9. FORM USED TO REPORT FOLLOWUP INVESTIGATION OR SUPPLEMENTAL INFORMATION ☐	10. CORRECT OFFENSE OR INCIDENT CLASSIFICATION	CHANGED ☐ YES

11. KIND OF REPORT CONTINUED ☐ OFFENSE ☐ TRAFFIC ACCIDENT ☐ ARREST ☐ VEHICLE ☐ OTHER	12. MULTIPLE CLEARANCE ☐ YES (LIST OTHER COMPLAINT NUMBERS IN NARRATIVE) ☐ NO

13. INSTRUCTIONS FOR FOLLOWUP OR SUPPLEMENTAL USAGE.	UNDER NARRATIVE RECORD YOUR ACTIVITY AND ALL DEVELOPMENTS IN THE CASE SUBSEQUENT TO LAST REPORT. DESCRIBE AND RECORD VALUE OF ANY PROPERTY RECOVERED, NAMES AND ARREST NUMBERS OF PERSONS ARRESTED. EXPLAIN ANY OFFENSE CLASSIFICATION CHANGE. CLEARLY SHOW DISPOSITION OF RECOVERED PROPERTY AND INVENTORY NO. RECOMMEND TO SUPERVISOR CASE STATUS AND TO REVIEWER UCR DISPOSITION. INDICATE "ITEM NUMBER CONTINUED" AT LEFT, IF ANY.

ITEM NO.

instructions as to how to mail the records. She was told to call the Lab and give them the information about physical description and jewelry description. She advised that she would get the information to the Lab as quick as possible.

At 11:25 am Investigator Chandler called Clark Russell's residence and spoke with Mrs. Russell's sister. Investigator Chandler asked that she get Clark's dental records and Express Mail them to the Lab and she said that she would. Investigator Chandler asked her to call the Lab and give them the physical description and jewelry description as soon as she could get them together. She told Investigator Chandler that she would.

At 11:40 am Investigator Chandler was called by Andy Chapins' brother-in-law. An earlier attempt to call Andy Chapin's residence had been unsuccessful due to a busy circuit. Mr. Chapin's brother-in-law asked what he could do to assist Investigator Chandler. Investigator Chandler told him of the need for the dental records, physical and jewelry descriptions. He advised that he was in Las Vegas, Nevada, but was going to fly to Los Angeles as soon as he got off the phone with Investigator Chandler. He told Investigator Chandler that he would get all the information and get it to the Lab. He told Investigator Chandler that the plane had been having problems since the Band started using it and they never could get the problems fixed.

14.	MONEY	JEWELRY	CLOTHING	FURS	AUTO ACCESS.	BICYCLES	MISCELL.
STOLEN	$	$	$	$	$	$	$
15.	MONEY	JEWELRY	CLOTHING	FURS	AUTO ACCESS.	BICYCLES	MISCELL.
RECOVERED	$	$	$	$	$	$	$

16. REPORTING OFFICER NO.	18. CASE STATUS (STATUS MUST BE INDICATED FOR ALL CASES, INCLUDING NON-CRIMINAL INCIDENTS)	OFFICE USE ONLY
280		19. DATE/TIME TYPED NO	20. REPRODUCED BY NO
R&I OFFICER NO.	☐ OPEN (PENDING) ☐ CLOSED ☐ SUSPENDED	21. UNIT REFERRED TO:	22. UCR DISPOSITION
	CASE DISPOSITION (DISPOSITION OF CRIMINAL CASES MAY BE INDICATED AS APPROPRIATE)	
17. SUPERVISOR APPROVING NO.	☐ UNFOUNDED ☐ CLEARED BY ARREST ☐ CLEARED EXCEP.	23. REVIEWER NO.	PAGE NO. 8 OF 13

SUPPLEMENTAL REPORT

1. EVIDENCE NUMBER	2. ARREST, CITATION, OR SUMMONS NO.	3. COMPLAINT NO

4. NAME OF COMPLAINANT, DRIVER #1, VICTIM OR ARRESTEE	5. DATE OF THIS REPORT	6. DATE OF ORIGINAL OCCURRENCE
Plane Crash	01-01-86	12-31-85

7. FORM USED AS CONTINUATION SHEET FOR CURRENT REPORT ☐	8. OFFENSE, CHARGE OR INCIDENT ON ORIGINAL REPORT

9. FORM USED TO REPORT FOLLOWUP INVESTIGATION OR SUPPLEMENTAL INFORMATION ☐	10. CORRECT OFFENSE OR INCIDENT CLASSIFICATION	CHANGED ☐ YES

11. KIND OF REPORT CONTINUED ☐ OFFENSE ☐ TRAFFIC ACCIDENT ☐ ARREST ☐ VEHICLE ☐ OTHER	12. MULTIPLE CLEARANCE ☐ YES (LIST OTHER COMPLAINT NUMBERS IN NARRATIVE) ☐ NO

13. INSTRUCTIONS FOR FOLLOWUP OR SUPPLEMENTAL USAGE.	UNDER NARRATIVE RECORD YOUR ACTIVITY AND ALL DEVELOPMENTS IN THE CASE SUBSEQUENT TO LAST REPORT. DESCRIBE AND RECORD VALUE OF ANY PROPERTY RECOVERED, NAMES AND ARREST NUMBERS OF PERSONS ARRESTED. EXPLAIN ANY OFFENSE CLASSIFICATION CHANGE. CLEARLY SHOW DISPOSITION OF RECOVERED PROPERTY AND INVENTORY NO. RECOMMEND TO SUPERVISOR CASE STATUS AND TO REVIEWER UCR DISPOSITION. INDICATE "ITEM NUMBER CONTINUED" AT LEFT, IF ANY.

ITEM NO.

Mr. Chapin's brother-in-law indicated that he was already considering civil action in reference to the maintenance of the plane.

At 11:55 am Investigator Chandler call Greg McDonald and spoke with him. Mr. McDonald revealed that he and Rick were best friends as well as business associates. Mr. McDonald stated that he had talked to David Nelson earlier and that if the Department needed any more information that we should call him and not the family. Investigator Chandler gave Mr. McDonald all the information that had been given to the families in case they should call him for clarity. Mr. McDonald stated that he had Ricks' dental records and that Helen had seen Ricks' dentist about a month ago and he would get that information to the Lab. Mr. McDonald stated that Rick only wore two (2) pieces of jewelry; a small gold cross and a pinky ring with the initials "ERN". He stated that Helen would be wearing a similiar ring with the initial "H" and a diamond solitaire engagement ring. Mr. McDonald was given the Bowie County Sheriff Department phone number, as all the families were, and told to call if he needed any further assistance. Investigator Chandler got the telephone number for Patrick Woodward's wife in Dallas, Texas from Mr. McDonald.

At 12:19 pm Investigator Chandler spoke with Jody Woodward briefly and then spoke with her cousin who advised that another member of the Band's family had called and

14.	MONEY	JEWELRY	CLOTHING	FURS	AUTO ACCESS.	BICYCLES	MISCELL.
STOLEN	$	$	$	$	$	$	$
15. RECOVERED	MONEY $	JEWELRY $	CLOTHING $	FURS $	AUTO ACCESS. $	BICYCLES $	MISCELL. $

16. REPORTING OFFICER NO.	18. CASE STATUS (STATUS MUST BE INDICATED FOR ALL CASES, INCLUDING NON-CRIMINAL INCIDENTS)	OFFICE USE ONLY

2ND OFFICER   NO.

☐ OPEN (PENDING) ☐ CLOSED ☐ SUSPENDED

19. DATE/TIME TYPED NO	REPRODUCED BY NO

CASE DISPOSITION (DISPOSITION OF CRIMINAL CASES MAY BE INDICATED AS APPROPRIATE)

21. UNIT REFERRED TO.	22. UCR DISPOSITION

17. SUPERVISOR APPROVING   NO.

☐ UNFOUNDED
☐ CLEARED BY ARREST ☐ CLEARED EXCEP.

23. REVIEWER NO.	PAGE NO. 9 OF 13

SUPPLEMENTAL REPORT

1. EVIDENCE NUMBER	2. ARREST, CITATION, OR SUMMONS NO.	3. COMPLAINT NO

4. NAME OF COMPLAINANT, DRIVER #1, VICTIM OR ARRESTEE	5. DATE OF THIS REPORT	6. DATE OF ORIGINAL OCCURRENCE
Plane Crash	01-01-86	12-31-85

7. FORM USED AS CONTINUATION SHEET FOR CURRENT REPORT ☐

8. OFFENSE, CHARGE OR INCIDENT ON ORIGINAL REPORT

9. FORM USED TO REPORT FOLLOWUP INVESTIGATION OR SUPPLEMENTAL INFORMATION ☐

10. CORRECT OFFENSE OR INCIDENT CLASSIFICATION — CHANGED ☐ YES

11. KIND OF REPORT CONTINUED ☐ OFFENSE ☐ TRAFFIC ACCIDENT ☐ ARREST ☐ VEHICLE ☐ OTHER

12. MULTIPLE CLEARANCE ☐ YES (LIST OTHER COMPLAINT NUMBERS IN NARRATIVE) ☐ NO

13. INSTRUCTIONS FOR FOLLOWUP OR SUPPLEMENTAL USAGE. UNDER NARRATIVE RECORD YOUR ACTIVITY AND ALL DEVELOPMENTS IN THE CASE SUBSEQUENT TO LAST REPORT. DESCRIBE AND RECORD VALUE OF ANY PROPERTY RECOVERED, NAMES AND ARREST NUMBERS OF PERSONS ARRESTED. EXPLAIN ANY OFFENSE CLASSIFICATION CHANGE. CLEARLY SHOW DISPOSITION OF RECOVERED PROPERTY AND INVENTORY NO. RECOMMEND TO SUPERVISOR CASE STATUS AND TO REVIEWER UCR DISPOSITION. INDICATE "ITEM NUMBER CONTINUED" AT LEFT, IF ANY.

ITEM NO.

given them the information about the dental records and descriptions needed. She advised that her husband was enroute to the Dallas Lab with a dental mold and the other information.

After contacting all the families involved Investigator Chandler returned to the crash site and checked with Chief Deputy Huggins to see if his help was needed there. Chief Huggins advised it was not and that Investigator Chandler should get some rest. The crash site was in the hands of the NTSB and FAA Investigators and all the BCSO was doing was providing security and traffic control. As investigator Chandler was leaving the crash scene he was advised to call the BIC that they had a long distant phone call for him to return. Investigator Chandler returned to J.P. Dunn's office and got the phone number. The number was David Nelson's number. Investigator Chandler called the number and spoke with David Nelson. Mr Nelson also said that he had spoke with Greg McDonald. Mr. Nelson stated that Mr. McDonald had passed along Investigator Chandlers' concern about David Nelson or his mother coming to the crash site. Investigator Chandler told Mr. Nelson that while he understood Mr. Nelson's feelings and his desire to learn about the tragedy, Investigator Chandler thought that it would be in their best interest that they not come. Mr. Nelson said that he had thought it might be faster if he hand carried Rick's dental records to the Dallas

	MONEY	JEWELRY	CLOTHING	FURS	AUTO ACCESS.	BICYCLES	MISCELL.
14. STOLEN	$	$	$	$	$	$	$
15. RECOVERED	$	$	$	$	$	$	$

16. REPORTING OFFICER — NO.

2ND OFFICER — NO.

17. SUPERVISOR APPROVING — NO.

18. CASE STATUS (STATUS MUST BE INDICATED FOR ALL CASES, INCLUDING NON-CRIMINAL INCIDENTS)
☐ OPEN (PENDING) ☐ CLOSED ☐ SUSPENDED

CASE DISPOSITION (DISPOSITION OF CRIMINAL CASES MAY BE INDICATED AS APPROPRIATE)
☐ UNFOUNDED
☐ CLEARED BY ARREST ☐ CLEARED EXCEP.

OFFICE USE ONLY

19. DATE/TIME TYPED NO. 20. REPRODUCED BY NC

21. UNIT REFERRED TO: 22. UCR DISPOSITION

23. REVIEWER — NO.

PAGE NO. 10 OF 13

SUPPLEMENTAL REPORT

1. EVIDENCE NUMBER	2. ARREST, CITATION, OR SUMMONS NO.	3. COMPLAINT NO

4. NAME OF COMPLAINANT, DRIVER #1, VICTIM OR ARRESTEE	5. DATE OF THIS REPORT	6. DATE OF ORIGINAL OCCURRENCE
Plane Crash	01-01-86	12-31-85

7. FORM USED AS CONTINUATION SHEET FOR CURRENT REPORT ☐

8. OFFENSE, CHARGE OR INCIDENT ON ORIGINAL REPORT

9. FORM USED TO REPORT FOLLOWUP INVESTIGATION OR SUPPLEMENTAL INFORMATION ☐

10. CORRECT OFFENSE OR INCIDENT CLASSIFICATION CHANGED ☐ YES

11. KIND OF REPORT CONTINUED ☐ OFFENSE ☐ TRAFFIC ACCIDENT ☐ ARREST ☐ VEHICLE ☐ OTHER _____

12. MULTIPLE CLEARANCE ☐ YES (LIST OTHER COMPLAINT NUMBERS IN NARRATIVE) ☐ NO

13. INSTRUCTIONS FOR FOLLOWUP OR SUPPLEMENTAL USAGE.

UNDER NARRATIVE RECORD YOUR ACTIVITY AND ALL DEVELOPMENTS IN THE CASE SUBSEQUENT TO LAST REPORT. DESCRIBE AND RECORD VALUE OF ANY PROPERTY RECOVERED, NAMES AND ARREST NUMBERS OF PERSONS ARRESTED. EXPLAIN ANY OFFENSE CLASSIFICATION CHANGE. CLEARLY SHOW DISPOSITION OF RECOVERED PROPERTY AND INVENTORY NO. RECOMMEND TO SUPERVISOR CASE STATUS AND TO REVIEWER UCR DISPOSITION. INDICATE "ITEM NUMBER CONTINUED" AT LEFT, IF ANY.

ITEM NO.

Lab. Investigator Chandler advised Mr. Nelson that putting the records in Express Mail should be sufficient. Mr. Nelson then mentioned the fact that his 74 year old Mother had heard the news on television. Investigator Chandler apologized for this and told Mr. Nelson that when the story began to appear at the crash site that Investigator Chandler had checked and been told twice that the families had been notified. Investigator Chandler told Mr. Nelson that the information that the families had been notified came from the Texas Department of Public Safety. After again apologizing for the problem Investigator Chandler ended the conversation.

Investigator Chandler then returned to the crash site to see if his assistance was needed. It was not and Investigator Chandler left the crash site.

	MONEY	JEWELRY	CLOTHING	FURS	AUTO ACCESS.	BICYCLES	MISCELL.
14. STOLEN	$	$	$	$	$	$	$
15. RECOVERED	$	$	$	$	$	$	$

16. REPORTING OFFICER   NO.

2ND OFFICER   NO.

17. SUPERVISOR APPROVING   NO.

18. CASE STATUS (STATUS MUST BE INDICATED FOR ALL CASES, INCLUDING NON-CRIMINAL INCIDENTS)
☐ OPEN (PENDING) ☐ CLOSED ☐ SUSPENDED

CASE DISPOSITION (DISPOSITION OF CRIMINAL CASES MAY BE INDICATED AS APPROPRIATE)
☐ UNFOUNDED
☐ CLEARED BY ARREST ☐ CLEARED EXCEP.

OFFICE USE ONLY

19. DATE/TIME TYPED NO.   20. REPRODUCED BY NO

21. UNIT REFERRED TO: 22. UCR DISPOSITION

23. REVIEWER   NO.   PAGE NO.   11 OF 13

SUPPLEMENTAL REPORT

	1. EVIDENCE NUMBER	2. ARREST, CITATION, OR SUMMONS NO.	3. COMPLAINT NO

4. NAME OF COMPLAINANT, DRIVER #1, VICTIM OR ARRESTEE	5. DATE OF THIS REPORT	6. DATE OF ORIGINAL OCCURRENCE
Plane Crash	01-03-86	12-31-85

7. FORM USED AS CONTINUATION SHEET FOR CURRENT REPORT ☐

8. OFFENSE, CHARGE OR INCIDENT ON ORIGINAL REPORT

9. FORM USED TO REPORT FOLLOWUP INVESTIGATION OR SUPPLEMENTAL INFORMATION ☐

10. CORRECT OFFENSE OR INCIDENT CLASSIFICATION — CHANGED ☐ YES

11. KIND OF REPORT CONTINUED ☐ OFFENSE ☐ TRAFFIC ACCIDENT ☐ ARREST ☐ VEHICLE ☐ OTHER _____

12. MULTIPLE CLEARANCE ☐ YES (LIST OTHER COMPLAINT NUMBERS IN NARRATIVE) ☐ NO

13. INSTRUCTIONS FOR FOLLOWUP OR SUPPLEMENTAL USAGE. UNDER NARRATIVE RECORD YOUR ACTIVITY AND ALL DEVELOPMENTS IN THE CASE SUBSEQUENT TO LAST REPORT. DESCRIBE AND RECORD VALUE OF ANY PROPERTY RECOVERED, NAMES AND ARREST NUMBERS OF PERSONS ARRESTED. EXPLAIN ANY OFFENSE CLASSIFICATION CHANGE, CLEARLY SHOW DISPOSITION OF RECOVERED PROPERTY AND INVENTORY NO. RECOMMEND TO SUPERVISOR CASE STATUS AND TO REVIEWER UCR DISPOSITION. INDICATE "ITEM NUMBER CONTINUED" AT LEFT, IF ANY.

ITEM NO.

On 01-02-86 Investigator Chandler returned to the crash site. Investigator Chandler met with Investigator McFall and offered his assistance to the NTSB and FAA. Investigator McFall advised that they needed assistance in contacting some of the witness's to the crash. Investigator Chandler did this and assisted around the crash site the rest of the day.

On 01-04-86 Investigator Chandler again assisted the NTSB at the crash site. Investigator Chandler took Investigator McFall to the Blackmon air strip and located several other small private air strips in the area of western Bowie County.

01-05-86 Investigator Chandler transported two body parts found in the wreckage to the Dallas County Medical Examiners office in Dallas, Texas.

01-06-86 Investigator Chandler assisted by Investigator Gillispie, Deputy Calhoun, Deputy Mike Boling assisted the NTSB in sifting through the wrechage while Air Salvage of Dallas began to load the wrechage for removal from the area. All personal items found in t he sifting of the wreckage were inventoried and turned to Sheriff Hodge.

14.	MONEY	JEWELRY	CLOTHING	FURS	AUTO ACCESS.	BICYCLES	MISCELL.
STOLEN	$	$	$	$	$	$	$
15. RECOVERED	MONEY $	JEWELRY $	CLOTHING $	FURS $	AUTO ACCESS. $	BICYCLES $	MISCELL. $

16. REPORTING OFFICER NO.	18. CASE STATUS (STATUS MUST BE INDICATED FOR ALL CASES, INCLUDING NON-CRIMINAL INCIDENTS)	OFFICE USE ONLY
2ND OFFICER NO.	☐ OPEN (PENDING) ☐ CLOSED ☐ SUSPENDED	19. DATE/TIME TYPED NO. 20. REPRODUCED BY NO.
	CASE DISPOSITION (DISPOSITION OF CRIMINAL CASES MAY BE INDICATED AS APPROPRIATE)	21. UNIT REFERRED TO: 22. UCR DISPOSITION
17. SUPERVISOR APPROVING NO.	☐ UNFOUNDED ☐ CLEARED BY ARREST ☐ CLEARED EXCEP.	23. REVIEWER NO. PAGE NO. 13 OF 13

WU Telegram **WU** Telegram **WU**
western union   western union   western union

```
IPM62TX
1-015886A003 01/03/86
ICS IPMRYND RNO
06581 RENO NV.01-03 0220P PST RYNC
ICS IPM62TX

4-036176S003 01/03/86
ICS IPMRNCZ CSP
  2138518396 TDRN LOS ANGELES CA 59 01-03 0511P EST
PMS SHERIFF THOMAS HODGE BOWIE COUNTY SHERIFF DEPT BI-STATE JUSTICE
BLDG, URGENT, DLR
100 STATELINE AVE
TEXARKANA TX 75501
THIS IS WRITTEN NOTICE AUTHORIZING YOU TO SEND ALL ACCIDENT REPORT
INFORMATION REGARDING DECEMBER 31, DC #3, N711Y, CRASH IN WHICH MY
FATHER, ERIC H. NELSON ALSO KNOW AS RICK NELSON PERISHED TO GM
PERSONAL MANAGEMENT. 899 AVENIDA PALMAS, PALM SPRING, CA. 92262. IF
POSSIBLE SEND VIA FEDERAL EXPRESS BILLING GM PERSONAL MANAGEMENT
ACCOUNT #109995836 FOR COLLECT MAILING. SINCERELY,
  MATTHEW NELSON SON OF ERIC NELSON

1716 EST

1720 EST

IPM62TX
```

FORM APPROVED—OMB No. 004-R-5713

NATIONAL TRANSPORTATION SAFETY BOARD

WASHINGTON, D.C. 20594

STATEMENT OF WITNESS

he purpose of this statement is intended solely for use in determining the facts, conditions and circumstances,
nd the probable cause of the subject accident.

Date _2-2-86_

. Place of accident _DE KALB, TX_   Date _12-31-85_   Hour _5:17 PM_

. Type of vehicle _AIRCRAFT_

. Identification of vehicle _N7114_

. What is your name _L. B. BARRETT_   Age _60_

. Address _BOX 462   DE KALB, TX_

. Occupation _GROCER_   By whom employed _SELF_

. Where were you at the time of the accident _FEEDING CATTLE._

. Tell in your own words what you saw or heard before and at the time the accident occurred.

I WAS FEEDING CATTLE AND SAW AIRPLANE PULL-UP AND GO
BACK DOWN BEHIND TREES. MY SON AND I DROVE TO GATE AND WENT
TO AIRPLANE. APPROACHED AIRPLANE FROM FRONT AND SAW A MAN
WALKING AWAY FROM LEFT SIDE OF CABIN. THE AIRPLANE WAS RESTING
ON THE LANDING GEAR WITH THE LEFT ENGINE RUNNING + PROPELLER
TURNING. THE FIRE WAS ON THE FRONT RIGHT SIDE AROUND THE
RIGHT ENGINE. THE FIRE WAS FIERCE AND SPRED RAPIDLY. THE LEFT
ENGINE CONTINUED TO RUN FOR "10-15 MIN UNTIL THE AIRPLANE
FELL DOWN TO THE GROUND. SHORTLY AFTER SEEING THE FIRST
MAN WE SAW THE SECOND MAN COME OUT OF THE TALL GRASS

L. B. Barrett Jr
(Signature)

SB FORM 6120.11 (Rev. 10/77)   (Use reverse side of sheet for diagram and additional statement)

VERY BADLY BURNED. THE FIRST MAN TOLD US THERE WERE 9 PEOPLE ON THE AIRPLANE AND THAT WE COULDN'T GET THE OTHER PEOPLE OUT.

SIGNATURE ON FRONT

I AM THE SON OF MR. BARRETT. MY OBSERVATIONS WERE THE SAME. FROM MY VIEW IT LOOKED LIKE THE FIRST MAN WE SAW CAME OUT FROM THE RIGHT SIDE OF THE AIRPLANE AND UNDER IT RUNNING TO THE LEFT AWAY ~~FEB~~ FROM THE BURNING AIRPLANE.

Randy Barrett

AS WE APPROACHED THE AIRPLANE THERE WAS AN ARM HANGING OUT OF A FRONT WINDOW OR OPENING ON THE FRONT LEFT SIDE OF THE AIRPLANE. THE ARM NEVER MOVED.

L.B.B.
R.B.B.

Budget Bureau No. 39-R024.2.

NATIONAL TRANSPORTATION SAFETY BOARD

DEPARTMENT OF TRANSPORTATION
WASHINGTON, D.C. 20591

STATEMENT OF WITNESS

The purpose of this statement is intended solely for use in determining the facts, conditions and circumstances, and the probable cause of the subject accident.

Date __1/5/86__

I. Place of accident __DeKalb, Tx__ Date __12/31/85__ Hour __5:17 p.m.__

II. Aircraft _____ FAA Certificate No. _____

III. What is your name __Debbie Foster__ Age __22__

IV. Address __Rt 3 Box 16 AA   DeKalb, Tx. 75559__

V. Occupation __Teacher__ By whom employed __DeKalb Independent School__

VI. Where were you at the time of the accident __~~South~~ North end and west window of home__

VII. Tell in your own words what you saw or heard before and at the time the accident occurred.

4 pages attached

__Debbie Foster__
(Signature)

NTSB Form 6120.11   (Use reverse side of sheet for diagram and additional statement)

110

At about 5:17 p.m. Tuesday, December 31, my two year old daughter, Tiffany and I were in her bedroom playing dolls. Her room is on the north end of the house facing west. She began to cry saying that a noise was hurting her ears. About that time all I could here was a terrible rumble throughout the house. This noise, which I assume was the engines, shook our entire home. I told Tiffany it was probably just a big truck coming down the road. I went to her window to show her that it was just a truck and all I could see was the wheel of the plane. I grabbed Tiffany and told her the plane was going to crash. When we looked at the plane, we could see it dropping fire from somewhere. It looked like it was coming from near the wheel but I was so scared that I am not sure of the

111

location from where the fire was
coming. I must have just froze
because all I remember is watching
the plane until it to a stop in the
trees.

As the plane descended over
our house, all I could really
see was the landing gear and
the tail section. I felt that if
I had reached out Tiffany's window
I could have touched the plane.
The next thing I remember seeing
was the plane hitting the fence
on Mr. Jones' land. His cows were
in the pasture lying down where the
plane first hit. They all jumped
and ran. The plane then went
airborne a short distance before
finally coming to rest in the trees.

The plane was on fire, or
at least it was dropping fire
all of the way down while I was
watching it! The plane never burst
into flames nor did it blow-up.
The flames just gradually got larger. 113

I immediately ran to the phone to call the fire department but the plane had taken down my phone lines and my electrical lines.

Bowie-Cass is our electrical company. When they came to hook our electricity back up, Mike Childers of Bowie Cass, told my husband, Jeff, that it missed our roof by no more than six feet. The electrical pole is about fifteen feet from the back of our home. It has a black connecting wire that goes to our house. The plane jerked the black connecting wire from our home but did not disturb the pole. The NTSB investigators told us that they felt that it had missed our home by no more than 3 feet.

When I realized that I had no electricity or a phone, I grabbed my daughter and we left. I realized that all of the firemen would be at the crash and they would never notice the fire behind our house, beside our house and in our front yard. When I got back from _ _ _ taking my daughter to my aunts, there were friends of our family fighting the fires in our yard. The fire did burn up our water meter but thanks to our friends it did not get very close to our house. I also did not know what might have fallen on our home and I was worried about my daughter safety.

Debbie Foster

NATIONAL TRANSPORTATION SAFETY BOARD *page one*

WASHINGTON, D.C. 20594

STATEMENT OF WITNESS

The purpose of this statement is intended solely for use in determining the facts, conditions and circumstances, and the probable cause of the subject accident.

Date _____ 1-4-85 _____

. Place of accident ½ *Miles SE of* DeKalb, TX, Date _12-31-85_ Hour _5:05 P.M._
    BETWEEN 5:00 & 5:15 P.M.

. Type of vehicle _BIG PLANE_

. Identification of vehicle _I KNEW IT WAS A BIG PLANE_ WHITE 2 ENGINES

. What is your name _~~Donna~~ Donald E Lewis_ Age _53_

. Address _402 SE SOUTH STREET DEKALB, TX_

. Occupation _ENGINEER + OPERATOR_ By whom employed _R R A D_
    RED RIVER ARMY DEPOT

. Where were you at the time of the accident _1 3/10 Mile SE of DEKALB, TX_

Tell in your own words what you saw or heard before and at the time the accident occurred.

I was at My Farm on My Tractor (above site) headed Due East. I heard the sound of the aircraft and looked up. I saw the above aircraft headed due North below tree top level. about 30 or 40 feet High. (less than 100 feet) It flew north for 150 acres. He Banked right, pulled up and headed northeast bound. I then lost sight of the aircraft. The Window looked Black. The smoke was coming from under the wing on the other Side of the aircraft. This Side of the aircraft was white. Black smoke was Bellowing from the right side / far Side of the aircraft. No Flame, Just smoke. No Sparks. The aircraft was 300 To 400 yards in Front of me. The wheels under the wing was down. _Donald E Lewis_
(Signature)

ISB FORM 6120.11 (Rev. 10/77)   (Use reverse side of sheet for diagram and additional statement)   —

(over)   115

Music's Broken Wings

I don't remember the tail wheel being down. The Tail looked up. The aircraft was in sight for approximately 2 minutes. 3 to 5 minutes elapsed and then I saw the smoke. As the aircraft went out of Sight I drove my Tractor to the accident Site as hard as I could go. When I arrived at the Aircraft Both tires were up. I could have driven My Tractor under the Aircraft if it ~~hadn't~~ hadn't been on fire. (My Tractor is a 10-20 John Deere and the ~~Hood is chest high~~) When I arrived at the Aircraft the left engine was still running. The right engine was Stopped. Alot of fire ~~was~~ and mostly Black Smoke ~~was in~~ the area of the right engine. (Mostly Black Smoke) Alot of Black Smoke, very Thick was coming from the Right engine and main Body of the right side of the Aircraft. I heard both tires Blow individually. I am a volunteer Fireman and have been on the Fire Department for 24 almost 25 years. The gasoline never did blow. MR. L. B. Barrett and His Son Randy were the only people there Before me. The first person I saw was the Co-Pilot. The pilot was about 20 feet from the Copilot. About this time MR. Don Ruggles set down in his Helicopter. The pilot told me there was a ~~totle~~ of nine people on the aircraft. The pilot ask me to call his wife and tell her the Aircraft had crashed, but that he was O.K. I then went to the road (at the Woodards Home) and directed the Ambulence to the ~~Aircraft~~ P10T&Co R10T. About this time the Air Life Helicopter landed. The following Department of Public Safety officers were at the Site. Messers Williams Estes, Longo Butler and Ronnie Fincher.

116

See attached Sketch explains this Statement.

See Page Three More

(Page three)

When I went BACK to the Aircraft the
Body of the Aircraft had dropped
to the ground. This was after the
Ambulance had taken the Pilot
and Co-Pilot to the Hospital.

FORM APPROVED—OMB No. 004-R-5713

NATIONAL TRANSPORTATION SAFETY BOARD

WASHINGTON, D.C. 20594

STATEMENT OF WITNESS

The purpose of this statement is intended solely for use in determining the facts, conditions and circumstances, and the probable cause of the subject accident.

Date _January 6 1986_

. Place of accident _De Kalb Texas_   Date _December 31, 85_ Hour _5:10 pm_

. Type of vehicle _aircraft   DC 3_

. Identification of vehicle _____

. What is your name _Dean Waters_   Age _49_

. Address _Rt 1 Box 23   De Kalb Texas 75559_

. Occupation _thoroughbred trainer_ By whom employed _Self_

. Where were you at the time of the accident _on my farm_

. Tell in your own words what you saw or heard before and at the time the accident occurred.

I had just finished evening feeding and heard an aircraft - engines had been idled back - I looked up to see the DC 3 descending he was approximately 500 feet flying east at approx 90 mph, he was trailing smoke, I was unable to tell where the smoke was coming from, whether it was the fuselage or the right engine - I could tell it was not the left engine - at this point he was obviously looking for a place to land - we jumped into our pick up to try to be of assistance when we turned North on 990 we could see the smoke & flames from the _Dean Waters_ (Signature)
pto

FSB FORM 6120.11 (Rev. 10/77)   (Use reverse side of sheet for diagram and additional statement)

grass field burning — I proceeded to the point of impact where we parked our vehicle and ran to the aircraft (I met 2 of my employees in the field) We approached the aircraft from the left side - it was evident the entire interior was engulfed in flames from the rear cargo door forward to the cockpit — the left engine only was running fanning the flames to great intensity. the engine ran for 8 to 10 minutes — there were 3 explosions 2 minor which I assumed were tires on major that I assumed to be a fuel cell I didn't see the pilot or copilot escape from the aircraft — I assumed that no one got out. a helicopter landed about 8-10 minutes after the crash there were some people near it — about 200 feet in front of the aircraft — the aircraft burned with intense red & blue flames and heavy black smoke — the flames were most intense in the cockpit area due to the air movement of the engine — (prop wash)

Dean   at this time the heavy flames were
in the cockpit area — the fuseloge had
already been heavily damaged by the
fire

Pat   the flames appeared to the worst in the
area right at the trailing edge of the wing
the planes structure showing, the skin was
gone — the flames yellow orange & blue with black smoke

120

Arizona
BUILDING MAINTENANCE

1507 WEST McDOWELL ROAD, PHOENIX, AZ 85007, (602) 257-0020

and occasionally fluffy gray smoke —
the intensity of the flames sounded like
a blow torch — I heard 3 explosions
I assumed it was hot oil trapped in
the engines system — I was later told
it was probably tires — it makes sense —

Pat Waters

FORM APPROVED—OMB No. 004-R-5713

NATIONAL TRANSPORTATION SAFETY BOARD

WASHINGTON, D.C. 20594

STATEMENT OF WITNESS

The purpose of this statement is intended solely for use in determining the facts, conditions and circumstances, and the probable cause of the subject accident.

Date _January 6 1986_

. Place of accident _DeKalb texas_ Date _Dec 31, 1985_ Hour _5¹⁰ pm_

. Type of vehicle _Aircraft DC 3_

. Identification of vehicle _____

. What is your name _Pat Waters_ Age _45_

. Address _Rt 1 Box 23 DeKalb texas 75559_

. Occupation _asst trainer_ By whom employed _self_

. Where were you at the time of the accident _on our farm_

. Tell in your own words what you saw or heard before and at the time the accident occurred.

my husband called for me to look at a plane coming over our farm - it was decending noticably. & trailing smoke it started to nose toward FM 990 - we knew it was going to crash so we jumped in our truck to follow it hoping to help the pilot & who ever - when we reached 990 we saw fire everywhere the plane was down the power poles were in pieces we ran to the plane "it was fire so intense I could not believe it - the tip of the left wing was in a tree crumpled up. We couldn't help at all -

Pat Waters
(Signature)

FSB FORM 6120.11 (Rev. 10/77)   (Use reverse side of sheet for diagram and additional statement)

**US Department
of Transportation**

**Federal Aviation
Administration**

Memorandum

FORT WORTH ARTC CENTER
13800 FAA Road
Euless, TX 76040

Subject: <u>INFORMATION</u>: Transcription concerning the accident involving N711Y, a Douglas DC-3, on December 31, 1985, at 2315 UTC

Date: January 3, 1986

From: James D. Howden
Manager, Fort Worth ARTC Center

Reply to
Attn. of:

To This transcription covers the time period from December 31, 1985, 2222:22 UTC to December 31, 1985, 2320 UTC.

Agencies making Transmissions	Abbreviations
Fort Worth ARTCC Texarkana Low Altitude Radar Position	TXK R
Fort Worth ARTCC Texarkana Low Altitude Manual Position	TXK D
Texarkana Municipal Airport Tower, Texarkana, Arkansas	TXK TWR
Douglas N711Y	11Y
Eagle Express 1756	MEX1756
Helicopter 2625N	25N
Life Guard Helicopter 3174S	74S

I hereby certify that the following is a true transcription of the recorded conversation pertaining to the subject aircraft accident:

Leland H. Berlekamp
Leland H. Berlekamp
Air Traffic Assistant

(2222:00)

(2223:00)

(2224:00)

(2225:00)

(2226:00)

(2227:00)

2227:22	11Y	Fort Worth Center Douglas seven eleven yankee with you we're level at six thousand
2227:27	TXK R	Douglas seven one one Yankee Fort Worth Center roger the Texarkana altimeter three zero zero eight
2227:32	11Y	Three zero zero eight

(2228:00)

(2229:00)

(2230:00)

(2231:00)

(2232:00)

(2233:00)

(2234:00)

(2235:00)

(2236:00)

(2237:00)

(2238:00)

2238:10	11Y	Fort Worth Center seven eleven yankee
2238:19	TXK R	Douglas seven one yankee go ahead
2238:21	11Y	I'm sorry just hadn't heard anything for awhile was afraid I'd lost you
2238:26	TXK R	Douglas seven one yankee tell you what got an amendment to your clearance if you're ready to copy
2238:30	11Y	Standby one
2238:40	11Y	Okay ready to copy

Chapter 34: Rick Nelson

2238:42	TXK R	And Douglas seven uh one one Yankee uh cleared to the Dallas Love Airport via after Texarkana victor two seventy eight to Blue Ridge then the Blue Ridge nine arrival maintain six thousand
2238:57	11Y	Okay after Texarkana be victor two seventy eight to Blue Ridge nine arrival maintain six
2239:05	TXK R	Uh Douglas uh one one yankee that's affirmative
(2240:00)		
(2241:00)		
(2242:00)		
(2243:00)		
(2244:00)		
(2245:00)		
(2246:00)		
(2247:00)		
(2248:00)		
(2249:00)		
(2250:00)		
2251:18	TXK D	Go ahead
2251:19	TXK TWR	Eagle Express seventeen fifty six DFW taxiing out
2251:25	TXK D	Eagle Express seventeen fifty six cleared to DFW Airport via victor two seventy eight to Blue Ridge Blue Ridge nine arrival climb and maintain five thousand squawk five one four zero
2251:35	TXK TWR	Roger
(2252:00)		
(2253:00)		

Music's Broken Wings

2254:11	TXK D	Go ahead
2254:12	TXK TWR	Eagle Express seventeen fifty six off at five five JG
2255:52	TXK D	Tower Texarkana
2255:54	TXK TWR	Go ahead
2255:55	TXK D	Eagle Express uh has he started to turn yet
2255:58	TXK TWR	Yeah he's already talking to you all
2256:00	TXK D	Okay
2256:01	TXK TWR	Alright (unintelligible)
2256:15	MEX1756	Fort Worth Eagle Express seventeen fifty six is with you out of one point five for five thousand
2256:20	TXK R	Eagle Express seventeen fifty six uh Fort Worth Center radar contact three miles north of Texarkana airport uh fly heading uh three four zero vector climb and maintain five thousand say altitude
2256:31	MEX1756	We're out of two thousand you want us back to three forty to five seventeen fifty six
2256:38	TXK R	And Eagle Express seventeen fifty six we can leave you on course but we got traffic at six thousand just west of the vortac now proceeding westbound to Dallas he's doing a hundred sixty knots we'd have to hold you at five for quite awhile unless you want to vector off course for the climb
2256:51	MEX1756	Fine whatever you wanna do
2256:55	TXK R	Uh its up to you sir if you want to stay at five we can leave you there or if you wanna go on up to twelve we can take you off course
2257:05	MEX1756	We'll go for five for awhile
2257:07	TXK R	Eagle Express seventeen fifty six roger resume own navigation on course maintain five thousand
2257:11	MEX1756	Up to five thousand on course seventeen fifty six

Chapter 34: Rick Nelson   *399*

2258:19	MEX1756	Fort Worth seventeen fifty six is that our traffic about eleven o'clock there
2258:23	TXK R	Eagle seventeen fifty six uh that's affirmative eleven o'clock about five miles westbound at six thousand
2258:29	MEX1756	We got him in sight
(2259:00)		
(2300:00)		
(2301:00)		
2302:49	TXK R	Douglas uh one one yankee you'll have a uh...Douglas one one yankee you'll have a HP thirteen uh going underneath you westbound level at five thousand
2303:03	11Y	Uh we just saw him he's going by us pretty quick there
(2304:00)		
(2305:00)		
2306:39	TXK R	Eagle Express seventeen fifty six climb and maintain one two thousand
2306:42	MEX1756	(Yes sir)* we're out of five we'd like ten for a final (unintelligible)
2306:46	TXK R	Eagle seventeen fifty six climb and maintain one zero thousand
2306:49	MEX1756	(Unintelligible) for ten we're out of five seventeen fifty six
(2307:00)		
2308:40	11Y	Fort Worth Douglas seven eleven yankee
2308:44	TXK R	Douglas seven one one yankee go ahead
2308:48	11Y	I think I'd like to turn around uh head for Texarkana here I've got a little problem
2308:53	TXK R	Yeah Douglas uh seven one one yankee uh roger cleared to Texarkana airport via direct and advise of any assistance you need

Music's Broken Wings

2309:00	11Y	Kay give me a vector for starters
2309:06	11Y	(Unintelligible) Texarkana's the closest decent airport there is that affirmative
2309:12	TXK R	Uh seven one one yankee uh that's the closest uh fairly good sized airport
2309:19	TXK R	OK uh seven one yankee uh need heading of uh zero nine zero degrees for uh Texarkana
2309:26	11Y	Zero nine zero
2309:38	11Y	Uh Fort Worth just any field will do we've got a problem here
2309:54	TXK R	Okay one one yankee can you make it back to Texarkana
2309:58	11Y	Negative we got to get on the ground
2310:03	25N	Uh Fort Worth Center this is helicopter (unintelligible)
2310:10	TXK R	OK uh helicopter standby just a second one one yankee I've got Red River County Airport that's back at your uh six o'clock position now and nineteen miles uh that would be the nearest airport to you Mount Pleasant is south of you off at uh about hundred eighty degree heading and twenty two miles if you want to attempt Mount Pleasant
2310:29	11Y	We've got uh...smoke in the cockpit
2310:34	TXK R	One one yankee you're breaking up uh can you state your nature of the emergency
2310:40	MEX1756	Said he had smoke in the cockpit Center seventeen fifty six relaying
2310:44	TXK R	Eagle Express seventeen fifty six thank you much and Eagle Express seventeen fifty six ask him if he can make it to Mount Pleasant
2310:51	MEX1756	Douglas seven eleven yankee can you make it to Mount Pleasant airport
2311:01	11Y	Seven one yankee we don't know where it is we've lost our chart

2311:05	MEX1756	(Unintelligible) right on your tail and seventeen miles is an airport
2311:14	11Y	Can't do it
2311:18	TXK R	Eagle Express seventeen fifty six tell him the Mount Pleasant airport would be hundred eighty degree heading and uh twenty miles if he wanted to make it to that
2311:25	MEX1756	One eight zero heading and twenty miles Douglas
2311:29	11Y	Negative we can't do it
2311:33	TXK R	Okay one one yankee uh those would be the two closest airports I have to you behind you twenty miles and to the south of you twenty miles
2311:40	MEX1756	Says he can't make it have you got anything closer at all even shorter
2311:44	TXK R	That's uh the closest two airports
2311:49	11Y	(Unintelligible) smoke in the cockpit have smoke in the cockpit
2311:53	UNK	--on oxygen
2312:02	MEX1756	And uh maybe we ought to try to lead him in someplace huh what do you think
2312:06	MEX1756	Got gas enough to do that
2312:08	MEX1756	Yeah we do
2312:10	MEX1756	Hey Center can uh seventeen fifty six be of any assistance we'll pull up on his wing and lead him someplace if we have to
2312:16	TXK R	Eagle Express seventeen fifty six that'll be fine if the aircraft will agree to it you might want to inquire to see if you could do that
2312:21	MEX1756	Think he's ready for anything give us a vector direct his position please

2312:25	TXK R	Eagle Express seventeen fifty six roger he's reversed course he's heading back to the east now you'd have to make a uh one hundred eighty turn proceed back towards Texarkana
2312:32	MEX1756	Fine whatever it takes
2312:34	TXK R	Roger sir turn uh right or left your choice and fly heading of uh zero seven five
2312:39	MEX1756	Left heading zero seven five seventeen fifty six roger
2312:41	TXK R	And Eagle Express seventeen fifty six I don't believe you're gonna uh be able to catch him in time I show his Mode C now six hundred feet so that would put him just a couple hundred feet above ground level
2312:50	MEX1756	And we want to follow him anyway if we can help him out
2312:52	TXK R	Okay that'll be fine I can vector you to where the aircraft is at this time
2312:55	MEX1756	Do it...how many miles
2313:00	TXK R	And Eagle Express seventeen fifty six he's immediately behind you now at twenty six miles
2313:05	MEX1756	Proceeding uh..his position
2313:07	TXK R	Roger fly heading of zero eight zero
2313:10	MEX1756	New heading zero eight zero seventeen fifty six
2313:14	UNK	Hey Dave
2313:15	25N	Seventeen fifty six you copy the helicopter
2313:17	MEX1756	Affirmative go ahead
2313:18	25N	Uh we have the aircraft in sight looks like he's gone down uh you need to call Texarkana for the Air Life helicopter

2313:27	MEX1756	Texarkana looks like the (unintelligible) is going down uh can you roll some emergency equipment for him
2313:27	UNK	Unintelligible
2313:28	TXK D	Texarkana tower Texarkana low
2313:31	TXK R	Eagle Express seventeen fifty six roger we're on the phone right now
2313:32	TXK TWR	Go ahead
2313:34	TXK D	Okay we got 'an aircraft going down its a Dee Cee three he's uh on Texarkana west of Texarkana about twenty miles you have an Air Life helicopter
2313:36	MEX1756	(Yes sir)*
2313:38	25N	And helicopter two five november we'll go to his location and give you a uh latitude and longitude on it
2313:44	TXK TWR	Yeah we sure do I'll get in touch with him
2313:46	TXK D	Okay when he gets airborne let us know
2313:48	TXK TWR	Okay JG
2313:48	TXK R	And Eagle Express seventeen fifty six his last radar position was the Texarkana two six three radial twenty five mile fix
2313:55	MEX1756	Two six three at twenty five seventeen fifty six
2314:00	25N	Seventeen fifty six uh (contact)* Texarkana for uh alert the Air Life helicopter uh from Texarkana and get them on the way
2314:07	TXK R	Okay and what (is your position)* exactly helicopter
2314:11	25N	It looks like uh..roger standby
2314:16	25N	Okay our-our position now is thirty three twenty five point nine and (unintelligible) thirty one point seven
2314:26	MEX1756	Rog Center uh they say a position now is thirty three twenty five point nine and ninety four thirty one point seven

2314:35	TXK R	Roger I copy that and uh we've marked him on the radar at the Texarkana two sixty three radial twenty five mile fix
2314:41	MEX1756	Roger thank you
2314:46	TXK R	And does the helicopter have the aircraft in sight
2314:49	25N	Uh that's affirmative we're uh uh ten out on the uh site
2314:54	TXK R	Roger sir uh are you able to contact the aircraft..helicopter over Texarkana
2315:01	TXK R	And Eagle Express I have communication now with the helicopter and the helicopter at uh inbound to the uh Douglas site do you have uh communications with the Douglas
2315:10	25N	Uh negative they've already gone down looks like there's a quite a bit of smoke so you need to call the uh Air Life helicopter to get on their way from Texarkana
2315:19	TXK R	Roger
2315:20	TXK TWR	Texarkana low D Texarkana
2315:22	TXK D	Okay go ahead
2315:23	TXK TWR	Okay we I called there and informed them where is the guy can you get us a better ide-idea
2315:25	MEX1756	Uh seventeen fifty six did you read that from the helicopter
2315:27	TXK R	Eagle Express seventeen fifty six affirm
2315:30	25N	Seventeen fifty six it might be a good idea to alert that Care-Flite out of Dallas it uh looks like uh they're pretty close to a little town up here but I don't know what the name of the town is
2315:30	TXK D	Okay (unintelligible) crash (unintelligible)
2315:35	TXK TWR	He has already crashed
2315:37	TXK D	Yeah (unintelligible) vectors to the site

Chapter 34: Rick Nelson

2315:40	TXK TWR	Okay thank you JG
2315:41	MEX1756	Have a frequency we could call them direct
2315:46	25N	(Unintelligible) Care Flite of Dallas is located at uh uh Methodist Hospital
2315:52	MEX1756	Roger will do
2315:54	TXK R	And uh helicopter could I have your call sign
2316:01	TXK R	Roger and the helicopter could we have your full call sign
2316:04	25N	Uh roger this is two six two five november and we're not medical there just uh two of us on board I-I'm a medical person on board land and give whatever assistance I can
2316:14	TXK R	Two five november thank you very much and uh does it appear that the aircraft was able to land at a uh private strip or just out in a in an open field
2316:22	25N	(Unintelligible) looks like he's in an open field but uh we're still about five miles away
2316:27	TXK R	Roger thank you very much
2316:30	25N	Seventeen fifty six uh what's your location
2316:35	MEX1756	Seventeen fifty six is thirty eight point four on the two six three radial inbound to your position
2316:35	TXK D	Texarkana tower Texarkana low
2316:37	TXK TWR	Go ahead
2316:38	TXK D	(Unintelligible) off the Texarkana Vortac two six six radial at twenty three miles
2316:41	25N	Okay uh we're still about uh four miles south and we're reading now thirty three twenty seven and ninety four thirty four

2316:44	TXK TWR	Okay I'll tell him as soon as he gets airborne I've called him and I'll let you know as soon as they're airborne...we'll you know we'll send him over to you as soon as we get him
2316:49	MEX1756	Kay
2316:51	TXK D	Okay
2316:51	TXK TWR	Okay JG
2317:02	TXK R	And Eagle Express seventeen fifty six the uh crash site should be now twelve o'clock to you and lemme give you a distance from where I last marked it on the radar showing uh twelve miles twelve o'clock twelve miles
2317:15	MEX1756	Seventeen fifty six
2317:21	25N	Seventeen fifty six do you see the smoke
2317:24	MEX1756	Yeah we see fire too
2317:26	25N	Okay we're just now over the site and uh we're gonna go ahead and land and uh oh uh see if they've got some local assistance down here
2317:37	MEX1756	Kay we'll stay up here and uh relay anything that you may have for us
2317:40	25N	Okay
2317:42	TXK R	And two five november and Eagle Express seventeen fifty six we appreciate the help
2317:47	MEX1756	Glad to
2317:50	25N	And seventeen fifty six double check and make sure that helicopter is on their way from Texarkana
2317:55	MEX1756	Yeah we called uh our company they're calling for Texarkana as well as Dallas sir
2317:59	25N	Okay look like uh looks like a little town here probably is DeKalb
2318:21	MEX1756	Chopper let's go to a different frequency uh want to do that

2318:53	MEX1756	And helicopter seventeen fifty six are you sure that's DeKalb maybe we can have them uh pull some fire trucks outa there
2318:59	25N	Okay seventeen fifty six uh yeah---here---
2319:12	TXK R	And Eagle Express seventeen fifty six I'm not able to to receive the helicopter any longer he's below my radio communication uh coverage uh just feel free to relay any information you've got going
2319:22	MEX1756	Okay if you can you might scramble a fire truck out of DeKalb that seems to be the nearest town it's just southeast corner of DeKalb he says it's totally engulfed in flames and uh...(went)* over the crash site at this time
2319:36	TXK R	And Eagle Express seventeen fifty six uh we copied that and we will do
2319:41	MEX1756	Thank you very much
2319:43	74S	Fort Worth Center this is Life Guard helicopter uh three one seven four sierra over
2319:45	TXK D	Texarkana tower this is Texarkana low
2319:50	TXK TWR	Texarkana
2319:52	TXK D	(Okay at this crash site we need some fire trucks they say DeKalb is the nearest place)*
2319:55	TXK TWR	DeKalb yeah (unintelligible)

*This portion of the recording is not entirely clear, but this represents the best interpretation possible under the circumstances.

END OF TRANSCRIPT

PERSONNEL STATEMENT

FEDERAL AVIATION ADMINISTRATION
FORT WORTH ARTC CENTER
EULESS, TX

February 18, 1986

The following is a report concerning the accident to aircraft N711Y at two miles south of DeKalb, Texas, December 31, 1985, at approximately 2315 UTC.

My name is Lawrence R. Jones (JX). I am employed as an Air Traffic Control Specialist by the Federal Aviation Administration at the Fort Worth Air Route Traffic Control Center, Euless, Texas.

During the period 1745 UTC, December 31, 1985, to 0145 UTC, January 1, 1986, I was on duty in the Fort Worth Air Route Traffic Control Center. I was working the Texarkana low altitude manual/radar position combined from 2207 UTC to 2310 UTC under the supervision of Air Traffic Control Specialist W. D. Powers. I was working the Texarkana low altitude manual position from 2311 UTC to 2338 UTC.

At approximately 2309 UTC, N711Y requested to proceed to Texarkana because of a problem. I cleared N711Y to the Texarkana Airport. N711Y asked if Texarkana was the nearest airport. I advised N711Y that Texarkana was the nearest good-sized airport. N711Y asked for a vector to Texarkana. I assigned N711Y heading 090 to Texarkana. At approximately 2310 UTC, N711Y said that just any field would do. The Texarkana low altitude radar position was assumed by Air Traffic Control Specialist W. D. Powers.

I had no further communication with N711Y.

_____
LAWRENCE R. JONES, ATCS

PERSONNEL STATEMENT

FEDERAL AVIATION ADMINISTRATION
FORT WORTH ARTC CENTER
EULESS, TX

January 15, 1986

The following is a report concerning the accident to aircraft N711Y at two miles south of DeKalb, Texas, December 31, 1985, at approximately 2315 UTC.

My name is William D. Powers (DP). I am employed as an Air Traffic Control Specialist by the Federal Aviation Administration at the Fort Worth Air Route Traffic Control Center, Euless, Texas.

During the period 1945 UTC, December 31, 1985, to 0145 UTC, January 1, 1986, I was on duty in the Fort Worth Air Route Traffic Control Center. I was working Texarkana low sector radar position from 2154 UTC to 2341 UTC. I was providing radar training to ATCS Jones from 2207 UTC to 2310 UTC.

At approximately 2227 UTC, N711Y reported on my frequency at 6,000 feet. At approximately 2309 UTC, N711Y requested to turn around and proceed to Texarkana because of a problem. I heard Mr. Jones clear N711Y to Texarkana Airport and provide a radar vector to Texarkana. At approximately 2310 UTC, N711Y stated, "...Just any field will do, we've got a problem here." I asked N711Y if it was possible to go to Texarkana. N711Y replied, "Negative." I advised N711Y of Red River County and Mt. Pleasant Airports and gave N711Y the location and distance to each airport. N711Y's next transmission was broken. I advised N711Y that the transmissions were broken and requested N711Y state the nature of the emergency. MEX1756 relayed to me that N711Y reported smoke in the cockpit. I then gave a position and distance to Mt. Pleasant Airport and heard MEX1756 relay the information to N711Y. I heard N711Y reply, "Negative, we can't do it," and state that there was smoke in the cockpit. I had no further communication with N711Y. I gave MEX1756 a radar vector to the last radar position I had on N711Y. At approximately 2313 UTC, N2625N reported having N711Y in sight and stated, "It looks like he's gone down." MEX1756 orbited over the accident site and relayed information from N2625N.

WILLIAM D. POWERS, ATCS

National Transportation Safety Board
PRELIMINARY REPORT
AVIATION

2 NTSB Accident/Incident No.	DC A 8 6 A A Ø L 2
3 Investigation By	1 ✓ NTSB 2 ☐ FAA delegated

1 — 1 ✓ Accident 2 ☐ Incident	**4 I.C.A.O. Preliminary Report Submitted** (NTSB only) 1 ☐ Yes 2 ✓ No
5 Report Status	1 ☐ Initial report 2 ✓ Preliminary Report

Location/Date

6 Nearest City/Place	7 State	8 Zip Code (First 5 Nos.)	9 Date (Nos. for M, D, Y)	10 Local time (24 hour clock)	11 Time Zone
DEKALB	TX	7557	12-31-85	1715	CST

Aircraft Information

12 Registration No.	13 Aircraft Manufacturer	14 Model/Series No.
N 711 Y	DOUGLAS	DC-3C

15 Type of Aircraft
1 ☒ Airplane 3 ☐ Glider 5 ☐ Blimp/Dirigible 7 ☐ Gyroplane
2 ☐ Helicopter 4 ☐ Balloon 6 ☐ Ultralight A ☐ Specify _____

16 Home Built
1 ☐ Yes
2 ☒ No

Other Aircraft—Collision Between Aircraft

17 Registration No.	18 Aircraft Manufacturer	19 Model/Series No.

Accident Information

20 Aircraft Damage
1 ☐ None
2 ☐ Minor
3 ☐ Substantial
4 ☒ Destroyed

21 Property Damage (Multiple entry)
1 ☐ None 6 ☐ Airport Facility
2 ☐ Residence 7 ☒ Trees
3 ☐ Residential area 8 ☐ Crops
4 ☐ Commercial Bldg. 9 ☒ Wires, Poles
5 ☐ Vehicle 10 ☒ Other property

22 Accident/Incident Phase of Operation
1 ☐ Standing 6 ☐ Descent
2 ☐ Taxi 7 ☐ Approach
3 ☐ Takeoff 8 ☐ Landing
4 ☐ Climb 9 ☐ Maneuvering
5 ☒ Cruise 10 ☐ Hover
A ☐ Specify _____

23 Injury Index (Most critical injury)
1 ☐ None
2 ☐ Minor
3 ☐ Serious
4 ☒ Fatal

Injury Summary

24 Fatal	25 Serious	26 Minor	27 None
7	2		

Crew A Name	B Address (City, State only)	C Certificate No.	D Injury Code	Passenger A Name	B Injury Code
BRADLEY S. RANK	—	355 465 073	3	ERIC NELSON	4
KENNETH FERGUSON	—	1879921	3	HELEN BLAIR	4
				PATRICK WOODWARD	4
				ANDY CHASIN	4
				CLARK RUSSELL	4
				RICK INVELD	4
				BOBBY NEAL	4

Ground Personnel A Name / B Injury Code

Injury Codes None—1   Minor—2   Serious—3   Fatal—4

Operator Information

42 Name	43 Operator Designator Code	44 Doing Business as (dba)
STONE CANYON BAND		

45 Street Address	46 City	47 State	48 Zip Code
Box 9528	PALM SPRINGS	CA.	92263

Type of Certificate(s) Held

49 ☐ None (Go to Block 53)

50 Air Carrier Operating Certificate (Check all applicable)
1 ☐ Flag carrier/domestic (121) 4 ☐ Large helicopter (127)
2 ☐ Supplemental 5 ☐ Commuter air carrier
3 ☐ All cargo (418) 6 ☐ On-demand air taxi

51 Operating Certificate
☒ Other operator of large aircraft

52 Operator Certificate
1 ☐ Rotorcraft—external load operator (133)
2 ☐ Agricultural aircraft operator (137)

Regulation Flight Conducted Under

53
1 ☒ 14 CFR 91 (only) 4 ☐ 14 CFR 105 7 ☐ 14 CFR 127 10 ☐ 14 CFR 137 A Specify _____
2 ☐ 14 CFR 91D 5 ☐ 14 CFR 121 8 ☐ 14 CFR 133 11 ☐ 14 CFR 129
3 ☐ 14 CFR 103 6 ☐ 14 CFR 125 9 ☐ 14 CFR 135 (Foreign flag)

PRELIMINARY INFORMATION — SUBJECT TO CHANGE

NTSB Form 6120.19A (1-84) This form supersedes NTSB Form 6120.19 (Rev. 1-83)

Page 1

National Transportation Safety Board
PRELIMINARY REPORT
AVIATION
ACCIDENT/INCIDENT

NTSB Accident/Incident Number

D C A 8 6 A A 0 L 4

Type of Flight Operation Conducted

(Complete 54, 55, 56 ONLY if flight was a revenue operation conducted under 121, 125, 127, 129, 135)

54		55		56			
1 ☐ Scheduled		1 ☐ Domestic		1 ☐ Passenger	3 ☐ Passenger/cargo		
2 ☐ Non-scheduled		2 ☐ International		2 ☐ Cargo	4 ☐ Mail contract ONLY		

(Complete 57 ONLY if 54, 55, 56 not applicable)

57

1 ☐ Personal	4 ☐ Executive/corporate	7 ☐ Other work use	
2 ☒ Business	5 ☐ Aerial application	8 ☐ Public use	10 ☐ Positioning
3 ☐ Instructional (Including air carrier training)	6 ☐ Aerial observation	9 ☐ Ferry	A Specify _____

Flight Plan/Itinerary

58 Flight Plan Filed

1 ☐ None   2 ☐ VFR   3 ☒ IFR   4 ☐ IFR/VFR   5 ☐ Company (VFR)   6 ☐ Military (VFR)

59 Itinerary—Last Departure Point	60 State	61 Airport I.D.	62 Destination (If "local," mark X here 1 ☐)	63 State	64 Airport I.D.
1 ☐ Same as accident/incident location. Nearest city/place A GUNTRSVILLE	ALABAMA	GTS	Nearest city/place A DALLAS, TE	TE	DAL

Weather Information

65 Source	67 Sky/Lowest Cloud Condition	68 Lowest Ceiling	69 Visibility (decimals)
1 ☒ Accident site (Pilot/witness)	1 ☒ Clear	1 ☑ None	**5** SM
2 ☐ Weather Observation Facility	2 ☐ Scattered	2 ☐ Broken	
	3 ☐ Thin broken	3 ☐ Overcast	**70 Temperature**
A Facility Identifier _____	4 ☐ Thin overcast	4 ☐ Obscured	**56** °F
	5 ☐ Partial obscuration		
66 Time of Weather Observation			**71 Dew Point**
1715 (local)	A _____ Ft. AGL	A _____ Ft. AGL	**54** °F

72 Wind Direction	73 Wind Speed	74 Gusts	75 Altimeter	76 Weather Conditions (at accident site)	77 Precipitation
340 Degrees (Mag.)	**10** Kts.	_____ Kts	_____ "Hg	1 ☒ VMC 2 ☐ IMC	1 ☐ Yes 2 ☒ No

Narrative

78 (Brief resume of facts. The information shall not contain opinion, conjecture, or statements reflecting on the character or integrity of the persons involved.)

The flight departed Gunterville, Alabama, at about 1345 e.s.t. en route to Love Field, Dallas, Texas. At about 1708, c.s.t., N711Y contacted Fort Worth Center stating, "I think I would like to turn-around and head for Texarkana here, I've got a little problem." Fort Worth cleared the aircraft to Texarkana and gave the crew a heading of 090°. One minute later N711Y transmitted, "Fort Worth just any field will do, we've got a problem here." Fort Worth asked the crew if they could reach Texarkana to which they responded, "Negative, we got to get on the ground." Fort Worth then advised the crew of 2 other airports, one 19 miles away and the other 22 miles. Twenty-one seconds later, N711Y transmitted, "We've got uh...smoke in the cockpit." For the next minute another airplane assisted Fort Worth relaying transmissions to and from N711Y regarding alternate airports in the vicinity. At 2311:49, N711Y made its last recorded transmission; "smoke in the cockpit, black smoke in the cockpit...on oxygen." The assisting aircraft and a helicopter continued to assist Fort

(Please continue to next page.)

PRELIMINARY INFORMATION — SUBJECT TO CHANGE

NTSB Form 6120.19A (1-84) This form supersedes NTSB Form 6120.19 (Rev. 1-83)   Page 2

PRELIMINARY REPORT
AVIATION
ACCIDENT/INCIDENT

NTSB Accident/Incident Number

U|C|A|8|6|A|A|0|7|2|

Narrative (continued)

Worth Center. At 2313:20, the helicopter transmitted that the DC-3 was in sight and recommended that Fort Worth notify Air Life, a local helicopter emergency medical rescue service.

Fort Worth Center furnished an NTAP (National Track Analysis Program) with a start time of 1700 and a stop time of 1714 c.s.t. The initial altitude is 6,100 feet m.s.l. on a westerly heading. At 1709:47, the radar return descends through 6,000 feet in a left turn to a southeasterly heading. At 1712 c.s.t., the return is descending through 1,800 feet m.s.l. turning left to a north-northwesterly course. The last return for the target was at 1712:36 c.s.t. descending through 600 feet m.s.l. Elevation at the site was approximately 440 feet.

Witnesses stated that the airplane flew a left descending turn to the field on a westerly heading trailing smoke and "sparks." Small fires erupted in fields as the airplane overflew them, ignited by the falling hot pieces of metal. The aircraft flew low over a house, struck and severed 2 power lines about 30 feet AGL, collided with and broke 2 telephone poles, and landed gear down in an unimproved field. The aircraft came to rest about 1,260 feet from wire contact and was consumed by fire.

(Attach additional pages if necessary.)

Administrative Data

79 Notification From		80 Date (Nos. for M. D. Y)	81 Local Time (24 hour clock)	82 Time Zone
FAA COMM CTR		12-13-85	2000	EST

83 FAA District Office/Coordinator	84 Other Federal Agencies Involved in Investigation		
D. ELAM	1 ☐ FBI 2 ☐ USCG	3 ☐ DEA 4 ☐ DOD	5 ☐ Customs A Specify _____

Investigator(s) Assigned

85 Investigator-In-Charge	86 Form Preparation Date (Nos. for M. D. Y)	87 Form Receipt Date (For NTSB use only)
R. KAPUSTIN	1/24/86	

88 Other NTSB Personnel Assigned

A	D. KUHNS	D	F. SHERERTZ	G	M. MARKS
B		E	D. JOHNS	H	
C	T. McFALL	F	M. BIRKY	I	

PRELIMINARY INFORMATION — SUBJECT TO CHANGE

NTSB Form 6120.19A (1-84) This form supersedes NTSB Form 6120.19 (Rev. 1-83)

Page 3

National Transportation Safety Board

PRELIMINARY REPORT
AVIATION
ACCIDENT/INCIDENT

NTSB Accident/Incident Number

| D | C | 4 | 8 | 6 | A | A | 0 | L | 2 |

Accident/Incident Phase of Operation

500 Standing
501 Pre Flight
502 Starting engine(s)
503 Engine(s) operating
504 Engine(s) not operating
505 Idling rotors
510 Taxi
511 Pushback/tow
512 To takeoff
513 From landing
514 Aerial taxi
520 Takeoff
521 Ground run
522 Initial climb
530 Climb
531 To cruise
540 Cruise
541 Normal
542 Holding (IFR)
550 Descent
551 Normal
552 Emergency
553 Uncontrolled
560 Approach
561 VFR pattern—downwind
562 VFR pattern—base turn
563 VFR pattern—base to final
564 VFR pattern—final approach
565 Go Around (VFR)
566 IAF to FAF/outer marker (IFR)
567 FAF/outer marker to threshold (IFR)
568 Circling (IFR)
569 Missed approach (IFR)
570 Landing
571 Flare/touchdown
572 Landing roll
580 Maneuvering
581 Aerial application maneuver
582 Turn to reverse direction
583 Turn to landing area (Emergency)
590 Hover
600 Other
610 Unknown

Occurrence

100 Abrupt maneuver
110 Altitude deviation, uncontrolled
120 Cargo shift
130 Airframe/component/system failure/malfunction
140 Decompression
150 Ditching
160 Dragged wing, rotor, pod, or float
170 Fire/explosion
171 Fire
172 Explosion
180 Forced landing
190 Gear collapsed
191 Main gear collapsed
192 Nose gear collapsed
193 Tail gear collapsed
194 Complete gear collapsed
195 Other gear collapsed
196 Gear not extended
200 Hard landing
210 Hazardous materials leak/spill (fumes/smoke)
220 In flight collision with object
230 In flight collision with terrain
240 In flight encounter with weather
250 Loss of control—in flight
260 Loss of control—on ground
270 Midair collision
280 Near collision between aircraft
290 Nose down
300 Nose over
310 On ground collision with object
320 On ground collision with terrain
330 On ground encounter with weather
340 Overrun
350 Loss of power
351 Loss of power (total)—mech failure/malfunction
352 Loss of power (partial)—mech failure/malfunction
353 Loss of power (total)—non-mechanical
354 Loss of power (partial)—non-mechanical
355 Engine tearaway
360 Propeller blast or jet exhaust/suction
370 Propeller/rotor contact
380 Roll over
390 Undershoot
400 Undetermined
410 Vortex turbulence encountered
420 Missing aircraft
430 Miscellaneous/other

89 Phase of Operation (Enter code)
1 540
2 552
3 _____
4 _____
5 _____

90 Occurrence (Enter code)
1 171
2 180
3 _____
4 _____
5 _____

91 Altitude MSL (Inflight occurrence)
1 6000
2 _____
3 _____
4 _____
5 _____

PRELIMINARY INFORMATION — SUBJECT TO CHANGE

NTSB Form 6120.19A (1-84) This form supersedes NTSB Form 6120.19 (Rev. 1-83)

Page 4

COUNTY OF BOWIE

ALFRED F. WELCH
JUSTICE OF THE PEACE
PRECINCT 2
601 E. NORTH FRONT
NEW BOSTON, TEXAS 75570
214-628-5567

January 1, 1986

I, ALFRED F. WELCH, JUSTICE OF THE PEACE, Precinct 2, Place 1, New Boston, Bowie County, Texas, do hereby order the Dallas Mortuary Services, of   St., Dallas, Texas to transport the bodies of Rick Nelson, believed to be the age of 45, Helen Blair, believed to be the age of 27, Patrick Woodard, believed to be the age of 35, Rick Intveld, believed to be the age of 32, Andy Chaplain, believed to be the age of 30, Clark Russell, believed to be the age of 35, and Bobby Neal, believed to be the age of 38, present addresses unknown, all apparently killed as a result of an airplane crash near DeKalb, Texas, to the Southwest Institute of Forensic Science of Dallas, Texas, for the purpose of performing an autopsy and identifying such persons more postively. Upon the completion of said autopsies being performed by the Southwest Institute of Forensic Science you are hereby ordered to release the bodies of each of such persons *to the next of kin or* to Bates-Rolf Funeral Home or their Representative of DeKalb, Texas to be transported back to DeKalb, Texas for the purposes of burial at direction of next of kin.

SIGNED this the 1st day of January, 1986.

A.F.W. delete
this at 10:20 A.M.
1/1/86

Alfred F. Welch
ALFRED F. WELCH
JUSTICE OF THE PEACE
PRECINCT 2, PLACE 1
BOWIE COUNTY, TEXAS

GLOSSARY OF TOXICOLOGICAL TERMS

acetaminophen: analgesic, active ingedient in over-the-counter drug such. as Tylenol

benzoylecgonine: metabolite of cocaine

COHb: carboxyhemoglobin that results from the inhalation of carbon monoxide which combines with the hemoglobin in the blood

cyanide: hydrogen cyanide is a toxic gas that is produced during the combustion of certain nitrogen containing polymeric materials

delta-9-tetrahydrocannabinol: psychoactive component of marihuana sometimes referred to as THC

delta-9-tetrahydrocannabinolic acid: non-psychoactive acid metabolite of THC

ethanol: alcohol present in alcoholic drinks

norpropoxyphene: metabolite of propoxyphene

propoxyphene: a narcotic analgesic, active ingredient of Darvon

pseudoephedrine: constituent in over-the-counter cold remedy as a nasal decongestant

TOXICOLOGICAL EXERPTS
from
SOUTHWESTERN INSTITUTE OF FORENSIC SCIENCES
AT DALLAS

Blair, Helen
    Blood: Alcohol screen - negative
            Alkaline screen - Quantity Not Sufficient (QNS)
            Carbon monoxide - 60% saturation
            Cyanide - QNS
            Thiocyanate - QNS
            Benzene - 0.29 ugm/ml
            Narcotics - negative
    Liver: Alkaline screen - 0.13 mg/kg propoxyphene
                              7.40 mh/kh norpropoxyphene

Chapin, Andrew
    Blood: Alcohol screen - negative
            Alkaline screen - negative
            Carbon monoxide - 80% saturation
            Cyanide - 1.2 mg/L
            Thiocyanate - 7.5 mg/L
            Benzene - 0.86 ugm/ml
    Urine: Narcotics - negative
            Alkaline screen - negative
            Cocaine - postive by EMIT

Intveld, Rick
    Blood: Alcohol screen - 0.08% ethanol
            Alkaline screen - negative
            Carbon monoxide - 57% saturation
            Cyanide - 0.44 mg/L
            Thiocyanate - 11.0 mg/L
            Benzene - 1.40 ugm/ml
            Narcotics - negative
    Vitreous:
            Alcohol screen - 0.10% ethanol

Neal, Bobby
    Blood: Alcohol screen - negative
            Alkaline screen - negative
            Carbon monoxide - 33% saturation
            Cyanide - 0.9 mg/L
            Thiocyanate - 8.5 mg/L
            Benzene - 0.21 ugm/ml
    Urine: Alcohol - negative
            Opiates - negative by EMIT
            Cocaine - postive by EMIT
            Alkaline drug screen - negative
    Vitreous:
            Alcohol- negative

TOXICOLOGICAL EXERPTS
continued

Nelson, Rick
        Blood: Alcohol screen - negative
        Alkaline screen -
                0.05 mg/L propoxyphene
                0.66 mg/L norpropoxyphene
                0.01 mg/L cocaine
                Carbon monoxide - 56% saturation
                Cyanide - 0.43 mg/L
                Thiocyanate - 10.5 mg/L
                Benzene - 1.06 ugm/ml
        Vitreous:
                Alcohol screen - negative
        Urine: Narcotics - negative
                Cocaine, propoxyphen, norpropoxyphene detected
                in urine
                Positive cocaine by EMIT

Russell, Donald C.
        Blood: Carbon Monoxide - 48% saturation
                Benzene - 0.43 ugm/ml
        Urine: Alcohol - negative
                Alkaline screen - negative
                Cocaine - negative by EMIT
                Narcotics - negative

Woodward, Patrick
        Blood: Alcohol screen - negative
                Alkaline screen - negative
                Carbon monoxide - 64% saturation
                Cyanide - 0.95mg/L
                Thiocyanate - 8.5 mg/L
                Benzene - 1.19ugm/ml
        Urine: Alcohol - negative
                Opiates - negative
                Cocaine - postive by EMIT
                Alkaline drug screen - negative

DEPARTMENT OF TRANSPORTATION
FEDERAL AVIATION ADMINISTRATION
MIKE MONRONEY AERONAUTICAL CENTER
TOXICOLOGY REPORT (RIS: AC 8025-2)

DATE: January 23, 1986	CASE NO. 5882	PILOT: Brad Rank (nonfatal) COPILOT: Kenneth Ferguson (nonfatal)

ACCIDENT OR EVENT:

Aircraft accident which occurred near DeKalb, Texas, on December 31, 1985.

RECEIVED BY:

P. A. Roberts from Federal Express at 9:30 a.m. on January 3, 1986, (first shipment).
Jesse Williams Jr. from Federal Express at 12:20 p.m. on January 4, 1986, (second shipment).

SAMPLES:

First shipment:
Two tubes of blood identified with 0006-86, Unk/M.
Two tubes of blood identified with 0007-86, Unk/M.
Two tubes of blood identified with 0008-86, Unk/M.
Two tubes of blood and one bottle of urine identified with 0009-86.
One bottle of heat coagulated blood and one bag of liver identified with
    0010-86, Blair.
Two tubes of blood identified with 0011-85. (86?)
Two tubes of blood identified with 0012-86.
Specimens were cold.

Second shipment:
Two tubes of blood identified with the name Brad Rank.
Two tubes of blood identified with the name Kenneth Ferguson
Specimens were placed in the CAMI freezer upon arrival.

Identification of the numbered specimens was provided by the
Dallas County Medical Examiner's Office:

        0006-86 - Clark Russell
        0007-86 - Bobby Neal
        0008-86 - Patrick Woodward
        0009-86 - Rick Nelson
        0010-86 - Helen Blair
        0011-86 - Andy Chapin
        0012-86 - Rich Intzeld

RESULTS:

ACIDIC & NEUTRAL DRUGS (Acid-Ether Extractions, UV Scan, Confirmation by
    Gas Chromatography):

    Rank - None detected - blood
    Ferguson - None detected - blood
    Russell - Quantity not sufficient.
    Neal - None detected - blood
    Woodward - None detected - blood
    Nelson - None detected - urine and blood
    Blair - None detected - heat coagulated blood homogenate
    Chapin - None detected - blood
    Intzeld - None detected - blood

000003

Page 1 of 4

DEPARTMENT OF TRANSPORTATION
FEDERAL AVIATION ADMINISTRATION
MIKE MONRONEY AERONAUTICAL CENTER

TOXICOLOGY REPORT (RIS: AC 8025-2)

Date: January 23, 1986   Case No. 5882 Pilot: Brad Rank (Nonfatal)
                               (Continued)   Copilot: Kenneth Ferguson (Nonfatal)

RESULTS: (Continued)

BASIC DRUGS (Alkaline-Ether Extraction, UV Scan, Confirmation by
  Gas Chromatography):

    Rank   — None detected — blood
    Ferguson — None detected — blood
    Russell   — Quantity not sufficient for testing.
    Neal   — None detected — blood
    Woodward — None detected — blood
    Nelson   — 0.082 mg/L cocaine in blood; 0.131 mg/L cocaine in urine;
                trace of propoxyphene in urine.
    Blair   — None detected — heat coagulated blood homogenate and
                bloody fluid from liver.
    Chapin   — None detected — blood
    Intzeld   — None detected — blood

ETHYL ALCOHOL (Gas Chromatography):

    Rank   — None detected — blood
    Ferguson — None detected — blood
    Russell   — None detected — blood
    Neal   — None detected — blood
    Woodward — None detected — blood
    Nelson   — None detected — blood and urine
    Blair   — None detected — heat coagulated blood homogenate
    Chapin   — None detected — blood
    Intzeld   — None detected — blood

CARBON MONOXIDE (Conway Diffusion, Palladium Chloride; Confirmation by
  Gas Chromatography):

    Rank   — None detected in blood containing 13.7 gm% hemoglobin.
    Ferguson — 9% saturation in blood containing 14.7 gm% hemoglobin.
    Russell — 35% saturation in blood containing 22.6 gm% hemoglobin.
    Neal   — 28% saturation in blood containing 10.5 gm% hemoglobin.
    Woodward — 44% saturation in blood containing 18.9 gm% hemoglobin.
    Nelson   — 38% saturation in blood containing 16.8 gm% hemoglobin.
    Blair   — 32% saturation in blood homogenate containing 6.2 gm% hemoglobin.
    Chapin   — 58% saturation in blood containing 16.5 gm% hemoglobin.
    Intzeld — 46% saturation in blood containing 17.2 gm% hemoglobin.

000004

Music's Broken Wings

DEPARTMENT OF TRANSPORTATION
FEDERAL AVIATION ADMINISTRATION
MIKE MONRONEY AERONAUTICAL CENTER

TOXICOLOGY REPORT (RIS: AC 8025-2)

Date: January 23, 1986	Case No. 5882 (Continued)	Pilot: Brad Rank (Nonfatal) Copilot: Kenneth Ferguson (Nonfatal)

RESULTS: (Continued)

CYANIDE (Conway Diffusion, Sodium Hydroxide):

    Rank   - None detected - blood
    Ferguson - None detected - blood
    Russell   - 0.94 µg/ml - blood
    Neal   - 0.45 µg/ml - blood
    Woodward - 1.42 µg/ml - blood
    Nelson   - 0.50 µg/ml - blood
    Blair   - 0.28 µg/ml - blood homogenate
    Chapin   - 1.23 µg/ml - blood
    Intzeld   - 0.50 µg/ml - blood

Signature and Title:

Delbert J. Lacefield
Delbert J. Lacefield, Ph.D.
Supervisor, Forensic Toxicology Research Unit, AAM-114B

cc: АА ПІ-132;
Dr. Barnes, RFS, FAA, ASW-300; Fran Sherertz & Rudolf Kapustin, NTSB, Wash., D.C.;
Dallas County Medical Examiner, Dallas, TX; Dr. Horne, AAM-510, Frank DelGandio, ASF-110, &
Dr. Frank Austin, AAM-1, FAA, Washington,D.C.;Dr. Colangelo, AAM-114 & Dr. Dille, AAM-100, OK

-1 (Rev. 4-26-78)

REPORT
of the

FEDERAL BUREAU OF INVESTIGATION
WASHINGTON, D. C. 20535

February 13, 1986

To: National Transportation Safety Board
800 Independence Avenue, S.W.
Washington, D. C. 20594

FBI FILE NO.

Attention: Dr. Merritt M. Birky

LAB. NO.   60116028 S/D LY VY TY

Re: DC-3 (N711Y)
DEKALB, TEXAS;
AIRCRAFT CRASH

YOUR NO.

Examination requested by: Addressee

Reference: Letter dated January 15, 1986

Examination requested: Instrumental Analyses - Chemical Analyses -
Document

Specimens personally delivered by Mr. Spencer Phillips on
January 16, 1986:

Q1   Five-gallon can

Q2-Q4   Three one-gallon cans

Q5-Q6   Two one-quart cans (rectangular)

Q7   Quart can (round)

Q8-Q9   Two round cans

Q10-Q14   Five round cans

Q15-Q34   Twenty aerosol cans

Q35-Q38   Four small bottles

Page 1   (over)

Result of Examination:

This report confirms the information telephonically furnished to Mr. Spencer Phillips of your organization on January 23, 1986, and completes the requested Laboratory examinations.

The submitted items were examined in an effort to determine the contents of the cans and bottles. During the examination, it was noted that all the items had been subjected to intense heat and exhibited extensive heat damage.

Attempts to restore labeling information on the enclosed items were unsuccessful.

A limited amount of labeling material was noted on some of the items. Information remaining on the Q7 specimen, a round, quart-size container, described the contents as being a polishing material for fiberglass, plexiglass, aluminum, chrome, magnesium, and other surfaces. The name FLITZ appeared in several places and is apparently the trade name for this material.

Examination of the contents of specimens Q8 and Q9, two containers of the size of some wax cans, reflects that these were containers for some type of polishing compound; however, there was no labeling information remaining on either of these items.

The one-gallon container designated Q3 had the lettering "KEEP" and "CAU" remaining on it. There was no other labeling information present and the intended use of this container is not known to the Laboratory.

The aerosol can designated Q19 had labeling remaining which suggests this may have been a PLEDGE furniture polish container.

The aerosol can designated Q30 had lettering "de" remaining on it; however, the intended use of this item is not known to the Laboratory.

The remaining cans from specimens Q2 through Q34 did not possess any identifying data, and the identity of any contents of these items is not known to the Laboratory.

Page 2
60116028 S/D LY

(over)

Residues of hydrocarbons characteristic of creosote (coal tar) were identified in Q1.

The contents Q8, Q10, Q14 and Q35 through Q38 were not identified; however, no drugs were found.

Specimens Q1, Q8, Q10, Q14, and Q35 through Q38 were containers that had not been completely opened before or during the fire.

The Q36, Q37, and Q35 bottles appear to be some type of paint or cosmetic (make-up) containers.

The submitted items will be retained in the FBI Laboratory until called for by a representative of your department.

NATIONAL TRANSPORTATION SAFETY BOARD
Bureau of Technology
Washington, D. C.

January 15, 1986

Materials Laboratory
Report No. 86-31

METALLURGIST'S FACTUAL REPORT

A. ACCIDENT

Place   : De Kalb, Texas
Date   : December 31, 1985
Aircraft   : DC-3, N711Y
NTSB No.   : DCA 86-A-A012
Investigator: Thomas McFall (FTW)

B. COMPONENTS EXAMINED

Pieces and particulate samples reported found on root tops and along
grass in the flightpath of the accident aircraft.

C. DETAILS OF EXAMINATION

A bag containing numerous samples was submitted to the National
Transportation Safety Board's Materials Laboratory on January 3, 1986.
Although no documentation accompanied the samples, subsequent telephone
communications with Mr. Thomas McFall established that these samples were
found along the accident aircraft flightpath on root tops and grass and
apparently had started ground fires. The exact as-found locations of the
samples were not communicated or established. The investigator requested
that the Materials Laboratory identify the material samples for metallic
chemical content.

As received, the pieces and particulate samples were segregated
into groups by physical shape, color, and surface texture. Seven
individual groups were established. Most of one group was obviously
large flakes of blistered paint (light tan to beige in color), although
two of the large flake pieces in this group contained fabric structure
having a side with an intact white enamel-type paint. Since the primary
concern was for establishing metallic substances in the pieces, this
paint flake group was not considered further for analysis.

Of the remaining six particulate groups, the following was established by X-ray energy dispersive analysis of selected samples. Five of the six groups had high concentrations of magnesium with moderate or small amounts of aluminum. The remaining group was predominately aluminum having some magnesium. One of the pieces high in aluminum appeared to be a piece of aluminum alloy sheet with zinc chromate on one surface.

Michael L. Marx
Senior Metallurgist

UNITED STATES OF AMERICA

NATIONAL TRANSPORTATION SAFETY BOARD

SUBPOENA

To __President/Chief Executive Officer_____

_____Duncan Aviation, P.O. Box 81887, Lincoln, Nebraska 68501_____

At the instance of __Frances Sherertz, Investigator_____

you are hereby required to ~~appear before~~ produce copies of all records, workorders,_____

_receipts, descriptions of completed work, photographs and drawings_____

_relating to Douglas DC-3 N711Y_____

~~of the National Transportation Safety Board XXXX~~_____

_____

_____

_____

~~in the XXXXX~~_____
by
~~on~~ the _21_ day of _March_____ 19_86_ at _12_ o'clock _p_.M. ~~XX~~

~~there day XX testify in the Matter of~~ _ Materials to be addressed to:_____

____Investigator Sherertz, TE-10, National Transportation Safety Board,_____

_Washington, D.C. 20594_____

~~And you are hereby required to bring with you and produce at said time and place the following~~
~~books, papers, documents, and records:~~_____

_____

_____

_____

_____

Fail not at your peril.

IN TESTIMONY WHEREOF, the undersigned, a member of the said National Transportation Safety Board, or an officer designated by it, has hereunto set his hand at _____Washington, D.C._____
this __6__ day of _March_____ 19_86_.

NTSB FORM 6100.1 (REV. 5/84)

NATIONAL TRANSPORTATION SAFETY BOARD,
800 INDEPENDENCE AVE., S.W.
WASHINGTON, DC 20594

Duncan Aviation, Inc.

March 13, 1986

Investigator Frances Sherertz
TE-10
National Transportation Safety Board
Washington, D.C. 20594

    RE: Douglas DC-3, N711Y

Dear Investigator Sherertz:

In response to your subpoena I am enclosing copies of the documents you requested. I numbered them, and a brief description of each follows.

1. Mechanic's on the job work order indicating squawks and corrective action, with the mechanic's initials and time spent on each job.

2. Copy of the actual customer billing for the work order in No. 1.

3. Our front counter receipt for payment of the work order No. SN720, plus fuel, plus 3 small items not identified.

4. Our deposit ticket, indicating we were paid in full by a check signed by Rick Nelson

5. Our mechanic's narrative report of the work he accomplished and his actions in general. I believe this report was previously sent to the NTSB.

6. This is a print I requested of our service shop for reference purposes only, to get an idea of where the aft cabin heater was located in the fuselage.

7. Our statement of account at October 1985 month end indicating a debit and credit for the work order.

I did not include copies of the complaints and summons on each of the three lawsuits which have been instigated against us so far. If you need these, please advise.

          Sincerely,

          Wayne L. Matthes
          Vice President-Administration

Post Office Box 81887   Lincoln Municipal Airport   Lincoln, Nebraska 68501   (402) 475-2611   Telex: 48-4365   (800) 228-4277

AIRCRAFT SERVICE REPORT

Registration No.: N711Y
Make: DC-3

On October 22, 1985, N711Y, a DC-3 owned or operated by SCB Records, Inc. landed at Duncan Aviation. The pilot, Brad Rank, requested that we work on his plane. He was told that we had a good working knowledge of Janitrol heaters and were somewhat familiar with DC-3's and we would try to help him out. He said that was OK that he would assist us, which he did.

We worked on two problems with the plane. First, a hydraulic leak in the area of the left engine. A cracked AN fitting on the hydraulic pump was at fault, it was replaced.

The second problem was the cabin heater was inoperative. I had the pilot turn the heater on, and I checked the electrical circuits at the heater, all seemed to be in order. I checked to see if the ignition unit was supplying spark to the plug, it was. I checked the fuel filter to see if it was clean and open, it was. I had the pilot turn on the fuel pump to be sure there was an adequate supply of fuel to the heater, there was. The combustion air blower was very noisy and didn't seem to be running fast enough. I removed the blower, we did not have a new motor in stock so I cleaned the old one up, lubricated the bearings and reinstalled. I then had the pilot turn the heater on for a functional check. The heater lit off and started putting out heat to the cabin. It didn't seem to be very much but the pilot said it was a lot better than it had been and that he would take it like it was. I closed up the aircraft and it left the following morning.

Ed Carter
Duncan Aviation, Inc.
P.O. Box 81887
Lincoln, NE   68501

ORIGINAL

TESTIMONY IN THE MATTER OF

DCA.86AA012

Douglas Aircraft

DC-3 N711Y

NATIONAL TRANSPORTATION SAFETY BOARD

TESTIMONY OF KENNETH REINHARD FERGUSON

March 19th, 1986, 10:50 o'clock p.m.

APPEARANCES:

Rudolf Kapustin, Hearing Officer, National Transportation Safety Board, Aviation Accident Division, Washington, D.C., 20594.

Frances A. Sherertz, Investigator, National Transportation Safety Board, 800 Independence Avenue Southwest, Washington, D.C., 20594.

Frode C. Jespersen, Principal Operations Inspector, Department of Transportation, Federal Aviation Administration, 6201 - 34th Avenue South, Minneapolis, Minnesota, 55450.

Tyrone P. Bujold, Esq., Robins Zelle Larson & Kaplan, 1800 International Centre, 900 Second Avenue South, Minneapolis, Minnesota, 55402.

Leo R. Kniebel, RPR
ASK, ZENDER, MAC PHAIL & KNIEBEL
Suite 500, 701 Fourth Avenue South
Minneapolis, Minnesota   55415
(612) 332-2603

BEST COPY AVAILABLE

1   (Wednesday, March 19th, 1986, 10:50 a.m.)

2   HEARING OFFICER KAPUSTIN: In accordance with Section

3   304 of the Federal Aviation Act, this will be sworn testimony

4   taken from Mr. Kenneth Ferguson in connection with the

5   accident involving November 711 Yankee which occurred near

6   DeKalb, D-e-K-a-l-b, Texas on December 31st, 1985.

7   I'm Rudy Kapustin, Hearing Officer, investigating

8   and in charge of the case. There will be no objections

9   during any of this proceeding. Admissibility questions will

10 be ruled on by me, and my rulings will be final.

11   I would like for the record all of the appearances

12 here starting with the gentleman on my left. State your

13 name.

14   MR. JESPERSEN: Frode Jespersen.

15   HEARING OFFICER KAPUSTIN: You're with --

16   MR. JESPERSEN: And I'm with the Air Carrier District

17 Office FAA here in Minneapolis.

18   MR. BUJOLD: My name is Tyrone Bujold, and I'm an

19 attorney practicing in Minneapolis, and I represent Kenneth

20 Ferguson.

21   HEARING OFFICER KAPUSTIN: Frances Sherertz is the

22 senior investigator on the case with me. She will being

23 asking the bulk the questions.

24   THE WITNESS: And I guess I don't have to be

25 introduced.

BEST COPY AVAILABLE

BEST COPY AVAILABLE

```
 1
 2                      KENNETH REINHARD FERGUSON,
 3   being first duly sworn, testifies as follows:
 4
 5          HEARING OFFICER KAPUSTIN:      Frances, proceed with the
 6   questioning.
 7
 8                           EXAMINATION
 9   BY MS. SHERERTZ:
10       Q.    Would you state your name and your legal address?
11       A.    My name is -- Do you want full middle name?
12   Kenneth Reinhard, that's R-e-i-n-h-a-r-d, Ferguson, and my
13   legal address is 26427, Olive Drive, Apartment A, and that's
14   Hemet, California, H-e-m-e-t, California.  I believe the zip
15   is 92344.  I can't quite swear to that.
16       Q.    By whom were you most recently employed?
17       A.    Most recently by the corporation named Rick
18   Nelson-SCB Records, Inc.  At least that's where my paychecks
19   came from, so I consider them the employer.
20       Q.    And how long have you been employed with them?
21       A.    Well, it's very close to two years.  I would say 20
22   months, 22 months, about 20, 21 months.
23       Q.    Are you still employed by them?
24       A.    I don't know.  I hadn't thought about that.  There
25   is no longer an airplane.  There is no longer a Rick Nelson.
```

1   I honestly don't know. I guess I hadn't considered myself

2   still employed by them, but I haven't talked to the manager,

3   so I really don't know what they consider my status to be.

4   Q.   Okay. How were you paid for your services? That

5   is, did they pay you by the day, or the month or the trip, or

6   what?

7   A.   I was paid by the day. A daily wage, plus we

8   received per diem on the road, as expense money on the road.

9   Q.   And in what amounts did they pay you?

10   A.   I received a hundred dollars a day wages for my

11   piloting, and the per diem was $25 a day.

12   Q.   Who set those amounts, and how were they

13   negotiated?

14   A.   Oh, gosh. Initially, the very first trip I took

15   was one of those deals where they call, you know, on short

16   notice, and they needed someone, and could I come and

17   whatnot. And at that time, I said, "What do you pay," and he

18   said a hundred a day. This was Brad Rank that I was speaking

19   to on the phone who at that time I did not know and I hadn't

20   met him.

21   And it was -- frankly, it was less than I was used

22   to working for under the circumstances, but I wanted to meet

23   Rick Nelson. So I went, and we just never renegotiated. I

24   kind of worked out and became their regular man, and it just

25   was never renegotiated.

BEST COPY AVAILABLE

1   Q.   What aeronautical certificates and licenses do you

2 hold?

3   A.   All right. I hold a commercial pilot's license, I

4 believe it's 1879921. I've even got trouble remembering

5 that, my pilot's license number. I believe that's correct,

6 though. You'd have to check the records. The license -- let

7 me divert here for a moment.

8   All my licenses were in my wallet, which either was

9 lost at the scene of the crash or by the hospitals, or it

10 went up in flames in the airplane. I don't know. All I know

11 is that my clothes were not returned to me by the people who

12 had cut them off of me. And if my wallet was in them, then

13 it went with them. So I do not have the certificates

14 currently in my possession, and that's why I'm having a

15 little trouble with the number. Do you want all the ratings

16 on the license?

17   Q.   Yes, please.

18   A.   Okay. It was commercial pilot's license with

19 single and multi-engine planned NC plane ratings; instrument

20 airplane rating; Citation jet type rating. I believe that's

21 it on the license.

22   Then I had a certified flight instructor's license

23 of the same number carrying single and multi-engine ratings

24 and instrument airplane ratings.

25   I had a ground instructor's certificate numbered my

BEST COPY AVAILABLE

1 social security number, which is 469-46-5080, and that had

2 both advanced and instrument ratings on it.

3   I also carried a first-class medical certificate.

4   Q.   What was the date and location of either your last

5 flight check or your last biennial flight review?

6   A.   Well, let me see. Which was the last biennial?

7 Would be -- I renewed my flight instructor license in -- let

8 me see, when did I renew that? Well, I can tell you the

9 examiner and the place it was renewed at Sail Plane

10 Enterprises at the Hemet Airport in Hemet, California, by our

11 designated examiner John Tempest, and it was late this past

12 summer, July or August, that approximately time period. I

13 don't remember exactly now what date. I can certainly find

14 out easily enough.

15   Q.   We can call. When he renewed your -- re-validated

16 your CFI ticket, did he do that by flight check?

17   A.   Yes. That was by flight check and oral examination

18 both. That's my most recent one. I had had one in the

19 spring, too, but that was my most recent.

20   Q.   Approximately what's your total flight time?

21   A.   Oh, around numbers about 4,500 hours.

22   Q.   4,500?

23   A.   Yes, including co-pilot time. All time, total

24 time.

25   Q.   And how much DC-3?

BEST COPY AVAILABLE

ASK, ZENDER, MAC PHAIL & KNIEBEL

1   A.   Round numbers again, about 150 to 180 hours.

2   Q.   Were you flying the DC-3 for Rick Nelson as a

3   full-time job, or doing other things?

4   A.   Well, it was my primary job. I had a part-time job

5   at Hemet at Sail Plane Enterprises that I used to fill in

6   when I wasn't flying for Rick. There were months when Rick

7   didn't go out that much and I needed something else, so I

8   filled in with that. But Rick was my primary employer, and I

9   was on call to him so that he took precedence over the other

10 job, I guess would be the way to say it.

11 Q.   Have you flown any other large transport category

12 airplane other than DC-3?

13 A.   Not any large ones, no.

14 Q.   Did you fly the Jet Commander when the band had

15 that?

16 A.   I was co-pilot on that also, yes.

17 Q.   We would like to examine your pilot logbook. Is

18 that available?

19 A.   In the airplane. I have some ancient ones, but

20 they wouldn't be pertinent to the current --

21 Q.   None in the last 24 months?

22 A.   No.

23 Q.   I'd like to review now some of the circumstances

24 and conditions that surrounded just the general operation of

25 November 711 Yankee.

BEST COPY AVAILABLE

ASK, ZENDER, MAC PHAIL & KNIEBEL

1 A. Okay.

2 Q. Do you know what regulation it was being operated

3 under?

4 A. To the best of my knowledge, we were operating

5 under Part 91.

6 Q. Have you, yourself, actually seen the airplane's

7 airworthiness certificate?

8 A. Personally examined it, no.

9 Q. Do you know where it was kept?

10 A. It was supposed to be in a pocket in the pilot's

11 compartment in the aircraft.

12 Q. Meaning that it was your understanding that that's

13 where it was?

14 A. It was my understanding, right.

15 Q. Have you actually personally seen the airplane's

16 registration certificate?

17 A. No, I have not.

18 Q. Do you know where it was kept?

19 A. Again, it was my understanding it was kept in the

20 same packet of papers in the pilot's compartment.

21 Q. Okay. To the best of your knowledge, who owned the

22 airplane?

23 A. Well, that's kind of in a way sort of hard to say,

24 because there were corporations involved. But as I

25 understood it, the airplane was originally purchased by Rick

BEST COPY AVAILABLE

ASK, ZENDER, MAC PHAIL & KNEBEL

1   Nelson-SCB Records, Inc., that corporation. And then there

2   was later an intent -- I don't know if it was ever carried

3   out -- to create a corporation called 711 Yankee, Inc., and

4   that the airplane would be placed in that corporation, the

5   ownership of the airplane would be placed in that

6   corporation, because we had found that maintenance costs and

7   other things tend to go up when people found out the airplane

8   was owned by Rick Nelson. So they wanted to put a buffer

9   between his name and FBOs and maintenance people who tended

10   to charge generously when they found out who owned the

11   airplane.

12   HEARING OFFICER KAPUSTIN: Let me just ask a question

13   here on 711, this corporation. When did you first hear about

14   the fact that they may have formed a separate corporation?

15   THE WITNESS: Oh, late summer, early fall

16   approximately.

17   HEARING OFFICER KAPUSTIN: So this was before the

18   accident?

19   THE WITNESS: Say a couple of months before the

20   accident, something in that general area.

21   HEARING OFFICER KAPUSTIN: Thanks, go ahead.

22   BY MS. SHERERTZ:

23   Q. Were the weight and balance papers for the airplane

24   actually on the airplane?

25   A. Yes, they were. Those I have seen and worked --

BEST COPY AVAILABLE

ASK, ZENDER, MAC PHAIL & KNIEBEL

10

1   personally worked with.

2   Q.   But they were normally stored on the airplane?

3   A.   Yes.

4   Q.   What about the airplane operating manual or some

5   other source of operating limitations?

6   A.   We had two of them on board.

7   Q.   Two manuals?

8   A.   Yes, we did.

9   Q.   Current, as far as you knew?

10   A.   To the best of my knowledge, there were revisions

11   in them of quite recent date.

12   Q.   Where were the airframe and engine logbooks

13   normally kept?

14   A.   Well, when we got the airplane, they were in a

15   beautiful leather holding thing that I guess were originally

16   kept in the office of the people who previously owned the

17   airplane. We carried them in the airplane for a while, and

18   then Brad Rank, the pilot, took them out and took them with

19   him on a trip, not in the airplane, but a trip they went on

20   commercial airline transportation with, and they were -- at

21   that time they were lost. I have not seen them since -- I

22   have not seen them since the aircraft went down with that

23   engine change. That was the last -- That was June, I

24   believe.

25   Q.   Subsequent to that then, was a new set of engineer

BEST COPY AVAILABLE

ASK, ZENDER, MAC PHAIL & KNIEBEL

Chapter 34: Rick Nelson

1   frame logbooks started?

2   A.   Considering that I had nothing to do with the

3   maintenance, I can't swear to that. I certainly would assume

4   so. We had an engine change and various maintenance things

5   going on that Brad was in charge of. I don't know. I simply

6   assumed that there would be.

7   Q.   Okay. Were there any principal airports where most

8   of the maintenance was done?

9   A.   Yes, Orange County Airport. UCO Jet was the FBO,

10   the name of the fixed base operator where we had most of our

11   maintenance done. Did that make sense to you? It made sense

12   to you, didn't it, I trust? Okay.

13   Q.   What have been the most outstanding recurrent

14   maintenance problems with 711 Yankee?

15   A.   Most outstanding recurrent. I'm sorry, I'm

16   thinking out loud. Well, No. 1 would be oil leakage from the

17   engines, especially the left engine. That was a constant

18   problem that you just fiddled with, you know, on every flight

19   -- in between every flight. It was a continuing thing. The

20   main cabin heater was a frequent and continuous maintenance

21   problem.

22   Q.   Were there problems that were anything other than

23   unusual in getting money to pay for these things and paying

24   for maintenance?

25   A.   Well, that's a perfectly legitimate question. I

BEST COPY AVAILABLE

ASK, ZENDER, MAC PHAIL & KNIEBEL

1 have to qualify my answer by pointing out that I was not

2 privy in any way, shape, or form to any of the management or

3 policy decisions made on the airplane, on its maintenance, or

4 on its operation. I was purely a daily-wage,

5 call-when-wanted pilot.

6   Now with that in mind, it seemed to me at times as

7 though money were rather slow in coming forth for some of

8 these things. But as I said, not being privy to the

9 decisions of management, I cannot, you know, it's difficult

10 to give a real hard and fast answer on that.

11   To the best of my knowledge, the aircraft was

12 always airworthy in the legal sense. I know the inspections

13 were pulled, and I helped Brad pull some of them. The

14 pre-flights and so on that we conducted always indicated to

15 me that the airplane was airworthy.

16   As for the payment of the bills to the maintenance

17 people, it was beyond my ken. I wasn't involved in it.

18   Q.   Okay.

19   HEARING OFFICER KAPUSTIN: Off the record for a

20 second.

21   (Off the record discussion)

22 BY MS. SHERERTZ:

23   Q.   Was there -- We are still back in the maintenance

24 area. Was there an incident involving an in-flight engine

25 seizure last summer?

BEST COPY AVAILABLE

ASK, SEIDER, MAC PHAIL & KNISBER

1   A.   Yes, there was.

2   Q.   Would you elaborate on it?

3   A.   Elaborate on it? Well, we --

4   Q.   Specifically on things that happened, the previous

5   maintenance cycles, or the previous few days that may have

6   contributed to the seizure of the engine.

7   A.   Well, let me think. We made the trip in May

8   without any incident. The aircraft, I don't know from

9   personal knowledge, that is from on-the-scene knowledge, what

10   maintenance was pulled on the airplane between that trip and

11   the one in June when the in-flight engine failure took place.

12   The maintenance, if you wish to call it that, that

13   I personally pulled on the airplane consisted of checking and

14   adding oil to the oil tanks, which consisted largely of

15   cleaning up the mess I made when I did it.

16   Maintenance, I can't speak to what maintenance

17   might have been involved that might have contributed to

18   problems on that engine. I don't know about maintenance.

19   Q.   Okay. There have been --

20   HEARING OFFICER KAPUSTIN: Let me interrupt you. I

21   think that requires a conclusion as to what contributed to

22   it. You do you have any recollection what maintenance was

23   done to the engine prior to the failure?

24   THE WITNESS: Wasn't done?

25   HEARING OFFICER KAPUSTIN: What was done to the

BEST COPY AVAILABLE

ASK, ZENDER, MAC PHAIL & KNIEBEL   14

1   engine that you're aware of.

2   THE WITNESS: I'm aware of none.

3   HEARING OFFICER KAPUSTIN: You're aware of no

4   specific maintenance operations done?

5   THE WITNESS: No, sir. No, none.

6   HEARING OFFICER KAPUSTIN: Any conversations between

7   you and Brad regarding the condition of the engine prior to

8   the failure?

9   THE WITNESS: No, sir. None, no, not prior to that

10 flight, no.

11   HEARING OFFICER KAPUSTIN: Okay, go ahead.

12 BY MS. SHERERTZ:

13   Q.   One individual to whom -- that we talked to said

14 that he believed that the airplane -- or that that engine had

15 been run with the oil shut off at the time at the cockpit

16 pull which worked the unit?

17   A.   That's right.

18   Q.   Is there anything to this? Do you know anything

19 about it? Has Brad said anything about it?

20   A.   Okay. On the night of the flight, okay, at the

21 time we started that engine with the ground power unit --

22   (Off the record discussion)

23   A.   At the time the engine was started, the firewall

24 shutoff valves for that engine were in the closed position.

25 Because of -- This is in the nature of an explanation rather

BEST COPY AVAILABLE

1 than excusing. Because the ground personnel got involved in

2 -- they had trouble getting the power unit disconnected and

3 out of the way, and we got involved in watching that and

4 missed the fact that the oil pressure light did not go out.

5   Then following that a couple of really -- to me,

6 an afterthought, pretty unbelievable things happened

7 considering the level of experience. When I drew to Brad's

8 attention that we had no oil pressure showing, the first

9 thing he said was check the circuit breakers. Now, both he

10 and I were former turbine engine pilots where the oil

11 pressure gauges are activated by AC electricity, and there

12 are circuit breakers and fuses and all kinds of things

13 involved.

14   All I can say is I got up out of my seat with a

15 flashlight, and I went back to the circuit breaker board, and

16 a little thing in my mind kept saying something's not right

17 about this, but I don't know what it is. And I spent a lot

18 of time looking for circuit breakers, non-existent circuit

19 breakers on the oil pressure system.

20   Eventually, I turned around and noticed that the

21 light had gone out, and I said, "What happened?" You know, I

22 guess I didn't know. And Brad said that the valves had been

23 closed, and he shoved them open.

24   The exact amount of time that the engine ran in

25 that condition, I do not know. I cannot say how many minutes

BEST COPY AVAILABLE

1 were involved.

2   Q.   Was it this flight following that incident that the

3 seizure occurred?

4   A.   Yes, it is.   That's the other, to me, unbelievable

5 thing about that incident is that neither one of us, our

6 alarm bells didn't go off and say, "Don't fly this thing till

7 you've checked it out after that."

8   We looked at the guages, the temperatures, the

9 pressures, the run-up of engine.   Everything was normal.

10 Everything was perfect when we were in the airplane.   No

11 alarm bells.

12   Q.   Okay.   I would like you to think now about the

13 three days or four days or so preceding the accident.   And

14 those would have been Saturday, which was December 28th, and

15 then Sunday the 29th, Monday the 30th, and of course New

16 Year's Eve, December 31st.

17   On Saturday and Sunday, that's the 28th and 29th,

18 tell me what you did those days, where you were, what flying

19 occurred.

20   A.   Okay.   I'm going to have to ask you to tell me

21 where we were on those days.   I don't remember.

22   Q.   You don't know, okay.   I don't know where you were.

23   A.   Okay.   We were -- On the 31st, we were in

24 Guntersville, Alabama.   That's the day we left there.   So we

25 were there on the 30th.   How did that work out?   Did we -- It

BEST COPY AVAILABLE

Chapter 34: Rick Nelson

1 all runs together in my head. See, I'm not even absolutely

2 positive where we played just prior to Guntersville. I think

3 it was Detroit. I have to talk to the office and find out.

4 Do you know?

5   MR. BUJOLD: I might be able to help you. Try

6 thinking in terms of being in the Twin Cities at Jan Sayer's

7 home.

8   THE WITNESS: Right. Well, during Christmas, yes,

9 of course.

10   MR. BUJOLD: Right. And then flying down to Memphis.

11   THE WITNESS: Correct.

12   MR. BUJOLD: And then going on down -- Didn't you go

13 to Orlando or someplace in Florida?

14   THE WITNESS: No, no. That was one of the last

15 things that we had on the --

16   MR. BUJOLD: Then I'm mistaken. Pardon me.

17   THE WITNESS: I'm sorry. We did go there. It's

18 getting all screwed up in my mind.

19 BY MS. SHERERTZ:

20   Q.   That's okay. Tell you what, let's just start

21 talking about --

22   A.   The last part of your question is that the majority

23 of that time we were on the ground in Guntersville, and the

24 airplane was not being flown.

25   Q.   Okay. December 30th, which was a Monday. It was

BEST COPY AVAILABLE

1   the day before the accident.   Did you do any flying that day?

2   A.   No.

3   Q.   What did you do during the day?

4   A.   Well, there was a show that evening.   If there are

5   not specific demands on days like that, my time's my own.   I

6   go for hikes if the weather is suitable, and I just entertain

7   myself.

8   On that day, I believe we -- Brad and I spent part

9   of the day at the airplane doing wash and polish kinds of

10   thing and messing around with the urinal which we had had

11   problems with.   I know we spent one of those days doing that,

12   and I think it was that day.   All right?

13   We had several free, non-flying days in

14   Guntersville, and on one of those, Brad and I spent a half

15   day out at the airplane.   I think that was the 30th.

16   Q.   Did you go to the show that night?

17   A.   Yes.

18   Q.   And about what time does the show get out?

19   A.   Roughly midnight, approximately.   The second show.

20   Q.   And then did you retire for the evening?

21   A.   Yes.

22   Q.   And about what time on the next morning do you

23   think you got up?

24   A.   Between 8:00 and 9:00, something like that.

25   Q.   Okay.   After you got up, did you go immediately to

BEST COPY AVAILABLE

1   the airport, or did you have other duties in Guntersville?

2   A.   Well, I always helped with the baggage, helped

3   getting people moving and all that kind of stuff. They were

4   informal duties. They weren't required. It was just things

5   I always did.

6   Both Brad and I went to the airport prior to the

7   passengers arriving on that particular day. Frequently, I

8   went to the airport alone and, you know, got the oiling and

9   got the baggage loaded and got things opened up and the

10   engines pulled through and all that sort of thing. But on

11   that particular day, Brad and I went out together around

12   10:00 a.m., I think. I can't swear to the exact time, but

13   that would be approximately.

14   Q.   What events occurred at the airport? What was done

15   in the way of servicing the airplane fueling, oiling? What

16   actually had to be done that day?

17   A.   Here's where I get a little confused. We serviced

18   the body. I think we did that on that day when we went out

19   on free time. We had attempted to repair the -- what I call

20   the cross-country tube, the in-flight urinal, and I believe

21   we did some work on that.

22   The servicing was done. I believe I had gotten --

23   Whatever oil was to be put on board and so on I'd done on

24   whatever day we were out there together. So it would have

25   been baggage loading; pulling the engines through; I believe

BEST COPY AVAILABLE

1   we did a run-up, a warm-up prior to the passengers arriving.

2   Then, as I'm sure you know, after the passengers

3   arrived when we attempted to depart, the left engine wouldn't

4   start because we'd had -- recently we'd had problems with the

5   priming system on that engine. Essentially it was just the

6   jets were plugging up. And so we took off the appropriate

7   section of cowling, and Brad blew out one of the primer jets,

8   re-installed it, and we were able to start the engine.

9   Aside from that, I don't recall now. There again,

10 whether it was that day or the previous day that we were out

11 there together, Brad did investigate the main cabin heater,

12 which we did frequently, finding nothing of note. The darn

13 thing had a habit of running beautifully on the ground while

14 we were parked. But there again, whether that was on

15 departure day or the previous day that we were out there

16 together, I'm not sure. One or the other.

17   The major maintenance, if you will, was fixing the

18 primer so the engine would start, and that was the main thing

19 that was done on departure day.

20   Q.   In-flight, was the heater activated from the

21 cockpit?

22   A.   Yes.

23   Q.   Turned on from the cockpit?

24   A.   Yeah. Just a simple toggle switch.

25   Q.   Could the passengers regulate the cold air or hot

BEST COPY AVAILABLE

1 air mix themselves?

2   A.   There was -- In the passenger cabin, there was a

3 thermostatic control located about mid point in the cabin.   I

4 should add there were two cockpit switches.   There was an

5 on-off, and then -- Three.   There was an on-off; there was a

6 mode switch which you could place either in automatic or in

7 manual; and then there was a third switch that when the mode

8 switch was in manual, you could select colder or hotter

9 manually with this third toggle switch.   When the mode switch

10 was in automatic, then, at least in theory, the thermostat

11 back in the cabin controlled how much the -- produced what

12 the mix was.

13   Q.   When there were problems with the cabin heater, was

14 it a regulatory problem in that it ran when it shouldn't

15 have, or was it -- were there problems in it shutting down

16 when you didn't want it to shut down, or did it not turn on?

17 What did those problems consist of?

18   A.   We were not -- Did all of those things.   A couple

19 of times, perhaps three times, it turned on and ran to the

20 point of turning the place into a sauna without ever showing

21 any overheat light or any indication of problem whatsoever.

22 Turn it off, it would shut down, it would cool down.   Try it

23 again, and it would work normally.

24   The most common recurrent problem was that it would

25 show -- We had two warning lights.   We had one that said

BEST COPY AVAILABLE

ASK, ZENDER, MAC PHAIL & KNIEBEL

22

1 Janitrol Overheat. We had another that said Janitrol Fire.

2 The overheat light would come on with no great temperature in

3 the cabin, in fact, with no great temperature on the unit

4 itself, because we had experimented on the ground, and you

5 could lay your hand on the thing. It wasn't -- But this

6 overheat light would come on. If you did not turn off the

7 heater when that overheat light came on, eventually it would

8 pop a circuit breaker that I believe was called Janitrol

9 Override, I think it was called. It was located in the main

10 circuit breaker panel behind the captain's seat in some

11 cabinetry there that was part of the galley and all that.

12   Again, without ever any overt signs of heat, of

13 overheating, that was the most common problem. However, at

14 other times, yes, it would simply shut down by itself and

15 just quit working.

16   Q. Were those problems resolved at all after the

17 heater was worked on by Duncan?

18   A. Not really. It would seem like it for a while, but

19 we just -- they just came back. There was -- It seemed for

20 perhaps the first day or two that there was an improvement

21 after that work was done, but they didn't -- There was no

22 lasting improvement.

23   HEARING OFFICER KAPUSTIN: Just back up a little bit.

24 You said when the Janitrol overheat light came on that you

25 could put your hand on the heater and not feel any high

BEST COPY AVAILABLE

ASK, ZENDER, MAC PHAIL & KNIEBEL

1 temperatures?

2   THE WITNESS: Yeah. I mean there was warmth, but it

3 wasn't something that was --

4   HEARING OFFICER KAPUSTIN: Was this a routine way of

5 determining if it was in fact overheating, or not?

6   THE WITNESS: No. We just experimented with it one

7 day.

8   HEARING OFFICER KAPUSTIN: Where would he put his

9 hand? Would it be you, or --

10   THE WITNESS: No, it was Brad. And I can't say. I

11 don't know where he was --

12   HEARING OFFICER KAPUSTIN: You couldn't say

13 specifically where he would put his hand in trying to feel --

14   THE WITNESS: No. He simply stated that it was not

15 unnaturally hot. There was no --

16   HEARING OFFICER KAPUSTIN: And then to correct the

17 overheat indication, you would shut it off?

18   THE WITNESS: Correct, yeah. As I say, if you didn't

19 shut it off, then it would pop this circuit breaker

20 eventually, although again, not right away. It might not do

21 it for five minutes.

22   HEARING OFFICER KAPUSTIN: Do you recall any

23 instances where it did pop the circuit breaker?

24   THE WITNESS: You mean immediately? I don't recall

25 any. There may have been, but there aren't any that stick in

BEST COPY AVAILABLE

ASK, ZENDER, MAC PHAIL & KNIEBEL

1 my mind where it blew the circuit breaker right away as soon

2 as the light came on.

3   The other thing, you could always tell when the

4 circuit breaker had blown, because when you turned the

5 operating switch off, then the overheat light would stay on

6 as long as that circuit breaker was popped. I don't know

7 why, but it did.

8 BY MS. SHERERTZ:

9   Q.   Okay. Were the passengers, the people who were

10 regular passengers on the airplane, knowledgeable about the

11 fire extinguishers that were associated with -- either the

12 cabin fire extinguisher or the two that were dedicated for

13 the heater?

14   A.   They would not have been familiar with those

15 dedicated for the heater, as they were located -- the

16 switches were up in the cockpit. Well, of course, there was

17 the little manual one back in the tail. But they had been

18 briefed -- I want to qualify this. They had been briefed on

19 the cabin fire extinguishers, the emergency exits, and so on.

20 How much of that was retained in less meaningful knowledge, I

21 can't say.

22   Q.   Did that airplane also have an overhead hatch?

23   A.   In the cockpit.

24   MS. SHERERTZ: I would like a break now. It's about

25 time for him to have a break, and I think it's a good time to

BEST COPY AVAILABLE

ASK, ZEIDER, MAC PHAIL & KNIEBEL

25

1 do it.

2   HEARING OFFICER KAPUSTIN: What time do you want to

3 go back?

4   MS. SHERETZ: What times a good time for you?

5   THE WITNESS: I'll be ready approximately noon. I

6 don't need that long.

7   (Recess at approximately 11:30 a.m.)

8 (12:15 p.m.)

9   HEARING OFFICER KAPUSTIN: Mr. Ferguson, let me

10 remind you that you're still under oath.

11   THE WITNESS: All right. I understand that.

12   HEARING OFFICER KAPUSTIN: Please proceed.

13 BY MS. SHERERTZ:

14   Q.   Before we go into anything new, I want to just

15 review some areas where there was either uncertainty on my

16 part or on the part of Mr. Kapustin.

17   A.   Sure.

18   Q.   When you began flying the DC-3 November 711 Yankee,

19 was that your first experience in the DC-3?

20   A.   Correct.

21   Q.   Who trained you in DC-3?

22   A.   Brad.

23   Q.   Brad? Was it formal dual?

24   A.   Yes. Well, it was my understanding it was formal

25 dual, yeah.

BEST COPY AVAILABLE

ASK, ZEIDER, MAC PHAIL & KNIEBEL

1   Q.   Okay. Are you type rated in the DC-3?

2   A.   No, ma'am. I wished I had. That was supposed to

3   be part of the deal. I was eventually supposed to get a

4   check ride and a type rating out of it, but it just never

5   materialized.

6   Q.   Did you take any instrument competency checks or

7   biennials or any type of flight checks in the DC-3?

8   A.   No. Just the required Part 91 familiarity with the

9   aircraft for a co-pilot in it.

10   Q.   At the time of the accident, were you current in

11   the aircraft? That is, in terms of takeoffs and landings?

12   A.   Yes. Brad wasn't real generous with takeoffs and

13   landings, but I got a few and easily enough to stay current,

14   yes.

15   Q.   And were you current as a PIC on instruments? Not

16   necessarily in that airplane, but were you instrument

17   current?

18   A.   Yeah, I think so. I'd have to check, but I believe

19   so.

20   Q.   Earlier we discussed the ownership of the airplane

21   and Stone Canyon Band and Stone Canyon Band, Inc. and 711

22   Yankee, Inc. Is your use of the words "corporation" and

23   "incorporated" with regards to any of those entities based on

24   the fact that that was what they called themselves and it was

25   the popular jargon, or do you have some knowledge that there

BEST COPY AVAILABLE

ASK, ZENDER, MAC PHAIL & KNIEBEL

27

1   was in fact a legal corporate structure?

2   A.   I have no knowledge of any legal corporate

3   structure. That was just common usage and assumption, I

4   guess. As I say now, as I sit here and picture one of my

5   checks, I could have sworn it said "Inc." at the end of it.

6   But Ty says it doesn't, so -- which, as I say, rattles me a

7   little, considering I was drawing those checks for some

8   substantial period of time.

9   For instance, when we went into Canada, we told the

10   Canadian customs that the aircraft -- customs or immigration

11   that asks, that the owner was SCB Records, Inc. Now, maybe

12   we told them an untruth, I don't know. But that was the way

13   referred to it.

14   Q.   Okay. I want you to begin to give me a history of

15   the flight for December 31st, beginning with say about the

16   time that the passengers were boarded and preparations made

17   for the takeoff, and culminating with the landing in DeKalb.

18   Structure it as you will. I have a sectional of the DeKalb

19   area with me and also a low altitude L-13 and L-14 chart if

20   you want them to use. What I'll do is just let you kind of

21   tell me how events happened, and then we'll fill in the holes

22   with questioning after.

23   A.   All right, that sounds reasonable. And let me see,

24   starting with the time the passengers were boarded, we had a

25   couple of false boardings due to weather. About the time

BEST COPY AVAILABLE

ASK, ZENDER, MAC PHAIL & KNIEBEL

1 we'd decide to go, the visibility at Guntersville would go so

2 low with either rain or low-lying cloud that we'd have to

3 postpone. Everybody would go back inside again and sit

4 around some more and wait for it to lift.

5 Then, of course, when it finally lifted, then the

6 left engine wouldn't start, and we had to clear that primer

7 and get that squared away. So there may have been three

8 postponements before finally the weather and the engine all

9 cooperated at once, and we took off.

10 Now without -- if you had a sectional showing

11 Guntersville, it would help, because I'm not remembering for

12 sure. I think whatever I say is probably going to be wrong.

13 Seems to me the runway there ran approximately -- what would

14 that be -- northwest-southeast. In any event, we took off

15 out over the lake, whichever end of the runway the lake was

16 on.

17 I had previously called the local flight service

18 and obtained a clearance and a void time, because we couldn't

19 get anyone on the ground. And we took off well within our

20 void time and contacted -- who would that have been probably?

21 Gee, I can't remember big towns near there now. Anyway,

22 whoever the appropriate controlling authority was, and climb

23 to our assigned altitude and proceeded en route in a very

24 normal manner.

25 The question was previously asked by you, and

BEST COPY AVAILABLE

ASK, ZENDER, MAC PHAIL & KNIEBEL

29

1 others have asked whether Brad put on his coveralls before

2 the flight or after -- or during. I still can't swear to it,

3 but it seems to me, as he was the one cleaning the primer out

4 of that engine that he would have had his coveralls on at

5 that time and probably didn't take them off, which was

6 common. We weren't under any formal dress code in the

7 airplane. We tried to dress appropriately when occasion

8 allowed, but there was so much dirty work to do on that

9 airplane that sometimes it was kind of hard to wear your coat

10 and tie and stuff and still make everything work. That's why

11 I happened to be in jeans and tennis shoes, because I was

12 always the guy who got to do the oil and the fun stuff like

13 that. That comes with being No. 2.

14   Somewhere en route, at some point en route, the

15 heater, the main cabin heater started to act up. We would

16 get the Janitrol overheat light, turn it off, wait for a

17 while, turn it on. It would work for a while, and it would

18 either quit working, that is, it would start blowing cold

19 air, or it would turn on the overheat light again.

20   At some point, exactly when or where I can't say,

21 Brad decided to go aft of the tail and see if there was

22 anything he could do to get it to function correctly, the

23 main cabin heater. He then came back into the cabin. And

24 now I don't remember. There was several times involved here,

25 and exact times when he did exactly what and I did exactly

BEST COPY AVAILABLE

1 what are jumbled. He may have signaled for me to turn it on

2 from in back going, you know, turn the switch on

3 (indicating), or he may have come up front and told me to

4 turn it on or whatever. This happened several times.

5   When he came forward again, I -- Well, what

6 happened was one of the times I refused to turn it on. I

7 didn't turn it on. I was getting nervous. I didn't think

8 that we should be messing with the heater en route. I had

9 discussed this with Brad previously on previous flights. And

10 of course, as time goes on and nothing goes wrong, one's

11 arguments become weaker.

12   But nontheless, he came forward, and I said, "Brad"

13 -- this isn't an exact quote, but words to the effect of, "I

14 don't like it. Let's just leave it off and just quit messing

15 with it." And he said, "Rick wants heat," and he turn it

16 back on again.

17   Once again, after some length of time, it either

18 shut off or turned the overheat light on, I'm not sure which;

19 went through the same cycle. How many times this happened, I

20 can't say. Three or four, perhaps five times. The last time

21 Brad went aft in the tail, he was aft for not very long, came

22 out and signaled me to turn it on again, which I did, and it

23 was several minutes after that that Pat Woodward, one of the

24 band members, came forward to me and said, "There is smoke

25 back here back in the cabin."

1   At that point, I turned off the heater switch,

2   looked aft, and Brad was standing back by Rick's chair, which

3   we've previously discussed the location of, and he was

4   signaling me to turn it off, which I had already done. I

5   could see some slight smoke back in the aft part of the cabin

6   at that time, and it was at that time that I called Fort

7   Worth Center and told them that we had a problem and we

8   wanted to return to Texarkana.

9   I initiated a turn back towards Texarkana while

10   they were giving me the vector. And at that time, Brad came

11   forward and sat down in the pilot's seat and remained there

12   then for the rest of the flight.

13   As you can tell from the transcripts of the radio

14   communication, the smoke volume built very rapidly, became

15   impossible to breathe, impossible to see inside the aircraft

16   more than inches. It's very difficult for me to even

17   describe the density of the smoke. It was roiling, boiling

18   black smoke that was just -- I don't know. You couldn't see

19   the instrument panel of the aircraft, it was that heavy. And

20   on the DC-3, they're pretty close.

21   At that time, Brad and I both opened our cockpit

22   side windows both in order to be able to breathe and in order

23   to be able to see. There was nothing else to see. I

24   continued the conversation with Center until Brad signaled

25   that we were going down. I attempted to say that. I think

BEST COPY AVAILABLE

ASK, ZENDER, MAC PHAIL & KNIEBEL

32

1   all I got out was "down," and we proceeded to descend as

2   rapidly as possible. Brad made the entire descent and

3   landing visually with his head out the left cockpit side

4   window. I spent some time outside and some time inside doing

5   co-pilot duties, securing the gear and putting the flaps down

6   and preparing for landing.

7   As I mentioned before when we talked, I had

8   unbuckled my seat belt, because when you open the window, it

9   acted like a chimney, and it was drawing flames up around me.

10   So I undid my seat belt so I could jam my body far enough in

11   the window to stop the chimney effect.

12   Well, after I'd put the gear and flaps down --

13   Well, let me correct that. Brad called for gear down. I

14   went to do it, and he had already put the lever in the down

15   position. So I merely followed up when they showed ful 1 down

16   by locking the -- latching the locking lever down and

17   verifying that they were down.

18   I had -- In putting the flaps down, I had so

19   severely burned my hands that I couldn't re-fasten my seat

20   belt, and I had to decide whether I wanted to make the

21   landing jammed in the window or some other way, and I opted,

22   as I told you before, to get out of my seat and place my back

23   and head against the windshield and instrument panel in a

24   brace position, and that's the way I was when we landed.

25   The landing was better than normal. It was

BEST COPY AVAILABLE

ASK, ZENDER, MAC PHAIL & KNIEBEL

33

1 probably the best one he ever made. I told my sister later

2 that I think the airplane landed itself. It was very nearly

3 a three-point, which was something we never did. We always

4 wheel-landed the airplane.

5 After the roll-out, which I recall being very

6 short, I secured, shut down my engine. Why I didn't do both

7 as was my normal habit, I don't know. I know I didn't want

8 my propeller blades turning when I went out that window, and

9 I shut them down. I looked at the skylight or the hatch, as

10 you called it, and realized that I didn't really -- that I'd

11 never personally opened it and wasn't familiar enough with

12 the latch and just made the mental decision to forget it.

13 I tore my side window open again and went out head

14 first, as I have described before. My engine had stopped

15 turning. There was no flame on the outside of the airplane

16 on my side, on the right side of the aircraft. It was free

17 of flame. The aircraft was in a normal three-point attitude

18 on the landing. As I think I mentioned, I fell head first on

19 a pile of brush which acted as a cushion, and I rolled over

20 onto my back and up on my feet and took a few steps away from

21 the airplane and looked back.

22 The cabin of the aircraft through the windows

23 appeared to be an inferno. Flames and smoke was all that one

24 could see. I couldn't see Brad or anyone else at that time.

25 The left engine of the aircraft was still running. The left

BEST COPY AVAILABLE

ASK, ZENDER, MAC PHAIL & KNIEBEL

34

1   side of the fuselage was in flames at that time.

2   I decided that I'd best get away from the airplane.

3   I was afraid of explosion, and I could see no one moving. I

4   could not believe that anyone was alive in the cabin due to

5   the smoke and the fact that they hadn't had any fresh air

6   back there.

7   In any event, my hands were useless. And so that's

8   when I simply walked away and tried to get to high ground

9   where I though that rescue people would find me more easily.

10 My eyes had been burned. I was not seeing very well. I

11 could see dimly. I could see the aircraft and that the

12 engine was running and the fire.

13   While walking, I sort of ran into Brad. I just

14 kind of bumped into him. And he took me and calmed me down

15 and sat me down on the hill, and we sat and waited. There

16 was a helicopter overhead, which I understand was a private

17 helicopter that happened to be in the area and had seen us go

18 down and was in contact, I believe, with both Center, and as

19 I understand it, with some local authorities. Now, how he

20 did that, I don't know. But I was told that he got some

21 people to come out from DeKalb, a sheriff and an ambulance or

22 something. I don't know. That's just what I have been told.

23   After really quite a short period of time, the

24 helicopters were there, and they took me away first, because

25 I was damaged rather more than Brad was. And of course,

BEST COPY AVAILABLE

ASK, ZENDER, MAC PHAIL & KNIEBEL

35

1   that's the last I saw of him. I do seem to recall that when

2   they took me away in the helicopter that left engine was

3   still running completely surrounded by flames. I'd heard the

4   fuel tanks on that side go. I'd watched and heard them go.

5   And that's essentially it.

6   Q.   Okay. Were there open flames in the cockpit prior

7   to either you or Rank opening any windows?

8   A.   No. Just dense smoke. In fact, if I may add, and

9   now this is not certainty. But it seems to me that the major

10   flames in the cockpit did not come until we went into a

11   descent, into a nose-down attitude. And it's then that I

12   recall that the flames were there and that I suddenly was --

13   that I was burning. Prior to that, it had been just this

14   incredibly dense smoke to deal with.

15   Q.   Were you wearing a full ear cover type head set?

16   A.   Yes, a David Clark earmuff type of head set.

17   Q.   Could you hear any passenger activity in the cabin?

18   A.   No.

19   Q.   Do you have any knowledge of any passenger activity

20   in the cabin from the time say that Rank signaled you to turn

21   the heater off? Any time after that, do you have any

22   understanding of what they were doing?

23   A.   No, I have no clear understanding. It seems to me,

24   and here again, things were dim. I was, you know, under

25   stress, to say the least. My eyes had been burned. The

BEST COPY AVAILABLE

ASK, ZEIDER, MAC PHAIL & KNIEBEL

3⁶

1 cockpit was full of smoke. But it seemed to me that just

2 before I went out the side window that a person, a shape that

3 reminded me of Pat Woodward, came up and was attempting to --

4 I don't know what, was on Brad's side of the cockpit doing

5 something; trying get Brad's attention or trying to get help

6 or what, I don't know. It's unclear to me. It's unclear

7 exactly what that was, or if it was anything at all.

8   Q.   Do you have any ideas, even if they aren't things

9 that you know to be as facts, but ideas about what the origin

10 of that fire was?

11   A.   Well, I've developed a theory that may be just

12 conjecture. But remembering, thinking that I remembered that

13 the flames came when we started the descent, when the nose

14 went down, the flames in the cockpit, I remember an incident

15 a number of years when I was flight instructing in a Cessna

16 152 aircraft. And I had been up with a student, and I

17 noticed quite a strong gasoline smell in the airplane. So

18 after we landed, I'd gone and gotten one of mechanics and

19 told him. When he examined the airplane, he found that the

20 usual shutoff valve, which is down on the floor between the

21 seats in a 152, was leaking fuel into the belly of the 152

22 where it was sloshing back and forth. Wonderful.

23   Now, my theory, if you will, is that the fire was

24 most assuredly originally a gasoline fire from the color and

25 density of the smoke. If you've ever seen gasoline burn

BEST COPY AVAILABLE

ASK, ZENDER, MAC PHAIL & KNIEBEL

37

1 without enough air, it produces thick, black smoke. It only

2 burns clean if it has lots and lots of air. But if it

3 doesn't have enough air, you get these clouds of thick, black

4 smoke.

5   The apparent fact that the flames arrived in the

6 cockpit when we went into a nose-down attitude just makes me

7 think that perhaps at that point, fuel in the belly of the

8 aircraft which was on fire slid forward when the nose went

9 down. For whatever it's worth, that's what it seems like in

10 remembrance to me.

11   As to an ignition source for the fire, perhaps the

12 heater, perhaps a passenger's cigarette, perhaps static

13 electricity, I don't know. It is interesting that throughout

14 the smoke and the fire, neither the Janitrol overheat nor the

15 Janitrol fire light ever came on, for whatever that means. I

16 don't know what it means.

17   Q. Okay.

18 HEARING OFFICER KAPUSTIN: You said after the last

19 time after the smoke started that you turned the heater off?

20   THE WITNESS: Correct.

21 HEARING OFFICER KAPUSTIN: And was it the history was

22 either that when you turned it off after an overheat light

23 would come on, that the light would still stay on?

24   THE WITNESS: No. The light would stay on only if

25 the circuit breaker had been popped. Then it would stay on.

BEST COPY AVAILABLE

ASK, ZENDER, MAC PHAIL & KNIEBEL

1 If the circuit breaker had not been popped, it went out when

2 you turned heater switch on.

3   HEARING OFFICER KAPUSTIN: So after you turned it

4 off, you wouldn't have expected anything like that to happen?

5   THE WITNESS: Well, I guess I wouldn't have expected

6 an overheat light, but I guess I just assumed that the fire

7 warning sensor would sense fire. Maybe I misunderstand the

8 system. But in any event, it never came on.

9   HEARING OFFICER KAPUSTIN: That's one of the

10 questions I had. I don't know if you asked it. But there

11 are two separate lights, an overheat, and then the fire

12 warning?

13   THE WITNESS: Yes, sir. Right next to each other.

14   HEARING OFFICER KAPUSTIN: And to make sure I

15 understood you correctly, neither one of them came on?

16   THE WITNESS: Neither one, no, which I remember

17 thinking was sort of ironic.

18 BY MS. SHERERTZ:

19   Q. In your emergency treatment in Texarkana, you

20 commented to some of the emergency room personnel that it

21 flared up on us. Can you tell me what you meant by that?

22   A. Things I said in emergency and intensive care, a

23 lot of them were in the nature of ravings. Much of that

24 period is completely lost to me as far as any conscious

25 remembrance, including that statement. Perhaps I meant the

BEST COPY AVAILABLE

1 flames that appeared when they did, whether it was when we

2 started our descent, or whether they just simply appeared.

3 But suddenly at some point, there were flames in the cockpit.

4 Now, perhaps that's what I meant.

5   I am going to state right now that statements I

6 made in Texarkana and Little Rock were under the influence of

7 drugs, under the influence of shock, under the influence of

8 pain like I've never experienced before. I refuse to take

9 responsibility for anything I said at that time.

10   Q.   That's okay, but I have to ask anyway.

11   A.   Okay.

12   Q.   What color was your shirt?

13   A.   Khaki.

14   Q.   Was it a polyester cotton kind of thin material?

15   A.   Blend, yes.

16   Q.   Jeans? Levis?

17   A.   Calvin Kleins. And I had a blue sleeveless sweater

18 vest on top of the shirt, none of which were ever returned to

19 me.

20   Q.   What kind of relationship did you have with Brad

21 Rank prior to the accident?

22   A.   That's kind of a tough question. Brad is a very

23 difficult man to get to know and a very difficult man to like

24 at times. He's short tempered, he is sort of dictatorial.

25 Some people think of him as nasty.

BEST COPY AVAILABLE

ASK, ZENDER, MAC PHAIL & KNIEBEL

40

1   But I was his friend. I was a good co-pilot, I

2   think just about the best damn co-pilot in private industry.

3   Professionally, I did my best to support him in every way

4   that I could. I viewed that as my job. Some people think of

5   the co-pilot's job as being splitting in flying the airplane

6   50-50. Well, if that's what the captain wants. But I saw it

7   as being to supporting him in whatever he was doing to the

8   best of my ability so long as what he was doing was at least

9   fairly reasonable.

10   The relationship, I mean it wasn't -- there was no

11   enmity between us. As I say, he could be difficult to get

12   along with at times, but he knew it, and he would

13   occasionally let me know that he knew it, you know.

14   I don't know what more there is to say. We were

15   not close friends. I didn't socialize with him. When we

16   went on a trip, I had my own circle of friends. But we

17   coordinated well in the airplane. I'm a darn good navigator

18   and an excellent radio operator, and he very quickly and just

19   simply abandoned those duties to me, which was fine. I enjoy

20   doing them. And that was more -- We split the workload more

21   on a, I guess perhaps it's a traditional basis. I did the

22   pre-flight planning, the navigating, and the radio work, most

23   of the en route flying; he did most of the takeoffs and

24   landings, most of the approaches, and then, of course, made

25   all the decisions. I had no right to make any decisions in

BEST COPY AVAILABLE

Chapter 34: Rick Nelson

1   that airplane. And I did my best to support him in those

2   decisions.

3   Q. Has there been any direct contact between the two

4   of you since the accident?

5   A. Only once. He got through to me on the phone in

6   Little Rock during a brief period when they had released me

7   from intensive care but before my pneumonia became extreme

8   and I had to go back in.

9   Q. What was the content of that conversation?

10   A. He wanted to know if I'd talked to you folks yet.

11   I said no. And he said, "Well, don't."

12   Q. Okay. Has there been any indirect contacts, that

13   is, third-party contacts where he has sent messages to you or

14   you sent messages to him through a third party?

15   A. I don't think "sent messages" is correct. He has

16   called both my sister and friends of mine who have taken over

17   the organization of my personal affairs while I've been in

18   here numerous times, sometimes just to talk, often to inquire

19   how I'm doing, what I'm doing. He has expressed an interest

20   in directly contacting me, but my people have not allowed him

21   to, or anyone as far as that goes. Like you said, you were

22   told I wasn't here. I'm a man who didn't exist as far as a

23   lot of people are concerned. The only other contact was he

24   sent me a letter about his new baby, and that's been all.

25   Q. Anything in that letter that relates to this

BEST COPY AVAILABLE

ASK, ZENDER, MAC PHAIL & KNIEBEL

1   accident or to your relationship with him?

2   A.   Nothing whatsoever. Not even a mention.

3   Q.   Okay. Talk to us about Greg McDonald, your

4   relationship with him?

5   A.   Well, my relationship with him is very superficial.

6   I mean I know the man. I've seen him dozens and dozens and

7   dozens of times. I have had dinner with him occasionally

8   when we have been on the road or whatever.

9   I can in honesty tell you nothing very specific

10   about the man. He's personal and fun to be around, but I

11   always used to kind of mentally check my pockets after I left

12   his presence. He's a Hollywood huckster. He's kind of a

13   fast mover, and he's a fast talker, and he's always got deals

14   going and that kind of thing.

15   He was in charge of the operation that paid me,

16   that I got my paycheck from. My paychecks were normally

17   signed by someone else other than him. They were signed by

18   the bookkeeper or the treasurer or whoever took care of those

19   things. I really had very little business contact with Greg.

20   I had no reason to. The scheduling for trips was done by

21   Annie, the secretary in the office. And so when I wanted to

22   know where the next trip was going or when I called her, she

23   was the one who had the information.

24   Most of the booking was done by Rick Nelson's

25   cousin Willie Nelson. So I might talk to him. My most often

BEST COPY AVAILABLE

ASK, ZENDER, MAC PHAIL & KNIEBEL

43

1 reason for calling was looking for my paycheck, in which case

2 I'd talk to the bookkeeper or whatever. So I can't tell you

3 much about Greg other than he was Rick's manager. I had been

4 led to believe that he had Rick's power of attorney, but I

5 don't know that as a fact. I know that he acted as -- I have

6 been told that he acted as booking agent on our big shows

7 like at the Amphitheater and when we were with Fats Domino

8 and some of these things. That's just really all I know.

9   Q. What was the relationship between you and Rick

10 Nelson?

11   A. We were real close, and I was real close with both

12 he and his fiancee. And on the road, I acted as their escort

13 or their informal security, if you will. We were kind of

14 like family. The whole group was like family. We were a

15 road company, but we were real, real close. And there again,

16 I didn't socialize with Rick at home. We moved in different

17 circles. I was invited to his birthday party, and I was

18 invited for Thanksgiving and Christmas. And of course, I had

19 my own family for the holidays. It happened that on his

20 birthday I wasn't -- or at the time of his birthday party, I

21 was not feeling well and was unable to go. What else can I

22 say. We were very, very close.

23   Q. Okay. I want to ask you again about another one of

24 these comments that was made in the hospital. Some of the

25 persons who visited you in Little Rock after you were moved

BEST COPY AVAILABLE

ASK, ZENDER, MAC PHAIL & KNIEBEL

1 there attributed the following statement to you. "I'm going

2 to make certain that son of a bitch never does that to anyone

3 again." Do you remember the statement, and if you remember

4 it, can you tell me what was behind it?

5   A. Frankly, I do not remember the statement, ~~and~~

6 that's the truth, although I am willing to believe that in

7 the condition I was in there that I said something to that

8 effect. I was at that time emotionally very upset, to say

9 the least. And it seemed to me likely that Brad's actions

10 with the heater had been the cause of our problem, and I was

11 very angry with him about it.

12   You know, in more rational reflection, I realize

13 that they may have been, and they may not have been, and that

14 it's not up to me to say anything. You know, I can tell you

15 people what I know, and you people can establish what you can

16 and find out what you can. I no longer feel as though it's

17 up to me to do anything to anyone.

18   Q. To do anything to what?

19   A. Anyone.

20   Q. Oh, okay.

21   A. All right?

22   Q. Do you know which of the passengers were smokers?

23 Pipes, cigarettes, cigars, who smoked what?

24   A. Okay. Rick and Helen Blair, his fiancee who

25 traveled with us, both smoked cigarettes; Pat Woodward smoked

BEST COPY AVAILABLE

ASK, ZENDER, MAC PHAIL & KNIEBEL

45

1   cigarettes; Clark Russell, the sound engineer, smoked

2   cigarettes; I cannot remember if Andy Chapin, the piano

3   player, if he smoked or not, I don't think he did; and

4   neither Bobby Neal nor Rick Intveld smoked as a regular

5   thing. They were not regular tobacco smokers. To the best

6   of my knowledge, no one smoked either pipes or cigars that I

7   can recall.

8   Q. Okay. Are you aware of any drug use that has

9   occurred on that airplane at any time that you have flown in

10   it?

11   A. Well, I have smelled things that I would have

12   thought smelled like marijuana smoke.

13   Q. Okay. Any that trip?

14   A. Probably, but I can't swear to it one way or the

15   other.

16   Q. Were Rick and Helen seated in the aft section of

17   club seating?

18   A. The last I saw them, they were, yes. And that was

19   their normal, their accustomed place to sit.

20   Q. Did the other people have a usual place that they

21   normally staked out?

22   A. Pat usually staked out one of the sofas up front.

23   Bobby Neal, the guitar player, kind of floated. Sometimes

24   he'd sit with Rick and Helen sometimes. Often when Brad was

25   in back, Bobby would come up and sit with me. So he didn't

BEST COPY AVAILABLE

ASK, ZENDER, MAC PHAIL & KNIEBEL

         Music's Broken Wings

1 really have a staked out place, and I don't remember that

2 Little Rick or Andy did, either. But Rick and Helen

3 habitually occupied the aft two forward-facing club seats,

4 and Pat pretty habitually occupied the starboard side sofa.

5 It was kind of his home.

6   Q.   Okay. All through.

7

8   EXAMINATION

9 BY HEARING OFFICER KAPUSTIN:

10   Q.   If I may, I would like to go back to the heater

11 problem a little bit. Were you with the airplane and Rick

12 when he had the work done on the heater in Lincoln, Nebraka?

13   A.   Yes, I was.

14   Q.   Was that a scheduled trip? Did you plan to go in

15 there?

16   A.   Into Lincoln?

17   Q.   Yes.

18   A.   No. We had a day off, and we decided to see if we

19 could get some kind of permanent solution to this heater

20 problem. And I think there was a couple of other squawks on

21 the airplane that were taken care of at that time, too.

22   Q.   Were you personally familiar with exactly what they

23 did to the heater?

24   A.   No, I was not. I treated it as a day off for

25 myself, which it was supposed to have been.

BEST COPY AVAILABLE

ASK, ZENDER, MAC PHAIL & KNIEBEL

1   Q.   You just helped them fly the airplane in, and you

2 went off on your own?

3   A.   Essentially after we got it hangared and put to

4 bed, I went to the motel, and Brad stayed to supervised the

5 maintenance.   But there was nothing for me to do there.

6   Q.   Did you acquire any firsthand knowledge before the

7 airplane went in -- or after it went into Lincoln exactly

8 what they did?

9   A.   Firsthand, no.   It was explained to me by Brad.

10   Q.   What did he tell you?

11   A.   Okay.   He said that they had, you know, broken it

12 down into its constituent parts, both the igniter plug and so

13 on, and essentially cleaned everything and adjusted

14 everything and tried to look for obvious breakages or obvious

15 faults and found none; reassembled it in a cleaned and

16 adjusted condition and tested it, and it worked fine on the

17 ground.

18   Q.   Well, after the stop at Lincoln, did you have

19 anybody else, or do you know if anybody else worked on the

20 heater after that?

21   A.   I don't know, other than Brad himself, who was a

22 licensed mechanic.

23   Q.   Do you have any idea exactly what he did in-flight

24 during the time when he asked you to turn it on and turn it

25 off, turn it on and turn it off?

BEST COPY AVAILABLE

ASK, ZENDER, MAC PHAIL & KNIEBEL

1   A.   No. I know he went aft. He did tell me once --

2   Now, I'm not certain this was that trip, but that he had

3   adjusted the air intake vanes for the heater. I remembered

4   recalling him saying once that he'd listened to or felt the

5   igniter box or something like that. But no, I don't think

6   that trip that he ever mentioned exactly what he was doing.

7   Q.   He just went back into the cabin, did some work as

8   far as you know, and then told you to turn it on?

9   A.   Exactly.

10   Q.   And then told you to turn it off again? Or you

11   turned it off, and the overheat light came on?

12   A.   Correct.

13   Q.   To the best of your knowledge, did he have tools on

14   the airplane with him?

15   A.   There were tools. There was a tool box in the

16   baggage compartment, which of course was where he would have

17   stood. I mean the heater was just aft of the baggage

18   compartment. So yes, there would have been tools back in the

19   tail.

20   Q.   During the time that he was working on the heater,

21   or at any time during the flight, did you hear any unusual

22   noises that you could attribute to the heater?

23   A.   No, I did not. No, I honestly did not.

24   Q.   I would like to pursue this just a little bit more.

25   A.   Sure, by all means.

BEST COPY AVAILABLE

ASK, BENDER, MAC PHAIL & KNIEBEL

Chapter 34: Rick Nelson

1   Q.   If you can give us, you know, some guidance. We

2 have the heater in the laboratory, and I guess the

3 investigation on that part is still not complete. Can you

4 give us any guidance, you know, from your contact with Brad

5 Rank and the operation as to what we should be looking for?

6   A.   What we should be looking for. Golly. A source of

7 fuel leakage. I really -- That's a very difficult question.

8   Q.   I know.

9   A.   I have literally looked at the heater. That's how

10 involved I got with it. I held tools for Brad while he tried

11 to -- this is on the ground, of course. We weren't both back

12 in the tail. Let the guitar player fly the airplane while we

13 work on it.

14   I'm not a mechanic, and I make no pretense at being

15 one. My usefulness was in holding things, whatever muscle of

16 which I could apply. I'm sorry. I can't be of any help.

17   Q.   That's okay. In order to work on the heater at

18 times where you held tools for him or flashlights, was it

19 necessary for him to open up any access plates?

20   A.   Yeah. We removed the -- There was a metal, or I

21 guess it's supposed to be a steel sheet alongside of the

22 heater, and that had screw-type fasteners, and we would

23 remove that.

24   Q.   And that had to be removed in order to do anything

25 on the heater?

BEST COPY AVAILABLE

ASK, ZENDER, MAC PHAIL & KNIEBEL

1   A.   I don't know if that's a correct statement. It had

2   to be removed to do things like remove the spark plug or get

3   into the burner or things like that. Now, it didn't have to

4   be removed, for instance, to adjust the air controls. That

5   could be done without removing it. I don't know for sure

6   what else could be done without removing it. I'm just not

7   that familiar with it.

8   Q.   I know this might be difficult for you. I want to

9   go back over something that you already discussed as far as

10   during the flight on the 31st. Before you knew there was

11   something radically wrong, you saw smoke. And did you smell

12   any fuel?

13   A.   No, I did not. I wish I could say I had, but I did

14   not. In fact, up until the moment that smoke was reported,

15   the airplane was running and flying as well as it ever had.

16   It was performing beautifully. There was no warning other

17   than the smoke.

18   Q.   Is there a fire extinguishing discharge switch,

19   fire extinguishing agent discharge switch on the heater panel

20   in the cockpit?

21   A.   It's not on the heater panel up here. Behind my

22   seat was first the hydrolic systems, tank and plumbing, and

23   then aft of that was a circuit breaker board that had a lot

24   of the avionic circuits on it. And on the bottom of that was

25   a safety toggle switch that was part of the fire extinguisher

BEST COPY AVAILABLE

1   system for the heater. It could not be reached from my seat.

2   Now, I'm not sure if the captain's seat could reach it or

3   not. I could not reach it without getting out of my seat.

4   Q. Do you know if that was discharged in-flight?

5   A. I do not know. By the time I wanted to discharge

6   it, I couldn't find it. I could hardly find the control

7   wheel. It had gone beyond that for me at that point.

8   HEARING OFFICER KAPUSTIN: Let's go around the room

9   and see if anybody else has any questions. Do you have any

10   questions?

11   MR. DUJOLD: No, I don't right now. I might want to

12   take just a minute, if we can take a little recess and give

13   Ken a minute to rest up, and I can visit with him if you'd

14   like.

15   HEARING OFFICER KAPUSTIN: How about Mr. Jespersen

16   with the FAA? Do you have any questions?

17   MR. JESPERSEN: No.

18   HEARING OFFICER KAPUSTIN: Okay. Why don't we take a

19   couple minute recess?

20   (Short recess)

21   HEARING OFFICER KAPUSTIN: Back on the record.

22   Again, I remind you that you are still under oath.

23   THE WITNESS: All right.

24   HEARING OFFICER KAPUSTIN: Did you say you had some

25   additional questions, Fran?

BEST COPY AVAILABLE

ASK, ZENDER, MAC PHAIL & KNIEBEL

52

1 BY MS. SHERERTZ:

2   Q.   I would like for you to go back to that section in

3 the flight of the 31st where the heater was going through its

4 cycles and Brad Rank was out of the cockpit in the cabin area

5 trying to r(late it better there, especially if you could

6 develop again for us the chronology of what you did, what he

7 did, what the heater did, what you did, what he did, what the

8 heater did, those kinds of things, what he asked you to do.

9   A.   Okay. Now, here again, we are working on best of

10 recollection. I seem to recall three, four, or perhaps five

11 trips into the tail. Now, I'm not talking about the cabin.

12 I mean back into tail cone where the heater was located,

13 follow by a hand signal like this, indicating flip the switch

14 up, turn the heater on. Let's just say four for sake of

15 argument. It's close enough, anyway. Each time I did so,

16 the same thing would happen. Either the heater would run for

17 a while and show the overheat light, or it would run for a

18 while and just started blowing cold air, one or the other.

19   On one of those times, one of those four times, I

20 didn't turn it on. I was becoming nervous. I don't like

21 combustion heaters. This is a personal thing. I've had

22 trouble with them in a dozen airplanes, and I hate them.

23 They're terrible things. I've had them blow smoke at me;

24 I've had them melt pitot tubes so that ? lost my air speed

25 indicator. It's still sort of a source of amazement to me

BEST COPY AVAILABLE

1   that they're certified for use on aircraft. But anyway.

2   So when he came up and asked me why I hadn't turned

3   it on, or something to that effect, I just said, "Brad, I

4   don't like it. Let's leave it alone. I'm nervous about it.

5   Let's wait till we get on the ground." And at that time,

6   whichever one of those several incidences it was, he just

7   simply said, "Rick wants heat," and he reached over -- I

8   guess I never mentioned all of the heater controls are on the

9   overhead panel on my side of the cockpit, which is why I

10   always ended up doing the turning on and then off because

11   they were right over my head up here (indicating). But in

12   this instance, he simply reached over and turned it on.

13   Then there were one or two more incidences prior to

14   the smoke appearing. The smoke did not appear

15   instantaneously upon the heater being turned on. It was

16   matter of some minutes, two, three, perhaps. That's hard to

17   say. When you're flying the airplane and maybe talking to

18   Center and doing some other things, getting an exact handle

19   on how much time has passed is difficult. But let's say

20   three or four minutes, perhaps two to four minutes elapsing

21   between the last time I turned the heater on and the smoke

22   appearing.

23   During that time. I was alone in the cockpit.

24   Bobby Neal had been up earlier sitting with me and chatting,

25   but he'd gone back in the cabin. And Brad, as I say, I

BEST COPY AVAILABLE

1 recall seeing him standing next to Rick's chair and

2 apparently talking with him. And then, as I say, from then

3 on, of course, the smoke developed and so on.

4 BY HEARING OFFICER KAPUSTIN:

5   Q. A couple of logistic questions that I'm not clear

6 on.

7   A. Sure.

8   Q. You said you used hand signals. How did you manage

9 to see these hand signals or know when he was ready to give

10 you hand signals?

11   A. Oh, well, he would come out of -- See, there was a

12 closet that connected with the tail cone. Boy, you had to be

13 skinny to go back and through it, too. He would emerge from

14 the closet and signal me.

15   Q. You would have to be looking back?

16   A. True enough.

17   Q. Turning around?

18   A. Which I guess I must have done periodically.

19   Q. You just periodically turned around to see if he

20 was -- You were expecting him?

21   A. Remember, I said Bobby Neal was sitting with me

22 chatting. And yes, of course, I was expecting him because I

23 knew he was working on it. But I have a habit when I'm

24 chatting with a guy in the other seat, I sit over leaning on

25 the arm rest towards the middle anyway, and I probably

BEST COPY AVAILABLE

ASK, ZENDER, MAC PHAIL & KNIEBEL

55

1 periodically checked the cabin. And yes, it's correct, I was

2 expecting him anyway. But there was no -- there was no

3 communication. There is a telephone from aft to forward with

4 a buzzer on it. Now, I can't remember if he used it once or

5 not. Might have. I don't remember.

6   HEARING OFFICER KAPUSTIN: There was one other thing

7 about your position in the cockpit during the landing. Did

8 you want to ask it?

9

10   EXAMINATION

11 BY MR. JESPERSEN:

12   Q. Well, yes. I was just curious. I understand you

13 were turned, and you had your back --

14   A. Jammed up against my windshield and my butt jammed

15 up against the instrument panel between the -- kind of above

16 the power quadrant. There again, exactly what I was pushing

17 againt is kind of hard to say.

18   Q. But the yoke was still free?

19   A. Oh, absolutely, yeah. You bet. It may not have

20 been the smartest solution, but it was the only one I could

21 think of.

22   Q. That airplane has the flat panel and the gear

23 handle again on the left?

24   A. Yes, sir, right next to my seat.

25   Q. And when you burned your hand, you said they were

BEST COPY AVAILABLE

ASK, ZENDER, MAC PHAIL & KNIEBEL

54

1 worse on the left?

2 A.   That seemed to be where the worse flames were. All

3 of my serious burns are on my left side. So apparently,

4 that's where the worse of the flames were.

5 Q.   But you had the flaps down, and you had the **gear**

6 down before you got up and sat up?

7 A.   Oh, yes. The flap thing went this way. When I

8 went down to put the flaps down, my original thought had been

9 to shove the lever down, leave it down, and let them come

10 out. We apparently were quite fast, and I couldn't see any

11 air speed indicator or anything. I was guestimating

12 everything I was doing.

13 We started to balloon a lot, and I didn't want to

14 screw up whatever Brad was doing. So I stopped at 25 degrees

15 and then just kept milking them down as I was able until I

16 couldn't stand it anymore. It seems to me that I got about

17 three quarters extension before I just simply couldn't keep

18 my hand on there anymore.

19 In any event, it helped slow the airplane, and it

20 worked out. But that's how that particular sequence came

21 about. And then as I say, I simply could not re-fasten my

22 seat belt, and I just picked an option, I guess.

23 Q.   Did you have your feet up? Were your feet up on

24 the seat, or where?

25 A.   I honestly don't remember.

BEST COPY AVAILABLE

1   Q.   but anyway, you were in that position when the

2   airplane landed?

3   A.   Yes. And it was probably one of the gentlist

4   landings we've ever made. It felt -- I don't recall the tail

5   coming down. It darn near felt like he three-pointed, or it

6   three-pointed itself.

7   Q.   And your window was closed at this time?

8   A.   Yeah. It acted like such a chimney when I wasn't

9   out it, I shut it just because it just drew the flames up

10   over the seat. I didn't need that. I didn't need that at

11   all.

12   BY MS. SHERERTZ:

13   Q.   I'm not certain I followed this. After the time

14   when Brad signaled you that he wanted you turn the heater on

15   and you didn't do it, are there an additional two to three

16   times after that that you had to turn the heater on for him?

17   A.   No. This is so difficult, because it's so

18   imprecise. If we make an odd number, it would be real easy.

19   Let's say he went to the tail cone five times. On the third

20   time, I refused to turn the switch on. I am making that as

21   an analagy, if you will. So somewhere in about the middle of

22   the messing with the heater was when I refused to turn it on,

23   or when I just simply didn't, and he came up and turned it on

24   himself.

25   Q.   And then did it cycle on and off and had to be

BEST COPY AVAILABLE

1 turned back on additional times?

2   A.   Yes, but not another four. Another couple let's

3 say.

4 BY HEARING OFFICER KAPUSTIN:

5   Q.   Let's see if we can fill something in here.

6   A.   Sure.

7   Q.   Had this type of thing with the heater happened

8 before prior to your going to take it to Lincoln for repairs?

9   A.   Yeah. Now, as I mentioned when we first started

10 discussing the heater, it's displayed every kind of faulty

11 behavior that one of those things can, as we've already

12 mentioned. But yeah, to the best of my recollection, it was

13 doing the overheat light business prior to being serviced in

14 Lincoln.

15   Q.   Did it ever produce smoke?

16   A.   No, it never did. It never did. Never even

17 produced a smell.

18   Q.   Well, what was this -- If you can can't answer,

19 just tell me. Was this procedure, was it his practice to

20 write discrepancies in the logbook?

21   A.   No. We wrote up -- See, he was in charge of the

22 maintenance. So we just simply wrote up on a slip of paper

23 towards the end of a trip the squawks, and then when we

24 parked the airplane at the end of the trip back at Orange

25 County or wherever we were then leaving it, we'd clip the

BEST COPY AVAILABLE

ASK, ZENDER, MAC PHAIL & KNIEBEL

1   squawk sheet to his -- to the left side yoke which had a

2   built-in clip board on it, and then that would be his

3   reminder of what needed to be worked on during the layover,

4   you know, during the period when we weren't out on a trip.

5   Q.   Was there such a thing as a maintenance log on the

6   airplane?

7   A.   I don't believe so.

8   Q.   Do you know why he didn't write the discrepancies

9   into the airplane log?

10   A.   Well, the airplane logs were lost.

11   Q.   And it was your testimony or your recollection that

12 they had gotten a new one?

13   A.   I never saw any new ones. I never personally saw

14 them. But considering there was, you know, a new engine and

15 whatnot on the airplane, all these entries were somewhere.

16 Now, whether they were in a formal log book or what kind of

17 thing, surely Brad has the answer to that.

18 BY MS. SHERERTZ:

19   Q.   During this whole sequence of work in the -- in and

20 for the heater, were there any telephone calls between -- on

21 the interphone between you and Rank?

22   A.   See, that's what I'm not absolutely sure of. We

23 used that interphone infrequently. In fact, it hadn't worked

24 for a long time. He finally fixed it one day on either a

25 layover or something. He found a connection or whatever and

BEST COPY AVAILABLE

1 made them work. All I can say is he might have called me. I

2 don't remember.

3   In any event, it just wouldn't have been important

4 enough to register, but he could have. He certainly could

5 have. There were several stations with phones back there.

6   Q. There were several stations with phones?

7   A. (Witness nods head)

8   Q. Where were they?

9   A. Well, there was one at the club seating table, and

10 there was one then near the next set of the little club

11 seats; on the starboard side, there was one there; and I'm

12 not sure, but I think there was one across from it on the

13 port side, but I won't swear to that. I know there were at

14 least the two on the starboard side, and they were just black

15 hand sets on a hard stand with the push buttons on them where

16 you push the button and it buzzed a thing up in the cockpit

17 when it worked right.

18   Q. Okay. Go back now to the timeframe immediately

19 after you left the airplane.

20   A. Okay.

21   Q. When you said you wandered around and kind of

22 bumped into Brad.

23   A. That's essentially right.

24   Q. Between then and the time that you left the field

25 in the helicopter to go to the hospital, what things did Brad

BEST COPY AVAILABLE

ASK, ZENDER, MAC PHAIL & KNIEBEL

61

Chapter 34: Rick Nelson

1 say to you?

2 A. Well, let me see. When he first ran him into me or

3 I ran into him or whatever, he grabbed my arm, and I tried to

4 pull away from him. I don't remember which arm he had. If

5 he had this arm, it's no wonder I tried to pull away from

6 him. He was grabbing a lot of bare muscle and stuff. But he

7 held me, and he kept saying, "Ferg, Ferg, you're hurt, sit

8 down, sit down," and I kept trying to back away from him.

9 And finally he just kind of pushed me down, and we sat down

10 on this hill.

11 And somewhere along there he said, which I told you

12 before, the comment about, "I started out with nine, and now

13 all I've got left is Ferg." He started out with nine, which

14 of course would have included himself in the total. And he

15 said, "Now all I have left is Ferg." That was my name to the

16 company was Ferg. I mean that's what people called me. And

17 he also said, "Don't say anything about the heater. Don't

18 say anything about the heater. Don't say anything about the

19 heater."

20 Q. And that's it until you left for the helicopter?

21 A. Yeah. Now, again, I have to equivocate to this

22 extent. It might have been, "Don't tell anyone about the

23 heater," but it was -- I'm trying to quote as closely as I

24 can. It was one or the other of those two things.

25 Q. Okay. Was he, "he" meaning Brad, was he afraid of

BEST COPY AVAILABLE

ASK, ZENDER, MAC PHAIL & KNIEBEL

1   that airplane?

2   A.   That is a question asking for an opinion.   I will

3   give you an opinion if you want one.

4   Q.   That's what I'm asking.

5   A.   But it has to be understood that it's an opinion.

6   I think he was.

7   BY HEARING OFFICER KAPUSTIN:

8   Q.   Let me try to elaborate on that a little bit.   In

9   some of the interviews, we also got the distinct impression,

10 and this also goes for your impression and characterization

11 of the heater, you were concerned about that type of heater?

12   A.   Yes, sir, I was.

13   Q.   And was he. Was Captain Rank maybe overly

14 concerned or quite concerned about the heater, to the best of

15 your understanding of his attitude towards the thing?

16   A.   It seemed to me -- Well, I think I was more afraid

17 of the heater in the sense of the misbehavior, because I did

18 all of my early flying in the far north regions here, and I

19 have been living with those bloody things for longer than I

20 care to remember, and they're terrible; whereas most of his

21 flying career has been in southern regions or in Leer jets

22 and Commanders and things that have air cycle machines and

23 don't have combustion heaters. I really don't -- I never

24 felt that -- I did 't think he had a proper respect for the

25 darn thing, frankly.

BEST COPY AVAILABLE

1   You know, friends of mine in aviation, I mean we

2 don't call them combustion heaters. We call this explosion

3 heaters. And I'm going to have difficulty flying airplanes

4 equipped with them after this. They're -- Well, it's not

5 germane.

6   HEARING OFFICER KAPUSTIN: Off the record for just a

7 second.

8   (Off the record discussion)

9   HEARING OFFICER KAPUSTIN: Go ahead. Back on the

10 record.

11 BY MS. SHERERTZ:

12   Q. The two times that, or whatever --

13   A. Approximately.

14   Q. -- it is necessary to turn on the heater after the

15 one time where you didn't do it and Brad came back up and

16 turned it on himself, anyway, the times that you turned it on

17 after that, were those times that Rank indicated to you,

18 either through his customary hand signals or through telling

19 you, that he wanted that turned back on?

20   A. Yes.

21   Q. Was that at his direction?

22   A. That's correct.

23   HEARING OFFICER KAPUSTIN: I think that's been

24 answered before. You testified to that before, didn't you?

25   THE WITNESS: I believe I did, yes, sir.

BEST COPY AVAILABLE

ASK, ZENDER, MAC PHAIL & KNIEBEL

64

1   HEARING OFFICER KAPUSTIN: I think that's clear on
2 the record.

3   MS. SHERERTZ: I'm through, Mr. Kapustin.

4   HEARING OFFICER KAPUSTIN: Unless anybody else has
5 any questions, I'll let this proceeding end. However, the
6 investigation will remain open, and you're subject to recall
7 at any time.

8   THE WITNESS: Certainly.

9   HEARING OFFICER KAPUSTIN: It will be recessed
10 indefinitely.

11   (Whereupon, the hearing was recessed
12   at approximately 1:50 p.m.)

13

14

15

16

17

18

19

20

21

22

23

24

25

BEST COPY AVAILABLE

65

ASK, ZENDER, MAC PHAIL & KNIEBEL

STATE OF MINNESOTA)
)
COUNTY OF ANOKA)

1 | STATE OF MINNESOTA)
2 | COUNTY OF ANOKA)

             BE IT KNOWN THAT I, Leo R. Kniebel, the
undersigned, a duly commissioned and qualified Notary Public
within and for the County and State of aforesaid, do hereby,
certify that before the giving of his testimony, the said
Kenneth Ferguson was by me first duly sworn upon his oath
to depose the whole truth and nothing but the truth; that the
foregoing is a true and correct copy of my original stenotype
notes taken at said hearing; that I am neither a relative of,
nor attorney for, any of the parties to the cause and have no
interest whatever in the result of the same.

             WITNESS MY HAND AND SEAL this 21st day of
March, 1986.

                    Leo R. Kniebel
                    _____
                    Leo R. Kniebel, RPR
                    Notary Public, Anoka County, Minnesota
                    My commission expires June 8, 1990.

BEST COPY AVAILABLE

Music's Broken Wings

National Transportation Safety Board
800 Independence Avenue, S.W.
Washington, D.C. 20594

In the matter of Aviation Accident DCA86AA012
Douglas DC-3, N711Y
De Kalb, Texas
December 31, 1985

INTERROGATORY - SUPPLEMENT TO SWORN TESTIMONY

1. Did the airplane, N711Y, contain any placards relating to the operation of the forward (Stewart-Warner) heater, or to its operation following illumination of the overtemp light? If so, what was the wording or approximate wording on the placard?

No PLACARD, NOR WAS THERE ANY SHADOW OR GLUE SPOT WHERE ONE MIGHT HAVE BEEN IN THE PAST.

2. Did the airplane contain any placard relating to the operation of the aft (Janitrol) heater, or to its operation following illumination of the overtemp light? If so, what was the wording or approximate wording on the placard?

SAME AS ABOVE, NO PLACARD OR SHADOW OF ONE.

Page 1 of 2

In the matter of Aviation Accident DCA86AA012
            Douglas DC-3, N711Y
            De Kalb, Texas
            December 31, 1985

    3. What was the inventory of band equipment on board N711Y
    at the time of the accident?

several 5 guitars
    1 drum cymbals
    1 snare drum,
    2 small amplifiers
Misc. equipment (stands, pedals, stool)
    1 upright bass fiddle (located in
                        passenger comp.

I certify that my answers to these three questions are true to
the best of my knowledge.

                Kenneth Reinhard Ferguson

SUBSCRIBED AND SWORN to before me this 2ND day of JUNE , 1986.

                NOTARY PUBLIC

My Commission expires:

    DOROTHEA E. JOHNS
    NOTARY PUBLIC - MINNESOTA
    HENNEPIN COUNTY
    My Commission Expires July 13, 1991

                                    Page 2 of 2

National Transportation Safety Board
800 Independence Avenue, S.W.
Washington, D.C. 20594

In the matter of Aviation Accident DCA86AA012
Douglas DC-3, N711Y
De Kalb, Texas,
December 31, 1985

INTERROGATORY - SUBSTITUTE FOR SWORN STATEMENT

1. Did you, Ed Carter, inspect or work on the aft (Janitrol) cabin heater of N711Y between October 15, 1985 and October 31, 1985?

Answer:

Yes. I performed an exterior inspection and minor repair of the subject aft cabin heater during the evening of October 22, 1985.

2. Was Pilot Bradley Rank present for all or part of this work?

Answer:

Mr. Rank was present and assisted me during the exterior inspection and minor repair of the aft cabin heater.

3. Describe the procedures performed.

Answer:

I performed the tasks necessary to troubleshoot Mr. Rank's complaint that the aft cabin heater was inoperative. The heater was turned on and all electrical circuits were checked for electrical power to verify that the pilot's complaint was not the result of a lack of electrical power to the unit. I removed and inspected the unit's spark plug and found same to be servicable. I functionally tested the ignition system and found power to the spark plug. I removed and cleaned the fuel filter and verified that there was fuel flow to unit. I noted that the combustion air blower was noisy and sluggish. I removed and bench checked the blower and cleaned the motor and brushes. I lubricated and reinstalled the blower and functionally checked the unit. The blower operated satisfactorily. I visually inspected the exterior of the heater and the intake air duct and found no discrepancy. I performed a functional check of the unit. The unit operated successfully on repetitive cycles to Mr. Rank's satisfaction. The fuel connections were inspected for leaks and none were found. The aircraft was then returned to service.

4. During these procedures was the ignitor removed from its mountings?

Answer:

No, only the spark plug was removed.

5. Were any discrepancies or unusual conditions seen on the cold air plenum? If so, describe or include a sketch.

Answer:

I assume you are referring to the cold air intake ducting. No discrepancies or unusual conditions were noted.

6. Describe the general condition of the cold air plenum.

Answer:

The cold air intake ducting appeared servicable.

I certify that my answers to these six questions are true to the best of my knowledge.

Edward W. Carter Jr.
Ed Carter

SUBSCRIBED AND SWORN to before me this 18ᵀʰ day of JULY, 1986

David C. Bornemeier
NOTARY PUBLIC

DAVID C. BORNEMEIER
GENERAL NOTARIAL
SEAL
STATE OF NEBRASKA

My Commission expires:
June 27, 1987

Music's Broken Wings

NATIONAL TRANSPORTATION SAFETY BUREAU
Bureau of Technology
Washington, D.C. 20594

May 30, 1986

Structures/Powerplants Group Chairman's Factual Report

A. ACCIDENT

Owner/Operator: Century Equipment Co./Rick Nelson

Airplane   : Douglas DC-3C, N711Y, MSN 13658

Location   : Near De Kalb, Texas

Date   : December 31, 1985

NTSB No.   : DCA 86AA012

B. STRUCTURES/POWERPLANTS GROUP

Donald Kuhns - NTSB - Washington, D.C. - Chairman
Charles Burge - FAA - Little Rock, Ark. - Member
Lawrence Fogg - McDonnell - Douglas - Member
Phillip Laber - McDonnell-Douglas - Member

C. SUMMARY

No evidence was discovered during the on-site investigation or subsequent examination of selected accident components to indicate that the airplane structure or power plants had suffered any pre-impact failures or malfunctions. Examination of the suspected final landing approach path, however, revealed melted globules of aluminum, magnesium, and control surface fabric. The source of the materials was not readily apparent. During the enroute segment of a flight between Gunthersville, Alabama, and Dallas, Texas, the flight crew reported smoke in the cockpit/cabin area and that they would attempt an emergency landing. The airplane was destroyed during the landing in a farmer's field near De Kalb, Texas. The fuselage was destroyed by fire after the airplane came to rest. The pilot and co-pilot were seriously injured; 7 passengers were killed.

D. DETAILS OF THE EXAMINATION

1.   The chart attached depicts the probable approach path, the landing area, and the main wreckage site. The following paragraph summarizes the observations made by the Structures/Powerplants Group.

The airplane approached the landing site from the south then turned left onto a westerly heading for the final approach. Several grass fires were started beneath the approach path and molten globules of magnesium and aluminum were found in the burned areas. The airplane just cleared a home on the east side of Texas Route 990 (two lane), then struck two utility poles and a powerline before touching down in a farmer's field just inside the eastern perimeter fence (125 feet west of the highway centerline). The imprints of the main landing gear tires indicated a left wing low attitude. The left imprint was 42 feet long while the right was 30 feet in length. Both main gear imprints were shallow and there was no evidence of tail wheel contact noted. The next ground contact discovered was about 750 feet west of the highway centerline and was about 50 feet long, shallow, and there was no evidence of tail wheel contact. The airplane then entered a small group of large diameter trees where the outer wing sections, left and right, separated during tree contact. The airplane came to rest upright on its landing gear and was consumed by fire. The main wreckage area was about 1200 feet from the highway centerline.

2. Fuselage Damage

The fuselage was completely destroyed by fire from the nose, fuselage stations (F.S.)-0 aft to about F.S.-568 (baggage compartment door area). The only identifiable structure in this area was the main entry door and a small section of the baggage compartment door, both located on the left side of the airplane. It was noted that the main entry door locking pins were in the retracted position (unlocked).

3. Empennage

This fuselage structure was intact from about F.S.-583 aft. The vertical stabilizer, with rudder and trim tab attached, was in place with minimal fire damage noted. The vertical stabilizer leading edge had been forced aft in the area immediately below the anti-collision light. Black smudges were observed in and adjacent to the compressed area. With the exception of the above damage, the vertical stabilizer de-icer boot was intact with no fire damage. The left and right stabilizers, elevators, and trim tabs were attached to the empennage. The following damage was noted:

Left Stabilizer - The de-icer boot was in place but it was noted that, in addition to heat damage (blistering) on the leading edge, metal spattering had occurred on both the upper and lower surfaces along the span. The boot was subsequently removed and delivered to the NTSB metallurgical laboratory, Washington, D.C., for detailed examination. Results of the examination are to be documented in a metallurgical factual report. Minimal damage was noted on the upper and lower surfaces of the stabilizer. The lower surface of the elevator fabric was burned away. The outboard 2-3 feet of fabric from the upper surface was burned; the remainder was intact. Several small burn holes with metal splatter were noted on the elevator upper surface at the inboard end. One of these areas was removed for subsequent examination in the metallurgical laboratory. The metal elevator trim tab was intact and faired.

Right Stabilizer - The inboard leading edge of the de-icer boot exhibited fire damage and was blistered from the heat. Minimal damage was observed on the upper and lower surfaces of the stabilizer. The fabric on the elevator was completely burned away. The metal trim tab was intact and faired.

Smoke/Heat Pattern - A pattern was noted on the lower inboard surface of the right stabilizer. The paint on the stabilizer root to empennage fairing was heat damaged and some of the paint near the leading edge was peeled off. The smoke/heat pattern appeared to be a continuation of the pattern which was evident on the skin of the lower aft fuselage and included the area of the aft cabin heater exhaust stack, fuel drain line, and tail landing gear wheel well. Traces of soot were also evident trailing rivet patterns located on the lower right side of the vertical stabilizer. The above patterns were documented with photographs and video-tape. The tail cone was intact as well as the position light and anti-collision light.

4. Left Wing

The outboard 25 foot section of wing including the wing tip and position light was located at the base of a large diameter tree which was situated at the western perimeter fence line of the farmer's field. The lower surface of the wing section exhibited sooting and heat damage from the tip inboard to the separation. The wing leading edge, front, and center spars had been compressed and deformed in the wing separation area due to tree impact. The aileron was attached to the rear spar area through its hinges with the exception of a 2-3-foot inboard section which had separated and was located about 75 feet forward. A 12-15-foot left wing section (from immediately outboard of the engine nacelle outboard to the above mentioned separation) was suspended in a tree forward of the 25-foot section and about 20 feet south of the empennage. There was no evidence of heat or fire damage but the section was badly compressed and deformed, fore to aft, from tree contact. This wing section included the outboard split trailing edge flap which was not damaged.

5. Center Wing Section

The center wing section was completely destroyed by fire down to the lower skin surface from inboard of the No. 1 engine nacelle to the left fuselage wing root. Very little of the wing structure was identifiable in the center wing area.

6. Right Wing

Wing root to outboard of No. 2 engine nacelle - the front spar was evident in the nacelle area; the center spar had been burned away from the outboard edge of the nacelle inboard to the wing root with the exception of 7-8-foot section of the cap. In the area of the center to front spar the cap and lower skin had melted down. The bottom portion of the aft fuel tank was identified; the inboard end had burned away. The forward tank was completely destroyed by fire. The upper wing skin exhibited fire damage inboard to the wing root and over the complete chord. The trailing edge area was intact.

Outboard Wing Section - the outboard wing section attach angles were intact. This wing section from just outboard of the attach angles to the wing tip separated as a unit and was located adjacent to and aft of the No. 2 engine nacelle area. The most inboard portion of the wing section had been compressed aft across about 80 percent of the chord (front spar in rear spar area). The remainder of this 36-foot wing section exhibited minimal damage with no evidence of heat or fire. Two leading edge indentations near the tip were noted and associated with tree contact. The fabric covered aileron and metal trim tab were attached and the tab was faired. The outboard split trailing edge flap was intact and not damaged. The wing tip, including the position light, was intact.

7. Nacelles

Left - The firewall and outboard nacelle were intact but exhibited heat and fire damage. The main landing gear truss/sway brace assembly, retract cylinder, and tension bar were intact and exhibited heat and fire damage.

Right - The upper and outboard side of the wheel well were identified with heat and fire damage noted. The firewall was intact. The main landing gear truss/sway brace assembly, retract cylinder, and tension bar were intact with heat and fire damage noted.

8. Landing Gear

Left - The landing gear tire and rim were destroyed by heat and fire. Remnants of the exposed brake drum were visible and appeared to be in good condition. The gear was in the down and locked position.

Right - The landing gear tire and rim were destroyed by heat and fire. The exposed brake drum appeared to be in good condition. The gear was in the down and locked position.

Tail - The tire and rim were intact on the tail strut; the tire was flat. The tail wheel frame, strut, and shock absorber were intact in the forward end of the empennage.

9. Flight Controls

The mechanical control system was examined in an effort to establish continuity. All cable runs were intact from the cockpit controls aft through the fire damaged fuselage area. It was noted that the brass barrel portion on numerous turnbuckle fittings had melted from the heat. Pulleys and bracketry were consumed in the fire. A detailed continuity check was made of the elevator cable control system. Continuity existed from the cockpit control column aft through the tail cone to the elevators. All elevator pulleys and brackets had been destroyed by fire in the cabin area.

10. Other

Aft Cabin Heater Area

The Janitrol heater, located on the right side of the fuselage immediately aft of the F.S.-596 bulkhead, was examined with the Systems Group. It was noted that the heater fuel system filter located below the heater fire shield had separated from its mounting bracket. Both male inlet and outlet filter fittings had fractured in their threaded area. The filter, containing the fractured fittings, along with a section of heater fuel line, were delivered to the NTSB metallurgical laboratory for detailed examination of the fractured surfaces. The heater fuel supply selector valve area aft to the fractured fitting at the fuel filter inlet was continuous.

Flight Path Debris

Small molten droplets of a metallic like substance were recovered from grass fire areas which were located beneath the suspected final approach path. These were found east of Texas Route 990 and also in the back yard, the roof, and the front yard of the house east of the highway. In addition, a small piece of metal (aluminum) about the size of a half dollar, was found in the area of the largest grass fire which was also located east and south of the house. A substance similar in appearance to paint flakes was also found in the grass fire areas and near the house. Samples of the above mentioned materials were delivered to the NTSB metallurgical laboratory for analysis.

POWERPLANTS

The airplane was powered by two Pratt and Whitney R-1830-75 reciprocating engines. The following damage was noted by the Group during the on-site investigation.

No. 1 Engine
SN BP 600902

The engine and nacelle area exhibited extensive heat and fire damage. The engine remained attached to the firewall. The accessory case and most of the engine driven accessories were consumed by the fire. The cylinder heads on cylinders No.1 through 7 were melted off in place. Cylinders 8 through 14 were intact. The exhaust system was complete except for the short extension which attached to No. 3 cylinder. It had separated but was found directly below its normally installed location. The engine cowling and most of the cowl flap system was destroyed by fire. The propeller dome, hub, and the three blades were intact. The blades were complete, fire damaged and appeared to be near the low pitch stop position. There was no evidence of gross leading edge or chord-wise damage noted on any of the blades.

Following part numbers and serial numbers were documented for No. 1 engine from the data plates of those accessories not destroyed by fire.

Component	Part/Model No. and Serial No.
Left Magneto	SF 14LN-8-AN-M-4 SN 209349
Right Magneto	SF 14LN-8-AN-M-4 SN 232273
Prop Governor	NN 12264 SN4G8-G67M
Generator	2 CM63C7 SN 11001
Starter (Eclipse Pioneer)	DWG NO. 141616-B E 1602-1
Propeller Assembly	Hamilton Standard Data Plates Destroyed

No. 2 Engine
SN BP 600487

The No. 2 engine nacelle was supported by the fire damaged landing gear. The engine, however, had separated from the firewall through the engine mount tubes and fell to the ground directly beneath and slightly outboard of its installed position. The engine suffered less fire and heat damage than No. 1 and was essentially intact. All 14 cylinders were examined and the following damage noted. The No. 10 cylinder was lifted upward about 1/4 inch from the case; all hold down studs were fractured. The visible fractured surfaces appeared to be the result of an overstress condition. The exhaust valve rocker box cover on this cylinder has been knocked free and exhibited heat damage. The push rod housings and push rods on cylinders 6 through 8 had been exposed to high temperatures (some melting). A small diameter hole (burn through) was located in the nose section casing directly forward of the No. 10 cyclinder. The engine's exhaust system was intact. The propeller dome, hub, and three blades were intact. A small puncture was noted in the propeller dome. All three of the blades were slightly bent and appeared to be near the low stop position. Spanwise scrape marks were evident on all three blades. Initially one blade was buried in the ground with no rotational marks noted. It was later exposed with no gross damage noted. The engine main oil screen was removed and found to be free of metal contaminants. Several globules of molten metal were located on the screen but were associated with heat generated by the post crash fire. The engine cowling was damaged but intact around the engine except for the lower section. The outboard cowling section had evidence of a light contact mark on its leading edge (located at the 9 o'clock position looking forward).

The following part numbers and serial numbers were documented from the accessories installed on the No. 2 engine.

Component	Part/Model No. and Serial No.
Carburetor (Stromberg)	37027-2 SN 287089
Starter (Eclipse Pioneer)	36E004D SN NQ28
Generator (Wagner Electric)	2GM3C7 SN 1593
Hydraulic Pump (Pesco)	1 P582CA-2 SN PE 500-37
Vacuum Pump (Pesco)	207 JE SN PE 10682
Prop Feathering Motor (Pesco)	280 3BA SN V1054193
Prop Feathering Pump	C 22936 BB SN Unknown

Prop Governor (Hamilton-Standard)   4G8-630
                                       SN Unknown

Left Magneto   SF14LN-8-AN-M-4
                                       SN 224713

Right Magneto   SF 14LN-8-AN-M-4
                                       SN 210226

GENERAL

Both of the engine exhaust system outlets were examined in detail for indications of localized hot spots and/or metal splatter; none was found. The following control positions were documented from the No. 2 engine components. It should be recognized that the mechanical engine and prop controls separated when the engine fell to the ground and the positions should be reviewed in that context.

Engine Throttle Position   -Near Idle
Prop Control (cockpit)   -High Pitch/Low RPM
Mixture Control   -Auto-Lean
Hydraulic By-pass Valve   -Closed

The above documents the observations made by the Structures/Powerplants Group during the on-site portion of the investigation.

Donald Kuhns
Donald Kuhns
Group Chairman

DOUGLAS DC-3C ~ DE KALB, TEXAS ~ DECEMBER 31, 1985 ~ N711Y

AIRPLANE DAMAGE

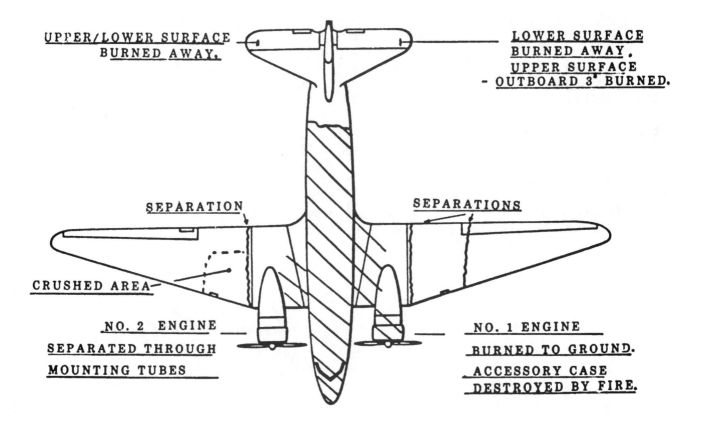

UPPER/LOWER SURFACE
BURNED AWAY.

LOWER SURFACE
BURNED AWAY.
UPPER SURFACE
- OUTBOARD 3' BURNED.

SEPARATION

SEPARATIONS

CRUSHED AREA

NO. 2 ENGINE
SEPARATED THROUGH
MOUNTING TUBES

NO. 1 ENGINE
BURNED TO GROUND.
ACCESSORY CASE
DESTROYED BY FIRE.

LEGEND

 - COMPLETELY DESTROYED BY FIRE

BEST COPY AVAILABLE

38

Music's Broken Wings

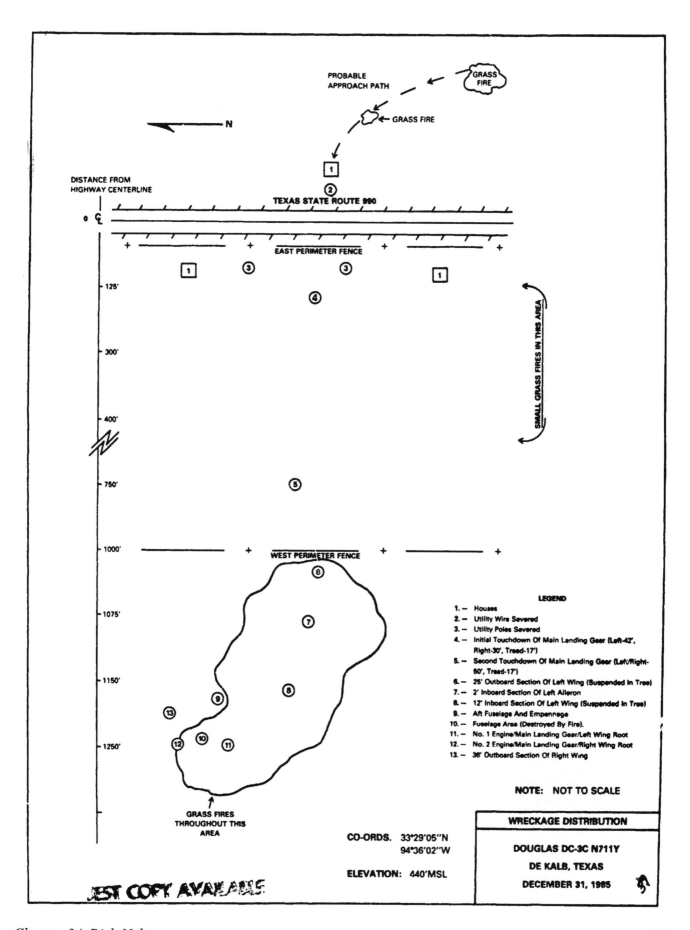

LEGEND
1. — Houses
2. — Utility Wire Severed
3. — Utility Poles Severed
4. — Initial Touchdown Of Main Landing Gear (Left-42', Right-30', Tread-17')
5. — Second Touchdown Of Main Landing Gear (Left/Right-50', Tread-17')
6. — 25' Outboard Section Of Left Wing (Suspended In Tree)
7. — 2' Inboard Section Of Left Aileron
8. — 12' Inboard Section Of Left Wing (Suspended In Tree)
9. — Aft Fuselage And Empennage
10. — Fuselage Area (Destroyed By Fire).
11. — No. 1 Engine/Main Landing Gear/Left Wing Root
12. — No. 2 Engine/Main Landing Gear/Right Wing Root
13. — 36' Outboard Section Of Right Wing

NOTE: NOT TO SCALE

WRECKAGE DISTRIBUTION

DOUGLAS DC-3C N711Y

DE KALB, TEXAS

DECEMBER 31, 1985

CO-ORDS.   33°29'05"N
94°36'02"W

ELEVATION: 440'MSL

EST COPY AVAILABLE

NATIONAL TRANSPORTATION SAFETY BOARD
Bureau of Technology
Washington, D.C. 20594

May 30, 1986

SYSTEMS GROUP CHAIRMAN'S FACTUAL REPORT

A. Accident

Owner/Operator:	Century Equipment Co./Rick Nelson
Aircraft:	Douglas DC-3C, N711Y
Location:	Near Dekalb, Texas
	33°29'05" N
	94°36'02" W
Date:	December 31, 1985, approximately 1715 CST
NTSB No.:	DCA-86-A-A012

B. Systems Group Members

David K. Johns   Group Chairman
                             National Transportation Safety Board
                             Washington, D.C.
                             202-382-6766

Larry L. Fogg   Senior Staff Engineer Design
                             Assistance & Safety
                             Douglas Aircraft Co.
                             Long Beach, Ca.
                             213-593-6742

Charles Burge   Federal Aviation Administration
                             FSDO 65
                             Little Rock, Arkansas
                             501-378-5565

C. Summary

        At approximately 1700 1/, while enroute from Guntersville, Alabama, to Dallas Love Field, the flightcrew of the DC-3 reported experiencing inflight difficulties near Texarkana, Arkansas. A request for vectors to the Texarkana (TXK) airport was acknowledged and granted by the Air Route Traffic Control Center (ARTCC)Fort Worth, Texas. Immediately thereafter the DC-3 flight crew requested the distance and bearing to airports closer than TXK, which was forty miles behind the aircraft. Vectors were given to two other airports. During the ensuing conversation the crew reported smoke in the cockpit.

1/ All times herein are expressed in military time for the Central Standard Time (CST) zone.

They indicated they would not be able to reach any of the airports recommended by ATC, but would have to land immediately. Subsequently the flight crew attempted to land in a farm pasture. The aircraft struck utility poles and wires and continued into a small stand of mature trees. The accident resulted in substantial impact damage and fire. Seven passengers, including Rick Nelson and members of his Stone Canyon Band, were fatally injured during the crash and/or post crash fire. The pilot and co-pilot escaped the burning wreckage and survived.

D.   **On Scene Investigation**

   1.   **Cockpit Instrumentation**

The cockpit instrument panels including the two forward panels, overhead panels, pedestal panels, and eyebrow panels were unidentifiable in the wreckage because of extreme post crash fire damage. The majority of the cockpit instruments recovered were severely burned and distorted from heat. (See Photo No. 1 and 2) Those instruments that were identified had questionable readings; two exceptions were a directional gyro indicator and a cockpit clock.

The face of the directional gyro indicator was frozen at approximately 250°. This corresponded roughly to the heading of the final resting position of the wreckage.

The cockpit clock showed signs of heat damage. The hour hand was either missing or had melted into the face. The minute hand was intact and indicated fourteen (14) minutes past the hour. This corresponds approximately to the time of the accident as established by ATC information and witness statements.

   2.   **Radio Rack Equipment**

The radio rack was located just aft of the cockpit/cabin bulkhead, behind the co-pilots seat. Remnants of the equipment were recovered in the wreckage near their installed position. Because of the extreme heat and fire damage the part number or serial number of the "black boxes" could not be identified. Some functional identification was possible; one communications transceiver was identified and one distance measuring equipment transceiver was identified.

   3.   **Electrical System**

The aircraft batteries (2) were located in the wreckage in their normal position. Both batteries had sustained substantial post-impact fire damage which precluded identificati of part number or manufacturer.

Lamps were removed from the left wing navigation light assembly, the tail navigation light assembly, and the lower rotating beacon assembly. All lamps were returned to the Safety Board's lab facilities in Washington, D.C., to determine if power was on at impact.

Two aircraft rotary inverters were found mounted in their proper positions in the tail section of the aircraft. Neither unit had sustained any impact damage, however, both units were heavily sooted from the outside. The inverters were removed from their mounts and the cooling fan shrouds were removed. The fan blades were examined and there was no evidence of damage from ingestion of foreign matter.

The aircraft engine driven electrical generating components on the left (number 1) engine were severely damaged by postcrash fire. The right engine components (number 2) were intact and mounted on their appropriate pads.

4.   Environmental Systems

The aircraft was equipped with two supplemental breathing oxygen bottles of approximately thirty-two cubic feet capacity each. The bottles were located in the wreckage near their normal positions aft of the co-pilot's seat. The bottles showed no evidence of impact damage; heat discoloration was the extent of damage to the bottles. The bottle heads and valving had suffered moderate impact damage. The position of the shutoff valves was determined to be as follows:

Crew bottle - fully open.
Passenger bottle - one turn from closed toward open.

An air conditioning system had been installed in the aircraft. The major components of the system were located in the wreckage at their appropriate locations as indicated by the Form 337 Major Repair or Alteration paperwork initiated at their installation. The main frame, which constituted the major bulk of the system, was substantially damaged from both impact and fire.

Heating of the cabin and cockpit was accomplished by use of two gasoline fired combustion can type heaters. A twenty-thousand BTU unit supplied heated air to the cockpit. This heater, manufactured by Stewart-Warner, was located near its installed position behind the co-pilots seat area. (See Photo No. 3). All ducts, fans, shrouds and electrical wiring for the unit were found intact. The system had sustained minor to substantial impact damage and heat discoloration from post-crash fire. During the on-site investigation a representative of Stewart-Warner participated in a teardown of the heater. During the teardown the burner can assembly was scrutinized for cracks, but none were found. The forward heater assembly was determined to be in satisfactory condition with the exception of impact damage.

A heater manufactured by Janitrol was installed in the tail area of the aircraft aft of the rear baggage closet. (See Photo No. 4 and 5). This 200,000 BTU system provided heated air for the cabin. This unit had sustained minor impact damage and some heat discoloration; numerous hoses and wires were melted during the post crash fire. The entire unit was removed from the wreckage and shipped to NTSB Headquarters for further examination.

5.   Fire Protection Capabilities

The engine fire extinguishing system consists of a single bottle equipped with valving to select either number one or number two engine. After engine selection has been made, the bottle is fired by hand operated controls. The bottle was located near its proper position in the cockpit wreckage. Impact damage prevented a determination of which engine had been selected, however, examination of the activation control valve indicated it had not been fired.

Two hand held fire extinguishers were found in the cockpit area still attached to their mounts. Both units are of the type that require removal from the mount for activation. It was not determined where these two units were normally mounted in the airplane.

The forward gasoline fired heater system described in part 4 "Environmental Systems" was protected by one dedicated fire extinguisher. The output of the extinguisher is plumbed directly into the heater's shrouded enclosure. The safety pin must be removed and the handle squeezed to activate the unit. The extinguisher was found in the wreckage still attached to its mount on the front of the heater enclosure; the safety pin was still installed.

The aft gasoline fired heater system described in part 4 "Environmental Systems" was protected by two dedicated fire extinguishers of different sizes. Both extinguishers were located in the wreckage near their proper positions at the aft wall of the rear baggage enclosure. (See Photo 6). The agent from either extingusher could have been discharged into the aft heater system enclosure through braided lines. The smaller bottle was identical in operation to the unit used on the forward heater system, i.e. the safety pin must be pulled and the handle squeezed. The safety pin for the small bottle was found amid the debris and not attached to the bottle. Both the safety pin and the bottle were returned to NTSB Headquarters for further examination.

The larger bottle was equipped with a "squib" charge at the top of the bottle. The "squib" charge, when electrically activated fires a projectile which perforates the diaphrgam permitting the fire extinguishing agent to leave the bottle and enter the braided lines under pressure. The firing of the "squib" charge would be accomplished remotely from the cockpit. The "squib" charge and diaphragm of the larger bottle were examined at the accident site. It was determined that the squib charge had not been fired and the diaphragm had not been perforated.

6. Miscellaneous Observations

The cockpit hydraulic system control panel was found in the wreckage aft of where the copilot's seat would normally have been located. This is the standard position for this panel. The panel has controls for the actuation of the wing flaps, the landing gear and a hydraulic by-pass valve. Only the position of the by-pass valve could be determi with any certainty because of heat and impact damage. The by-pass valve was in the non-by-pass position.

The aircraft was equipped with a Collins Type AP-101E Autopilot System. All three of the autopilot flight control surface servos (aileron, elevator and rudder) were located within the wreckage in their intended positions. All bridle cables were intact.

Remnants of an airplane emergency locator transmitter (ELT) were recovered in the cockpit area of the wreckage. Identification of manufacturer and/or part number was not possible because of severe fire damage.

The aft lavatory installation was examined in the wreckage. It had suffered excessive heat damage and moderate impact damage.

E. Laboratory Examinations

1. The aft heater assembly (manufactured by Janitrol) including most of the heater enclosure was removed from the wreckage and shipped to NTSB Headquarters in Washington, D.C. On January 15, 1986, the System Group reconvened in the laboratory facilities to disassemble the heater.

The Federal Aviation Administration and Douglas Aircraft representatives who participated as members of the Systems Group during the field investigation were unavailable for this examination. The following representatives were present in their places:

William F. O'Brien

FAA AFS-340
Airworthiness Inspector
Washington, D.C.

Steve Lund

Douglas Aircraft Co.
Air Safety Investigator
Long Beach, Ca.

Also present for the disassembly were:

Tom Roberts

Janitrol-Midland Ross
Quality Control Manager
Columbus, Ohio

Merritt M. Birky

NTSB, TE-50
Fire Group Chairman
Washington, D.C.

Photographic documentation of the examination with accompanying captions is provided as Attachment I. First the heater can assembly was removed from the enclosure. This was done by loosening the marmon clamps at the top and bottom of the can assembly, cutting the fuel inlet line at the outside of the can shroud and the fuel drain line at the bottom of the can assembly, and then disconnecting the marmon clamps at the combustion air inlet connection and the exhaust output nozzle. The igniter was then removed and examined for abnormalities. None were noted. The fuel inlet filter assembly was then removed from the top of the can. The assembly was further dismantled for examination of the filter screen and orifice. No discrepancies were noted.

The shroud which surrounds the burner can was then removed. This was accomplished by cutting the top and bottom retaining rings of the shroud and spreading the shroud circumferentially to enable the burner can to slide out.

The inside of the shroud was examined for evidence of abnormal heating patterns. One such pattern was found near the bottom of the can at approximately the seven o'clock position when viewed from the top. (See photographs in Attachment I) The significance of this area of discoloration is questionable at this time. The burner can was examined for evidence of cracks, dents, abnormal heating/cooling patterns and general condition; none was found. At this point, with the agreement of all involved, the disassembly of the heater assembly was terminated.

The following day Rudy Kapustin, the NTSB IIC, requested that the burner can be pressure checked to be sure that the can did not contain non-visible fractures. A telephone conference with the Janitrol and FAA representatives concluded that it would not be necessary to reconvene the Systems Group unless the pressure check resulted in signficiant findings. Subsequently the burner can was sealed at the fuel inlet, the exhaust outlet and the combustion air inlet. A pressure gauge was attached to the fuel drain fitting and approximately ten pounds per square inch of air was then introduced through a fitting on the igniter plug orifice. The pressurized can was sprayed with a mixture of tap water and liquid soap to detect cracks or pin holes. No holes or cracks were observed on the can surface. The can was free of leaks except for several small leaks around the combustion air inlet and the exhaust outlet seals. These findings were then reported to the Systems Group representatives and Mr. Kapustin and all agreed that further testing would not be necessary.

2. Reports of the laboratory examinations of the aircraft lamps and the aft heater enclosure fire extinguisher are still in process at this time.

David K. Johns
Systems Group Chairman

NATIONAL TRANSPORTATION SAFETY BOARD
BUREAU OF TECHNOLOGY
Washington, D.C. 20594
July 24, 1986

SURVIVAL FACTORS/OPERATIONS/WITNESS GROUPS FACTUAL REPORT

A.   Accident   : DCA86AA012
      Operator   : Rick Nelson
      Aircraft   : Douglas DC-3, N711Y
      Location   : De Kalb, Texas
      Date   : December 31, 1985
      Time   : 1714 CST[1]

B.   Survival Factors/Operations/Witness Group
      Frances A. Sherertz, Group Chairman
      National Transportation Safety Board

      Tommy McFall
      NTSB - Fort Worth

      Ernie Colvard
      FAA - Dallas/Fort Worth FSDO

      Max Young
      FAA - Dallas/Fort Worth FSDO

      Thomas Hodge
      Sheriff, Bowie County, Texas

----
1. All times herein are Central Standard Time and are based on the 24-hour clock unless otherwise noted.

C. Synopsis
     This flight originated in Guntersville, Alabama on December
31, 1985 at approximately 1300 CST on an IFR flight plan to
Dallas, Texas, Love Field. The airplane, a Douglas DC-3
registered to Century Equipment Company but operated by Rick
Nelson, was occupied by a pilot, a copilot, and 7 adult
passengers. At 1708, while operating in daylight visual
meteorological conditions, the flight advised Fort Worth Center
that it had a "little problem" and wanted to reverse course and
proceed to the Texarkana airport. The flight was unable to make
Texarkana and the crew executed an off-airport landing in a farm
field near De Kalb, Texas, approximately 1714. The airplane came
to rest at 33·29'5"N, 94·36'2"W. A fire consumed the
airplane. Both crewmembers exited the airplane and were
seriously burned. None of the passengers exited the airplane and
none of them survived.

D. Details of the Investigation
1. History of Flight
     Ramp service personnel at the Guntersville Airport stated
that on the date of the accident, the crew arrived at the airport
between 0830 and 0900 Under the direction of the crew, 345.6
gallons of 100 octane low lead fuel were added to the airplane.
This fuel was sufficient to fill both main fuel tanks and to fill
the left and right auxiliary tanks to within approximately 6 to 8
inches of their respective filler necks. The crew members and
ramp personnel loaded the passengers' personal luggage and
musical equipment consisting of a standup base, an electric base,
3 or 4 guitars, 2 small amplifiers, a snare drum, some drum
cymbals, and the miscellaneous accessory equipment.
     Prior to boarding the passengers, both crewmembers boarded
the airplane and performed an uneventful start and runup of both
engines. The engines were then secured and passengers boarded.
During the engine start which followed, the left engine was
cranked but would not start. Fuel was observed to be coming out
of the engine case drain line. The right engine was then started
and the crew again attempted to start the left engine. The crew
and passengers disembarked, the engine primer line was cleared
using compressed air. Instead of reboarding the passengers, the
crew elected to delay takeoff because of deteriorating weather.
At approximately 1240 the crew and passengers reboarded the
airplane, both engines started normally, and the airplane taxied
for takeoff.
     At 1708 N711Y contacted Fort Worth Center stating, "I think
I'd like to turn around, uh, head for Texarkana here, I've got a
little problem." A complete transcript of communications between
Fort Worth Center and N711Y is contained in Attachment A.
Several communications between the airplane and the Center were
made regarding the heading and distance to various airports where
the flight could land. At 1711, N711Y transmitted, "...smoke in
the cockpit, have smoke in the cockpit." No further
transmissions were received from the flight. At 1712, N711Y's

transponder transmitted an altitude of 600 feet Mean Sea Level, and at 1714 radar contact was lost.

Witnesses, local farmers and their families, persons on the roadway, and local law enforcement observers stated that the airplane flew a left descending turn to it's final approach course, and appeared to line up on a farm field, trailing smoke and "sparks". Small fires erupted in fields overflown by the airplane, ignited by falling pieces or droplets of hot metal. The airplane flew low over a house, struck and severed 2 power lines about 30 feet AGL (Above Ground Level), collided with and broke 2 telephone poles, and landed, gear down, in a field. The airplane came to rest about 1260 feet from the point of contact with the wires. The airplane was subsequently enveloped in fire.

2. Injuries to Persons

Table 1. Injury Table

	Cockpit Crew	Passengers	Total
Fatal	0	7	9
Serious	2	0	0
Minor	0	0	0
None	0	0	0
TOTAL	2	7	9

Neither crewmember could provide information on the condition of the passengers during the landing sequence and moments immediately following, except that they were aware of at least one passenger standing in the cockpit doorway. Pilot Bradley Rank reported that prior to exiting his cockpit window, he felt one passenger behind him in the cockpit. Pilot Rank pulled this individual toward the cockpit window as he exited, and reported that he could see the individual silhouetted in the window after he, Rank, reached the ground. Pilot Rank reported that he was unable to reach or assist the person in the window from his position on the ground. Early witnesses on the scene also reported seeing a person in the cockpit's left window.

The pilot and copilot reported exiting the airplane by falling from their respective cockpit windows. This represents a drop of approximately 10 feet, depending on the exact attitude of the airplane at the time. Neither crewmember received injuries from this fall.

Autopsies were conducted by the Dallas County, Texas, Forensic Laboratory on all of the passengers. The causes of death were reported to be smoke inhalation and thermal burns. Toxicological studies were conducted incident to the autopsies to ascertain the levels of carbon monoxide and cyanide. Among the fatally injured, carbon monoxide levels ranged from 33% to 80%, and cyanide from .43 mg/L to 1.2 mg/L. Both crewmembers were hospitalized for treatment of burns and inhalation injuries. Copies of all toxicological studies conducted are contained in Attachment B.

3.   Damage to Airplane
     During the landing sequence, the airplane struck utility poles and wires, touched down in a field, and then continued into a small stand of mature trees. The airplane was totally destroyed by the combination of inflight fire, impact damage and postflight fire. However, witness statements indicated that the airplane's exterior was largely intact immediately after landing, and that the airplane was upright on its gear. Several witnesses stated that the left engine was still running after the airplane came to rest.
     Destruction of the cabin seat materials and seat belt webbing by fire precluded determination of seat belt use or seat occupancy. Only seat frames and attachment hardware remained for the single-unit and double-unit cabin seats. Seat frames showed no evidence of impact deformation, and were still attached to their floor attachment hardware although the floor had burned away. None of the divan structure (seats 1,2,3 left and right, see Figure 1, page 7) remained.
     Supplemental oxygen systems had not been used by either crew or passengers. The hand-held fire extinguisher located in the cockpit had not been used.
     See the Systems/Structures Group Chairman's Factual Report for details concerning the wreckage.

4.   Other Damage
     Several trees, telephone poles and brush were damaged from impact with the airplane. Additionally, a number of fields were subjected to grass fires.

5.   Crew Information
     The crew consisted of a pilot, Bradley Scott Rank, and a copilot, Kenneth Reinhard Ferguson. There was no flight attendant on board and none was required.

Table 2.   Crew Summary

	Pilot Rank	Copilot Ferguson
Date of birth	9-17-53	5-03-41
Date/Class physical	2-04-85/2nd	7-09-85/1rst
Total time (approx)	5,700 hours	4,500 hours
Time in Type (approx)	150 hours	150 hours
Biennial/Flight Check	5-02-85	11-05-85

     Pilot Rank possessed an airline transport pilot rating, certificate number 555465073, and an airframe and powerplant mechanic's certificate bearing the same number. He held type ratings for Lear Jet, IA Jet, and the DC-3. Pilot Rank also held a flight instructor certificate. His type rating in the DC-3 was awarded on May 3, 1985. Because his DC-3 type rating had been awarded in the previous 24 calendar months, Pilot Rank was not required to have a biennial flight review. He also held commercial pilot privileges for single-engine land airplanes and helicopters. His medical certificate, issued February 4, 1985, as a First Class medical had reverted, through the passage of time, to a Second Class medical. Pilot Rank's medical certificate contained no waivers or limitations.

Pilot Rank reported that his pilot logbook was destroyed in N711Y. During sworn testimony, Pilot Rank reported his total flight time as approximately 5,700 hours. On applications for previously issued medical certificates and for various aeronautical ratings, Rank reported his pilot times as shown in Table 3.

Table 3.   Reported Pilot Times - Pilot Rank.

Date		Hours	Time in Last 6 Months
01-22-86	:	5,700 TT	NR
02-04-85	:	5,000	300
01-10-84	:	5,700	310
01-03-83	:	5,500	300
01-12-82	:	5,500	400
04-10-81	:	2,663	NR
03-16-81	:	2,598	NR
02-09-81	:	3,000	570
11-01-79	:	925	NR
05-16-79	:	592	NR
05-08-78	:	327	NR
04-18-78	:	272	NR
02-30-78	:	208	NR
12-13-75	:	51	NR

(NR = not reported)

On his application for the DC-3 type rating (May 3, 1985), Pilot Rank reported that he had 55.0 hours pilot experience in DC-3. The pilot examiner who granted Pilot Rank the DC-3 type rating also gave Pilot Rank 4 to 5 hours dual in N711Y prior to the flight check. Contrary to Rank's statement, the examiner stated that Pilot Rank had no experience as a pilot of DC-3 prior to the dual given in preparation for the checkride.

Pilot Rank was employed by Mr. Rick Nelson (Eric Hilliard Nelson), doing business as Stone Canyon Band Records, in October, 1982, to perform services as a corporate pilot and to provide maintenance services on Mr. Nelson's Jet Commander, N333SV. When N333SV was replaced by N711Y, Pilot Rank continued as the command pilot and supervisor of maintenance. He previously had been employed by Aerojet General as a mechanic.

Copilot Ferguson possessed a commercial pilot certificate, single- and multi-engine land and sea, and a type rating for Cessna CE-500. He had been hired by Stone Canyon Band Records as a copilot in March, 1984. His flight instructor certificate was revalidated by a flight check on November 5, 1985. Therefore, he did not require a biennial flight review. Copilot Ferguson possessed a valid first class medical certificate dated July 9, 1985. His medical certificate contained no waivers of limitations.

6. Crew History.

The trip from Guntersville to Dallas was to be the next-to-last trip the crew was to fly on a multi-legged, multiple-stop series of performances for Rick Nelson and for his band. The crewmembers flew N711Y (occupied by Mr. Nelson, the band members and Mr. Nelson's fiancee, Ms Blair) into Guntersville on December 27, 1985. During December 28 through 30, the crewmembers attended to personal matters, and did no flying. On December 30, both crewmembers attended to light maintenance duties for N711Y at the Guntersville airport. They attended Mr. Nelson's show that night, and retired for the evening approximately midnight. Both crew members awakened between 0700 and 0800 on December 31, 1985, and left for the airport between 0830 and 0900.

7. Airplane Information

The airplane was a twin-engine Douglas DC-3, N711Y, manufactured and certificated as a C-47 in 1944, serial number 13650. The airplane was equipped with an aft passenger/crew entrance door. An emergency exit was located over each wing. Cockpit windows could be opened from the inside and were also designated as emergency exits. There was also a top hatch in the cockpit area which could be used as an emergency exit. Emergency exits could be opened only from inside the airplane.

In 1959, the airplane was converted from a C-47 to a DC-3 and its interior was refurbished and equipped with an executive interior which included 14 passenger seats (4 single seat units, 2 double seat units, and 2 triple seat divans), and 2 crew seats. The passenger seats were equipped with seatbelts of the metal-to-fabric type. Both crew seats were equipped with seatbelts with metal-to-metal fasteners. Crew seats were not equipped with shoulder harnesses. The airplane was not pressurized, but contained 2 supplemental oxygen systems of 32 cubic feet each: 1 for the cockpit crew and 1 for use by passengers. Both supplemental oxygen systems were of the rebreather type. There were no smoke goggles aboard the airplane.

The airplane included 2 gasoline heaters, one for heating the cockpit and a cabin heater located aft of the lavatory. Both heaters were activated from the cockpit; the aft cabin heater could be adjusted with a thermostat once the heater was activated. The aft heater was equipped with 2 dedicated fire extinguishers, activated from the heater area itself. The forward (cockpit) heater was not equipped with dedicated extinguishers. A hand-held portable fire extinguisher was located in the cockpit. The airplane was also equipped with engine fire extinguishers.

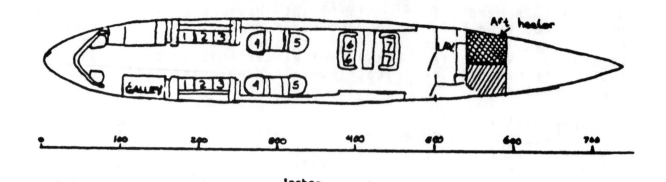

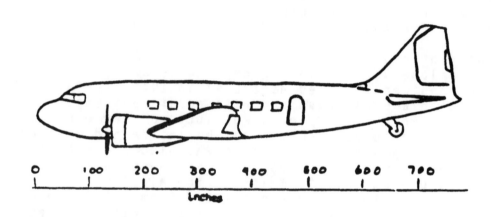

Music's Broken Wings

8 Airplane Operations

N711Y was registered to Century Equipment Company of Los Angeles, California, on March 13, 1981. Century Equipment personnel stated that N711Y was sold to Mr. Nelson on May 2, 1985. Century's claim of having sold the airplane was substantiated by a copy of a bill of sale, a copy of Mr. Nelson's check for the down payment, a promissory note signed by Mr. Nelson for the purchase price of the airplane less the down payment, and a record of at least 1 monthly payment made by Nelson. Copies of these documents are included as Attachment C. No application for change of registration was ever received by the FAA, and the registration of record at the time of the accident was still Century Equipment Company. FAA regulations (14 CFR 47.3) require that "no person may operate an aircraft... unless that aircraft (1) Has been registered by its owner, (2) Is carrying aboard the ... authorization required."

In May, 1981, Century Equipment applied for, and received, a waiver to conduct operations under 14 CFR 91, and to perform inspections and maintenance under an FAA approved program. The waiver received by Century Equipment Company did not .ransfer to Mr. Nelson. No application from Mr. Nelson for such a waiver or application for approval of an inspection and maintenance program has been received by the FAA. The airplane was not operated under either 14 CFR 125 (Certification and Operation of Airplanes Having a Seating Capacity of 20 or More Passengers or a Maximum Payload Capacity of 6,000 pounds or More) or under 14 CFR 91 subpart D (General Operating and Flight Rules, Large and Turbine-Powered Multiengine Airplanes).

N711Y's empty weight, as established by Remmert-Warner, Inc. when the airplane was converted from C-47 to DC-3, was 20610 pounds. The maximum gross weight in all configurations was 26,900 pounds. Allowances for an estimated fuel supply of 680 gallons, full anti-ice alcohol, full lavatory water supply and 100 pounds of baggage and cargo and allowances for passengers and crew result in an estimated takeoff weight of 26,519 pounds.

None of the required documents (Airworthiness Certificate, Registration, Radio Transmitter License, and Weight and Balance Information) were recovered from the wreckage.

9. Crew Statements.

Sworn testimony was taken from Pilot Rank on January 22, 1986. Pilot Rank described the prestart and pretakeoff activities noted earlier, and described an uneventful takeoff. He stated that during the latter stages of the flight, he left the cockpit to check on the passengers and see to their needs. Pilot Rank stated that he was standing approximately midcabin, talking to passenger Woodward, when he noticed smoke in the area occupied by Mr. Nelson and Ms. Blair (seats 66 and 77 on Figure 1). He did not investigate the smoke at that location but states that, instead, he proceeded directly through the baggage compartment to the cabin heater. The heater was cool to his touch. He saw neither smoke nor fire. However, Pilot Rank

Chapter 34: Rick Nelson

activated the smaller of the 2 fire extinguishers permanently attached to the heater. He then left the heater area, and moved through the cabin opening the cabin fresh air inlets on his way back to the cockpit, and directing passenger Woodward to open other fresh air inlets. When Pilot Rank reached the cockpit and regained his seat, Copilot Ferguson had already begun communications with air traffic control relative to the location of the nearest airports. Pilot Rank donned his headset, resumed control of the airplane, and opened his own cockpit window. Thereupon, "things rapidly got worse... I started a slow descending turn... and the window was open, and from there, things went completely blacked out. The smoke came through the cabin... it stained the windows, the cockpit glass, everything... We had to land right now.". Subsequently, Pilot Rank directed Copilot Ferguson to open his window as well. According to Pilot Rank's statement, vision inside the cockpit was so badly obscured that he could not see through the forward windows to land the airplane. He leaned through the opened cockpit window to obtain sufficient visual references to select a landing site, achieve the desired pitch attitude, and land the airplane. After the airplane rolled to a stop, the pilot exited the airplane through his cockpit window. He states that he then opened the aft passenger entrance door and ascended the stairs in order to look into the cabin of 711Y. He further states that he could see in the smoke and that there was a small flame or fire in the area of the aft club seating (seats 66 and 77) at the location where smoke had originally been seen. There was no response to his calls, and Pilot Rank abandoned the airplane to search outside for his employer and the other passengers.

Sworn testimony was obtained from Copilot Ferguson on March 19, 1986. Copilot Ferguson stated that on December 30, 1985, the day previous to the accident, Pilot Rank had checked over the cabin heater and found nothing of note. On the accident day, takeoff was postponed because of weather and because of problems starting the left engine. The engine problems were cleared up, and after the weather improved the flight taxied out and departed Guntersville. After the flight was airborne, the cabin heater began to "act up". The overheat light would come on in the cockpit, the crew would turn the heater off, wait for a while, and then turn the heater back on again. According to Copilot Ferguson, "At some point, ...Brad (Pilot Rank) decided to go aft of the tail to see if there was anything he could do to get it to function correctly... there were several times involved here...he ... signaled for me to turn it on or he ... came up front and told me to turn it on or whatever. This happened several times. One of the times I refused to turn it on, I didn't turn it on. I was getting nervous. I didn't think that we should be messing with that heater enroute. I had discussed this with Brad on previous flights... and he turned it on again... Once, again, it either shut off or the overheat light came on, (it) went through the same cycle... How many times this happened... three, four, perhaps five times. The last time Brad went aft in the tail, he was aft for not very long, came out and signaled me to turn it on again, which I did. Several minutes after that, Pat Woodward,... came forward to me and said, "There is smoke back here in the cabin"." Copilot Ferguson stated that the time interval between the last time he turned the heater on and the appearance of the smoke was approximately 4 minutes.

In response to questions concerning the fire, Copilot Ferguson stated, "It is interesting that throughout the smoke and the fire, neither the Janitrol overheat nor the Janitrol fire light ever came on." However, Copilot Ferguson did state that the Janitrol cabin heater had been turned "off" prior to Pilot Rank's return to the cockpit. Pilot Rank directed Copilot Ferguson to open his cockpit window, but Copilot Ferguson stated that it "acted like such a chimney... I shut it."

After the airplane landed, Copilot Ferguson stated that he reopened the right cockpit window, and then exited through it, and fell to the ground below. "My engine (the right engine) had stopped turning, there was no flame on the outside of the airplane on my side, on the right side of the aircraft... The cabin of the aircraft through the windows appeared to be an inferno. Flames and smoke was all that one could see. " Copilot Ferguson moved away from the airplane, fearing an explosion. He encountered Pilot Rank, who sat Ferguson on the ground, and Pilot Rank said, "Don't tell anyone about the heater, don't tell anyone about the heater, don't tell anyone about the heater."

10. Passengers.

The 7 adult passengers included 1 female and 6 males. They were identified as:

Helen Blair, age 29
Andy Chapin, age 30
Rick Intveld, age 23
Bobby Neal, age 38
Rick Nelson, age 45
Clark Russell, age 35
Patrick Woodward, age 35

Ms. Blair and Mr. Nelson were reported to have been seated in seats 66 and 77. Pilot Rank stated that they had been sleeping prior to the crew's decision to land. Pilot Rank stated that a passenger he believed was Woodward was standing in the cockpit area immediately prior to the landing. Seating locations for the other passengers, or their positions in the cabin during landing, could not be reconstructed. The bodies of passengers Russell and Neal were found together in the approximate position of the cabin/cockpit companionway. The bodies of passengers Woodward, Nelson and Blair were found together in the forward cabin, and the bodies of passengers Chapin and Intveld were found slightly forward of midcabin.

11. Emergency Procedures.
    The Operating Manual for this airplane requires the completion of the following emergency checklist for inflight fire:
    (1) Close all hatches, doors and ventilating ducts.
    (2) Oxygen masks - ON, and oxygen regulator controls - 100% oxygen.
    (3) Combat the fire with hand fire extinguishers.

12. Crash/Fire/Rescue
    Initiation of the Crash/Fire/Rescue response was made by several organizations or individuals almost simultaneously. A helicopter pilot who was in flight in the vicinity assisted in the alert of the local hospital-based ambulance, and then proceeded to the location of N711Y to render what assistance was possible pending the arrival of air and ground emergency medical services personnel.
    A police officer for De Kalb, Texas, witnessed some of the prelanding sequence from his patrol car, and requested fire equipment and ambulance services from the public safety dispatcher. Several neighboring jurisdiction's officers became aware of the De Kalb dispatch and initiated dispatch of their own fire and rescue units, including the equipment available at Texarkana Airport, since it was the only quickly available unit with foam. This is an Oshkosh P-19 unit, which supplied 130 gallons of foam concentrate, 1000 gallons of water, and 500 pounds of dry powder.
    After the 2 surviving crew members were enroute to Texarkana's St. Michael Hospital, officers attached to the City of De Kalb and to Texarkana, Texas, to Bowie County, Texas, and to the Texas Department of Public Safety remained on scene to assist fire suppression efforts and to look for additional survivors. When none were found, the Bowie County Sheriff's Department maintained security at the site, pending arrival of the National Transportation Safety Board.

Frances A. Sherertz
Group Chairman

NATIONAL TRANSPORTATION SAFETY BOARD	ACCIDENT IDENTIFICATION NUMBER
RELEASE OF AIRCRAFT WRECKAGE	DCA86AA012

PART I — RELEASE OF AIRCRAFT WRECKAGE

REGISTERED OWNER (name and address)	REGISTRATION NUMBER—N
Century Equipment Company 2126 Cotner Avenue Los Angeles, California 90025	N711Y
	MAKE
	Douglas

MODEL	DATE OF ACCIDENT	LOCATION
DC-3	12-31-85	DeKalb, Texas

The National Transportation Safety Board has ☒ has not ☐ completed its investigation of the aircraft wreckage described above. All wreckage except that listed on the reverse side is hereby released to the registered owner, or owner's representative, for appropriate disposition. (If no parts are retained, insert NONE.)

NONE

SIGNATURE OF NTSB REPRESENTATIVE	TITLE	DATE
Frances A. Sherertz	Investigator	8-31-86

(This section may be signed by a person, not the owner or owner's representative, who has knowledge of the disposition of the aircraft wreckage and its parts. Such signature does not place a responsibility for disposition of the wreckage upon that person.)

I HEREBY ACKNOWLEDGE:

☐ Receipt of the above described aircraft wreckage.

☐ Removal of the parts, if any, listed on the reverse side of this form.

SIGNATURE	TITLE	DATE

REMARKS:

NTSB FORM 6120.15 (Rev. 5/79)

National Transportation Safety Board
Washington, D.C. 20594

Brief of Accident

DCA86AA012
FILE NO. 2932   12/31/85   DEKALB,TX   AIRCRAFT REG. NO. N711Y   TIME (LOCAL) - 17:14 CST

MAKE/MODEL   - DOUGLAS DC-3
ENGINE MAKE/MODEL   - P&W R-1830-75   FATAL   SERIOUS   MINOR/NONE
AIRCRAFT DAMAGE   - Destroyed   CREW   0   2   0
NUMBER OF ENGINES   - 2   PASS   7   0   0

OPERATING CERTIFICATES   - None
TYPE OF FLIGHT OPERATION   - Executive/corporate
REGULATION FLIGHT CONDUCTED UNDER - 14 CFR 91

LAST DEPARTURE POINT   - GUNTERSVILLE,AL   CONDITION OF LIGHT - Daylight
DESTINATION   - DALLAS,TX
                                                     WEATHER INFO SOURCE- Witness
AIRPORT PROXIMITY   - Off airport/airstrip
                                                     BASIC WEATHER   - Visual (VMC)
                                                     LOWEST CEILING   - None
                                                     VISIBILITY   - 0015.000 SM
                                                     WIND DIR/SPEED   - Unk/Nr
                                                     TEMPERATURE (F)   - 65
                                                     OBSTR TO VISION   - None
                                                     PRECIPITATION   - None

PILOT-IN-COMMAND   AGE - 33   FLIGHT TIME (Hours)

CERTIFICATES/RATINGS   TOTAL ALL AIRCRAFT   - 5700
  Commercial, Airline transport, Flight instructor   LAST 90 DAYS   - Unk/Nr
  Single-engine land, Multiengine land   TOTAL MAKE/MODEL   - 150
  Helicopter   TOTAL INSTRUMENT TIME - Unk/Nr
INSTRUMENT RATINGS
  Airplane

AT 1708:48, WHILE CRUISING AT 6000', A PILOT OF N711Y ADVISED ATC, "I THINK I"D LIKE TO TURN AROUND, HEAD FOR TEXARKANA
HERE, I"VE GOT A LITTLE PROBLEM." HE WAS PROVIDED A VECTOR & ADVISED OF CLOSEST AIRPORTS. SHORTLY AFTER, HE STATED HE
WOULD BE UNABLE TO REACH THE AIRPORTS. AT 1711:49, HE SAID THERE WAS SMOKE IN THE COCKPIT. WHILE LANDING IN A FIELD AT
1714, THE AIRCRAFT HIT WIRES & A POLE. THEN CONTINUED INTO TREES WHERE IT WAS EXTENSIVELY DAMAGED BY IMPACT & FIRE. THE
CREW EGRESSED THRU THE COCKPIT WINDOWS. THE PASSENGERS DID NOT ESCAPE. DURING FLIGHT, THE CREW WAS UNABLE TO START THE
CABIN HEATER; DESPITE REPEATED ATTEMPTS BY THE CAPTAIN. SMOKE THEN ENTERED THE CABIN. FRESH AIR VENTS & COCKPIT WINDOWS
WERE OPENED, BUT SMOKE BECAME DENSE. THE CREW HAD DIFFICULTY SEEING. THE OXYGEN SYSTEM & HAND HELD FIRE EXTINGUISHERS
WERE NOT USED. FASTENERS FOR THE HEATER DOOR WERE FOUND UNFASTENED. EXAMINATION INDICATED THE FIRE ORIGINATED IN THE AFT
CABIN AREA, RIGHT HAND SIDE, AT OR NEAR THE FLOOR LINE. THE IGNITION AND FUEL SOURCES WERE NOT DETERMINED.

Brief of Accident (Continued)

DCA86AA012
FILE NO. 2932   12/31/85   DEKALB,TX   AIRCRAFT REG. NO. N711Y   TIME (LOCAL) - 17:14 CST

Occurrence# 1   FIRE
Phase of Operation   CRUISE

Findings
    1. - FUSELAGE,CABIN - FIRE
    2. - REASON FOR OCCURRENCE UNDETERMINED
    3. - FUSELAGE,CABIN - SMOKE
    4. - FUSELAGE,CREW COMPARTMENT - SMOKE
    5. - EMERGENCY PROCEDURE - NOT FOLLOWED - PILOT-IN-COMMAND
    6. - CHECKLIST - NOT USED
    7. - OXYGEN SYSTEM - NOT USED

Occurrence# 2   FORCED LANDING
Phase of Operation   DESCENT - EMERGENCY

Occurrence# 3   IN-FLIGHT COLLISION WITH OBJECT
Phase of Operation   LANDING - FLARE/TOUCHDOWN

Findings
    8. - OBJECT - WIRE,TRANSMISSION
    9. - OBJECT - UTILITY POLE

Occurrence# 4   ON GROUND/WATER COLLISION WITH OBJECT
Phase of Operation   LANDING - ROLL

Findings
    10. - TERRAIN CONDITION - TREE(S)

---Probable Cause--

CAUSES   1 2 5 6 7 8 9 10
FACTORS   3 4

Format Revision 4/97

NTSB Identification: **DCA86AA012** For details, refer to NTSB microfiche number **29185A**

Accident occurred DEC-31-85 at DEKALB, TX
Aircraft: DOUGLAS DC-3, registration: N711Y
Injuries: 7 Fatal, 2 Serious.

AT 1708:48, WHILE CRUISING AT 6000', A PILOT OF N711Y ADVISED ATC, "I THINK I"D LIKE TO TURN AROUND, HEAD FOR TEXARKANA HERE, I"VE GOT A LITTLE PROBLEM." HE WAS PROVIDED A VECTOR & ADVISED OF CLOSEST AIRPORTS. SHORTLY AFTER, HE STATED HE WOULD BE UNABLE TO REACH THE AIRPORTS. AT 1711:49, HE SAID THERE WAS SMOKE IN THE COCKPIT. WHILE LANDING IN A FIELD AT 1714, THE AIRCRAFT HIT WIRES & A POLE THEN CONTINUED INTO TREES WHERE IT WAS EXTENSIVELY DAMAGED BY IMPACT & FIRE. THE CREW EGRESSED THRU THE COCKPIT WINDOWS. THE PASSENGERS DID NOT ESCAPE. DURING FLIGHT, THE CREW WAS UNABLE TO START THE CABIN HEATER; DESPITE REPEATED ATTEMPTS BY THE CAPTAIN. SMOKE THEN ENTERED THE CABIN. FRESH AIR VENTS & COCKPIT WINDOWS WERE OPENED, BUT SMOKE BECAME DENSE. THE CREW HAD DIFFICULTY SEEING. THE OXYGEN SYSTEM & HAND HELD FIRE EXTINGUISHERS WERE NOT USED. FASTENERS FOR THE HEATER DOOR WERE FOUND UNFASTENED. EXAMINATION INDICATED THE FIRE ORIGINATED IN THE AFT CABIN AREA, RIGHT HAND SIDE, AT OR NEAR THE FLOOR LINE. THE IGNITION AND FUEL SOURCES WERE NOT DETERMINED.

Probable Cause

Fuselage,cabin..Fire
Reason for occurrence undetermined..no modifier specified..no person specified

Contributing Factors

Fuselage,cabin..Smoke
Fuselage,crew compartment..Smoke
Emergency procedure..Not followed..Pilot in command
Checklist..Not used..no person specified
Oxygen system..Not used..no person specified
Object..Wire,transmission
Object..Utility pole
Terrain condition..Tree(s)

Amulets, Saints and Final Thoughts

Nearly all pilots will tell you that there has been at least one time in their flying career when they have successfully brought a particularly tense flight to its completion and, breathing with great relief, uttered something like "There must be someone watching over me." Whether it be unforecasted weather, wind shear, mechanical problems or a near miss with another aircraft, almost all pilots have experienced the flushed face, knock knees and trembling hands associated with such a stressful flight. It does not matter what the expertise level of the pilot is. Student pilots sometimes experience this feeling within the safety of the airport traffic pattern with an event such as their first solo crosswind landing. Seasoned airline and military pilots can certainly tell stories about tense flights regarding bad weather, equipment faliure or the anxiety that comes with flying an aircraft into a war zone.

From an early age nearly every child is taught about or exposed to stories about mythical, Biblical and make-believe characters who can fly. These characters include Santa Claus, the Tooth Fairy, Peter Pan, angels, dragons and witches. Perhaps this is the reason why, from an early age, the whole idea of flight so overwhelmingly captures our imagination. A child's innocent pretend play usually does not include any hint that flying can be frightening. To the older person, however, the risks of aviation are more evident.

Often developing in tandem with this awareness is a psychological need to have something lucky, or safe, to hold onto. A rabbit's foot, four-leaf clover and horseshoe are the most common lucky charms that we cling to, but within aviation there are only a few amulets or characters to calm earthly fears. Most of these are not well known.

Since the Catholic Church has a patron saint for nearly every vocation imaginable, it should not be surprising that there are saints dedicated to aviation as well. Additionally, there are minerals that, while less well-known as a source of good luck, some believe have the power to counteract certain natural forces that can afflict pilots. I have included information on some of these saints and "power rocks" in this text with the intent that anyone who flies can hold onto (either literally or figuratively) the particular saint or "lucky force" that provides personal comfort and calm. I suppose one only has to believe in order for the positive energy to work.

With regard to minerals, there are over 20 guardian stones which, according to the experts who subscribe to this kind of information, supposedly can help pilots with everything from altitude sickness to vertigo problems. The most common minerals believed to invoke protective energy for aviators are malachite, black tourmaline, lapis lazuli and various quartz crystals. For the person who is more inclined to look to a saint to find calm, there are three who the Catholic church recognizes. Two of these saints are Saint Therese of Lisieux and Saint Joseph Cupertino. Saint Joseph Cupertino was said to possess powers of prolonged levitation. However, there is another saint who, although well-known, is not usually associated with aviation. She is a Lady who nearly everyone learns about from a young age. Her official title in this aeronautical protective role is Our Lady of Loreto, Patroness of Aviators and Air Travelers. She is better known to Catholics as the Blessed Virgin Mary, the mother of Jesus Christ.

The small town of Loreto, Italy is not a commonly visited tourist location. Located just south of the larger town of Ancona, on Italy's eastern Adriatic coast, Loreto harbors a legend and a truth that are two of the more remarkable, yet lesser-told, stories that have come to be associated with aviation.

The historical record shows that around the year 1294 A.D., the European Crusaders found the house in Nazareth in which Mary was born, had lived as a child, and where it is believed she received the visit from the archangel Gabriel announcing that she would be the mother of Christ. The Crusaders, not wanting the house to be destroyed by the invading Moslems, dismantled the three-wall, stone-built portion of the house (the fourth wall of the house being a grotto cut into solid rock) and transported the pieces to the hill of Loreto where they were carefully reconstructed. Finally, around this new location of the holy house, a church was constructed. However, the legend surrounding this story is that angels came down from heaven and lifted the house from its original site with the power of their wings and flew it out of the Holy Land, and from assured destruction, to the site in Loreto. This angelic legend is the basis for Mary, mother of Jesus, being appointed as the patroness of aviators.

The basilica that stands today in Loreto still houses the original three walls that the Crusaders rescued. Modern day archaeologists have examined the walls and have determined that the stones and the construction techniques originated in the Holy Land, around the same time period when Mary was born. Within this church, like so many large churches in Italy, there is a large main sanctuary as well as smaller chapels around the inside periphery of the structure. Within one of these smaller chapels the theme of aviation is depicted. This particular chapel is known by two names: the Chapel of the Assumption, as well as the American Chapel. There are two large frescoes within the chapel, which span from floor to ceiling, on the right and left walls. The fresco on the right wall is dedicated to aviation.

It was on March 24, 1920, that Pope Benedict XV declared, "By Our supreme authority We appoint and declare the Most Blessed Virgin, under her title of Loreto, to be the chief Patron before God of all aviators." Since then, the Lady has naturally become the patron saint of astronauts as well. The fresco clearly depicts astronauts. Even Laika, the Russian dog, which was the first living creature to orbit the Earth, is shown. This fresco also illustrates the Wright brothers' 1903 Flyer, a modern jet airplane and the likenesses of commercial pilots. Directly above all of the figures in the fresco is the representation of angels carrying a house through the air. The fresco was painted in 1970 by Guiseppe Steffanina.

For those not able to journey to Italy for a pilgrimmage to aviation's religious shrine, there is a church named Our Lady of Loreto in Worcester, Massachusetts. One of the stained glass windows in the Worcester church portrays the Loreto story, complete with a depiction of the legend of the house being flown by angels, as well as an entire aviation theme. Some of the other figures portrayed on the stained glass window are the likenesses of Lindbergh, an air traffic controller and an astronaut. Above the people depicted in this window are images of the Spirit of St. Louis airplane and a modern space shuttle.

So here is where the first fifty years of aviation accidents that have somehow affected the music industry comes to an end. Sadly, there is already enough material to write a second volume about this genre of air crashes. After compiling these reports and completing this first volume, I have gained an enhanced love for life and all its simple joys. I also still love to fly and perform my job. I am fortunate to go to work each day as a professional pilot, take people where they want to go, put them on the ground safely and afterwards rest well at night.

It is my wish that everyone who has read this book, and subsequently embarks on a flight, will do so with more knowledge, confidence, and perhaps, a greater feeling of relaxation knowing that from these events, much has been learned for the future of aviation safety. For those who have the dream of learning to fly I have simple yet emphatic words for you, "Go and do it!" For those who might endeavor to write a song someday, I remind you that in this activity there is absolutely nothing to lose. Songs can be written with one's feet planted firmly on the ground.

"Because thou hast been my help, therefore in the shadow
of thy wings will I rejoice."
Psalms 63:7

BIBLIOGRAPHY
(in alphabetical order)

Print References:

Aeronautical Information Manual. US Department of Transportation. Federal Aviation Administration. 2002.

Airplane Flying Handbook. US Department of Transportation, Federal Aviation Administration. Flight Standards Service. FAA-H-8083-3. Revised 1999.

A Star Is Dead. Time, 69(17): 34. April 1957.

Bateman, Don. Flight Into Terrain And The Ground Proximity Warning System. Allied Signal, Inc. 1995.

Bramson, Alan. The Book Of Flight Tests. Blitz Editions. Leicester, England. 1990.

Brickell, Sean and Rich Rothschild. On This Day In Rock 'n Roll. The Donning Company. Norfolk, Virginia. 1983.

Clarke, Bill. The Illustrated Buyer's Guide To Used Airplanes. TAB Books, Inc. Blue Ridge Summit, Pennsylvania. 1985.

Clarke, Bill. The Piper Indians. TAB Books, Inc. Blue Ridge Summit, Pennsylvania. 1988.

Clark, Hedy. Limelights And Footlights. Theatre Arts, 40(15): 15-16. May 1956.

Death From Above. The Burg. Lynchburg, Virginia. April 5, 2000.

Erlewine, Michael, Vladimir Bogdanov, Chris Woodstra and Stephen Thomas Erlewine, Editors. All Music Guide To Country: The Experts' Guide To The Best Recordings In Country Music. Miller Freeman Books. San Francisco, California. 1997.

Fein, Seth. Infante, Pedro: 1917-57: Film Actor And Singer. Encyclopedia Of Mexico: History, Society And Culture. Fitzroy Dearborn Publishers. Chicago. 1997.

Frazier, George. Glenn Miller. Radio Corporation Of America. 1954.

Gero, David. Military Aviation Disasters: Significant Losses Since 1908. Patrick Stephens Limited. United Kingdom. 1999.

Graham, Don. No Name On The Bullet: A Biography Of Audie Murphy. Viking Penguin. New York, New York. 1989.

Green, Melody and David Hazard. No Compromise: The Life Story Of Keith Green. Sparrow Press. Chatsworth, California. 1989.

Gregory, Hugh. Soul Music A-Z: Revised Editon. Da Capo Press, Inc. New York, New York. 1995.

Haynes, Don W. Minus One. Unpublished Diary of the Executive Officer of the American Band of the Supreme Allied Command, Directed by Major Glenn Miller. June 1944 - August 1945.

Hemphill, Paul. The Nashville Sound: Bright Lights And Country Music. Simon and Schuster. New York, New York. 1970.

Ide, Stephen A. Stan Rogers A Tribute. The Patriot Ledger. Boston, Massachusetts. July 1991.

Infante, Quintanilla, Jose Ernesto. Pedro Infante, el Maximo Idolo de Mexico: (Vida, Obra, Muerte y Leyenda). Ediciones Castillo. Monterrey, Nuevo Leon, Mexico. 1992.

Jennings, Waylon and Lenny Kaye. Waylon: An Autobiography. Warner Books. New York, New York. 1996.

Jordanoff, Assen. Your Wings. Funk & Wagnalls Company. New York, New York. 1940.

Jud Strunk: A Memorial Note To His Creativity. The Rangeley Highlander. Rangeley, Maine. October 9, 1981.

Jud Strunk. Farmington Bicentennial. Lewiston, Maine. June 26, 1994.

Kleimenhagen, Verdon, Ron Keones and James Szajkovics of FAA and Ken Patz of MN/DOT Office of Aeronautics. 178 Seconds To Live: Spatial Disorientation Can Be A Killer. FAA Aviation News, 32(1): 8-10. January-February 1993.

Lisheron, Mark. Cause Of Fatal Crash Being Investigated. Tyler Morning Telegraph. Tyler, Texas. July 29, 1982.

Lisheron, Mark. Too Much Weight A Factor In Fatal Airplane Crash. Tyler Morning Telegraph. Tyler, Texas. July 30, 1982.

Lucas, Jim. Boeing 747: The First Twenty Years. Browcom Group Plc. London, England. 1988.

Mann, Alan. The A-Z Of Buddy Holly. Aurum Press Ltd. London, England. 1996.

McBrien, Richard P. Lives Of The Saints: From Mary And St. Francis Of Assisi To John XXIII And Mother Teresa. HarperCollins Publishers, Inc. New York, New York. 2001.

McDermott, John with Eddie Kramer. Hendrix: Setting The Record Straight. Warner Books. New York, New York. 1992.

Melody. Love Is In The Earth: A Kaleidoscope Of Crystals Updated. Earth-Love Publishing House. Wheat Ridge, Colorado. 1995.

Mondey, David. The Concise Guide To American Aircraft Of World War II. Chartwell Books, Inc. Edison, New Jersey. 1982.

Montgomery, M. R. and Gerald L. Foster. A Field Guide To Airplanes Of North America. Houghton Mifflin Company. New York, New York. 1992.

Myrick, Tom. In Search Of: What Happened To Major Glenn Miller. The Record Finder, 1(9): 3-4. November 1980.

Nassour, Ellis. Honky Tonk Angel: The Intimate Story Of Patsy Cline. St. Martin's Press. New York, New York. 1993.

Nesbit, Roy. What Happened To Glenn Miller. Aeroplane Monthly. January 1987.

Nesbit, Roy. What Happened To Glenn Miller. Aeroplane Monthly. February 1987.

Pareles, Jon and Patricia Romanowski, Editors. The Rolling Stone Encyclopedia Of Rock & Roll. Rolling Stone Press/Summit Books. New York, New York. 1983.

Pike, Jeff. The Death Of Rock 'n Roll: Untimely Demises, Morbid Preoccupations, And Premature Forecasts Of Doom In Pop Music. Faber and Faber, Inc. Winchester, Massachusetts. 1993.

Pilot Safety And Warning Supplements. Cessna Aircraft Company. Wichita, Kansas. 1985.

Pilot's Handbook Of Aeronautical Knowledge. US Department of Transportation, Federal Aviation Administration. Flight Standards Service. AC 61-23C. Revised 1997.

Pilot's Weight And Balance Handbook. US Department of Transportation, Federal Aviation Administration. Flight Standards Service. AC 91-23A. Revised 1977.

Raper, Jim. Singers Win Rock Fans, Lose Plane. The Virginian-Pilot. Norfolk, Virginia. September 2, 1974.

Rees, Dafydd and Luke Crampton. Encyclopedia Of Rock Stars. DK Publishing, Inc. London, England. 1996.

Sanville, Jim. Sons Make Video Tribute. Portland, Maine Press Herald. Portland, Maine. December 6, 1985.

Smith, Howard. Dick And Jud What Can You Say. Kingfeld, Maine Irregular. Kingfeld, Maine. October 7, 1981.

Two 747s Require Additional Bulkhead Repair. Aviation Week & Space Technology, 123(14): 28-29. October 1985.

Varley, Helen, Editor. The Air Traveler's Handbook, The Complete Guide To Air Travel, Airplanes And Airports. Simon and Schuster. New York, New York. 1978.

Vicenzi, Ugo. Early American Jetliners: Boeing 707, Douglas DC-8 And Convair CV-880. MBI Publishing Co. Osceola, Wisconsin. 1999.

Watson, Margaret. Friends Mourn Death. Tyler Morning Telegraph. Tyler, Texas. July 29, 1982.

Worth, Fred, L. Thirty Years Of Rock 'n Roll Trivia. Warner Books. New York, New York. 1980.

Internet References (www):

aero-web.org
aeroweb.brooklyn.cuny.edu
airdisaster.com
airliners.de
airliners.net
airsafe.com
albany.net
altavista.com
all4one.com
alphainter.net
amex.com
angelfire.com
aol.com
arbiterrecords.com
arkairmuseum.org/engines.html
arlingtoncemetery.org
aros.net
artistinformation.com
ask.com
audiemurphy.com
austinoldies.com
aviation-history.com
aviation.ntmsc.ca
aviation-safety.net
avstop.com
bigbandmusic.com
biography.com
bird.cn
blackwoodbrothers.com
boeing.com
bonanza.org
britannica.com
bushplane.com
canada.com
catholic-forum.com
celebratetoday.com/airceleb.html
cmcsb.com
cmt.com
corazon.com
country.org
crashpages.com
crosslink.net
dogpile.com
doobiebros.com
dynax.co.jp

eb.com
ebay.com
elibrary.com
elvispelvis.com/airplanecrash.htm
encyklopedia.pl
everything2.com
excite.com
findagrave.com
flash.net
flyaow.com/planes.htm
freei.net
galenet.com
geocities.com
getmusic.com
gmmy.com
go.com
goldrecord.com
google.com
gotonet.com
great-music.com
homepages.ihug.com.au/~rtester/index.htm
hotbot.com
hotshotdigital.com
imaginethat.com
imdb.com
infoseek.com
jaba.net/aviation/clipper.htm
jacksonville.com
jamesintveld.com
japanorama.com
jets.dk
jim-croce.com
jimsden.com
kyoto-su.ac.jp
lastdaysministries.org
latinoculture.about.com
letsfindout.com
lonester.utsa.edu
looksmart.com
lycaeum.org
lycos.com
mainichi.co.jp
manasepro.co.jp/kyu
members.surfsouth.com/~mnash
miningco.com

mitmusic.com
msmta.org
mtsu.edu
mufi.org.mx
myprimetime.com
navyband.navy.mil
northernlight.com
ntsb.gov
nviclassical.com
officialbigbopper.com
oldies.com
oldiesmusic.com
onweb.com
ourworld.compuserve.com
panam.com
patsycline.com
patsy.nu
pavarottiinconcert.com
planecrashinfo.com
police999.com/drugs/crack.html
prop-liners.com
raycharles.com
ricknelson.com
risingup.com

rockabillyhall.com
rockhall.com
rockin50s.com
rockmine.music.co.uk
santuarioloreto.it
search.eb.com
seeleymusic.com
skynyrd.com
starlightroof.com
system.missouri.edu
summerfolk.org
sunstudio.com
tbs.co.jp
tennessean.com
thenelsonbrothers.com
todotango.com
topedge.com
trade-a-plane.com
tripod.com
usdoj.gov/dea/concern/cocaine.htm
webcrawler.com
yahoo.com
zem.co.uk

Audio/Visual Reference:

Williams, Peter, Executive Producer; David Capey, Producer; David Hutt, Director. Gentleman Jim Reeves: The Story Of A Legend. TVS, Picture Parade, Kultur, White Star, BMG Video. 50 minutes. 1990.